Power of Language; Language of Power: A Collection of Readings

CUSTOM EDITION
for Ozarks Technical Community College
OTC Composition I & II

Custom Publishing

New York   Boston   San Francisco
London   Toronto   Sydney   Tokyo   Singapore   Madrid
Mexico City   Munich   Paris   Cape Town   Hong Kong   Montreal

**Pearson
Custom Publishing**
is a division of

www.pearsonhighered.com

ISBN 10: 0-558-32079-1
ISBN 13: 978-0-558-32079-9

Contents

CONTENTS

CONTENTS

Power of Language
Composition I

A Letter to America

Margaret Atwood

Margaret Atwood (1939–), born in Ottawa, Canada, attended the University of Toronto, Radcliffe, and Harvard. At a young age she decided to become a writer, and she has published a remarkable list of novels, poetry, and essays, along with forays into other genres such as children's stories and television scripts. She is best known, however, for her novels: The Edible Woman *(1969),* Surfacing *(1972),* Lady Oracle *(1976),* Life Before Man *(1979),* Bodily Harm *(1982)* The Handmaid's Tale *(1985),* Cat's Eye *(1989),* The Robber Bride *(1994),* Alias Grace *(1996),* The Blind Assassin *(2000),* Oryx and Crake *(2003), which was shortlisted for the Giller Prize and the Man Booker Prize,* The Penelopiad *(2005), and* The Tent *(2006). In this letter published in the* International Herald Tribune, *Atwood expresses her deep concerns regarding the direction of United States domestic and foreign policy in the first years of the twenty-first century.*

1 Dear America:

This is a difficult letter to write, because I'm no longer sure who you are.

Some of you may be having the same trouble. I thought I knew you: We'd become well acquainted over the past 55 years. You were the Mickey Mouse and Donald Duck comic books I read in the late 1940s. You were the radio shows—Jack Benny, Our Miss Brooks. You were the music I sang and danced to: the Andrews Sisters, Ella Fitzgerald, the Platters, Elvis. You were a ton of fun.

You wrote some of my favorite books. You created Huckleberry Finn, and Hawkeye, and Beth and Jo in *Little Women*, courageous in their different ways. Later, you were my beloved Thoreau, father of environmentalism, witness to individual conscience; and Walt Whitman, singer of the great Republic; and Emily Dickinson, keeper of the private soul. You were Hammett and Chandler, heroic walkers of mean streets; even later, you were the amazing trio, Hemingway, Fitzgerald, and Faulkner, who traced the dark labyrinths of your hidden heart. You were Sinclair Lewis and Arthur Miller, who, with their own American idealism, went after the sham in you, because they thought you could do better.

5   You were Marlon Brando in *On The Waterfront*, you were   5 Humphrey Bogart in *Key Largo*, you were Lillian Gish in *Night of the Hunter*. You stood up for freedom, honesty and justice; you protected the innocent. I believed most of that. I think you did, too. It seemed true at the time.

You put God on the money, though, even then. You had a way of thinking that the things of Caesar were the same as the things of God: that gave you self-confidence. You have always wanted to be a city upon a hill, a light to all nations, and for a while you were. Give me your tired, your poor, you sang, and for a while you meant it.

We've always been close, you and us. History, that old entangler, has twisted us together since the early 17th century. Some of us used to be you; some of us want to be you; some of you used to be us. You are not only our neighbors: In many cases—mine, for instance—you are also our blood relations, our colleagues, and our personal friends. But although we've had a ringside seat, we've never understood you completely, up here north of the 49th parallel.

We're like Romanized Gauls—look like Romans, dress like Romans, but aren't Romans—peering over the wall at the real Romans. What are they doing? Why? What are they doing now? Why is the haruspex eyeballing the sheep's liver? Why is the soothsayer wholesaling the Bewares?

Perhaps that's been my difficulty in writing you this letter: I'm not sure I know what's really going on. Anyway, you have a huge posse of experienced entrail-sifters who do nothing but analyze your every vein and lobe. What can I tell you about yourself that you don't already know?

10   This might be the reason for my hesitation: embarrassment,   10 brought on by a becoming modesty. But it is more likely to be

embarrassment of another sort. When my grandmother—from a New England background—was confronted with an unsavory topic, she would change the subject and gaze out the window. And that is my own inclination: Mind your own business.

But I'll take the plunge, because your business is no longer merely your business. To paraphrase Marley's Ghost, who figured it out too late, mankind is your business. And vice versa: When the Jolly Green Giant goes on the rampage, many lesser plants and animals get trampled underfoot. As for us, you're our biggest trading partner: We know perfectly well that if you go down the plug-hole, we're going with you. We have every reason to wish you well.

I won't go into the reasons why I think your recent Iraqi adventures have been—taking the long view—an ill-advised tactical error. By the time you read this, Baghdad may or may not look like the craters of the Moon, and many more sheep entrails will have been examined. Let's talk, then, not about what you're doing to other people, but about what you're doing to yourselves.

You're gutting the Constitution. Already your home can be entered without your knowledge or permission, you can be snatched away and incarcerated without cause, your mail can be spied on, your private records searched. Why isn't this a recipe for widespread business theft, political intimidation, and fraud? I know you've been told all this is for your own safety and protection, but think about it for a minute. Anyway, when did you get so scared? You didn't used to be easily frightened.

You're running up a record level of debt. Keep spending at this rate and pretty soon you won't be able to afford any big military adventures. Either that or you'll go the way of the USSR: lots of tanks, but no air conditioning. That will make folks very cross. They'll be even crosser when they can't take a shower because your short-sighted bulldozing of environmental protections has dirtied most of the water and dried up the rest. Then things will get hot and dirty indeed.

You're torching the American economy. How soon before the answer to that will be, not to produce anything yourselves, but to grab stuff other people produce, at gunboat-diplomacy prices? Is the world going to consist of a few megarich King Midases, with the rest being serfs, both inside and outside your country? Will the biggest business sector in the United States be the prison system? Let's hope not.

If you proceed much further down the slippery slope, people around the world will stop admiring the good things about you.

They'll decide that your city upon the hill is a slum and your democracy is a sham, and therefore you have no business trying to impose your sullied vision on them. They'll think you've abandoned the rule of law. They'll think you've fouled your own nest.

The British used to have a myth about King Arthur. He wasn't dead, but sleeping in a cave, it was said; in the country's hour of greatest peril, he would return. You, too, have great spirits of the past you may call upon: men and women of courage, of conscience, of prescience. Summon them now, to stand with you, to inspire you, to defend the best in you. You need them.

The Lesson

Toni Cade Bambara

Toni Cade Bambara (1939–1995) was born in New York City and attended Queens College, the University of Florence, the City University of New York, and the New School for Social Research, as well as dance studios and other institutes. Her professional life was as varied as her education, including social work and teaching in women's studies and literature programs. She wrote much fiction and many essays for a wide range of magazines as well as several books. Her short stories are collected into three books: Gorilla, My Love *(1972),* The Sea Birds Are Still Alive *(1977), and* The Salt Eaters *(1980). Her novel* If Blessing Comes *was published in 1987. The story "The Lesson" was printed in* Gorilla, My Love. *Like a personal essay, this story leads the reader through an experience that grows to a larger significance than the event itself may first suggest.*

1   Back in the days when everyone was old and stupid or young and foolish and me and Sugar were the only ones just right, this lady moved on our block with nappy hair and proper speech and no makeup. And quite naturally we laughed at her, laughed the way we did at the junk man who went about his business like he was some big-time president and his sorry-ass horse his secretary. And we kinda hated her too, hated the way we did the winos who cluttered up our parks and pissed on our handball walls and stank up our hallways and stairs so you couldn't halfway play hide-and-seek without a goddamn gas mask. Miss Moore was her name. The only woman on the block with no first name. And she was black as hell, cept for her feet, which were fish-white and spooky. And she was always planning these

boring-ass things for us to do, us being my cousin, mostly, who lived on the block cause we all moved North the same time and to the same apartment then spread out gradual to breathe. And our parents would yank our heads into some kinda shape and crisp up our clothes so we'd be presentable for travel with Miss Moore, who always looked like she was going to church, though she never did. Which is just one of things the grown-ups talked about when they talked behind her back like a dog. But when she came calling with some sachet she'd sewed up or some gingerbread she'd made or some book, why then they'd all be too embarrassed to turn her down and we'd get handed over all spruced up. She'd been to college and said it was only right that she should take responsibility for the young ones' education, and she not even related by marriage or blood. So they'd go for it. Specially Aunt Gretchen. She was the main gofer in the family. You got some ole dumb shit fool-ishness you want somebody to go for, you send for Aunt Gretchen. She been screwed into the go-along for so long, it's a blood-deep nat-ural thing with her. Which is how she got saddled with me and Sugar and Junior in the first place while our mothers were in a la-de-da apartment up the block having a good ole time.

So this one day Miss Moore rounds us all up at the mailbox and it's puredee hot and she's knockin herself out about arithmetic. And school suppose to let up in summer I heard, but she don't never let up. And the starch in my pinafore scratching the shit outta me and I'm really hating this nappy-head bitch and her goddamn college degree. I'd much rather go to the pool or to the show where it's cool. So me and Sugar leaning on the mailbox being surly, which is a Miss Moore word. And Flyboy checking out what everybody brought for lunch. And Fat Butt already wasting his peanut-butter-and-jelly sandwich like the pig he is. And Junebug punchin on Q.T.'s arm for potato chips. And Rosie Giraffe shifting from one hip to the other waiting for somebody to step on her foot or ask her if she from Georgia so she can kick ass, preferably Mercedes'. And Miss Moore asking us do we know what money is, like we a bunch of retards. I mean real money, she say, like it's only poker chips or monopoly papers we lay on the grocer. So right away I'm tired of this and say no. And would much rather snatch Sugar and go to the Sunset and terrorize the West In-dian kids and take their hair ribbons and their money too. And Miss Moore files that remark away for next week's lesson on brotherhood, I can tell. And finally I say we oughta get to the subway cause it's cooler and besides we might meet some cute boys. Sugar done swiped her mama's lipstick, so we ready.

So we heading down the street and she's boring us silly about what things cost and what our parents make and how much goes for rent and how money ain't divided up right in this country. And then she gets to the part about we all poor and live in the slums, which I don't feature. And I'm ready to speak on that, but she steps out in the street and hails two cabs just like that. Then she hustles half the crew in with her and hands me a five-dollar bill and tells me to calculate 10 percent tip for the driver. And we're off. Me and Sugar and Junebug and Flyboy hangin out the window and hollering to everybody, putting lipstick on each other cause Flyboy a faggot anyway, and making farts with our sweaty armpits. But I'm mostly trying to figure how to spend this money. But they all fascinated with the meter ticking and Junebug starts laying bets as to how much it'll read when Flyboy can't hold his breath no more. Then Sugar lays bets as to how much it'll be when we get there. So I'm stuck. Don't nobody want to go for my plan, which is to jump out at the next light and run off to the first bar-b-que we can find. Then the driver tells us to get the hell out cause we there already. And the meter reads eighty-five cents. And I'm stalling to figure out the tip and Sugar say give him a dime. And I decide he don't need it bad as I do, so later for him. But then he tries to take off with Junebug foot still in the door so we talk about his mama something ferocious. Then we check out that we on Fifth Avenue and everybody dressed up in stockings. One lady in a fur coat, hot as it is. White folks crazy.

"This is the place," Miss Moore say, presenting it to us in the voice she uses at the museum. "Let's look in the windows before we go in."

5   "Can we steal?" Sugar asks very serious like she's getting the   5
ground rules squared away before she plays. "I beg your pardon," says Miss Moore, and we fall out. So she leads us around the windows of the toy store and me and Sugar screamin, "This is mine, that's mine, I gotta have that, that was made for me, I was born for that," till Big Butt drowns us out.

"Hey, I'm goin to buy that there."

"That there? You don't even know what it is, stupid."

"I do so," he say punchin on Rosie Giraffe. "It's a microscope."

"Watcha gonna do with a microscope, fool?"

10   "Look at things."   10

"Like what, Ronald?" ask Miss Moore. And Big Butt ain't got the first notion. So here go Miss Moore gabbing about the thousands of bacteria in a drop of water and the somethin or other in a speck of blood and the million and one living things in the air around us is invisible to the naked eye. And what she say that for? Junebug go to town on that "naked" and we rolling. Then Miss Moore ask what it cost. So we all jam into the window smudgin it up and the price tag say $300. So then she ask how long'd take for Big Butt and Junebug to save up their allowances. "Too long," I say. "Yeh," adds Sugar, "outgrown it by that time." And Miss Moore say no, you never outgrow learning instruments. "Why, even medical students and interns and," blah, blah, blah. And we ready to choke Big Butt for bringing it up in the first damn place.

"This here costs four hundred eighty dollars," say Rosie Giraffe. So we pile up all over her to see what she pointin out. My eyes tell me it's a chunk of glass cracked with something heavy, and different-color inks dripped into the splits, then the whole thing put into a oven or something. But the $480 it don't make sense.

"That's a paperweight made of semi-precious stones fused together under tremendous pressure," she explains slowly, with her hands doing the mining and all the factory work.

"So what's a paperweight?" asks Rosie Giraffe.

"To weigh paper with, dumbbell," say Flyboy, the wise man from the East.

"Not exactly," say Miss Moore, which is what she say when you warm or way off too. "It's to weigh paper down so it won't scatter and make your desk untidy." So right away me and Sugar curtsy to each other and then to Mercedes who is more the tidy type.

"We don't keep paper on top of the desk in my class," say Junebug, figuring Miss Moore crazy or lyin one.

"At home, then," she say. "Don't you have a calendar and a pencil case and a blotter and a letter-opener on your desk at home where you do your homework?" And she know damn well what our homes look like cause she nosys around in them every chance she gets.

"I don't even have a desk," say Junebug. "Do we?"

"No. And I don't get no homework neither," say Big Butt.

"And I don't even have a home," say Flyboy like he do at school to keep the white folks off his back and sorry for him. Send this poor kid to camp posters, is his specialty.

"I do," says Mercedes. "I have a box of stationery on my desk and a picture of my cat. My godmother bought the stationery and the desk. There's a big rose on each sheet and the envelopes smell like roses."

"Who wants to know about your smelly-ass stationery," say Rosie Giraffe fore I can get my two cents in.

"It's important to have a work area all your own so that . . . "

25 "Will you look at this sailboat, please," say Flyboy, cuttin her off 25 and pointin to the thing like it was his. So once again we tumble all over each other to gaze at this magnificent thing in the toy store which is just big enough to maybe sail two kittens across the pond if you strap them to the posts tight. We all start reciting the price tag like we in assembly. "Handcrafted sailboat of fiberglass at one thousand one hundred ninety-five dollars."

"Unbelievable," I hear myself say and am really stunned. I read it again for myself just in case the group recitation put me in a trance. Same thing. For some reason this pisses me off. We look at Miss Moore and she lookin at us, waiting for I dunno what.

"Who'd pay all that when you can buy a sailboat set for a quarter at Pop's, a tube of glue for a dime, and a ball of string for eight cents? It must have a motor and a whole lot else besides," I say. "My sailboat cost me about fifty cents."

"But will it take water?" say Mercedes with her smart ass.

"Took mine to Alley Pond Park once," say Flyboy. "String broke. Lost it. Pity."

30 "Sailed mine in Central Park and it keeled over and sank. Had to 30 ask my father for another dollar."

"And you got the strap," laugh Big Butt. "The jerk didn't even have a string on it. My old man wailed on his behind."

Little Q.T. was staring hard at the sailboat and you could see he wanted it bad. But he too little and somebody'd just take it from him. So what the hell. "This boat for kids, Miss Moore?"

"Parents silly to buy something like that just to get all broke up," say Rosie Giraffe.

"That much money it should last forever," I figure.

35 "My father'd buy it for me if I wanted it." 35

"Your father, my ass," say Rosie Giraffe getting a chance to finally push Mercedes.

"Must be rich people shop here," say Q.T.

"You are a very bright boy," say Flyboy. "What was your first clue?" And he rap him on the head with the back of his knuckles, since Q.T. the only one he could get away with. Though Q.T. liable to come up behind you years later and get his licks in when you half expect it.

"What I want to know," I says to Miss Moore though I never talk to her, I wouldn't give the bitch that satisfaction, "is how much a real boat costs? I figure a thousand'd get you a yacht any day."

40 "Why don't you check that out," she says, "and report back to the group?" Which really pains my ass. If you gonna mess up a perfectly good swim day least you could do is have some answers. "Let's go in," she say like she got something up her sleeve. Only she don't lead the way. So me and Sugar turn the corner to where the entrance is, but when we get there I kinda hang back. Not that I'm scared, what's there to be afraid of, just a toy store. But I feel funny, shame. But what I got to be shamed about? Got as much right to go in as anybody. But somehow I can't seem to get hold of the door, so I step away for Sugar to lead. But she hangs back too. And I look at her and she looks at me and this is ridiculous. I mean, damn, I have never ever been shy about doing nothing or going nowhere. But then Mercedes steps up and then Rosie Giraffe and Big Butt crowd in behind and shove, and next thing we all stuffed into the doorway with only Mercedes squeezing past us, smoothing out her jumper and walking right down the aisle. Then the rest of us tumble in like a glued-together jigsaw done all wrong. And people lookin at us. And it's like the time me and Sugar crashed into the Catholic church on a dare. But once we got in there and everything so hushed and holy and the candles and the bowin and the handkerchiefs on all the drooping heads, I just couldn't go through with the plan. Which was for me to run up to the altar and do a tap dance while Sugar played the nose flute and messed around in the holy water. And Sugar kept givin me the elbow. Then later teased me so bad I tied her up in the shower and turned it on and locked her in. And she'd be there till this day if Aunt Gretchen hadn't finally figured I was lyin about the boarder takin a shower.

Same thing in the store. We all walkin on tiptoe and hardly touchin the games and puzzles and things. And I watched Miss Moore who is steady watchin us like she waitin for a sign. Like Mama Drewery watches the sky and sniffs the air and takes note of just how much slant is in the bird formation. Then me and Sugar bump smack into each other, so busy gazing at the toys, specially the sailboat. But we don't laugh and go into our fat-lady bump-stomach routine. We just stare at that price tag. Then Sugar run a finger over the whole boat. And I'm jealous and want to hit her. Maybe not her, but I sure want to punch somebody in the mouth.

"Watcha bring us here for, Miss Moore?"

"You sound angry, Sylvia. Are you mad about something?" Givin me one of them grins like she tellin a grown-up joke that never turns out to be funny. And she's lookin very closely at me like maybe she plannin to do my portrait from memory. I'm mad, but I won't give her that satisfaction. So I slouch around the store bein very bored and say, "Let's go."

Me and Sugar at the back of the train watchin the tracks whizzin by large then small then gettin gobbled up in the dark. I'm thinkin about this tricky toy I saw in the store. A clown that somersaults on a bar then does chin-ups just cause you yank lightly at his leg. Cost $35. I could see me askin my mother for a $35 birthday clown. "You wanna who that costs what?" she'd say, cocking her head to the side to get a better view of the hole in my head. Thirty-five dollars could buy new bunk beds for Junior and Gretchen's boy. Thirty-five dollars and the whole household could visit Grandaddy Nelson in the country. Thirty-five dollars would pay for the rent and the piano bill too. Who are these people that spend that much for performing clowns and $1,000 for toy sailboats? What kinda work they do and how they live and how come we ain't in on it? Where we are is who we are, Miss Moore always pointin out. But it don't necessarily have to be that way, she always adds then waits for somebody to say that poor people have to wake up and demand their share of the pie and don't none of us know what kind of pie she talkin about in the first damn place. But she ain't so smart cause I still got her four dollars from the taxi and she ain't gettin it. Messin up my day with this shit. Sugar nudges me in my pocket and winks.

45   Miss Moore lines us up in front of the mailbox where we started 45
from, seem like years ago, and I got a headache for thinkin so hard. And we lean all over each other so we can hold up under the draggy-ass lecture she always finishes us off with at the end before we thank her for borin us to tears. But she just looks at us like she readin tea leaves. Finally she say, "Well, what did you think of F.A.O. Schwarz?"

Rosie Giraffe mumbles, "White folks crazy."

"I'd like to go there again when I get my birthday money," says Mercedes, and we shove her out the pack so she has to lean on the mailbox by herself.

"I'd like a shower. Tiring day," say Flyboy.

Then Sugar surprises me by sayin, "You know, Miss Moore, I don't think all of us here put together eat in a year what that sailboat costs." And Miss Moore lights up like somebody goosed her. "And?" she say, urging Sugar on. Only I'm standin on her foot so she don't continue.

50   "Imagine for a minute what kind of society it is in which some people can spend on a toy what it would cost to feed a family of six or seven. What do you think?"

"I think," say Sugar pushing me off her feet like she never done before, cause I whip her ass in a minute, "that this is not much of a democracy if you ask me. Equal chance to pursue happiness means an equal crack at the dough, don't it?" Miss Moore is besides herself and I am disgusted with Sugar's treachery. So I stand on her foot one more time to see if she'll shove me. She shuts up, and Miss Moore looks at me, sorrowfully I'm thinkin. And somethin weird is goin on, I can feel it in my chest.

"Anybody else learn anything today?" lookin dead at me. I walk away and Sugar has to run to catch up and don't even seem to notice when I shrug her arm off my shoulder.

"Well, we got four dollars anyway," she says.

"Uh hunh."

55   "We could go to Hascombs and get half a chocolate layer and then go to the Sunset and still have plenty money for potato chips and ice-cream sodas."

"Uh hunh."

"Race you to Hascombs," she say.

We start down the block and she gets ahead which is O.K. by me cause I'm going to the West End and then over to the Drive to think this day through. She can run if she want to and even run faster. But ain't nobody gonna beat me at nuthin.

The Case Against College

Caroline Bird

Caroline Bird (1915-) was born in New York City. In addition to writing about business issues affecting women, she has taught at Vassar College and worked in public relations. Her books include Born Female *(1968),* What Women Want *(1979),* The Two-Paycheck Marriage *(1982),* The Good Years: Your Life in the 21st Century *(1983), and* Lives of Our Own: Secrets of Salty Old Women *(1995). In this essay, which was excerpted from* The Case Against College *(1975), Bird questions the value of college and a college education.*

1   The case *for* college has been accepted without question for more than a generation. All high school graduates ought to go, says Conventional Wisdom and statistical evidence, because college will help them earn more money, become "better" people, and learn to be more responsible citizens than those who don't go.

But college has never been able to work its magic for everyone. And now that close to half our high school graduates are attending, those who don't fit the pattern are becoming more numerous, and more obvious. College graduates are selling shoes and driving taxis; college students sabotage each other's experiments and forge letters of recommendation in the intense competition for admission to graduate school. Others find no stimulation in their studies, and drop out— often encouraged by college administrators.

Some observers say the fault is with the young people themselves— they are spoiled, stoned, overindulged, and expecting too much. But that's mass character assassination, and doesn't explain all campus unhappiness. Others blame the state of the world, and they are partly right. We've been told that young people have to go to college because our economy can't absorb an army of untrained eighteen-year-olds. But disillusioned graduates are learning that it can no longer absorb an army of trained twenty-two-year-olds, either. . . .

The ultimate defense of college has always been that while it may not teach you anything vocationally useful, it will somehow make you a better person, able to do anything better, and those who make it through the process are initiated into the "fellowship of educated men and women." In a study intended to probe what graduates seven years out of college thought their colleges should have done for them, the Carnegie Commission found that most alumni expected the "development of my abilities to think and express myself." But if such respected educational psychologists as Bruner and Piaget are right, specific learning skills have to be acquired very early in life, perhaps even before formal schooling begins.

5   So, when pressed, liberal-arts defenders speak instead about something more encompassing, and more elusive. "College changed me inside," one graduate told us fervently. The authors of a Carnegie Commission report, who obviously struggled for a definition, concluded that one of the common threads in the perceptions of a liberal education is that it provides "an integrated view of the world which can serve as an inner guide." More simply, alumni say that college should have "helped me to formulate the values and goals of my life," 5

In theory, a student is taught to develop these values and goals himself, but in practice, it doesn't work quite that way. All but the wayward and the saintly take their sense of the good, the true, and the beautiful from the people around them. When we speak of students acquiring "values" in college, we often mean that they will acquire the values—and sometimes that means only the tastes—of their professors. The values of professors may be "higher" than many students will encounter elsewhere, but they may not be relevant to situations in which students find themselves in college and later.

Of all the forms in which ideas are disseminated, the college professor lecturing a class is the slowest and most expensive. You don't have to go to college to read the great books or learn about the great ideas of Western Man. Today you can find them everywhere—in paperbacks, in the public libraries, in museums, in public lectures, in adult-education courses, in abridged, summarized, or adapted form in magazines, films, and television. The problem is no longer one of access to broadening ideas; the problem is the other way around: how to choose among the many courses of action proposed to us, how to edit the stimulations that pour into our eyes and ears every waking hour. A college experience that piles option on option and stimulation on stimulation merely adds to the contemporary nightmare.

What students and graduates say that they did learn on campus comes under the heading of personal, rather than intellectual, development. Again and again I was told that the real value of college is learning to get along with others, to practice social skills, to "sort out my head," and these have nothing to do with curriculum.

For whatever impact the academic experience used to have on college students, the sheer size of many undergraduate classes . . . dilutes faculty-student dialogue, and, more often than not, they are taught by teachers who were hired when colleges were faced with a shortage of qualified instructors, during their years of expansion and when the big rise in academic pay attracted the mediocre and the less than dedicated.

10   On the social side, colleges are withdrawing from responsibility 10 for feeding, housing, policing, and protecting students at a time when the environment of college may be the most important service it could render. College officials are reluctant to "intervene" in the personal lives of the students. They no longer expect to take over from parents, but often insist that students—who have, most often, never lived away from home before—take full adult responsibility for their plans, achievements, and behavior.

Most college students do not live in the plush, comfortable country-clublike surroundings their parents envisage, or, in some cases, remember. Open dorms, particularly when they are coeducational, are noisy, usually overcrowded, and often messy. Some students desert the institutional "zoos" (their own word for dorms) and move into run-down, overpriced apartments. Bulletin boards in student centers are littered with notices of apartments to share and the drift of conversation suggests that a lot of money is dissipated in scrounging for food and shelter.

Taxpayers now provide more than half of the astronomical sums that are spent on higher education. But less than half of today's high school graduates go on, raising a new question of equity: Is it fair to make all the taxpayers pay for the minority who actually go to college? We decided long ago that it is fair for childless adults to pay school taxes because everyone, parents and nonparents alike, profits by a literate population. Does the same reasoning hold true for state-supported higher education? There is no conclusive evidence on either side.

Young people cannot be expected to go to college for the general good of mankind. They may be more altruistic than their elders, but no great numbers are going to spend four years at hard intellectual labor, let alone tens of thousands of family dollars, for "the advancement of human capability in society at large," one of the many purposes invoked by the Carnegie Commission report. Nor do any considerable number of them want to go to college to beat the Russians to Jupiter, improve the national defense, increase the Gross National Product, lower the crime rate, improve automobile safety, or create a market for the arts—all of which have been suggested at one time or other as benefits taxpayers get for supporting higher education.

One sociologist said that you don't have to have a reason for going to college because it's an institution. His definition of an institution is something everyone subscribes to without question. The burden of proof is not on why you should go to college, but why anyone thinks there might be a reason for not going. The implication—and some educators express it quite frankly—is that an eighteen-year-old high school graduate is still too young and confused to know what he wants to do, let alone what is good for him.

15   Mother knows best, in other words.   15

It had always been comfortable for students to believe that authorities, like Mother, or outside specialists, like educators, could determine what was best for them. However, specialists and authorities no longer enjoy the credibility former generations accorded them. Patients talk back to doctors and are not struck suddenly dead. Clients question the lawyer's bills and sometimes get them reduced. It is no longer self-evident that all adolescents must study a fixed curriculum that was constructed at a time when all educated men could agree on precisely what it was that made them educated.

The same with college. If high school graduates don't want to continue their education, or don't want to continue it right away, they may perceive more clearly than their elders that college is not for them.

College is an ideal place for those young adults who love learning for its own sake, who would rather read than eat, and who like nothing better than writing research papers. But they are a minority, even at the prestigious colleges, which recruit and attract the intellectually oriented.

The rest of our high school graduates need to look at college more closely and critically, to examine it as a consumer product, and decide if the cost in dollars, in time, in continued dependency, and in future returns, is worth the very large investment each student—and his family—must make.

Casa: A Partial Remembrance of a Puerto Rican Childhood

Judith Ortiz Cofer

Judith Ortiz Cofer (1952–) was born in Hormigueros, Puerto Rico, and emigrated to the United States when she was four. Cofer attended Augusta College and Florida Atlantic University; she was also a Scholar of the English Speaking Union at Oxford University. She has worked as a bilingual teacher in the Florida public schools, and as a visiting writer at Vanderbilt University and the University of Michigan, Ann Arbor. Cofer is currently the Franklin Professor of English and Creative Writing at The University of Georgia. An award-winning poet, Cofer has received grants from the Witter Bynner Foundation and the National Endowment for the Arts. Her books include The Line of the Sun *(1989),* Silent Dancing *(1990),* The Latin Deli *(1993),* Reaching for the Mainland and Selected New Poems *(1995),* The Year of Our Revolution *(1998),* Woman In Front of the Sun: On Becoming a Writer *(2000),* A Love Story Beginning in Spanish: Poems *(2005), as well as a children's book,* Call Me Maria *(2004). Cofer, who has also written for* Glamour *and* The Kenyon Review, *often combines her love of language with her interest in the lives and traditions of Puerto Ricans. In this essay, Cofer reveals the beauty and knowledge contained in family stories.*

From *Prairie Schooner* 62, No. 2 (Fall 1989). Copyright © 1989 by the University of Nebraska Press.

¹

At three or four o'clock in the afternoon, the hour of *café con leche*, the women of my family gathered in Mamá's living room to speak of important things and retell familiar stories meant to be overheard by us young girls, their daughters. In Mamá's house (everyone called my grandmother Mamá) was a large parlor built by my grandfather to his wife's exact specifications so that it was always cool, facing away from the sun. The doorway was on the side of the house so no one could walk directly into her living room. First they had to take a little stroll through and around her beautiful garden where prize-winning orchids grew in the trunk of an ancient tree she had hollowed out for that purpose. This room was furnished with several mahogany rocking chairs, acquired at the births of her children, and one intricately carved rocker that had passed down to Mamá at the death of her own mother.

It was on these rockers that my mother, her sisters, and my grandmother sat on these afternoons of my childhood to tell their stories, teaching each other, and my cousin and me, what it was like to be a woman, more specifically, a Puerto Rican woman. They talked about life on the island, and life in *Los Nueva Yores,* their way of referring to the United States from New York City to California: the other place, not home, all the same. They told real-life stories though, as I later learned, always embellishing them with a little or a lot of dramatic detail. And they told *cuentos,* the morality and cautionary tales told by the women in our family for generations: stories that became a part of my subconscious as I grew up in two worlds, the tropical island and the cold city, and that would later surface in my dreams and in my poetry.

One of these tales was about the woman who was left at the altar. Mamá liked to tell that one with histrionic intensity. I remember the rise and fall of her voice, the sighs, and her constantly gesturing hands, like two birds swooping through her words. This particular story usually would come up in a conversation as a result of someone mentioning a forthcoming engagement or wedding. The first time I remember hearing it, I was sitting on the floor at Mamá's feet, pretending to read a comic book. I may have been eleven or twelve years old, at that difficult age when a girl was no longer a child who could be ordered to leave the room if the women wanted freedom to take their talk into forbidden zones, nor really old enough to be considered a part of their conclave. I could only sit quietly, pretending to be in another world, while absorbing it all in a sort of unspoken agreement of my status as silent auditor. On this day, Mamá had taken my long, tangled mane of hair into her ever-busy hands. Without looking down at me and with no interruption of her flow of words, she began braiding my hair, working at it with the quickness and determination that characterized all her actions. My mother was watching us impassively from her rocker across the room. On her lips played a little ironic smile. I would never sit still for *her* ministrations, but even then, I instinctively knew that she did not possess Mamá's matriarchal power to command and keep everyone's attention. This was never more evident than in the spell she cast when telling a story.

"It is not like it used to be when I was a girl," Mamá announced. "Then, a man could leave a girl standing at the church altar with a bouquet of fresh flowers in her hands and disappear off the face of the earth. No way to track him down if he was from another town. He could be a married man, with maybe even two or three families all over the island. There was no way to know. And there were men who did this. Hombres with the devil in their flesh who would come to a pueblo, like this one, take a job at one of the haciendas, never meaning to stay, only to have a good time and to seduce the women."

5 The whole time she was speaking, Mamá would be weaving my hair into a flat plait that required pulling apart the two sections of hair with little jerks that made my eyes water; but knowing how grandmother detested whining and *boba* (sissy) tears, as she called them, I just sat up as straight and stiff as I did at La Escuela San Jose, where the nuns enforced good posture with a flexible plastic ruler they bounced off of slumped shoulders and heads. As Mamá's story progressed, I noticed how my young Aunt Laura lowered her eyes, refusing to meet Mamá's meaningful gaze. Laura was seventeen, in her last year of high school, and already engaged to a boy from another town who had staked his claim with a tiny diamond ring, then left for Los Nueva Yores to make his fortune. They were planning to get married in a year. Mamá had expressed serious doubts that the wedding would ever take place. In Mamá's eyes, a man set free without a legal contract was a man lost. She believed that marriage was not something men desired, but simply the price they had to pay for the privilege of children and, of course, for what no decent (synonymous with "smart") woman would give away for free.

"María La Loca was only seventeen when *it* happened to her." I listened closely at the mention of this name. María was a town character, a fat middle-aged woman who lived with her old mother on the outskirts of town. She was to be seen around the pueblo delivering the meat pies the two women made for a living. The most peculiar thing about María, in my eyes, was that she walked and moved like a little girl though she had the thick body and wrinkled face of an old woman. She would swing her hips in an exaggerated, clownish way, and sometimes even hop and skip up to someone's house. She spoke to no one. Even if you asked her a question, she would just look at you and smile, showing her yellow teeth. But I had heard that if you got close enough, you could hear her humming a tune without words. The kids yelled out nasty things at her, calling her *La Loca,* and the men who hung out at the bodega playing dominoes sometimes whistled mockingly as she passed by with her funny, outlandish walk. But María seemed impervious to it all, carrying her basket of *pasteles* like a grotesque Little Red Riding Hood through the forest.

María La Loca interested me, as did all the eccentrics and crazies of our pueblo. Their weirdness was a measuring stick I used in my serious quest for a definition of normal. As a Navy brat shuttling between New Jersey and the pueblo, I was constantly made to feel like an oddball by my peers, who made fun of my two-way accent: a Spanish accent when I spoke English, and when I spoke Spanish I was told that I sounded like a *Gringa.* Being the outsider had already turned my brother and me into cultural chameleons. We developed early on the ability to blend into a crowd, to sit and read quietly in a fifth story apartment building for days and days when it was too bitterly cold to play outside, or, set free, to run wild in Mamá's realm, where she took charge of our lives, releasing Mother for a while from the intense fear for our safety that our father's absences instilled in her. In order to keep us from harm when Father was away, Mother kept us under strict surveillance. She even walked us to and from Public School No. 11, which we attended during the months we lived in Paterson, New Jersey, our home base in the states. Mamá freed all three of us like pigeons from a cage. I saw her as my liberator and my model. Her stories were parables from which to glean the *Truth.*

"María La Loca was once a beautiful girl. Everyone thought she would marry the Méndez boy." As everyone knew, Rogelio Méndez was the richest man in town. "But," Mamá continued, knitting my hair with the same intensity she was putting into her story, "this *macho* made a fool out of her and ruined her life." She paused for the effect of her use of the word "macho," which at that time had not yet become a popular epithet for an unliberated man. This word had for us the crude and comical connotation of "male of the species," stud; a *macho* was what you put in a pen to increase your stock.

I peeked over my comic book at my mother. She too was under Mamá's spell, smiling conspiratorially at this little swipe at men. She was safe from Mamá's contempt in this area. Married at an early age, an unspotted lamb, she had been accepted by a good family of strict Spaniards whose name was old and respected, though their fortune had been lost long before my birth. In a rocker Papá had painted sky blue sat Mamá's oldest child, Aunt Nena. Mother of three children, stepmother of two more, she was a quiet woman who liked books but had married an ignorant and abusive widower whose main interest in life was accumulating wealth. He too was in the mainland working on his dream of returning home rich and triumphant to buy the *finca* of his dreams. She was waiting for him to send for her. She would leave her children with Mamá for several years while the two of them slaved away in factories. He would one day be a rich man, and she a sadder woman. Even now her life-light was dimming. She spoke little, an aberration in Mamá's house, and she read avidly, as if storing up spiritual food for the long winters that awaited her in Los Nueva Yores without her family. But even Aunt Nena came alive to Mamá's words, rocking gently, her hands over a thick book in her lap.

10   Her daughter, my cousin Sara, played jacks by herself on the tile   10 porch outside the room where we sat. She was a year older than I. We shared a bed and all our family's secrets. Collaborators in search of answers, Sara and I discussed everything we heard the women say, trying to fit it all together like a puzzle that, once assembled, would reveal life's mysteries to us. Though she and I still enjoyed taking part in boys' games—chase, volleyball, and even *vaqueros*, the island version of cowboys and Indians involving cap-gun battles and violent shootouts under the mango tree in Mamá's backyard—we loved best the quiet hours in the afternoon when the men were still at work, and the boys had gone to play serious baseball at the park. Then Mamá's house belonged only to us women. The aroma of coffee perking in the kitchen, the mesmerizing creaks and groans of the rockers, and the women telling their lives in *cuentos* are forever woven into the fab-

ric of my imagination, braided like my hair that day I felt my grand-mother's hands teaching me about strength, her voice convincing me of the power of storytelling.

That day Mamá told how the beautiful María had fallen prey to a man whose name was never the same in subsequent versions of the story; it was Juan one time, José, Rafael, Diego, another. We under-stood that neither the name nor any of the *facts* were important, only that a woman had allowed love to defeat her. Mamá put each of us in María's place by describing her wedding dress in loving detail: how she looked like a princess in her lace as she waited at the altar. Then, as Mamá approached the tragic denouement of her story, I was dis-tracted by the sound of my Aunt Laura's violent rocking. She seemed on the verge of tears. She knew the fable was intended for her. That week she was going to have her wedding gown fitted, though no firm date had been set for the marriage. Mamá ignored Laura's obvious discomfort, digging out a ribbon from the sewing basket she kept by her rocker while describing María's long illness, "a fever that would not break for days." She spoke of a mother's despair: "that woman climbed the church steps on her knees every morning, wore only black as a *promesa* to the Holy Virgin in exchange for her daughter's health." By the time María returned from her honeymoon with death, she was ravished, no longer young or sane. "As you can see, she is almost as old as her mother already," Mamá lamented while tying the ribbon to the ends of my hair, pulling it back with such force that I just knew I would never be able to close my eyes completely again.

"That María's getting crazier every day." Mamá's voice would take a lighter tone now, expressing satisfaction, either for the perfection of my braid, or for a story well told—it was hard to tell. "You know that tune María is always humming?" Carried away by her enthusiasm, I tried to nod, but Mamá still had me pinned between her knees.

"Well, that's the wedding march." Surprising us all, Mamá sang out, "Da, da, dara . . . da, da, dara." Then lifting me off the floor by my skinny shoulders, she would lead me around the room in an impromptu waltz—another session ending with the laughter of women, all of us caught up in the infectious joke of our lives.

Understanding Natural Selection

Charles Darwin

*Charles Darwin (1809–1892), the famed scientist cred-
ited with discovering natural selection, was born in
Shrewsbury, England. The grandson of a noted physi-
cian/scientist, Darwin studied medicine at Edinburgh,
then biology at Cambridge. In 1835, at age 26, he embarked on a 5-year scientific survey of South American waters. In 1839, he married a cousin, Emma Wedgewood;
shortly after, Darwin began a period of intensive research
and writing. By the mid-1840s, he had published several
works on his geological and zoological discoveries and had
become recognized as one of the leading scientists of the day.
Darwin's best-known work,* On the Origin of Species by
Means of Natural Selection *(1859), received mixed reaction initially, but over time it has become known as a central document of scientific writing. This essay, which comes
from that work, presents some of the basic theories of the
scientist whose concept of evolution has become a household
world—Darwinism. As you read the essay, be alert to the
various rhetorical strategies Darwin uses to transform hard
science into good reading.*

1   It may be said that natural selection is daily and hourly scrutiniz-
ing, throughout the world, every variation, even the slightest; rejecting that which is bad, preserving and adding up all that is
good; silently and insensibly working, whenever and wherever opportunity offers, at the improvement of each organic being in relation to
its organic and inorganic conditions of life. We see nothing of these
slow changes in progress, until the hand of time has marked the long
lapses of ages, and then so imperfect is our view into long past
geological ages, that we only see that the forms of life are now different from what they formerly were.

Although natural selection can act only through and for the good of each being, yet characters and structures, which we are apt to consider as of very trifling importance, may thus be acted on. When we see leaf-eating insects green, and bark-feeders mottled-grey; the alpine ptarmigan white in winter, the red-grouse the color of heather, and the black-grouse that of peaty earth, we must believe that these tints are of service to these birds and insects in preserving them from danger. Grouse, if not destroyed at some period of their lives, would increase in countless numbers; they are known to suffer largely from birds of prey; and hawks are guided by eyesight to their prey—so much so, that on parts of the Continent persons are warned not to keep white pigeons, as being the most liable to destruction. Hence I can see no reason to doubt that natural selection might be most effective in giving the proper color to each kind of grouse, and in keeping that color, when once acquired, true and constant. Nor ought we to think that the occasional destruction of an animal of any particular color would produce little effect: we should remember how essential it is in a flock of white sheep to destroy every lamb with the faintest trace of black. In plants the down on the fruit and the color of the flesh are considered by botanists as characters of the most trifling importance: yet we hear from an excellent horticulturist, Downing, that in the United States smooth-skinned fruits suffer far more from a beetle, a curculio, than those with down; that purple plums suffer far more from a certain disease than yellow plums; whereas another disease attacks yellow-fleshed peaches far more than those with other colored flesh. If, with all the aids of art, these slight differences make a great difference in cultivating the several varieties, assuredly, in a state of nature, where the trees would have to struggle with other trees and with a host of enemies, such differences would effectually settle which variety, whether a smooth or downy, a yellow or purple fleshed fruit, should succeed.

In looking at many small points of difference between species, which, as far as our ignorance permits us to judge, seem to be quite unimportant, we must not forget that climate, food, and so on probably produce some slight and direct effect. It is, however, far more necessary to bear in mind that there are many unknown laws of correlation to growth, which, when one part of the organization is modified through variation, and the modifications are accumulated by natural selection for the good of the being, will cause other modifications, often of the most unexpected nature.

As we see that those variations which under domestication appear at any particular period of life, tend to reappear in the offspring of the same period; for instance, in the seeds of the many varieties of our culinary and agricultural plants; in the caterpillar and cocoon stages of the varieties of the silkworm; in the eggs of poultry, and in the color of the down of their chickens; in the horns of our sheep and cattle when nearly adult; so in a state of nature, natural selection will be enabled to act on and modify organic beings at any age, by the accumulation of profitable variations at that age, and by their inheritance at a corresponding age. If it profit a plant to have its seeds more and more widely disseminated by the wind, I can see no greater difficulty in this being effected through natural selection, than in the cotton-planter increasing and improving by selection the down in the pods on his cotton-trees. Natural selection may modify and adapt the larva of an insect to a score of contingencies, wholly different from those which concern the mature insect. These modifications will no doubt affect, through the laws of correlation, the structure of the adult; and probably in the case of those insects which live only for a few hours, and which never feed, a large part of their structure is merely the correlated result of successive changes in the structure of their larvae. So, conversely, modifications in the adult will probably often affect the structure of the larva; but in all cases natural selection will ensure that modifications consequent on other modifications at a different period of life, shall not be in the least degree injurious: for if they became so, they would cause the extinction of the species.

5   Natural selection will modify the structure of the young in relation to the parent, and of the parent in relation to the young. In social animals it will adapt the structure of each individual for the benefit of the community; if each in consequence profits by the selected change. What natural selection cannot do, is to modify the structure of one species, without giving it any advantage, for the good of another species; and though statements to this effect may be found in works of natural history, I cannot find one case which will bear investigation. A structure used only once in an animal's whole life, if of high importance to it, might be modified to any extent by natural selection; for instance, the great jaws possessed by certain insects, and used exclusively for opening the cocoon; or the hard tip to the beak of nestling birds, used for breaking the egg. It has been asserted, that of the best short-beaked tumbler-pigeons more perish in the egg than are able to get out of it; so that fanciers assist in the act of hatching. Now,

if nature had to make the beak of a full-grown pigeon very short for the bird's own advantage, the process of modification would be very slow, and there would be simultaneously the most rigorous selection of the young birds within the egg, which had the most powerful and hardest beaks, for all with weak beaks would inevitably perish: or, more delicate and more easily broken shells might be selected, the thickness of the shell being known to vary like every other structure.

Sexual Selection

Inasmuch as peculiarities often appear under domestication in one sex and become hereditarily attached to that sex, the same fact probably occurs under nature, and if so, natural selection will be able to modify one sex in its functional relations to the other sex, or in relation to wholly different habits of life in the two sexes, as is sometimes the case with insects. And this leads me to say a few words on what I call sexual selection. This depends, not on a struggle for existence, but on a struggle between the males for possession of the females; the result is not death to the unsuccessful competitor, but few or no offspring. Sexual selection is, therefore, less rigorous than natural selection. Generally, the most vigorous males, those which are best fitted for their places in nature, will leave most progeny. But in many cases, victory will depend not on general vigor, but on having special weapons, confined to the male sex. A hornless stag or spurless cock would have a poor chance of leaving offspring. Sexual selection by always allowing the victor to breed might surely give indomitable courage, length to the spur, and strength to the wing to strike in the spurred leg, as well as the brutal cock-fighter, who knows well that he can improve his breed by careful selection of the best cocks. How low in the scale of nature this law of battle descends, I know not; male alligators have been described as fighting, bellowing, and whirling round, like Indians in a war dance, for the possession of the females; male salmons have been seen fighting all day long; male stag-beetles often bear wounds from the huge mandibles of other males. The war is, perhaps, severest between the males of polygamous animals, and these seem oftenest provided with special weapons. The males of carnivorous animals are already well armed; though to them and to others, special means of defence may be given through means of sexual selection, as the mane to the lion, the shoulder-pad to the boar, and the hooked jaw to the male salmon; for the shield may be as important for victory, as the sword or spear.

Amongst birds, the contest is often of a more peaceful character. All those who have attended to the subject, believe that there is the severest rivalry between the males of many species to attract by singing the females. The rock-thrush of Guiana, birds of Paradise, and some others, congregate; and successive males display their gorgeous plumage and perform strange antics before the females, which standing by as spectators, at last choose the most attractive partner. Those who have closely attended to birds in confinement well know that they often take individual preferences and dislikes: thus Sir R. Heron has described how one pied peacock was eminently attractive to all his hen birds. It may appear childish to attribute any effect to such apparently weak means: I cannot here enter on the details necessary to support this view; but if man can in a short time give elegant carriage and beauty to his bantams, according to his standard of beauty, I can see no good reason to doubt that female birds, by selecting, during thousands of generations, the most melodious or beautiful males, according to their standard of beauty, might produce a marked effect. I strongly suspect that some well-known laws with respect to the plumage of male and female birds, in comparison with the plumage of the young, can be explained on the view of plumage having been chiefly modified by sexual selection, acting when the birds have come to the breeding age or during the breeding season; the modifications thus produced being inherited at corresponding ages or seasons, either by the males alone, or by the males and females; but I have not space here to enter on this subject.

Thus it is, as I believe, that when the males and females of any animal have the same general habits of life, but differ in structure, color, or ornament, such differences have been mainly caused by sexual selection; that is, individual males have had, in successive generations, some slight advantage over other males, in their weapons, means of defence, or charms; and have transmitted these advantages to their male offspring. Yet, I would not wish to attribute all such sexual differences to this agency: for we see peculiarities arising and becoming attached to the male sex in our domestic animals (as the wattle in male carriers, horn-like protuberances in the cocks of certain fowls, and so on), which we cannot believe to be either useful to the males in battle, or attractive to the females. We see analogous cases under nature, for instance, the tuft of hair on the breast of the turkey-cock, which can hardly be either useful or ornamental to this bird; indeed, had the tuft appeared under domestication, it would have been called a monstrosity.

Illustration of the Action of Natural Selection

. . . Let us take the case of a wolf, which preys on various animals, securing some by craft, some by strength, and some by fleetness; and let us suppose that the fleetest prey, a deer for instance, had from any change in the country increased in numbers, or that other prey had decreased in numbers, during that season of the year when the wolf is hardest pressed for food. I can under such circumstances see no reason to doubt that the swiftest and slimmest wolves would have the best chance of surviving, and so be preserved or selected—provided always that they retained strength to master their prey at this or at some other period of the year, when they might be compelled to prey on other animals. I can see no more reason to doubt this, than that man can improve the fleetness of his greyhounds by careful and methodical selection, or by that unconscious selection which results from each man trying to keep the best dogs without any thought of modifying the breed.

10　　　Even without any change in the proportional numbers of the animals on which our wolf preyed, a cub might be born with an innate tendency to pursue certain kinds of prey. Nor can this be thought very improbable; for we often observe great differences in the natural tendencies of our domestic animals; one cat, for instance, taking to catch rats, another mice; one cat . . . bringing home winged game, another hares or rabbits, and another hunting on marshy ground and almost nightly catching woodcocks or snipes. The tendency to catch rats rather than mice is known to be inherited. Now, if any slight innate change of habit or of structure benefited an individual wolf, it would have the best chance of surviving and of leaving offspring. Some of its young would probably inherit the same habits or structure, and by the repetition of this process, a new variety might be formed which would either supplant or coexist with the parent-form of wolf. Or, again, the wolves inhabiting a mountainous district, and those frequenting the lowlands, would naturally be forced to hunt different prey; and from the continued preservation of the individuals best fitted for the two sites, two varieties might slowly be formed. These varieties would cross and blend where they met; but to this subject of intercrossing we shall soon have to return. I may add, that . . . there are two varieties of the wolf inhabiting the Catskill Mountains in the United States, one with a light greyhound-like form, which pursues deer, and the other more bulky, with shorter legs, which more frequently attacks the shepherd's flocks.

On Going Home

Joan Didion

Joan Didion (1934–) was born in Sacramento, Califor-
nia. She received a B.A. at the University of California at
Berkeley in 1956, then moved to New York City, where she
spent 7 years as an associate editor at Vogue *and as a con-*
tributor to Esquire, The National Review, *and* The Saturday Evening Post. *In 1964, Didion married writer*
John Gregory Dunne and returned home to California,
where she began to write the essays and fiction that became
her genre: personal commentaries on contemporary events
that expose social disintegration. Her published works in-
clude the collections of essays Slouching Towards Bethlehem *(1968),* The White Album *(1970), and* After
Henry *(1992); the novels* Run River *(1963),* Play It As
It Lays *(1970),* A Book of Common Prayer *(1977), and*
Democracy *(1984); and the nonfiction books* Salvador
(1983), Miami *(1987),* Political Fictions *(2001),* Where
I Was From *(2003), and* The Year of Magical Thinking
(2005), for which she won the National Book Award for
nonfiction. Didion often applies her spare style—frequently
edged with tension—to personal recollections. Look for her
restless discomfort in this essay about going home but never
really arriving.

1 I am home for my daughter's first birthday. By "home" I do not 1
mean the house in Los Angeles where my husband and I and the
baby live, but the place where my family is, in the Central Valley of
California. It is a vital although troublesome distinction. My husband
likes my family but is uneasy in their house, because once there I fall
into their ways, which are difficult, oblique, deliberately inarticulate,

not my husband's ways. We live in dusty houses ("D-U-S-T," he once wrote with his finger on surfaces all over the house, but no one noticed it) filled with mementos quite without value to him (what could the Canton dessert plates mean to him? how could he have known about the assay scales, why should he care if he did know?), and we appear to talk exclusively about people we know who have been committed to mental hospitals, about people we know who have been booked on drunk-driving charges, and about property, particularly about property, land, price per acre and C-2 zoning and assessments and freeway access. My brother does not understand my husband's inability to perceive the advantage in the rather common real-estate transaction known as "sale-leaseback," and my husband in turn does not understand why so many of the people he hears about in my father's house have recently been committed to mental hospitals or booked on drunk-driving charges. Nor does he understand that when we talk about sale-leasebacks and right-of-way condemnations we are talking in code about the things we like best, the yellow fields and the cottonwoods and the rivers rising and falling and the mountain roads closing when the heavy snow comes in. We miss each other's points, have another drink and regard the fire. My brother refers to my husband, in his presence, as "Joan's husband." Marriage is the classic betrayal.

Or perhaps it is not anymore. Sometimes I think that those of us who are now in our thirties were born into the last generation to carry the burden of "home," to find in family life the source of all tension and drama. I had by all objective accounts a "normal" and a "happy" family situation, and yet I was almost thirty years old before I could talk to my family on the telephone without crying after I had hung up. We did not fight. Nothing was wrong. And yet some nameless anxiety colored the emotional charges between me and the place that I came from. The question of whether or not you could go home again was a very real part of the sentimental and largely literary baggage with which we left home in the fifties; I suspect that it is irrelevant to the children born of the fragmentation after World War II. A few weeks ago in a San Francisco bar I saw a pretty young girl on crystal take off her clothes and dance for the cash prize in an "amateur-topless" contest. There was no particular sense of moment about this, none of the effect of romantic degradation, of "dark journey," for which my generation strived so assiduously. What sense could that girl possibly make of, say, *Long Day's Journey into Night?* Who is beside the point?

That I am trapped in this particular irrelevancy is never more apparent to me than when I am home. Paralyzed by the neurotic lassitude engendered by meeting one's past at every turn, around every corner, inside every cupboard, I go aimlessly from room to room. I decide to meet it head-on and clean out a drawer, and I spread the contents on the bed. A bathing suit I wore the summer I was seventeen. A letter of rejection from *The Nation,* an aerial photograph of the site for a shopping center my father did not build in 1954. Three teacups hand-painted with cabbage roses and signed "E.M.," my grandmother's initials. There is no final solution for letters of rejection from *The Nation* and teacups handpainted in 1900. Nor is there any answer to snapshots of one's grandfather as a young man on skis, surveying around Donner Pass in the year 1910. I smooth out the snapshot and look into his face, and do and do not see my own. I close the drawer, and have another cup of coffee with my mother. We get along very well, veterans of a guerrilla war we never understood.

Days pass. I see no one. I come to dread my husband's evening call, not only because he is full of news of what by now seems to me our remote life in Los Angeles, people he has seen, letters which require attention, but because he asks what I have been doing, suggests uneasily that I get out, drive to San Francisco or Berkeley. Instead I drive across the river to a family graveyard. It has been vandalized since my last visit and the monuments are broken, over-turned in the dry grass. Because I once saw a rattlesnake in the grass I stay in the car and listen to a country-and-Western station. Later I drive with my father to a ranch he has in the foothills. The man who runs his cattle on it asks us to the roundup, a week from Sunday, and although I know that I will be in Los Angeles I say, in the oblique way my family talks, that I will come. Once home I mention the broken monuments in the graveyard. My mother shrugs.

5   I go to visit my great-aunts. A few of them think now that I am   5 my cousin, or their daughter who died young. We recall an anecdote about a relative last seen in 1948, and they ask if I still like living in New York City. I have lived in Los Angeles for three years, but I say that I do. The baby is offered a horehound drop, and I am slipped a dollar bill "to buy a treat." Questions trail off, answers are abandoned, the baby plays with the dust motes in a shaft of afternoon sun.

It is time for the baby's birthday party: a white cake, strawberry-marshmallow ice cream, a bottle of champagne saved from another party. In the evening, after she has gone to sleep, I kneel beside the crib and touch her face, where it is pressed against the slats, with mine. She is an open and trusting child, unprepared for and unaccustomed to the ambushes of family life, and perhaps it is just as well that I can offer her little of that life. I would like to give her more. I would like to promise her that she will grow up with a sense of her cousins and of rivers and of her great-grandmother's teacups, would like to pledge her a picnic on a river with fried chicken and her hair uncombed, would like to give her *home* for her birthday, but we live differently now and I can promise her nothing like that. I give her a xylophone and a sundress from Madeira, and promise to tell her a funny story.

On Self-Respect

Joan Didion

Joan Didion (1934–) was born in Sacramento, Califor-
nia. She received a B.A. at the University of California at
Berkeley in 1956, then moved to New York City, where she
spent seven years working as an associate editor at Vogue
and as a contributor to Esquire, *the* National Review,
and the Saturday Evening Post. *In 1964, Didion mar-*
ried writer John Gregory Dunne and went back to Cali-
fornia, where she began to write the essays and fiction that
became her genre: personal commentaries on contemporary
events that expose social disintegration. Her published
works include the collections of essays Slouching Towards
Bethlehem *(1968),* The White Album *(1970), and*
After Henry *(1992); the novels* Run River *(1963),* Play
It As It Lays *(1970),* A Book of Common Prayer
(1977), and Democracy *(1984); and the nonfiction*
books Salvador *(1983),* Miami *(1987),* Political Fictions
(2001), Where I Was From *(2003), and* The Year of
Magical Thinking *(2005), for which she won the National*
Book Award for nonfiction. Didion looks inward in this
essay, leveling her sometimes terse, always sharp commen-
tary on herself and on the rest of us.

1   Once, in a dry season, I wrote in large letters across two pages   1
of a notebook that innocence ends when one is stripped of
the delusion that one likes oneself. Although now, some years
later, I marvel that a mind on the outs with itself should have nonetheless made painstaking record of its every tremor, I recall with embar-
rassing clarity the flavor of those particular ashes. It was a matter of
misplaced self-respect.

I had not been elected to Phi Beta Kappa. This failure could scarcely have been more predictable or less ambiguous (I simply did not have the grades), but I was unnerved by it; I had somehow thought myself a kind of academic Raskolnikov, curiously exempt from the cause-effect relationships which hampered others. Although even the humorless nineteen-year-old that I was must have recognized that the situation lacked real tragic stature, the day that I did not make Phi Beta Kappa nonetheless marked the end of something, and innocence may well be the word for it. I lost the conviction that lights would always turn green for me, the pleasant certainty that those rather passive virtues which had won me approval as a child automatically guaranteed me not only Phi Beta Kappa keys but happiness, honor, and the love of a good man; lost a certain touching faith in the totem power of good manners, clean hair, and proven competence on the Stanford-Binet scale. To such doubtful amulets had my self-respect been pinned, and I faced myself that day with the nonplused apprehension of someone who has come across a vampire and has no crucifix at hand.

Although to be driven back upon oneself is an uneasy affair at best, rather like trying to cross a border with borrowed credentials, it seems to me now the one condition necessary to the beginnings of real self-respect. Most of our platitudes notwithstanding, self-deception remains the most difficult deception. The tricks that work on others count for nothing in that very well-lit back alley where one keeps assignations with oneself: no winning smiles will do here, no prettily drawn lists of good intentions. One shuffles flashily but in vain through one's marked cards—the kindness done for the wrong reason, the apparent triumph which involved no real effort, the seemingly heroic act into which one had been shamed. The dismal fact is that self-respect has nothing to do with the approval of others—who are, after all, deceived easily enough; has nothing to do with reputation, which, as Rhett Butler told Scarlett O'Hara, is something people with courage can do without.

To do without self-respect, on the other hand, is to be an unwilling audience of one to an interminable documentary that details one's failings, both real and imagined, with fresh footage spliced in for every screening. *There's the glass you broke in anger, there's the hurt on X's face; watch now, this next scene, the night Y came back from Houston, see how you muff this one.* To live without self-respect is to lie awake some night, beyond the reach of warm milk, phenobarbital, and the sleeping hand on the coverlet, counting up the sins of commission and omission, the trusts betrayed, the promises subtly broken, the gifts irrevocably wasted through sloth or cowardice or carelessness. However long we postpone it, we eventually lie down alone in that notoriously uncomfortable bed, the one we make ourselves. Whether or not we sleep in it depends, of course, on whether or not we respect ourselves.

To protest that some fairly improbable people, some people who *could not possibly respect themselves,* seem to sleep easily enough is to miss the point entirely, as surely as those people miss it who think that self-respect has necessarily to do with not having safety pins in one's underwear. There is a common superstition that "self-respect" is a kind of charm against snakes, something that keeps those who have it locked in some unblighted Eden, out of strange beds, ambivalent conversations, and trouble in general. It does not at all. It has nothing to do with the face of things, but concerns instead a separate peace, a private reconciliation. Although the careless, suicidal Julian English in *Appointment in Samarra* and the careless, incurably dishonest Jordan Baker in *The Great Gatsby* seem equally improbable candidates for self-respect, Jordan Baker had it, Julian English did not. With that genius for accommodation more often seen in women than in men, Jordan took her own measure, made her own peace, avoided threats to that peace: "I hate careless people," she told Nick Carraway. "It takes two to make an accident."

Like Jordan Baker, people with self-respect have the courage of their mistakes. They know the price of things. If they choose to commit adultery, they do not then go running, in an excess of bad conscience, to receive absolution from the wronged parties; nor do they complain unduly of the unfairness, the undeserved embarrassment, of being named correspondent. In brief, people with self-respect exhibit a certain toughness, a kind of moral nerve; they display what was once called *character,* a quality which, although approved in the abstract, sometimes loses ground to other, more instantly negotiable virtues. The measure of its slipping prestige is that one tends to think of it only in connection with homely children and United States senators who have been defeated, preferably in the primary, for reelection. Nonetheless, character—the willingness to accept responsibility for one's own life—is the source from which self-respect springs.

Self-respect is something that our grandparents, whether or not they had it, knew all about. They had instilled in them, young, a certain discipline, the sense that one lives by doing things one does not particularly want to do, by putting fears and doubts to one side, by weighing immediate comforts against the ability of larger, even intangible, comforts. It seemed to the nineteenth century admirable, but not remarkable, that Chinese Gordon put on a clean white suit and held Khartoum against the Mahdi; it did not seem unjust that the way to free land in California involved death and difficulty and dirt. In a diary kept during the winter of 1846, an emigrating twelve-year-old named Narcissa Cornwall noted coolly: "Father was busy reading and did not notice that the house was being filled with strange Indians until Mother spoke about it." Even lacking any clue as to what Mother said, one can scarcely fail to be impressed by the entire incident: the father reading, the Indians filing in, the mother choosing the words that would not alarm, the child duly recording the event and noting further that those particular Indians were not, "fortunately for us," hostile. Indians were simply part of the *donnée*.

In one guise or another, Indians always are. Again, it is a question of recognizing that anything worth having has its price. People who respect themselves are willing to accept the risk that the Indians will be hostile, that the venture will go bankrupt, that the liaison may not turn out to be one in which *every day is a holiday because you're married to me*. They are willing to invest something of themselves; they may not play at all, but when they do play, they know the odds.

That kind of self-respect is a discipline, a habit of mind that can never be faked but can be developed, trained, coaxed forth. It was once suggested to me that, as an antidote to crying, I put my head in a paper bag. As it happens, there is a sound physiological reason, something to do with oxygen, for doing exactly that, but the psychological effect alone is incalculable: it is difficult in the extreme to continue fancying oneself Cathy in *Wuthering Heights* with one's head in a Food Fair bag. There is a similar case for all the small disciplines, unimportant in themselves; imagine maintaining any kind of swoon, commiserative or carnal, in a cold shower.

10   But those small disciplines are available only insofar as they represent larger ones. To say that Waterloo was won on the playing fields of Eton is not to say that Napoleon might have been saved by a crash program in cricket; to give formal dinners in the rain forest would be pointless did not the candlelight flickering on the liana call forth deeper, stronger disciplines, values instilled long before. It is a kind of

ritual, helping us to remember who and what we are. In order to re-member it, one must have known it.

To have that sense of one's intrinsic worth which constitutes self-respect is potentially to have everything: the ability to discriminate, to love and to remain indifferent. To lack it is to be locked within one-self, paradoxically incapable of either love or indifference. If we do not respect ourselves, we are on the one hand forced to despise those who have so few resources as to consort with us, so little perception as to remain blind to our fatal weaknesses. On the other, we are peculiarly in thrall to everyone we see, curiously determined to live out—since our self-image is untenable—their false notions of us. We flatter our-selves by thinking this compulsion to please others an attractive trait: a gist for imaginative empathy, evidence of our willingness to give. Of *course* I will play Francesca to your Paolo, Helen Keller to anyone's Annie Sullivan: no expectation is too misplaced, no role too ludicrous. At the mercy of those we cannot but hold in contempt, we play roles doomed to failure before they are begun, each defeat generating fresh despair at the urgency of divining and meeting the next demand made upon us.

It is the phenomenon sometimes called "alienation from self." In its advanced stages, we no longer answer the telephone, because some-one might want something; that we could say *no* without drowning in self-reproach is an idea alien to this game. Every encounter de-mands too much, tears the nerves, drains the will, and the specter of something as small as an unanswered letter arouses such dispropor-tionate guilt that answering it becomes out of the question. To assign unanswered letters their proper weight, to free us from the expecta-tions of others, to give us back to ourselves—there lies the great, the singular power of self-respect. Without it, one eventually discovers the final turn of the screw: one runs away to find oneself, and finds no one at home.

The Death of a Moth

Annie Dillard

Annie Dillard (1945–) was born in Pittsburgh, Pennsylvania. She received a B. A. (1967) and an M. A. (1968) from Hollins College and then embarked on a career as a writer and teacher. Dillard has worked as a columnist for The Living Wilderness *and a contributing editor for* Harper's, *and taught at Western Washington University and Wesleyan University in Connecticut. Fascinated with the intricacies of the natural world and blessed with an introspective, poetic mind, Dillard has developed a reputation for exploring the relationships between humans and nature, physically and spiritually. She has been compared to Henry David Thoreau, and her work has been compared to his* Walden. *An accomplished writer, Dillard has published nonfiction, poetry, literary criticism, essays, autobiographies, and a novel. Her published work includes* Pilgrim at Tinker Creek *(1974), observations about nature for which she received the Pulitzer Prize;* Tickets for a Prayer Wheel *(1974), a volume of poetry;* Living By Fiction *(1982), a collection of literary criticism;* Teaching a Stone to Talk *(1982), a collection of essays;* An American Childhood *(1987), an account of her youth in Pittsburgh;* The Writing Life, *(1989), reflections on the process of writing; and* The Living, *(1992), a novel. In this essay, Dillard applies her powers of description and introspection to her life alone, to a spider, and to a transfigured moth.*

Transfiguration in a Candle Flame

1   I live alone with two cats, who sleep on my legs. There is a yellow one, and a black one whose name is Small. In the morning I joke

to the black one, Do you remember last night? Do you remember? I throw them both out before breakfast, so I can eat.

There is a spider, too, in the bathroom, of uncertain lineage, bulbous at the abdomen and drab, whose six-inch mess of web works, works somehow, works miraculously, to keep her alive and me amazed. The web is in a corner behind the toilet, connecting tile wall to tile wall. The house is new, the bathroom immaculate, save for the spider, her web, and the sixteen or so corpses she's tossed to the floor.

The corpses appear to be mostly sow bugs, those little armadillo creatures who live to travel flat out in houses, and die round. In addition to sow-bug husks, hollow and sipped empty of color, there are what seem to be two or three wingless moth bodies, one new flake of earwig, and three spider carcasses crinkled and clenched.

I wonder on what fool's errand an earwig, or a moth, or a sow bug, would visit that clean corner of the house behind the toilet; I have not noticed any blind parades of sow bugs blundering into corners. Yet they do hazard there, at a rate of more than one a week, and the spider thrives. Yesterday she was working on the earwig, mouth on gut; today he's on the floor. It must take a certain genius to throw things away from there, to find a straight line through that sticky tangle to the floor.

Today the earwig shines darkly, and gleams, what there is of him: a dorsal curve of thorax and abdomen, and a smooth pair of pincers by which I knew his name. Next week, if the other bodies are any indication, he'll be shrunk and gray, webbed to the floor with dust. The sow bugs beside him are curled and empty, fragile, a breath away from brittle fluff. The spiders lie on their sides, translucent and ragged, their legs drying in knots. The moths stagger against each other, headless, in a confusion of arcing strips of chitin like peeling varnish, like a jumble of buttresses for cathedral vaults, like nothing resembling moths, so that I would hesitate to call them moths, except that I have had some experience with the figure Moth reduced to a nub.

Two summers ago I was camped alone in the Blue Ridge Mountains of Virginia. I had hauled myself and gear up there to read, among other things, *The Day on Fire*, by James Ullman, a novel about Rimbaud that had made me want to be a writer when I was sixteen; I was hoping it would do it again. So I read every day sitting under a tree by my tent, while warblers sang in the leaves overhead and bristle worms trailed their inches over the twiggy dirt at my feet; and I read every night by candlelight, while barred owls called in the forest and pale moths seeking mates massed round my head in the clearing, where my light made a ring.

Moths kept flying into the candle. They would hiss and recoil, reeling upside down in the shadows among my cooking pans. Or they would singe their wings and fall, and their hot wings, as if melted, would stick to the first thing they touched—a pan, a lid, a spoon—so that the snagged moths could struggle only in tiny arcs, unable to flutter free. These I could release by a quick flip with a stick; in the morning I would find my cooking stuff decorated with torn flecks of moth wings, ghostly triangles of shiny dust here and there on the aluminum. So I read, and boiled water, and replenished candles, and read on.

One night a moth flew into the candle, was caught, burnt dry, and held. I must have been staring at the candle, or maybe I looked up where a shadow crossed my page; at any rate, I saw it all. A golden female moth, a biggish one with a two-inch wingspread, flapped into the fire, dropped abdomen into the wet wax, stuck, flamed, and frazzled in a second. Her moving wings ignited like tissue paper, like angels' wings, enlarging the circle of light in the clearing and creating out of the darkness the sudden blue sleeves of my sweater, the green leaves of jewelweed by my side, the ragged red trunk of a pine; at once the light contracted again and the moth's wings vanished in a fine, foul smoke. At the same time, her six legs clawed, curled, blackened, and ceased, disappearing utterly. And her head jerked in spasms, making a spattering noise; her antennae crisped and burnt away and her heaving mouthparts cracked like pistol fire. When it was all over, her head was, so far as I could determine, gone, gone the long way of her wings and legs. Her head was a hole lost to time. All that was left was the glowing horn shell of her abdomen and thorax—a fraying, partially collapsed gold tube jammed upright in the candle's round pool.

And then this moth-essence, this spectacular skeleton, began to act as a wick. She kept burning. The wax rose in the moth's body from her soaking abdomen to her thorax to the shattered hole where her head should have been, and widened into flame, a saffron-yellow flame that robed her to the ground like an immolating monk. That candle had two wicks, two winding flames of identical light, side by side. The moth's head was fire. She burned for two hours, until I blew her out.

10   She burned for two hours without changing, without swaying or   10 kneeling—only glowing within, like a building fire glimpsed through silhouetted walls, like a hollow saint, like a flame-faced virgin gone to

God, while I read by her light, kindled, while Rimbaud in Paris burnt out his brain in a thousand poems, while night pooled wetly at my feet.

So. That is why I think those hollow shreds on the bathroom floor are moths. I believe I know what moths look like, in any state.

I have three candles here on the table which I disentangle from the plants and light when visitors come. The cats avoid them, although Small's tail caught fire once; I rubbed it out before she noticed. I don't mind living alone. I like eating alone and reading. I don't mind sleeping alone. The only time I mind being alone is when something is funny; then, when I am laughing at something funny, I wish someone were around. Sometimes I think it is pretty funny that I sleep alone.

So This Was Adolescence

Annie Dillard

Annie Dillard (1945–) was born in Pittsburgh, Pennsylvania. She received a B.A. (1967) and an M.A. (1968) from Hollins College and then embarked on a career as a writer and teacher. Dillard has worked as a columnist for The Living Wilderness *and a contributing editor for* Harper's *and has taught at Western Washington University and Wesleyan University in Connecticut. Fascinated with the intricacies of the natural world and blessed with an introspective, poetic mind, Dillard has earned a reputation for insightful descriptions of the relationships between humans and nature, physically and spiritually. She has been compared to Henry David Thoreau, and her work has been compared to his* Walden. *An accomplished writer, Dillard has published non-fiction, poetry, literary criticism, essays, autobiographies, and a novel. Her published work includes* Pilgrim at Tinker Creek *(1974), observations about nature for which she received a Pulitzer Prize;* Tickets for a Prayer Wheel *(1974), a volume of poetry;* Living By Fiction *(1982), a collection of literary criticism;* Teaching a Stone to Talk *(1982), a collection of essays;* An American Childhood *(1987), an account of her youth in Pittsburgh;* The Writing Life *(1983), reflections on the process of writing; and* The Living *(1992), a novel. This essay, taken from* An American Childhood, *is a lively and passionate description of Dillard's sensations of adolescence.*

1 **W**hen I was fifteen, I felt it coming; now I was sixteen, 1
and it hit.

My feet had imperceptibly been set on a new path, a fast path into a long tunnel like those many turnpike tunnels near Pittsburgh, turnpike tunnels whose entrances bear on brass plaques a roll call of those men who died blasting them. I wandered witlessly forward and found myself going down, and saw the light dimming; I adjusted to the slant and dimness, traveled further down, adjusted to greater dimness, and so on. There wasn't a whole lot I could do about it, or about anything. I was going to hell on a handcart, that was all, and I knew it and everyone around me knew it, and there it was.

I was growing and thinning, as if pulled. I was getting angry, as if pushed. I morally disapproved most things in North America, and blamed my innocent parents for them. My feelings deepened and lingered. The swift moods of early childhood—each formed by and suited to its occasion—vanished. Now feelings lasted so long they left stains. They arose from nowhere, like winds or waves, and battered at me or engulfed me.

When I was angry, I felt myself coiled and longing to kill someone or bomb something big. Trying to appease myself, during one winter I whipped my bed every afternoon with my uniform belt. I despised the spectacle I made in my own eyes—whipping the bed with a belt, like a creature demented!—and I often began halfheartedly, but I did it daily after school as a desperate discipline, trying to rid myself and the innocent world of my wildness. It was like trying to beat back the ocean.

5 Sometimes in class I couldn't stop laughing; things were too funny 5
to be borne. It began then, my surprise that no one else saw what was so funny.

I read some few books with such reverence I didn't close them at the finish, but only moved the pile of pages back to the start, without breathing, and began again. I read one such book, an enormous novel, six times that way—closing the binding between sessions, but not between readings.

On the piano in the basement I played the maniacal "Poet and Peasant Overture" so loudly, for so many hours, night after night, I damaged the piano's keys and strings. When I wasn't playing this crashing overture, I played boogie-woogie, or something else, anything else, in octaves—otherwise, it wasn't loud enough. My fingers were so strong I could do push-ups with them. I played one piece with my

fists. I banged on a steel-stringed guitar till I bled, and once on a particularly piercing rock-and-roll downbeat I broke straight through one
of Father's snare drums.

I loved my boyfriend so tenderly, I thought I must transmogrify
into vapor. It would take spectroscopic analysis to locate my molecules
in thin air. No possible way of holding him was close enough. Nothing could cure this bad case of gentleness except, perhaps, violence:
maybe if he swung me by the legs and split my skull on a tree? Would
that ease this insane wish to kiss too much his eyelids' outer corners
and his temples, as if I could love up his brain?

I envied people in books who swooned. For two years I felt myself continuously swooning and continuously unable to swoon; the
blood drained from my face and eyes and flooded my heart; my hands
emptied, my knees unstrung, I bit at the air for something worth
breathing—but I failed to fall, and I couldn't find the way to black
out. I had to live on the lip of a waterfall, exhausted.

10   When I was bored I was first hungry, then nauseated, then furious   10
and weak. "Calm yourself," people had been saying to me all my life.
Since early childhood I had tried one thing and then another to calm
myself, on those few occasions when I truly wanted to. Eating helped;
singing helped. Now sometimes I truly wanted to calm myself. I couldn't
lower my shoulders; they seemed to wrap around my ears. I couldn't
lower my voice although I could see the people around me flinch. I
waved my arm in class till the very teachers wanted to kill me.

I was what they called a live wire. I was shooting out sparks that
were digging a pit around me, and I was sinking into that pit. Laughing with Ellin at school recess, or driving around after school with
Judy in her jeep, exultant, or dancing with my boyfriend to Louis
Armstrong across a polished diningroom floor, I got so excited I
looked around wildly for aid; I didn't know where I should go or what
I should do with myself. People in books split wood.

When rage or boredom reappeared, each seemed never to have
left. Each so filled me with so many years' intolerable accumulation it
jammed the space behind my eyes, so I couldn't see. There was no
room left even on my surface to live. My rib cage was so taut I couldn't
breathe. Every cubic centimeter of atmosphere above my shoulders and
head was heaped with last straws. Black hatred clogged my very blood.
I couldn't peep, I couldn't wiggle or blink; my blood was too mad to flow.

For as long as I could remember, I had been transparent to myself, unselfconscious, learning, doing, most of every day. Now I was in

my own way; I myself was a dark object I could not ignore. I couldn't remember how to forget myself. I didn't want to think about myself, to reckon myself in, to deal with myself every livelong minute on top of everything else—but swerve as I might, I couldn't avoid it. I was a boulder blocking my own path. I was a dog barking between my own ears, a barking dog who wouldn't hush.

So this was adolescence. Is this how the people around me had died on their feet—inevitably, helplessly? Perhaps their own selves eclipsed the sun for so many years the world shriveled around them, and when at last their inescapable orbits had passed through these dark egoistic years it was too late, they had adjusted.

15   Must I then lose the world forever, that I had so loved? Was it all, 15 the whole bright and various planet, where I had been so ardent about finding myself alive, only a passion peculiar to children, that I would outgrow even against my will?

The Brown Wasps

Loren Eiseley

*Loren Eiseley (1907–1977) was born in Lincoln, Ne-
braska. A noted anthropologist, educator, poet, and author,
Eiseley was lauded for his beautiful prose and his ability to
make science interesting and entertaining to lay readers.
Eiseley taught at the University of Kansas at Lawrence,
Oberlin College, and the University of Pennsylvania. His
books include* The Immense Journey *(1957),* Darwin's
Century *(1958),* The Firmament of Time *(rev.
ed. 1960), and* Night Country *(1971). In this essay, Eiseley notes the ability of humans as well as other animals to
hold an image in the mind—the homing instinct—despite
the proof of reality.*

1   There is a corner in the waiting room of one of the great Eastern stations where women never sit. It is always in the shadow
and overhung by rows of lockers. It is, however, always
frequented—not so much by genuine travelers as by the dying. It is
here that a certain element of the abandoned poor seeks a refuge out
of the weather, clinging for a few hours longer to the city that has fa-
thered them. In a precisely similar manner I have seen, on a sunny day
in midwinter, a few old brown wasps creep slowly over an abandoned
wasp nest in a thicket. Numbed and forgetful and frost-blackened, the
hum of the spring hive still resounded faintly in their sodden tissues.
Then the temperature would fall and they would drop away into the
white oblivion of the snow. Here in the station it is in no way different save that the city is busy in its snows. But the old ones cling to
their seats as though these were symbolic and could not be given up.
Now and then they sleep, their gray old heads resting with painful
awkwardness on the backs of the benches.

Also they are not at rest. For an hour they may sleep in the gasping exhaustion of the ill-nourished and aged who have to walk in the night. Then a policeman comes by on his round and nudges them upright.

"You can't sleep here," he growls.

A strange ritual then begins. An old man is difficult to waken. After a muttered conversation the policeman presses a coin into his hand and passes fiercely along the benches prodding and gesturing toward the door. In his wake, like birds rising and settling behind the passage of a farmer through a cornfield, the men totter up, move a few paces and subside once more upon the benches.

One man, after a slight, apologetic lurch, does not move at all. Tubercularly thin, he sleeps on steadily. The policeman does not look back. To him, too, this has become a ritual. He will not have to notice it again officially for another hour.

Once in a while one of the sleepers will not awake. Like the brown wasps, he will have had his wish to die in the great droning center of the hive rather than in some lonely room. It is not so bad here with the shuffle of footsteps and the knowledge that there are others who share the bad luck of the world. There are also the whistles and the sounds of everyone, everyone in the world, starting on journeys. Amidst so many journeys somebody is bound to come out all right. Somebody.

Maybe it was on a like thought that the brown wasps fell away from the old paper nest in the thicket. You hold till the last, even if it is only to a public seat in a railroad station. You want your place in the hive more than you want a room or a place where the aged can be eased gently out of the way. It is the place that matters, the place at the heart of things. It is life that you want, that bruises your gray old head with the hard chairs; a man has a right to his place.

But sometimes the place is lost in the years behind us. Or sometimes it is a thing of air, a kind of vaporous distortion above a heap of rubble. We cling to a time and place because without them man is lost, not only man but life. This is why the voices, real or unreal, which speak from the floating trumpets at spiritualist seances are so unnerving. They are voices out of nowhere whose only reality lies in their ability to stir the memory of a living person with some fragment of the past. Before the medium's cabinet both the dead and the living revolve endlessly about an episode, a place, an event that has already been engulfed by time.

This feeling runs deep in life; it brings stray cats running over endless miles, and birds homing from the ends of the earth. It is as though all living creatures, and particularly the more intelligent, can survive only by fixing or transforming a bit of time into space or by securing a bit of space with its objects immortalized and made permanent in time. For example, I once saw, on a flower pot in my own living room, the efforts of a field mouse to build a remembered field. I have lived to see this episode repeated in a thousand guises, and since I have spent a large portion of my life in the shade of a nonexistent tree, I think I am entitled to speak for the field mouse.

One day as I cut across the field which at the time extended on one side of our suburban shopping center, I found a giant slug feeding from a runnel of pink ice cream in an abandoned Dixie cup. I could see his eyes telescope and protrude in a kind of dim, uncertain ecstasy as his dark body bunched and elongated in the curve of the cup. Then, as I stood there at the edge of the concrete, contemplating the slug, I began to realize it was like standing on a shore where a different type of life creeps up and fumbles tentatively among the rocks and sea wrack. It knows its place and will only creep so far until something changes. Little by little as I stood there I began to see more of this shore that surrounds the place of man. I looked with sudden care and attention at things I had been running over thoughtlessly for years. I even waded out a short way into the grass and the wild-rose thickets to see more. A huge black-belted bee went droning by and there were some indistinct scurrying in the underbrush.

Then I came to a sign which informed me that this field was to be the site of a new Wanamaker suburban store. Thousands of obscure lives were about to perish, the spores of puffballs would go smoking off to new fields, and the bodies of little white-footed mice would be crunched under the inexorable wheels of the bulldozers. Life disappears or modifies its appearances so fast that everything takes on an aspect of illusion—a momentary fizzing and boiling with smoke rings, like pouring dissident chemicals into a retort. Here man was advancing, but in a few years his plaster and bricks would be disappearing once more into the insatiable maw of the clover. Being of an archaeological cast of mind, I thought of this fact with an obscure sense of satisfaction and waded back through the rose thickets to the concrete parking lot. As I did so, a mouse scurried ahead of me, frightened of my steps if not of that ominous Wanamaker sign. I saw him vanish in the general direction of my apartment house, his little body quivering with fear in the great open sun on the blazing concrete. Blinded and confused, he was running straight away from his field. In another week scores would follow him.

I forgot the episode then and went home to the quiet of my living room. It was not until a week later, letting myself into the apartment, that I realized I had a visitor. I am fond of plants and had several ferns standing on the floor in pots to avoid the noon glare by the south window.

As I snapped on the light and glanced carelessly around the room, I saw a little heap of earth on the carpet and a scrabble of pebbles that had been kicked merrily over the edge of one of the flower pots. To my astonishment I discovered a full-fledged burrow delving downward among the fern roots. I waited silently. The creature who had made the burrow did not appear. I remembered the wild field then, and the flight of the mice. No house mouse, no *Mus domesticus*, had kicked up this little heap of earth or sought refuge under a fern root in a flower pot. I thought of the desperate little creature I had seen fleeing from the wild-rose thicket. Through intricacies of pipes and attics, he, or one of his fellows, had climbed to this high green solitary room. I could visualize what had occurred. He had an image in his head, a world of seed pods and quiet, of green sheltering leaves in the dim light among the weed stems. It was the only world he knew and it was gone.

Somehow in his flight he had found his way to this room with drawn shades where no one would come till nightfall. And here he had smelled garden leaves and run quickly up the flower pot to dabble his paws in common earth. He had even struggled half the afternoon to carry his burrow deeper and had failed. I examined the hole, but no whiskered twitching face appeared. He was gone. I gathered up the earth and refilled the burrow. I did not expect to find traces of him again.

15   Yet for three nights thereafter I came home to the darkened room 15
and my ferns to find the dirt kicked gaily about the rug and the burrow reopened, though I was never able to catch the field mouse within it. I dropped a little food about the mouth of the burrow, but it was never touched. I looked under beds or sat reading with one ear cocked for rustlings in the ferns. It was all in vain; I never saw him. Probably he ended in a trap in some other tenant's room.

But before he disappeared I had come to look hopefully for his evening burrow. About my ferns there had begun to linger the insubstantial vapor of an autumn field, the distilled essence, as it were, of a mouse brain in exile from its home. It was a small dream, like our dreams, carried a long and weary journey along pipes and through spider webs, past holes over which loomed the shadows of waiting cats, and finally, desperately, into this room where he had played in the shuttered daylight for an hour among the green ferns on the floor. Every day these invisible dreams pass us on the street, or rise from beneath our feet, or look out upon us from beneath a bush.

Some years ago the old elevated railway in Philadelphia was torn down and replaced by a subway system. This ancient El with its barnlike stations containing nut-vending machines and scattered food scraps had, for generations, been the favorite feeding ground of flocks of pigeons, generally one flock to a station along the route of the El. Hundreds of pigeons were dependent upon the system. They flapped in and out of its stanchions and steel work or gathered in watchful little audiences about the feet of anyone who rattled the peanut-vending machines. They even watched people who jingled change in their hands, and prospected for food under the feet of the crowds who gathered between trains. Probably very few among the waiting people who tossed a crumb to an eager pigeon realized that this El was like a food-bearing river, and that the life which haunted its banks was dependent upon the running of the trains with their human freight.

I saw the river stop.

The time came when the underground tubes were ready; the traffic was transferred to a realm unreachable by pigeons. It was like a great river subsiding suddenly into desert sands. For a day, for two days, pigeons continued to circle over the El or stand close to the red vending machines. They were patient birds, and surely this great river which had flowed through the lives of unnumbered generations were merely suffering from some momentary drought.

20   They listened for the familiar vibrations that had always heralded   20 an approaching train; they flapped hopefully about the head of an occasional workman walking along the steel runways. They passed from one empty station to another, all the while growing hungrier. Finally they flew away.

I thought I had seen the last of them about the El, but there was a revival and it provided a curious instance of the memory of living things for a way of life or a locality that has long been cherished. Some weeks after the El was abandoned workmen began to tear it down. I went to work every morning by one particular station, and the time came when the demolition crews reached this spot. Acetylene torches showered passersby with sparks, pneumatic drills hammered at the base of the structure, and a blind man who, like the pigeons, had clung with his cup to a stairway leading to the change booth, was forced to give up his place.

It was then, strangely, momentarily, one morning that I witnessed the return of a little band of the familiar pigeons. I even recognized one or two members of the flock that had lived around this particular station before they were dispersed into the streets. They flew bravely in and out among the sparks and the hammers and the shouting workmen. They had returned—and they had returned because the hubbub of the wreckers had convinced them that the river was about to flow once more. For several hours they flapped in and out through the empty windows, nodding their heads and watching the fall of girders with attentive little eyes. By the following morning the station was reduced to some burned-off stanchions in the street. My bird friends had gone. It was plain, however, that they retained a memory for an insubstantial structure now compounded of air and time. Even the blind man clung to it. Someone had provided him with a chair, and he sat at the same corner staring sightlessly at an invisible stairway where, so far as he was concerned, the crowds were still ascending to the trains.

I have said my life has been passed in the shade of a nonexistent tree, so that such sights do not offend me. Prematurely I am one of the brown wasps and I often sit with them in the great droning hive of the station, dreaming sometimes of a certain tree. It was planted sixty years ago by a boy with a bucket and a toy spade in a little Nebraska town. That boy was myself. It was a cottonwood sapling and the boy remembered it because of some words spoken by his father and because everyone died or moved away who was supposed to wait and grow old under its shade. The boy was passed from hand to hand, but the tree for some intangible reason had taken root in his mind. It was under its branches that he sheltered; it was from this tree that his memories, which are my memories, led away into the world.

After sixty years the mood of the brown wasps grows heavier upon one. During a long inward struggle I thought it would do me good to go and look upon that actual tree. I found a rational excuse in which to clothe this madness. I purchased a ticket and at the end of two thousand miles I walked another mile to an address that was still the same. The house had not been altered.

25   I came close to the white picket fence and reluctantly, with great 25 effort, looked down the long vista of the yard. There was nothing there to see. For sixty years that cottonwood had been growing in my mind. Season by season its seeds had been floating farther on the hot prairie winds. We had planted it lovingly there, my father and I, because he had a great hunger for soil and live things growing, and because none of these things had long been ours to protect. We had planted the little sapling and watered it faithfully, and I remembered that I had run out with my small bucket to drench its roots the day we moved away. And all the years since it had been growing in my mind, a huge tree that somehow stood for my father and the love I bore him. I took a grasp on the picket fence and forced myself to look again.

A boy with the hard bird eye of youth pedaled a tricycle slowly up beside me.

"What'cha lookin' at?" he asked curiously.

"A tree," I said.

"What for?" he said.

30   "It isn't there," I said, to myself mostly, and began to walk away 30 at a pace just slow enough not to seem to be running.

"What isn't there?" the boy asked. I didn't answer. It was obvious I was attached by a thread to a thing that had never been there, or certainly not for long. Something that had to be held in the air, or sustained in the mind, because it was part of my orientation in the universe and I could not survive without it. There was more than an animal's attachment to a place. There was something else, the attachment of the spirit to a grouping of events in time; it was part of our morality.

So I had come home at last, driven by a memory in the brain as surely as the field mouse who had delved long ago into my flower pot or the pigeons flying forever amidst the rattle of nut-vending machines. These, the burrow under the greenery in my living room and the red-bellied bowls of peanuts now hovering in midair in the minds of pigeons, were all part of an elusive world that existed nowhere and yet everywhere. I looked once at the real world about me while the persistent boy pedaled at my heels.

It was without meaning, though my feet took a remembered path. In sixty years the house and street had rotted out of my mind. But the tree, the tree that no longer was, that had perished in its first season, bloomed on in my individual mind, unblemished as my father's words. "We'll plant a tree here, son, and we're not going to move any more. And when you're an old, old man you can sit under it and think how we planted it here, you and me, together."

I began to outpace the boy on the tricycle.

35   "Do you live here, Mister?" he shouted after me suspiciously I 35 took a firm grasp on airy nothing—to be precise, on the bole of a great tree. "I do," I said. I spoke for myself, one field mouse, and several pigeons. We were all out of touch but somehow permanent. It was the world that had changed.

HIV Sufferers Have a Responsibility

Amitai Etzioni

Amitai Etzioni (1929–) was born in Cologne, Germany. Educated at Hebrew University in Jerusalem (B.A., 1954) and the University of California at Berkeley (M.A., 1956, and Ph.D., 1958), Etzioni has directed the Center for Policy Research at Columbia University and taught at George Washington University. Published widely, Etzioni has written for both scholarly and lay audiences. He also has edited a journal, Responsive Community. *His books include* The Spirit of Community: Rights, Responsibilities, and the Communitarian Agenda *(1993). In this essay, which appeared in* Newsweek *in 1993, Etzioni argues that HIV sufferers must disclose their illness for the good of society, regardless of the personal consequences.*

1   A major drive to find a cure for AIDS was announced last week by Donna Shalala, President Clinton's Secretary of Health and Human Services. Researchers from the private sector, gay activists and government officials were teamed up to accelerate the search for an effective treatment. Yet even highly optimistic observers do not expect a cure to be found before the end of this century. Still, as the Shalala announcement's exclusive focus on cure highlights, it is not acceptable to explore publicly the measures that could curb the spread of the disease by slowing the transmission of HIV, the virus that causes it. Indeed, before you can say What about prevention? the politically correct choir chimes in: You cannot call it a plague! You are feeding the fires of homophobia! Gay basher!

Case in point: a panel of seven experts fielded questions from 4,000 personnel managers at a conference in Las Vegas. "Suppose you work for medical records. You find out that Joe Doe, who is driving the company's 18-wheeler, is back on the bottle. Will you violate confidentiality and inform his supervisor?" The panel stated unanimously, "I'll find a way." Next question: "Joe Smith is HIV positive; he is intimate with the top designer of the company but did not tell; will *you?*" "No way," the panel agreed in unison.

We need to break the silence. It is not antigay but fully compassionate to argue that a massive prevention drive is a viable way to save numerous lives in the very next years. We must lay a moral claim on those who are likely to be afflicted with HIV (gays, drug addicts who exchange needles and anyone who received a blood transfusion before 1985) and urge them as a social obligation to come forward to be tested. If the test is positive, they should inform their previous sexual contacts and warn all potential new ones. The principle is elementary, albeit openly put: the more responsibly HIV sufferers act, the fewer dead they will leave in their trail.

HIV testing and contact tracing amount to "a cruel hoax," claims a gay representative from the West Coast. "There are not enough beds to take care of known AIDS patients. Why identify more?" Actually, testing is cruel only in a world where captains of sinking ships do not warn passengers because the captains cannot get off. We must marshal the moral courage to tell those infected with HIV: It is truly tragic that currently we have no way to save your life, but surely you recognize your duty to try to help save the lives of others.

5   "Warning others is unnecessary because everybody should act safely all the time anyhow," argues Rob Teir, a gay activist in Washington. But human nature is such, strong data show, that most people cannot bring themselves to act safely all the time. A fair warning that they are about to enter a highly dangerous situation may spur people to take special precautions. The moral duty of those already afflicted, though, must be clearly articulated: being intimate without prior disclosure is like serving arsenic in a cake. And not informing previous contacts (or not helping public authorities trace them without disclosing your name) leaves the victims, unwittingly, to transmit the fatal disease to uncounted others.

Testing and contact tracing may lead to a person's being deprived of a job, health insurance, housing and privacy, many civil libertarians fear. These are valid and grave concerns. But we can find ways to protect civil rights without sacrificing public health. A major AIDS-prevention campaign ought to be accompanied by intensive public education about the ways the illness is not transmitted, by additional safeguards on data banks and by greater penalties for those who abuse HIV victims. It may be harsh to say, but the fact that an individual may suffer as a result of doing what is right does not make doing so less of an imperative. Note also that while society suffers a tremendous loss of talent and youth and is stuck with a gargantuan bill, the first victims of nondisclosure are the loved ones of those already afflicted with HIV, even—in the case of infected women—their children.

"Not cost effective," intone the bean counters. Let's count. Take, for example, a suggestion by the highly regarded Centers for Disease Control and Prevention that hospitals be required to ask patients whose blood is already being tested whether they would consent to having it tested for HIV as well. The test costs $60 or less and routinely identifies many who were unaware they had the virus. If those who are thus identified were to transmit the disease to only one less person on average, the suggested tests would pay for themselves much more readily than a coronary bypass, PSA tests and half the pills we pop. And society could continue to enjoy the lifelong earnings and social contributions of those whose lives would be saved.

There are other excuses and rationalizations. But it is time for some plain talk: if AIDS were any other disease—say, hepatitis B or tuberculosis—we would have no trouble (and indeed we have had none) introducing the necessary preventive measures. Moreover, we should make it clear that doing all you can to prevent the spread of AIDS or any other fatal disease is part and parcel of an unambiguous commandment: Thou shalt not kill.

It's a Girl

Kathleen Fackelmann

> *Kathleen Fackelmann writes regularly for the weekly mag-*
> *azine* Science News *and is a health and behavior reporter*
> *for* USA Today. *She investigates groups of related research*
> *studies and writes essays on a variety of topics; issues she has*
> *reported on include genetics, diet and nutrition, medical*
> *discoveries, and disease. In this November 1998 article,*
> *Fackelmann reports on recent research that has effectively*
> *pre-determined the female sex of babies and discusses the*
> *ethics of such research.*

1   Some parents-to-be hope for a girl. Some wish for a boy. The outcome, however, has always been pretty much a matter of
chance.

Researchers at the Genetics & IVF Institute in Fairfax, Va., recently announced a technique that helps stack the odds in favor of
parents getting what they want. Using a mechanical sperm sorter, the
Fairfax team reported that nearly 93 percent of the babies born were
of the desired sex.

All the couples in this study wanted girls. However, the technique
also can easily help those who desire a boy. Will such technology lead
to a United States overpopulated by one sex? Most ethicists don't think
that will happen any time soon. Nonetheless, the new technology
raises some concerns about the future, they say.

Before getting to the ethical debate about sex selection, consider
the research itself. Reproductive biologist Edward F. Fugger and his
colleagues at the Genetics & IVF Institute began their study by
recruiting 119 couples who wanted a baby girl. In most cases, the

"It's a Girl," by Kathleen Fackelmann published in *Science News*, Volume 154,
November 28, 1998.

couples already had a boy or boys, and they wanted a girl for variety—
to balance their family, as the scientists say. In a few cases, couples
faced the risk of giving birth to a child with a genetic disorder that
strikes boys only.

5   The patented sperm sorter used by Fugger and his team helps par-   5
ents pick out the child's gender before fertilization of the egg. The
technology, developed during animal studies by Lawrence A. Johnson
of the U.S. Department of Agriculture in Beltsville, Md., exploits the
difference in amounts of DNA in X and Y chromosomes. Sperm bearing the X, or female, chromosome have more DNA than sperm carrying the Y, or male, chromosome.

An embryo resulting from the merger of an egg, which always carries an X chromosome, and a sperm carrying an X chromosome will
have two Xs and, therefore, develop into a girl. An egg fertilized by a
sperm carrying a Y chromosome becomes a boy.

In the September issue of HUMAN REPRODUCTION, Fugger and
his colleagues describe their use of the method. Each couple provided
a sperm sample, which the researchers treated with a dye that attaches
to DNA and glows under laser light. The team then exposed the
tagged sperm to a laser beam.

The researchers reasoned that the X-carrying sperm would glow
the brightest under the laser light. Sure enough, even though sperm
carrying an X chromosome—and 22 other chromosomes—contain
only 2.8 percent more DNA than those bearing a Y, the sorter separated the bright sperm from the dim sperm. It then directed most of
those bearing X chromosomes to swim down one collection tube, and
most of the Y-bearing sperm went down another tube.

When the researchers analyzed the sperm in the X collection tube,
they found that 85 percent had the X chromosome, as desired. The
researchers thus estimate that samples from the X collection tubes are
five to six times as likely to result in a girl baby than in a boy.

10   In 92 cases, the researchers inserted the sorted sperm directly into   10
the woman's uterus, a procedure called intrauterine insemination. In
this version of artificial insemination, the sperm must latch onto and
fertilize an egg in the woman's body for pregnancy to occur.

Some of the couples required more complex—and expensive—
techniques to achieve pregnancy. In 27 cases, the researchers united
sperm and egg in a laboratory dish and then transferred the resulting
embryos to the woman's uterus.

Out of 119 women, 29 got pregnant using the sorted sperm. In 8 women, the pregnancy ended in miscarriage or surgery, the latter because of a dangerous condition in which the fertilized egg starts to grow in a fallopian tube above the uterus. At the time the Fairfax researchers published their journal article, 12 women had ongoing pregnancies and 9 women had already delivered 11 babies, including two sets of twins. As of mid-November, Fugger and his colleagues had not released updated results.

Of the 14 pregnancies in which the gender of the child had been determined, 13 were girls, the researchers say.

Fugger and his team are also conducting a study with parents who want boys. In such cases, the sperm sorter is less effective at concentrating Y-bearing sperm. Still, the method yields a sperm sample in which 65 percent carry the Y chromosome, Fugger says. The team has not announced any results of that study yet.

15   The researchers identified no safety concerns in the published   15
study. "All of the babies born have been healthy," Fugger says. "That doesn't mean that all of the risk has been excluded," he says. "There's a lot that's not known."

The study raised more concerns than just the usual fear about side effects. For some people, a technology that could pick out the sex of a baby raises the specter of China's overabundance of baby boys.

Many Chinese couples opt for an abortion of a female fetus if they lose the natural-reproduction lottery by not conceiving a boy, notes ethicist R. Alta Charo of the University of Wisconsin-Madison. As a result, China has experienced some significant demographic shifts, Charo notes.

Most people in the United States recoil at the thought of a society so geared toward male offspring that abortion—and even infanticide—is the fate of some baby girls. Indeed, Arthur Caplan of the University of Pennsylvania's Center for Bioethics says most U.S. couples have only a moderate preference for a child of a given sex. If they lose the reproduction lottery for the gender they desire, they rarely opt for an abortion, he says.

Furthermore, Caplan says that only a small subset of the U.S. population would try to ensure their baby's gender with this expensive, difficult technique. Charo agrees, noting that a man must first produce a sperm sample for the doctor. Then, his partner must submit to artificial insemination or other techniques performed in a doctor's office or clinic.

20   Of course, Charo notes, for couples who can have children no other way, the difficulties of such high-tech reproductive methods are a small price to pay for a successful pregnancy. But for couples whose only concern is the gender of their baby, the rigmarole might very well put them off.

Caplan argues that sex selection to balance a family is ethically acceptable but that it won't be popular enough in the United States to change Mother Nature's gender sorting.

He wonders whether the preference for a boy or a girl stems from inherently sexist attitudes. Does a U.S. parent's desire for a boy or a girl mean that one sex is viewed as inferior to the other? "Sex selection doesn't bother us—sexism does," Caplan says.

Sex ratios and sexism aside, some ethicists worry about a culture where parents are driven to pick out any of the traits of their unborn children. "There's a notion now that parenting is a kind of consumer experience," says Barbara Katz Rothman, a sociologist at the City University of New York.

Rothman, for example, worries about parents who choose a sex because they are seeking to fill stereotypical, perhaps unrealistic roles. For example, a woman who hopes for a girl may say she wants to shop for a prom gown or go for manicures with a daughter. "You listen to this woman and think, 'This woman is not prepared for a 300-pound, 6-foot girl who wears denim and boots,'" Rothman says.

25   The trend toward more parental control over a child's characteristics will increase in the future, warns biomedical ethicist Thomas H. Murray, the director of the Center for Biomedical Ethics at Case Western Reserve University in Cleveland. Murray notes that scientists working on the human genome project soon will have methods of identifying disease-causing genes as well as the DNA that produces characteristics such as hair color, height, athletic ability, and perhaps some behaviors.

Most ethicists see no problem with parents trying to avoid a genetic disease in their offspring, but Murray and others say that parents should leave the selection of nondisease traits to fate.

"As consumers, we think, 'The more choice the better,'" he says. But even rudimentary attempts to pick one trait from column A and one from column B might encourage the belief that parents can design the perfect baby, Murray says. Substantially increased parental control over their tyke's personality may change the dynamics of the parent-child relationship, he adds.

Charo says that selecting a child's sex is a far cry from designing a baby. Indeed, while parents can now pay for sorting X- and Y-carrying sperm, the technology hasn't been invented that could guarantee a red-haired cellist with a genius-level IQ.

She adds that sex-selection techniques may be useful to limit the size of all-girl families where the parents might otherwise continue having babies until they get a son or of all-boy families intent on having a girl. "This technology would let couples up the odds that their next kid will be the last kid," Charo says.

30   Caplan and Charo both propose that regulation of the technol- 30 ogy is not necessary. "The presumption in the United States is that you let people do what they want unless there is a very god reason to stop them," Charo says. "In the United States today, the harm [of sex selection] is not that great."

Although lawmakers may never regulate sex-selection methods, Murray contends that genetic counselors should begin developing guidelines to steer couples away from the designer-baby concept. The harm to society from attempts to select human characteristics may be subtle, he says. For example, how will parents who think that they have designed a child act toward that offspring when a wrong trait shows up?

Rothman says that even with all the human reproductive genetic advances, one thing should remain the same: "When you parent, you get what you get."

McBastards: McDonald's and Globalization

Paul Feine

Paul Feine is associated with the Centre for Civil Society and is a program director at aWorldConnected.org. This essay takes a friendly and casual look at the much-criticized McDonald's empire. Feine describes the trials of traveling in Paris with a small child who will not eat French food and who also annoys the French when he appears in their presence. In such circumstances, nothing is as good as a McDonald's french fry, or pommes frites as the French would say, for keeping a child quiet and happy. The American traveler sighs with relief at the sight of those arches and a hot Quarter-Pounder.

1   On a recent trip to Paris with my family, I was standing inside a McDonald's restaurant gazing out at the street as my wife ordered Le Happy Meal for our two-year old. My son at the time was happily tugging away at my hair from his perch in his baby backpack (one of the most significant technological innovations in recent history, to my mind).

We hadn't traveled to Paris with the intention of eating at McDonald's, but we were looking for a quick fix for our hungry little boy, and McDonald's represented a cheap alternative to the more traditional cafés. Typical Paris cafés are not only far more expensive, but as previous experience made clear, they tend to be filled with Parisians who are less than charmed by the presence of toddlers.

As I pondered the differing cultural attitudes toward children and stared out onto the busy Paris street, my gaze rested on an elderly French man, whom I instantly categorized as quintessentially French, complete

Reprinted from *www.aworldconnected.org*, by permission of the author.

with black beret, long black trench coat, and a cane. The man hobbled by the entrance to McDonald's, stopped, turned to look inside, spat loudly, and sneered "bastards," or its rough equivalent in French.

I sipped my coffee, which was very good (Café Jacques Vabre, I learned later), while our son used his pommes frites as a ketchup delivery device and my wife drank from a bottle of Evian. We both chuckled as I shared with her the image of the authentic anti-McDonald's activist I had just witnessed.

McWhipping Boy

As the symbol for cultural imperialism and multinational corporate greed, McDonald's takes a lot of heat. *McSpotlight*, the anti-McDonald's website, for instance, boasts over one million hits per month. Critics demonize McDonald's for its unabashed pursuit of profits, its disregard for nutritional value and the environment, and the way it panders to children.

Most recently, McDonald's has been condemned for systematically seeking to addict naïve youngsters to its fatty fare, just like its evil older brothers in the cigarette business. In fact, crusading public interest lawyer John Banzhaf (whose van sports a license plate with a shortened version of "sue the bastards") is *suing McDonald's* in an attempt to hold them responsible for fast food addicts' health problems.

Indeed, though this multinational giant controls 43% of the US fast food market, the avarice of McDonald's seems to have no bounds. As Nick Gillespie of *Reason* magazine points out, "McDonald's is so desperate for customers that it's held prices essentially constant over the past two decades, while boosting portion sizes (burgers, fries, and drinks are all bigger than they used to be), expanding its menu, and building elaborate play structures for kids while simultaneously throwing increasingly sophisticated toys at them."

As anyone with small children knows, safe and secure McDonald's Playlands can be a dream come true, especially when you're stuck inside on a rainy day with kids who desperately need to burn some energy. Tiny plastic toys are received with as much delight as any large plastic toy they might have received last Christmas and, it must be emphasized, they're free.

Maybe, just maybe, McDonald's, in its unwavering pursuit of profits, has figured out the secret to succeeding in business—you've got to give the people what they want.

McCulture?

10 Okay, maybe McDonald's is fine for the U.S. Perhaps we're too value   10
conscious, gluttonous, and superficial to care that our landscapes are
littered with gleaming arches that have already polluted our bodies
and our minds. But surely the same cannot be said for other societies
around the world. Isn't it true that places that still have truly authentic dining experiences should be protected from the barbaric
McHordes that are clamoring at their gates?

Golden Arches East, a recent book edited by James Watson, seeks
to gain a better grasp on how McDonald's is affecting Asian culture.
The results of this inquiry are in many ways surprising. For instance,
one essay tells the story of an unintended and unanticipated consequence of McDonald's invasion of Hong Kong—the rest rooms in
the city became cleaner.

Before the first McDonald's opened up in the mid-1970s, restaurant restrooms in Hong Kong were notoriously dirty. Over time, the
cleanliness standards of McDonald's were replicated by other restaurants eager to out-compete the increasingly popular restaurant.

In Korea, McDonald's established the practice of lining up in an
orderly fashion to order food—the traditional custom, it seems, was
to mob the counter.

When the first McDonald's was opened in Moscow, it was necessary for an employee to stand outside the McDonald's with a blow
horn in order to explain to those in the queue that the smiling
employees were not laughing at them but, rather, were pleased to
serve them.

15 Moreover, and in contradistinction to the widespread assumption   15
that McDonald's is having an implacably homogenizing effect on
global culture, Golden Arches East is filled with examples of the pains
McDonald's takes to appeal to the unique local tastes and customs of
people around the world. My own experience with the decidedly
leisurely attitude of McDonald's employees in southern Spain further
attests to McDonald's ability to adapt to the local culture.

Is It True That No Two Countries with McDonald's Have Ever Gone to War?

Long before I'd enjoyed the Andalucian version of McDonald's, I
traveled to Belgrade, in what was then Yugoslavia, and I must admit

that I was ecstatic to see a sign for a recently opened McDonald's. I'd just spent a couple of months consuming nothing but souvlaki, salad, and Ouzo in Greece, and the very thought of a Quarter-Pounder and a Coke made my mouth water.

My traveling buddy and I proceeded to wait in line for more than an hour and, as I stood happily munching on a french fry that brought back sweet memories of childhood Sunday-after-church treats, I looked across a sea of dark haired Yugoslavians into the eyes of two beautiful, blonde, obviously American women (actually it turned out they were Canadian nurses, but who am I to complain?). Absurdly, we waved to each other and fought through the crowd to greet one other like dear old friends. The memory of that day in Belgrade still brings a smile to my face.

Although you often hear people say it, it's not quite true that no two countries with McDonald's have ever gone to war—both the U.S. and Serbia, for example, had McDonald's during the conflict between the two nations. But even if McDonald's isn't a kind of multinational for-profit god of peace, McDonald's does provide cheap food, decent coffee, and free entertainment for kids, not to mention a salad-in-a-cup for health-conscious parents.

Around the world, this increasingly popular symbol (like it or not) of America is encouraging healthy competition—competition that, in many cases, is leading to improved sanitation standards and civility. And sometimes, just sometimes, McDonald's even brings people together and creates a few smiles . . . just like its commercials say it does.

The bastards.

High School Students Fight Anti-Cheating Firm

Maria Glod

Maria Glod was born in 1971 in Wilkes-Barre, Pennsylvania. She graduated from Bucknell University in 1993. She has worked at the Washington Post *since 1997, and has been its Metro/Virginia desk writer since 2005, covering a broad range of education-related topics such as mandated tutoring, testing, enrollment, math, reading and writing, and many other issues. The following selection deals with students at a Virginia high school who are protesting the school's use of databases intended to deter plagiarism as well as expose instances of it. Enterprises such as Turnitin.com, the students assert, create an atmosphere of assumed guilt. Also, the students contend that having student essays in the database constitutes a violation of intellectual property rights.*

1   When McLean High School students write this year about Othello or immigration policy, their teachers won't be the only ones examining the papers. So will a California company that specializes in catching cheaters.

The for-profit service, Turnitin, checks student work against a database of more than 22 million papers written by students around the world and online sources and electronic archives of journals. Administrators at the Northern Virginia school said the service, which they will start using this week, is meant to deter plagiarism at a time the Internet makes it easy to copy someone else's words.

But some McLean High students are rebelling. Members of the new Committee for Students' Rights said they do not cheat or

Reprinted from *The Seattle Times*, September 24, 2006, by permission of The Washington Post Writers Group.

condone cheating. But they object to Turnitin's automatically adding their essays to the massive database, calling it an infringement of intellectual property rights. And they contend the school's action will tar students at one of Fairfax County's academic powerhouses.

"It irked a lot of people because there's an implication of assumed guilt," said Ben Donovan, 18, a senior who helped collect 1,190 student signatures on a petition against mandatory use of the service. "It's like if you searched every car in the parking lot or drug-tested every student."

5   Questions about the legality and effectiveness of plagiarism-   5
detection services such as Turnitin are being asked beyond McLean High, another sign of the challenge educators face as they navigate benefits and problems the Internet has brought.

School and Turnitin officials said lawyers for the company and various universities have concluded the paper-checking system does not violate student rights. Many educators agree. Turnitin, a leader in the field, lists Georgetown University and the University of Maryland's University College among its clients.

But three professors at Grand Valley State University in Michigan this month posted a letter online arguing that Turnitin "makes questionable use of student intellectual property."

The University of Kansas recently decided to let its contract with Turnitin expire because of cost and intellectual-property concerns. The intellectual-property caucus of the Conference on College Composition and Communication, an organization of 6,000 college-level educators, is debating whether such services "undermine students' authority over the uses of their own writing" and make them feel "guilty until proven innocent," according to a draft position statement.

"There's a lot of debate out there," said Rebecca Ingalls, a University of Tampa English professor who has analyzed Turnitin.

10   "These students are giving their work to a company that's making   10
money and they are getting no compensation."

Kimberly Carney, an assistant principal at McLean High, said there have been isolated cases of plagiarism at the 1,770-student school. The main reason administrators will use Turnitin is to teach students how to give proper credit to sources, Carney said.

The Fairfax County system began using Turnitin in 2003. More than three-fourths of the county's high schools use the service.

The Center for Academic Integrity, affiliated with Duke University's Kenan Institute for Ethics, surveyed 18,000 public and private high-school students over four years and found that more than 60 percent admitted to some form of plagiarism, according to a 2005 report.

Turnitin charges about 80 cents a student a year, according to a company official. Fairfax County paid between $24,000 and $30,000 in the last school year for the service, school-system officials said.

15   Founder John Barrie said Turnitin evolved out of a Web site he created to facilitate peer review when he was a graduate student at the University of California, Berkeley. When fellow students complained about cheating classmates, Barrie helped develop a system to catch them. Turnitin's parent company, iParadigms, opened 10 years ago.

The service has grown dramatically, Barrie said, and is used by more than 6,000 academic institutions in 90 countries. He said 60,000 student assignments are added to the database daily. He said no student has ever pursued a legal challenge.

Members of the Committee for Students' Rights want the school to allow students to opt out. They said they can learn about plagiarism directly from teachers and there are other ways to catch cheaters.

They also said fees paid to Turnitin would be better spent on other educational matters.

The Company Man

Ellen Goodman

*Ellen Goodman (1941–), was born in Newton, Massa-
chusetts. A graduate of Radcliffe College (1963), Goodman
worked for* Newsweek *and* The Detroit Free Press *before
joining* The Boston Globe *in 1967. In addition to writing a regular column for the* Globe, "At Large," *which has
been syndicated since 1976, Goodman also is a frequent
radio and television commentator. The recipient of a
Pulitzer Prize for distinguished commentary in 1980,
Goodman has published a number of collections of her
columns—including* Close to Home *(1979) and* At Large
*(1981)—as well as an interview-based review of the im-
pact of the feminist movement—* Making Sense *(1989).
Goodman's essays, which often probe very personal aspects of
late 20th century America, are generally a blend of irony
and satire. Note how Goodman uses her skills of observation and description to quickly dispatch the workaholic
company man in this classic Goodman-style essay.*

1   He worked himself to death, finally and precisely, at 3:00 A.M.   1
Sunday morning.
The obituary didn't say that, of course. It said that he died
of a coronary thrombosis—I think that was it—but everyone among
his friends and acquaintances knew it instantly. He was a perfect Type
A, a workaholic, a classic, they said to each other and shook their
heads—and thought for five or ten minutes about the way they lived.

This man who worked himself to death finally and precisely at
3:00 A.M. Sunday morning—on his day off—was fifty-one years old
and a vice-president. He was, however, one of six vice-presidents, and

one of three who might conceivably—if the president died or retired soon enough—have moved to the top spot. Phil knew that.

He worked six days a week, five of them until eight or nine at night, during a time when his own company had begun the four-day week for everyone but the executives. He worked like the Important People. He had no outside "extracurricular interests," unless, of course, you think about a monthly golf game that way. To Phil, it was work. He always ate egg salad sandwiches at his desk. He was, of course, overweight, by 20 or 25 pounds. He thought it was okay, though, because he didn't smoke.

5   On Saturdays, Phil wore a sports jacket to the office instead of a suit, because it was the weekend.

He had a lot of people working for him, maybe sixty, and most of them liked him most of the time. Three of them will be seriously considered for his job. The obituary didn't mention that.

But it did list his "survivors" quite accurately. He is survived by his wife, Helen, forty-eight years old, a good woman of no particular marketable skills, who worked in an office before marrying and mothering. She had, according to her daughter, given up trying to compete with his work years ago, when the children were small. A company friend said, "I know how much you will miss him." And she answered, "I already have."

"Missing him all these years," she must have given up part of herself which had cared too much for the man. She would be "well taken care of."

His "dearly beloved" eldest of the "dearly beloved" children is a hard-working executive in a manufacturing firm down South. In the day and a half before the funeral, he went around the neighborhood researching his father, asking the neighbors what he was like. They were embarrassed.

10   His second child is a girl, who is twenty-four and newly married. She lives near her mother and they are close, but whenever she was alone with her father, in a car driving somewhere, they had nothing to say to each other.

The youngest is twenty, a boy, a high-school graduate who has spent the last couple of years, like a lot of his friends, doing enough odd jobs to stay in grass and food. He was the one who tried to grab at his father, and tried to mean enough to him to keep the man at home. He was his father's favorite. Over the last two years, Phil stayed up nights worrying about the boy.

The boy once said, "My father and I only board here."

At the funeral, the sixty-year-old company president told the forty-eight-year-old widow that the fifty-one-year-old deceased had meant much to the company and would be missed and would be hard to replace. The widow didn't look him in the eye. She was afraid he would read her bitterness and, after all, she would need him to straighten out the finances—the stock options and all that.

Phil was overweight and nervous and worked too hard. If he wasn't at the office, he was worried about it. Phil was a Type A, a heart-attack natural. You could have picked him out in a minute from a lineup.

15   So when he finally worked himself to death, at precisely 3:00 A.M.   15 Sunday morning, no one was really surprised.

By 5:00 P.M. the afternoon of the funeral, the company president had begun, discreetly of course, with care and taste, to make inquiries about his replacement. One of three men. He asked around: "Who's been working the hardest?"

The Beatles: They Changed Rock, Which Changed the Culture, Which Changed US

Jeff Greenfield

Jeff Greenfield (1943–) was born in New York City. A graduate of the University of Wisconsin and Yale University School of Law, he has worked as legislative aide and speechwriter (notably for former New York City Mayor John Lindsay and for the late Senator Robert Kennedy), a television correspondent and commentator for ABC, and a syndicated columnist. His books, which frequently focus on sports, politics, and the media, include Where Have You Gone, Joe DiMaggio? *(1973),* The World's Greatest Team: A Portrait of the Boston Celtics *(1976),* Television: The First Fifty Years *(1977),* Playing to Win: An Insider's Guide to Politics *(1980),* The Real Campaign: How the Media Missed the Story of the 1980 Campaign *(1982), and* The People's Choice *(1995). He also coauthored (with Jack Newfield)* A Populist Manifesto *(1972). Greenfield contemplates the impact of the Beatles on rock, culture, and a large generation of "baby boomers" in this 1975 essay. As you read, try to identify another popular person or group that has had a similar impact on your life.*

1   They have not performed together on stage for more than eight years. They have not made a record together in five years. The formal dissolution of their partnership in a London courtroom last month was an echo of an ending that came long ago. Now each of them is seeking to overcome the shadow of a past in which

they were bound together by wealth, fame and adulation of an intensity unequaled in our culture. George Harrison scorns talk of reunion, telling us to stop living in the past. John Lennon told us years ago that "the dream is over."

He was right: When the Beatles broke up in 1970 in a welter of lawsuits and recriminations, the sixties were ending as well—in spirit as well as by the calendar. Bloodshed and bombings on campus, the harsh realities beneath the facile hopes for a "Woodstock nation," the shabby refuse of counterculture communities, all helped kill the dream.

What remains remarkable now, almost 20 years after John Lennon started playing rock 'n' roll music, more than a decade after their first worldwide conquest, is how appealing this dream was: how its vision of the world gripped so much of a generation; how that dream reshaped our recent past and affects us still. What remains remarkable is how strongly this dream was triggered, nurtured and broadened by one rock 'n' roll band of four Englishmen whose entire history as a group occurred before any of them reached the age of 30.

Their very power guarantees that an excursion into analysis cannot fully succeed. Their songs, their films, their lives formed so great a part of what we listened to and watched and talked about that everyone affected by them still sees the Beatles and hears their songs through a personal prism. And the Beatles themselves never abandoned a sense of self-parody and put-on. They were, in Richard Goldstein's phrase, "the clown-gurus of the sixties." Lennon said more than once that the Beatles sometimes put elusive references into their songs just to confuse their more solemn interpreters. "I am the egg man," they sang, not "egghead."

5   Still, the impact of the Beatles cannot be waved away. If the Marx   5
they emulated was Groucho, not Karl, if their world was a playground instead of a battleground, they still changed what we listened to and how we listened to it; they helped make rock music a battering ram for the youth culture's assault on the mainstream, and that assault in turn changed our culture permanently. And if the "dream" the Beatles helped create could not sustain itself in the real world, that speaks more to our false hopes than to their promises. They wrote and sang songs. We turned it into politics and philosophy and a road map to another way of life. The Beatles grew up as children of the first generation of rock 'n' roll, listening to and imitating the music of Little Richard, Larry Williams, Chuck Berry, Elvis Presley, and the later,

more sophisticated sounds of the Shirelles and the Miracles. It was the special genius of their first mentor, Brian Epstein, to package four Liverpool working-class "rockers" as "mods," replacing their greasy hair, leather jackets, and onstage vulgarity with jackets, ties, smiles and carefully groomed, distinctive haircuts. Just as white artists filtered and softened the raw energy of black artists in the nineteen-fifties, the Beatles at first were softer, safer versions of energetic rock 'n' roll musicians. The words promised they only wanted to hold hands—the rhythm was more insistent.

By coming into prominence early in 1964, the Beatles probably saved rock 'n' roll from extinction. Rock in the early nineteen-sixties existed in name only; apart from the soul artists, it was a time of "shlock rock," with talentless media hypes like Fabian and Frankie Avalon riding the crest of the American Bandstand wave. By contrast, the Beatles provided a sense of musical energy that made successful a brilliant public-relations effort. Of course, the $50,000 used to promote the Beatles' first American appearance in February, 1964, fueled some of the early hysteria; so did the timing of their arrival.

Coming as it did less than a hundred days after the murder of John Kennedy, the advent of the Beatles caught America aching for any diversion to replace the images of a flag-draped casket and a riderless horse in the streets of Washington.

I remember a Sunday evening in early February, standing with hundreds of curious collegians in a University of Wisconsin dormitory, watching these four longhaired (!) Englishmen trying to be heard over the screams of Ed Sullivan's audience. Their music seemed to me then derivative, pleasant and bland, a mixture of hard rock and the sounds of the black groups then popular. I was convinced it would last six months, no more.

The Beatles, however, had more than hype; they had talent. Even their first hits, "I Want to Hold Your Hand," "She Loves You," "Please Please Me," "I Saw Her Standing There," had a hint of harmonies and melodies more inventive than standard rock tunes. More important, it became immediately clear that the Beatles were hipper, more complicated, than the bovine rock stars who could not seem to put four coherent words together.

10   In the spring of 1964, John Lennon published a book, "In His 10 Own Write," which, instead of a ghost-written string of "groovy guides for keen teens," offered word plays, puns and black-humor satirical sketches. A few months later came the film "A Hard Day's

Night," and in place of the classic let's-put-on-a-prom-and-invite-the-TeenChords plot of rock movies, the Beatles and director Richard Lester created a funny movie parodying the Beatles's own image.

I vividly recall going to that film in the midst of a National Student Association Congress: at that time, rock 'n' roll was regarded as high-school nonsense by this solemn band of student-body presidents and future C.I.A. operatives. But after the film, I sensed a feeling of goodwill and camaraderie among that handful of rock fans who had watched this movie: The Beatles were media heroes without illusion, young men glorying in their sense of play and fun, laughing at the conventions of the world. They were worth listening to and admiring.

The real surprise came at the end of 1965, with the release of the "Rubber Soul" album. Starting with that album, and continuing through "Revolver" and "Sgt. Pepper's Lonely Hearts Club Band," the Beatles began to throw away the rigid conventions of rock 'n' roll music and lyrics. The banal abstract, second-hand emotions were replaced with sharp, sometimes mordant portraits of first-hand people and experiences, linked to music that was more complicated and more compelling than rock had ever dared attempt. The Beatles were drawing on their memories and feelings, not those cut from Tin Pan Alley cloth.

"Norwegian Wood" was about an unhappy, inconclusive affair ("I once had a girl/or should I say/she once had me"). "Michelle" and "Yesterday" were haunting, sentimental ballads, and Paul McCartney dared sing part of "Michelle" in French—most rock singers regarded English as a foreign language. "Penny Lane" used cornets to evoke the suggestion of a faintly heard band concert on a long-ago summer day. Staccato strings lent urgency to the story of "Eleanor Rigby."

These songs were different from the rock music that our elders had scorned with impunity. Traditionally, rock 'n' roll was rigidly structured: 4/4 tempo, 32 bars, with a limited range of instruments. Before the Beatles, rock producer Phil Spector had revolutionized records by adding strings to the drums, bass, sax and guitar, but the chord structure was usually limited to a basic blues or ballad pattern. Now the Beatles, with the kind of visibility that made them impossible to ignore, were expanding the range of rock, musically and lyrically. A sitar—a harpsichord effect—a ragtime piano—everything was possible.

15   With the release of "Sgt. Pepper" in the spring of 1967, the era of   15
rock as a strictly adolescent phenomenon was gone. One song, "A Day in the Life," with its recital of an ordinary day combined with a

dreamlike sense of dread and anxiety, made it impossible to ignore the skills of Lennon and McCartney. A decade earlier, Steve Allen mocked the inanity of rock by reading "Hound Dog" or "Tutti-Frutti" as if they were serious attempts at poetry. Once "Sgt. Pepper" was recorded, *Partisan Review* was lauding the Beatles, Ned Rorem proclaimed that "She's Leaving Home" was "equal to any song Schubert ever wrote," and a *Newsweek* critic meant it when he wrote: " 'Strawberry Fields Forever' [is] a superb Beatleizing of hope and despair in which the four minstrels regretfully recommend a Keatsian lotus-land of withdrawal from the centrifugal stresses of the age."

"We're so well established," McCartney had said in 1966, "that we can bring fans along with us and stretch the limits of pop." By using their fame to help break through the boundaries of rock, the Beatles proved that they were not the puppets of backstage manipulation or payola or hysterical 14-year-olds. Instead, they helped make rock music *the* music of an entire international generation. Perhaps for the first time in history, it was possible to say that tens of millions of people, defined simply by age, were all doing the same thing: they were listening to rock 'n' roll. That fact changed the popular culture of the world.

Rock 'n' roll's popularity had never been accompanied by respectability, even among the young. For those of us with intellectual pretenses, rock 'n' roll was like masturbation: exciting, but shameful. The culturally alienated went in for cool jazz, and folk music was the vehicle for the politically active minority. (The growth of political interest at the start of the sixties sparked something of a folk revival.)

Along with the leap of Bob Dylan into rock music, the Beatles destroyed this division. Rock 'n' roll was now broad enough, free enough, to encompass every kind of feeling. Its strength had always been rooted in the sexual energy of its rhythms; in that sense, the outraged parents who had seen rock as a threat to their children's virtue were right. Rock 'n' roll made you want to move and shake and get physically excited. The Beatles proved that this energy could be fused with a sensibility more subtle than the "let's-go-down-to-the-gym-and-beat-up-the-Coke-machine" quality of rock music.

In 1965, Barry McGuire recorded the first "rock protest" song (excluding the teen complaints of the Coasters and Chuck Berry). In his "Eve of Destruction," we heard references to Red China, Selma, Alabama, nuclear war and middle-class hypocrisy pounded out to heavy rock rythms. That same year came a flood of "good time" rock music, with sweet, haunting melodies by groups like the Lovin'

Spoonful and the Mamas and the Papas. There *were* no limits to what could be done; and the market was continually expanding.

20   The teenagers of the nineteen-fifties had become the young adults   20
of the nineteen-sixties, entering the professions, bringing with them a cultural frame of reference shaped in good measure by rock 'n' roll. The "youth" market was enormous—the flood of babies born during and just after World War II made the under-25 population group abnormally large; their tastes were more influential than ever before. And because the music had won acceptability, rock 'n' roll was not judged indulgently as a "boys will be boys" fad. Rock music was expressing a sensibility about the tangible world—about sensuality, about colors and sensations, about the need to change consciousness. And this sensibility soon spilled over into other arenas.

Looking back on the last half of the last decade, it is hard to think of a cultural innovation that did not carry with it the influence of rock music, and of the Beatles in particular: the miniskirt, discothèques, the graphics of Peter Max, the birth of publications like *Rolling Stone,* the "mindbending" effects of TV commercials, the success of "Laugh-In" on television and "Easy Rider" in the movies—all of these cultural milestones owe something to the emergence of rock music as the most compelling and pervasive force in our culture.

This is especially true of the incredible spread of drugs—marijuana and the hallucinogens most particularly—among the youth culture. From "Rubber Soul" through "Sgt. Pepper," Beatle music was suffused with a sense of mystery and mysticism: odd choral progressions, mysterious instruments, dreamlike effects, and images that did not seem to yield to "straight" interpretation. Whether specific songs ("Lucy in the Sky with Diamonds," "A Little Help From My Friends") were deliberately referring to drugs is beside the point. The Beatles were publicly recounting their LSD experiences, and their music was replete with antirational sensibility. Indeed, it was a commonplace among my contemporaries that Beatle albums could not be understood fully without the use of drugs. For "Rubber Soul," marijuana; for "Sgt. Pepper," acid. When the Beatles told us to turn off our minds and float downstream, uncounted youngsters assumed that the key to this kind of mind-expansion could be found in a plant or a pill. Together with "head" groups like Jefferson Airplane and the Grateful Dead, the Beatles were, consciously or not, a major influence behind the spread of drugs.

In this sense, the Beatles are part of a chain: (1) the Beatles opened up rock; (2) rock changed the culture; (3) the culture changed us. Even limited to their impact as musicians, however, the Beatles were as powerful an influence as any group or individual; only Bob Dylan stands as their equal. They never stayed with a successful formula; they were always moving. By virtue of their fame, the Beatles were a giant amplifier, spreading "the word" on virtually every trend and mood of the last decade.

They were never pure forerunners. The Yardbirds used the sitar before the Beatles; the Beach Boys were experimenting with studio enhancement first; the Four Seasons were using elaborate harmonies before the Beatles. They were never as contemptuously antimiddle-class or decadent as the Kinks or the Rolling Stones; never as lyrically compelling as Dylan; never as musically brilliant as the Band; never as hallucinogenic as the San Francisco groups. John Gabree, one of the most perceptive of the early rock writers, said that "their job, and they have done it well, has been to travel a few miles behind the avant-garde, consolidating gains and popularizing new ideas."

25   Yet this very willingness meant that new ideas did not struggle and   25 die in obscurity; instead, they touched a hundred million minds. Their songs reflected the widest range of mood of any group of their time. Their openness created a kind of salon for a whole generation of people, idea exchange into which the youth of the world was wired. It was almost inevitable that, even against their will, their listeners shaped a dream of politics and lifestyle from the substance of popular music. It is testament both to the power of rock music, and to the illusions which can be spun out of impulses.

The Beatles were not political animals. Whatever they have done since going their separate ways, their behavior as a group reflected cheerful anarchy more than political rebellion. Indeed, as editorialists, they were closer to *The Wall Street Journal* than to *Ramparts*. "Taxman" assaults the heavy progressive income tax ("one for you, 19 for me"), and "Revolution" warned that "if you go carrying pictures of Chairman Mao/you ain't gonna make it with anyone anyhow."

The real political impact of the Beatles was not in any four-point program or in an attack on injustice or the war in Vietnam. It was instead in the counterculture they had helped to create. Somewhere in the nineteen-sixties, millions of people began to regard themselves as a class separate from mainstream society *by virtue of their youth and the sensibility that youth produced.*

The nineteen-fifties had produced the faintest hint of such an attitude in the defensive love of rock 'n' roll; if our parents hated it, it had to be good. The sixties had expanded this vague idea into a battle cry. "Don't trust anyone over 30!"—shouted from a police car in the first massive student protest of the decade at Berkeley—suggested an outlook in which the mere aging process was an act of betrayal in which youth itself was a moral value. *Time* magazine made the "under-25 generation" its Man of the Year in 1967, and politicians saw in the steadily escalating rebellion among the middle-class young a constituency and a scapegoat.

The core value of this "class" was not peace or social injustice; it was instead a more elusive value, reflected by much of the music and by the Beatles' own portrait of themselves. It is expressed best by a scene from their movie "Help!" in which John, Paul, George and Ringo enter four adjoining row houses. The doors open—and suddenly the scene shifts inside, and we see that these "houses" are in fact one huge house; the four Beatles instantly reunite.

30   It is this sense of commonality that was at the heart of the youth   30 culture. It is what we wished to believe about the Beatles, and about the possibilities in our own lives. If there is one sweeping statement that makes sense about the children of the last decade, it is that the generation born of World War II was saying "no" to the atomized lives their parents had so feverishly sought. The most cherished value of the counterculture—preached if not always practiced—was its insistence on sharing, communality, a rejection of the retreat into private satisfaction. Rock 'n' roll was the magnet, the driving force, of a shared celebration. From Alan Freed's first mammoth dance parties in Cleveland in 1951, to the Avalon Ballroom in San Francisco, to the be-ins in our big cities, to Woodstock itself. Spontaneous gathering was the ethic: Don't plan it, don't think about it, *do* it—you'll get by with a little help from your friends.

In their music, their films, their sense of play, the Beatles reflected this dream of a ceaseless celebration. If there *was* any real "message" in their songs, it was the message of Charles Reich: that the world would be changed by changing the consciousness of the new generation. "All you need is love," they sang. "Say the word [love] and you'll be free." "Let it be." "Everything's gonna be all right."

As a state of mind, it was a pleasant fantasy. As a way of life, it was doomed to disaster. The thousands of young people who flocked to California or to New York's Lower East Side to join the love generation found the world filled with people who did not share the ethic of mutual trust. The politicization of youth as a class helped to divide natural political allies and make politics more vulnerable to demagogues. As the Beatles found in their own personal and professional lives, the practical outside world has a merciless habit of intruding into fantasies; somebody has to pay the bills and somebody has to do the dishes in the commune and somebody has to protect us from the worst instincts of other human beings. John Lennon was expressing some very painful lessons when he told *Rolling Stone* shortly after the group's breakup that "nothing happened except we all dressed up . . . the same bastards are in control, the same people are runnin' everything."

Shame

Dick Gregory

Dick Gregory (1932–) grew up in St. Louis, Missouri. He attended Southern Illinois University and became a well-known comedian and entertainer. He was active in the civil rights movement of the 1960s and the movement against the Vietnam War. As a candidate in the Peace and Freedom Party, Gregory campaigned for president in 1968. His books include Dick Gregory's Political Primer; From the Back of the Bus, No More Lies; *and his autobiography,* Nigger *(1964), from which the following selection is excerpted. In this episode about his early childhood, Gregory writes about one of poverty's destructive psychological effects on children.*

1   I never learned hate at home, or shame. I had to go to school for that. I was about seven years old when I got my first big lesson. I was in love with a little girl named Helene Tucker, a light-complected little girl with pigtails and nice manners. She was always clean and she was smart in school. I think I went to school then mostly to look at her. I brushed my hair and even got me a little old handkerchief. It was a lady's handkerchief, but I didn't want Helene to see me wipe my nose on my hand. The pipes were frozen again, there was no water in the house, but I washed my socks and shirt every night. I'd get a pot, and go over to Mister Ben's grocery store, and stick my pot down into his soda machine. Scoop out some chopped ice. By evening the ice melted to water for washing. I got sick a lot that winter because the fire would go out at night before the clothes were dry. In the morning I'd put them on, wet or dry, because they were the only clothes I had.

From *Nigger: An Autobiography* by Dick Gregory. Published by Dutton, an imprint of New American Library, a division of Penguin Books USA Inc. Copyright © 1964 by Dick Gregory Enterprises, Inc.

Everybody's got a Helene Tucker, a symbol of everything you want. I loved her for her goodness, her cleanness, her popularity. She'd walk down my street and my brothers and sisters would yell, "Here comes Helene," and I'd rub my tennis sneakers on the back of my pants and wish my hair wasn't so nappy and the white folks' shirt fit me better. I'd run out on the street. If I knew my place and didn't come too close, she'd wink at me and say Hello. That was a good feeling. Sometimes I'd follow her all the way home, and shovel the snow off her walk and try to make friends with her Momma and her aunts. I'd drop money on her stoop late at night on my way back from shining shoes in the taverns. And she had a Daddy, and he had a good job. He was a paper hanger.

I guess I would have gotten over Helene by summertime, but something happened in that classroom that made her face hang in front of me for the next twenty-two years. When I played the drums in high school it was for Helene and when I broke track records in college it was for Helene and when I started standing behind microphones and heard applause I wished Helene could hear it, too. It wasn't until I was twenty-nine years old and married and making money that I finally got her out of my system. Helene was sitting in that classroom when I learned to be ashamed of myself.

It was on a Thursday. I was sitting in the back of the room, in a seat with a chalk circle drawn around it. The idiot's seat, the troublemaker's seat.

5   The teacher thought I was stupid. Couldn't spell, couldn't read,   5
couldn't do arithmetic. Just stupid. Teachers were never interested in finding out that you couldn't concentrate because you were so hungry, because you hadn't had any breakfast. All you could think about was noontime, would it ever come? Maybe you could sneak into the cloakroom and steal a bite of some kid's lunch out of a coat pocket. A bite of something. Paste. You can't really make a meal of paste, or put it on bread for a sandwich, but sometimes I'd scoop a few spoonfuls out of the paste jar in the back of the room. Pregnant people get strange tastes. I was pregnant with poverty. Pregnant with dirt and pregnant with smells that made people turn away, pregnant with cold and pregnant with shoes that were never bought for me, pregnant with five other people in my bed and no Daddy in the next room, and pregnant with hunger. Paste doesn't taste too bad when you're hungry.

The teacher thought I was a troublemaker. All she saw from the front of the room was a little black boy who squirmed in his idiot's seat and made noises and poked the kids around him. I guess she couldn't see a kid who made noises because he wanted someone to know he was there.

It was on a Thursday, the day before the Negro payday. The eagle always flew on Friday. The teacher was asking each student how much his father would give to the Community Chest. On Friday night, each kid would get the money from his father, and on Monday he would bring it to the school. I decided I was going to buy me a Daddy right then. I had money in my pocket from shining shoes and selling papers, and whatever Helene Tucker pledged for her Daddy I was going to top it. And I'd hand the money right in. I wasn't going to wait until Monday to buy me a Daddy.

I was shaking, scared to death. The teacher opened her book and started calling out names alphabetically.

"Helene Tucker?"

"My Daddy said he'd give two dollars and fifty cents."

"That's very nice, Helene. Very, very nice indeed."

That made me feel pretty good. It wouldn't take too much to top that. I had almost three dollars in dimes and quarters in my pocket. I stuck my hand in my pocket and held onto the money, waiting for her to call my name. But the teacher closed her book after she called everybody else in the class. I stood up and raised my hand.

"What is it now?"

"You forgot me."

She turned toward the blackboard. "I don't have time to be playing with you, Richard."

"My Daddy said he'd . . . "

"Sit down, Richard, you're disturbing the class."

"My Daddy said he'd give . . . fifteen dollars."

She turned around and looked mad. "We are collecting this money for you and your kind, Richard Gregory. If your Daddy can give fifteen dollars you have no business being on relief."

"I got it right now, I got it right now, my Daddy gave it to me to turn in today, my Daddy said . . . "

"And furthermore," she said, looking right at me, her nostrils getting big and her lips getting thin and her eyes opening wide, "we know you don't have a Daddy."

Helene Tucker turned around, her eyes full of tears. She felt sorry for me. Then I couldn't see her too well because I was crying, too.

"Sit down, Richard."

And I always thought the teacher kind of liked me. She always picked me to wash the blackboard on Friday, after school. That was a big thrill, it made me feel important. If I didn't wash it, come Monday the school might not function right.

"Where are you going, Richard?"

I walked out of school that day, and for a long time I didn't go back very often. There was shame there.

Now there was shame everywhere. It seemed like the whole world had been inside that classroom, everyone had heard what the teacher had said, everyone had turned around and felt sorry for me. There was shame in going to the Worthy Boys Annual Christmas Dinner for you and your kind, because everybody knew what a worthy boy was. Why couldn't they just call it the Boys Annual Dinner, why'd they have to give it a name? There was shame in wearing the brown and orange and white plaid mackinaw the welfare gave to 3,000 boys. Why'd it have to be the same for everybody so when you walked down the street the people could see you were on relief? It was a nice warm mackinaw and it had a hood, and my Momma beat me and called me a little rat when she found out I stuffed it in the bottom of a pail full of garbage way over on Cottage Street. There was shame in running over to Mister Ben's at the end of the day and asking for his rotten peaches, there was shame in asking Mrs. Simmons for a spoonful of sugar, there was shame in running out to meet the relief truck. I hated that truck, full of food for you and your kind. I ran into the house and hid when it came. And then I started to sneak through alleys, to take the long way home so the people going into White's Eat Shop wouldn't see me. Yeah, the whole world heard the teacher that day, we all know you don't have a Daddy.

It lasted for a while, this kind of numbness. I spent a lot of time feeling sorry for myself. And then one day I met this wino in a restaurant. I'd been out hustling all day, shining shoes, selling newspapers, and I had goo-gobs of money in my pocket. Bought me a bowl of chili for fifteen cents, and a cheeseburger for fifteen cents, and a Pepsi for five cents, and a piece of chocolate cake for ten cents. That was a good meal. I was eating when this old wino came in. I love winos because they never hurt anyone but themselves.

The old wino sat down at the counter and ordered twenty-six cents worth of food. He ate it like he really enjoyed it. When the owner, Mister Williams, asked him to pay the check, the old wino didn't lie or go through his pocket like he suddenly found a hole.

30   He just said: "Don't have no money."   30

The owner yelled: "Why in hell you come in here and eat my food if you don't have no money? That food cost me money."

Mister Williams jumped over the counter and knocked the wino off his stool and beat him over the head with a pop bottle. Then he stepped back and watched the wino bleed. Then he kicked him. And he kicked him again.

I looked at the wino with blood all over his face and I went over. "Leave him alone, Mister Williams. I'll pay the twenty-six cents."

The wino got up, slowly, pulling himself up to the stool, then up to the counter, holding on for a minute until his legs stopped shaking so bad. He looked at me with pure hate. "Keep your twenty-six cents. You don't have to pay, not now. I just finished paying for it."

35   He started to walk out, and as he passed me, he reached down and 35 touched my shoulder. "Thanks, sonny, but it's too late now. Why didn't you pay it before?"

I was pretty sick about that. I waited too long to help another man.

Salvation

Langston Hughes

Langston Hughes (1902–1967), a poet, short-story writer, essayist, and playwright, was born in Joplin, Missouri, and grew up in Kansas and Ohio. After graduating from high school (where he began writing poetry), Hughes spent 15 months in Mexico with his father, attended Columbia University for a year, worked as a seaman on cargo ships bound to Africa and Europe, and bused tables at a hotel in New York City. Later, he returned to school and graduated from Lincoln University (1929). Part of the "Harlem Renaissance" or "New Negro Renaissance"—and fiercely proud of his African-American heritage—Hughes often drew from Negro spirituals and blues and jazz in his literary work. Hughes was published in Amsterdam News, Crisis, The New Negro, *and many other periodicals. His books include the novel* Not Without Laughter *(1930); the short story collection* The Ways of White Folks *(1934); the play* The Mulatto *(1935); his autobiography* The Big Sea *(1940); and his poetry collections* The Weary Blues *(1926),* Shakespeare of Harlem *(1942),* Montage of a Dream Deferred *(1951), and* Ask Your Mama *(1961). This selection, which appeared first in* The Big Sea, *dramatizes an important event in Hughes's life.*

1   I was saved from sin when I was going on thirteen. But not really saved. It happened like this. There was a big revival at my Auntie Reed's church. Every night for weeks there had been much preaching, singing, praying, and shouting, and some very hardened sinners had been brought to Christ, and the membership of the church had

grown by leaps and bounds. Then just before the revival ended, they held a special meeting for children, "to bring the young lambs to the fold." My aunt spoke of it for days ahead. That night I was escorted to the front row and placed on the mourners' bench with all the other young sinners, who had not yet been brought to Jesus.

My aunt told me that when you were saved you saw a light, and something happened to you inside! And Jesus came into your life! And God was with you from then on! She said you could see and hear and feel Jesus in your soul. I believed her. I had heard a great many old people say that same thing and it seemed to me they ought to know. So I sat there calmly in the hot, crowded church, waiting for Jesus to come to me.

The preacher preached a wonderful rhythmical sermon, all moans and shouts and lonely cries and dire pictures of hell, and then he sang a song about the ninety and nine safe in the fold, but one little lamb was left out in the cold. Then he said: "Won't you come? Won't you come to Jesus? Young lambs, won't you come?" And he held out his arms to all us young sinners there on the mourners' bench. And the little girls cried. And some of them jumped up and went to Jesus right away. But most of us just sat there.

A great many old people came and knelt around us and prayed, old women with jet-black faces and braided hair, old men with work-gnarled hands. And the church sang a song about the lower lights are burning, some poor sinners to be saved. And the whole building rocked with prayer and song.

5   Still I kept waiting to *see* Jesus.   5

Finally all the young people had gone to the altar and were saved, but one boy and me. He was a rounder's son named Westley. Westley and I were surrounded by sisters and deacons praying. It was very hot in the church, and getting late now. Finally Westley said to me in a whisper: "God damn! I'm tired o' sitting here. Let's get up and be saved." So he got up and was saved.

Then I was left all alone on the mourners' bench. My aunt came and knelt at my knees and cried, while prayers and song swirled all around me in the little church. The whole congregation prayed for me alone in a mighty wail of moans and voices. And I kept waiting serenely for Jesus, waiting, waiting—but he didn't come. I wanted to see him, but nothing happened to me. Nothing! I wanted something to happen to me, but nothing happened.

I heard the songs and the minister saying: "Why don't you come? My dear child, why don't you come to Jesus? Jesus is waiting for you. He wants you. Why don't you come? Sister Reed, what is this child's name?"

"Langston," my aunt sobbed.

10 "Langston, why don't you come? Why don't you come and be 10 saved? Oh, Lamb of God! Why don't you come?"

Now it was really getting late. I began to be ashamed of myself, holding everything up so long. I began to wonder what God thought about Westley, who certainly hadn't seen Jesus either, but who was now sitting proudly on the platform, swinging his knickerbockered legs and grinning down at me, surrounded by deacons and old women on their knees praying. God had not struck Westley dead for taking his name in vain or for lying in the temple. So I decided that maybe to save further trouble, I'd better lie, too, and say that Jesus had come, and get up and be saved.

So I got up.

Suddenly the whole room broke into a sea of shouting, as they saw me rise. Waves of rejoicing swept the place. Women leaped in the air. My aunt threw her arms around me. The minister took me by the hand and led me to the platform.

When things quieted down, in a hushed silence, punctuated by a few ecstatic "Amens," all the new young lambs were blessed in the name of God. Then joyous singing filled the room.

15 That night, for the last time in my life but one—for I was a big 15 boy twelve years old—I cried. I cried, in bed alone, and couldn't stop. I buried my head under the quilts, but my aunt heard me. She woke up and told my uncle I was crying because the Holy Ghost had come into my life, and because I had seen Jesus. But I was really crying because I couldn't bear to tell her that I had lied, that I had deceived everybody in the church, that I hadn't seen Jesus, and that now I didn't believe there was a Jesus any more, since he didn't come to help me.

Why We Crave Horror Movies

Stephen King

Stephen King (1947 –) was born in Portland, Maine. After graduating from the University of Maine in 1970, King held a number of jobs—knitting mill worker, janitor, high school English teacher—before gaining fame and fortune as a mystery writer. A prolific and widely popular writer (his book sales have surpassed 20 million copies), King has become synonymous with horror stories and movies. His many books include Carrie *(1974),* Salem's Lot *(1975),* The Shining *(1977),* The Dead Zone *(1979),* Firestarter *(1980),* Christine *(1983),* Pet Sematery *(1983),* Tommy-knockers *(1984),* Misery *(1987),* Needful Things *(1991),* Insomnia *(1994),* Bag of Bones *(1998),* The Green Mile *(2000),* The Plant *(2000)—a serial novel which he published online,* The Colorado Kid *(2005), and* Cell *(2006). First published in* Playboy *in 1982, this essay explains, in the master's words, why we crave good horror shows.*

1   I think that we're all mentally ill; those of us outside the asylums only   1
hide it a little better—and maybe not all that much better, after all.
We've all known people who talk to themselves, people who sometimes squinch their faces into horrible grimaces when they believe no one is watching, people who have some hysterical fear—of snakes, the dark, the tight place, the long drop . . . and, of course, those final worms and grubs that are waiting so patiently underground.

When we pay our four or five bucks and seat ourselves at tenth-row center in a theater showing a horror movie, we are daring the nightmare.

From *Playboy* (1982). Copyright © 1982 Stephen King.

101

Why? Some of the reasons are simple and obvious. To show that we can, that we are not afraid, that we can ride this roller coaster. Which is not to say that a really good horror movie may not surprise a scream out of us at some point, the way we may scream when the roller coaster twists through a complete 360 or plows through a lake at the bottom of the drop. And horror movies, like roller coasters, have always been the special province of the young; by the time one turns 40 or 50, one's appetite for double twists or 360-degree loops may be considerably depleted.

We also go to re-establish our feelings of essential normality; the horror movie is innately conservative, even reactionary. Freda Jackson as the horrible melting woman in *Die, Monster, Die!* confirms for us that no matter how far we may be removed from the beauty of a Robert Redford or a Diana Ross, we are still light-years from true ugliness.

5   And we go to have fun.   5

Ah, but this is where the ground starts to slope away, isn't it? Because this is a very peculiar sort of fun indeed. The fun comes from seeing others menaced—sometimes killed. One critic has suggested that if pro football has become the voyeur's version of combat, then the horror film has become the modern version of the public lynching.

It is true that the mythic, "fairytale" horror film intends to take away the shades of gray. . . . It urges us to put away our more civilized and adult penchant for analysis and to become children again, seeing things in pure blacks and whites. It may be that horror movies provide psychic relief on this level because this invitation to lapse into simplicity, irrationality and even outright madness is extended so rarely. We are told we may allow our emotions a free rein . . . or no rein at all.

If we are all insane, then sanity becomes a matter of degree. If your insanity leads you to carve up women like Jack the Ripper or the Cleveland Torso Murderer, we clap you away in the funny farm (but neither of those two amateur-night surgeons was ever caught, heh-heh-heh); if, on the other hand your insanity leads you only to talk to yourself when you're under stress or to pick your nose on your morning bus, then you are left alone to go about your business . . . though it is doubtful that you will ever be invited to the best parties.

The potential lyncher is in almost all of us (excluding saints, past and present; but then, most saints have been crazy in their own ways), and every now and then, he has to be let loose to scream and roll around in the grass. Our emotions and our fears form their own body, and we recognize that it demands its own exercise to maintain proper muscle tone.

Certain of these emotional muscles are accepted—even exalted—in civilized society; they are, of course, the emotions that tend to maintain the status quo of civilization itself. Love, friendship, loyalty, kindness—these are all the emotions that we applaud, emotions that have been immortalized in the couplets of Hallmark cards and in the verses (I don't dare call it poetry) of Leonard Nimoy.

10   When we exhibit these emotions, society showers us with positive reinforcement; we learn this even before we get out of diapers. When, as children, we hug our rotten little puke of a sister and give her a kiss, all the aunts and uncles smile and twit and cry, "Isn't he the sweetest little thing?" Such coveted treats as chocolate-covered graham crackers often follow. But if we deliberately slam the rotten little puke of a sister's fingers in the door, sanctions follow—angry remonstrance from parents, aunts and uncles; instead of a chocolate-covered graham cracker, a spanking.

But anticivilization emotions don't go away, and they demand periodic exercise. We have such "sick" jokes as, "What's the difference between a truckload of bowling balls and a truckload of dead babies?" (You can't unload a truckload of bowling balls with a pitchfork . . . a joke, by the way, that I heard originally from a ten-year-old.) Such a joke may surprise a laugh or a grin out of us even as we recoil, a possibility that confirms the thesis: If we share a brotherhood of man, then we also share an insanity of man. None of which is intended as a defense of either the sick joke or insanity but merely as an explanation of why the best horror films, like the best fairy tales, manage to be reactionary, anarchistic, and revolutionary all at the same time.

The mythic horror movie, like the sick joke, has a dirty job to do. It deliberately appeals to all that is worst in us. It is morbidity unchained, our most base instincts let free, our nastiest fantasies realized . . . and it all happens, fittingly enough, in the dark. For those reasons, good liberals often shy away from horror films. For myself, I like to see the most aggressive of them—*Dawn of the Dead,* for instance—as lifting a trap door in the civilized forebrain and throwing a basket of raw meat to the hungry alligators swimming around in that subterranean river beneath.

Why bother? Because it keeps them from getting out, man. It keeps them down there and me up here. It was Lennon and McCartney who said that all you need is love, and I would agree with that.

As long as you keep the gators fed.

I Have a Dream

Martin Luther King, Jr.

*Martin Luther King, Jr. (1929–1968) was born in At-
lanta, Georgia, the son and grandson of Baptist ministers.
His college and postgraduate studies took him from Moorhouse College to Crozer Theological Seminary to Boston
University, where he received a Ph.D. (1955) and met his
future wife, Coretta Scott. King's active involvement in the
civil rights movement began in 1955, when he led a boycott of segregated buses in Montgomery, Alabama. From the
mid-1950s until he was shot and killed in Memphis, Tennessee, while supporting striking city workers, King organized boycotts, sit-ins, mass demonstrations, and other
protest activities. As a black civil rights leader, King was arrested, jailed, stoned, stabbed, and beaten; his house was
bombed; and he was placed under secret surveillance by
Federal Bureau of Investigation (FBI) director J. Edgar
Hoover. Through his leadership—always underscored by his
nonviolent beliefs—King's name has become synonymous
with the watersheds of the civil rights movement in the
United States: Rosa Parks, the Southern Christian Leadership Conference, Selma, Alabama, the Civil Rights Act,
and the Voting Rights Act. His crowning moment occurred
during the August 1963 civil rights march on Washington,
D.C., when King, standing in front of the Lincoln Memorial, delivered his most famous speech, this essay. A year later
he would receive the Nobel Peace Prize. As you read King's
words, spoken nearly a century after Lincoln signed the
Emancipation Proclamation, listen to this great orator; try
to feel the emotion that hundreds of thousands of black
Americans carried to the Esplanade that memorable day.*

1   I am happy to join with you today in what will go down in history   1
     as the greatest demonstration for freedom in the history of our
     nation.
          Five score years ago, a great American, in whose symbolic shadow
     we stand today, signed the Emancipation Proclamation. This mo-
     mentous decree came as a great beacon light of hope to millions of
     Negro slaves who had been seared in the flames of withering injustice.
     It came as a joyous daybreak to end the long night of their captivity.
     But one hundred years later, the Negro is still not free. One hundred
     years later, the life of the Negro is still sadly crippled by the manacles
     of segregation and the chains of discrimination. One hundred years
     later, the Negro lives on a lonely island of poverty in the midst of a
     vast ocean of material prosperity. One hundred years later, the Negro
     is still anguished in the corners of American society and finds himself
     in exile in his own land. And so we have come here today to drama-
     tize a shameful condition.
          In a sense we have come to our nation's capital to cash a check.
     When the architects of our republic wrote the magnificent words of
     the Constitution and the Declaration of Independence, they were
     signing a promissory note to which every American was to fall heir.
     This note was the promise that all men—yes, Black men as well as
     white men—would be guaranteed the inalienable rights of life, liberty,
     and the pursuit of happiness.
          It is obvious today that America has defaulted on this promissory
     note insofar as her citizens of color are concerned. Instead of honoring
     this sacred obligation, America has given the Negro people a bad check,
     a check which has come back marked "insufficient funds." But we
     refuse to believe that the bank of justice is bankrupt. We refuse to be-
     lieve that there are insufficient funds in the great vaults of opportunity
     of this nation; and so we have come to cash this check, a check that will
     give us upon demand the riches of freedom and the security of justice.
5   We have also come to this hallowed spot to remind America of   5
     the fierce urgency of *now*. This is no time to engage in the luxury of
     cooling off or to take the tranquilizing drug of gradualism. Now is the
     time to make real the promises of democracy. Now is the time to rise
     from the dark and desolate valley of segregation to the sunlit patch of
     racial justice. Now is the time to lift our nation from the quicksands
     of racial injustice to the solid rock of brotherhood. Now is the time to
     make justice a reality for all of God's children.

It would be fatal for the nation to overlook the urgency of the moment. This sweltering summer of the Negro's legitimate discontent will not pass until there is an invigorating autumn of freedom and equality. Nineteen Sixty-three is not an end, but a beginning. And those who hope that the Negro needed to blow off steam and will now be content will have a rude awakening if the nation returns to business as usual. There will be neither rest nor tranquility in America until the Negro is granted his citizenship rights. The whirlwinds of revolt will continue to shake the foundations of our nation until the bright day of justice emerges.

But there is something that I must say to my people who stand on the warm threshold which leads into the palace of justice. In the process of gaining our rightful place, we must not be guilty of wrongful deeds. Let us not seek to satisfy our thirst for freedom by drinking from the cup of bitterness and hatred. We must forever conduct our struggle on the high plane of dignity and discipline. We must not allow our creative protest to degenerate into physical violence. Again and again we must rise to the majestic heights of meeting physical force with soul force. And the marvelous new militancy which has engulfed the Negro community must not lead us to a distrust of all white people; for many of our white brothers, as evidenced by their presence here today, have come to realize that their destiny is tied up with our destiny, and they have come to realize that their freedom is inextricably bound to our freedom.

We cannot walk alone. And as we walk we must make the pledge that we shall always march ahead. We cannot turn back. There are those who are asking the devotees of civil rights, "When will you be satisfied?" We can never be satisfied as long as the Negro is the victim of the unspeakable horrors of police brutality. We can never be satisfied as long as our bodies, heavy with the fatigue of travel, cannot gain lodging in the motels of the highways and the hotels of the cities. We cannot be satisfied as long as the Negro's basic mobility is from a smaller ghetto to a larger one. We can never be satisfied as long as our children are stripped of their selfhood and robbed of their dignity by signs stating "For Whites Only." We cannot be satisfied as long as the Negro in Mississippi cannot vote and a Negro in New York believes he has nothing for which to vote. No, no, we are not satisfied, and we will not be satisfied until justice rolls down like waters and righteousness like a mighty stream.

I am not unmindful that some of you have come here out of great trials and tribulations. Some of you have come fresh from narrow jail cells. Some of you have come from areas where your quest for freedom left you battered by the storms of persecution and staggered by the winds of police brutality. You have been the veterans of creative suffering. Continue to work with the faith that unearned suffering is redemptive.

10   Go back to Mississippi, and go back to Alabama. Go back to 10 South Carolina. Go back to Georgia. Go back to Louisiana. Go back to the slums and ghettos of our Northern cities, knowing that somehow this situation can and will be changed. Let us not wallow in the valley of despair.

I say to you today, my friends, even though we face the difficulties of today and tomorrow, I still have a dream. It is a dream deeply rooted in the American dream. I have a dream that one day this nation will rise up and live out the true meaning of its creed: "We hold these truths to be self-evident, that all men are created equal." I have a dream that one day, on the red hills of Georgia, sons of former slaves and the sons of former slave owners will be able to sit down together at the table of brotherhood. I have a dream that one day even the state of Mississippi, a state sweltering with the heat of injustice, sweltering with the heat of oppression, will be transformed into an oasis of freedom and justice. I have a dream that my four little children will one day live in a nation where they will not be judged by the color of their skin, but by the content of their character.

I have a dream today. I have a dream that one day down in Alabama—with its vicious racists, with its governor's lips dripping with the words of interposition and nullification—one day right there in Alabama, little Black boys and Black girls will be able to join hands with little white boys and white girls as sisters and brothers.

I have a dream today. I have a dream that one day every valley shall be exalted and every hill and mountain shall be made low, the rough places will be made plain and the crooked places will be made straight, and the glory of the Lord shall be revealed, and all flesh shall see it together.

This is our hope. This is the faith that I go back to the South with. And with this faith we will be able to hew out of the mountain of despair a stone of hope. With this faith we will be able to transform the jangling discords of our nation into a beautiful symphony of brotherhood. With this faith we will be able to work together, to play together, to struggle together, to go to jail together, to stand up for freedom together, knowing that we will be free one day.

15   And this will be the day—this will be the day when all of God's 15 children will be able to sing with new meaning.

My country, 'tis of thee,
Sweet land of liberty,
  Of thee I sing;
Land where my fathers died,
Land of the Pilgrims' pride,
From every mountainside
Let freedom ring.

And if America is to be a great nation, this must become true.

And so let freedom ring from the prodigious hilltops of New Hampshire. Let freedom ring from the mighty mountains of New York. Let freedom ring from the heightening Alleghenies of Pennsylvania. Let freedom ring from the snow-capped Rockies of Colorado. Let freedom ring from the curvaceous slopes of California.

But not only that. Let freedom ring from Stone Mountain of Georgia. Let freedom ring from Lookout Mountain of Tennessee. Let freedom ring from every hill and molehill of Mississippi. "From every mountainside let freedom ring."

And when this happens—when we allow freedom to ring, when we let it ring from every village and every hamlet, from every state and every city—we will be able to speed up that day when all of God's children, Black men and white men, Jews and Gentiles, Protestants and Catholics, will be able to join hands and sing in the words of the old Negro spiritual: "Free at last! Free at last! Thank God Almighty. We are free at last!"

Shitty First Drafts

Anne Lamott

Anne Lamott (1954–), a writer who writes on writing, among many other subjects, is both a creator of fiction and nonfiction and a commentator on religious subjects. She acquired her interest in writing from her father, Kenneth Lamott, the model and inspiration for her first novel, Hard Laughter *(1987).* Bird by Bird: Some Instructions on Writing and Life, *from which the following excerpt has been taken, is a much read and taught book that looks at the experiences of a writer at work. She is also known for her works on family life, including* Operating Instructions: A Journal of My Son's First Year *(1994) and* Crooked Little Heart *(1997) about the stuff that keeps a family together. Her religious works include* Traveling Mercies: Some Thoughts on Faith *(2000),* Plan B: Further Thoughts on Faith *(2005), and* Grace (Eventually): Thoughts on Faith *(2007). Lamott writes the books she would like to have discovered to read, and helps other aspiring writers to do the same.*

Most writers write terrible stuff in their first drafts, and sometimes the fear of those drafts keeps writers from writing at all. In this humorous book chapter, Lamott tells how to go right ahead and write no matter how bad the first try.

1   Now, practically even better news than that of short assignments is the idea of shitty first drafts. All good writers write them. This is how they end up with good second drafts and terrific third drafts. People tend to look at successful writers, writers who are getting their books published and maybe even doing well

Reprinted from *Bird By Bird: Some Instructions on Writing and Life* (1995), by permission of Pantheon Books, a division of Random House, Inc.

financially, and think that they sit down at their desks every morning feeling like a million dollars, feeling great about who they are and how much talent they have and what a great story they have to tell; that they take in a few deep breaths, push back their sleeves, roll their necks a few times to get all the cricks out, and dive in, typing fully formed passages as fast as a court reporter. But this is just the fantasy of the uninitiated. I know some very great writers, writers you love who write beautifully and have made a great deal of money, and not *one* of them sits down routinely feeling wildly enthusiastic and confident. Not one of them writes elegant first drafts. All right, one of them does, but we do not like her very much. We do not think that she has a rich inner life or that God likes her or can even stand her. [(Although when I mentioned this to my priest friend Tom, he said you can safely assume you've created God in your own image when it turns out that God hates all the same people you do.)]

Very few writers really know what they are doing until they've done it. Nor do they go about their business feeling dewy and thrilled. They do not type a few stiff warm-up sentences and then find themselves bounding along like huskies across the snow. One writer I know tells me that he sits down every morning and says to himself nicely, "It's not like you don't have a choice, because you do— you can either type or kill yourself." We all often feel like we are pulling teeth, even those writers whose prose ends up being the most natural and fluid. The right words and sentences just do not come pouring out like ticker tape most of the time. Now, Muriel Spark is said to have felt that she was taking dictation from God every morning—sitting there, one supposes, plugged into a Dictaphone, typing away, humming. But this is a very hostile and aggressive position. One might hope for bad things to rain down on a person like this.

For me and most of the other writers I know, writing is not rapturous. In fact, the only way I can get anything written at all is to write really, really shitty first drafts.

The first draft is the child's draft, where you let it all pour out and then let it romp all over the place, knowing that no one is going to see it and that you can shape it later. You just let this childlike part of you channel whatever voices and visions come through and onto the page. If one of the characters wants to say, "Well, so what, Mr. Poopy Pants?," you let her. No one is going to see it. If the kid wants to get into really sentimental, weepy, emotional territory, you let him. Just get it all down on paper, because there may be something great in those six crazy pages that you would never have gotten to by more rational, grown-up means. There may be something in the very last line of the very last paragraph on page six that you just love, that is so beautiful or wild that you now know what you're supposed to be writing about, more or less, or in what direction you might go—but there was no way to get to this without first getting through the first five and a half pages.

5   I used to write food reviews for *California* Magazine before it folded. (My writing food reviews had nothing to do with the magazine folding, although every single review did cause a couple of canceled subscriptions. Some readers took umbrage at my comparing mounds of vegetable puree with various ex-presidents' brains.) These reviews always took two days to write. First I'd go to a restaurant several times with a few opinionated, articulate friends in tow. I'd sit there writing down everything anyone said that was at all interesting or funny. Then on the following Monday I'd sit down at my desk with my notes, and try to write the review. Even after I'd been doing this for years, panic would set in. I'd try to write a lead, but instead I'd write a couple of dreadful sentences, XX them out, try again, XX everything out, and then feel despair and worry settle on my chest like an x-ray apron. It's over, I'd think, calmly. I'm not going to be able to get the magic to work this time. I'm ruined. I'm through. I'm toast. Maybe, I'd think, I can get my old job back as a clerk-typist. But probably not. I'd get up and study my teeth in the mirror for a while. Then I'd stop, remember to breathe, make a few phone calls, hit the kitchen and chow down. Eventually I'd go back and sit down at my desk, and sigh for the next ten minutes. Finally I would pick up my one-inch picture frame, stare into it as if for the answer, and every time the answer would come: all I had to do was to write a really shitty first draft of, say, the opening paragraph. And no one was going to see it.

So I'd start writing without reining myself in. It was almost just typing, just making my fingers move. And the writing would be *terrible*. I'd write a lead paragraph that was a whole page, even though the entire review could only be three pages long, and then I'd start writing up descriptions of the food, one dish at a time, bird by bird, and the critics would be sitting on my shoulders, commenting like cartoon characters. They'd be pretending to snore, or rolling their eyes at my overwrought descriptions, no matter how hard I tried to tone those descriptions down, no matter how conscious I was of what a friend said to me gently in my early days of restaurant reviewing. "Annie," she said, "it is just a piece of *chicken*. It is just a bit of *cake*."

But because by then I had been writing for so long, I would eventually let myself trust the process—sort of, more or less. I'd write a first draft that was maybe twice as long as it should be, with a self-indulgent and boring beginning, stupefying descriptions of the meal, lots of quotes from my black-humored friends that made them sound more like the Manson girls than food lovers, and no ending to speak of. The whole thing would be so long and incoherent and hideous that for the rest of the day I'd obsess about getting creamed by a car before I could write a decent second draft. I'd worry that people would read what I'd written and believe that the accident had really been a suicide, that I had panicked because my talent was waning and my mind was shot.

The next day, though, I'd sit down, go through it all with a colored pen, take out everything I possibly could, find a new lead somewhere on the second page, figure out a kicky place to end it, and then write a second draft. It always turned out fine, sometimes even funny and weird and helpful. I'd go over it one more time and mail it in.

Then, a month later, when it was time for another review, the whole process would start again, complete with the fears that people would find my first draft before I could rewrite it.

10 Almost all good writing begins with terrible first efforts. You need 10 to start somewhere. Start by getting something—anything down on paper. A friend of mine says that the first draft is the down draft—you just get it down. The second draft is the up draft—you fix it up. You try to say what you have to say more accurately. And the third draft is the dental draft, where you check every tooth, to see if it's loose or cramped or decayed, or even, God help us, healthy.

What I've learned to do when I sit down to work on a shitty first draft is to quiet the voices in my head. First there's the vinegar-lipped Reader Lady, who says primly, "Well, *that's* not very interesting, is it?" And there's the emaciated German male who writes these Orwellian memos detailing your thought crimes. And there are your parents, agonizing over your lack of loyalty and discretion; and there's William Burroughs, dozing off or shooting up because he finds you as bold and articulate as a houseplant; and so on. And there are also the dogs: let's not forget the dogs, the dogs in their pen who will surely hurtle and snarl their way out if you ever *stop* writing, because writing is, for some of us, the latch that keeps the door of the pen closed, keeps those crazy ravenous dogs contained.

Quieting these voices is at least half the battle I fight daily. But this is better than it used to be. It used to be 87 percent. Left to its own devices, my mind spends much of its time having conversations with people who aren't there. I walk along defending myself to people, or exchanging repartee with them, or rationalizing my behavior, or seducing them with gossip, or pretending I'm on their TV talk show or whatever. I speed or run an aging yellow light or don't come to a full stop, and one nanosecond later am explaining to imaginary cops exactly why I had to do what I did, or insisting that I did not in fact do it.

I happened to mention this to a hypnotist I saw many years ago, and he looked at me very nicely. At first I thought he was feeling around on the floor for the silent alarm button, but then he gave me the following exercise, which I still use to this day.

Close your eyes and get quiet for a minute, until the chatter starts up. Then isolate one of the voices and imagine the person speaking as a mouse. Pick it up by the tail and drop it into a mason jar. Then isolate another voice, pick it up by the tail, drop it in the jar. And so on. Drop in any high-maintenance parental units, drop in any contractors, lawyers, colleagues, children, anyone who is whining in your head. Then put the lid on, and watch all these mouse people clawing at the glass, jabbering away, trying to make you feel like shit because you won't do what they want—won't give them more money, won't be more successful, won't see them more often. Then imagine that there is a volume-control button on the bottle. Turn it all the way up for a minute, and listen to the stream of angry, neglected, guilt-mongering voices. Then turn it all the way down and watch the frantic mice lunge at the glass, trying to get to you. Leave it down, and get back to your shitty first draft.

A writer friend of mine suggests opening the jar and shooting them all in the head. But I think he's a little angry, and I'm sure nothing like this would ever occur to you.

All's Not Well in Land of "The Lion King"

Margaret Lazarus

Margaret Lazarus is an Oscar-winning filmmaker with Cambridge Documentary Films in Massachusetts. One of her documentaries, Strong at the Broken Places: Turning Trauma into Recovery *(1998), deals with people's ability to overcome trauma and use their experience to help society.*

In her review of The Lion King, *Lazarus ignores typical film criteria—such as acting, directing, and cinematography—and focuses on the cultural stereotypes in the film that are communicated to the impressionable children in the audience. The "Disney magic," argues Lazarus, reinforces and reproduces bigoted and stereotyped views of minorities and women in our society.*

1   It's Official: Walt Disney's *The Lion King* is breaking box-office   1
records. Unfortunately, it's not breaking any stereotypes.

My sons, along with millions of other kids around the world, joyously awaited *The Lion King.* I was intrigued because this time Disney appeared to be skipping the old folk-tales with their traditional and primal undercurrents.

I hoped Disney had grown weary of reinforcing women's subordinate status by screening fables about a beauty who tames an angry male beast or a mermaid who gives up her glorious voice and splits her body to be with a prince.

So off we went to the movies, figuring we would enjoy all original, well-animated story about animals on the African plain. Even before the title sequence, however, I started to shudder.

5   Picture this (and I apologize for spilling the plot): The golden-   5
maned—that is, good—lion is presenting his first born male child to his

---

Reprinted by permission of the author.

subjects. All the animals in the kingdom, known as Pride Lands, are paying tribute to the infant son that will someday be their king. These royal subjects are basically lion food—zebras, monkeys, birds, etc.—and they all live together in supposed harmony in the "circle of life."

Outside the kingdom, in a dark, gloomy, and impoverished elephant graveyard, are the hyenas. They live dismally jammed together among bones and litter. The hyenas are dark—mostly black—and they are nasty, menacing the little lion prince when he wanders into their territory.

One of their voices is done by Whoopie Goldberg, in a clearly inner-city dialect. If this is not the ghetto, I don't know what is.

All is not perfect inside Pride Lands, however. The king's evil brother Scar has no lionesses or cubs. Scar has a black mane, and speaks in an effeminate, limp-pawed, British style done by Jeremy Irons—seemingly a gay caricature.

Scar conspires with the hyenas to kill the king and send the prince into exile. In exchange for their support, Scar allows the hyenas to live in Pride Lands. But property values soon crash: The hyenas overpopulate, kill all the game, and litter the once-green land with bones.

10   Already Disney has gays and blacks ruining the "natural order,"   10
and the stereotypes keep rolling. The lionesses never question whether they should be serving Scar and the hyenas—they just worry a lot. They are mistreated, but instead of fighting back these powerful hunters passively await salvation. (Even my 7-year-old wondered why the young, strong lioness didn't get rid of Scar.)

The circle of life is broken; disaster awaits everyone. But then the first-born male returns to reclaim power. The royal heir kills the gay usurper, and sends the hyenas back to the dark, gloomy, bone-filled ghetto. Order is restored and the message is clear: Only those born to privilege can bring about change.

This is not a story about animals—we know animals don't behave like this. This is a metaphor for society that originated in the minds of Disney's creators. These bigoted images and attitudes will lodge deeply in children's consciousness.

I'm not sure I always understand the law of the Hollywood jungle, but my boys definitely don't. Scared and frightened by *The Lion King*, they were also riveted, and deeply affected. But entranced by the "Disney magic," they and millions of other children were given hidden messages that can only do them—and us—harm.

The Ones Who Walk Away from Omelas

Ursula K. Le Guin

Ursula K. Le Guin (1929–), born Ursula Kroeber in Berkeley, California, enjoyed an intellectually stimulating childhood with her parents, anthropologist Alfred Kroeber and writer Theodora Kroeber, author of Ishi. *She received her undergraduate degree from Radcliffe College and did graduate work at Columbia University. In Paris in 1953, she married Charles A. Le Guin, a historian; in 1958 they moved to Portland, Oregon. Ursula Le Guin writes poetry and prose, especially science fiction and fantasy. Her best known fantasy works are the first four books of* Earthsea. *Her science fiction novel,* The Left Hand of Darkness *(1969), investigates gender roles with great complexity.* The Dispossessed *(1974) and* Always Coming Home *(1985) provide a new view of utopian fiction. Her* Lathe of Heaven *(1971) was made into a powerful and artistically successful science fiction movie. Recent publications include* Changing Planes *(2003);* The Wave in the Mind: Talks and Essays on the Reader, the Writer, and the Imagination *(2004); and* Gifts, *a fantasy novel, published in September 2004.*

This science fiction story introduces the reader to a planned community in which all are happy and well fed. Under the city, however, lies something so hideous that young people of conscience walk away when they see the truth.

First appeared in *New Dimensions*. Reprinted by permission from the author and the Virginia Kidd Literary Agency, Inc. Copyright © 1973, 2001 by Ursula K. Le Guin.

1   With a clamor of bells that set the swallows soaring, the   1
Festival of Summer came to the city. Omelas, bright-
towered by the sea. The rigging of the boats in harbor
sparkled with flags. In the streets between houses with red roofs and
painted walls, between old moss-grown gardens and under avenues of
trees, past great parks and public buildings, processions moved. Some
were decorous: old people in long stiff robes of mauve and grey, grave
master workmen, quiet, merry women carrying their babies and chat-
ting as they walked. In other streets the music beat faster, a shimmering of gong and tambourine, and the people went dancing, the
procession was a dance. Children dodged in and out, their high calls
rising like the swallows' crossing flights over the music and the singing.
All the processions wound towards the north side of the city, where on
the great water-meadow called the Green Fields boys and girls, naked
in the bright air, with mud-stained feet and ankles and long, lithe
arms, exercised their restive horses before the race. The horses wore no
gear at all but a halter without bit. Their manes were braided with
streamers of silver, gold, and green. They flared their nostrils and
pranced and boasted to one another; they were vastly excited, the
horse being the only animal who has adopted our ceremonies as his
own. Far off to the north and west the mountains stood up half encir-
cling Omelas on her bay. The air of morning was so clear that the
snow still crowning the Eighteen Peaks burned with white gold fire
across the miles of sunlit air, under the dark blue of the sky. There was
just enough wind to make the banners that marked the racecourse
snap and flutter now and then. In the silence of the broad green mead-
ows one could hear the music winding through the city streets, farther
and nearer and ever approaching, a cheerful faint sweetness of the air
that from time to time trembled and gathered together and broke out
into the great joyous clanging of the bells.

     Joyous! How is one to tell about joy? How describe the citizens of
Omelas?

     They were not simple folk, you see, though they were happy. But we
do not say the words of cheer much any more. All smiles have become
archaic. Given a description such as this one tends to make certain
assumptions. Given a description such as this one tends to look next for
the King, mounted on a splendid stallion and surrounded by his noble
knights, or perhaps in a golden litter borne by great-muscled slaves. But
there was no king. They did not use swords, or keep slaves. They were
not barbarians. I do not know the rules and laws of their society, but I

suspect that they were singularly few. As they did without r
slavery, so they also got on without the stock exchange, t
ment, the secret police, and the bomb. Yet I repeat that the
simple folk, nor dulcet shepherds, noble savages, bland utop
were not less complex than us. The trouble is that we have a
encouraged by pedants and sophisticates, of considering happiness as
something rather stupid. Only pain is intellectual, only evil interesting.
This is the treason of the artist: a refusal to admit the banality of evil and
the terrible boredom of pain. If you can't lick 'em, join 'em. If it hurts,
repeat it. But to praise despair is to condemn delight, to embrace violence is to lose hold of everything else. We have almost lost hold; we can
no longer describe a happy man, nor make any celebration of joy. How
can I tell you about the people of Omelas? They were not naïve and
happy children—though their children were, in fact, happy. They were
mature, intelligent, passionate adults whose lives were not wretched.
O miracle! but I wish I could describe it better. I wish I could convince
you. Omelas sounds in my words like a city in a fairy tale, long ago and
far away, once upon a time. Perhaps it would be best if you imagined it
as your own fancy bids, assuming it will rise to the occasion, for certainly
I cannot suit you all. For instance, how about technology? I think that
there would be no cars or helicopters in and above the streets; this follows from the fact that the people of Omelas are happy people. Happiness is based on a just discrimination of what is necessary, what is neither
necessary nor destructive, and what is destructive. In the middle category, however—that of the unnecessary but indestructive, that of comfort, luxury, exuberance, etc.—they could perfectly well have central
heating, subway trains, washing machines, and all kinds of marvelous
devices not yet invented here, floating light-sources, fuelless power, a
cure for the common cold. Or they could have none of that it doesn't
matter. As you like it. I incline to think that people from towns up and
down the coast have been coming in to Omelas during the last days
before the Festival on very fast little trains and double-decked trams and
that the train station of Omelas is actually the handsomest building in
town, though plainer than the magnificent Farmers' Market. But even
granted trains, I fear that Omelas so far strikes some of you as goody-
goody. Smiles, bells, parades, horses, bleh. If so, please add an orgy. If an
orgy would help, don't hesitate. Let us not, however, have temples from
which issue beautiful nude priests and priestesses already half in ecstasy
and ready to copulate with any man or woman, lover or stranger, who
desires union with the deep godhead of the blood, although that was my

first idea. But really it would be better not to have any temples in Omelas—at least, not manned temples. Religion yes, clergy no. Surely the beautiful nudes can just wander about, offering themselves like divine soufflés to the hunger of the needy and the rapture of the flesh. Let them join the processions. Let tambourines be struck above the copulations, and the glory of desire be proclaimed upon the gongs, and (a not unimportant point) let the offspring of these delightful rituals be beloved and looked after by all. One thing I know there is none of in Omelas is guilt. But what else should there be? I thought at first there were no drugs, but that is puritanical. For those who like it, the faint insistent sweetness of *drooz* may perfume the ways of the city, drooz which first brings a great lightness and brilliance to the mind and limbs, and then after some hours a dreamy languor, and wonderful visions at last of the very arcana and inmost secrets of the Universe, as well as exciting the pleasure of sex beyond all belief; and it is not habit-forming. For more modest tastes I think there ought to be beer. What else, what else belongs in the joyous city? The sense of victory, surely, the celebration of courage. But as we did without clergy, let us do without soldiers. The joy built upon successful slaughter is not the right kind of joy; it will not do; it is fearful and it is trivial. A boundless and generous contentment, a magnanimous triumph felt not against some outer enemy but in communion with the finest and fairest in the souls of all men everywhere and the splendor of the world's summer: this is what swells the hearts of the people of Omelas, and the victory they celebrate is that of life. I really don't think many of them need to take *drooz*.

Most of the processions have reached the Green Fields by now. A marvelous smell of cooking goes forth from the red and blue tents of the provisioners. The faces of small children are amiably sticky; in the benign grey beard of a man a couple of crumbs of rich pastry are entangled. The youths and girls have mounted their horses and are beginning to group around the starting line of the course. An old woman, small, fat, and laughing, is passing out flowers from a basket, and tall young men wear her flowers in their shining hair. A child of nine or ten sits at the edge of the crowd, alone, playing on a wooden flute. People pause to listen, and they smile, but they do not speak to him, for he never ceases playing and never sees them, his dark eyes wholly rapt in the sweet, thin magic of the tune.

He finishes, and slowly lowers his hands holding the wooden flute.

As if that little private silence were the signal, all at once a trumpet sounds from the pavillion near the starting line: imperious, melancholy, piercing. The horses rear on their slender legs, and some of them neigh in answer. Sober-faced, the young riders stroke the horses' necks and soothe them, whispering, "Quiet, quiet, there my beauty, my hope. . . ." They begin to form in rank along the starting line. The crowds along the racecourse are like a field of grass and flowers in the wind. The Festival of Summer has begun.

Do you believe? Do you accept the festival, the city, the joy? No? Then let me describe one more thing.

In a basement under one of the beautiful public buildings of Omelas, or perhaps in the cellar of one of its spacious private homes, there is a room. It has one locked door, and no window. A little light seeps in dustily between cracks in the boards, secondhand from a cobwebbed window somewhere across the cellar. In one corner of the little room a couple of mops, with stiff, clotted, foul-smelling heads, stand near a rusty bucket. The floor is dirt, a little damp to the touch, as cellar dirt usually is. The room is about three paces long and two wide: a mere broom closet or disused tool room. In the room a child is sitting. It could be a boy or a girl. It looks about six, but actually is nearly ten. It is feeble-minded. Perhaps it was born defective, or perhaps it has become imbecile through fear, malnutrition, and neglect. It picks its nose and occasionally fumbles vaguelly with its toes or genitals, as it sits hunched in the corner farthest from the bucket and the two mops. It is afraid of the mops. It finds them horrible. It shuts its eyes, but it knows the mops are still standing there; and the door is locked; and nobody will come. The door is always locked; and nobody ever comes, except that sometimes—the child has no understanding of time or interval—sometimes the door rattles terribly and opens, and a person, or several people, are there. One of them may come in and kick the child to make it stand up. The others never come close, but peer in at it with frightened, disgusted eyes. The food bowl and the water jug are hastily filled, the door is locked, the eyes disappear. The people at the door never say anything, but the child, who has not always lived in the tool room, and can remember sunlight and its mother's voice, sometimes speaks. "I will be good," it says. "Please let me out. I will be good!" They never answer. The child used to scream for help at night, and cry a good deal, but now it only makes a kind of whining, "eh-haa, eh-haa," and it speaks less and less often. It is so thin there are no calves to its legs; its belly protrudes; it lives on a half-bowl of corn meal and grease a day. It is naked. Its buttocks and thighs are a mass of festered sores, as it sits in its own excrement continually.

They all know it is there, all the people of Omelas. Some of them have come to see it, others are content merely to know it is there. They all know that it has to be there. Some of them understand why, and some do not, but they all understand that their happiness, the beauty of their city, the tenderness of their friendships, the health of their children, the wisdom of their scholars, the skill of their makers, even the abundance of their harvest and the kindly weathers of their skies, depend wholly on this child's abominable misery.

10   This is usually explained to children when they are between eight   10 and twelve, whenever they seem capable of understanding; and most of those who come to see the child are young people, though often enough an adult comes, or comes back, to see the child. No matter how well the matter has been explained to them, these young spectators are always shocked and sickened at the sight. They feel disgust, which they had thought themselves superior to. They feel anger, outrage, impotence, despite all the explanations. They would like to do something for the child. But there is nothing they can do. If the child were brought up into the sunlight out of that vile place, if it were cleaned and fed and comforted, that would be a good thing, indeed; but if it were done, in that day and hour all the prosperity and beauty and delight of Omelas would wither and be destroyed. Those are the terms. To exchange all the goodness and grace of every life in Omelas for that single, small improvement: to throw away the happiness of thousands for the chance of the happiness of one: that would be to let guilt within the walls indeed.

The terms are strict and absolute; there may not even be a kind word spoken to the child.

Often the young people go home in tears, or in a tearless rage, when they have seen the child and faced this terrible paradox. They may brood over it for weeks or years. But as time goes on they begin to realize that even if the child could be released, it would not get much good of its freedom: a little vague pleasure of warmth and food, no doubt, but little more. It is too degraded and imbecile to know any real joy. It has been afraid too long ever to be free of fear. Its habits are too uncouth for it to respond to humane treatment. Indeed, after so long it would probably be wretched without walls about it to protect it, and darkness for its eyes, and its own excrement to sit in. Their tears at the bitter injustice dry when they begin to perceive the terrible justice of reality and to accept it. Yet it is their tears and anger, the trying of their generosity and the acceptance of their helplessness, which are perhaps the true source of the splendor of their lives. Theirs is no vapid, irresponsible happiness. They know that they, like the child, are not free. They know compassion. It is the existence of the child, and their knowledge of its existence, that makes possible the nobility of their architecture, the poignancy of their music, the profundity of their science. It is because of the child that they are so gentle with children. They know that if the wretched one were not there snivelling in the dark, the other one, the flute-player, could make no joyful music as the young riders line up in their beauty for the race in the sunlight of the first morning of summer.

Now do you believe in them? Are they not more credible? But there is one more thing to tell, and this is quite incredible.

At times one of the adolescent girls or boys who go to see the child does not go home to weep or rage, does not, in fact, go home at all. Sometimes also a man or woman much older falls silent for a day or two, and then leaves home. These people go out into the street, and walk down the street alone. They keep walking, and walk straight out of the city of Omelas, through the beautiful gates. They keep walking across the farmlands of Omelas. Each one goes alone, youth or girl, man or woman. Night falls; the traveler must pass down village streets, between the houses with yellow-lit windows, and on out into the darkness of the fields. Each alone, they go west or north, towards the mountains. They go on. They leave Omelas, they walk ahead into the darkness, and they do not come back. The place they go towards is a place even less imaginable to most of us than the city of happiness. I cannot describe it at all. It is possible that it does not exist. But they seem to know where they are going, the ones who walk away from Omelas.

Snoop's Devil Dogg: African American Ghostlore and *Bones*

Richard Ravalli

1 The 2001 motion picture *Bones*, starring gangsta rapper-turned-actor Snoop Dogg, is perhaps not the most "serious" horror movie ever made. Near the end, while on his bloody rampage to destroy the murderers who turned him into a revenant, lead character Jimmy Bones, played by Snoop, decapitates his victims and carries about their still-talking severed heads, providing what some feel is an awkward sequence of comic relief. Yet the film also less humorously portrays popular elements of the African American sacred world, ones Snoop Dogg himself to some extent incorporates. Among other things, *Bones* leads us to consider the history of ghost dogs in black folklore.[1]

The spectral hound in *Bones*, part vengeful spirit, part corporeal dog, acts as a familiar and helps bring about the resurrection of Jimmy Bones. Their symbiotic relationship signifies distinct, layered connections between Snoop and earlier properties of African American culture. The dog is no exception to the complexity of folk processes in ultimately being more than a scary story uprooted from a haunted countryside and placed in the film. In *Bones*, ghost dog lore is urbanized and ghettocentricized, representing the horrors of the turn-of-the-millennium inner city. Equally important to this study is how this symbol has developed. With Snoop, the devil dog blends with secular

Reprinted from *The Journal of American Culture* 30, no. 3 (2007).

Richard Ravalli is a doctoral student in World Cultures and History at University of California, Merced. His interests include American cultural history, American film, and the Pacific frontier. He is currently researching the Pacific sea otter trade and the early years of George Lucas.
The Journal of American Culture, 30:3 ©2007, Copyright the Authors, Journal compilation ©2007, Blackwell Printing, Inc.

"badman" folklore and "dogg" iconography in black tradition. Popular conceptions of dangerous masculinity and the dogg persona help provide for a unique manifestation of the modern supernatural canine. I rely here on Eithne Quinn's works, which interrogate the gangsta rapper as badman as well as African American vernacular uses of "dog," the latter remaining underexplored by scholars (Quinn 1999, 2005). Her grounding of Snoop Dogg in the black cultural past has influenced the following analysis. Finally, *Bones* is not the only recent movie to suggest the ghost dog amidst filmic conventions of the hood. The subtle spectral environment of *Ghost Dog: The Way of the Samurai* (2000) is highlighted and compared.

Origins[2]

The devil dog, or black dog, has a rich history in western culture. The Egyptian god of death Anubis was pictured with a dog's head, while "[t]he Greeks and Romans associated dogs with Hecate, goddess of the infernal regions and of witchcraft" (Woods 230). Large black hounds with fiery eyes haunt locations and follow people at night in German folklore. In Britain, the Barguest is a shape shifting demon dog, although other specters are viewed as less-antagonistic ghosts of human beings or of dogs (Briggs 115). The supernatural creature survived the trip across the Atlantic and appears in the "wonder" records of early New England. At Salem, Sarah Carrier was promised a black dog for her witchcraft. During a trip into the woods, William Barker encountered "the Shape of a black dog w'ch looked Verry fercly Upon him" (Hall 88).

While African animistic and ancestor beliefs (and tales about dogs) played some role in the existence of the ghost dog in African American lore, European sources likely provided a larger inspiration than what has heretofore been recognized. In his article on black spirits, Elliott Gorn correctly notes the amalgamation of traditions that shaped slave ghost stories (Gorn 551–52). However, I feel that the dog ghost is mistakenly identified as African in origin due to his reliance on J. Mason Brewer, who was unaware of the motif's larger existence in America beyond black usage. Also, Brewer's focus was on tales of benevolent canine spirits, hence his citation of an African myth about the dog as a helper to man (Brewer 3). To be sure, non-Anglo ethnic sources should not be ignored. Jennifer Hildebrand has recently argued that Igbo belief in the transmigration of spirits lay behind tales of humans in animal form (Hildebrand 127–52). But to the best of my knowledge, the question of a specific West African tradition involving ghost dogs, or humans as dogs, remains an open one.

5   The current lack of early ghost dog records from the South complicates a master–slave transmission origin but does not contradict it. As Christine Leigh Heyrman suggests, southern Christians may not have excelled as their New England counterparts did in accounts of the Devil and preternatural entities until the evangelical revivals of the mid-eighteenth century, even if clergy in the region grew increasingly skeptical about elements of wonder lore in subsequent decades (Heyrman ch. 1). Yet some measure of popular occult fascination took root there and sustained throughout the antebellum period. In a variety of ways and in diverse locations, beliefs about malevolent beings taking physical or quasi-physical forms were passed to slaves as their spirits became increasingly diabolical (Sobel 66–71). African elements were indeed retained, and Brewer's dog ghosts are perhaps evidence of that, but at this moment it is fair to say that Euro-American influences are at least equally responsible for the ghost dog in African American folklore. Many (if not most) of the examples lead in that cultural direction.

Whatever the case may be about ethnic origins, by the early twentieth century the ghost dog was an often-told tale among African Americans in the South. It may be possible to claim, without complete exaggeration, that such lore among southern whites today owes as much to black storytelling as it does to Anglo myth. For example, in his 1926 study titled *Folk Beliefs of the Southern Negro,* Newbell Niles Puckett recorded tales of huge, calf-sized dog spirits with fiery red eyes (128–29). Hallie Hanson from Augusta, Georgia told WPA researchers in 1938 of an encounter with a frightening headless white dog near a tree when she was around ten years old. She ran to her house and looked back, only to find that the "ha'nt" had disappeared (Brown 43). Friends believed that legendary Delta blues musician Robert Johnson sold his soul to the Devil at a crossroads to gain his musical talent (Guralnick 17–18). His song "Hell Hound On My Trail" can be read as a consequence of his supposed Faustian bargain.[3] Mary Richardson told folklorist Richard Dorson of the time she met with a "colored" Devil who also appeared as a hound that chased her into a field: "Why he struck my track to run me in there I don't know, 'cept that was just before I got converted" (Dorson 137). Such examples can be multiplied.

Stories of the black dog continued to be told well into the twentieth century. Mark Chester (a white informant) related a high school experience from 1978 in a written account to a paranormal magazine.[4] He and a friend were custodians at a bank chain in Atlanta, Georgia when, on their way to their second location, a huge spectral hound appeared:

> Suddenly, about seventy-five yards ahead, a large black dog, about the size and shape of a Labrador Retriever, trotted out into the road. I could see it plainly as the road was well lit by streetlights, and I wasn't concerned for its safety because it was a good distance in front of us and there weren't any other cars nearby. Then a strange thing occurred! As the dog was about three quarters of the way across the road, it simply vanished! Just as it was about to step on the broken white line on our side of the four lane, it simply disappeared. (Rowlett 50)

The setting here, an urban location, suggests that the tradition has traveled from the shadows of the backwoods to the shadows of the city. Evidence in this paper supports the notion that twentieth-century black migration played a role in an urbanization of the ghost dog.[5] In the 1990s, a Los Angeles gang member named Lo-Jo lost his pet pit bull to a stray drive-by bullet. While he and friends planned a revenge attack against another local gang, he saw his dog in an alley behind a pawn shop: "I told everybody to look but when they did he was gone. Now everybody was thinking I was crazy and shit so they told me to come on" (Freak-o-Pedia). His concern for the spectral dog may have saved his life, as Lo-Jo's friends who left were soon thereafter shot. The ghettocentric theme of this type of account is shared with the setting in *Bones*. The urban ghost dog's role as a protective agent is similar to stories such as those in Brewer's collection and is returned to below.

One may wonder about the popularity of the supernatural dog in black folklore. In the antebellum era, slave dogs provided numerous benefits for their owners, including companionship during hunting. Many masters allowed the practice until laws prohibiting dog ownership for slaves intensified in areas of the South just before the Civil War (Campbell 53–76). Perhaps the substantial psychic bonds that developed helped shape "good" dog ghost stories, yet seemingly more influential was the use of the animals for slave patrols and chasing runaways as reasons why the canine was prone to be imbued with frightening spiritual qualities well beyond emancipation.[6] I cannot offer an in depth analysis of major factors relating to origins here, but the special place of the dog in African American thought and the disparate responses it elicited are also mirrored in secular expressive culture. The "dogg" that Snoop utilizes in his performance career is drawn from a milieu of colorful dog personification and hypermasculine themes.

The D-O-Double-G and the Badman

10 Quinn traces the noun *dog* in black vernacular discourse to examples 10
in early twentieth-century music, from female artists such as Bessie Smith and Big Mama Thornton. The "low down dirty dog" was often employed pejoratively to refer to laid-back, devious player types (Quinn 1999: 191–92). Dog, or dogg, also developed a heroic connotation. Used largely by African American men, a "supersexual and street-identified black male," according to Quinn, was signified by its use in funk and gangsta rap. In the gangsta subculture of the 1990s, lyrics such as the following helped Snoop Dogg gain credibility as a lion-ized pimp figure: "How many hoes in ninety-four will I be bangin'?/ Every single one, to get the job done" (Quinn 1999: 193). The dogg is meant to alarm both the white and black "Post-Soul" middle class, representing a critical response to civil-rights era masculinity during a time of increasing pressures on inner-city male youths, but by others his prowess is admired. This dual nature of the dogg is highlighted in Snoop's breakthrough video for "Who Am I (What's My Name)?," in which a supernormal Snoop causes havoc by morphing into a menac-ing Doberman pinscher, yet is hailed as a neighborhood hero (Quinn 2005: 141–42). Neither are the predations of Jimmy Bones seen as entirely diabolical. According to director Ernest Dickerson, "There's a righteousness in what he's doing . . . I wanted the audience to root for him at first" (*Digging Up Bones*).

Snoop is a type of badman. In her recent volume *Nuthin' but a "G" Thang: The Culture and Commerce of Gangsta Rap,* Quinn discusses the relationship between the toasts of black outlaws such as Stackolee and Dolemite in tradition and the lyrics of gangsta. If, according to Julius Lester, Stackolee was "the baddest nigger that ever lived," then the rapper's boasts in NWA's 1988 "Straight Outta Compton" pro-vide a similar folk reputation. As Quinn writes, "[T]he rhyme evokes the randomness of the badman's gratuitous violence and anonymous sex. MC Ren, the 'crazy-ass nigga' here, unleashes his ire at all the usual suspects, boasting about street toughness, criminal activity, and sexual dominance" (Quinn 2005: 97). Snoop himself is "clockin' a grip like my name is Dolemite" in he and Dr. Dre's G-Funk classic. It is this connection to "black anti-heroes" that helped inspire the creation of Snoop Dogg as Jimmy Bones, as *Bones* coscreenwriter Adam Simon explained in a recent e-mail (Simon). While qualifications partly in relation to the dogg's heroism are noted below, Snoop becomes a spectral badman on the big screen, committing devious, otherworldly deeds. His dogg persona and its literal adaptations, complete with supernatural suggestions, are linked with the badman and are natural inclusions in the film. Thus, if only partially recognized, the hell hound is incorporated into a rich cultural landscape in *Bones*.[7] The urban gothic environment provides an ideal place for Snoop's devilish dogg to materialize.

Spooking the Ghetto

The creature appears in roughly the first half of the film. In *Bones,* a mixed-race group of young entrepreneurs from a Chicago suburb decide to purchase a decaying brownstone in the inner-city to renovate into a nightclub. They soon discover a strange dog inside the building and adopt it as a pet. As the hellish hound begins attacking them within the finished establishment, its predations aid the reanimation of Jimmy Bones, buried in the basement after having been murdered in the building years earlier. We discover through flashback that Bones was a well-respected pimp during the neighborhood's Soul years, idealized in the film as a time of togetherness and civil-rights era optimism. Bones refused to push crack and was taken out by neighborhood rivals, including a crooked cop. He returns to the now-soulless ghetto to take his revenge. The revenant is eventually dispatched by Bones's former lover, played by Pam Grier (formerly "Foxy Brown").

The film is partially a blaxploitation homage that criticizes conditions in the postindustrial hood. Scholars have differed on whether the horror genre is appropriate for addressing concerns about social equality (see Briefel and Ngai; Benshoff). Movies such as *Blackula* (1972) and *Candyman* (1992), both featuring supernatural badmen similar to Bones, can be read as both subverting and justifying dominant racial dialogues.[8] This debate is not fully engaged here, but *Bones* does at least attempt to present the turn-of-the-millennium black city as a troubling (yet stylized) place, utilizing conventions similar to those of earlier ghettocentric/hood films (Watkins 196–231; Massood 145–74). A run-down neighborhood, corrupt law enforcement, black middle-class flight, and the damaging effects crack in the 1980s help set the stage for a haunted, dark environment dominated by the spirit of Jimmy Bones. Dickerson summarizes, "You see the difference. When Bones is alive, the neighborhood is alive, you see kids playing. When Bones is dead, the neighborhood is dead. It's a ghost town. You don't see anybody there" (*Digging Up Bones*).

Snoop's dogg persona assumes mythological status as it terrorizes this dystopian environment. Yet the devil dog in *Bones* is not viewed as a completely evil spirit. After a terrifying opening sequence, it appears as a somewhat normal animal. The dog can be fed by and act friendly to the youths who take it in, yet its dangerous, spectral nature is acknowledged throughout.[9] Perhaps like Snoop as a *dogg*, it exists somewhere between good and evil, friend and foe. It is a frightening being created by the realities of the hood, but it gains a level of acceptance from those who surround it. This and other evidence intimates that Jimmy Bones and his familiar remain distinct from earlier badmen in black culture. Ultimately the dogg may only be out for his own nefarious pleasure, but his handiwork is admired. However, according to Lawrence Levine in his classic study of African American folk thought, postbellum bandits were never pictured in tales as good, gentlemen miscreants:

> Black legend did not portray good bad men or noble outlaws. The brutality of Negro bad men was allowed to speak for itself without extenuation. Their badness was described without the excuse of socially redeeming qualities. They preyed upon the weak as well as the strong, women as well as men. They killed not merely in self-defense but from sadistic need and sheer joy. . . . Coming from the depths of society, representing the most oppressed and deprived strata, these bandits are manifestations of the feeling that, within the circumstances in which they operate, to assert any power at all is a triumph. (417–18)

15   While storytellers and listeners no doubt received a degree of pleasure   15
from the exploits of Stackolee and Dolemite, "black folk refused to romantically embellish or sentimentalize them" (Levine 415). By contrast, the revenant in *Bones* brings well-deserved justice to the corruptors of the ghetto, poor souls who make up a majority of his victims. Thus the film's reliance on white outlaw conventions is revealed. Bones

may not be the quintessential badman partially because producers invoke a *good* badman, noting Clint Eastwood's supernatural avenger in *High Plains Drifter* (1973) as inspiration (Simon; *Digging Up Bones*). Bones' western-style duster helps establish his quasi-heroic image.

Of all the black outlaws, perhaps Railroad Bill most resembles Jimmy Bones and his ghost dog. Based on the exploits of a turpentine worker in Alabama who killed a policeman in 1893, Railroad Bill survived by robbing trains for three years. He stole canned food and forced poor blacks who lived along the tracks to buy it. According to Levine, legend includes that he was a conjure man and could transform himself into an animal in order to elude capture: "With posses close behind him, he would turn himself into a sheep, a brown dog, a red fox and watch them ride by" (411). The dog in *Bones* also appears in multiple forms; early on, a shadow informs of us a transformation into a rat, and a succubus precedes the gory attack in the nightclub. Tales about bandits such as Bill remind us that supernormal badmen are not reserved for the modern likes of Blackula and Bones, and suggest intricate connections within the black sacred world.[10]

Despite the movie's ambivalence about its central character, he remains an unsavory presence who graphically reminds the neighborhood of its sins. Bones and his canine familiar stalk a romanticized gothic ghetto and reflect its recent evil past. This "dead" neighborhood may not be an ideal place for evocative political commentary. Future scholars should address this question and include consideration of *Bones* as it relates to tensions between inner city and suburban blacks, an issue it attempts to raise. I offer that the dog ghost is incorporated into the film's ghettocentric landscape and marks an urbanization of the motif. It is mediated by distinct and interconnected black cultural traditions, as well as by white storytelling. Thus the devil dog's origins in *Bones* (by no means completely examined here) mirrors similarly complex patterns in the creature's earlier American history. Through this process the spectral hound emerges to spook the hood and warn those who may enter its domain. If the rural South once gripped African Americans with dangers both physical and spiritual, now the city contains special dangers to be heeded and devils to chase you.

The moral message of African American ghostlore also remains in its inner city manifestations. Jacqueline Fulmer argues that the specters of *Tales From the Hood* (1995) act as reminders of proper group behavior: "Specifically, elements of African American folklore that emphasize one's responsibility to the community, the weak overcoming the strong, and the wisdom of elders appear to have influenced this particular example of movie making" (Fulmer 422–23). Similarly, *Bones* criticizes not only those who have left for the suburbs, but those white and black who are guilty of infecting the hood with drugs. The film's spirits prey upon villains who turned their backs on a proud ghetto and whites who profit from and purchase illicit substances. Gorn's description of slave ghost accounts as "a subtle form of in-group communication, a dramatic way of conveying essential social meanings" (565) is therefore applicable to the twenty-first century. *Bones* helps demonstrate that the "ha'nts" of African American horror function at certain levels to address wrongs and promote cohesion in the black community.

Jim Jarmusch's *Ghost Dog* (1999) has received more critical attention. Set in a contemporary urban environment, it is the story of a loner assassin named Ghost Dog, played by the well-renowned, low-key Forest Whitaker. Ghost Dog is half gangsta, half Eastern-inspired warrior, living by a feudal code known as *Hagakure: The Way of the Samurai* (by Yamamoto Tsunetomo in the seventeenth century) as he carries out Mafia hits. As Ingrid Walker Fields describes:

> Juxtaposed against an impotent Mafia (the cartoonish and cartoon-obsessed Vargo family) and a ghostly urban world, Ghost Dog radiates the power and serenity inherent to the strict observance of a code. The warrior's skill and art become the logical evolution and refinement of gangsta culture: more than a mode of survival of inner-city life, it is the path to self-fulfillment. (615)

20   It is ultimately the code that leads to the downfall of this tough *dogg*   20 after Ghost Dog deems it just that his gangster "master" Louie—who earlier saved Ghost Dog's life and is the only mobster with whom he communicates—should kill him to avenge the deaths of Vargo family bosses. They meet in an Old West standoff where Ghost Dog sacrifices himself, allowing Louie to shoot him dead. *Ghost Dog* presents a cultural pastiche (billed as "East meets West") with a rich variety of characters and symbols. After learning of his existence, the mob bosses associate both gangsta-naming and Native American traditions with Ghost Dog's name. Like Jimmy Bones, he is a noble badman, yet unlike Bones's revenant, his relaxed, likable demeanor gains him open respect in the ghetto. As Fields notes, Ghost Dog's life and eventual death may

therefore go farther in complicating conceptions of gangsta nihilism and masculinity (Fields 622–30). The film also plays with an eclectic spirituality. I believe it is in this context where we witness a spectral canine.

Beyond the name "Ghost Dog" and the character's prowess as a mysterious, ghost-like assassin, Jarmusch includes a subtle animism that compliments his use of Eastern philosophy. Birds, bears, and cartoon animals reappear throughout the production, and at two-key moments a mysterious brown dog stares at Ghost Dog. The first time is as he sits on a park bench near a young Jamaican girl named Pearline. He is surprised by the sudden appearance of the animal and its odd, stoic behavior, yet Pearline sees it too. The dog allows Ghost Dog and the girl to strike up a conversation then instantly heeds his command to leave. It returns as Ghost Dog heads out for his final, nocturnal hit, shortly before the fatal faceoff with Louie. Once again the dog simply gazes at him in a dark alley, waiting for him to walk away. Whatever its possible, seemingly non-European origin (Native American, Asian, African), the animal is similar to a spirit guide aiding Ghost Dog on his path. It plays a role in helping him reach Pearline, to whom he ultimately passes on his interests in literature, including *Hagakure*. Does it strengthen him in his final mission toward his eventual death, the fulfillment of the samurai's code? Is it an urban canine spirit, akin to the devil dogg but also reminiscent of Brewer's *friendly* dog ghosts? *Ghost Dog* points to a connection with folklore, but I leave it to future inquiry to further explore such a spectral interpretation.

Notes

1. For the most part, I interchangeably use ghost dog, dog ghost, black dog, devil dog, etc., to refer to a general body of spectral canine lore. Distinctions are recognized elsewhere (see Russell and Barnett xi–xii, for example).

2. Much more can be said on origins than space here permits, which I plan for in a longer treatment of the ghost dog in America.

3. For a skeptical treatment of the Johnson Devil story, see Wald 265–76.

4. I wish to thank the late Mark Chorvinsky of *Strange Magazine* for sharing his interest in dog ghosts. I also thank Curt Rowlett for this story, published in the 1990s.

5. Black supernatural belief in the twentieth-century urban north can be found in McCall, in Dundes 419–27.

6. See Derr 85, 150–55.

7. While Simon noted devil dog folklore as an inspiration for *Bones,* he claims to have been unaware of the African American traditions (Simon). It is unclear to me whether Snoop Dogg consciously invokes the ghost dog, although given his familial connection to the South and his involvement with spectrally suggestive imagery, it is not unlikely.

8. Recently, Jacqueline Fulmer noted the contributions of *Tales From the Hood* (1995) in challenging stereotypes of black masculinity, something that Snoop Dogg's gangsta-fied spirit world outlaw in *Bones* may not be helpful in accomplishing (Fulmer).

9. The pseudophysicality of the dog is reflected in other folklore examples. See Stein 65–66; Brewer 93–95.

10. For more on supernatural elements of the badman, see Roberts 199–203.

Filmography

Blackula. Dir. William Crain. Perf. William Marshall, Venetia McGee, and Denise Nicholas. American International Pictures, 1972.

Bones. Dir. Ernest Dickerson, Perf. Snoop Dogg and Pam Grier. New Line Cinema, 2001.

Candyman. Dir. Bernard Rose, Perf. Virginia Madsen and Tony Todd. Poly-Gram Filmed Entertainment, 1992.

Ghost Dog: The Way of the Samurai. Dir. Jim Jarmusch. Perf. Forest Whitaker and John Tormey. Artisan Entertainment, 1999.

High Plains Drifter. Dir. Clint Eastwood. Perf. Clint Eastwood, Verna Bloom, Marianna Hill, and Mitch Ryan. Universal Studios, 1973.

Tales From the Hood. Dir. Rusty Cundieff. Perf. Clarence Williams III, Joe Torry, De'aundre Bonds, and Samuel Monroe, Jr. 40 Acres and a Mule Filmworks/Savoy Pictures, 1995.

Works Cited

Benshoff, Harry. "Blaxploitation Horror Films: Generic Reappropriation or Reinscription?" *Cinema Journal* 39.2 (Winter 2000): 31–50.

Brewer, Mason J. *Dog Ghosts and Other Texas Negro Folktales.* Austin: U of Texas P, 1958.

Briefel, Aviva, and Sistine Ngai. "'How much did you Pay for this Place?' Fear, Entitlement, and Urban Space in Bernard Rose's *Candyman.*" *Camera Obscura: A Journal of Feminism, Culture, and Media Studies* 37 (January 1996): 71–91.

Briggs, Katharine. *British Folk Tales.* New York: Pantheon Books, 1970.

Brown, Alan. *Shadows and Cypress: Southern Ghost Stories.* Jackson: UP of Mississippi, 2000.

Campbell, John. "'My Constant Companion': Slaves and Their Dogs in the Antebellum South." *Working Toward Freedom: Slave Society and Domestic Economy in the American South.* Ed. Larry E. Hudson. Rochester: U of Rochester P, 1994.

Derr, Mark. *A Dog's History of America: How Our Best Friend Explored, Conquered, and Settled a Continent.* New York: North Point Press, 2004.

Digging Up Bones. Production Documentary. *Bones* New Line Platinum Series DVD, 2004.

Dorson, Richard M. *American Negro Folktales.* New York: Fawcett Premier, 1967.

Fields, Ingrid Walker. "Family Values and Feudal Codes: The Social Politics of America's Twenty-First Century Gangster." *The Journal of Popular Culture* 37.4 (2004): 611–33.

Freak-o-Pedia (online). "Gang Banger Ghost Dog." Freaky Links, date unknown. 29 Mar. 2006 (http://www.haxan.com/portfolio/freakylinks/WWWFRE-l.COM/FREAKO-1/NECROP-1/GANG_D-1.HTM).

Fulmer, Jacqueline. "'Men Ain't All'—A Reworking of Masculinity in Tales From the Hood, or, Grandma Meets the Zombie." *Journal of American Folklore* 115 (2002): 422–42.

Gorn, Elliott J. "Black Spirits: The Ghostlore of Afro-American Slaves." *American Quarterly* 36.4 (Spring-Winter 1984): 549–65.

Guralnick, Peter. *Searching for Robert Johnson.* New York: Dutton, 1989.

Hall, David D. *Worlds of Wonder, Days of Judgment: Popular Religious Belief In Early New England.* Cambridge, MA: Harvard UP, 1989.

Heyrman, Christine Leigh. *Southern Cross: The Beginnings of the Bible Belt.* Chapel Hill, NC: The U of North Carolina P, 1997.

Hildebrand, Jennifer. "'Dere Were No Place in Heaven For Him, An' He Were Not Desired In Hell: Igbo Cultural Beliefs in African American Folk Expressions." *The Journal of African American History* 91.2 (Spring 2006): 127–52.

Levine, Lawrence W. *Black Culture and Black Consciousness: Afro-American Folk Thought from Slavery to Freedom.* Oxford: Oxford UP, 1977.

Massood, Paula J. *Black City Cinema: African American Urban Experiences in Film.* Philadelphia: Temple UP, 2003.

McCall, George J. "Symbiosis: The Case of Hoodoo & the Numbers Racket." *Mother Wit from the Laughing Barrel: Readings in the Interpretation of Afro-American Folklore.* Ed. Alan Dundes. Jackson: UP of Mississippi, 1990.

Puckett, Newbell Niles. *Folk Beliefs of the Southern Negro.* Chapel Hill, NC: U of North Carolina P, 1926.

Quinn, Eithne. "'It's a Doggy-Dogg World': Black Cultural Politics, Gangsta Rap and the 'Post Soul Man'." *Gender and the Civil Rights Movement.* Eds. Peter J. Ling and Sharon Monteith. New Brunswick, NJ: Rutgers UP, 1999. 187–213.

———. *Nuthin' But a "G" Thang: The Culture and Commerce of Gangsta Rap.* New York: Columbia UP, 2005.

Roberts, John W. *From Trickster to Badman: The Black Folk Hero in Slavery and Freedom.* Philadelphia: U of Pennsylvania P, 1989.

Rowlett, Curtis A. "Phantom Black Dog." *Strange Magazine* 13 (date unknown): 28; 50.

Russell, Randy and Janet Barnett. *Ghost Dogs of the South.* Winston-Salem, NC: John F. Blair, 2001.

Simon, Adam. E-mail to author. 9 Aug. 2005.

Sobel, Mechal. *Trabelin' On: The Slave Journey to an Afro-Baptist Faith.* West-port, CT: Greenwood Press, 1979.

Stein, Gordon. "Black Dogs: Fact of Fancy?" *Fate* (June 1990): 65–73.

Wald, Elijah. *Escaping the Delta: Robert Johnson and the Invention of the Blues.* New York: Amistad, 2004.

Watkins, Craig S. *Representing: Hip Hop Culture and the Production of Black Cinema.* Chicago: The U of Chicago P, 1998.

Woods, Barbara Allen. "The Devil in Dog Form." *Western Folklore* 13 (October 1954): 229–35.

How to Say Nothing in 500 Words

Paul Roberts

Paul Roberts (1917–1967) wrote clear and helpful writ-
ing textbooks, among them English *Syntax (1954),* Patterns of English *(1956),* Understanding English *(1958)*
and English Sentences *(1962). He approached writing*
with the scientific discipline of a linguist. In the following
excerpt from Understanding English, *note his tendency to*
categorize and classify, to write descriptions and rules. In
this way, the "art" of writing is transformed to the science
(Latin for knowledge) of composition.

Nothing About Something

1   It's Friday afternoon, and you have almost survived another week
of classes. You are just looking forward dreamily to the weekend when
the English instructor says: "For Monday you will turn in a five-
hundred-word composition on college football."

Well, that puts a good big hole in the weekend. You don't have
any strong views on college football one way or the other. You get
rather excited during the season and go to all the home games and find
it rather more fun than not. On the other hand, the class has been
reading Robert Hutchins in the anthology and perhaps Shaw's
"Eighty-Yard Run," and from the class discussion you have got the
idea that the instructor thinks college football is for the birds. You are
no fool, you. You can figure out what side to take.

After dinner you get out the portable typewriter that you got for
high school graduation. You might as well get it over with and enjoy
Saturday and Sunday. Five hundred words is about two double-spaced

From *Understanding English* by Paul Roberts. Published by HarperCollins Publishers,
Inc. Copyright © 1958 by Paul Roberts, copyright by Prentice Hall, a Pearson
Education Company.

pages with normal margins. You put in a sheet of paper, think up a title, and you're off:

Why College Football Should Be Abolished

College football should be abolished because it's bad for the school and also bad for the players. The players are so busy practicing that they don't have any time for their studies.

5   This, you feel, is a mighty good start. The only trouble is that it's only thirty-two words. You still have four hundred and sixty-eight to go, and you've pretty well exhausted the subject. It comes to you that you do your best thinking in the morning, so you put away the typewriter and go to the movies. But the next morning you have to do your washing and some math problems, and in the afternoon you go to the game. The English instructor turns up too, and you wonder if you've taken the right side after all. Saturday night you have a date, and Sunday morning you have to go to church. (You shouldn't let English assignments interfere with your religion.) What with one thing and another, it's ten o'clock Sunday night before you get out the typewriter again. You make a pot of coffee and start to fill out your views on college football. Put a little meat on the bones.

Why College Football Should Be Abolished

In my opinion, it seems to me that college football should be abolished. The reason why I think this to be true is because I feel that football is bad for the colleges in nearly every respect. As Robert Hutchins says in his article in our anthology in which he discusses college football, it would be better if the colleges had race horses and had races with one another, because then the horses would not have to attend classes. I firmly agree with Mr. Hutchins on this point, and I am sure that many other students would agree too.

One reason why it seems to me that college football is bad is that it has become too commercial. In the olden times when people played football just for the fun of it, maybe college football was all right, but they do not play football just for the fun of it now as they used to in the old days. Nowadays college football is what you might call a big business. Maybe this is not true at all schools, and I don't think it is especially true here at State, but certainly this is the case at most colleges and universities in America nowadays, as Mr. Hutchins points out in his very interesting article. Actually the coaches and alumni go around to the high schools and offer the high school stars large salaries to come to their colleges and play football for them. There was one case where a high school star was offered a convertible if he would play football for a certain college.

Another reason for abolishing college football is that it is bad for the players. They do not have time to get a college education, because they are so busy playing football. A football player has to practice every afternoon from three to six, and then he is so tired that he can't concentrate on his studies. He just feels like dropping off to sleep after dinner, and then the next day he goes to his classes without having studied and maybe he fails the test.

(Good ripe stuff so far, but you're still a hundred and fifty-one words from home. One more push.)

Also I think college football is bad for the colleges and the universities because not very many students get to participate in it. Out of a college of ten thousand students only seventy-five or a hundred play football, if that many. Football is what you might call a spectator sport. That means that most people go to watch it but do not play it themselves.

(Four hundred and fifteen. Well, you still have the conclusion, and when you retype it, you can make the margins a little wider.)

10   These are the reasons why I agree with Mr. Hutchins   10
that college football should be abolished in American colleges and universities.

On Monday you turn it in, moderately hopeful, and on Friday it comes back marked "weak in content" and sporting a big "D."

This essay is exaggerated a little, not much. The English instructor will recognize it as reasonably typical of what an assignment on college football will bring in. He knows that nearly half of the class will contrive in five hundred words to say that college football is too commercial and bad for the players. Most of the other half will inform him that college football builds character and prepares one for life and brings prestige to the school. As he reads paper after paper all saying the same thing in almost the same words, all bloodless, five hundred words dripping out of nothing, he wonders how he allowed himself to get trapped into teaching English when he might have had a happy and interesting life as an electrician or a confidence man.

Well, you may ask, what can you do about it? The subject is one on which you have few convictions and little information. Can you be expected to make a dull subject interesting? As a matter of fact, this is precisely what you are expected to do. This is the writer's essential task. All subjects, except sex, are dull until somebody makes them interesting. The writer's job is to find the argument, the approach, the angle, the wording that will take the reader with him. This is seldom easy, and it is particularly hard in subjects that have been much discussed: College Football, Fraternities, Popular Music, Is Chivalry Dead?, and the like. You will feel that there is nothing you can do with such subjects except repeat the old bromides. But there are some things you can do which will make your papers, if not throbbingly alive, at least less insufferably tedious than they might otherwise be.

Avoid the Obvious Content

Say the assignment is college football. Say that you've decided to be against it. Begin by putting down the arguments that come to your mind: it is too commercial, it takes the students' minds off their studies, it is hard on the players, it makes the university a kind of circus instead of an intellectual center, for most schools it is financially ruinous. Can you think of any more arguments just off hand! All right. Now when you write your paper, *make sure that you don't use any of the material on this list.* If these are the points that leap to your mind, they will leap to everyone else's too, and whether you get a "C" or a "D" may depend on whether the instructor reads your paper early when he is fresh and tolerant or late, when the sentence "In my opinion, college football has become too commercial," inexorably repeated, has brought him to the brink of lunacy.

15   Be against college football for some reason or reasons of your own.   15
If they are keen and perceptive ones, that's splendid. But even if they
are trivial or foolish or indefensible, you are still ahead so long as they
are not everybody else's reasons too. Be against it because the colleges
don't spend enough money on it to make it worth while, because it is
bad for the characters of the spectators, because the players are forced
to attend classes, because the football stars hog all the beautiful women,
because it competes with baseball and is therefore un-American and
possibly Communist inspired. There are lots of more or less unused
reasons for being against college football.

Sometimes it is a good idea to sum up and dispose of the trite and
conventional points before going on to your own. This has the advantage of indicating to the reader that you are going to be neither
trite nor conventional. Something like this:

> We are often told that college football should be abol-
> ished because it has become too commercial or because it is
> bad for the players. These arguments are no doubt very co-
> gent, but they don't really go to the heart of the matter. Then
> you go to the heart of the matter.

Take the Less Usual Side

One rather simple way of getting interest into your paper is to
take the side of the argument that most of the citizens will want to
avoid. If the assignment is an essay on dogs, you can, if you choose,
explain that dogs are faithful and lovable companions, intelligent, useful as guardians of the house and protectors of children, indispensable
in police work—in short, when all is said and done, man's best friends.
Or you can suggest that those big brown eyes conceal, more often than
not, a vacuity of mind and an inconstancy of purpose; that the dogs
you have known most intimately have been mangy, ill-tempered
brutes, incapable of instruction; and that only your nobility of mind
and fear of arrest prevent you from kicking the flea-ridden animals
when you pass them on the street.

Naturally, personal convictions will sometimes dictate your approach. If the assigned subject is "Is Methodism Rewarding to the individual?" and you are a pious Methodist, you have really no choice.
But few assigned subjects, if any, will fall in this category. Most of
them will lie in broad areas of discussion with much to be said on both

sides. They are intellectual exercises and it is legitimate to argue now one way and now another, as debaters do in similar circumstances. Always take the side that looks to you hardest, least defensible. It will almost always turn out to be easier to write interestingly on that side.

20   This general advice applies where you have a choice of subjects. If 20 you are to choose among "The Value of Fraternities" and "My Favorite High School Teacher" and "What I Think About Beetles," by all means plump for the beetles. By the time the instructor gets to your paper, he will be up to his ears in tedious tales about the French teacher at Bloombury High and assertions about how fraternities build character and prepare one for life. Your views on beetles, whatever they are, are bound to be a refreshing change.

Don't worry too much about figuring out what the instructor thinks about the subject so that you can cuddle up with him. Chances are his views are no stronger than yours. If he does have convictions and you oppose them, his problem is to keep from grading you higher than you deserve in order to show he is not biased. This doesn't mean that you should always cantankerously dissent from what the instructor says; that gets tiresome too. And if the subject assigned is "My Pet Peeve," do not begin, "My pet peeve is the English instructor who assigns papers on 'my pet peeve.'" This was still funny during the War of 1812, but it has sort of lost its edge since then. It is in general good manners to avoid personalities.

Slip out of Abstraction

If you will study the essay on college football . . . you will perceive that one reason for its appalling dullness is that it never gets down to particulars. It is just a series of not very glittering generalities: "football is bad for the colleges," "it has become too commercial," "football is a big business," "it is bad for the players," and so on. Such round phrases thudding against the reader's brain are unlikely to convince him, though they may well render him unconscious.

If you want the reader to believe that college football is bad for the players, you have to do more than say so. You have to display the evil. Take your roommate, Alfred Simkins, the second-string center. Picture poor old Alfy coming home from football practice every evening, bruised and aching, agonizingly tired, scarcely able to shovel the mashed potatoes into his mouth. Let us see him staggering up to the room, getting out his econ textbook, peering desperately at it with his good eye, falling asleep and failing the test in the morning. Let us share his unbearable tension as Saturday draws near. Will he fail, be demoted, lose his monthly allowance, be forced to return to the coal mines? And if he succeeds, what will be his reward? Perhaps a slight ripple of applause when the third-string center replaces him, a moment of elation in the locker room if the team wins, of despair if it loses. What will he look back on when he graduates from college? Toil and torn ligaments. And what will be his future? He is not good enough for pro football, and he is too obscure and weak in econ to succeed in stocks and bonds. College football is tearing the heart from Alfred Simkins and, when it finishes with him, will callously toss aside the shattered hulk.

This is no doubt a weak enough argument for the abolition of college football, but it is a sight better than saying, in three or four variations, that college football (in your opinion) is bad for the players.

25   Look at the work of any professional writer and notice how consistently he is moving from the generality, the abstract statement, to the concrete example, the facts and figures, the illustration. If he is writing on juvenile delinquency, he does not just tell you that juveniles are (it seems to him) delinquent and that (in his opinion) something should be done about it. He shows you juveniles being delinquent, tearing up movie theatres in Buffalo, stabbing high school principals in Dallas, smoking marijuana in Palo Alto. And more than likely he is moving toward some specific remedy, not just a general wringing of the hands.   25

It is no doubt possible to be *too* concrete, too illustrative or anecdotal, but few inexperienced writers err this way. For most the soundest advice is to be seeking always for the picture, to be always turning general remarks into seeable examples. Don't say, "Sororities teach girls the social graces." Say "Sorority life teaches a girl how to carry on a conversation while pouring tea, without sloshing the tea into the saucer." Don't say, "I like certain kinds of popular music very much." Say, "Whenever I hear Gerber Spinklittle play 'Mississippi Man' on the trombone, my socks creep up my ankles."

Get Rid of Obvious Padding

The student toiling away at his weekly English theme is too often tormented by a figure: five hundred words. How, he asks himself, is he to achieve this staggering total? Obviously by never using one word when he can somehow work in ten.

He is therefore seldom content with a plain statement like "Fast driving is dangerous." This has only four words in it. He takes thought, and the sentence becomes:

> In my opinion, fast driving is dangerous.

30   Better, but he can do better still: 30

> In my opinion, fast driving would seem to be rather dangerous.

If he is really adept, it may come out:
> In my humble opinion, though I do not claim to be an expert on this complicated subject, fast driving, in most circumstances, would seem to be rather dangerous in many respects, or at least so it would seem to me.

Thus four words have been turned into forty, and not an iota of content has been added.

35   Now this is a way to go about reaching five hundred words, and   35 if you are content with a "D" grade, it is as good a way as any. But if you aim higher, you must work differently. Instead of stuffing your sentences with straw, you must try steadily to get rid of the padding, to make your sentences lean and tough. If you are really working at it, your first draft will greatly exceed the required total, and then you will work it down, thus:

> It is thought in some quarters that fraternities do not contribute as much as might be expected to campus life.
> Some people think that fraternities contribute little to campus life.

> The average doctor who practices in small towns or in the country must toil night and day to heal the sick.
> Most country doctors work long hours.

40   When I was a little girl, I suffered from shyness and em-   40 barrassment in the presence of others.
> I was a shy little girl.

It is absolutely necessary for the person employed as a marine fireman to give the matter of steam pressure his undivided attention at all times.

The fireman has to keep his eye on the steam gauge.

You may ask how you can arrive at five hundred words at this rate. Simply. You dig up more real content. Instead of taking a couple of obvious points off the surface of the topic and then circling warily around them for six paragraphs, you work in and explore, figure out the details. You illustrate. You say that fast driving is dangerous, and then you prove it. How long does it take to stop a car at forty and at eighty? How far can you see at night? What happens when a tire blows?! What happens in a head-on collision at fifty miles an hour! Pretty soon your paper will be full of broken glass and blood and headless torsos, and reaching five hundred words will not really be a problem.

Call a Fool a Fool

45   Some of the padding in freshman themes is to be blamed not on   45
anxiety about the word minimum but on excessive timidity. The student writes, "In my opinion, the principal of my high school acted in ways that I believe every unbiased person would have to call foolish." This isn't exactly what he means. What he means is, "My high school principal was a fool." If he was a fool, call him a fool. Hedging the thing about with "in-my-opinion's" and "it-seems-to-me's" and "as-I-see-it's" and "at-least-from-my-point-of-view's" gains you nothing. Delete these phrases whenever they creep into your paper.

The student's tendency to hedge stems from a modesty that in other circumstances would be commendable. He is, he realizes, young and inexperienced, and he half suspects that he is dopey and fuzzy-minded beyond the average. Probably only too true. But it doesn't help to announce your incompetence six times in every paragraph. Decide what you want to say and say it as vigorously as possible, without apology and in plain words.

Linguistic diffidence can take various forms. One is what we call *euphemism*. This is the tendency to call a spade "a certain garden implement" or women's underwear "unmentionables." It is stronger in some eras than others and in some people than others but it always operates more or less in subjects that are touchy or taboo: death, sex, madness, and so on. Thus we shrink from saying "He died last night" but say instead "passed away," "left us," "joined his Maker," "went to his reward." Or we try to take off the tension with a lighter cliché: "kicked the bucket," "cashed in his chips," "handed in his dinner pail." We have found all sorts of ways to avoid saying *mad*: "mentally ill," "touched," "not quite right upstairs," "feeble-minded," "innocent," "simple," "off his trolley," "not in his right mind. "Even such a now plain word as *insane* began as a euphemism with the meaning "not healthy."

Modern science, particularly psychology, contributes many polysyllables in which we can wrap our thoughts and blunt their force. To many writers there is no such thing as a bad schoolboy. Schoolboys are maladjusted or unoriented or misunderstood or in need of guidance or lacking in continued success toward satisfactory integration of the personality as a social unit, but they are never bad. Psychology no doubt makes us better men or women, more sympathetic and tolerant, but it doesn't make writing any easier. Had Shakespeare been confronted with psychology, "To be or not to be" might have come out, "To continue as a social unit or not to do so. That is the personality problem. Whether 'tis a better sign of integration at the conscious level to display a psychic tolerance toward the maladjustments and repressions induced by one's lack of orientation in one's environment or—" But Hamlet would never have finished the soliloquy.

Writing in the modern world, you cannot altogether avoid modern jargon. Nor, in an effort to get away from euphemism, should you salt your paper with four-letter words. But you can do much if you will mount guard against those roundabout phrases, those echoing polysyllables that tend to slip into your writing to rob it of its crispness and force.

Beware of the Pat Expression

50   Other things being equal, avoid phrases like "other things being equal." Those sentences that come to you whole, or in two or three doughy lumps, are sure to be bad sentences. They are no creation of yours but pieces of common thought floating in the community soup.

Pat expressions are hard, often impossible, to avoid, because they come too easily to be noticed and seem too necessary to be dispensed with. No writer avoids them altogether, but good writers avoid them more often than poor writers.

By "pat expressions" we mean such tags as "to all practical int and purposes," "the pure and simple truth," "from where I sit," the time of his life," "to the ends of the earth," "in the twinkling of an eye," "as sure as you're born," "over my dead body," "under cover of darkness," "took the easy way out," "when all is said and done," "told him time and time again," "parted the best of friends," "stand up and be counted," "gave him the best years of her life," "worked her fingers to the bone." Like other clichés, these expressions were once forceful. Now we should use them only when we cant possibly think of anything else.

Some pat expressions stand like a wall between the writer and thought. Such a one is "the American way of life." Many student writers feel that when they have said that something accords with the American way of life or does not they have exhausted the subject. Actually, they have stopped at the highest level of abstraction. The American way of life is the complicated set of bonds between a hundred and eighty million ways. All of us know this when we think about it, but the tag phrase too often keeps us from thinking about it.

So with many another phrase dear to the politician: "this great land of ours," "the man in the street," "our national heritage." These may prove our patriotism or give a clue to our political beliefs, but otherwise they add nothing to the paper except words.

Colorful Words

55   The writer builds with words, and no builder uses a raw material   55
more slippery and elusive and treacherous. A writer's work is a constant struggle to get the right word in the right place, to find that particular word that will convey his meaning exactly, that will persuade the reader or soothe him or startle or amuse him. He never succeeds altogether—sometimes he feels that he scarcely succeeds at all—but such successes as he has are what make the thing worth doing.

There is no book of rules for this game. One progresses through everlasting experiment on the basis of ever-widening experience. There are few useful generalizations that one can make about words as words, but there are perhaps a few.

Some words are what we call "colorful." By this we mean that they are calculated to produce a picture or induce an emotion. They are dressy instead of plain, specific instead of general, loud instead of soft. Thus, in place of "Her heart beat," we may write "Her heart *pounded, throbbed, fluttered, danced.*" Instead of "He sat in his chair," we may say, "He *lounged, sprawled, coiled.*" Instead of "It was hot," we may say, "It was *blistering, sultry, muggy, suffocating, steamy, wilting.*"

However, it should not be supposed that the fancy word is always better. Often it is as well to write "Her heart beat" or "It was hot" if that is all it did or all it was. Ages differ in how they like their prose. The nineteenth century liked it rich and smoky. The twentieth has usually preferred it lean and cool. The twentieth-century writer, like all writers, is forever seeking the exact word, but he is wary of sounding feverish. He tends to pitch it low, to understate it, to throw it away. He knows that if he gets too colorful, the audience is likely to giggle.

See how this strikes you: "As the rich, golden glow of the sunset died away along the eternal western hills, Angela's limpid blue eyes looked softly and trustingly into Montague's flashing brown ones, and her heart pounded like a drum in time with the joyous song surging in her soul." Some people like that sort of thing, but most modern readers would say, "Good grief," and turn on the television.

Colored Words

60 Some words we would call not so much colorful as colored—that 60 is, loaded with associations, good or bad. All words—except perhaps structure words—have associations of some sort. We have said that the meaning of a word is the sum of the contexts in which it occurs. When we hear a word, we hear with it an echo of all the situations in which we have heard it before.

In some words, these echoes are obvious and discussable. The word *mother,* for example, has, for most people, agreeable associations. When you hear *mother* you probably think of home, safety, love, food, and various other pleasant things. If one writes, "She was like a *mother* to me," he gets an effect which he would not get in "She was like an aunt to me." The advertiser makes use of the associations of *mother* by working it in when he talks about his product. The politician works it in when he talks about himself.

So also with such words as *home, liberty, fireside, contentment, patriot, tenderness, sacrifice, childlike, manly, bluff, limpid.* All of these words are loaded with favorable associations that would be rather hard to indicate in a straightforward definition. There is more than a literal difference between "They sat around the fireside" and "They sat around the stove." They might have been equally warm and happy around the stove, but *fireside* suggests leisure, grace, quiet tradition, congenial company, and *stove* does not.

Conversely, some words have bad associations. *Mother* suggests pleasant things, but *mother-in-law* does not. Many mothers-in-law are heroically lovable and some mothers drink gin all day and beat their children insensible, but these facts of life are beside the point. The thing is that *mother* sounds good and *mother-in-law* does not.

Or consider the word *intellectual*. This would seem to be a complimentary term, but in point of fact it is not, for it has picked up associations of impracticality and ineffectuality and general dopiness. So also with such words as *liberal, reactionary, Communist, socialist, capitalist, radical, schoolteacher, truck driver, undertaker, operator, salesman, huckster, speculator*. These convey meanings on the literal level, but beyond that—sometimes, in some places—they convey contempt on the part of the speaker.

65   The question of whether to use loaded words or not depends on   65 what is being written. The scientist, the scholar, try to avoid them; for the poet, the advertising writer, the public speaker, they are standard equipment. But every writer should take care that they do not substitute for thought. If you write, "Anyone who thinks that is nothing but a Socialist (or Communist or capitalist)," you have said nothing except that you don't like people who think that, and such remarks are effective only with the most naive readers. It is always a bad mistake to think your readers more naive than they really are.

Colorless Words

But probably most student writers come to grief not with words that are colorful or those that are colored but with those that have no color at all. A pet example is *nice*, a word we would find it hard to dispense with in casual conversation but which is no longer capable of adding much to a description. Colorless words are those of such general meaning that in a particular sentence they mean nothing. Slang adjectives, like *cool* ("That's real cool") tend to explode all over the language. They are applied to everything, lose their original force, and quickly die.

Beware also of nouns of very general meaning, like *circumstances, cases, instances, aspects, factors, relationships, attitudes, eventualities,* etc.

In most circumstances you will find that those cases of writing which contain too many instances of words like these will in this and other aspects have factors leading to unsatisfactory relationships with the reader resulting in unfavorable attitudes on his part and perhaps other eventualities, like a grade of "D." Notice also what "etc." means. It means "I'd like to make this list longer, but I can't think of any more examples."

The Proper Place for Sports

Theodore Roosevelt

Theodore Roosevelt (1858–1919) was born in New York City where he was taught at home by his parents and by private tutors. He was then sent to Harvard, and then Columbia Law School. He entered politics after leaving law school in 1881. He became Assistant Secretary of the Navy in 1896, but left to form his Rough Riders to fight in the Spanish-American War. It was with this group that he led the famous charge in the Battle of San Juan for which he won the Congressional Medal of Honor. In 1899 he was elected Vice President of the United States, and then became the youngest president in 1901 when McKinley was assassinated. Roosevelt was a champion of peace and equality, being the first president to invite an African American (Booker T. Washington) to the White House and becoming the first American to win the Nobel Peace Prize for mediating the Russo-Japanese War (1901). Roosevelt championed conservation in the United States and elsewhere and promoted progress with the building of the Panama Canal. This letter to his son shows his balanced view of what a healthy life entails.

White House, Oct. 4, 1903.

Dear Ted:

1   In spite of the "Hurry! Hurry!" on the outside of your envelope, I did   1
not like to act until I had consulted Mother and thought the matter
over; and to be frank with you, old fellow, I am by no means sure that
I am doing right now. If it were not that I feel you will be so bitterly
disappointed, I would strongly advocate your acquiescing in the decision to leave you off the second squad this year. I am proud of your
pluck, and I greatly admire football—though it was not a game I was

---

"The Proper Place for Sports," by Theodore Roosevelt, October 4th, 1903.

ever able to play myself, my qualities resembling Kermit's rather than yours. But the very things that make it a good game make it a rough game, and there is always the chance of your being laid up. Now, I should not in the least object to your being laid up for a season if you were striving for something worth while, to get on the Groton school team, for instance, or on your class team when you entered Harvard— for of course I don't think you will have the weight to entitle you to try for the 'varsity. But I am by no means sure that it *is* worth your while to run the risk of being laid up for the sake of playing in the second squad when you are a fourth former, instead of when you are a fifth former. I do not know that the risk is balanced by the reward. However, I have told the Rector that as you feel so strongly about it, I think that the chance of your damaging yourself in body is out-weighed by the possibility of bitterness of spirit if you could not play. Understand me, I should think mighty little of you if you permitted chagrin to make you bitter on some point where it was evidently right for you to suffer the chagrin. But in this case I am uncertain, and I shall give you the benefit of the doubt. If, however, the coaches at any time come to the conclusion that you ought not to be in the second squad, why you must come off without grumbling.

I am delighted to have you play football. I believe in rough, manly sports. But I do not believe in them if they degenerate into the sole end of any one's existence. I don't want you to sacrifice standing well in your studies to any over-athleticism; and I need not tell you that character counts for a great deal more than either intellect or body in winning success in life. Athletic proficiency is a mighty good servant, and like so many other good servants, a mighty bad master. Did you ever read Pliny's letter to Trajan, in which he speaks of [it] being advisable to keep the Greeks absorbed in athletics, because it distracted their minds from all serious pursuits, including soldiering, and prevented their ever being dangerous to the Romans? I have not a doubt that the British officers in the Boer War had their efficiency partly reduced because they had sacrificed their legitimate duties to an inordinate and ridiculous love of sports. A man must develop his physical prowess up to a certain point; but after he has reached that point there are other things that count more. In my regiment nine-tenths of the men were better horsemen than I was, and probably two-thirds of them better shots than I was, while on the average they were certainly hardier and more enduring. Yet after I had had them a very short while they all knew, and I knew too, that nobody else could command them as I could. I am glad you should play football; I am glad that you should box; I am glad that you should ride and shoot and walk and row as well as you do. I should be very sorry if you did not do these things. But don't ever get into the frame of mind which regards these things as constituting the end to which all your energies must be devoted, or even the major portion of your energies.

Yes, I am going to speak at Groton on prize day. I felt that while I was President, and while you and Kermit were at Groton I wanted to come up there and see you, and the Rector wished me to speak, and so I am very glad to accept.

By the way, I am working hard to get Renown accustomed to automobiles. He is such a handful now when he meets them that I seriously mind encountering them when Mother is along. Of course I do not care if I am alone, or with another man, but I am uneasy all the time when I am out with Mother. Yesterday I tried Bleistein over the hurdles at Chevy Chase. The first one was new, high and stiff, and the old rascal never rose six inches, going slap through it. I took him at it again and he went over all right.

I am very busy now, facing the usual endless worry and discouragement, and trying to keep steadily in mind that I must not only be as resolute as Abraham Lincoln in seeking to achieve decent ends, but as patient, as uncomplaining, and as even-tempered in dealing, not only with knaves, but with the well-meaning foolish people, educated and uneducated, who by their unwisdom give the knaves their chance.

Anatomy of a Hangover

Donald G. Ross

In this article, readers who have not yet experienced the af-tereffects of too much alcohol will be horrified, while read-ers who have experienced a hangover may be edifed to learn about the chemical causes of their misery. As you read, note particularly the way Ross uses cause and effect, description, and process analysis. Ross's techniques are fa-miliar to readers and writers of scientific reports, but he has toned down the technicality of science and applied it to a well-known experience.

Fred awakens with a pounding headache. The room seems to be spinning. Feeling nauseated and sweating profusely, he stumbles into the kitchen for a drink of water. As he glances around the room, he spots the empty bottles of red wine. "Did I really drink that much?" he asks himself. Shaking his head, he is overcome with an-other wave of piercing head pains and nausea. Fred is in the throws of a substantial hangover. But why do some people get hangovers while others seemingly are able to drink with abandon?

What Is a Hangover?

A hangover typically begins several hours after a person stops drink-ing, when the blood alcohol level is falling. Symptoms usually peak around the time it hits zero and persist for up to 24 hours. The un-pleasant symptoms that commonly follow a heavy bout of drinking can range from a mild headache and upset stomach to a feeling of se-vere illness—raging headache, nausea, dizziness, and extreme sensitiv-ity to light and sound (see Table 1). The specific symptoms and their intensity may vary widely—from person to person, from drinking

Reprinted from *Healthline* (October 1999), by permission of the author. Copyright © 1999 by Donald G. Ross.

bout to drinking bout, and with the type and amount of alcohol consumed.

In general, the more alcohol one consumes, the more likely that one will suffer a hangover. A 1993 survey found that 75 percent of the people who drank to intoxication had hangovers at least some of the time. A study of 2,160 Finnish men found that over 43.8 percent of the heaviest drinkers, those who drank about nine drinks per week, had one or more hangovers every month, compared to 6.6 percent for the rest of the study group. Yet individual differences are large. Some people have hangovers after drinking only one to three alcoholic drinks, while others drink heavily without any morning-after misery.

What Causes a Hangover?

Scientists blame hangover symptoms on several different factors. Alcohol directly affects the brain and other organs, and its withdrawal may be a culprit. Toxic compounds produced as the body processes alcohol may also be responsible. Alcoholic drinks often contain non-alcoholic, yet biologically active, components. Concurrent use of other drugs, restricted eating, and going to bed later than normal can contribute to the intensity of the hangover. Personal traits, such as temperament, personality, and family history of alcoholism, can also be cofactors. Evidence suggest that an interaction of more than one of these factors is responsible for the myriad of hangover symptoms.

Direct Effects of Alcohol

5   Since its diuretic properties increase urinary output and send drinkers on regular visits to the bathroom, alcohol commonly causes dehydration and electrolyte imbalance. Consumption of about four drinks of alcohol and water (about 250 milliliters) causes the excretion of 600 to 1,000 milliliters of urine! During a hangover, the sweating, vomiting, and diarrhea cause further fluid loss and electrolyte imbalance. Symptoms of dehydration—thirst, weakness, dryness of mucous membranes, dizziness, and lightheadedness—are also typical symptoms of a hangover.

Alcohol directly irritates and inflames the lining of the stomach and intestines. It also triggers increased production of gastric acid and increased pancreatic and intestinal secretions. Beverages with high alcohol content delay stomach emptying. And high alcohol consumption produces fatty acids in liver cells and can cause a fatty liver. An interplay of all these factors commonly causes the upper abdominal pain, nausea, and vomiting of a hangover.

Alcohol alters the body's normal metabolic processes and can cause low blood sugar levels (hypoglycemia). Alcohol-induced hypoglycemia usually occurs in diabetics, as well as alcoholics who binge drink for several days without eating. Hypoglycemia may or may not contribute to a hangover, but the two conditions have similar symptoms—headache, fatigue, weakness, and mood disturbances.

Alcohol has sedating effects that put one to sleep. But it is a disturbed sleep, and rebound effects can lead to insomnia. Drinking often takes place at night in competition with normal sleeping hours, so it reduces sleep time. Alcohol also decreases the amount of dreaming and deep sleep. You may have heard the sonorous sounds of someone snoring away the night after a bout of drinking. Alcohol relaxes the soft palate, increasing snoring and possibly causing sleep apnea.

Alcohol upsets circadian rhythms, and the effects persist into the hangover period. It alters the normal ebb and flow of body temperature, abnormally lowering it during intoxication and abnormally raising it during a hangover, thus promoting sweating the next morning. Alcohol also disrupts the nighttime release of growth hormone and the rise and fall of cortisol levels. The overall disruption of circadian rhythms is similar to "jet lag" and makes hangover symptoms worse.

10   Alcohol intoxication leads to the dilation of blood vessels, a possible cause of headaches. It also affects the activity of neurotransmitters and hormones, such as histamine, serotonin, and prostaglandins, which have been implicated in head pain.   10

Alcohol Withdrawal and Toxic Byproducts

A hangover may be a mild manifestation of alcohol withdrawal. Overlapping symptoms include nausea and vomiting, tremor, sweating, anxiety, agitation, and headache. Since consuming additional alcohol can alleviate the immediate unpleasantness of both alcohol withdrawal and hangover, they may share a common underlying mechanism. (Further alcohol use—the "hair of the dog that bit you" hangover remedy—should be avoided. Additional drinking only enhances the toxicity of the alcohol previously consumed and extends the recovery time.)

Your body gets rid of alcohol as fast as it can. The liver converts alcohol to acetaldehyde, which the enzyme aldehyde dehydrogenase (ALDH) quickly converts to a harmless substance that is used for energy or stored as fat. Acetaldehyde is highly toxic, and most people's bodies rapidly and efficiently convert it to avoid its accumulation. Despite this effort, small amounts of acetaldehyde are found in the bloodstream during intoxication.

The ability to convert acetaldehyde varies between women and men and has a strong genetic component. For nonalcoholics, the ALDH enzyme in the stomach lining of women is 40 percent less active than in men. About half the people of Asian descent have low levels of ALDH and experience flushing on the face and neck after drinking alcohol, probably due to high blood acetaldehyde levels. In alcohol aversion therapy, the medication disulfiram (Antabuse) deliberately blocks the conversion of acetaldehyde, allowing even small amounts of alcohol to trigger a highly unpleasant reaction, which includes a throbbing headache, breathing difficulties, nausea, copious vomiting, flushing, vertigo, confusion, and a drop in blood pressure.

Which Drinks Are More Likely To Cause a Hangover?

Gin and vodka are mostly pure ethanol, while brandy, whiskey, and red wine contain other biologically active compounds known as congeners. Congeners contribute to the distinctive taste, smell, and appearance of alcoholic beverages, but they have a dark side. Beverages containing congeners are more likely to cause a hangover than beverages of mostly pure ethanol. Congeners also may enhance the alcoholic beverage's intoxicating effects and worsen a subsequent hangover.

One congener, methanol, is a particularly vicious villain. Although it is a type of alcohol, its chemical structure differs slightly from ethanol's. When the body metabolizes methanol, it produces highly toxic compounds that in high concentrations cause blindness and even death.

The distilled spirits most frequently associated with hangovers, such as brandies and whiskeys, contain the highest concentrations of methanol. In addition, a study of red-wine consumption found that methanol persisted in the blood for several hours after ethanol was metabolized—a time period that matches the course of a hangover.

Some people suffer aftereffects from drinking red wine but not white wine or vodka. While red wine can increase serotonin and histamine levels, triggering pounding headaches in susceptible people, white wine and vodka do not affect the production of these substances.

Personal Factors

People with certain personality traits, such as neuroticism, anger, and defensiveness, seem to suffer hangovers more frequently than others. Hangovers also are associated with negative life events and feelings of guilt about drinking. People who have a personality risk for alcoholism tend to have more severe hangover symptoms and may drink in an attempt to find relief.

Treating a Hangover

So what can one do about a hangover? Innumerable folk remedies purport to prevent, shorten, or cure a hangover, but few have undergone rigorous, scientific investigation. Time is the most effective remedy—symptoms usually disappear within 8 to 24 hours. Consumption of fruits, fruit juices, or other fructose-containing foods has been reported to decrease a hangover's intensity, but this has not been well studied. Eating bland foods containing complex carbohydrates, such as toast or crackers, can combat low blood sugar levels and possibly nausea. Sleep can ease fatigue, and drinking nonalcoholic, noncaffeinated beverages can alleviate dehydration (caffeine is a diuretic and increases urine production).

20   Certain medications can provide symptom relief. Antacids may   20 relieve nausea and stomach pains. Aspirin may reduce headache and muscle aches, but it could increase stomach irritation. Acetaminophen should be avoided because alcohol metabolism enhances its toxicity to the liver. People who drink three or more alcoholic beverages per day should avoid all over-the-counter pain relievers and fever reducers. These heavy drinkers may have an increased risk of liver damage and stomach bleeding from these medicines, which contain aspirin, other salicylates, acetaminophen (Tylenol), ibuprofen (Advil), naproxen sodium (Aleve), or ketoprofen (Orudis KT and Actron).

As the Old Adage Says, Prevention Is the Best Medicine

A person who drinks only small, nonintoxicating amounts of alcohol is less likely to suffer a hangover than a person who drinks to get drunk. Even among intoxicated people, the ones who drink the most are the most likely to wake up in misery.

TABLE 1: SYMPTOMS OF A HANGOVER

Class of Symptoms	Type
Constitutional	Fatigue, weakness, and thirst
Pain	Headache and muscle aches
Gastrointestinal	Nausea, vomiting, and stomach pain
Sleep and biological rhythms	Decreased duration and quality of sleep
Sensory	Vertigo and sensitivity to light and sound
Cognitive	Decreased attention and concentration
Mood	Depression, anxiety, and irritability
Sympathetic hyperactivity	Tremor, sweating, and increased pulse and systolic blood pressure

No Compromise: Couples Dealing with Issues for Which They Do Not See a Compromise

Paul C. Rosenblatt and Samantha J. Rieks

Department of Family Social Science,
University of Minnesota, St. Paul, Minnesota, USA

This is a conceptual exploration of what may be involved when a couple cannot resolve an important difference because they do not see a compromise (for example, whether or not to have a child). There may be creative ways of constructing a compromise or defusing the issue, but crucial to the resolution is how the two partners perceive matters, what they gain by being stuck, and the value and meanings to them of various ways of dealing with the impasse. It may be of importance to explore linked or underlying issues, such as cultural or family of origin differences, and resolving an impasse may transform binds associated with the linked or underlying issues. Beyond these issues, the paper explores a number of conceptual issues that might arise in therapy with these couples and indicates some possibly helpful tools for working with the couples.

Sometimes couples seem to themselves to have encountered decision differences about which compromise is not possible. In order to be clear about our starting place, we offer a working definition of *compromise:* "a settlement in which each side gives up some demands

Reprinted from *American Journal of Family Therapy* 37, no. 3 (May 2009), by permission of Taylor and Francis.

or makes concessions." Of course, in therapy, a working definition of compromise may need to be subordinated to the definition of a client couple. Examples of issues on which a couple might not be able to find a compromise include whether or not to have a child, what to name a child, whether to live in Los Angeles or Boston, whether to buy or rent, or whether to have a TV set in the bedroom. If the issue were whether to save 10% of income or 0% of income, there is a quantitative midpoint that could be where partners compromise. But many issues seem to have no quantitative midpoint, no "in between." This is a conceptual exploration of what may be involved for a couple that finds themselves in a situation that seems to have no compromise.

In couple relationships one partner's self-interests may conflict with the interests of the other. Sometimes, conflict may be resolved through concessions at the expense of one's own immediate self-interests for the interest of the partner or relationship, but then the concession may be made with the expectation that the partner will make comparable concessions in the future. Related to that, another approach to dealing with a decision issue in which compromise seems impossible at the moment is that if the issue comes up repeatedly, like whether to visit one partner's family at Christmas or the other partner's family, the couple might compromise by taking turns, one year with one partner's family, the next with the other partner's family. But such compromises might not work for one or both partners because the turn taking could move them half the time into a situation that they felt was unacceptable. Also, many issues cannot be dealt with by turn taking; they are what Thomas (1977, p. 118) called "nonrecurring decision issues," issues that will only occur once. Among examples of nonrecurring decision issues are whether to have a big wedding and whether to have a child. Some nonrecurring issues may be trivial to both partners, but others can be of enormous importance.

If an issue is such that one partner can do one thing and one can do another (for example, one could join the local Catholic church and one does not) that might be seen as a compromise by a couple, unless for one or both of the partners the issue is "what church should we go to together as a couple?" Partner compromise by individuating enough to do different things is only a compromise if individuating in that way is acceptable to both partners.

Potentially, what a couple does with issues for which there seems to them to be no compromise (or no way to create or collaborate on a resolution of the disagreement) is extremely important to their future as a couple. A decision (or no decision) may grate at one or both of the partners as long as they are together, may add tones of anger, pain, resentment, sorrow, disappointment, or vengefulness to the couple relationship. It may leave partners in an intolerable situation. It may establish a pattern that by the standards of one or both partners is not good. It may even lead to the dissolution of the relationship.

5   Perhaps issues in which compromise seems impossible differ at different stages of a couple's relationship. New couples may encounter more issues for which it seems to them that there are no compromises. They will have less experience working together to find compromises or other solutions to standoffs. If the couple has rarely or never experienced an argument or disagreement, an issue on which they disagree may seem a terrifying test of the relationship. But there may be other concerns. They may be more concerned about the possibility that what they do now will set up a pattern that will be a burden for many years, such as Partner A always giving in to Partner B. Perhaps there are more issues a new couple faces that seem to one or both of them to be central to their long-term identity as individuals and to their long-term future as a couple. That may be one reason why some couples who are thinking of marrying tangle over what last name one or both partners will take when they marry.

Couples who are together longer may routinize decision issue domains so each has areas in which she or he is the sole decision maker. By doing so they may encounter relatively few issues on which they might disagree. For example, Partner A might be in charge of figuring out how to entertain guests; Partner B might be in charge of deciding when to pay bills and which bills have highest priority to be paid. But couples who are together longer may still lack relevant experience when facing a new issue that seems to them to have no compromise.

Compromisability Is a Matter of Perception

We believe that for the two partners in a couple, compromise and compromisability are matters of perception. It does not matter what outside observers see as possibilities for compromise. Well-meaning advice from friends and family, writings by experts, and other input from outside the couple might be helpful, but ultimately it is the perceptions of the two partners that matter. Perhaps partners might change their minds about compromisability if they can find different ways of understanding the issues, if they can back away from relevant cultural and family meanings, if they move toward greater personal flexibility, if they can change key values, if they can invest less in having their way on the issue, or if they hang in there with each other through a long and difficult discussion process. But that is not necessarily going to happen.

Compromise means different things to different people. Either in general or in certain situations compromise can be seen in a negative light or a positive one. Compromise can have negative meanings for some decision makers if, for example, the person feels that compromise on the issue is also compromise on principles or morals, if the person feels that if one compromises one lacks the willpower to hang tough or to stand up for oneself or to resist bullying, or if compromise means that she or he is too passive. Compromise can also have negative meanings to a person who feels that she or he has agreed to something that is harmful, painful, demeaning, immoral, or otherwise not good. Compromise can also have positive meanings. For example, compromise might mean that one is a constructive problem solver and a good negotiator, one who respects the other's interests while taking care of self, and one who is flexible or a good partner.

The degree of compromisability of an issue is to some extent inherent in the issues, but it is also dependent on how the people involved understand the issues. Symbolic interaction theory would suggest that it is the couple's shared meanings regarding the issue and their interactions around it that will play the most important role in their relationship and future decisions (LaRossa & Reitzes, 1993). And in this regard there may be very substantial cultural differences in the interpretation of an issue, its compromisability, or its significance to the couple. So what seems to many outsiders to be an issue where compromise is possible may not seem to the couple to be compromisable by their cultural realities. For example, a Chinese woman partnered with a European man may not want to compromise about sending money to her needy parents or observing the proper birth ritual (Rosenblatt & Stewart, 2004).

10   It is also true that an issue that might seem to many observers to   10
be one for which there is no compromise may be compromised by some couples. For example, a couple struggling over whether the architecture of the home they want to build should be Classical or Gothic might not seem to observers to have any way to compromise, but one couple came to a compromise by building the front half of the house

(outside and inside) in Classical style and the back half of the house (outside and inside) in Gothic style (DeBotton, 2006, pp. 44–46).

Perhaps many couples find ways to compromise when compromise seems to outsiders to be impossible. One way that could be done is to add one or more issues to the one on which there is an impasse. Thus, instead of continuing to struggle about a single issue on which they differ, the couple could decide on a way to compromise by adding a second issue: "You win on this issue if you let me win on that issue."

"Big" Issues versus "Small"

An outsider might rate some issues on which couples have differences that they cannot see how to compromise as big and others as small and think that the big issues are most important in trying to understand a couple's relationship. The big issues could be seen as matters of life direction ("in what part of the country should we live"), matters central to individual and couple identity ("how close should we be to our families of origin"), or matters that in the culture(s) of one or both partners have great importance and meaning ("should we circumcise our infant son"). By someone's standards, the big issues are those which can have a major life impact for years, a lifetime, or all eternity. The big issues, by someone's standards, might involve major upheavals, expenditures, and changes in social relationships and self. No doubt there are also little issues each day that are not compromisable, like whether to watch this program or that, whether to make macaroni or a salad for supper for the family.

However, it would be wise to pay attention to what is a "big" issue by the standards of one or both partners. What could be taken by an observer to be a small issue could be big to a partner because it is tied to things that the partner experiences as big, like feeling one never gets one's way or that one's partner discounts what one says. Some seemingly small decisions are about matters that are toxic to some people (for example, for some people, watching television in the bedroom at bedtime is very upsetting, possibly even upsetting enough to contribute to a decision to divorce—Rosenblatt, 2006, p. 52). And what is small in one culture may be enormous in another, for example, whether in a heterosexual married couple the woman walks behind the man or not. The analysis in this paper may focus a great deal on what seems to be "big" issues by some standards, but issues that might seem to be "small" can be as challenging, difficult, and significant in the relationship of some couples as "big" issues are for other couples.

Compromise Processes

Perhaps most couples deal satisfactorily by their standards with many issues on which they at first feel that there is no compromise. One partner decides that an issue is more important to the other and gives in. One partner decides that the risks are too high if she or he does not give in. An issue that seems like a couple issue becomes an individual one because one of the partners decides to pull away from the situation (for example, instead of arguing about which TV program to watch, one of the partners decides to do something other than watch TV). Even though a couple may focus on the issue on which compromise seems impossible, the process of coming to compromise (or not) may be as significant to the couple as what they do about the issue.

15   One might think that the process of dealing with seemingly uncompromisable issues in couple relationships would have been well studied, but we have searched extensively and have not found such research. One might imagine that John Gottman has researched the matter, but after searching his body of publications carefully we have turned up nothing. The closest thing to it is that Gottman and Silver (1994) described three types of couples who may deal with conflict successfully in their relationships. They were validating couples, volatile couples, and conflict-avoidant couples. Each of these three relationship types were said to have different processes for dealing with inevitable conflict, but only validating couples were described as compromising. However, Gottman and Silver did not explain how a validating couple may find compromise or when.

An Exchange Theory Perspective

Perhaps compromise is often possible if couples can think the way exchange theory (e.g., Sabatelli & Shehan, 1993) says people think. In an exchange theory perspective, people in relationships work at exchanging one thing of value for another, maintaining a balance of exchange. What they exchange may be whatever they have, in a sense, commodified. So over the course of an evening, a day, or a week, Partner A and Partner B may exchange affection, good listening, smiles, approval, help, and touching. Partner A might do some shopping for

Partner B, as well as household repairs that benefit both of them. Partner B might provide emotional support to Partner A as Partner A faces a difficult issue at work and might also help Partner A find something that had been lost.

From the perspective of exchange theory, willingness to give in to one's partner on a difficult issue could be balanced by the partner giving in on other issues, by the partner taking on more of certain chores, by the partner paying with love, approval, sex, favors, gifts, or other commodity exchanges. However, exchange theory gives us reasons to think things are not necessarily that easy. Partners may differ in how they perceive the value of this or that. For example, one may consider that giving in on a decision issue is worth 100 units of exchange credit (if we may make up a metric to include in this exchange theory discussion) while the other thinks it is only worth 10 units. Similarly, one may think that picking up some of the chores the partner formerly did is worth many more units of exchange credit than the partner thinks it is worth.

Some exchange theorists (e.g., Blau, 1964) have said that the exchange relationship is weighted by status, so that when two people in an exchange relationship differ in status, the one who is lower in status has to do more in order to achieve exchange balance in relationship to the one of higher status. From that perspective, issues on which there is no apparent compromise may be harder to resolve if the partners do not see their relative status in the same way. ("Even though you are older, male, and bring in more income, we are equals . . . or I am higher status because I have more friends and superior social skills.") Thus, it is possible that with some couples dealing with an issue that they cannot compromise, it is not just the issue at focus that they are stuck on, but also how to sort out their relative power/status. If they step away from the issue to define and negotiate their relative power/ status in the relationship, they may see that the underlying issue of power/status is actually what is keeping them stuck.

Exchange theory comes from a culture in which many things are commodified, many things can be priced, a what's-in-it-for-me perspective is appropriate moral thinking, and where people want good value for their investments of labor, energy, money, caring, and time. There are other cultures in which this kind of thinking makes little or no sense. For example, there are cultures in which family loyalty or moral obligations are dominant values. In cultures like those, there may be much less possibility of finding an appropriate exchange for, say, acting contrary to one's family or to cultural morality, and hence much less possibility of finding an exchange-based compromise on those issues.

Getting to "Yes": A Collaborative Model

20   In their book *Getting to Yes,* Fisher and Ury (1981) advocated invent-   20
ing options for mutual gain, so no matter what the issue, the outcomes are sufficiently good for both partners. The invention might often be options for oneself, but ideally one would want to support the other in the negotiation in inventing options, since it is in one's best interests to get to "yes." Thus, the getting-to-yes process involves both sides not closing prematurely on a single option and not assuming there is a single, fixed pie. It involves a collaborative process that makes the situation less one of conflict and more one of working together. (For example, instead of arguing about how to divide this one pie, let's add other pies and a loaf of bread.) As a result, the negotiation process involves brainstorming rather than interminable arguing, and in the end the two parties may not only have found a way to deal with the issue that was the focus of their discussion but may have learned how to deal with many of their interpersonal conflicts through collaborative, creative compromise.

The Meaning of An Ongoing Unresolved Difference

On some issues, no decision is a decision. The partner who did not want a new kitchen table wins because they never resolve whether to get a new table or which table to get. Or if she wants to have a baby and he does not, and they keep wrangling about the issue until it is no longer possible for her to become pregnant, he wins. So for some couples on some issues the meaning of ongoing unresolved conflict is that someone is winning; a decision is being made de facto.

Related to this, sometimes a couple may go a long time without any overt conflict or disagreement. That might mean that they have not encountered decision issues on which they disagree or that they find it easy to resolve differences in a way that works for both of them. But it may also mean that one is always getting her or his way.

One can think of a decision situation in terms of goals. The partners may have many goals, for example, general goals such as getting along well, spending within their means, having a good sexual relationship, and having a house that feels comfortable. On any decision issue, each may have issue-specific goals. For example, if the issue is what to name a child, Partner A may have the goal of giving the child a name that sounds good and that will not lead to the child being teased as it grows up. Partner B may have the goal of giving the child a name that connects the child to Partner B's family. Both partners may want to win on the issue, to have the other give in. With disparate goals and both wanting to win, compromise is not so likely to have positive meanings for the two. With identical goals, but different ideas about how to achieve those goals, compromise might be easier.

Long-term unresolved conflicts may sustain a couple relationship, since if one were to give in to the other, that might make staying together intolerable. For example, each partner might want to live close to her or his family of origin. Their ongoing arguing may mark how much each cares about her or his family of origin and how uncomfortable each would feel being close to the other's family of origin. Thus, the ongoing disagreement expresses important values and feelings and giving in to the partner might be a great betrayal of self and family of origin. There are also couples for whom ongoing unresolved conflict is painful or even intolerable to one or both partners. For them, the conflict could mean that they are fundamentally incompatible, or that there is no hope or future in the relationship. Perhaps a single issue of disagreement could do this. One hears, for example, of couples who break up because one wants a baby and the other does not or one wants to go back to school and the other cannot tolerate it. But it also may be that what appears to be a single difficult decision issue is entangled in much more. Entangled in the overtly expressed decision issue may be the fact that one or both partners is fighting to maintain self-esteem. Or it may be that the issue at the focus is linked to broad power battles in the couple, battles that are present on many different issues. It may be that the couple differs culturally, and the one issue of disagreement is linked to broad cultural differences, for example, what is appropriate for women and men in their two cultures, or differing cultural understandings of loyalty to family of origin.

The Possible Wounds of Compromise

25 What if one of the partners feels that a "compromise" the couple has 25
agreed to is not actually a compromise in the sense that each has gained

from it? What seems to an observer to be an appropriate compromise and good for both partners may have negative, even harmful meanings to one of the partners. Perhaps over time he or she may become more accepting of a compromise that was painful at first, or more tolerant of living with the tension of unresolved issues. She or he may sufficiently grieve what was lost when the compromise was made or may come to see the wisdom of the compromise. Or maybe the person does not become accustomed to the state of affairs, and it remains a sore point, a source of anger, emotional distance, criticism, and resentment. Whitton, Stanley, and Markman (2007) found that when a person in a relationship perceives a sacrifice for their partner as harmful, there is a strong link to depressive symptomology. That fits Beck's cognitive theory of depression (e.g., Wright & Beck, 1983), which asserts that negative interpretations of life events are central to the development of depression. Our focus here is not on mental health or depression, but on how compromise plays out. If one partner is depressed, what might that say about the compromise? What damage could be done to the relationship or the partners if a compromise is internalized as sacrifice, coercion, or betrayal?

A compromise on a major issue may set up an ongoing pattern, perhaps one of resentment and passive aggressiveness by the one who gave in. ("Yes, we have moved to Boston so you can have the job you want, but I will be emotionally distant and resentful. I will spend lots of our money to connect with my family in Los Angeles. I will expect you to give in to me on everything that comes up.") Such a pattern may taint future decision situations with dispositions one ideally would rather not see in couple relationships: bullying, for example, or nagging, threats, and emotional blackmail.

Do These Couples Need Therapy?

Perhaps all couples struggle at times with difficult decision issues on which compromise seems impossible. Perhaps all couples at times get stuck on such issues. Perhaps all couples at times resolve a difficult decision issue in a way that leaves one or both partners feeling unhappy, resentful, depressed, or otherwise not in a good place. Assuming these things are normal in the sense of occurring widely, perhaps any of these experiences is not an indication that therapy is needed. And perhaps one thing a therapist can do with a couple whose presenting problem revolves around a difficult decision issue is to normalize what they are experiencing.

Although couple therapy might ordinarily be thought of as being about deep issues with broad ramifications, it is possible that some couples come to a therapist when they are stuck on a single, big issue. And for them, the consultation might be beneficial if it helps them with that single issue. For example, if they cannot agree on whether to have a baby, the therapist may help simply by being a referee, mentor, coach, information source, and communication facilitator on that issue.

What if a couple claims to need help because they are stuck on a big issue but the couple's stuckness on that issue seems symptomatic of something deeper? For example, the therapist believes that the single presenting problem is entangled in ongoing power battles, fear of deciding, persisting resentments about past issues, or battles to maintain self-esteem. If there are those underlying factors, they may be holding the couple back from resolving issues, and couple therapy might be of real help in making issues more resolvable. Helping the couple to explore the presenting problem issue and to go deeper into more complex patterns and processes may take some finesse depending on the urgency of the issue on which they are stuck and the flexibility of the clients. Suggesting alternative reasons for difficulty compromising on the issue may be helpful but it may also be more challenging for the clients than they can handle.

30   On the other hand, resolving an issue that had seemed impossi-   30
ble to compromise may be wonderfully beneficial to a couple. The underlying issues may diminish in significance in the couple's relationship if the couple finds a path that gets them through to a decision both feel good about. Relieving the pressure of the specific situation may give the couple freedom from or new perspectives on the broader patterns in their relationship.

Similarly, couples who do not seem ever to be stuck on decisions issues may be that way because of an underlying difficulty which allows one partner always to win. They may benefit from couple therapy because something may be going on (bullying by one partner, for example, or low self-esteem by the other) that is not good for the couple relationship. Likewise, couples who hardly ever seem to encounter decision situations might need help to the extent that the infrequency of decisions may mean that important decision issues are being ignored or avoided, to the detriment of the couple, or that one partner wins by shutting off discussion, which may be a sign that the couple needs to work on safety issues, communication, honesty, knowing feelings, expressing feelings, and being comfortable with difference and disagreement. In this interpretation, assuming all couples face decision impasses at some point, never to have an uncompromisable issue could be seen as a possible indicator of relationship trouble.

We anticipate many different therapeutic contexts, strategies, and outcomes around working with couples on issues for which compromise seems to the couple to be impossible. In general, however, we imagine that there would be two common ways this might present in therapy: either the couple explicitly discusses a scenario in which they cannot come to an agreement, or the couple does not discuss any issues in which they feel stuck. Below we suggest questions that may be helpful for a therapist to consider in dealing with clients who seem to have a problem with an issue that they cannot compromise or with compromising in general.

Meanings of Being at an Impasse

- What are the cultural meanings of compromising and not compromising to each partner?
- Do the partners perceive the issue in the same way?
- What are the gains and losses from not compromising?
- Might not compromising be keeping the relationship together?
- Are there ways that being stuck on an issue feels familiar and easy to the partners?
- Has conflict around an impasse ever helped the partners to respect each other and to improve their conflict resolution skills?
- How might the partners see the patterns established in their families of origin and their history as a couple playing into how they are dealing with the impasse?

Couple Processes of Compromise and of Remaining at an Impasse

- Have there been impasses that were resolved by agreeing to do different things?
- Have there been compromises when the partners took turns getting what they wanted?

- Have there been impasses on which one of the partners gave in or gave up? If so, what were the consequences of giving in or giving up?
- Has any impasse been resolved by negotiating an exchange around other issues?
- Has either of the partners ever felt that an impasse was not about the issue on which the two disagreed but about one of them wanting to win?
- Have the partners ever resolved an impasse by collaborating and coming up with a creative solution? If so, what did that resolution feel like to each of them?
- Have there been times when it seemed that a partner has used emotional blackmail, bullying, or another power strategy to get their way in an impasse?
- Can the couple remember compromises that felt really good to both partners?

Wounds of Being Stuck or of Compromising

- How is the tone of the relationship and the emotional life of each partner affected by not being able to compromise on an important issue or by compromising?
- Has either partner ever felt they lost something important because of an impasse or a compromise in the relationship?
- Have there been times when the relationship has felt intolerable because of an impasse or a compromise?
- Do either of the partners worry that the two of them are fundamentally incompatible because of an impasse or because of the ways a compromise has played out?

Avoidance versus Engagement

- Have there been times when by avoiding the conflict around a seeming impasse, a decision was made de facto?
- On important issues that have never been discussed or discussed fully, is someone getting their way and the other not?
- Does either partner feel that it was good to air differences in values and feelings even if they remain at an impasse on an issue?

Conclusion

We conclude where we started. There are issues on which as a couple views things, compromise cannot be achieved. These issues may be linked to culture, underlying individual and couple matters, and much more. They may be issues that many couples confront, but there will also be issues that are unique to a specific couple. What a couple does with an impasse where there does not seem to be a compromise, even if it is nothing, could be significant for the partners individually and for the couple. These issues may be linked to culture, underlying individual and couple matters, and more. For some couples, the resistance of the issues to resolution may be great, and a seeming resolution of the issue may have long-term negative consequences, because the underlying problems and feelings, the cultural perspectives, and so on, have not gone away. On the other hand, effectively dealing with an issue may have very positive long-term effects for a couple because it brings them to different places as individuals and as a pair. Therapeutic work on an issue on which a couple cannot find a compromise might be wonderfully helpful, but then sometimes it might be more helpful to explore matters that are attached to or underlie the issue on which the couple is stuck. Our interpretation is that issues on which a couple cannot compromise might often be wrapped up in the complexity of who they are and how they are in relationship, and so therapeutic work might need to extend well beyond the issue of not being able to compromise on a specific, important matter.

References

Blau, P. M. (1964). *Exchange and power in social life.* New York: Wiley.

DeBotton, A. (2006). *The architecture of happiness.* New York: Pantheon.

Fisher, R., & Ury, W. (1981). *Getting to yes: Negotiating agreement without giving in.* New York: Houghton Mifflin.

Gottman, J., & Silver, N. (1994). What makes marriage work? *Psychology Today, 27* (2), 38–44.

LaRossa, R., & Reitzes, D. C. (1993). Symbolic interactionism and family studies. In P. G. Boss, W. J. Doherty, R. LaRossa, W. R. Schumm, & S. K. Steinmetz (Eds.), *Sourcebook of family theories and methods: A contextual approach* (pp. 135–163). New York: Plenum.

Rosenblatt, P. C. (2006). *Two in a bed: The social system of couple bed sharing.* Albany, NY: State University of New York Press.

Rosenblatt, P. C., & Stewart, C. C. (2004). Challenges in cross-cultural marriage: When she is Chinese and he Euro-American. *Sociological Focus, 37,*
43–58.

Sabatelli, R. M., & Shehan, C. L. (1993). Exchange and resource theories.
In P. G. Boss, W. J. Doherty, R. LaRossa, W. R. Schumm, & K. Steinmetz (Eds.), *Sourcebook of family theories and methods. A contextual
approach* (pp. 385–411). New York: Plenum.

Thomas, E. J. (1977). *Marital communication and decision making.* New York:
Free Press.

Whitton, S. W., Stanley, S. M., & Markman, H. J. (2007). If I help my partner, will it hurt me? Perceptions of sacrifice in romantic relationships.
Journal of Social and Clinical Psychology, 26, 64–91,

Wright, J. H., & Beck, A. T. (1983). Cognitive therapy of depression: Theory and practice. *Hospital and Community Psychiatry, 34,* 1119–1127.

Of Ideas and Data

Theodore Roszak

*The proliferation of information made possible by com-
puter technology can lead us to believe that more facts will
result in better ideas. Theodore Roszak contends that technology enthusiasts—especially those who stand to gain from
it—actively promote this stance, one that he insists is both
intellectually and morally damaging.*

The following essay is an excerpt from Roszak's book
The Cult of Information: The Folklore of Computers
and the True Art of Thinking *(1986), which examines
our fascination with information and the distortions such
a fascination can bring to our pursuit of ideas. He writes,
"Is our capacity to think creatively being undermined by
the very 'information' that is supposed to help us? Is information processing being confused with science or even
beginning to replace thought? And are we in danger of
blurring the distinction between what machines do when
they process information and what minds do when they
think?" From Roszak's perspective, if we undermine the
deepest ways the human mind works, we will lose the
source of our greatest ideas, from scientific theory to moral
concepts such as justice.*

*A professor of history and director of the Ecopsychology
Institute of California State University, Hayward, Roszak
has gained national recognition as a social commentator.
His 1969 book,* The Making of a Counterculture: Reflections on the Technocratic Society and Its Youthful
Opposition, *is regarded as a key commentary on the
1960s. His writings include fiction,* The Memoirs of Elizabeth Frankenstein *(1995), as well as nonfiction, such as*
Ecopsychology: Restoring the Earth, Healing the Mind

Reprinted from *The Cult of Information: The Folklore of Computers and the True Art of
Thinking,* Pantheon Books, a division of Random House.

(1995), and Where the Wasteland Ends *(1995). He has received a Guggenheim Fellowship and has been nominated twice for the National Book Award.*

Ideas Come First

1   In raising these questions about the place of the computer in our   1
schools, it is not my purpose to question the value of information in
and of itself. For better or worse, our technological civilization needs
its data the way the Romans needed their roads and the Egyptians of
the Old Kingdom needed the Nile flood. To a significant degree, I share
that need. As a writer and teacher, I must be part of the 5 to 10 percent of our society which has a steady professional appetite for reliable,
up-to-date information. I have long since learned to value the services
of a good reference library equipped with a well-connected computer.

Nor do I want to deny that the computer is a superior means of
storing and retrieving data. There is nothing sacred about the typed
or printed page when it comes to keeping records; if there is a faster
way to find facts and manipulate them, we are lucky to have it. Just
as the computer displaced the slide rule as a calculating device, it has
every right to oust the archive, the filing cabinet, the reference book,
if it can prove itself cheaper and more efficient.

But I do want to insist that information, even when it moves at
the speed of light, is no more than it has ever been: discrete little bundles of fact, sometimes useful, sometimes trivial, and never the substance of thought. I offer this modest, common-sense notion of
information in deliberate contradiction to the computer enthusiasts
and information theorists who have suggested far more extravagant
definitions. In the course of this chapter . . . , as this critique unfolds,
it will be my purpose to challenge these ambitious efforts to extend the
meaning of information to nearly global proportions. That project, I
believe, can only end by distorting the natural order of intellectual priorities. And insofar as educators acquiesce in that distortion and agree
to invest more of their limited resources in information technology,
they may be undermining their students' ability to think significantly.

That is the great mischief done by the data merchants, the futur-
ologists, and those in the schools who believe that computer literacy
is the educational wave of the future: They lose sight of the paramount
truth that *the mind thinks with ideas, not with information.* Informa-

tion may helpfully illustrate or decorate an idea; it may, where it works under the guidance of a contrasting idea, help to call other ideas into question. But information does not create ideas; by itself it does not validate or invalidate them. An idea can only be generated, revised, or unseated by another idea. A culture survives by the power, plasticity, and fertility of its ideas. Ideas come first, because ideas define, contain, and eventually produce information. The principal task of education, therefore, is to teach young minds how to deal with ideas: how to evaluate them, extend them, adapt them to new uses. This can be done with the use of very little information, perhaps none at all. It certainly does not require data processing machinery of any kind. An excess of information may actually crowd out ideas, leaving the mind (young minds especially) distracted by sterile, disconnected facts, lost among shapeless heaps of data.

5   It may help at this point to take some time for fundamentals.   5

The relationship of ideas to information is what we call a *generalization*. Generalizing might be seen as the basic action of intelligence; it takes two forms. *First,* when confronted with a vast shapeless welter of facts (whether in the form of personal perceptions or secondhand reports), the mind seeks for a sensible, connecting pattern. *Second,* when confronted with very few facts, the mind seeks to create a pattern by enlarging upon the little it has and pointing it in the direction of a conclusion. The result in either case is some general statement which is not in the particulars, but has been imposed upon them by the imagination. Perhaps, after more facts are gathered, the pattern falls apart or yields to another, more convincing possibility. Learning to let go of an inadequate idea in favor of a better one is part of a good education in ideas.

Generalizations may take place at many levels. At the lowest level, they are formulated among many densely packed and obvious facts. These are cautious generalizations, perhaps even approaching the dull certainty of a truism. At another level, where the information grows thinner and more scattered, the facts less sharp and certain, we have riskier generalizations which take on the nature of a guess or hunch. In science, where hunches must be given formal rigor, this is where we find theories and hypotheses about the physical world, ideas that are on trial, awaiting more evidence to strengthen, modify, or subvert them. This is also the level at which we find the sort of hazardous generalizations we may regard as either brilliant insights or reckless prejudices, depending upon our critical response: sweeping statements perhaps asserted as unassailable truths, but based upon very few instances.

Generalizations exist, then, along a spectrum of information that stretches from abundance to near absence. As we pass along that spectrum, moving away from a secure surplus of facts, ideas tend to grow more unstable, therefore more daring, therefore more controversial. When I observe that women have been the homemakers and child minders in human society, I make a safe but uninteresting generalization that embraces a great many data about social systems past and present. But suppose I go on to say, "And whenever women leave the home and forsake their primary function as housewives, morals decline and society crumbles." Now I may be hard pressed to give more than a few questionable examples of the conclusion I offer. It is a risky generalization, a weak idea.

In Rorschach psychological testing, the subject is presented with a meaningless arrangement of blots or marks on a page. There may be many marks or there may be few, but in either case they suggest no sensible image. Then, after one has gazed at them for a while, the marks may suddenly take on a form which becomes absolutely clear. But where is this image? Not in the marks, obviously. The eye, searching for a sensible pattern, has projected it into the material; it has imposed a meaning upon the meaningless. Similarly in Gestalt psychology, one may be confronted with a specially contrived perceptual image: an ambiguous arrangement of marks which seems at first to be one thing but then shifts to become another. Which is the "true" image? The eye is free to choose between them, for they are both truly there. In both cases—the Rorschach blots and the Gestalt figure—the pattern is in the eye of the beholder; the sensory material simply elicits it. The relationship of ideas to facts is much like this. The facts are the scattered, possibly ambiguous marks; the mind orders them one way or another by conforming them to a pattern of its own invention. *Ideas are integrating patterns* which satisfy the mind when it asks the question, What does this mean? What is this all about?

10   But, of course, an answer that satisfies me may not satisfy you.   10
We may see different patterns in the same collection of facts. And then we disagree and seek to persuade one another that one or the other of these patterns is superior, meaning that it does more justice to the facts at hand. The argument may focus on this fact or that, so that we will seem to be disagreeing about particular facts—as to whether they really *are* facts, or as to their relative importance. But even then, we are prob-

ably disagreeing about ideas. For as I shall suggest further on, facts are themselves the creations of ideas.

Those who would grant information a high intellectual priority often like to assume that facts, all by themselves, can jar and unseat ideas. But that is rarely the case, except perhaps in certain turbulent periods when the general idea of "being skeptical" and "questioning authority" is in the air and attaches itself to any dissenting, new item that comes along. Otherwise, in the absence of a well-formulated, intellectually attractive, new idea, it is remarkable how much in the way of dissonance and contradiction a dominant idea can absorb. There are classic cases of this even in the sciences. The Ptolemaic cosmology* that prevailed in ancient times and during the Middle Ages had been compromised by countless contradictory observations over many generations. Still, it was an internally coherent, intellectually pleasing idea; therefore, keen minds stood by the familiar old system. Where there seemed to be any conflict, they simply adjusted and elaborated the idea, or restructured the observations in order to make them fit. If observations could not be made to fit, they might be allowed to stand along the cultural sidelines as curiosities, exceptions, freaks of nature. It was not until a highly imaginative constellation of ideas about celestial and terrestrial dynamics, replete with new concepts of gravitation, inertia, momentum, and matter, was created that the old system was retired. Through the eighteenth and nineteenth centuries, similar strategies of adjustment were used to save other inherited scientific ideas in the fields of chemistry, geology, and biology. None of these gave way until whole new paradigms were invented to replace them, sometimes with relatively few facts initially to support them. The minds that clung to the old concepts were not necessarily being stubborn or benighted; they simply needed a better idea to take hold of.

No Ideas, No Information

From the viewpoint of the strict, doctrinaire empiricism which lingers on in the cult of information, the facts speak for themselves. Accumulate enough of them, and they will conveniently take the shape of knowledge. But how do we recognize a fact when we see one? Pre-

---

*Ptloemaic cosmology: A geocentric view of the universe formulated by the Greek-speaking geographer and astronomer Claudius Ptolemaeus (90–168 A.D.) that was widely accepted until it was superseded to the heliocentric solar system of Copernicus.

sumably, a fact is not a mental figment or an illusion; it is some small, compact particle of truth. But to collect such particles in the first place, we have to know what to look for. There has to be the idea of a fact.

The empiricists were right to believe that facts and ideas are significantly connected, but they inverted the relationship. *Ideas create information,* not the other way around. Every fact grows from an idea; it is the answer to a question we could not ask in the first place if an idea had not been invented which isolated some portion of the world, made it important, focused our attention, and stimulated inquiry

Sometimes an idea becomes so commonplace, so much a part of the cultural consensus, that it sinks out of awareness, becoming an invisible thread in the fabric of thought. Then we ask and answer questions, collecting information without reflecting upon the underlying idea that makes this possible. The idea becomes as subliminal as the grammar that governs our language each time we speak.

15   Take an example. The time of day, the date. These are among the   15 simplest, least ambiguous facts. We may be right or wrong about them, but we know they are subject to a straightforward true or false decision. It is either 2:15 P.M. in our time zone, or it is not. It is either March 10, or it is not. This is information at its most irreducible level.

Yet behind these simple facts, there lies an immensely rich idea: the idea of time as a regular and cyclical rhythm of the cosmos. Somewhere in the distant past, a human mind invented this elegant concept, perhaps out of some rhapsodic or poetic contemplation of the bewilderingly congested universe. That mind decided the seemingly shapeless flow of time can be ordered in circles, the circles can be divided into equal intervals, the intervals can be counted. From this insight, imposed by the imagination on the flux of experience, we derive the clock and the calendar, the minutes, days, months, seasons we can now deal with as simple facts.

Most of our master ideas about nature and human nature, logic and value eventually become so nearly subliminal that we rarely reflect upon them as human inventions, artifacts of the mind. We take them for granted as part of the cultural heritage. We live off the top of these ideas, harvesting facts from their surface. Similarly, historical facts exist as the outcroppings of buried interpretive or mythic insights which make sense of, give order to the jumbled folk memory of the past. We pick up a reference book or log on to a data base and ask for some simple information. When was the Declaration of Independence signed and who signed it? Facts. But behind those facts there lies a major cultural paradigm. We date the past (not all societies do) because we inherit a Judeo-Christian view of the world which tells us that the world was created in time and that it is getting somewhere in the process of history. We commemorate the names of people who "made history" because (along other lines) we inherit a dynamic, human-centered vision of life which convinces us that the efforts of people are important, and this leads us to believe that worthwhile things can be accomplished by human action.

When we ask for such simple points of historical information, all this stands behind the facts we get back as an answer. We ask and we answer the questions within encompassing ideas about history which have become as familiar to us as the air we breathe. But they are nonetheless human creations, each capable of being questioned, doubted, altered. The dramatic turning points in culture happen at just that point—where new idea rises up against old idea and judgment must be made.

What happens, then, when we blur the distinction between ideas and information and teach children that information processing is the basis of thought? Or when we set about building an "information economy" which spends more and more of its resources accumulating and processing facts? For one thing, we bury even deeper the substructures of ideas on which information stands, placing them further from critical reflection. For example, we begin to pay more attention to "economic indicators"—which are always convenient, simple-looking numbers—than to the assumptions about work, wealth, and well-being which underlie economic policy. Indeed, our orthodox economic science is awash in a flood of statistical figments that serve mainly to obfuscate basic questions of value, purpose, and justice. What contribution has the computer made to this situation? It has raised the flood level, pouring out misleading and distracting information from every government agency and corporate boardroom. But even more ironically, the hard focus on information which the computer encourages must in time have the effect of crowding out new ideas, which are the intellectual source that generates facts.

20   In the long run, no ideas, no information.   20

Academic Discourse: Community or Communities?

David R. Russell

Students in university writing programs are often unaware that their course work has grown out of heated, ongoing debates about how writing should be taught. David R. Russell became a key voice in the debates with the publication of Writing in the Academic Disciplines, 1870–1990 *(1991), which explores the historical context for understanding why teaching writing on the university level presents so many challenges. In the following excerpt from his book, Russell identifies what he considers to be one of the core challenges, tying it to particular developments in the emergence of the modern university.*

In Russell's view, the shift from the traditional liberal-arts education provided before 1870 to the modern focus on professional preparation fragmented the academic community, a development that complicated the task of initiating students into a "discourse community." Instead of working with a uniform approach to academic and professional writing, students—and their writing teachers—now contend with "competing discourse communities," each requiring a specialized approach to communication.

Through his research, Russell has become a central figure in the development of "writing across the curriculum" or "communication across the curriculum," a teaching approach that seeks to use writing as a tool for learning, even as it addresses the diverse composing and speaking demands of specialized academic and professional fields. Among Russell's current interests are genre theory and how various kinds of writing grow out of systems of activity in which authors and readers find themselves.

Reprinted from *Writing in the Academic Disciplines, 1870–1990* (1991), by permission of Southern Illinois University Press.

Russell, a professor of English at Iowa State University, teaches in the PhD program in rhetoric and professional communication in addition to teaching undergraduate courses in writing and rhetoric. A prolific writer and frequent speaker, Russell also collaborates on program development and has edited several collections of essays on writing and writing instruction.

1   The complex origins of mass education in America made it difficult for academia to view learning to write as an initiation into a discourse community, a process of gradually coming to use language in a certain way to become accepted, "literate," or, as is often the case in modern American higher education, credentialed in some profession. Before the advent of the modern university in the 1870s, academia was indeed a single discourse community. Institutions of higher learning built an intellectual and social community by selecting students primarily on the basis of social class (less than 1 percent of the population was admitted), which guaranteed linguistic homogeneity, and by initiating them intellectually through a series of highly language-dependent methods—the traditional recitation, disputation, debate, and oral examination of the old liberal curriculum. Equally important, most students shared common values (Christian, often sectarian) with their teachers (primarily ministers). They pursued a uniform course of study and were then duly welcomed as full members of the nation's governing elite.[1]

The modern university changed all that. It provided the specialized knowledge that drove the new urban-industrial economy and a new class of specialized *professionals* (the term came into use during the period) who managed that economy, with its secular rationale and complex bureaucratic organization—what Burton J. Bledstein has aptly called "the culture of professionalism." Beginning with the land-grant colleges of the late nineteenth century and continuing with the rise of the modern university on the German model, the academic discourse community became fragmented. Numbers swelled, with enrollments tripling as a percentage of the population between 1900 and 1925 alone. Students from previously excluded social groups were admitted, destroying linguistic homogeneity. The new elective curriculum was introduced to prepare students for a host of emerging professional careers in the new industrial society. The elective curriculum compartmentalized knowledge and broke one relatively stable academic discourse community into many fluctuating ones. And the active, personal, language-dependent instructional methods of the old curriculum were replaced by passive, rather impersonal methods borrowed from Germany or, later, from scientific management: lecture, objective testing, and the like. Ultimately, the professional faculty who replaced the gentlemen scholars and divines of the old curriculum came to see secondary and undergraduate education as only one of several competing responsibilities (along with graduate teaching, research, and professional service). And the teaching of writing—initiating the neophytes into a discourse community—suffered accordingly.

Because it is tempting to recall academia's very different past and hope for a very different future, the term *academic community* has powerful spiritual and political connotations, but today academia is a *discourse* community only in a context so broad as to have little meaning in terms of shared linguistic forms, either for the advancement of knowledge (which now goes on in disciplinary communities and subcommunities) or for the initiation of new members (who are initiated into a specific community's discourse). Thus, to speak of the academic community as if its members shared a single set of linguistic conventions and traditions of inquiry is to make a categorical mistake. In the aggregate of all the tightly knit, turf-conscious disciplines and departments, each of its own discourse community, the modern university consists. Many have wished it otherwise.

Despite these profound changes, American educators have continued to think of the academic community as holding out a single compositional norm, which would speak intelligently about the multiform new knowledge to a "general reader." In their complaints about student writing, academics hark back nostalgically to a golden age of academic community where Johnny could both read and write the "plain English" that purists enshrine. But that golden age never existed in the modern university (and writing per se was not valued or even evaluated in the old college). As Daniel P. and Lauren B. Resnick have observed, "There is little to go back to in terms of pedagogical method, curriculum, or school organization. The old tried and true approaches, which nostalgia today prompts us to believe might solve current problems, were designed neither to achieve the literacy standards sought today nor to assure successful literacy for everyone . . . there is no simple past to which we can return."[2] Though academia held onto a generalized ideal of an academic community sharing a single advanced literacy, there was never any consensus in the modern university about the nature of that community or its language. Academic discourse, like academia itself, continued its drive toward increasing specialization. The university became an aggregate of competing discourse communities; it was not a single community. But the myth of a single academic discourse community—and a golden age of student writing—endured.

5   American academia today (and for the last hundred years or so) is a community primarily in a broad institutional sense, a collection of people going about a vast enterprise, in much the same way that we speak of the "business community" as a sector of national life. The academic disciplines are in one sense united through their common missions: teaching, research, and service. But disciplines have been so diverse, so independent, and so bound up with professional communities outside academia that they require no common language or even shared values and methods within the university in order to pursue those missions. Those genres and conventions of writing that are shared by all academic disciplines are also shared by professional communities outside academia. And within academia, the conventions (and beyond them the assumptions and methodologies) of the various disciplines are characterized more by their differences than by their similarities. The various disciplines have grown to constitute the modern university through accretion, as Gerald Graff has forcefully argued, and through their relevance to concerns in the wider society, not through their logical relation to each other—so much so that "interdisciplinary" study is always a notable (and often suspect) exception.[3] Indeed, an academic is likely to have more linguistic common ground with a fellow professional in the corporate sector than with another academic in an unrelated field, except in regard to purely institutional matters (governance, academic freedom, teaching loads, etc.). As a leading sociologist of higher education, Burton Clark, puts it, academia is made up of "small worlds, different worlds."[4]

Notes

1. See Halloran, "Rhetoric" 249–56.

2. Daniel P. Resnick and Lauren B. Resnick, "The Nature of Literacy: An Historical Exploration," *Harvard Educational Review* 47 (1977): 385, qtd. in Rose 355. On the increasing and proliferating standards of literacy, see also Dell H. Hymes, "Foreword," in Wagner xi–xvii.

3. Gerald Graff, *Professing Literature* (Chicago: U of Chicago P, 1987) 6–15. See also theoretical discussions in *Interdisciplinary Relationships in the Social Sciences,* ed. Muzafer Sherif and Carolyn W. Sherif (Chicago: Aldine, 1969); and Stanley Fish, "Being Interdisciplinary Is So Very Hard To Do," *Profession* (1989): 15–22.

4. See Clark, *Academic Life* esp. chap. 5.

Works Cited

Clark, Burton R. *The Academic Life: Small Worlds, Different Worlds.* Princeton: Carnegie Foundation for the Advancement of Teaching, 1987.

Halloran, S. Michael. "Rhetoric in the American College Curriculum: The Decline of Public Discourse." *Pre/Text 3* (1982): 245–69.

Rose, Mike. "The Language of Exclusion: Writing Instruction at the University." *College English* 47 (1985): 341–59.

Wagner, Daniel A., ed. *The Future of Literacy in a Changing World.* Oxford: Pergamon, 1987.

Stereotyping of Arabs by the U.S. Ensures Years of Turmoil

Edward Said

Edward Said (1935–2003) was a distinguished Professor of Literature at Columbia University in New York. His most famous work, Orientalism *(1978) forms an important background for postcolonial studies. Said calls into question the underlying assumptions that form the foundation of Orientalist thinking. A rejection of Orientals entails a rejection of biological generalizations, cultural constructions of people, and racial and religious prejudices. For Said, Orientals can be found in American people's attitudes toward Arabs. Most recently, he published the* Edward Said Reader *(2000), which contains much of his writings. In 2000, he also published* The End of the Peace Process: Oslo and After. *Born in Jerusalem, he was an advocate of the Palestinian cause. In this selection, from the* Los Angeles Times, *Said is concerned that the United States and Israel have a blind eye—an Orientalist's view—denying Arabs the right to self-determination.*

1   The great modern empires have never been held together only by military power. Britain ruled the vast territories of India with only a few thousand colonial officers and a few more thousand troops, many of them Indians. France did the same in North Africa and Indochina, the Dutch in Indonesia, the Portuguese and Belgians in Africa. The key element was imperial perspective, that way of looking at a distant foreign reality by subordinating it in one's gaze, constructing its history from one's own point of view, seeing its people as subjects whose fate can be decided by what distant adminis-

trators think is best for them. From such willful perspectives ideas develop, including the theory that imperialism is a benign and necessary thing.

For a while this worked, as many local leaders believed—mistakenly—that cooperating with the imperial authority was the only way. But because the dialectic between the imperial perspective and the local one is adversarial and impermanent, at some point the conflict between ruler and ruled becomes uncontainable and breaks out into colonial war, as happened in Algeria and India. We are still a long way from that moment in American rule over the Arab and Muslim world because, over the last century, pacification through unpopular local rulers has so far worked.

At least since World War II, American strategic interests in the Middle East have been, first, to ensure supplies of oil and, second, to guarantee at enormous cost the strength and domination of Israel over its neighbors.

Every empire, however, tells itself and the world that it is unlike all other empires, that its mission is not to plunder and control but to educate and liberate. These ideas are by no means shared by the people who inhabit that empire, but that hasn't prevented the U.S. propaganda and policy apparatus from imposing its imperial perspective on Americans, whose sources of information about Arabs and Islam are woefully inadequate.

Several generations of Americans have come to see the Arab world mainly as a dangerous place, where terrorism and religious fanaticism are spawned and where a gratuitous anti-Americanism is inculcated in the young by evil clerics who are anti-democratic and virulently anti-Semitic.

In the United States, "Arabists" are under attack. Simply to speak Arabic or to have some sympathetic acquaintance with the vast Arab cultural tradition has been made to seem a threat to Israel. The media runs the vilest racist stereotypes about Arabs—see, for example, a piece by Cynthia Ozick in *The Wall Street Journal* in which she speaks of Palestinians as having "reared children unlike any other children, removed from ordinary norms and behaviors" and of Palestinian culture as "the life force traduced, cultism raised to a sinister spiritualism."

Americans are sufficiently blind that when a Middle Eastern leader emerges whom our leaders like—the shah of Iran or Anwar Sadat—it is assumed that he is a visionary who does things our way not because he understands the game of imperial power (which is to survive by humoring the regnant authority) but because he is moved by principles that we share.

Almost a quarter of a century after his assassination, Sadat is a forgotten and unpopular man in his own country because most Egyptians regard him as having served the United States first, not Egypt. The same is true of the shah in Iran. That Sadat and the shah were followed in power by rulers who are less palatable to the United States indicates not that Arabs are fanatics, but that the distortions of imperialism produce further distortions, inducing extreme forms of resistance and political self-assertion.

The Palestinians are considered to have reformed themselves by allowing Mahmoud Abbas, rather than the terrible Yasser Arafat, to be their leader. But "reform" is a matter of imperial interpretation. Israel and the United States regard Arafat as an obstacle to the settlement they wish to impose on the Palestinians, a settlement that would obliterate Palestinian demands and allow Israel to claim, falsely, that it has atoned for its "original sin."

10   Never mind that Arafat—whom I have criticized for years in the 10 Arabic and Western media—is still universally regarded as the legitimate Palestinian leader. He was legally elected and has a level of popular support that no other Palestinian approaches, least of all Abbas, a bureaucrat and longtime Arafat subordinate. And never mind that there is now a coherent Palestinian opposition, the Independent National Initiative; it gets no attention because the U.S. and the Israeli establishment wish for a compliant interlocutor who is in no position to make trouble. As to whether the Abbas arrangement can work, that is put off to another day. This is shortsightedness indeed— the blind arrogance of the imperial gaze. The same pattern is repeated in the official U.S. view of Iraq, Saudi Arabia, Egypt and the other Arab states.

Underlying this perspective is a long-standing view—the Orientalist view—that denies Arabs their right to national self-determination because they are considered incapable of logic, unable to tell the truth and fundamentally murderous.

Since Napoleon's invasion of Egypt in 1798, there has been an uninterrupted imperial presence based on these premises throughout the Arab world, producing untold misery—and some benefits, it is true. But so accustomed have Americans become to their own ignorance and the blandishments of U.S. advisers such as Bernard Lewis and Fouad Ajami, who have directed their venom against the Arabs in every possible way, that we somehow think that what we do is correct because "that's the way the Arabs are." That this happens also to be an Israeli dogma shared uncritically by the neo-conservatives who are at the heart of the Bush administration simply adds fuel to the fire.

We are in for many more years of turmoil and misery in the Middle East, where one of the main problems is, to put it as plainly as possible, U.S. power. What the United States refuses to see clearly it can hardly hope to remedy.

Speech on the Signing of the Treaty of Port Elliott, 1855

Chief Seattle

Chief Seattle (c.1788–1866), chief of the Suquamish and Duwamish tribes, was born near the location of Seattle, Washington. A warrior as a youth, he advocated peace with the white man and converted to Christianity in his later years. In 1852, the city of Seattle was named in his honor. In this address, delivered in 1855 (and translated by a white doctor fluent in Indian languages), Chief Seattle pleads for fair treatment of his people and asks that the government respect their cultural differences.

1   Yonder sky that has wept tears of compassion upon my people for centuries untold, and which to us appears changeless and eternal, may change. Today is fair. Tomorrow may be overcast with clouds. My words are like the stars that never change. Whatever Seattle says the great chief at Washington can rely upon with as much certainty as he can upon the return of the sun or the seasons. The White Chief says that Big Chief at Washington sends us greetings of friendship and goodwill. That is kind of him for we know he has little need of our friendship in return. His people are many. They are like the grass that covers vast prairies. My people are few. They resemble the scattering trees of a storm-swept plain. The great, and—I presume—good, White Chief sends us word that he wishes to buy our lands but is willing to allow us enough to live comfortably. This indeed appears just, even generous, for the Red Man no longer has rights that he need respect, and the offer may be wise also, as we are no longer in need of an extensive country. . . . I will not dwell on, nor mourn over, our untimely decay, nor reproach our paleface brothers with hastening it, as we too may have been somewhat to blame.

Youth is impulsive. When our young men grow angry at some real or imaginary wrong, and disfigure their faces with black paint, it denotes that their hearts are black, and then they are often cruel and relentless, and our old men and old women are unable to restrain them. Thus it has ever been. Thus it was when the white men first began to push our forefathers westward. But let us hope that the hostilities between us may never return. We would have everything to lose and nothing to gain. Revenge by young men is considered gain, even at the cost of their own lives, but old men who stay at home in times of war, and mothers who have sons to lose, know better.

Our good father at Washington—for I presume he is now our father as well as yours, since King George has moved his boundaries further north—our great good father, I say, sends us word that if we do as he desires he will protect us. His brave warriors will be to us a bristling wall of strength, and his wonderful ships of war will fill our harbors so that our ancient enemies far to the northward—the Hydas and Tsimpsians—will cease to frighten our women, children, and old men. Then in reality will he be our father and we his children. But can that ever be? Your God is not our God! Your God loves your people and hates mine. He folds his strong and protecting arms lovingly about the paleface and leads him by the hand as a father leads his infant son—but He has forsaken His red children—if they really are his. Our God, the Great Spirit, seems also to have forsaken us. Your God makes your people wax strong every day. Soon they will fill the land. Our people are ebbing away like a rapidly receding tide that will never return. The white man's God cannot love our people or He would protect them. They seem to be orphans who can look nowhere for help. How then can we be brothers? How can your God become our God and renew our prosperity and awaken in us dreams of returning greatness? If we have a common heavenly father He must be partial—for He came to his paleface children. We never saw Him. He gave you laws but He had no word for His red children whose teeming multitudes once filled this vast continent as stars fill the firmament. No; we are two distinct races with separate origins and separate destinies. There is little in common between us.

To us the ashes of our ancestors are sacred and their resting place is hallowed ground. You wander far from the graves of your ancestors and seemingly without regret. Your religion was written upon tables of stone by the iron finger of your God so that you could not forget. The Red Man could never comprehend nor remember it. Our religion is the traditions of our ancestors—the dreams of our old men, given them in solemn hours of night by the Great Spirit; and the visions of our sachems; and it is written in the hearts of our people.

5   Your dead cease to love you and the land of their nativity as soon as they pass the portals of the tomb and wander way beyond the stars. They are soon forgotten and never return. Our dead never forget the beautiful world that gave them being.

Day and night cannot dwell together. The Red Man has ever fled the approach of the White Man, as the morning mist flees before the morning sun. However, your proposition seems fair and I think that my people will accept it and will retire to the reservation you offer them. Then we will dwell apart in peace, for the words of the Great White Chief seem to be the words of nature speaking to my people out of dense darkness.

It matters little where we pass the remnant of our days. They will not be many. A few more moons; a few more winters—and not one of the descendants of the mighty hosts that once moved over this broad land or lived in happy homes, protected by the Great Spirit, will remain to mourn over the graves of a people once more powerful and hopeful than yours. But why should I mourn at the untimely fate of my people? Tribe follows tribe, and nation follows nation, like the waves of the sea. It is the order of nature, and regret is useless. Your time of decay may be distant, but it will surely come, for even the White Man whose God walked and talked with him as friend with friend, cannot be exempt from the common destiny. We may be brothers after all. We will see.

We will ponder your proposition, and when we decide we will let you know. But should we accept it, I here and now make this condition that we will not be denied the privilege without molestation of visiting at any time the tombs of our ancestors, friends and children. Every part of this soil is sacred in the estimation of my people. Every hillside, every valley, every plain and grove, has been hallowed by some sad or happy event in days long vanished. . . . The very dust upon which you now stand responds more lovingly to their footsteps than to yours, because it is rich with the blood of our ancestors and our bare feet are conscious of the sympathetic touch. . . . Even the little children who lived here and rejoiced here for a brief season will love these somber solitudes and at eventide they greet shadowy returning spirits. And when the last Red Man shall have perished, and the memory of my tribe shall have become a myth among the White Men, these shores will swarm with the invisible dead of my tribe, and when your children's children think themselves alone in the field, the store, the shop, upon the highway, or in the silence of the pathless woods, they will not be alone. . . . At night when the streets of your cities and villages are silent and you think them deserted, they will throng with the returning hosts that once filled and still love this beautiful land. The White Man will never be alone.

Let him be just and deal kindly with my people, for the dead are not powerless. Dead, did I say? There is no death, only a change of worlds.

Harrison Bergeron

Kurt Vonnegut Jr.

Kurt Vonnegut (1922–2007) was born in Indianapolis, Indiana. He was educated at Cornell, Carnegie-Mellon, and the University of Chicago, where his master's thesis was unanimously rejected by the department of anthropology. He served in the Army in World War II and was a prisoner of war in Dresden, Germany, during the Allied fire bombing of that city. He worked as a police reporter, a public relations writer, a Saab dealer, and a teacher. Vonnegut was that rarity, a popular writer who also has considerable standing among critics and intellectuals. The novels he wrote during the sixties, especially Cat's Cradle *(1963), found a cult following among students.* Slaughterhouse Five *(1969), perhaps his best, depicted the destruction by fire-bombing of Dresden. The satire and absurdity that are the trademarks of his novels occur also in "Harrison Bergeron," where Vonnegut sides with the non-conformist, the rule-breaker, the person who stands outside the narrow moral universe of conventional society.*

1   The year was 2081, and everybody was finally equal. They weren't only equal before God and the law. They were equal every which way. Nobody was smarter than anybody else. Nobody was better looking than anybody else. Nobody was stronger or quicker than anybody else. All this equality was due to the 211th, 212th, and 213th Amendments to the Constitution, and to the unceasing vigilance of agents of the United States Handicapper General.

Some things about living still weren't quite right, though. April, for instance, still drove people crazy by not being springtime. And it was in that clammy month that the H-G men took George and Hazel Bergeron's fourteen-year-old son, Harrison, away.

It was tragic, all right, but George and Hazel couldn't think about it very hard. Hazel had a perfectly average intelligence, which meant she couldn't think about anything except in short bursts. And George, while his intelligence was way above normal, had a little mental handicap radio in his ear. He was required by law to wear it at all times. It was tuned to a government transmitter. Every twenty seconds or so, the transmitter would send out some sharp noise to keep people like George from taking unfair advantage of their brains.

George and Hazel were watching television. There were tears on Hazel's cheeks, but she'd forgotten for the moment what they were about.

5   On the television screen were ballerinas.

A buzzer sounded in George's head. His thoughts fled in panic, like bandits from a burglar alarm.

"That was a real pretty dance, that dance they just did," said Hazel.

"Huh?" said George.

"That dance—it was nice," said Hazel.

10   "Yup," said George. He tried to think a little about the ballerinas. They weren't really very good—no better than anybody else would have been, anyway. They were burdened with sashweights and bags of birdshot, and their faces were masked, so that no one, seeing a free and graceful gesture or a pretty face, would feel like something the cat drug in. George was toying with the vague notion that maybe dancers shouldn't be handicapped. But he didn't get very far with it before another noise in his ear radio scattered his thoughts.

George winced. So did two out of the eight ballerinas.

Hazel saw him wince. Having no mental handicap herself, she had to ask George what the latest sound had been.

"Sounded like somebody hitting a milk bottle with a ball peen hammer," said George

"I'd think it would be real interesting, hearing all the different sounds," said Hazel, a little envious. "All the things they think up."

15   "Um," said George.

"Only, if I was Handicapper General, you know what I would do?" said Hazel. Hazel, as a matter of fact, bore a strong resemblance to the Handicapper General, a woman named Diana Moon Glampers. "If I was Diana Moon Glampers," said Hazel, "I'd have chimes on Sunday—just chimes. Kind of in honor of religion."

"I could think, if it was just chimes," said George.

"Well—maybe make 'em real loud," said Hazel. "I think I'd make a good Handicapper General."

"Good as anybody else," said George.

20 "Who knows better'n I do what normal is?" said Hazel.

"Right," said George. He began to think glimmeringly about his abnormal son who was now in jail, about Harrison, but a twenty-one-gun salute in his head stopped that.

"Boy!" said Hazel, "that was a doozy, wasn't it?"

It was such a doozy that George was white and trembling, and tears stood on the rims of his red eyes. Two of the eight ballerinas had collapsed to the studio floor, [and] were holding their temples.

"All of a sudden you look so tired," said Hazel. "Why don't you stretch out on the sofa, so's you can rest your handicap bag on the pillows, honeybunch." She was referring to the forty-seven pounds of birdshot in a canvas bag, which was padlocked around George's neck. "Go on and rest the bag for a little while," she said. "I don't care if you're not equal to me for a while."

25 George weighed the bag with his hands. "I don't mind it," he said. "I don't notice it any more. It's just a part of me."

"You been so tired lately—kind of wore out," said Hazel. "if there was just some way we could make a little hole in the bottom of the bag, and just take out a few of them lead balls. Just a few."

"Two years in prison and two thousand dollars fine for every ball I took out," said George. "I don't call that a bargain."

"If you could just take a few out when you came home from work," said Hazel. "I mean—you don't compete with anybody around here. You just set around."

"If I tried to get away with it," said George, "then other people'd get away with it—and pretty soon we'd be right back to the dark ages again, with everybody competing against everybody else. You wouldn't like that, would you?"

30 "I'd hate it," said Hazel.

"There you are," said George. "The minute people start cheating on laws, what do you think happens to society?"

If Hazel hadn't been able to come up with an answer to this question George couldn't have supplied one. A siren was going off in his head.

"Reckon it'd fall all apart," said Hazel.

"What would?" said George blankly.

35 "Society," said Hazel uncertainly. "Wasn't that what you just said?"

"Who knows?" said George.

The television program was suddenly interrupted for a news bulletin. It wasn't clear at first as to what the bulletin was about, since the announcer, like all announcers, had a serious speech impediment. For about half a minute, and in a state of high excitement, the announcer tried to say, "Ladies and gentlemen—"

He finally gave up, handed the bulletin to a ballerina to read.

"That's all right—" Hazel said of the announcer, "he tried. That's the big thing. He tried to do the best he could with what God gave him. He should get a nice raise for trying so hard."

40   "Ladies and gentlemen—" said the ballerina, reading the bulletin. She must have been extraordinarily beautiful, because the mask she wore was hideous. And it was easy to see that she was the strongest and most graceful of all the dancers, for her handicap bags were as big as those worn by two-hundred-pound men.

And she had to apologize at once for her voice, which was a very unfair voice for a woman to use. Her voice was a warm, luminous, timeless melody. "Excuse me—" she said, and she began again, making her voice absolutely uncompetitive.

"Harrison Bergeron, age fourteen," she said in a grackle squawk, "has just escaped from jail, where he was held on suspicion of plotting to overthrow the government. He is a genius and an athlete, is under-handicapped, and should be regarded as extremely dangerous."

A police photograph of Harrison Bergeron was flashed on the screen upside down, then sideways, upside down again, then right side up. The picture showed the full length of Harrison against a background calibrated in feet and inches. He was exactly seven feet tall.

The rest of Harrison's appearance was Halloween and hardware. Nobody had ever borne heavier handicaps. He had outgrown hindrances faster than the H-G men could think them up. Instead of a little ear radio for a mental handicap, he wore a tremendous pair of earphones, and spectacles with thick wavy lenses. The spectacles were intended to make him not only half blind, but to give him whanging headaches besides.

45   Scrap metal was hung all over him. Ordinarily, there was a certain symmetry, a military neatness to the handicaps issued to strong people, but Harrison looked like a walking junkyard. In the race of life, Harrison carried three hundred pounds.

And to offset his good looks, the H-G men required that he wear at all times a red rubber ball for a nose, keep his eyebrows shaved off, and cover his even white teeth with black caps at snaggle-tooth random.

"If you see this boy," said the ballerina, "do not—I repeat, do not—try to reason with him."

There was the shriek of a door being torn from its hinges.

Screams and barking cries of consternation came from the television set. The photograph of Harrison Bergeron on the screen jumped again and again, as though dancing to the tune of an earthquake.

50   George Bergeron correctly identified the earthquake, and well he might have—for many was the time his own home had danced to the same crashing tune. "My God—" said George, "that must be Harrison!"

The realization was blasted from his mind instantly by the sound of an automobile collision in his head.

When George could open his eyes again, the photograph of Harrison was gone. A living, breathing Harrison filled the screen.

Clanking, clownish, and huge, Harrison stood in the center of the studio. The knob of the uprooted studio door was still in his hand. Ballerinas, technicians, musicians, and announcers cowered on their knees before him, expecting to die.

"I am the Emperor!" cried Harrison. "Do you hear? I am the Emperor! Everybody must do what I say at once!" He stamped his foot and the studio shook.

55   "Even as I stand here——" he bellowed, "crippled, hobbled, sickened—I am a greater ruler than any man who ever lived. Now watch me become what I *can* become!"

Harrison tore the straps of his handicap harness like wet tissue paper, tore straps guaranteed to support five thousand pounds.

Harrison's scrap-iron handicaps crashed to the floor.

Harrison thrust his thumbs under the bar of the padlock that secured his head harness. The bar snapped like celery. Harrison smashed his headphones and spectacles against the wall.

He flung away his rubber-ball nose, revealed a man that would have awed Thor, the god of thunder.

60   "I shall now select my Empress!" he said, looking down on the cowering people. "Let the first woman who dares rise to her feet claim her mate and her throne!"

A moment passed, and then a ballerina arose swaying like a willow.

Harrison plucked the mental handicap from her ear, snapped off her physical handicaps with marvelous delicacy. Last of all, he removed her mask.

She was blindingly beautiful.

"Now—" said Harrison, taking her hand, "shall we show the people the meaning of the word dance? Music!" he commanded.

65   The musicians scrambled back into their chairs, and Harrison 65 stripped them of their handicaps, too. "Play your best," he told them, "and I'll make you barons and dukes and earls."

The music began. It was normal at first—cheap, silly, false. But Harrison snatched two musicians from their chairs, waved them like batons as he sang the music as he wanted it played. He slammed them back into their chairs.

The music began again and was much improved.

Harrison and his Empress merely listened to the music for a while—listened gravely, as though synchronizing their heartbeats with it.

They shifted their weights to their toes.

70   Harrison placed his big hands on the girl's tiny waist, letting her 70 sense the weightlessness that would soon be hers.

And then, in an explosion of joy and grace, into the air they sprang!

Not only were the laws of the land abandoned, but the law of gravity and the laws of motion as well.

They reeled, whirled, swiveled, flounced, capered, gamboled, and spun.

They leaped like deer on the moon.

75   The studio ceiling was thirty feet high, but each leap brought the 75 dancers nearer to it.

It became their obvious intention to kiss the ceiling.

They kissed it.

And then, neutralizing gravity with love and pure will, they remained suspended in air inches below the ceiling, and they kissed each other for a long, long time.

It was then that Diana Moon Glampers, the Handicapper General, came into the studio with a double-barreled ten-gauge shotgun. She fired twice and the Emperor and the Empress were dead before they hit the floor.

80   Diana Moon Glampers loaded the gun again. She aimed it at the
musicians and told them they had ten seconds to get their handicaps
back on.

It was then that the Bergerons' television tube burned out. Hazel
turned to comment about the blackout to George. But George had
gone out into the kitchen for a can of beer.

George came back in with the beer, paused while a handicap signal shook him up. And then he sat down again.

"You been crying?" he said to Hazel.

"Yup," she said.

85   "What about?" he said.

"I forget," she said. "Something real sad on television."

"What was it?" he said.

"It's all kind of mixed up in my mind," said Hazel.

"Forget sad things," said George.

90   "I always do," said Hazel.

"That's my girl," said George. He winced. There was the sound
of a riveting gun in his head.

"Gee— I could tell that one was a doozy," said Hazel.

"You can say that again," said George.

"Gee—" said Hazel, "I could tell that one was a doozy."

Beauty: When the Other Dancer Is the Self

Alice Walker

Alice Walker (1944–) was born in Georgia to sharecrop-per parents. She attended Spelman College and Sarah Lawrence College and was active in the civil rights move-ment of the 1960s. Publishing her first novel, The Third Life of Grange Copeland, *at the age of 26, she has been a prolific writer since. In all, she has published five novels, two short story collections, two collections of essays, and sev-eral books of poems. Her novel* The Color Purple *(1982) is perhaps her best known, having won the American Book Award, the Pulitzer Prize, and the Candace Award of the National Coalition of 100 Black Women. The novel was also made into a prize-winning film by director Steven Spielberg. Walker's topics run the gamut of human experi-ence and include some harsh realities such as incest and racial violence as well as relationships within families and society. In the following essay, published in* In Search of Our Mothers' Gardens: Womanist Prose *(1983), Walker examines an important aspect of her childhood that, while more personal than social, appears in an inevitable context of poorer blacks in the rural South.*

1 It is a bright summer day in 1947. My father, a fat, funny man with beautiful eyes and a subversive wit, is trying to decide which of his eight children he will take with him to the county fair. My mother, of course, will not go. She is knocked out from getting most of us ready: I hold my neck stiff against the pressure of her knuckles as she hastily completes the braiding and then be-ribboning of my hair.

My father is the driver for the rich old white lady up the road. Her name is Miss Mey. She owns all the land for miles around, as well as the house in which we live. All I remember about her is that she once offered to pay my mother thirty-five cents for cleaning her house, raking up piles of her magnolia leaves, and washing her family's clothes, and that my mother—she of no money, eight children, and a chronic earache—refused it. But I do not think of this in 1947. I am two and a half years old. I want to go everywhere my daddy goes. I am excited at the prospect of riding in a car. Someone has told me fairs are fun. That there is room in the car for only three of us doesn't faze me at all. Whirling happily in my starchy frock, showing off my biscuit-polished patent-leather shoes and lavender socks, tossing my head in a way that makes my ribbons bounce, I stand, hands on hips, before my father. "Take me, Daddy," I say with assurance; "I'm the prettiest!"

Later, it does not surprise me to find myself in Miss Mey's shiny black car, sharing the back seat with the other lucky ones. Does not surprise me that I thoroughly enjoy the fair. At home that night I tell the unlucky ones all I can remember about the merry-go-round, the man who eats live chickens, and the teddy bears, until they say: that's enough, baby Alice. Shut up now, and go to sleep.

It is Easter Sunday, 1950. I am dressed in a green, flocked, scalloped-hem dress (handmade by my adoring sister, Ruth) that has its own smooth satin petticoat and tiny hot-pink roses tucked into each scallop. My shoes, new T-strap patent leather, again highly biscuit-polished. I am six years old and have learned one of the longest Easter speeches to be heard that day, totally unlike the speech I said when I was two: "Easter lilies / pure and white / blossom in / the morning light." When I rise to give my speech I do so on a great wave of love and pride and expectation. People in the church stop rustling their new crinolines. They seem to hold their breath. I can tell they admire my dress, but it is my spirit, bordering on sassiness (womanishness), they secretly applaud.

5   "That girl's a little *mess*," they whisper to each other, pleased.   5

Naturally I say my speech without stammer or pause, unlike those who stutter, stammer, or, worst of all, forget. This is before the word "beautiful" exists in people's vocabulary, but "Oh, isn't she the *cutest* thing!" frequently floats my way. "And got so much sense!" they gratefully add . . . for which thoughtful addition I thank them to this day.

It was great fun being cute. But then, one day, it ended.

I am eight years old and a tomboy. I have a cowboy hat, cowboy boots, checkered shirt and pants, all red. My playmates are my brothers, two and four years older than I. Their colors are black and green, the only difference in the way we are dressed. On Saturday nights we all go to the picture show, even my mother; Westerns are her favorite kind of movie. Back home, "on the ranch," we pretend we are Tom Mix, Hopalong Cassidy, Lash LaRue (we've even named one of our dogs Lash LaRue); we chase each other for hours rustling cattle, being outlaws, delivering damsels from distress. Then my parents decide to buy my brothers guns. These are not "real" guns. They shoot "BBs," copper pellets my brothers say will kill birds. Because I am a girl, I do not get a gun. Instantly I am relegated to the position of Indian. Now there appears a great distance between us. They shoot and shoot at everything with their new guns. I try to keep up with my bow and arrows.

One day while I am standing on top of our makeshift "garage"— pieces of tin nailed across some poles—holding my bow and arrow and looking out toward the fields, I feel an incredible blow in my right eye. I look down just in time to see my brother lower his gun.

Both brothers rush to my side. My eye stings, and I cover it with my hand. "If you tell," they say, "we will get a whipping. You don't want that to happen, do you?" I do not. "Here is a piece of wire," says the older brother, picking it up from the roof; "say you stepped on one end of it and the other flew up and hit you." The pain is beginning to start. "Yes," I say. "Yes, I will say that is what happened." If I do not say this is what happened, I know my brothers will find ways to make me wish I had. But now I will say anything that gets me to my mother.

Confronted by our parents we stick to the lie agreed upon. They place me on a bench on the porch and I close my left eye while they examine the right. There is a tree growing from underneath the porch that climbs past the railing to the roof. It is the last thing my right eye sees. I watch as its trunk, its branches, and then its leaves are blotted out by the rising blood.

I am in shock. First there is intense fever, which my father tries to break using lily leaves bound around my head. Then there are chills: my mother tries to get me to eat soup. Eventually, I do not know how, my parents learn what has happened. A week after the "accident" they take me to see a doctor. "Why did you wait so long to come?" he asks, looking into my eye and shaking his head. "Eyes are sympathetic," he says. "If one is blind, the other will likely become blind too."

This comment of the doctor's terrifies me. But it is really how I look that bothers me most. Where the BB pellet struck there is a glob of whitish scar tissue, a hideous cataract, on my eye. Now when I stare at people—a favorite pastime, up to now—they will stare back. Not at the "cute" little girl, but at her scar. For six years I do not stare at anyone, because I do not raise my head.

Years later, in the throes of a mid-life crisis, I ask my mother and sister whether I changed after the "accident." "No," they say, puzzled. "What do you mean?"

15   *What do I mean?*   15

I am eight, and, for the first time, doing poorly in school, where I have been something of a whiz since I was four. We have just moved to the place where the "accident" occurred. We do not know any of the people around us because this is a different county. The only time I see the friends I knew is when we go back to our old church. The new school is the former state penitentiary. It is a large stone building, cold and drafty, crammed to overflowing with boisterous, ill-disciplined children. On the third floor there is a huge circular imprint of some partition that has been torn out.

"What used to be here?" I ask a sullen girl next to me on our way past it to lunch.

"The electric chair," says she.

At night I have nightmares about the electric chair, and about all the people reputedly "fried" in it. I am afraid of the school, where all the students seem to be budding criminals.

20   "What's the matter with your eye?" they ask, critically.   20

When I don't answer (I cannot decide whether it was an "accident" or not), they shove me, insist on a fight.

My brother, the one who created the story about the wire, comes to my rescue. But then brags so much about "protecting" me, I become sick.

After months of torture at the school, my parents decide to send me back to our old community, to my old school. I live with my grandparents and the teacher they board. But there is no room for Phoebe, my cat. By the time my grandparents decide there *is* room, and I ask for my cat, she cannot be found. Miss Yarborough, the boarding teacher, takes me under her wing, and begins to teach me to play the piano. But soon she marries an African—a "prince," she says—and is whisked away to his continent.

At my old school there is at least one teacher who loves me. She is the teacher who "knew me before I was born" and bought my first baby clothes. It is she who makes life bearable. It is her presence that finally helps me turn on the one child at the school who continually calls me "one-eyed bitch." One day I simply grab him by his coat and beat him until I am satisfied. It is my teacher who tells me my mother is ill.

25   My mother is lying in bed in the middle of the day, something I 25
have never seen. She is in too much pain to speak. She has an abscess in her ear. I stand looking down on her, knowing that if she dies, I cannot live. She is being treated with warm oils and hot bricks held against her cheek. Finally a doctor comes. But I must go back to my grandparents' house. The weeks pass but I am hardly aware of it. All I know is that my mother might die, my father is not so jolly, my brothers still have their guns, and I am the one sent away from home.

"You did not change," they say.

Did I imagine the anguish of never looking up?

I am twelve. When relatives come to visit I hide in my room. My cousin Brenda, just my age, whose father works in the post office and whose mother is a nurse, comes to find me. "Hello," she says. And then she asks, looking at my recent school picture, which I did not want taken, and on which the "glob," as I think of it, is clearly visible, "You still can't see out of that eye?"

"No," I say, and flop back on the bed over my book.

30   That night, as I do almost every night, I abuse my eye. I rant and 30
rave at it, in front of the mirror. I plead with it to clear up before morning. I tell it I hate and despise it. I do not pray for sight. I pray for beauty.

"You did not change," they say.

I am fourteen and baby-sitting for my brother Bill, who lives in Boston. He is my favorite brother and there is a strong bond between us. Understanding my feelings of shame and ugliness he and his wife take me to a local hospital, where the "glob" is removed by a doctor named O. Henry. There is still a small bluish crater where the scar tissue was, but the ugly white stuff is gone. Almost immediately I become a different person from the girl who does not raise her head. Or so I think. Now that I've raised my head I win the boyfriend of my dreams. Now that I've raised my head I have plenty of friends. Now that I've raised my head classwork comes from my lips as faultlessly as Easter speeches did, and I leave high school as valedictorian, most popular student, and *queen*, hardly believing my luck. Ironically, the girl who was voted most beautiful in our class (and was) was later shot twice through the chest by a male companion, using a "real" gun, while she was pregnant. But that's another story in itself. Or is it?

"You did not change," they say.

It is now thirty years since the "accident." A beautiful journalist comes to visit and to interview me. She is going to write a cover story for her magazine that focuses on my latest book. "Decide how you want to look on the cover," she says. "Glamorous, or whatever."

35   Never mind "glamorous," it is the "whatever" that I hear. Sud-   35
denly all I can think of is whether I will get enough sleep the night before the photography session: if I don't, my eye will be tired and wander, as blind eyes will.

At night in bed with my lover I think up reasons why I should not appear on the cover of a magazine. "My meanest critics will say I've sold out," I say. "My family will now realize I write scandalous books."

"But what's the real reason you don't want to do this?" he asks.

"Because in all probability," I say in a rush, "my eye won't be straight."

"It will be straight enough," he says. Then, "Besides, I thought you'd made your peace with that."

40   And I suddenly remember that I have.   40

I remember:

I am talking to my brother Jimmy, asking if he remembers anything unusual about the day I was shot. He does not know I consider that day the last time my father, with his sweet home remedy of cool lily leaves, chose me, and that I suffered and raged inside because of this. "Well," he says, "all I remember is standing by the side of the highway with Daddy, trying to flag down a car. A white man stopped, but when Daddy said he needed somebody to take his little girl to the doctor, he drove off."

I remember:

I am in the desert for the first time. I fall totally in love with it. I am so overwhelmed by its beauty, I confront for the first time, consciously, the meaning of the doctor's words years ago: "Eyes are sympathetic. If one is blind, the other will likely become blind too." I realize I have dashed about the world madly, looking at this, looking at that, storing up images against the fading of the light. *But I might have missed seeing the desert!* The shock of that possibility—and gratitude for over twenty-five years of sight—sends me literally to my knees. Poem after poem comes—which is perhaps how poets pray.

on sight

I am so thankful I have seen
The Desert
And the creatures in the desert
And the desert Itself.

The desert has its own moon
Which I have seen
With my own eye.

There is no flag on it.

Trees of the desert have arms
All of which are always up
That is because the moon is up
The sun is up
Also the sky
The stars
Clouds
None with flags.

If there *were* flags, I doubt
the trees would point.
Would you?

45   *But mostly, I remember this:*   45
    I am twenty-seven, and my baby daughter is almost three. Since her birth I have worried about her discovery that her mother's eyes are different from other people's. Will she be embarrassed? I think. What will she say? Every day she watches a television program called "Big Blue Marble." It begins with a picture of the earth as it appears from the moon. It is bluish, a little battered-looking, but full of light, with whitish clouds

swirling around it. Every time I see it I weep with love, as if it is a picture of Grandma's house. One day when I am putting Rebecca down for her nap, she suddenly focuses on my eye. Something inside me cringes, gets ready to try to protect myself. All children are cruel about physical differences, I know from experience, and that they don't always mean to be is another matter. I assume Rebecca will be the same.

But no-o-o-o. She studies my face intently as we stand, her inside and me outside her crib. She even holds my face maternally between her dimpled little hands. Then, looking every bit as serious and lawyerlike as her father, she says, as if it may just possibly have slipped my attention: "Mommy, there's a *world* in your eye." (As in, "Don't be alarmed, or do anything crazy.") And then, gently, but with great interest: "Mommy, where did you *get* that world in your eye?"

For the most part, the pain left then. (So what, if my brothers grew up to buy even more powerful pellet guns for their sons and to carry real guns themselves. So what, if a young "Morehouse man" once nearly fell off the steps of Trevor Arnett Library because he thought my eyes were blue.) Crying and laughing I ran to the bathroom, while Rebecca mumbled and sang herself off to sleep. Yes indeed, I realized, looking into the mirror. There *was* a world in my eye. And I saw that it was possible to love it: that in fact, for all it had taught me of shame and anger and inner vision, I *did* love it. Even to see it drifting out of orbit in boredom, or rolling up out of fatigue, not to mention floating back at attention in excitement (bearing witness, a friend has called it), deeply suitable to my personality, and even characteristic of me.

That night I dream I am dancing to Stevie Wonder's song "Always" (the name of the song is really "As," but I hear it as "Always"). As I dance, whirling and joyous, happier than I've ever been in my life, another bright-faced dancer joins me. We dance and kiss each other and hold each other through the night. The other dancer has obviously come through all right, as I have done. She is beautiful, whole and free. And she is also me.

Once More to the Lake

E.B. White

E.B. White (1899–1985) was born in Mt. Vernon, New York, and attended Cornell University. He was a career writer of newspaper pieces and essays for the magazines The New Yorker *and* Harper's. *His three children's books have become classics:* Stuart Little, Charlotte's Web, *and* The Trumpet of the Swan. *As an accomplished stylist, he revised the grammar book by Strunk that he had himself used as a student—which is now known universally as Strunk and White's* Elements of Style. *The essay "Once More to the Lake" was originally published in White's* One Man's Meat *in 1941. It examines what seems to be White's idyllic childhood of summers at a lake in Maine, revisited decades later by an older White who at first seems nostalgic. The essay gives us much more, however, than wistful memories of a happy time in a beautiful place.*

1   One summer, along about 1904, my father rented a camp on a lake in Maine and took us all there for the month of August. We all got ringworm from some kittens and had to rub Pond's Extract on our arms and legs night and morning, and my father rolled over in a canoe with all his clothes on; but outside of that the vacation was a success and from then on none of us ever thought there was any place in the world like that lake in Maine. We returned summer after summer—always on August 1st for one month. I have since become a salt-water man, but sometimes in summer there are days when the restlessness of the tides and the fearful cold of the sea water and the incessant wind which blows across the afternoon and into the evening make me wish for the placidity of a lake in the woods. A few weeks ago this feeling got so strong I bought myself a couple of

bass hooks and a spinner and returned to the lake where we used to go, for a week's fishing and to revisit old haunts.

I took along my son, who had never had any fresh water up his nose and who had seen lily pads only from train windows. On the journey over to the lake I began to wonder what it would be like. I wondered how time would have marred this unique, this holy spot— the coves and streams, the hills that the sun set behind, the camps and the paths behind the camps. I was sure the tarred road would have found it out, and I wondered in what other ways it would be desolated. It is strange how much you can remember about places like that once you allow your mind to return into the grooves which lead back. You remember one thing, and that suddenly reminds you of another thing. I guess I remembered clearest of all the early mornings, when the lake was cool and motionless, remembered how the bedroom smelled of the lumber it was made of and of the wet woods whose scent entered through the screen. The partitions in the camp were thin and did not extend clear to the top of the rooms, and as I was always the first up I would dress softly so as not to wake the others, and sneak out into the sweet outdoors and start out in the canoe, keeping close along the shore in the long shadows of the pines. I remembered being very careful never to rub my paddle against the gunwale for fear of disturbing the stillness of the cathedral.

The lake had never been what you would call a wild lake. There were cottages sprinkled around the shores, and it was in farming country although the shores of the lake were quite heavily wooded. Some of the cottages were owned by nearby farmers, and you would live at the shore and eat your meals at the farmhouse. That's what our family did. But although it wasn't wild, it was a fairly large and undisturbed lake and there were places in it which, to a child at least, seemed infinitely remote and primeval.

I was right about the tar: it led to within half a mile of the shore. But when I got back there, with my boy, and we settled into a camp near a farmhouse and into the kind of summertime I had known, I could tell that it was going to be pretty much the same as it had been before—I knew it, lying in bed the first morning, smelling the bedroom, and hearing the boy sneak quietly out and go off along the shore in a boat. I began to sustain the illusion that he was I, and therefore, by simple transposition, that I was my father. This sensation persisted, kept cropping up all the time we were there. It was not an entirely new feeling, but in this setting it grew much stronger. I seemed to be living a dual existence. I would be in the middle of some simple act, I would be picking up a bait box or laying down a table fork, or I would be saying something, and suddenly it would be not I but my father who was saying the words or making the gesture. It gave me a creepy sensation.

5   We went fishing the first morning. I felt the same damp moss covering the worms in the bait can, and saw the dragonfly alight on the tip of my rod as it hovered a few inches from the surface of the water. It was the arrival of this fly that convinced me beyond any doubt that everything was as it always had been, that the years were a mirage and there had been no years. The small waves were the same, chucking the rowboat under the chin as we fished at anchor, and the boat was the same boat, the same color green and the ribs broken in the same places, and under the floor-boards the same freshwater leavings and débris—the dead helgramite, the wisps of moss, the rusty discarded fishhook, the dried blood from yesterday's catch. We stared silently at the tips of our rods, at the dragonflies that came and went. I lowered the tip of mine into the water, tentatively, pensively dislodging the fly, which darted two feet away, poised, darted two feet back, and came to rest again a little farther up the rod. There had been no years between the ducking of this dragonfly and the other one—the one that was part of memory. I looked at the boy, who was silently watching his fly, and it was my hands that held his rod, my eyes watching. I felt dizzy and didn't know which rod I was at the end of.

We caught two bass, hauling them in briskly as though they were mackerel, pulling them over the side of the boat in a businesslike manner without any landing net, and stunning them with a blow on the back of the head. When we got back for a swim before lunch, the lake was exactly where we had left it, the same number of inches from the dock, and there was only the merest suggestion of a breeze. This seemed an utterly enchanted sea, this lake you could leave to its own devices for a few hours and come back to, and find that it had not stirred, this constant and trustworthy body of water. In the shallows, the dark, water-soaked sticks and twigs, smooth and old, were undulating in clusters on the bottom against the clean ribbed sand, and the track of the mussel was plain. A school of minnows swam by, each minnow with its small individual shadow, doubling the attendance, so clear and sharp in the sunlight. Some of the other campers were in swimming, along the shore, one of them with a cake of soap, and the water felt thin and clear and unsubstantial. Over the years there had been this person with the cake of soap, this cultist, and here he was. There had been no years.

Up to the farmhouse to dinner through the teeming, dusty field, the road under our sneakers was only a two-track road. The middle track was missing, the one with the marks of the hooves and the splotches of dried, flaky manure. There had always been three tracks to choose from in choosing which track to walk in; now the choice was narrowed down to two. For a moment I missed terribly the middle alternative. But the way led past the tennis court, and something about the way it lay there in the sun reassured me; the tape had loosened along the backline, the alleys were green with plantains and other weeds, and the net (installed in June and removed in September) sagged in the dry noon, and the whole place steamed with midday heat and hunger and emptiness. There was a choice of pie for dessert, and one was blueberry and one was apple, and the waitresses were the same country girls, there having been no passage of time, only the illusion of it as in a dropped curtain—the waitresses were still fifteen; their hair had been washed, that was the only difference—they had been to the movies and seen the pretty girls with the clean hair.

Summertime, oh summertime, pattern of life indelible, the fadeproof lake, the woods unshatterable, the pasture with the sweetfern and the juniper forever and ever, summer without end; this was the background, and the life along the shore was the design, the cottages with their innocent and tranquil design, their tiny docks with the flagpole and the American flag floating against the white clouds in the blue sky, the little paths over the roots of the trees leading from camp to camp and the paths leading back to the outhouses and the can of lime for sprinkling, and at the souvenir counters at the store the miniature birch-bark canoes and the post cards that showed things looking a little better than they looked. This was the American family at play, escaping the city heat, wondering whether the newcomers in the camp at the head of the cove were "common" or "nice," wondering whether it was true that the people who drove up for Sunday dinner at the farmhouse were turned away because there wasn't enough chicken.

It seemed to me, as I kept remembering all this, that those times and those summers had been infinitely precious and worth saving. There had been jollity and peace and goodness. The arriving (at the beginning of August) had been so big a business in itself, at the railway station the farm wagon drawn up, the first smell of the pine-laden air, the first glimpse of the smiling farmer, and the great importance of the trunks and your father's enormous authority in such matters, and the feel of the wagon under you for the long ten-mile haul, and at the top of the last long hill catching the first view of the lake after eleven months of not seeing this cherished body of water. The shouts and cries of the other campers when they saw you, and the trunks to be unpacked, to give up their rich burden. (Arriving was less exciting nowadays, when you sneaked up in your car and parked it under a tree near the camp and took out the bags and in five minutes it was all over, no fuss, no loud wonderful fuss about trunks.)

10   Peace and goodness and jollity. The only thing that was wrong 10 now, really, was the sound of the place, an unfamiliar nervous sound of the outboard motors. This was the note that jarred, the one thing that would sometimes break the illusion and set the years moving. In those other summertimes all motors were inboard; and when they were at a little distance, the noise they made was a sedative, an ingredient of summer sleep. They were one-cylinder and two-cylinder engines, and some were make-and-break and some were jump-spark, but they all made a sleepy sound across the lake. The one-lungers throbbed and fluttered, and the twin-cylinder ones purred and purred, and that was a quiet sound too. But now the campers all had outboards. In the daytime, in the hot mornings, these motors made a petulant, irritable sound; at night, in the still evening when the afterglow lit the water, they whined about one's ears like mosquitoes. My boy loved our rented outboard, and his great desire was to achieve singlehanded mastery over it, and authority, and he soon learned the trick of choking it a little (but not too much), and the adjustment of the needle valve. Watching him I would remember the things you could do with the old one-cylinder engine with the heavy flywheel, how you could have it eating out of your hand if you got really close to it spiritually. Motor boats in those days didn't have clutches, and you would make a landing by shutting off the motor at the proper time and coasting in with a dead rudder. But there was a way of reversing them, if you learned the trick, by cutting the switch and putting it on again exactly on the final dying revolution of the flywheel, so that it would kick back against compression and begin reversing. Approaching a dock in a strong following breeze, it was difficult to slow up sufficiently by the ordinary coasting method, and

if a boy felt he had complete mastery over his motor, he was tempted to keep it running beyond its time and then reverse it a few feet from the dock. It took a cool nerve, because if you threw the switch a twentieth of a second too soon you would catch the flywheel when it still had speed enough to go up past center, and the boat would leap ahead, charging bull-fashion at the dock.

We had a good week at the camp. The bass were biting well and the sun shone endlessly, day after day. We would be tired at night and lie down in the accumulated heat of the little bedrooms after the long hot day and the breeze would stir almost imperceptibly outside and the smell of the swamp drift in through the rusty screens. Sleep would come easily and in the morning the red squirrel would be on the roof, tapping out his gay routine. I kept remembering everything, lying in bed in the mornings—the small steamboat that had a long rounded stern like the lip of a Ubangi, and how quietly she ran on the moonlight sails, when the older boys played their mandolins and the girls sang and we ate doughnuts dipped in sugar, and how sweet the music was on the water in the shining night, and what it had felt like to think about girls then. After breakfast we would go up to the store and the things were in the same place—the minnows in a bottle, the plugs and spinners disarranged and pawed over by the youngsters from the boys' camp, the Fig Newtons and the Beeman's gum. Outside, the road was tarred and cars stood in front of the store. Inside, all was just as it had always been, except there was more Coca-Cola and not so much Moxie and root beer and birch beer and sarsaparilla. We would walk out with a bottle of pop apiece and sometimes the pop would backfire up our noses and hurt. We explored the streams, quietly, where the turtles slid off the sunny logs and dug their way into the soft bottom; and we lay on the town wharf and fed worms to the tame bass. Everywhere we went I had trouble making out which was I, the one walking at my side, the one walking in my pants.

One afternoon while we were there at that lake a thunderstorm came up. It was like the revival of an old melodrama that I had seen long ago with childish awe. The second-act climax of the drama of the electrical disturbance over a lake in America had not changed in any important respect. This was the big scene, still the big scene. The whole thing was so familiar, the first feeling of oppression and heat and a general air around camp of not wanting to go very far away. In midafternoon (it was all the same) a curious darkening of the sky, and a lull in everything that had made life tick; and then the way the boats suddenly swung the other way at their moorings with the coming of a breeze out of the new quarter, and the premonitory rumble. Then the kettle drum, then the snare, then the bass drum and cymbals, then crackling light against the dark, and the gods grinning and licking their chops in the hills. Afterward the calm, the rain steadily rustling in the calm lake, the return of light and hope and spirits, and the campers running out in joy and relief to go swimming in the rain, their bright cries perpetuating the deathless joke about how they were getting simply drenched, and the children screaming with delight at the new sensation of bathing in the rain, and the joke about getting drenched linking the generations in a strong indestructible chain. And the comedian who waded in carrying an umbrella.

When the others went swimming, my son said he was going in, too. He pulled his dripping trunks from the line where they had hung all through the shower, and wrung them out. Languidly, and with no thought of going in, I watched him, his hard little body, skinny and bare, saw him wince slightly as he pulled up around his vitals the small, soggy, icy garment. As he buckled the swollen belt, suddenly my groin felt the chill of death.

The Struggle to Be an All-American Girl

Elizabeth Wong

Elizabeth Wong, a playwright and television writer, grew up in Chinatown in Los Angeles. Although she resisted, her mother insisted that she learn the Chinese language and culture when she was in grade school. Educated at the University of Southern California (1980) and New York University (1991), Wong has worked as a reporter and taught in the theater department at Bowdoin College. In this essay, which was first published in the Los Angeles Times, *Wong recounts her childhood rebellion against learning Chinese and her adult regret of her assimilation into American culture.*

1   It's still there, the Chinese school on Yale Street where my brother and I used to go. Despite the new coat of paint and the high wire fence, the school I knew 10 years ago remains remarkably, stoically the same.

Every day at 5 P.M., instead of playing with our fourth- and fifth-grade friends or sneaking out to the empty lot to hunt ghosts and animal bones, my brother and I had to go to Chinese school. No amount of kicking, screaming, or pleading could dissuade my mother, who was solidly determined to have us learn the language of our heritage.

Forcibly, she walked us the seven long, hilly blocks from our home to school, depositing our defiant tearful faces before the stern principal. My only memory of him is that he swayed on his heels like a palm tree, and he always clasped his impatient twitching hands behind his back. I recognized him as a repressed maniacal child killer, and knew that if we ever saw his hands we'd be in big trouble.

Originally appeared in the *Los Angeles Times*.

We all sat in little chairs in an empty auditorium. The room smelled like Chinese medicine, an imported faraway mustiness. Like ancient mothballs or dirty closets. I hated that smell. I favored crisp new scents. Like the soft French perfume that my American teacher wore in public school.

There was a stage far to the right, flanked by an American flag and the flag of the Nationalist Republic of China, which was also red, white and blue but not as pretty.

Although the emphasis at the school was mainly language—speaking, reading, writing—the lessons always began with an exercise in politeness. With the entrance of the teacher, the best student would tap a bell and everyone would get up, kowtow, and chant, "Sing san ho," the phonetic for "How are you, teacher?"

Being ten years old, I had better things to learn than ideographs copied painstakingly in lines that ran right to left from the tip of a *moc but,* a real ink pen that had to be held in an awkward way if blotches were to be avoided. After all, I could do the multiplication tables, name the satellites of Mars, and write reports on *Little Women* and *Black Beauty.* Nancy Drew, my favorite book heroine, never spoke Chinese.

The language was a source of embarrassment. More times than not, I had tried to disassociate myself from the nagging loud voice that followed me wherever I wandered in the nearby American supermarket outside Chinatown. The voice belonged to my grandmother, a fragile woman in her seventies who could outshout the best of the street vendors. Her humor was raunchy, her Chinese rhythmless, patternless. It was quick, it was loud, it was unbeautiful. It was not like the quiet, lilting romance of French or the gentle refinement of the American South. Chinese sounded pedestrian. Public.

In Chinatown, the comings and goings of hundreds of Chinese on their daily tasks sounded chaotic and frenzied. I did not want to be thought of as mad, as talking gibberish. When I spoke English, people nodded at me, smiled sweetly, said encouraging words. Even the people in my culture would cluck and say that I'd do well in life. "My, doesn't she move her lips fast," they would say, meaning that I'd be able to keep up with the world outside Chinatown.

My brother was even more fanatical than I about speaking English. He was especially hard on my mother, criticizing her, often cruelly, for her pidgin speech—smatterings of Chinese scattered like chop suey in her conversation. "It's not 'What it is,' Mom," he'd say in exasperation. "It's 'What *is* it, what *is* it, what *is* it!' " Sometimes Mom might leave out an occasional "the" or "a," or perhaps a verb of being. He would stop her in mid-sentence: "Say it again, Mom. Say it right." When he tripped over his own tongue, he'd blame it on her: "See, Mom, it's all your fault. You set a bad example."

What infuriated my mother most was when my brother cornered her on her consonants, especially "r." My father had played a cruel joke on Mom by assigning her an American name that her tongue wouldn't allow her to say. No matter how hard she tried, "Ruth" always ended up "Luth" or "Roof."

After two years of writing with a *moc but* and reciting words with multiples of meanings, I finally was granted a cultural divorce. I was permitted to stop Chinese school.

I thought of myself as multicultural. I preferred tacos to egg rolls; I enjoyed Cinco de Mayo[1] more than Chinese New Year.

At last, I was one of you; I wasn't one of them.

15   Sadly, I still am.   15

---

[1]Fifth of May, Mexican national holiday marking Mexico's victory over France at Puebla in 1862.

Language of Power Composition II

Inventing the University

David Bartholomae

Education may well be, as of right, the instrument whereby every individual, in a society like our own, can gain access to any kind of discourse. But we well know that in its distribution, in what it permits and in what it prevents, it follows the well-trodden battle-lines of social conflict. Every educational system is a political means of maintaining or of modifying the appropriation of discourse, with the knowledge and the powers it carries with it.

—Foucault, *The Discourse on Language*

. . . the text is the form of the social relationships made visible, palpable, material.

—Bernstein, *Codes, Modalities and the Process of Cultural Reproduction: A Model*

I.

1   Every time a student sits down to write for us, he has to invent the university for the occasion—invent the university, that is, or a branch of it, like history or anthropology or economics or English. The student has to learn to speak our language, to speak as we do, to try on the peculiar ways of knowing, selecting, evaluating, reporting, concluding, and arguing that define the discourse of our community. Or perhaps I should say the *various* discourses of our community, since it is in the nature of a liberal arts education that a student, after the first year or two, must learn to try on a variety of voices and interpretive schemes—to write, for example, as a literary critic one day and as an experimental psychologist the next; to work within fields where the

Reprinted from *When A Writer Can't Write*, Guilford Press.

David Bartholomae, Department of English, University of Pittsburgh, Pittsburgh, Pennsylvania.

rules governing the presentation of examples or the development of an argument are both distinct and, even to a professional mysterious.

The student has to appropriate (or be appropriated by) a specialized discourse, and he has to do this as though he were easily and comfortably one with his audience, as though he were a member of the academy or an historian or an anthropologist or an economist; he has to invent the university by assembling and mimicking its language while finding some compromise between idiosyncrasy, a personal history, on the one hand, and the requirements of convention, the history of a discipline, on the other. He must learn to speak our language. Or he must dare to speak it or to carry off the bluff, since speaking and writing will most certainly be required long before the skill is "learned." And this, understandably, causes problems.

Let me took quickly at an example. Here is an essay written by a college freshman.

> In the past time I thought that an incident was creative was when I had to make a clay model of the earth, but not of the classical or your everyday model of the earth which consists of the two cores, the mantle and the crust. I thought of these things in a dimension of which it would be unique, but easy to comprehend. Of course, your materials to work with were basic and limited at the same time, but thought help to put this limit into a right attitude or frame of mind to work with the clay.
>
> In the beginning of the clay model, I had to research and learn the different dimensions of the earth (in magnitude, quantity, state of matter, etc.) After this, I learned how to put this into the clay and come up with something different than any other person in my class at the time. In my opinion, color coordination and shape was the key to my creativity of the clay model of the earth.
>
> Creativity is the venture of the mind at work with the mechanics relay to the limbs from the cranium, which stores and triggers this action. It can be a burst of energy released at a precise time a thought is being transmitted. This can cause a frenzy of the human body, but it depends on the characteristics of the individual and how they can relay the message clearly enough through mechanics of the body to us as an observer. Then we must determine if it is cre-

ative or a learned process varied by the individuals thought process. Creativity is indeed a tool which has to exist, or our world will not succeed into the future and progress like it should.

I am continually impressed by the patience and goodwill of our students. This student was writing a placement essay during freshman orientation. (The problem set to him was: "Describe a time when you did something you felt to be creative. Then, on the basis of the incident you have described, go on to draw some general conclusions about 'creativity.'") He knew that university faculty would be reading and evaluating his essay, and so he wrote for them.

5   In some ways it is a remarkable performance. He is trying on the discourse even though he doesn't have the knowledge that would make the discourse more than a routine, a set of conventional rituals and gestures. And he is doing this, I think, even though he *knows* he doesn't have the knowledge that would make the discourse more than a routine. He defines himself as a researcher working systematically, and not as a kid in a high school class: "I thought of these things in a dimension of . . ."; "I had to research and learn the different dimensions of the earth (in magnitude, quantity, state of matter, etc.)." He moves quickly into a specialized language (his approximation of our jargon) and draws both a general, textbook-like conclusion—"Creativity is the venture of the mind at work . . ."—and a resounding peroration— "Creativity is indeed a tool which has to exist, or our world will not succeed into the future and progress like it should." The writer has even picked up the rhythm of our prose with that last "indeed" and with the qualifications and the parenthetical expressions of the opening paragraphs. And through it all he speaks with an impressive air of authority.

There is an elaborate but, I will argue, a necessary and enabling fiction at work here as the student dramatizes his experience in a "setting"—the setting required by the discourse—where he can speak to us as a companion, a fellow researcher. As I read the essay, there is only one moment when the fiction is broken, when we are addressed differently. The student says, "Of course, your materials to work with were basic and limited at the same time, but thought help to put this limit into a right attitude or frame of mind to work with the clay." At this point, I think, we become students and he the teacher giving us a lesson (as in, "You take your pencil in your right hand and put your paper in front of you"). This is, however, one of the most characteristic slips of basic writers. (I use the term "basic writers" to refer to university students traditionally placed in remedial composition courses.) It is very hard for them to take on the role—the voice, the persona—of an authority whose authority is rooted in scholarship, analysis, or research. They slip, then, into a more immediately available and realizable voice of authority, the voice of a teacher giving a lesson or the voice of a parent lecturing at the dinner table. They offer advice or homilies rather than "academic" conclusions. There is a similar break in the final paragraph, where the conclusion that pushes for a definition ("Creativity is the venture of the mind at work with the mechanics relay to the limbs from the cranium") is replaced by a conclusion that speaks in the voice of an elder ("Creativity is indeed a tool which has to exist, or our world will not succeed into the future and progress like it should").

It is not uncommon, then, to find such breaks in the concluding sections of essays written by basic writers. Here is the concluding section of an essay written by a student about his work as a mechanic. He had been asked to generalize about work after reviewing an on-the-job experience or incident that "stuck in his mind" as somehow significant.

> How could two repairmen miss a leak? Lack of pride?
> No incentive? Lazy? I don't know.

At this point the writer is in a perfect position to speculate, to move from the problem to an analysis of the problem. Here is how the paragraph continues, however (and notice the change in pronoun reference).

> From this point on, I take *my* time, do it right, and don't let customers get under *your* skin. If they have a complaint, tell them to call your boss and he'll be more than glad to handle it. Most important, worry about yourself, and keep a clear eye on everyone, for there's always someone trying to take advantage of you, anytime and anyplace. (Emphasis added)

We get neither a technical discussion nor an "academic" discussion but a Lesson on Life.[1] This is the language he uses to address the general

question, "How could two repairmen miss a leak?" The other brand
of conclusion, the more academic one, would have required him to
speak of his experience in our terms; it would, that is, have required a
special vocabulary, a special system of presentation, and an interpretive scheme (or a set of commonplaces) he could have used to identify and talk about the mystery of human error. The writer certainly
had access to the range of acceptable commonplaces for such an explanation: "lack of pride," "no incentive," "lazy." Each commonplace
would dictate its own set of phrases, examples, and conclusions; and
we, his teachers, would know how to write out each argument, just as
we know how to write out more specialized arguments of our own. A
"commonplace," then, is a culturally or institutionally authorized concept or statement that carries with it its own necessary elaboration. We
all use commonplaces to orient ourselves in the world; they provide
points of reference and a set of "prearticulated" explanations that are
readily available to organize and interpret experience. The phrase "lack
of pride" carries with it its own account of the repairman's error, just
as at another point in time a reference to "original sin" would have provided an explanation, or just as in certain university classrooms a reference to "alienation" would enable writers to continue and complete
the discussion. While there is a way in which these terms are interchangeable, they are not all permissible: A student in a composition
class would most likely be turned away from a discussion of original
sin. Commonplaces are the "controlling ideas" of our composition textbooks, textbooks that not only insist on a set form for expository writing but a set view of public life.[2]

10   When the writer says, "I don't know," then, he is not saying that   10
he has nothing to say. He is saying that he is not in a position to carry
on this discussion. And so we are addressed as apprentices rather than
as teachers or scholars. In order to speak as a person of status or privilege, the writer can either speak to us in our terms—in the privileged
language of university discourse—or, in default (or in defiance) of that,
he can speak to us as though we were children, offering us the wisdom of experience.

I think it is possible to say that the language of the "Clay Model"
paper has come *through* the writer and not from the writer. The writer
has located himself (more precisely, he has located the self that is represented by the "I" on the page) in a context that is finally beyond him,
not his own and not available to his immediate procedures for inventing and arranging text. I would not, that is, call this essay an example

of "writer-based" prose. I would not say that it is egocentric or that it represents the "interior monologue or a writer thinking and talking to himself" (Flower, 1981, p. 63). It is, rather, the record of a writer who has lost himself in the discourse of his readers. There is a context beyond the intended reader that is not the world but a way of talking about the world, a way of talking that determines the use of examples, the possible conclusions, acceptable commonplaces, and key words for an essay on the construction of a clay model of the earth. This writer has entered the discourse without successfully approximating it.

Linda Flower (1981) has argued that the difficulty inexperienced writers have with writing can be understood as a difficulty in negotiating the transition between "writer-based" and "reader-based" prose. Expert writers, in other words, can better imagine how a reader will respond to a text and can transform or restructure what they have to say around a goal shared with a reader. Teaching students to revise for readers, then, will better prepare them to write initially with a reader in mind. The success of this pedagogy depends on the degree to which a writer can imagine and conform to a reader's goals. The difficulty of this act of imagination and the burden of such conformity are so much at the heart of the problem that a teacher must pause and take stock before offering revision as a solution. A student like the one who wrote the "Clay Model" paper is not so much trapped in a private language as he is shut out from one of the privileged languages of public life, a language he is aware of but cannot control.

II.

Our students, I've said, have to appropriate (or be appropriated by) a specialized discourse, and they have to do this as though they were easily or comfortably one with their audience. If you look at the situation this way, suddenly the problem of audience awareness becomes enormously complicated. One of the common assumptions of both composition research and composition teaching is that at some "stage" in the process of composing an essay a writer's ideas or his motives must be tailored to the needs and expectations of his audience. Writers have to "build bridges" between their point of view and the reader's. They have to anticipate and acknowledge the reader's assumptions and biases. They must begin with "common points of departure" before introducing new or controversial arguments. Here is what one of the most popular college textbooks says to students.

> Once you have your purpose clearly in mind, your next task
> is to define and analyze your audience. A sure sense of your
> audience—knowing who it is and what assumptions you
> can reasonably make about it—is crucial to the success of
> your rhetoric. (Hairston, 1978, p. 107)

It is difficult to imagine, however, how writers can have a purpose before they are located in a discourse, since it is the discourse with its projects and agendas that determines what writers can and will do. The writer who can successfully manipulate an audience (or, to use a less pointed language, the writer who can accommodate her motives to her reader's expectations) is a writer who can both imagine and write from a position of privilege. She must, that is, see herself within a privileged discourse, one that already includes and excludes groups of readers. She must be either equal to or more powerful than those she would address. The writing, then, must somehow transform the political and social relationships between students and teachers.

15   If my students are going to write for me by knowing who I am— 15 and if this means more than knowing my prejudices, psyching me out— it means knowing what I know; it means having the knowledge of a professor of English. They have, then, to know what I know and how I know what I know (the interpretive schemes that define the way I would work out the problems I set for them); they have to learn to write what I would write or to offer up some approximation of that discourse. The problem of audience awareness, then, is a problem of power and finesse. It cannot be addressed, as it is in most classroom exercises, by giving students privilege and denying the situation of the classroom—usually, that is, by having students write to an outsider, someone excluded from their privileged circle: "Write about 'To His Coy Mistress,' not for your teacher but for the students in your class"; "Describe Pittsburgh to someone who has never been there"; "Explain to a high school senior how best to prepare for college"; "Describe baseball to an Eskimo." Exercises such as these allow students to imagine the needs and goals of a reader, and they bring those needs and goals forward as a dominant constraint in the construction of an essay. And they argue, implicitly, what is generally true about writing—that it is an act of aggression disguised as an act of charity. What these assignments fail to address is the central problem of academic writing, where a student must assume the right of speaking to someone who knows more about baseball or "To His Coy Mistress" than the student does,

a reader for whom the general commonplaces and the readily available utterances about a subject are inadequate.

Linda Flower and John Hayes, in an often quoted article (1981), reported on a study of a protocol of an expert writer (an English teacher) writing about his job for readers of *Seventeen* magazine. The key moment for this writer, who seems to have been having trouble getting started, came when he decided that teenage girls read *Seventeen;* that some teenage girls like English because it is tidy ("some of them will have wrong reasons in that English is good because it's tidy—can be a neat tidy little girl"); that some don't like it because it is "prim" and that, "By God, I can change that notion for them." Flower and Hayes's conclusion is that this effort of "exploration and consolidation" gave the writer "a new, relatively complex, rhetorically sophisticated working goal, one which encompasses plans for a topic, a persona, and the audience" (p. 383).[3]

Flower and Hayes give us a picture of a writer solving a problem, and the problem as they present it is a cognitive one. It is rooted in the way the writer's knowledge is represented in the writer's mind. The problem resides there, not in the nature of knowledge or in the nature of discourse but in a mental state prior to writing. It is possible, however, to see the problem as (perhaps simultaneously) a problem in the way subjects are located in a field of discourse.

Flower and Hayes divide up the composing process into three distinct activities: "planning or goal-setting," "translating," and "reviewing." The last of these, reviewing (which is further divided into two subprocesses, "evaluating" and "revising"), is particularly powerful, for as a writer continually reviews his goals, plans, and the text he is producing, and as he continually generates new goals, plans, and text, he is engaging in a process of learning and discovery. Let me quote Flower and Hayes's conclusion at length.

> If one studies the process by which a writer uses a goal to generate ideas, then consolidates those ideas and uses them to revise or regenerate new, more complex goals, one can see this learning process in action. Furthermore, one sees why the process of revising and clarifying goals has such a broad effect, since it is through setting these new goals that the fruits of discovery come back to inform the continuing process of writing. In this instance, some of our most complex and imaginative acts can depend on the ele-

gant simplicity of a few powerful thinking processes. We feel that a cognitive process explanation of discovery, toward which this theory is only a start, will have another special strength. By placing emphasis on the inventive power of the writer, who is able to explore ideas, to develop, act on, test, and regenerate his or her own goals, we are putting an important part of creativity where it belongs—in the hands of the working, thinking writer. (1981, p. 386)

While this conclusion is inspiring, the references to invention and creativity seem to refer to something other than an act of writing—if writing is, finally, words on a page. Flower and Hayes locate the act of writing solely within the mind of the writer. The act of writing, here, has a personal, cognitive history but not a history as a text, as a text that is made possible by prior texts. When located in the perspective afforded by prior texts, writing is seen to exist separate from the writer and his intentions; it is seen in the context of other articles in *Seventeen,* of all articles written for or about women, of all articles written about English teaching, and so on. Reading research has made it possible to say that these prior texts, or a reader's experience with these prior texts, have bearing on how the text is read. Intentions, then, are part of the history of the language itself. I am arguing that these prior texts determine not only how a text like the *Seventeen* article will be read but also how it will be written. Flower and Hayes show us what happens in the writer's mind but not what happens to the writer as his motives are located within our language, a language with its own requirements and agendas, a language that limits what we might say and that makes us write and sound, finally, also like someone else. If you think of other accounts of the composing process—and I'm thinking of accounts as diverse as Richard Rodriguez's *Hunger or Memory* (1983) and Edward Said's *Beginnings* (1975)—you get a very different account of what happens when private motive enters into public discourse, when a personal history becomes a public account. These accounts place the writer in a history that is not of the writer's own invention; and they are chronicles of loss, violence, and compromise.

20   It is one thing to see the *Seventeen* writer making and revising his 20 plans for a topic, a persona, and an audience; it is another thing to talk about discovery, invention, and creativity. Whatever plans the writer had must finally have been located in language and, it is possible to argue, in a language that is persistently conventional and formulaic.

We do not, after all, get to see the *Seventeen* article. We see only the elaborate mental procedures that accompanied the writing of the essay. We see a writer's plans for a persona; we don't see that persona in action. If writing is a process, it is also a product; and it is the product, and not the plan for writing, that locates a writer on the page, that locates him in a text and a style and the codes or conventions that make both of them readable.

Contemporary rhetorical theory has been concerned with the "codes" that constitute discourse (or specialized forms of discourse). These codes determine not only what might be said but also who might be speaking or reading. Barthes (1974), for example, has argued that the moment of writing, where private goals and plans become subject to a public language, is the moment when the writer becomes subject to a language he can neither command nor control. A text, he says, in being written passes through the codes that govern writing and becomes "de-originated," becomes a fragment of something that has "always been *already* read, seen, done, experienced" (p. 21). Alongside a text we have always the presence of "off-stage voices," the oversound of all that has been said (e.g., about girls, about English). These voices, the presence of the "already written," stand in defiance of a writer's desire for originality and determine what might be said. A writer does not write (and this is Barthes's famous paradox) but is, himself, written by the languages available to him.

It is possible to see the writer of the *Seventeen* article solving his problem of where to begin by appropriating an available discourse. Perhaps what enabled that writer to write was the moment he located himself as a writer in a familiar field of stereotypes: Readers of *Seventeen* are teenage girls; teenage girls think of English (and English teachers) as "tidy" and "prim," and, "By God, I can change that notion for them." The moment of eureka was not simply a moment of breaking through a cognitive jumble in that individual writer's mind but a moment of breaking into a familiar and established territory—one with insiders and outsiders; one with set phrases, examples, and conclusions.

I'm not offering a criticism of the morals or manners of the teacher who wrote the *Seventeen* article. I think that all writers, in order to write, must imagine for themselves the privilege of being "insiders"— that is, the privilege both of being inside an established and powerful discourse and of being granted a special right to speak. But I think that right to speak is seldom conferred on us—on any of us, teachers or students—by virtue of that fact that we have invented or discovered an original idea. Leading students to believe that they are responsible for something new or original, unless they understand what those words mean with regard to writing, is a dangerous and counterproductive practice. We do have the right to expect students to be active and engaged, but that is a matter of continually and stylistically working against the inevitable presence of conventional language; it is not a matter of inventing a language that is new.

When a student is writing for a teacher, writing becomes more problematic than it was for the *Seventeen* writer (who was writing a version of the "Describe baseball to an Eskimo" exercise). The student, in effect, has to assume privilege without having any. And since students assume privilege by locating themselves within the discourse of a particular community—within a set of specifically acceptable gestures and commonplaces—learning, at least as it is defined in the liberal arts curriculum, becomes more a matter of imitation or parody than a matter of invention and discovery.

25   To argue that writing problems are also social and political problems is not to break faith with the enterprise of cognitive science. In a recent paper reviewing the tremendous range of research directed at identifying general cognitive skills, David Perkins (in press) has argued that "the higher the level of competence concerned," as in the case of adult learning, "the fewer *general* cognitive control strategies there are." There comes a point, that is, where "field-specific" or "domain-specific" schemata (what I have called "interpretive strategies") become more important than general problem-solving processes. Thinking, learning, writing—all these become bound to the context of a particular discourse. And Perkins concludes:

> Instruction in cognitive control strategies tends to be organized around problem-solving tasks. However, the isolated problem is a creature largely of the classroom. The nonstudent, whether operating in scholarly or more everyday contexts, is likely to find himself or herself involved in what might be called "projects"—which might be anything from writing a novel to designing a shoe to starting a business.

It is interesting to note that Perkins defines the classroom as the place of artificial tasks and, as a consequence, has to place scholarly projects outside the classroom, where they are carried out by the "nonstudent." It is true, I think, that education has failed to involve students in scholarly projects, projects that allow students to act as though they were colleagues in an academic enterprise. Much of the written work that students do is test-taking, report or summary—work that places them outside the official discourse of the academic community, where they are expected to admire and report on what we do, rather than inside that discourse, where they can do its work and participate in a common enterprise.[4] This, however, is a failure of teachers and curriculum designers, who speak of writing as a mode of learning but all too often represent writing as a "tool" to be used by an (hopefully) educated mind.

It could be said, then, that there is a bastard discourse peculiar to the writing most often required of students. Carl Bereiter and Marlene Scardamalia (in press) have written about this discourse (they call it "knowledge-telling"; students who are good at it have learned to cope with academic tasks by developing a "knowledge-telling strategy"), and they have argued that insistence on knowledge-telling discourse undermines educational efforts to extend the variety of discourse schemata available to students.[5] What they actually say is this:

> When we think of knowledge stored in memory we tend these days to think of it as situated in three-dimensional space, with vertical and horizontal connections between sites. Learning is thought to add not only new elements to memory but also new connections, and it is the richness and structure of these connections that would seem . . . to spell the difference between inert and usable knowledge. On this account, the knowledge-telling strategy is educationally faulty because it specifically avoids the forming of connections between previously separated knowledge sites.

It should be clear by now that when I think of "knowledge" I think of it as situated in the discourse that constitutes "knowledge" in a particular discourse community, rather than as situated in mental "knowledge sites." One can remember a discourse, just as one can remember an essay or the movement of a professor's lecture; but this discourse, in effect, also has a memory of its own, its own rich network of structures and connections beyond the deliberate control of any individual imagination.

There is, to be sure, an important distinction to be made between learning history, say, and learning to write as an historian. A student can learn to command and reproduce a set of names, dates, places, and canonical interpretations (to "tell" somebody else's knowledge); but this is not the same thing as learning to "think" (by learning to write) as an historian. The former requires efforts of memory; the latter requires a student to compose a text out of the texts that represent the primary materials of history and in accordance with the texts that define history as an act of report and interpretation.

30   Let me draw on an example from my own teaching. I don't expect 30 my students to *be* literary critics when they write about *Bleak House*. If a literary critic is a person who wins publication in a professional journal (or if he or she is one who could), the students aren't critics. I do, however, expect my students to be, themselves, invented as literary critics by approximating the language of a literary critic writing about *Bleak House*. My students, then, don't invent the language of literary criticism (they don't, that is, act on their own) but they are, themselves, invented by it. Their papers don't begin with a moment of insight, a "by God" moment that is outside of language. They begin with a moment of appropriation, a moment when they can offer up a sentence that is not theirs as though it were their own. (I can remember when, as a graduate student, I would begin papers by sitting down to write literally in the voice— with the syntax and the key words—of the strongest teacher I had met.)

What I am saying about my students' essays is that they are approximate, not that they are wrong or invalid. They are evidence of a discourse that lies between what I might call the students' primary discourse (what the students might write about *Bleak House* were they not in my class or in any class, and were they not imagining that they were in my class or in any class—if you can imagine any student doing any such thing) and standard, official literary criticism (which is imaginable but impossible to find). The students' essays are evidence of a discourse that lies between these two hypothetical poles. The writing is limited as much by a student's ability to imagine "what might be said" as it is by cognitive control strategies.[6] The act of writing takes the student away from where he is and what he knows and allows film to imagine something else. The approximate discourse, therefore, is evidence of a change, a change that, because we are teachers, we call "development." What our beginning students need to learn is to extend themselves, by successive approximations, into the commonplaces, set phrases, rituals and gestures, habits of mind, tricks of persuasion, obligatory conclusions and necessary connections that determine the "what might be said" and constitute knowledge within the various branches of our academic community.[7]

Pat Bizzell is, I think, one of the most important scholars writing now on "basic writers" (and this is the common name we use for students who are refused unrestrained access to the academic community) and on the special characteristics of academic discourse. In a recent essay, "Cognition, Convention, and Certainty: What We Need to Know about Writing" (1982a), she looks at two schools of composition research and the way they represent the problems that writing poses for writers.[8] For one group, the "inner-directed theorists," the problems are internal, cognitive, rooted in the way the mind represents knowledge to itself. These researchers are concerned with discovering the "universal, fundamental structures of thought and language" and with developing pedagogies to teach or facilitate both basic, general cognitive skills and specific cognitive strategies, or heuristics, directed to serve more specialized needs. Of the second group, the "outer-directed theorists," she says that they are "more interested in the social processes whereby language-learning and thinking capacities are shaped and used in particular communities."

> The staple activity of outer-directed writing instruction will be analysis of the conventions of particular discourse communities. For example, a main focus of writing-across-the-curriculum programs is to demystify the conventions of the academic discourse community. (1982a, pp. 218)

The essay offers a detailed analysis of the way the two theoretical camps can best serve the general enterprise of composition research and composition teaching. Its agenda, however, seems to be to counter the influence of the cognitivists and to provide bibliography and encouragement to those interested in the social dimension of language learning.

As far as basic writers are concerned, Bizzell argues that the cognitivists' failure to acknowledge the primary, shaping role of convention in the act of composing makes them "particularly insensitive to the problems of poor writers." She argues that some of those problems, like the problem of establishing and monitoring overall goals for a piece of writing, can be better understood in terms of their unfamiliarity with the academic discourse community, combined, perhaps, with such limited experience outside their native discourse communities that they are unaware that there is such a thing as a discourse community with conventions to be mastered. What is underdeveloped is their knowledge both of the ways experience is constituted and interpreted in the academic discourse community and of the fact that all discourse communities constitute and interpret experience. (1982a, p. 230)

35   One response to the problems of basic writers, then, would be to deter- 35 mine just what the community's conventions are, so that those conventions could be written out, "demystified" and taught in our classrooms. Teachers, as a result, could be more precise and helpful when they ask students to "think," "argue," "describe," or "define." Another response would be to examine the essays written by basic writers—their approximations of academic discourse—to determine more clearly where the problems lie. If we look at their writing, and if we look at it in the context of other student writing, we can better see the points of discord that arise when students try to write their way into the university.

The purpose of the remainder of this chapter will be to examine some of the most striking and characteristic of these problems as they are presented in the expository essays of first-year college students. I will be concerned, then, with university discourse in its most generalized form—as it is represented by introductory courses—and not with the special conventions required by advanced work in the various disciplines. And I will be concerned with the difficult, and often violent accommodations that occur when students locate themselves in a discourse that is not "naturally" or immediately theirs.

III.

I have reviewed 500 essays written, as the "Clay Model" essay was, in response to a question used during one of our placement exams at the University of Pittsburgh: "Describe a time when you did something you felt to be creative. Then, on the basis of the incident you have described, go on to draw some general conclusions about "creativity." Some of the essays were written by basic writers (or, more properly, those essays led readers to identify the writers as basic writers); some were written by students who "passed" (who were granted immediate access to the community of writers at the university). As I read these essays, I was looking to determine the stylistic resources that enabled writers to locate themselves within an "academic" discourse. My bias as a reader should be clear by now. I was not looking to see how a writer might represent the skills demanded by a neutral language (a language whose key features were paragraphs, topic sentences, transitions, and the like—features of a clear and orderly mind). I was looking to see what happened when a writer entered into a language to locate himself (a textual self) and his subject; and I was looking to see how, once entered, that language made or unmade the writer.

Here is one essay. Its writer was classified as a basic writer and, since the essay is relatively free of sentence level errors, that decision must have been rooted in some perceived failure of the discourse itself.

> I am very interested in music, and I try to be creative in my interpretation of music. While in highschool, I was a member of a jazz ensemble. The members of the ensemble were given chances to improvise and be creative in various songs. I feel that this was a great experience for me, as well as the other members. I was proud to know that I could use my imagination and feelings to create music other than what was written.
>
> Creativity to me, means being free to express yourself in a way that is unique to you, not having to conform to certain rules and guidelines. Music is only one of the many areas in which people are given opportunities to show their creativity. Sculpting, carving, building, art, and acting are just a few more areas where people can show their creativity.
>
> Through my music I conveyed feelings and thoughts which were important to me. Music was my means of showing creativity. In whatever form creativity takes, whether it be music, art, or science, it is an important aspect of our lives because it enables us to be individuals.

Notice the key gesture in this essay, one that appears in all but a few of the essays I read. The student defines as his own that which is a commonplace. "Creativity, to me, means being free to express yourself in a way that is unique to you, not having to conform to certain rules and guidelines." This act of appropriation constitutes his authority; it constitutes his authority as a writer and not just as a musician (that is, as someone with a story to tell). There were many essays in the set that told only a story—where the writer established his presence as a musician or a skier or someone who painted designs on a van, but not as a person at a remove from that experience interpreting it, treating it as a metaphor for something else (creativity). Unless those stories were long, detailed, and very well told—unless the writer was doing more than saying, "I am a skier" or a musician or a van-painter—those writers were all given low ratings.

40   Notice also that the writer of the "Jazz" paper locates himself and   40
his experience in relation to the commonplace (creativity is unique expression; it is not having to conform to rules or guidelines) regardless of whether the commonplace is true or not. Anyone who improvises "knows" that improvisation follows rules and guidelines. It is the power of the commonplace—its truth as a recognizable and, the writer believes, as a final statement—that justifies the example and completes the essay. The example, in other words, has value because it stands within the field of the commonplace.[9] It is not the occasion for what one might call an "objective" analysis or a "close" reading. It could also be said that the essay stops with the articulation of the commonplace. The following sections speak only to the power of that statement. The reference to "sculpting, carving, building, art, and acting" attest to the universality of the commonplace (and it attests the writer's nervousness with the status he has appropriated for himself—he is saying, "Now, I'm not the only one here who has done something unique"). The commonplace stands by itself. For this writer, it does not need to be elaborated. By virtue of having written it, he has completed the essay and established the contract by which we may be spoken to as equals: "In whatever form creativity takes, whether it be music, art, or science, it is an important aspect of *our* lives because it enables us to be individuals." (For me to break that contract, to argue that *my* life is not represented in that essay, is one way for me to begin as a teacher with that student in that essay.)

All of the papers I read were built around one of three commonplaces: (1) creativity is self-expression, (2) creativity is doing something new or unique, and (3) creativity is using old things in new ways. These are clearly, then, key phrases from the storehouse of things to say about creativity. I've listed them in the order of the students' ratings: A student with the highest rating was more likely to use number three than number one, although each commonplace ran across the range of possible ratings. One could argue that some standard assertions are more powerful than others, but I think the ranking simply represents the power of assertions within our community of readers. Every student was able to offer up an experience that was meant as an example of "creativity"; the lowest range of writers, then, was not represented by students who could not imagine themselves as creative people.[10]

I said that the writer of the "Jazz" paper offered up a commonplace regardless of whether it was true or not; and this, I said, was an instance of the power of a commonplace to determine the meaning of an example. A commonplace determines a system of interpretation that can be used to "place" an example within a standard system of belief. You call see a similar process at work in this essay.

> During the football season, the team was supposed to wear the same type of cleats and the same type socks, I figured that I would change this a little by wearing my white shoes instead of black and to cover up the team socks with a pair of my own white ones. I thought that this looked better than what we were wearing, and I told a few of the other people on the team to change too. They agreed that it did look better and they changed there combination to go along with mine. After the game people came up to us and said that it looked very good the way we wore our socks, and they wanted to know why we changed from the rest of the team.
>
> I feel that creativity comes from when a person lets his imagination come up with ideas and he is not afraid to express them. Once you create something to do it will be original and unique because it came about from your own imagination and if any one else tries to copy it, it won't be the same because you thought of it first from your own ideas.

This is not an elegant paper, but it seems seamless, tidy. If the paper on the clay model of the earth showed an ill fit between the writer and his project, here the discourse seems natural, smooth. You could reproduce this paper and hand it out to a class, and it would take a lot of prompting before the students sensed something fishy and one of the more aggressive ones said something like, "Sure he came up with the idea of wearing white shoes and white socks. Him and Billy 'White-

Shoes' Johnson. Come on. He copied the very thing he said was his own idea, 'original and unique.'"

The "I" of this text—the "I" who "figured," "thought," and "felt"—is located in a conventional rhetoric of the self that turns imagination into origination (I made it), that argues an ethic of production (I made it and it is mine), and that argues a tight scheme of intention (I made it because I decided to make it). The rhetoric seems invisible because it is so common. This "I" (the maker) is also located in a version of history that dominates classrooms, the "great man" theory: History is rolling along (the English novel is dominated by a central, intrusive narrative presence; America is in the throes of a Great Depression; during football season the team was supposed to wear the same kind of cleats and socks) until a figure appears, one who can shape history (Henry James, FDR, the writer of the "White Shoes" paper), and everything is changed. In the argument of the "White Shoes" paper, the history goes "I figured . . . I thought . . . I told . . . They agreed . . ." and, as a consequence, "I feel that creativity *comes from when* a person lets his imagination come up with ideas and he is not afraid to express them." The act of appropriation becomes a narrative of courage and conquest. The writer was able to write that story when he was able to imagine himself in that discourse: Getting him out of it will be a difficult matter indeed.

45   There are ways, I think, that a writer can shape history in the   45
very act of writing it. Some students are able to enter into a discourse but, by stylistic maneuvers, to take possession of it at the same time. They don't originate a discourse, but they locate themselves within it aggressively, self-consciously. Here is another essay on jazz, which for sake of convenience I've shortened. It received a higher rating than the first essay on jazz.

> Jazz has always been thought of as a very original creative field in music. Improvisation, the spontaneous creation of original melodies in a piece of music, makes up a large part of jazz as a musical style. I had the opportunity to be a member of my high school's jazz ensemble for three years, and became an improvisation soloist this year. Throughout the years, I have seen and heard many jazz players, both professional and amateur. The solos performed by these artists were each flavored with that particular individual's style and ideas, along with some of the conventional

premises behind improvisation. This particular type of solo work is creative because it is, done on the spur of the moment and blends the performer's ideas with basic guidelines.

I realized my own creative potential when I began soloing. . . .

My solos, just as all the solos generated by others, were original because I combined and shaped other's ideas with mine to create something completely new. Creativity is combining the practical knowledge and guidelines of a discipline with one's original ideas to bring about a new, original end result, one that is different from everyone else's. Creativity is based on the individual. Two artists can interpret the same scene differently. Each person who creates something does so by bringing out something individual in himself.

The essay is different in some important ways from the first essay on jazz. The writer of the second is more easily able to place himself in the context of an "academic" discussion. The second essay contains an "I" who realized his "creative potential" by soloing; the first contained an "I" who had "a great experience." In the second essay, before the phrase, "I had the opportunity to be a member of my high school's jazz ensemble," there is an introduction that offers a general definition of improvisation and an acknowledgment that other people have thought about jazz and creativity. In fact, throughout the essay the writer offers definitions and counterdefinitions. He is placing himself in the context of what has been said and what might be said. In the first paper, before a similar statement about being a member of a jazz ensemble, there was in introduction that locates jazz solely in the context of this individual's experience: "I am very interested in music." The writer of this first paper was authorized by who he is, a musician, rather than by what he can say about music in the context of what is generally said. The writer of the second essay uses a more specialized vocabulary; he talks about "conventional premises," "creative potential," "musical style," and "practical knowledge." And this is not just a matter of using bigger words, since these terms locate the experience in the context of a recognizable interpretive scheme—on the one hand there is tradition and, on the other, individual talent.

It could be said, then, that this essay is also framed and completed by a commonplace: "Creativity is combining the practical knowledge and guidelines of a discipline with one's original ideas to bring about a new, original end result, one that is different from everyone else's." Here, however, the argument is a more powerful one; and I mean "powerful" in the political sense, since it is an argument that complicates a "naive" assumption (it makes scholarly work possible, in other words), and it does so in terms that come close to those used in current academic debates (over the relation between convention and idiosyncrasy or between rules and creativity). The assertion is almost consumed by the pleas for originality at the end of the sentence; but the point remains that the terms "original" and "different," as they are used at the end of the essay, are problematic, since they must be thought of in the context of "practical knowledge and guidelines of a discipline."

The key distinguishing gesture of this essay, that which makes it "better" than the other, is the way the writer works against a conventional point of view, one that is represented within the essay by conventional phrases that the writer must then work against. In his practice he demonstrates that a writer, and not just a musician, works within "conventional premises." The "I" who comments in this paper (not the "I" of the narrative about a time when he soloed) places himself self-consciously within the context of a conventional discourse about the subject, even as he struggles against the language of that conventional discourse. The opening definition of improvisation, where improvisation is defined as spontaneous creation, is rejected when the writer begins talking about "the conventional premises behind improvisation." The earlier definition is part of the conventional language of those who "have always thought" of jazz as a "very original creative field in music." The paper begins with what "has been said" and then works itself out against the force and logic of what has been said, of what is not only an argument but also a collection of phrases, examples, and definitions.

I had a teacher who once told us that whenever we were stuck for something to say, we should use the following as a "machine" for producing a paper: "While most readers of _____ have said _____, a close and careful reading shows that _____." The writer of the second paper on jazz is using a standard opening gambit, even if it is not announced with flourish. The essay becomes possible when he sets himself against what must become a "naive" assumption—what "most people think." He has defined a closed circle for himself. In fact, you could say that he has laid the ground work for a discipline with its own key terms ("practical knowledge," "disciplinary guidelines," and "original ideas"), with its own agenda and with its own investigative procedures (looking for common features in the work of individual soloists).

50   The history represented by this student's essay, then, is not the history of a musician and it is not the history of a thought being worked out within an individual mind; it is the history of work being done within and against conventional systems.

In general, as I reviewed the essays for this study, I found that the more successful writers set themselves in their essays against what they defined as some more naive way of talking about their subject—against "those who think that . . ."—or against earlier, more naive versions of themselves—"once I thought that. . . ." By trading in one set of commonplaces at the expense of another, they could win themselves status as members of what is taken to be some more privileged group. The ability to imagine privilege enabled writing. Here is one particularly successful essay. Notice the specialized vocabulary, but notice also the way in which the text continually refers to its own language and to the language of others.

> Throughout my life, I have been interested and intrigued by music. My mother has often told me of the times, before I went to school, when I would "conduct" the orchestra on her records. I continued to listen to music and eventually started to play the guitar and the clarinet. Finally, at about the age of twelve, I started to sit down and to try to write songs. Even though my instrumental skills were far from my own high standards, I would spend much of my spare time during the day with a guitar around my neck, trying to produce a piece of music.
>
> Each of these sessions, as I remember them, had a rather set format. I would sit in my bedroom, strumming different combinations of the five or six chords I could play, until I heard a series of which sounded particularly good to me. After this, I set the music to a suitable rhythm, (usually dependent on my mood at the time), and ran through the tune until I could play it fairly easily. Only after this section was complete did I go on to writing lyrics, which generally followed along the lines of the current popular songs on the radio.
>
> At the time of the writing, I felt that my songs were, in themselves, an original creation of my own; that is, I, alone,

made them. However, I now see that, in this sense of the word, I was not creative. The songs themselves seem to be an oversimplified form of the music I listened to at the time.

In a more fitting sense, however, I *was* being creative. Since I did not purposely copy my favorite songs, I was, effectively, originating my songs from my own "process of creativity." To achieve my goal, I needed what a composer would call "inspiration" for my piece. In this case the inspiration was the current hit on the radio. Perhaps, with my present point of view, I feet that I used too much "inspiration" in my songs, but, at that time, I did not.

Creativity, therefore, it a process which, in my case, involved a certain series of "small creations" if you like. As well, it is something, the appreciation of which varies with one's point of view, that point of view being set by the person's experience, tastes, and his own personal view of creativity. The less experienced tend to allow for less originality, while the more experienced demand real originality to classify something a "creation." Either way, a term as abstract as this is perfectly correct, and open to interpretation.

This writer is consistently and dramatically conscious of herself forming something to say out of what has been said *and* out of what she has been saying in the act of writing this paper. "Creativity" begins in this paper as "original creation." What she thought was "creativity," however, she now says was imitation; and, as she says, "in this sense of the word" she was not "creative." In another sense, however, she says that she *was* creative, since she didn't purposefully copy the songs but used them as "inspiration."

While the elaborate stylistic display—the pauses, qualifications, and the use of quotation marks—is in part a performance for our benefit, at a more obvious level we as readers are directly addressed in the first sentence of the last paragraph: "Creativity, therefore, is a process which, in my case, involved a certain series of 'small creations' if you like." We are addressed here as adults who can share her perspective on what she has said and who can be expected to understand her terms. If she gets into trouble after this sentence, and I think she does, it is because she doesn't have the courage to generalize from her assertion. Since she has rhetorically separated herself from her younger "self," and since she argues that she has gotten smarter, she assumes that there is

some developmental sequence at work here and that, in the world of
adults (which must be more complete than the world of children) there
must be something like "real creativity." If her world is imperfect (if
she can only talk about creation by putting the word in quotation
marks), it must be because she is young. When she looks beyond herself to us, she cannot see our work as an extension of her project. She
cannot assume that we too will be concerned with the problem of
creativity and originality. At least she is not willing to challenge us on
those grounds, to generalize her argument, and to argue that even for
adults creations are really only "small creations." The sense of privilege that has allowed her to expose her own language cannot be
extended to expose ours.

The writing in this piece—that is, the work of the writer within
the essay—goes on in spite of, or against, the language that keeps pressing to give another name to her experience as a songwriter and to bring
the discussion to closure. (In comparison, think of the quick closure
of the "White Shoes" paper.) Its style is difficult, highly qualified. It
relies on quotation marks and parody to set off the language and attitudes that belong to the discourse (or the discourses) that it would
reject, that it would not take as its own proper location.

55   David Olson (1981) has argued that the key difference between   55
oral language and written language is that written language separates
both the producer and the receiver from the text. For my student
writers, this means that they had to learn that what they said (the code)
was more important than what they meant (the intention). A writer, in
other words, loses his primacy at the moment of writing and must begin
to attend to his and his words' conventional, even physical presence on
the page. And, Olson says, the writer must learn that his authority is
not established through his presence but through his absence—through
his ability, that is, to speak as a god-like source beyond the limitations
of any particular social or historical moment; to speak by means of
the wisdom of convention, through the oversounds of official or authoritative utterance, as the voice of logic or the voice of the community.
He concludes:

> The child's growing competence with this distinctive reg-
> ister of language in which both the meaning and the author-
> ity are displaced from the intentions of the speaker and
> lodged "in the text" may contribute to the similarly spe-

cialized and distinctive mode of thought we have come to associate with literacy and formal education. (1918, p. 110)

Olson is writing about children. His generalizations, I think I've shown, can be extended to students writing their way into the academic community. These are educated and literate individuals, to be sure, but they are individuals still outside the peculiar boundaries of the academic community. In the papers I've examined in this chapter, the writers have shown an increasing awareness of the codes (or the competing codes) that operate within a discourse. To speak with authority they have to speak not only in another's voice but through another's code; and they not only have to do this, they have to speak in the voice and through the codes of those of us with power and wisdom; and they not only have to do this, they have to do it before they know what they are doing, before they have a project to participate in, and before, at least in terms of our disciplines, they have anything to say. Our students may be able to enter into a conventional discourse and speak, not as themselves, but through the voice of the community; the university, however, is the place where "common" wisdom is only of negative values—it is something to work against. The movement toward a more specialized discourse begins (or, perhaps, best begins) both when a student can define a position of privilege, a position that sets him against a "common" discourse, and when he or she can work self-consciously, critically, against not only the "common" code but his or her own.

IV.

Pat Bizzell, you will recall, argues that the problems of poor writers can be attributed both to their unfamiliarity with the conventions of academic discourse and to their ignorance that there are such things as discourse communities with conventions to be mastered. If the latter is true, I think it is true only in rare cases. All the student writers I've discussed (and, in fact, most of the student writers whose work I've seen) have shown an awareness that something special or something different is required when one writes for an academic classroom. The essays that I have presented in this chapter all, I think, give evidence of writers trying to write their way into a new community. To some degree, however, all of them can be said to be unfamiliar with the conventions of academic discourse.

Problems of convention are both problems of finish and problems of substance. The most substantial academic tasks for students,
learning history or sociology or literary criticism, are matters of many
courses, much reading and writing, and several years of education. Our
students, however, must have a place to begin. They cannot sit through
lectures and read textbooks and, as a consequence, write as sociologists
or write literary criticism. There must be steps along the way. Some
of these steps will be marked by drafts and revisions. Some will be
marked by courses, and in an ideal curriculum the preliminary courses
would be writing courses, whether housed in an English department
or not. For some students, students we call "basic writers," these courses
will be in a sense the most basic introduction to the language and methods of academic writing.

Our students, as I've said, must have a place to begin. If the problem of a beginning is the problem of establishing authority, of defining rhetorically or stylistically a position from which one may speak,
then the papers I have examined show characteristic student responses
to that problem and show levels of approximation or stages in the
development of writers who are writing their way into a position of
privilege.

60   As I look over the papers I've discussed, I would arrange them in   60
the following order: the "White Shoes" paper; the first "Jazz" essay; the
"Clay Model" paper; the second "Jazz" essay; and, as the most successful paper, the essay on "Composing Songs." The more advanced essays
for me, then, are those that are set against the "naive" codes of "everyday"
life. (I put the terms "naive" and "everyday" in quotation marks because
they are, of course, arbitrary terms.) In the advanced essays one can see
a writer claiming an "inside" position of privilege by rejecting the language and commonplaces of a "naive" discourse, the language of "outsiders." The "I" of those essays locates itself against one discourse (what
it claims to be a naive discourse) and approximates the specialized language of what is presumed to be a more powerful and more privileged
community. There are two gestures present, then—one imitative and
one critical. The writer continually audits and pushes against a language
that would render him "like everyone else" and mimics the language
and interpretive systems of the privileged community.

At a first level, then, a student might establish his authority by simply stating his own presence within the field of a subject. A student,
for example, writes about creativity by telling a story about a time he
went skiing. Nothing more. The "I" on the page is a skier, and skiing

stands as a representation of a creative act. Neither the skier nor skiing are available for interpretation; they cannot be located in an essay that is not a narrative essay (where skiing might serve metaphorically as an example of, say, a sport where set movements also allow for a personal style). Or a student, as did the one who wrote the "White Shoes" paper, locates a narrative in an unconnected rehearsal of commonplaces about creativity. In both cases, the writers have finessed the requirement to set themselves against the available utterances of the world outside the closed world of the academy. And, again, in the first "Jazz" paper, we have the example of a writer who locates himself within an available commonplace and carries out only rudimentary procedures for elaboration, procedures driven by the commonplace itself and not set against it. Elaboration, in this latter case, is not the opening up of a system but a justification of it.

At a next level I would place student writers who establish their authority by mimicking the rhythm and texture, the "sound," of academic prose, without there being any recognizable interpretive or academic project under way. I'm thinking, here, of the "Clay Model" essay. At an advanced stage, I would place students who establish their authority as *writers;* they claim their authority, not by simply claiming that they are skiers or that they have done something creative, but by placing themselves both within and against a discourse, or within and against competing discourses, and working self-consciously to claim an interpretive project of their own, one that grants them their privilege to speak. This is true, I think, in the case of the second "Jazz" paper and, to a greater degree, in the case of the "Composing Songs" paper.

The levels of development that I've suggested are not marked by corresponding levels in the type or frequency of error, at least not by the type or frequency of sentence-level error. I am arguing, then, that a basic writer is not necessarily a writer who makes a lot of mistakes. In fact, one of the problems with curricula designed to aid basic writers is that they too often begin with the assumption that the key distinguishing feature of a basic writer is the presence of sentence-level error. Students are placed in courses because their placement essays show a high frequency of such errors, and those courses are designed with the goal of making those errors go away. This approach to the problems of the basic writer ignores the degree to which error is less often a constant feature than a marker in the development of a writer. A student who can write a reasonably correct narrative may fall to pieces when faced with a more unfamiliar assignment. More important, however, such courses fail to serve the rest of the curriculum. On every campus there is a significant number of college freshmen who require a course to introduce them to the kinds of writing that are required for a university education. Some of these students can write correct sentences and some cannot; but, as a group, they lack the facility other freshmen possess when they are faced with an academic writing task.

The "White Shoes" essay, for example, shows fewer sentence-level errors than the "Clay Model" paper. This may well be due to the fact that the writer of the "White Shoes" paper stayed well within safe, familiar territory. He kept himself out of trouble by doing what he could easily do. The tortuous syntax of the more advanced papers on my list is a syntax that represents a writer's struggle with a difficult and unfamiliar language, and it is a syntax that can quickly lead an inexperienced writer into trouble. The syntax and punctuation of the "Composing Songs" essay, for example, shows the effort that is required when a writer works against the pressure of conventional discourse. If the prose is inelegant (although I confess I admire those dense sentences) it is still correct. This writer has a command of the linguistic and stylistic resources—the highly embedded sentences, the use of parentheses and quotation marks—required to complete the act of writing. It is easy to imagine the possible pitfalls for a writer working without this facility.

65   There was no camera trained on the "Clay Model" writer while 65
he was writing, and I have no protocol of what was going through his mind, but it is possible to speculate on the syntactic difficulties of sentences like these: "In the past time I thought that an incident was creative was when I had to make a clay model of the earth, but not of the classical or your everyday model of the earth which consists of the two cores, the mantle and the crust. I thought of these things in a dimension of which it would be unique, but easy to comprehend." The syntactic difficulties appear to be the result of the writer's attempt to use an unusual vocabulary and to extend his sentences beyond the boundaries of what would have been "normal" in his speech or writing. There is reason to believe, that is, that the problem was with *this* kind of sentence, in this context. If the problem of the last sentence is that of holding together the units "I thought," "dimension," "unique" and "easy to comprehend," then the linguistic problem was not a simple matter of sentence construction. I am arguing, then, that such sentences fall apart not because the writer lacked the necessary syntax to glue the pieces together but because he lacked the full statement

within which these key words were already operating. While writing, and in the thrust of his need to complete the sentence, he had the key words but not the utterance. (And to recover the utterance, I suspect, he would need to do more than revise the sentence.) The invisible conventions, the prepared phrases remained too distant for the statement to be completed. The writer would have needed to get inside of a discourse that he could in fact only partially imagine. The act of constructing a sentence, then, became something like an act of transcription in which the voice on the tape unexpectedly faded away and became inaudible.

Shaughnessy (1977) speaks of the advanced writer as one who often has a more facile but still incomplete possession of this prior discourse. In the case of the advanced writer, the evidence of a problem is the presence of dissonant, redundant, or imprecise language, as in a sentence such as this: "No education can be *total,* it must be *continuous.*" Such a student, Shaughnessy says, could be said to hear the "melody of formal English" while still unable to make precise or exact distinctions. And, she says,

> the pre-packaging feature of language, the possibility of taking over phrases and whole sentences without much thought about them, threatens the writer now as before. The writer, as we have said, inherits the language out of which he must fabricate his own messages. He is therefore in a constant tangle with the language, obliged to recognize its public, communal nature and yet driven to invent out of this language his own statements. (1977, pp. 207–208)

For the unskilled writer, the problem is different in degree and not in kind. The inexperienced writer is left with a more fragmentary record of the comings and goings of academic discourse. Or, as I said above, he or she often has the key words without the complete statements within which they are already operating.

Let me provide one final example of this kind of syntactic difficulty in another piece of student writing. The writer of this paper seems to be able to sustain a discussion only by continually repeating his first step, producing a litany of strong, general, authoritative assertions that trail quickly into confusion. Notice how the writer seems to stabilize his movement through the paper by returning again and again to recognizable and available commonplace utterances. When he has

to move away from them, however, away from the familiar to statements that would extend those utterances, where he, too, must speak,
the writing—that is, both the syntax and the structure of the discourse—falls to pieces.

> Many times the times drives a person's life depends
> on how he uses it. I would like to think about if time is
> twenty-five hours a day rather than twenty-four hours. Some
> people think it's the boaring or some people might say it's
> the pleasure to take one more hour for their life. But I think
> the time is passing and coming, still we are standing on
> same position. We should use time as best we can use about
> the good way in our life. Everything we do, such as sleep,
> eat, study, play and doing something for ourselves. These
> take the time to do and we could find the individual abil-
> ity and may process own. It is the important for us and
> our society. As time going on the world changes therefor
> we are changing, too. When these situation changes we
> should follow the suitable case of own. But many times
> we should decide what's the better way to do so by using
> time. Sometimes like this kind of situation can cause the
> success of our lives or ruin. I think every individual of his
> own thought drive how to use time. These affect are done
> from environmental causes. So we should work on the bet-
> ter way of our life recognizing the importance of time.

There is a general pattern of disintegration when the writer moves off
from standard phrases. This sentence, for example, starts out coher-
ently and then falls apart: "*We should use time as best as we can* use about
the good way in our life." The difficulty seems to be one of extending
those standard phrases or of connecting them to the main subject reference, "time" (or "the time," a construction that causes many of the
problems in the paper). Here is an example of a sentence that shows,
in miniature, this problem of connection: "*I think every individual* of
his own thought drive how to use *time*."

70   One of the remarkable things about this paper is that, in spite of   70
all the synatic confusion, there is the hint of an academic project here.
The writer sets out to discuss how to creatively use one's time. The text
seems to allude to examples and to stages in an argument, even if in

the end it is all pretty incoherent. The gestures of academic authority, however, are clearly present, and present in a form that echoes the procedures in other, more successful papers. The writer sets himself against what "some people think"; he speaks with the air of authority: "But I think. . . . Everything we do. . . . When these situation changes. . . ." And he speaks as though there were a project underway, one where he proposes what he thinks, turns to evidence, and offers a conclusion: "These affect are done from environmental causes. So we should work. . . ." This is the case of a student with the ability to imagine the general outline and rhythm of academic prose but without the ability to carry it out, to complete the sentences. And when he gets lost in the new, in the unknown, in the responsibility of his own commitment to speak, he returns again to the familiar ground of the commonplace.

The challenge to researchers, it seems to me, is to turn their attention again to products, to student writing, since the drama in a student's essay, as he or she struggles with and against the languages of our contemporary life, is as intense and telling as the drama of an essay's mental preparation or physical production. A written text, too, can be a compelling model of the "composing process" once we conceive of a writer as at work within a text and simultaneously, then, within a society, a history, and a culture.

It may very well be that some students will need to learn to crudely mimic the "distinctive register" of academic discourse before they are prepared to actually and legitimately do the work of the discourse, and before they are sophisticated enough with the refinements of tone and gesture to do it with grace or elegance. To say this, however, is to say that our students must be our students. Their initial progress will be marked by their abilities to take on the role of privilege, by their abilities to establish authority. From this point of view, the student who wrote about constructing the clay model of the earth is better prepared for his education than the student who wrote about playing football in white shoes, even though the "White Shoes" paper is relatively error-free and the "Clay Model" paper is not. It will be hard to pry loose the writer of the "White Shoes" paper from the tidy, pat discourse that allows him to dispose of the question of creativity in such a quick and efficient manner. He will have to be convinced that it is better to write sentences he might not so easily control, and he will have to be convinced that it is better to write muddier and more confusing prose (in order that it may sound like ours), and this will be harder than convincing the "Clay Model" writer to continue what he has already begun.

Acknowledgements

Preparation of this chapter was supported by the Learning Research and Development Center of the University of Pittsburgh, which is supported in part by the National Institute of Education.

Notes

1. David Olson (1981) has made a similar observation about school-related problems of language learning in younger children. Here is his conclusion: "Hence, depending upon whether children assumed language was primarily suitable for making assertions and conjectures or primarily for making direct or indirect commands, they will either find school texts easy or difficult" (p. 107).

2. For Aristotle, there were both general and specific commonplaces. A speaker, says Aristotle, has a "stock of arguments to which he may turn for a particular need."

> If he knows the *topoi* (regions, places, lines or argument)—and a skilled speaker will know them—he will know where to find what he wants for a special case. The general topics, or *common*places, are regions containing arguments that are common to all branches of knowledge. . . . But there are also special topics (regions, places, *loci*) in which one looks for arguments appertaining to particular branches of knowledge, special sciences, such as ethics or politics. (1932, pp. 154–155)

And, he says, "the topics or places, then, may be indifferently thought of as in the science that is concerned, or in the mind of the speaker." But the question of location is "indifferent" *only* if the mind of the speaker is in line with set opinion, general assumption. For the speaker (or writer) who is not situated so comfortably in the privileged public realm, this is indeed not an indifferent matter at all. If he does not have the commonplace at hand, he will not, in Aristotle's terms, know where to go at all.

3. Pat Bizzell has argued that the *Seventeen* writer's process of goal-setting

> can be better understood if we see it in terms of writing for a discourse community. His initial problem . . . is to find a way to include these readers in a discourse community for which he is comfortable writing. He places them in the academic discourse community by imagining the girls as students. . . . Once he has included them in a familiar discourse community, he can find a way to address

them that is common in the community: he will argue with them, putting a new interpretation on information they possess in order to correct misconceptions. (1982a, p. 228)

4. See Bartholomae (1979, 1983) and Rose (1983) for articles on curricula designed to move students into university discourse. The movement to extend writing "across the curriculum" is evidence of a general concern for locating students within the work of the university; see Bizzell (1982a) and Maimon *et al.* (1981). For longer works directed specifically at basic writing, see Ponsot and Deen (1982) and Shaughnessy (1977). For a book describing a course for more advanced students, see Coles (1978).

5. In spite of my misgivings about Bereiter and Scardamalia's interpretation of the cognitive nature of the problem of "inert knowledge," this is an essay I regularly recommend to teachers. It has much to say about the dangers of what seem to be "neutral" forms of classroom discourse and provides, in its final section, a set of recommendations on how a teacher might undo discourse conventions that have become part of the institution of teaching.

6. Stanley Fish (1980) argues that the basis for distinguishing novice from expert readings is the persuasiveness of the discourse used to present and defend a given reading. In particular, see the chapter, "Demonstration vs. Persuasion: Two Models of Critical Activity" (pp. 356–373).

7. Some students, when they come to the university, can do this better than others. When Jonathan Culler says, "the possibility of bringing someone to see that a particular interpretation is a good one assumes shared points of departure and common notions of how to read," he is acknowledging that teaching, at least in English classes, has had to assume that students, to be students, were already to some degree participating in the structures of reading and writing that constitute English studies (quoted in Fish, 1980, p. 366).

Stanley Fish tells us "not to worry" that students will violate our enterprise by offering idiosyncratic readings of standard texts:

The fear of solipsism, of the imposition by the unconstrained self of its own prejudices, is unfounded because the self does not exist apart from the communal or conventional categories of thought that enable its operations (of thinking, seeing, reading). Once we realize that the conceptions that fill consciousness, including any conception of its own status, are culturally derived, the very notion of an unconstrained self, of a consciousness wholly and dangerously free, becomes incomprehensible. (1980, p. 335)

He, too, is assuming that students, to be students (and not "dangerously free"), must be members in good standing of the community whose immediate head is the English teacher. It is interesting that his parenthetical catalogue of the "operations" of thought, "thinking, seeing, reading," excludes writing, since it is only through written records that we have any real indication of how a student thinks, sees, and reads. (Perhaps "real" is an inappropriate word to use here, since there is certainly a "real" intellectual life that goes on, independent of writing. Let me say that thinking, seeing, and reading are valued in the academic community *only* as they are represented by extended, elaborated written records.) Writing, I presume, is a given for Fish. It is the card of entry into this closed community that constrains and excludes dangerous characters. Students who are excluded from this community are students who do poorly on written placement exams or in freshman composition. They do not, that is, move easily into the privileged discourse of the community, represented by the English literature class.

8. My debt to Bizzell's work should be evident everywhere in this essay. See also Bizzell (1978, 1982b) and Bizzell and Herzberg (1980).

9. Fish says the following about the relationship between student and an object under study:

> we are not to imagine a moment when my students "simply see" a physical configuration of atoms and *then* assign that configuration a significance, according to the situation they happen to be in. To be in the situation (this or any other) is to "see" with the eyes of its interests, its goals, its understood practices, values, and norms, and so to be conferring significance *by* seeing, not after it. The categories of my students' vision are the categories by which they understand themselves to be functioning as students . . . and objects will appear to them in forms related to that way of functioning rather than in some objective or preinterpretive form. (1980, p. 334)

10. I am aware that the papers given the highest rankings offer arguments about creativity and originality similar to my own. If there is a conspiracy here, that is one of the points of my chapter. I should add that my reading of the "context" of basic writers' essays is quite different from Lunsford's (1980).

References

Aristotle. (1932). *The "Rhetoric of Aristotle"* (L. Cooper, Trans.). Englewood Cliffs, NJ: Prentice-Hall.

Barthes, R. (1974). *S/Z*. (R. Howard, Trans.). New York: Hill & Wang.

Bartholomae, D. (1979). Teaching basic writing: An alternative to basic skills. *Journal of Basic Writing, 2*, 85–109.

Bartholomae, D. (1983). Writing assignments: Where writing begins. In P. Stock (Ed.), *Forum* (pp. 300–312). Montclair, NJ: Boynton/Cook.

Bereiter, C., & Scardamalia, M. (in press). Cognitive coping strategies and the problem of "inert knowledge." In S. S. Chipman, J. W. Segal, & R. Glaser (Eds.), *Thinking and learning skills: Research and open questions* (Vol. 2). Hillsdale, NJ: Erlbaum.

Bizzell, P. (1978). The ethos of academic discourse. *College Composition and Communication, 29,* 351–355.

Bizzell, P. (1982a). Cognition, convention, and certainty: What we need to know about writing. *Pre/text, 3,* 213–244.

Bizzell, P. (1982b). College composition: Initiation into the academic discourse community. *Curriculum Inquiry, 12,* 191–207.

Bizzell, P., & Herzberg, B. (1980). "Inherent" ideology, "universal" history, "empirical" evidence, and "context-free" writing: Some problems with E. D. Hirsch's *The Philosophy of Composition. Modern Language Notes, 95,* 1181–1202.

Coles, W. E., Jr. (1978). *The plural I.* New York: Holt, Rinehart & Winston.

Fish, S. (1980). *Is there a text in this class? The authority of interpretive communities.* Cambridge. MA: Harvard University Press.

Flower, L. S. (1981). Revising writer-based prose. *Journal of Basic Writing, 3,* 62–74.

Flower. L., & Hayes, J. (1981). A cognitive process theory of writing. *College Composition and Communication, 32,* 365–387.

Hairston, M. (1978). *A contemporary rhetoric.* Boston: Houghton Mifflin.

Lunsford, A. A. (1980). The content of basic writers' essays. *College Composition and Communication, 31,* 278–290.

Maimon, E. P., Belcher, G. L., Hearn, G. W., Nadine, B. F., & O'Connor, F. X. (1981). *Writing in the arts and sciences.* Cambridge, MA: Winthrop.

Olson, D. R. (1981). Writing: The divorce of the author from the text. In B. M. Kroll & R. J. Vann (Eds.), *Exploring speaking-writing relationships: Connections and contrasts.* Urbana, IL: National Council of Teachers of English.

Perkins, D. N. (in press). General cognitive skills: Why not? In S. S. Chipman, J. W. Segal, & R. Glaser (Eds.), *Thinking and learning skills: Research and open questions* (Vol. 2). Hillsdale, NJ: Earlbaum.

Ponsot, M., & Deen, R. (1982). *Beat not the poor desk.* Montclair, NJ: Boynton/Cook.

Rodriquez, R. (1983). *Hunger of memory.* New York: Bantam.

Rose, M. (1983). Remedial writing courses: A critique and a proposal. *College English, 45,* 109–128.

Said, E. W. (1975). *Beginnings: Intention and method.* Baltimore: The Johns Hopkins University Press.

Shaughnessy, M. (1977). *Errors and expectations.* New York: Oxford University Press.

Why I Want a Wife

Judy Brady

Judy Brady (1937–), born in San Francisco, studied painting and received a B.F.A. in 1962 in art from the University of Iowa. Then she married and raised a family in a traditional housewife role. She later commented that her male professors had talked her out of pursuing a career in education. In the late 1960s, she became active in the women's movement and began writing articles on feminism and other social issues. In 1990, she was the editor of Women and Cancer, *an anthology by women. The essay "Why I Want a Wife" appeared in the first issue of* Ms. *magazine in 1972.*

1   I belong to that classification of people known as wives. I am A 1 Wife. And, not altogether incidentally, I am a mother.

Not too long ago a male friend of mine appeared on the scene fresh from a recent divorce. He had one child, who is, of course, with his ex-wife. He is looking for another wife. As I thought about him while I was ironing one evening, it suddenly occurred to me that I, too, would like to have a wife. Why do I want a wife?

I would like to go back to school so that I can become economically independent, support myself, and, if need be, support those dependent upon me. I want a wife who will work and send me to school. And while I am going to school I want a wife to take care of my children. I want a wife to keep track of the children's doctor and dentist appointments. And to keep track of mine, too. I want a wife to make sure my children eat properly and are kept clean. I want a wife who will wash the children's clothes and keep them mended. I want a wife who is a good nurturant attendant to my children, who arranges for their schooling, makes sure that they have an adequate social life with their peers, takes them to the park, the zoo, etc. I want a wife who takes care of the children when they are sick, a wife who arranges to be around when the children need special care, because, of course, I cannot miss classes at school. My wife must arrange to lose time at work and not lose the job. It may mean a small cut in my wife's income from time to time, but I guess I can tolerate that. Needless to say, my wife will arrange and pay for the care of the children while my wife is working.

I want a wife who will take care of *my* physical needs. I want a wife who will keep my house clean, a wife who will pick up after me. I want a wife who will keep my clothes clean, ironed, mended, replaced when need be, and who will see to it that my personal things are kept in their proper place so that I can find what I need the minute I need it. I want a wife who cooks the meals, a wife who is a *good* cook. I want a wife who will plan the menus, do the necessary grocery shopping, prepare the meals, serve them pleasantly, and then do the cleaning up while I do my studying. I want a wife who will care for me when I am sick and sympathize with my pain and loss of time from school. I want a wife to go along when our family takes a vacation so that someone can continue to care for me and my children when I need a rest and change of scene.

5   I want a wife who will not bother me with rambling complaints   5
about a wife's duties. But I want a wife who will listen to me when I feel the need to explain a rather difficult point I have come across in my course of studies. And I want a wife who will type my papers for me when I have written them.

I want a wife who will take care of the details of my social life. When my wife and I are invited out by friends, I want a wife who will take care of the babysitting arrangements. When I meet people at school that I like and want to entertain, I want a wife who will have the house clean, will prepare a special meal, serve it to me and my friends, and not interrupt when I talk about the things that interest me and my friends. I want a wife who will have arranged that the children are fed and ready for bed before my guests arrive so that the children do not bother us. I want a wife who takes care of the needs of my guests so that they feel comfortable, who makes sure that they have an ashtray, that they are passed the hors d'oeuvres, that they are offered a second helping of the food, that their wine glasses are replenished when necessary, that their coffee is served to them as they like it. And I want a wife who knows that sometimes I need a night out by myself.

I want a wife who is sensitive to my sexual needs, a wife who makes love passionately and eagerly when I feel like it, a wife who makes sure that I am satisfied. And, of course, I want a wife who will not demand sexual attention when I am not in the mood for it. I want a wife who assumes the complete responsibility for birth control, because I do not want more children. I want a wife who will remain sexually faithful to me so that I do not have to clutter up my intellectual life with jealousies. And I want a wife who understands that *my* sexual needs may entail more than strict adherence to monogamy. I must, after all, be able to relate to people as fully as possible.

If, by chance, I find another person more suitable as a wife than the wife I already have, I want the liberty to replace my present wife with another one. Naturally, I will expect a fresh, new life; my wife will take the children and be solely responsible for them so that I am left free.

When I am through with school and have a job, I want my wife to quit working and remain at home so that my wife can more fully and completely take care of a wife's duties.

10   My God, who *wouldn't* want a wife?   10

The Art of Collaborative Learning: Making the Most of Knowledgeable Peers

Kenneth A. Bruffee

Most students pursue higher education as preparation for work in the "real world." As Kenneth A. Bruffee observes, the fact that the real world works primarily through collaboration has prompted teachers in colleges and universities to explore collaborative learning as a means for preparing students for professional life—and academic success. Studies indicate that not only do students learn the art of collaboration, they gain knowledge and judgment more quickly and effectively.

According to Bruffee, professional collaboration and collaborative learning work because knowledge itself is the result of our ongoing work with each other. In terms used by the social constructionists who have influenced Bruffee's thinking, knowledge is "socially constructed." For Bruffee, knowledge as a social construct means that "learning occurs among persons rather than between a person and things." This calls into question the authority we have traditionally assigned to some kinds of knowledge as being entirely objective and absolute and has us rethink the authority we traditionally grant to the teachers who convey that knowledge. Drawing on research in teaching and learning, Bruffee subscribes to the notion that learning "does not involve people's assimilation of knowledge, it involves people's assimilation into communities of knowledgeable peers" (par. 24).

Collaborative learning has been an area of specialization for Bruffee throughout his academic career. In

Reprinted by permission from *Change* 19, no. 2.

addition to publishing articles and books—including Collaborative Learning: Higher Education, Interdependence, and the Authority of Knowledge *(2nd ed., 1990)—he has led colloquia on collaborative learning, liberal education, and the authority of knowledge at a number of prominent colleges and universities. Bruffee is professor of English and director of the Scholars Program and the Honors Academy at Brooklyn College, City University of New York.*

The essay reprinted here was originally published in 1987 in Change, *a bimonthly magazine that focuses on contemporary issues in higher education. It was subsequently reprinted in 1994 in a special retrospective issue of* Change. *The author has kindly included a short bibliography that notes recent work on collaborative learning.*

1   Late last spring, a colleague of mine at a university out West—I'll   1
call him Jim—wrote and asked if I would read a manuscript of his. He felt he was finally ready for someone to take a close look at it.

Jim's an old friend. I dashed off a note saying of course I'd read it, with pleasure. At the beginning of June, which luckily for both of us was right at the end of exams, I got a weighty package in the mail—279 pages plus notes. I read it, scribbled clouds of barely decipherable marginal notes, and drafted a six-page letter to Jim congratulating him on first-rate work, suggesting a few changes and mentioning one or two issues he might think through a bit further.

He phoned to thank me when he got the letter and asked some questions. We then spent an hour or so discussing these questions and supporting AT&T in the manner to which it has become accustomed.

Before the snow blows, I expect I shall see some of Jim's manuscript again. I doubt that he needs another reading, but I'm happy to do it if he wants me to. I learned a lot reading his book. We both learned something talking out the few stickier points in it. Anyway, I owe him one. He did the same for me five years ago, when I was thrashing about in the terminal throes of the book I was finishing. His name appeared prominently on my acknowledgments page; I suppose mine will appear prominently on his.

5   The experience I have just described is familiar to most readers of   5
Change. To enjoy such an experience, you don't have to write a book.

All you have to do is work with an intelligent, compatible committee on an interesting grant proposal or a new development plan for your college. You know how it can go. Joe gets an idea and sketches it out in a couple of pages. Mary says, hey, wait a minute—that makes me think of. . . . Then Fred says, but look, if we change this or add that. . . . In the end everyone, with a little help from his and her friends, exceeds what anyone could possibly have learned or accomplished alone.

If I'm right that this kind of experience is familiar, then no one reading this article is a stranger to collaborative learning, however strange the term may be. Jim and I are peers. When Jim asked me to read his work and I agreed, we became an autonomous collaborative learning group of two with the task of revising and developing the written product of one of its members.

The term "collaborative learning" has become increasingly familiar today because it is applied not only to voluntary associations such as my work with Jim, but also to teaching that tries to imitate that experience in college and university classrooms. Teachers of writing at institutions throughout the country are discovering that teaching students in a variety of ways to work productively on their writing demonstrably improves students' work.

And it is not just writing teachers who are interested. Clark Bouton and Russell Y. Clark's useful book, *Learning in Groups,* reports on the way collaborative learning is being applied in subjects from business management to medicine to math. And there is at least one physics lab manual in the country (at Montana State University) that presents an extended rationale of collaborative learning on its front cover.

Perhaps more to the point for some of us, at least one trenchant article exists that explains collaborative learning for the benefit of faculty and administrators who find themselves evaluating teachers. Harvey S. Wiener's "Collaborative Learning in the Classroom: A Guide to Evaluation" (*College English* 48) suggests ways to tell when teachers are using collaborative learning most effectively. It is also, therefore, a useful guide to, effective use of collaborative learning for teachers.

10   Admittedly, there is not much research to date on the effects of 10 collaborative learning in college and university education. But recent work on its effect in primary and secondary schools is relevant. Surveys of research by David Johnson (*Psychological Bulletin* 89) and by Shlomo Sharan (*Review of Educational Research* 50) tend to support the experience of college and university instructors who have used collaborative learning. Students learn better through noncompetitive

collaborative group work than in classrooms that are highly individualized and competitive. Robert E. Slavin's *Cooperative Learning* reports similar results.

Interest in collaborative learning in colleges and schools is motivated in part by these results. It is motivated also by the observation that the rest of the world now works collaboratively almost as a universal principle. Japanese "Theory-Z" quality circles on the factory floor aside, there is hardly a bank, legal firm, or industrial management team that strives—much less dares—to proceed in the old-fashioned individualistic manner. Physicians are increasingly collaborative, too, although they prefer to call it "consultation." At Harvard Medical School, 25 percent of each entering class currently studies in collaborative groups, bypassing systematic lecture courses almost entirely.

Interest in collaborative learning is motivated also by recent challenges to our understanding of what knowledge is. This challenge is being felt throughout the academic disciplines. That is, collaborative learning is related to the social constructionist views promulgated by, among others, the philosophers Richard Rorty (*Philosophly and the Mirror of Nature*) and the anthropologist Clifford Geertz. These writers say (as Geertz puts it in his recent book, *Local Knowledge*) that "the way we think now" differs in essential ways from the way we thought in the past. Social constructionists tend to assume that knowledge is a social construct and that, as the historian of science Thomas Kuhn has put it, all knowledge, including scientific knowledge, "is intrinsically the common property of a group or else nothing at all." (See Bruffee, "Social Construction, Language, and the Authority of Knowledge: A Bibliographical Essay," *College English*, vol. 48, December 1986, pp. 773–90.)

Collaborative learning is related to these conceptual changes by virtue of the fact that it assumes learning occurs among persons rather than between a person and things. It even turns out that some teachers who are using collaborative learning have found that social constructionist assumptions enhance their understanding of what they are trying to do and give them a better chance of doing it well.

So, although the term *collaborative learning* may be unfamiliar for some, collaborative learning itself is not new. Our understanding of its importance to higher education began in the late 1950s with Theodore Newcomb's work on peer-group influence among college students (*College Peer Groups, The American College,* ed. Nevitt Sanford) and with M. L. J. Abercrombie's research on educating medical students at University Hospital, University of London. Newcomb demonstrated that peer-group influence is a powerful but wasted resource in higher education. Abercrombie's book, *The Anatomy of Judgment*, showed medical students learning the key element in successful medical practice, diagnosis—that is, medical judgment—more quickly and accurately when they worked collaboratively in small groups than when they worked individually.

15   Abercrombie began her important study by observing the scene 15
that most of us think is typical of medical education: the group of medical students with a teaching physician gathered around a ward bed to diagnose a patient. Then she made a slight but crucial change in the way that such a scene is usually played out. Instead of asking each individual medical student in the group to diagnose the patient on his or her own, Abercrombie asked the whole group to examine the patient together, discuss the case as a group, and arrive at a consensus—a single diagnosis agreed to by all.

When she did this, what she found was that students who learned diagnosis collaboratively in this way acquired better medical judgment faster than individual students working alone.

With the exception of small, recently instituted experimental programs at the medical schools of the University of New Mexico and Harvard University, Abercrombie's conclusion has had little impact as yet on medical school faculties anywhere, in Britain or America. But when I read the book in 1972, a dozen years or so after it was published, her conclusion had an immediate and, I believe, positive impact on my thinking about university instruction and, eventually, on the role I see myself in as a classroom instructor.

The aspect of Abercrombie's book that I found most illuminating was her evidence that learning diagnostic judgment is not an individual process but a social one. Learning judgment, she saw, patently occurs on an axis drawn not between individuals and things, but among people. But in making this observation, she had to acknowledge that there is something wrong with our normal cognitive assumptions about the nature of knowledge. Cognitive assumptions, she says, disregard "the biological fact that [the human being] . . . is a social animal." "How [do] human relationships," that is, relations among persons, she asked, "influence the receipt of information about apparently nonpersonal events?"

In trying to answer this question, Abercrombie makes the brilliant observation that, in general, people learn judgment best in groups;

she infers from this observation that we learn judgment well in groups because we tend to talk each other out of our unshared biases and presuppositions. And in passing, she drops an invaluable hint: The social process of learning judgment that she has observed seems to have something to do with language and with "interpretation."

20   These three principles underlie the practice of collaborative learn- 20
ing. One thing that college and university instructors most hope to do through collaborative learning is increase their students' ability to exercise judgment within the teacher's field of expertise, whatever that field is.

But there is today another thing that instructors hope to do through collaborative learning. They hope to raise their students' level of social maturity as exercised in their intellectual lives. In doing so, instructors are trying to prepare their students for the "real world." They are preparing them to enter law, medicine, architecture, banking, engineering, research science—any field, in fact, that depends on effective interdependence and consultation for excellence.

This discovery that excellent undergraduate education also depends on effective interdependence and consultation awaited the work of William Perry. Perry's book, *Forms of Intellectual and Ethical Development in the College Years,* has made an indelible impression on the thinking of many college and university instructors, but not in every instance for the right reason. Like Abercrombie, Perry makes cognitive assumptions about the nature of knowledge, and most readers to date have found his developmental "scheme" of greatest interest.

Yet Perry himself is not entirely, comfortable with the cognitive assumptions underlying his scheme. He has read Thomas Kuhn's *The Structure of Scientific Revolutions,* and he acknowledges that our current view that "knowledge is contextual and relative" is only the most recent phase in a tendency toward the assimilation of cultural diversity that needs for its fulfillment "a new social mind."

As a result, again like Abercrombie, Perry implies that the central educational issues today hinge on social relations, not on cognitive ones: relations among persons, not relations between persons and things. Learning as we must understand it today, he concludes, does not involve people's assimilation of knowledge, it involves people's assimilation into communities of knowledgeable peers. Liberal education today must be regarded as a process of leaving one community of knowledgeable peers and joining another.

25   Perry's discomfort with this conclusion when it comes to educa- 25
tional practice, however, suggests that he himself may never have quite
recognized the full implications of his study. He denies that the creating of communities of knowledgeable peers among students is a legitimate part of rationally and consciously organized university education.
He prefers to rely on "spontaneity" to organize knowledge communities among students. He politely dismisses as unprofessional attempts
to foster communities among students by using "particular procedures
or rituals." Students must independently manage their "identification
with the college community" as they go about "divorcing themselves"
from the communities they have left behind.

Fortunately, Perry quotes liberally from his raw material—
statements made by a sizable number of informants among the Harvard College undergraduate body. And these undergraduates are not at
all as ambivalent as Perry seems to be about regarding learning as a social
process. Many of them see their undergraduate education quite explicitly as a difficult, perhaps even treacherous passage from one homogeneous community—the one they came from—to another homogeneous
community—the college community of their student peers.

This "marrying into" the new community of students at college
is clearly, as the students describe it, an informal, autonomous variety
of collaborative learning that challenges students to define their indi-
viduality not as starkly and lonesomely independent, but as interdependent members of their new undergraduate community.

The more formal varieties of collaborative learning organized by
instructors in classrooms imitate this informal type. And they imitate the "real world" interdependence and consultation that goes on
in much business and professional work, including the work my friend
Jim and I did together on his book and mine. In classroom collaborative learning, typically, students organized by the teacher into small
groups discuss a topic proposed by the teacher with the purpose of
arriving at consensus, much as Abercrombie's medical students practiced diagnosis on patients chosen by the teaching physician. Or students may edit each other's writing, or tutor each other, or develop and
carry through assigned (or group-designed and teacher-approved) projects together.

But this classroom work, however collaborative, differs in striking ways from autonomous, "real world" interdependence. Classroom
collaborative learning is inevitably no more than semiautonomous,

because students don't usually organize their own groups or choose their own tasks, as Jim and I did. In most cases, teachers design and structure students' work for maximum learning as part of a course of study. And teachers evaluate the work when it is completed, comparing it with professional standards and the work other students have done, both currently and in the past.

30   Now, to be accurate to a fault, of course, Jim and I were not an absolutely autonomous group either, any more than any interdependent consultative professional work is. Like most independently organized groups—such as political clubs, golf foursomes, and sand-lot baseball teams—he and I organized our working group on our own initiative for our own purposes, but we played the game, so to speak, by a set of rules we held in common with many other such groups.

The mores, conventions, values, and goals of our professional organization (in our case, the Modern Language Association), of that motley class of human beings called "university faculty," of promotion and tenure committees whose values are probably similar at Jim's college and mine, and so on—these large institutional communities determine to some extent what Jim and I did and said, how we did it and said it, and in point of fact, that we were doing it and saying it at all. Institutional motives and constraints always apply when people prepare themselves to take a hand in what is going on in the prevailing economic, legal, and educational world.

Formed within the immediate confines of a college's institutional structure, however, working groups in a collaborative learning classroom are clearly *semi*autonomous. Like the New York Yankees, a Boy Scout troop, or the United States Supreme Court, their collaboration is organized by a larger institutional community and with its sanction. Group members abide by the conventions, mores, values, and goals of that institution. The autonomy of classroom groups derives from the fact that once the tasks are set and the groups organized, instructors step back, leaving peers to work in groups of pairs to organize, govern, and pace their work by themselves and to negotiate its outcome.

That this partial autonomy is the key to the impact of collaborative learning is evident when we compare semiautonomous work with work that is entirely nonautonomous. The work of nonautonomous groups cannot reasonably be called collaborative learning at all. Like life in a Trappist monastery or an army platoon, in which activity is rigorously controlled, classroom group work is nonautonomous whenever instructors do not step back from the groups of working students, but rather "sit in" on them or "hover," predetermining the outcome of the work and maintaining the students' direct dependency on the teacher's presence, resources, and expertise.

Degree of autonomy is the key to collaborative learning because the issue that collaborative learning addresses is the way authority is distributed and experienced in college and university classrooms. It would be disingenuous to evade the fact that collaborative learning challenges our traditional view of the instructor's authority in a classroom and the way that authority is exercised.

35   This issue is much too complex to go into here. But perhaps we   35 can get a provocative glimpse of the possible rewards that might accrue from pursuing it further if we take a brief look at the nature and source of the authority of knowledge in any autonomous working group. Return for a moment to my friend Jim and me at work together on his manuscript. What was the source of the authority exercised in that work? Where was it placed and how did it get there? Not to put too fine a point on it, where did I get the authority to comment on his writing?

The answer, of course, is that Jim and I together generated the authority in our group of two. And to occur at all in this way, that generation of authority required certain conditions. For starters, we like each other. We have read each other's stuff. We respect each other's intelligence. We have similar interests. We have worked together professionally in other circumstances. In short, we were *willing* to collaborate.

It was under these conditions that *Jim granted me* authority over his work by asking me to read it. The authority of my knowledge with regard to his manuscript originated primarily with him. I mean "primarily" here in the strongest possible sense. My authority began with his request, and the principal claim to the validity of my authority resulted from that request.

Furthermore, and equally important, when I responded positively, *I agreed to take on and assert* authority relative to him and his work. In that sense, the authority of my knowledge with regard to his manuscript originated primarily not only with his granting me the authority, but also with my accepting it, both, of course, in a context of friendliness and good grace.

Willingness to grant authority, willingness to take on and exercise authority, and a context of friendliness and good grace are the three ingredients essential to successful autonomous collaboration. If any of these three is missing or flags, collaboration fails. These three ingredients are essential also to successful semiautonomous collaboration, such as classroom collaborative learning.

40   But when instructors use semiautonomous groups in classes, the 40
stark reality is that willingness to grant authority, willingness to take it on and exercise it, and a context of friendliness and good grace are severely compromised. Classroom authority does not necessarily begin—as Jim's and mine began—with the participants' (that is, the students') willing consent to grant authority and exercise it. In a classroom, authority still begins in most cases with the representative or agent of the institution, the instructor. Furthermore, except in highly unusual classrooms, most students start the semester as relative strangers. They do not begin, as Jim and I did, as friends. It is not surprising that, as a result, in many classrooms students may at first be wary and not overly eager to collaborate.

That is, collaborative learning has to begin in most cases with an attempt to *reacculturate* students. Given most students' almost exclusively traditional experience of classroom authority, they have to learn, sometimes against considerable resistance, to grant authority to a peer ("What right has he got to . . . ?"), instead of the teacher. And students have to learn to take on the authority granted by a peer ("What right have I got to . . . ?"), and to exercise that authority responsibly and helpfully in the interest of a peer.

Skillfully organized, collaborative learning can itself reacculturate students in this way. Once the task is set and the groups organized, collaborative learning places students working in groups on their own to interpret the task and invent or adapt a language and means to get the work done. When the instructor is absent, the chain of hierarchical institutional authority is for the moment broken. Students are free to revert to the collaborative peership that they are quite used to exercising in other kinds of extracurricular activities from which faculty are usually absent.

Of course, students do not always exercise effective collaborative peership in classrooms, especially at first, because they have all so thoroughly internalized our long-prevailing academic prohibitions against it. And it need hardly be added that nonautonomus groups, in which the instructor insists on remaining in direct authority even after the task is set and the groups organized, cannot reacculturate students in these ways, because the chain of hierarchical institutional authority is never broken.

Because we usually identify the authority of knowledge in a classroom with the instructor's authority, the brief hiatus in the hierarchical chain of authority in the classroom that is at the heart of collaborative learning in the long run also challenges, willy-nilly, our traditional view of the nature and source of the knowledge itself. Collaborative learning tends, that is, to take its toll on the cognitive understanding of knowledge that most of us assume unquestioningly. Teachers and students alike may find themselves asking the sorts of questions Abercrombie asked. How can knowledge gained through a social process have a source that is not itself also social?

45   This is another aspect of collaborative learning too complex to go   45 into here. But raising it momentarily gives us a hint about why collaborative learning may empower students to work more successfully beyond the confines of college or university classrooms. Collaborative learning calls on levels of ingenuity and inventiveness that many students never knew they had. And it teaches effective interdependence in an increasingly collaborative world that today requires greater flexibility and adaptability to change than ever before.

Bibliography

Brown, John Seely, and Paul Duguid. *The Social Life of Information.* Boston: Harvard Business School Press, 2000.

Bruffee, Kenneth A. *A Short Course in Writing: Composition, Collaborative Learning, and Constructive Reading.* 5th ed. New York: Pearson Longman, 2006.

Cohen, Elizabeth G. *Designing Groupwork: Strategies for the Heterogeneous Classroom.* 2nd ed. New York: Teachers College, Columbia University Press, 1994.

Farrell, Michael P. *Collaborative Circles: Friendship Dynamics and Creative Work.* Chicago: University of Chicago Press, 2001.

Mazur, Eric. *Peer Instruction: A User's Manual.* Upper Saddle River, NJ: Prentice Hall, 1997.

What's So Great About America

Dinesh D'Souza

Dinesh D'Souza (1961–) was born in Bombay, India, and emigrated to the United States in 1978. A noted conservative, D'Souza edited The Dartmouth Review *(an independent, conservative student newspaper) while in college, and has edited* Prospect *and* Policy Review, *journals with a conservative focus. From 1987–1988 he was senior domestic policy analyst at the White House under President Reagan, and he continued to work as an adivser under the George H. W. Bush administration as well. D'Souza has held positions as Research Fellow at the American Enterprise Institute and the Hoover Institution. His areas of research include the economy and society, civil rights and affirmative action, cultural issues and politics, and higher education. D'Souza's books have had an influence on public policy, most notably* What's So Great About America *(2002),* The Virtue of Prosperity *(2000),* Ronald Reagan: How an Ordinary Man Became an Extraordinary Leader *(1997), and* The End of Racism *(1995). His writing has also appeared in numerous newspapers and magazines, such as* The New York Times, The Washington Post, Harper's, *the* Atlantic Monthly, The Boston Globe, The Wall Street Journal, Forbes, *and* The Los Angeles Times. *The following essay from 2002 appeared in* The Hoover Digest.

1   America has become an empire, a fact that Americans are reluctant to admit and that critics of America regard with great alarm. Since the end of the Cold War, America has exercised an unparalleled and largely unrivaled influence throughout the

Reprinted from *Hoover Digest* (2002), by permission. Copyright © 2002 by Hoover Institute Press.

world. No other nation has ever enjoyed such economic, political, cultural, and military superiority. Consequently the critics of America, both at home and abroad, are right to worry about how American power is being used.

The critics charge that America is no different from other large and rapacious empires that have trampled across the continents in previous centuries. Within the universities, intellectuals speak of American policies as "neo-imperialist" because they promote the goals of empire while eschewing the term. America talks about lofty ideals, the critics say, but in reality it pursues naked self-interest. In the Gulf War, for example, America's leaders asserted that they were fighting for human rights but in truth they were fighting to protect American access to oil. The critics point to longtime American support for dictators such as Somoza in Nicaragua, Pinochet in Chile, the Shah in Iran, and Marcos in the Philippines as evidence that Americans don't really care about the democratic ideals they give lip service to. Even now America supports unelected regimes in Pakistan, Egypt, and Saudi Arabia. No wonder, the critics say, that so many people around the world are anti-American and that some even resort to terrorism in order to lash out against the imperial exercise of American power.

Are the critics right? They are correct to note the extent of American influence but wrong to suggest that America is no different from colonial powers such as the British, the French, and the Spanish that once dominated the world. Those empires—like the Islamic empire, the Mongol empire, and the Chinese empire—were sustained primarily by force. The British, for example, ruled my native country of India with nearly 100,000 troops.

American domination is different in that it is not primarily sustained by force. This is not to deny that there are American bases in the Middle East and the Far East or that America has the military capacity to intervene just about anywhere in the world. The real power of America, however, extends far beyond its military capabilities. Walk into a hotel in Barbados or Bombay and the bellhop is whistling the theme song from *Titanic*. African boys in remote villages can be spotted wearing Yankees and Orioles baseball caps. Millions of people from all over the globe want to move to America. Countless people are drawn to American technology, American freedom, the American way of life. Some critics, especially from Europe, sneer that these aspirations are shortsighted, and perhaps they are right. People may be wrong to want the American lifestyle and may not foresee its disadvantages, but at least they are seeking it voluntarily.

5   What about the occasions, though, when America does exercise   5
its military power? Here we can hardly deny the critics' allegation that America acts to promote its self-interest. Even so, Americans can feel immensely proud of how often their country has served their interests while simultaneously promoting noble ideals and the welfare of others. Yes, America fought the Gulf War *in part* to protect its oil interests, but it *also* fought to liberate the Kuwaitis from Iraqi invasion.

But what about long-lasting U.S. backing for Latin American, Asian, and Middle Eastern dictators such as Somoza, Marcos, Pinochet, and the Shah? It should be noted that, in each of these cases, the United States eventually turned against the dictatorial regime and actively aided in its ouster. In Chile and the Philippines, the outcome was favorable: The Pinochet and Marcos regimes were replaced by democratic governments that have so far endured. In Nicaragua and Iran, however, one form of tyranny promptly gave way to another. Somoza was replaced by the Sandinistas, who suspended civil liberties and established a Marxist-style dictatorship, and the Shah of Iran was replaced by a harsh theocracy presided over by the Ayatollah Khomeini.

These outcomes help highlight a crucial principle of foreign policy: the principle of the lesser evil. This means that one should not pursue a thing that seems good if it is likely to result in something worse. A second implication of this doctrine is that one is usually justified in allying with a bad guy in order to oppose a regime that is even worse. The classic example of this occurred during World War II: The United States allied with a very bad man, Stalin, in order to defeat someone who posed a greater threat at the time, Hitler.

Once the principle of the lesser evil is taken into account, then many American actions in terms of supporting tin-pot dictators such as Marcos and Pinochet became defensible. These were measures taken to fight the Cold War. If one accepts what is today an almost universal consensus that the Soviet Union was indeed an "evil empire," then the United States was right to attach more importance to the fact that Marcos and Pinochet were anti-Soviet than to the fact that they were autocratic thugs.

But now the Cold War is over, so why does America support despotic regimes such as those of Musharaff in Pakistan, Mubarak in

Egypt, and the royal family in Saudi Arabia? Once again, we must apply the principle of the lesser evil and examine the practical alternative to those regimes. Unfortunately there do not seem to be viable liberal, democratic parties in the Middle East. The alternative to Mubarak and the Saudi royal family appears to be Islamic fundamentalists of the bin Laden stripe. Faced with the choice between "uncompromising medievals" and "corrupt moderns," America has no choice but to side with the corrupt moderns.

10   Empires have to make hard choices, but even if one disagrees with 10
American actions in a given case, one should not miss the larger context. America is the most magnanimous of all imperial powers that have ever existed. After leveling Japan and Germany during World War II, the United States rebuilt those countries. For the most part, America is an *abstaining* superpower: it shows no real interest in conquering and subjugating the rest of the world, even though it can. On occasion the United States intervenes in Grenada or Haiti or Bosnia, but it never stays to rule those countries. Moreover, when America does get into a war, it is supremely careful to avoid targeting civilians and to minimize collateral damage. Even as American bombs destroyed the infrastructure of the Taliban regime, American planes dropped rations of food to avert hardship and starvation of Afghan civilians. What other country does such things?

Jeane Kirkpatrick once said that "Americans need to face the truth about themselves, no matter how pleasant it is." The reason that many Americans don't feel this way is that they judge themselves by a higher standard than they judge anyone else. Thus if the Chinese, the Arabs, or the sub-Saharan Africans slaughter ten thousand of their own people, the world utters a collective sigh and resumes its normal business. By contrast, if America, in the middle of a war, accidentally bombs a school or a hospital and kills 200 civilians, there is an immediate uproar and an investigation is launched. What all this demonstrates, of course, is America's evident moral superiority. If this be the workings of empire, let us have more of it.

"Building a Mystery": Alternative Research Writing and the Academic Act of Seeking

Robert Davis and Mark Shadle

Robert Davis and Mark Shadle are associate professors of English–Writing at Eastern Oregon University in La Grande, where Davis directs the writing program and Shadle directs the Writing Lab. Davis's teaching and research interests include postmodern theory, ancient rhetoric, carnivalisque discourse, exploratory writing, and teacher education. He has published articles and book chapters on cultural simu- lations, multigenre approaches to writing pedagogy, and electronic writing. Shadle's teaching and research interests include writing center theory and practice, postmodern and post-colonial theory, exploratory writing, American and Caribbean Studies, environmental literature, multicultural and contemporary world literature. He has published arti- cles and book chapters on writing center staffing, online writing labs, blues/jazz, and the work of Wendell Berry, Ishmael Reed, David Rubadiri, and Simon Schama. Together, Davis and Shadle have spread the use of multi- writing in multiple genres, disciplines, cultures, and media from their own courses and campus throughout the Pacific Northwest and the country through conference presentations and National Writing Project workshops. Currently, they are at work on a textbook on research writing that presents multi-writing alongside traditional forms.

Reprinted from *College Composition and Communication* 51, no. 3 (2000) by permis- sion of the National Council of Teachers of English. This article culminated in a book that enlarges the article that the authors co-wrote: *Teaching Multiwriting: Researching and Composing with Multiple Genres, Media, Disciplines, and Cultures* (2006), South- ern Illinois University Press.

Alternative forms of research writing that displace those of modernism are unfolded, ending with "multi-writing," which incorporates multiple genres, disciplines, cultures, and media to syncretically gather post/modern forms. Such alternatives represent a shift in academic values toward a more exploratory inquiry that honors mystery.

1

R esearch writing is disrespected and omnipresent, trite and vital, central to modern academic discourse, yet a part of our own duties as teachers of writing that we seldom discuss.[1] For nearly thirty years, the conventional construct of research writing, the "research paper," has seemed ready to collapse, undercut by the charge that it is an absurd, "non-form of writing" (Larson). Still, the research paper goes on. In a 1982 survey, James Ford and Dennis R. Perry found that the research paper is taught in 84 percent of first-year composition courses and 40 percent of advanced composition courses (827). The survey has not been repeated, but our own informal research suggests that the research paper is still taught in most composition curriculums, typically at the end of a first-year composition course or course sequence, and thus it is positioned as the final, even climactic, step for students entering the communities of academic discourse.[2]

This notable status has not kept the research paper from being notoriously vacant, clichéd, and templated. Research writing textbooks, despite their earnest good intentions, tend to reinforce unoriginal writing by providing students not only with maps through the conventional routes of academic research, but also a standardized concept of how academic research writing should look and sound; textbooks typically provide sample papers, and stock advice on the "rules" of logical argumentation, linear organization, acceptable evidence, and the proper way to cite sources.

In this essay, we will present a series of alternatives to the modernist research paper: the argumentative research paper, the personal research paper, the research essay, and the multi-genre/media/disciplinary/cultural research paper. Part of our purpose is practical—we want to suggest new choices to teachers and students of research writing. However, we are also interested in the theoretical implications of alternative research writing strategies. We see in these strategies movement away from the modernist ideals of expertise, detachment, and certainty, and toward a new valuation of uncertainty, passionate exploration, and mystery. We also see an increased rhetorical sophistication. Alternative research writing often asks students to compose within a large range of strategies, genres, and media. Our students, whose work we will highlight at the end of this essay, create research projects that use, and mix, not only multiple genres and media, but also multiple disciplines and cultures. This work overcomes not only students' fear of, and boredom with, traditional research writing, but also some of the false oppositions prevalent in composition studies and academic culture. These include the divisions between: academic and expressive writing; competing canons; fiction and nonfiction; high, pop, and folk culture; and the methods and jargons of different fields.

Escaping Posusta

Research writing instruction in its current state has begun to spawn parasitic parodies. What "Cliff Notes" has done for literature, Steven Posusta's *Don't Panic: The Procrastinator's Guide to Writing an Effective Term Paper* (*You know who you are*) does for research writing manuals. Posusta is a snowboarder and mountain biker with an M.A. who tutored at UCLA. His book is at once a spoof of other research writing texts; an exposé of the emptiness of "academic discourse," at least as practiced by cynics; and perhaps the best guide to research writing in that it makes full, explicit use of the value that hovers at the edges of other, more polite, texts: sheer efficiency. The writing "process" Posusta outlines can be completed in just one night, although he admits that two are best.

5   This efficiency took time to develop. Posusta recounts his own   5
painful lessons as an academic outsider learning to, in David Bartholomae's phrase, "invent the university":

> Writing papers for college or university professors can be terrifying. The first paper I ever wrote came back to me flowing with red ink. A note on the first page read: "Why did you ignore my instructions? Rewrite!" I had unfortunately interpreted the professor's instructions as mere suggestions. Papers are personal, aren't they? If I answer the question and speak my mind, I'll do fine, right? Wrong. (7)

To better invent, Posusta had to learn the academy's customs, rules, and practices. He eventually did this well enough to become a writing tutor, where he encountered students like the one he had been, struggling to write in the ways of the academy. Further, he found that most students put off their writing until the last minute. Rather than attempt to help them enact longer writing processes, he instead suggested methods for quickly creating acceptable discourse.

His book is a continuation of his tutoring. At a sleek 62 pages (with large print), it claims a special ability to help students quickly get up to speed. Devices such as the Instant Thesis Maker help:

The Instant Thesis

#1. Although _____ ,
     (general statement, opposite opinion)
#2. nevertheless _____ ,
     (thesis, your idea)
#3. because _____ ,
     (examples, evidence, #1, #2 #3, etc.) (12)

The only thing more efficient would be to let an expert like Posusta or a computer program do the work for you, filling in the blanks in the Instant Thesis, Body, and Conclusion. Posusta, however, stands guard against forms of cheating even he considers too efficient. He cannot keep students from downloading research papers from the Internet, but he can foil their plans to pass off as their own the sample paper provided in *Don't Panic*. While other authors blather about the evils of plagiarism, Posusta takes protective measures. Instructors reading the photocopies of his sample paper handed in by students who have failed to read it, will find the following sentence in the midst of the competent prose: "I am plagiarizing, please fail me" (9).

As the many cases of plagiarism and Posusta's Instant Book suggest, the research paper has become a stationary target. We would like to believe that research writing teaches valuable skills and encourages students to commit to the academic ideals of inquiry and evidentiary reasoning. However, it may be as often the case that the research paper assignment teaches students little more than the act of producing, as effortlessly as possible, a drab discourse, vacant of originality or commitment.

10   Defenses of the research paper often rely on its preparatory func- 10
tion. We must teach the research paper, the argument goes, because students are likely to encounter it again in other courses across the disciplines. While this argument has validity, it can be countered by noting that teaching the research paper as the sole example of research

writing will fail to prepare students for a myriad of other research-based writings: lab reports, case studies, news stories, position papers, take-home exams, and research proposals. Further, one can argue, the research paper is solely academic. In a culture overrun with data, the public often remains uninterested in the detached perspective of the modernist research paper. As Sharon Crowley and Debra Hawhee point out, facts take on meaning within networks of interpretation, which enable and shape cultural debates (6).

Richard Larson's well-known criticism goes further, charging that, theoretically speaking, the research paper does not exist:

> Research can inform virtually any writing or speaking if the author wishes it to do so; there is nothing of substance or content that differentiates one paper that draws on data from outside the author's own self from another such paper—nothing that can enable one to say that this paper is a "research paper" and that paper is not. (Indeed even an ordered, interpretive reporting of altogether personal experiences and responses can, if presented purposively, be a reporting of research.) I would assert therefore that the so-called "research paper," as a generic, cross-disciplinary term, has no conceptual or substantive identity. If almost any paper is potentially a paper incorporating the fruits of research, the term "research paper" has virtually no value as an identification of a kind of substance in a paper. Conceptually, the generic term "research paper" is for practical purposes meaningless. (813)

Larson's erasure of the research paper's grounding, however, reveals the omnipresence and importance of research writing. He opens his essay with a defense of research-based learning as part of any literate education:

> Let me begin by assuring you that I do not oppose the assumption that student writers in academic and professional settings, whether they be freshmen or sophomores or students in secondary school or intend to be journalists or lawyers or scholars or whatever, should engage in research . . . and that appropriately informed people should help them learn to engage in research in whatever field these writers happen to be studying. (811)

Larson is joined by advocates of research writing, and the authors of sincere, non-Posusta research writing textbooks, in stressing the importance of research in our infoculture and the necessity of teaching research skills. Research writing, we are told, should teach students about how data is generated and expertise gained. It should also allow them to cultivate their intellectual curiosity and expand their knowledge. The issue becomes method and form—how to do research and how to write it in ways that will allow students to embrace academic ideals and escape the cynicism of Posusta.

In alternative research writing, Larson's claim that research can inform nearly all discourse becomes the ground on which research writing is re-made. The models of composing we will present often involve choosing among, mixing, and juxtaposing a grand variety of discourses. The field of composition is here constituted as the study of all utterances—communicative, persuasive, expressive—in any genre, media, discipline, or culture. Seen in this light, research writing begins to enact the vision of composition theorist Derek Owens:

> Feasibly, taken in this broadest sense, composition studies is a crossroads discipline, a catalytic zone where a motley assemblage of discourse communities and arenas for intellectual exploration converge, metamorphose, and regenerate. At the same time, we cannot study multiple disciplines without being brought back somehow to the art of composing: musically, syntactically, lexically, orally, dialogically, socially, politically, poetically. (160)

15   As well as a broadened field for composing, the practices of alter- 15
native research writing enact a revised understanding of the purposes of academic work. According to its original ideal, modern research writing was to inscribe an act of seeking by presenting the knowledge the act secured. Seeking was made to consist of creating the conditions under which knowledge could present itself to the mind ready to receive it. But, as critiques of modernism have shown, knowledge cannot "present itself" to the mind because the mind and the world around it cannot be separated. Research has never been the hollow act of recording dead facts in a static world, and research writing has never been a mirror of nature. As James Elkins says in *The Object Stares Back: On the Nature of Seeing*, the gaze into the mirror is always an act of desire:

When I say, "Just looking," I mean I am searching, I have my "eye out" for something. Looking is hoping, desiring, never just taking in light, never merely collecting patterns and data. Looking is possessing or the desire to possess— we eat food, we own objects, and we "possess" bodies—and there is no looking without thoughts of using, possessing, repossessing, owning, fixing, appropriating, keeping, remembering and commemorating, cherishing, borrowing, and stealing. I cannot look at *anything*—any object, any person— without the shadow of the thought of possessing that thing. Those appetites don't just accompany looking: they are looking itself. (22)

In the modern academy, the possessive gaze is expressed as the desire for expertise, which hides the passionate need to control the world. Werner Muensterberger has seen a similar drive in exacting and prestigious collectors. In *Collecting: An Unruly Passion*, he writes:

I have followed the trail of these emotional conditions in the life histories of many collectors. . . . They like to pose or make a spectacle of their possessions. But one soon realizes that these possessions, regardless of their value or significance, are but stand-ins for themselves. And while they use their objects for inner security and outer applause, their deep inner function is to screen off self-doubt and unassimilated memories. (13)

Alternative research writing may offer hope for resisting the will to possess without returning to illusory claims to detachment, objectivity, and pure reflection. Such research writing does not seek claims to constant truth or an unassailable perspective, but instead asks us to take comfort in contingency, and thrill at mystery. Desire here is enacted as a restlessness reversing the libidinal economy of ownership; instead of wanting to possess, or even "know" the other, we want to sustain the experiential excitement of not knowing, the seductive wonder we feel at discovering that the other is beyond us, unknown, inexhaustible. The ideal of alternative research writing is exploration freed from its historical weight of conquest and enslavement.

Alternative research writing then, is not only a set of pedagogic strategies, but also a series of expressions of an altered conception of inquiry. Knowledge here plays leapfrog with mystery; meanings are made to move beyond, and writing traces this movement. Research becomes seeking as a mode of being. As academic seekers, we journey toward a state of understanding that subsumes both ignorance and knowledge, a state in which we "know" more deeply our own incapacity for certainty and find that it is uncertainty that keeps us alive and thinking. Alternative research writing is what William Covino calls a form of wondering: a way not to end thinking, but to generate and sustain it.[3] This discursive inquiry has a literal parallel in many world cultures. Whether we think of Australian aborigines on walkabout or East Indian men on sunyata, intellectual wondering is enacted as physical wandering.

Alternative research writing is intensely academic, but it also strives to reconstitute the academy by reaching beyond the disciplinary thinking, logos-dominated arguing, and nonexpressive writing we have come to call "academic." Alternative research writing inscribes an inclusive cross-disciplinary academy, which mixes the personal and the public and values the imagination as much as the intellect. Such writing thus helps us to regather creative work as inquiry, recalling, for instance, the moral charge Milan Kundera has given the novel: it must operate within the unknown to rediscover our world and ourselves. The plight of the alternative research writer is like the one Donald Barthelme sees in the novelist beginning a work:

> Writing is a process of dealing with not-knowing, a forcing of what and how. We have all heard novelists testify to the fact that, beginning a new book, they are utterly baffled as to how to proceed, what should be written and how it might be written, even though they've done a dozen. At best there's a slender intuition, not much greater than an itch. (486)

20   Student research writers may be working on a writing project that is, in some ways, different from a novel—still, we want them to have, and heed, an itch.[4] We want them to use research writing to follow questions wherever they lead and write this winding trail in discourse that is dialogic, Protean, and playful, while also passionately engaged—in the act of seeking itself, the work of the restless, wandering mind.

Ours, then, is an Instant Thesis after vitamins:

1. The research paper may be a vacant (non) form;
2. nevertheless, research writing remains a valuable activity, central to the academy in an infoculture—
3. as evidenced by alternative research writing strategies, which we will discuss here.
4. Further, we want to suggest, these alternative strategies may be read as inscriptions of the field of composition and academic culture revising themselves, reclaiming mystery as the heart of academic experience and discourse.

The research paper as modernism diminished

But first, #0, some history. We will trace the research paper as a historical construct, in part to attach it to a modern era, now passing. We also want to suggest, however, a more complicated set of relations, in which the ghost of the original modern spirit lives on, rekindled in alternative research writing. At the advent of modern research writing, we find an egalitarian respect for the act of seeking, a desire to inscribe the passage into the unknown. Research writing was conceived in the modern era as a way of writing the making of knowledge, and this writing was, at least in theory, open to all.[5] Anyone, according to this modern mythology, was capable of making a breakthrough, given the right disposition, intelligence, and training. The research paper as we now teach it, like many things modern, scarcely lives up to this promise. It is, typically, an apprentice work, not making knowledge as much as reporting the known.

Curricular histories cast the research paper as the product of the modern American university and modern society. In *Writing in the Academic Disciplines, 1870–1990,* David R. Russell notes, "The research paper, like the American university itself, is a grafting of certain German traditions onto what was originally a British system of college education" (79). The idea of requiring students to do text-based scholarship, a thesis or dissertation, began to take hold in the United States as early as the 1860s. In many cases, theses supplanted the earlier forensic speechmaking toward which much of undergraduate education was geared. The change in forms signaled a change in values as well: "Oral performance for a local academic community demanded only a *display* of learning, but the new text-based standards demanded an *original contribution* to a disciplinary community in written form: a research paper" (Russell 80).

Research writing prospered in a climate favoring originality and calling for the creation of knowledge. Such writing was to demonstrate the writer's place in the society of knowers by increasing the society's store of knowledge. As a written embodiment of modernist values, research writing proliferated. By the early 20th century, it was central to college writing courses. Its widespread adoption, in these courses, however, may have stemmed from motivations very different from the stress on knowledge-making with which modern research writing began. In *Composition-Rhetoric,* Robert Connors writes:

> The rise of the "research paper" as a genre in freshman com-position is another way teachers tried to transcend the per-sonal writing that occupied the early stages of any course. Library research—often unconnected to any writing pur-pose other than amassing brute facts for regurgitation into a "research" paper—became wry popular around 1920 and has remained a staple in writing courses since. (321)

25   The research paper came to be chiefly a vehicle for training—not   25
in the creation of knowledge, but in the recording of existing knowledge. Connors describes the state-of-being of the student research paper writer:

> He is, finally, a medium, not an originator. His task is to explore the library or the words of the world, not timeless wisdom or his own experience. He is to be trained to pick and choose carefully among myriad facts, coming ideally to that selfless position of knowing secondary materials so well that he merges with them. As Canby et al. wrote in 1933, "Now if your paper is to be worth reading this must be the expression of information that has finally become so thoroughly digested that it truly comes from your own storehouse" (Canby et al., 300–01). The research writer is meant, in other words, to give himself up absolutely to a discourse community. (322–23)

A student writer given over to a discourse community may be ready for originality, ready to make the knowledge that will take the com-munity to a new place. However, this potential was often lost in a tangle of legalistic concerns. Freshman research writing was not only to introduce students to the already known, it also sought to enforce a set of rules about the ownership of the known. As Connors notes, the research paper assignment "meant to teach the entire process of 'ethical' research—giving proper space to varied sources and proper crediting of sources. These concerns were just a formalization of the growing concern with intellectual property that had become a notable part of nineteenth-century law and jurisprudence" (321). The emerging conventions of the research paper "presented teachers with a grateful mass of practical formal material for which they could hold students responsible—the minutiae of formats, footnotes, bibliographies, citation forms, and so on" (322).

Russell notes that teacher/regulators saw poor writing as caused by poor thinking, and saw poor thinking as a threat to the academy:

> The "undisciplined" gropings of student prose were of course far from the research ideal held up by the disciplines. As faculty never tired of pointing out, student papers were replete with ignorance and errors of all sorts, which could seemingly never be entirely eradicated. Because faculty tended to regard poor writing as evidence of poor thinking, not as evidence of a student's incomplete assimilation into a disciplinary community, faculty sensed that the discipline's "store of knowledge," acquired at great sacrifice, was "tarnished" by poor writing. (74)

The writing teacher thus becomes part guard, part dishwasher: "'Scouring' student writing for 'mistakes of fact and expression' became the goal, and writing instruction 'professional scullery'" (Wolverton 407, quoted in Russell, 74).

The history of research writing in the American university is one of failed promise for students, teachers, and discourse. Begun with the egalitarian ideal of the making of knowledge, modern research writing has become the fallen "research paper," an apprentice work piecing together what is known, and presenting this piecing in a form that is also known, at least by the teacher. The teaching of research writing has remained tied to a contrived and templated way of writing, and to the self-imposed charge of safeguarding the university's store of knowledge—from those who do not know, and may never know, the words and thoughts that will grant them admittance to the society of knowers.

30   Some students seem to experience the culture of expertise as Kafka's   30
land surveyor does the castle—as impenetrable, governed either by
inexplicable whims or rules that defy surveying. Those students who
learn the rules, however, often suffer another dilemma—an apparent
unwillingness or inability to think imaginatively or originally. Many
of the teachers we know complain that even advanced students are content to do what they know how to do: present the knowledge made
by others, write within set conventions, and produce what they have
been conditioned to believe teachers want. The teaching of research
writing is often part of this conditioning: by asking students to stick
to researching the known, we teach them to fear the unknown. We also
make possible Steven Posusta, who would make the research process
and product generic, repeatable, and instant.

The alternative ways of researching writing we survey below challenge the conditioned fear of the unknown and the banalities of "efficient" research writing. These methods embrace the modernist value
of collegial work within the unknown. At least two of the methods,
the research essay and the multi-genre/media/disciplinary/cultural
research project, recall the intellectual wandering of early modernists,
such as Montaigne. As ways of working within contingency, methods
that use multiple genres and media may seem in sync with postmodern literature and art.

Beyond this entwinement of the modern and postmodern, we prefer, however, to see these methods as neither modern nor postmodern, but instead as historical time-travelers, regathering habits of mind
and ways of writing, while attempting to stage intellectual experience
as seeking and saying in the heart of mystery.[6] Inside "heart" is the "ear"
and "hear"; it is thus what we heed in listening to poet Charles Olson's
call to pay attention to the life passing through us mysteriously.
Throughout *The Special View of History*, Olson also reminds us of the
consequences of practicing Herodotus's original translation of "'istorin
as "to find out for yourself." Such a perspective need not lead to a postmodern nihilism and relativism; instead, in an ever-changing world
where every person is imperfect, and each event is an incomplete
palimpsest we select or build from the shards at our disposal, the importance of the rhetorical process and critical thinking are amplified. When
no researcher can have the "best facts or interpretations," it becomes
crucial to carefully assess the audience, occasion, message, purpose, and
logic of our writing.

In teaching alternative research writing, we ask our students to practice not only this rhetorical sophistication, but also the gathering and syncretism found in so many cultures pre-dating and leaking into Western Civilization. In his novel *The Mapmaker's Dream*, James Cowan has his Italian Renaissance mapmaker monk, while researching the geography of earth, describe this syncretism of an either/and (rather than either/or) world/consciousness in these words:

> Every man who had ever lived became a contributor to the evolution of the earth, since his observations were a part of its growth. The world was thus a place entirely constructed from thought, ever changing, constantly renewing itself through the process of mankind's pondering its reality for themselves. (60)

Similarly we recall the "nomadic" thought of Deleuze and Guattari, which inscribes "plateaus" of intense conductivity without center or fixed form. This is the kind of practice we envision for, and begin to see enacted by, alternative research writing. Like the surprising transformation of traditional nomadic life into the itinerancy of our own, we see such research writing as committed, its practitioners engaged in a sustained, "lifelong" learning in which the spirit is always at stake precisely because the individual's journey does matter in a world that is always changing and uncertain.[7]

Survey of Alternative Research Writing Methods

When taken in turn, the alternative research writing methods we will present—the research argument, research essay, personal research paper, and multi-genre/media/disciplinary/cultural research project—enact a gradual reopening of the purpose of research writing, reminiscent of a closed fist opening finger-by-finger. Viewed consecutively, these methods trace a movement away from the templated discourse of the research paper and into an increasingly complex world of rhetorical choices. This movement also performs what Zygmunt Bauman calls a "re-enchantment of the world," supplanting the will to power with a sense of playfulness and wonder.[8] Alternative research writing, as we read and enact it, inscribes an enchanted world that is a continual source of wonder. The stunted will to know is here eclipsed by

its shadow: the academic act of seeking inspired by the endless seduc-
tions of mystery and the shimmering promise of syncretic mapping.

The Research Argument

Research writing has always *argued;* persuasion is needed, even in discourses aimed at exposition, to hold the writing together, and provide
an understanding of what the data means. Robert E. Schwegler and
Linda K. Shamoon, however, argue that research papers may contain
arguments, but are nonetheless distinct from persuasive writing. Instead,
they claim, the overall structure and aim of research papers fit the category James Kinneavy called scientific discourse: "writing that makes
interpretive statements about some aspect of reality . . . and demonstrates the validity of these statements" (Kinneavy 88–89, quoted in
Schwegler and Shamoon 818).

Still, most research writing textbooks now include some elements
of argumentation, often in complex relation to the informational and
interpretive intents of the modern research paper. In *The Craft of
Research,* Wayne C. Booth, Gregory G. Colomb, and Joseph M.
Williams suggest that copious notes and collections of facts take on
meaning only when writers discover the claims they want to make.
These authors then provide an explication of the Toulminian scheme
of claims, warrants, qualifications, and evidence. They further note that
arguing in research writing can shift the emphasis of the paper from
the information presented to the significance of the information, and
even the authorial self projected on the page. The authors recommend
that research writers imagine themselves in conversation with their
readers: ". . . you making claims, your readers asking good questions,
you answering them as best you can" (89).

In *Doing Research: The Complete Research Paper Guide,* Dorothy
Seyler delineates three modes of research writing: the expository research
paper, the analytic research paper, and the argumentative research essay.
Each is animated by different kinds of questions and yields different
sorts of discourse. She suggests the differences in a list of topics:

Expository:
Report on debate over relationship of modern birds to
    dinosaurs.
Report on recent literature on infant speech development.

Analytic:

Account of the processes used to identify and classify animals based on the fossil record.

Explanation of process of infant speech development.

Argumentative:

Support of claim that modern birds descended from dinosaurs.

Argument for specific actions by parents to aid infant speech development. (6)

Seyler's first argumentative topic would allow its writer to enter a current debate about evolution; far from reporting the known, this paper would stake a claim in a hotly contested area. The second topic functions on a personal level: it appeals to the parent, and/or future parent in its writer and reader. In each case, we can easily imagine that the student writer's claims would not be seen as pure knowledge, or even accepted as correct. Others in the class might suggest that birds evolved from another source, or that evolution does not make new families, phyla, or species. Advice about speech development could be supplemented or challenged by other research or the experience of the reader. Research and writing, here, become fodder for continuing debate.

40   The "research argument" constructs the academy as a site for   40
informed conversation. Writers of the research argument seek to become experts, taking in the research they need to formulate and support an intelligent position. They are not, however, charged with ending dialogue and establishing set truth. Instead, their responsibility is to use research to inform debate, and to position themselves as reasonable persuaders.

Further, the research argument can call on students to consider, and use, a range of rhetorical strategies. While some books may stress a fairly rigid approach to argumentation—stressing, for instance, the appeal to reason, using factual evidence or probabilities—teachers and students can also adopt a more varied approach, stressing diverse appeals and showing how they can be integrated.[9]

The research argument pushes toward, then, an academic environment that values debate, and calls for the appropriate and strategic use of a wide rhetorical repertoire. However, the research argument can also be criticized for requiring the defense of a claim or position, rather than a detached examination of data, as in the modernist research paper, or a more open exploration of a series of claims, as in the alternative methods of research writing explicated below. These methods allow writers to examine a range of viewpoints, but without forcing them to adopt a single position to defend. They make conversations not only communal, but also internal.

The Personal Research Paper

While the research argument asks students to at least simulate informed entry into public debate, the personal research paper allows students to research and inscribe a personal issue. In his textbook *Research: The Student's Guide to Writing Research Papers,* Richard Veit suggests that the advantage of the personal research paper is that it allows students to formally think about subjects to which they feel intimately connected. Veit acknowledges that his personal research paper is Macrorie's "I-Search" paper renamed and offers the same opportunity to answer existential, or practical needs; Veit and Macrorie's samples include papers on choosing the right camera and becoming a creative writer. Research sources include both written materials and interviews with those who can shed light on the question being pursued. In form, personal research papers often use a narrative structure and chronological order to recreate the writer's unfolding search. The papers typically end with either a tentative, perhaps temporary, conclusion, or the redirection of the question: "Should I be a writer?" becomes "Are the rewards of writing worth the sacrifices?"

The personal nature of these papers, it seems, might lead to writing that means much to the writer but little to readers. Veit and Macrorie, however, each stress that lively writing makes these papers captivating. Perhaps so, but the well-known criticism of Macrorie's approach—that it largely misses the social dimension of writing— still has force, even if the I-Search does seem a powerful method for helping students direct their own lives.[10]

45   Approaches are needed that preserve the spirit of the I-Search in   45 discourse that explores questions that are more explicitly intellectual and public. For instance, recasting "Should I be a disc jockey?" as "Why does radio fascinate?" may lead to interdisciplinary research that is both library and interview-based and writing that is more likely to apply to readers as well as its writer. Such public/private work preserves the

notion that learning is autobiographical, while also sustaining one of the chief lessons of rhetoric—that even the personal scripts in which we think are socially constructed and keep us connected to a shared, if conflicted, world. It also seems wise to preserve, while transforming, the idea that open questions are to be pursued and explored, rather than avoided, or terminally answered. As Theodore Zeldin argues in *An Intimate History of Humanity*, the ability and willingness to hold an open and continuing conversation is a defining act of consciousness, necessary for becoming human. We might add that it is what we may most need to escape from the current barbarisms in which our world abounds.

The alternative methods of research writing described below typically make use of open-ended questions that are both personal and public. These methods are notably inclusive, allowing writers to use material from different kinds of research as well as personal experience. Further, they are syncretic discourses—using a variety of modes, genres, and, in some cases, media, and bringing together material from a number of disciplines and perspectives. We cannot claim that any of these methods will save the world, but done well, they can help enliven the worlds of the students who use them.

The Research Essay

We refer to essaying in the Montaignian sense of attempting, wondering, or as Scott Russell Sanders puts it, creating "experiments in making sense of things" (*Paradise* xiii):

> The "essay is the closest thing we have, on paper, to a record of the individual mind at work and play . . . [it is] the spectacle of a single consciousness making sense of a part of the chaos" of experience. The essay works by "following the zigzag motions of the inquisitive mind. . . . The writing of an essay is like finding one's way through a forest without being quite sure what game you are chasing, what landmark you are seeking:" ("Singular" 660, quoted in Heilker 89)

Paul Heilker argues that the essay counters the "thesis/support form," which he finds restrictive to students' development as thinkers and writers, and in conflict with current theories of social epistemology and rhetoric. These theories, he notes, tend to see truth and reality as multiple, provisional, dialogic, and dialectical. The essay better fits such theories in that it allows for multiple viewpoints, puts these viewpoints into dialogue with one another, and arrives, like the I-Search, at a provisional conclusion to be questioned in the dialectic's next round, or a recasting of the question.

Potentially, the essay can include all of experience. As Susan Griffin suggests in "The Red Shoes," and enacts in many of her works, essays can make the private public, erasing the lines we draw between parts of our experience. In this way, Griffin says, the essay is like the novel, which she finds to have discovered the legitimacy of private worlds for public writing. In form, the essay also resembles the novel by being varied in structure and often radically mixed in form. As Lydia Fakundiny notes, "Every essay is the only one of its kind. There are no rules for making beginnings, or middles, or endings; it is a harder, a more original discipline than that" (2). Further, essays typically collect many different kinds of discourse: personal narratives, philosophic speculations, textual interpretations, parables, legends, folk wisdom, jokes, dialogues, complaints, rants, and arguments. Essay writing requires fluid thinking, rhetorical flexibility, and the ability to orchestrate.

50   The essay is brought to research writing in the work of Bruce Ballenger. In *The Curious Researcher*, Ballenger says that students who write research essays shape, and are shaped by, the information they encounter. A broad range of topics is possible, since the writer is not limited to arguing a single position. Topic development often leads to the expansion of thinking as the writer takes in and reflects on various viewpoints. It also offers an element of risk, as writers must mediate between views and work toward their own developing understanding. However, with risk can come intellectual growth—as well as academic enculturation. By inscribing themselves in the midst of a dialogue, debate, or search, students cast themselves within a culture of seeking.

An objection to assigning the research essay stems from compositionists' concerns with preparing students for college writing. Students are unlikely to write this hybrid, post-Montaignian, research-enhanced form (or collection of forms) in other courses. It may be, however, that the research essay prepares students for the diverse literacies of the academy precisely through its variety of information and discourse. It can be used to teach students various modes and genres, while also showing how this variety can function together. The research essay can prepare students for further academic and intellectual work by helping them to cultivate the ability and desire to engage multiple perspectives on issues that remain open for further inquiry.[11]

The Multi-Genre/Media/Disciplinary/ Cultural Research Project

The final alternative strategy we survey here, the multi-genre/media/ disciplinary/cultural research project, further expands the field of seeking. Here, students explore topics of interest or fascination and use a variety of sources to inform projects that combine multiple genres and, in some cases, different media, disciplines, and cultures. These projects often resist, suspend, and/or decenter the master consciousness or central perspective inscribed in the essay as a unifying voice. They instead suggest a wandering consciousness, the traces of which we read in the various, linked, echoing pieces it has left behind for us to find.

These traces may come in the form of words, or in other media. In *The Electronic Word,* Richard Lanham calls print "an act of perceptual self-denial," and says that electronic textuality makes us aware of that self-denial "at every point and in all the ways in which print is at pains to conceal" (74). Multi-media research writing also points out these denials, but offering a full world of expression and communication in which the visual arts, video, music, noise, textures, even smells and tastes work in complex relations with writing. Like Web sites and other electronic discourses, multi-media research writing enacts a process of intertextual linking that erases the boundaries between texts, and between author and audience. Multi-media research projects gather material from many sources and often inspire readers to contribute more, or to do related work.

The act of gathering can also go beyond genres and media. The wandering, and wondering, consciousness is connected to the traits Julie Thompson Klein ascribes to interdisciplinary thinkers: "reliability, flexibility, patience, resilience, sensitivity to others, risk-taking, a thick skin, and a preference for diversity and new social roles" (182–83). Klein also claims that "the tendency to follow problems across disciplinary boundaries" is ". . . a normal characteristic of highly active researchers" (183). The wandering/wondering consciousness knows no boundaries because its focus is on the questions it pursues. Such pursuit is not careless, for it requires great concentration as well as openness. Enacting such a mind is a sign of great "discipline," but not that which requires us to stick to bounded fields.

55　　　A combination of flexibility and focus is also often seen in the multi-　55
cultural codeswitchers who have finally begun to gain recognition as
the margins of culture become central sites for intellectual study. In
Borderlands/La Frontera, Gloria Anzaldúa writes of the new *mestiza,*
who "operates in a pluralistic mode—nothing is thrust out, the good,
the bad and the ugly, nothing rejected, nothing abandoned. Not only
does she sustain contradictions, she turns the ambivalence into something else" (79).

This "something else" is a state of consciousness and discourse that
the multi-genre/media/disciplinary/cultural/research project begins
to work toward. Such projects can create intellectual spaces that allow
for various information, mindsets, and ideas—as well as diverse methods of thinking and ways of expressing, arguing, and communicating—
to question and deepen one another and together make a greater, but
still dissonant, whole. These projects work by making, but not forcing, connections: as such, they model the holistic learning that most
formal schooling, with its disciplinary structure and many exclusions,
too often works against.

David Jolliffe's work on multi-genre inquiry offers a starting point
for considering how to enact multi-genre/disciplinary/cultural research
writing. Jolliffe asks students to make an "inquiry contract" in which
they agree to research and write several different pieces about a subject. Example topics, listed in Jolliffe's *Inquiry and Genre: Writing to
Learn in College,* include the history of the seeding system in tennis,
the relationship between the stock market and the defense industry,
and the roles of women in American wars. Students pursue their topics using a range of rhetorical strategies, including: the contract proposal; the clarification project, in which students write reflectively about
what they already know; the information project, in which they report
on things they learn; the exploration project, with an essay raising additional questions; and the working documents project, which results
in public writing designed to change people's minds.

Pieces within Jolliffe's method are reminiscent of the expository
modernist research paper, the research argument, and the research essay,
and—since each project begins with students' own interests—the overall agenda is similar to that of the personal research paper. By using
these varied strategies, students strive to build a rhetorical repertoire.
They also learn how to better recognize that their thinking is conditioned by the genres they write in, and that inquiry can extend across
a range of singular, but related, texts.

Tom Romano describes multi-genre research projects that are potentially even more student-driven and open-ended. Romano's idea for what he came to call the Multi-Genre Research Paper surfaced after reading Michael Ondaatje's multi-genre "novel," *The Collected Works of Billy the Kid,* the reading of which Romano compared to listening to jazz: ". . . the reader feels something satisfying and meaningful, but may not be able to articulate what it is right away" (124). Romano asked his high school students to make biographical research projects using a style similar to Ondaatje's. The students wrote on subjects including Elvis Presley, Jimi Hendrix, Jim Thorpe, Marilyn Monroe, and Maya Angelou. Romano reports on the results:

> I have never read anything like these papers. Although four or five [of 26] were disappointing, showing little depth, breadth, or commitment, the rest were good, genuinely interesting in style and content, with seven or eight papers astonishingly superior. The visions were complex, the writing versatile. (130–131)

60   These students' projects are portfolios of diverse writing on a com- 60 mon subject. Each piece echoes the others, as an inner dynamic or theme emerges. A sample paper on John Lennon focuses especially on Lennon's love for Yoko Ono. The project is linked, in part, by a continuing series of poems about Lennon's murder called "Unfinished Music." It also contains other genres, including a news story, several narratives, and a meditation on the number "9" and its repeating presence in John and Yoko's lives. The author, Brian McNight, calls the project a "play," perhaps because it manages multiple voices (132–37).

Our students at Eastern Oregon University have gone beyond the multi-genre research paper to compose research projects that incorporate multiple genres, media, disciplines, and cultures. This approach originated in a 200-level Applied Discourse Theory course. It came out of long meditation on the way our students often found research sterile and theory either incomprehensible or dry. While initial resistance to the multigenre/media/disciplinary/cultural approach was great—as the only thing more terrifying than slavery is sometimes freedom— students quickly found the excitement in research and theory directed toward projects that linked their academic and personal lives.

"Multi-writing," as we have come to call it, has now spread at our university to a 400-level capstone seminar in English/Writing;

300-level courses in Writing Theory, Electronic Literacy, and American Folklore; 200-level courses in Argumentation and Methods of Tutoring Writing, and a 100-level Exploratory Writing course. It has also expanded to courses in other disciplines, including a 100-level American Government course, and a 300-level Spanish Literature course. Next year, the university is planning a holistic revision of general education that will cast multi-writing as a central method for helping students to learn across disciplines and connect academic issues to their personal concerns. We see this sort of work early in college as an important retention effort, as well as a way of breaking intellectual ground for further work at the higher levels.

Through conference presentations and workshops, multi-writing has now been taken up on other campuses in our state and nationally and has moved into K–12 classes, especially those taught by fellows of the Oregon Writing Project, many of whom have participated in multi-writing workshops. At the primary and secondary levels, multi-writing helps students generate rich work samples, demonstrating multiple proficiencies for assessment.[12]

In teaching multi-writing in our discourse theory course, we first open students up to a sense of either a multi-dimensional self or multiple selves, in order to create in a postmodern world. We have used texts like Daniel Halpern's *Who's Writing This?*, where dozens of famous writers rewrite the little self-portrait of Jorge Luis Borges in their own surprisingly different ways. Often students move from writing traditional and summative autobiographical pieces, where the older and wiser narrator looks back, to multicultural and generative ones, where the writer creates a new incarnation to grow into. Also successful has been a variation of autoethnography where students interview three people about themselves, then affirm or rebut the comments. We even invented two new kinds of multi-autobiography: "ought-to" and "want-to" biography—where students with a difficult childhood they would rather not delve into can imagine a different past: struggling artist in Paris, Tibetan monk, Earth Goddess, architect, blues musician.

65 In our most recent term of teaching, multi-autobiography projects 65 included: Frank Kaminski's recycling box of personal obsessions from banal pop culture (*Star Wars,* the *Dukes of Hazzard,* the *Alien* movies); Katie McCann's cast-a-way project in which she imagines she is stranded on an island (her writings and drawings are contained in bottles); and Cara Kobernik's project on shoes. Shoes have been an important part

of the author's life since she was baby, due originally to medical problems with her feet. The project includes a mock shoe catalogue and an illuminated manuscript called "Shoe Stories," as well as a beloved pair of sandals. In another memorable project. Lisa Rodgers split herself into three emanations with very different personalities and had the three escape from the dictatorial "Lisa" and journey on an improbable adventure, reminiscent of *Thelma and Louise.*

To keep the self from becoming too abstract and imaginary, we then require a mini-body project. Texts like Diane Ackerman's *A Natural History of the Senses* help students see how to combine facts with stylish prose. Student projects on the body often counter the typical images of the body prevalent in our culture, searching for other, richer views. Recent examples include Aubree Tipton's study of the relation of mind to disease and Sherry McGeorge's elaborate project on a feminist philosophy of belly dancing.

Finally, students create their own "multi-research project" on a theme they select. Some of these projects are biographical, like those of Romano's students. Subjects of recent "multi-biographies" include Adrienne Rich, Howard Hughes, Georgia O'Keefe, and Kurt Cobain. Other students find different themes, including: angels, Schoedinger's cat experiment, theories of the end of the world, massage, autism, the mysteries of tea, the Grand Canyon, the color blue, the Shroud of Turin, the Taiwanese language/dialect, the religion of television, masks, islands, Proppian interpretation of dreams, the concept of the "soulmate," the birth of punk rock, and debates over the literary canon.

The works show remarkable syncretism. Aubree Tipton's project on the Grand Canyon brings together courses she has taken in history, geology, and literature. Linnea Simon's project on tea is a cross-cultural dialogue, while Jakob Curtis studies Taiwan as a multiculture. Shirley Crabtree's interdisciplinary/multicultural project on fleas inscribes the history of this tiny but durable animal as part of a wider narrative of attempts by various imperial and fascistic entities to kill those seen as lesser.

The projects are widely varied in form. Like Romano's students, ours typically employ a range of genres: narratives, interpretive essays, letters, poems, wills, employment applications, lab reports, ethnographic and archeological field notes, prophecies, aphorisms, monologues, and dialogues, to name just a few. Cara Kobernik's project on the meanings of spring includes poems, personal and historical narratives, myths, folk-tales, monologues (including one by the Easter bunny), scripture and scriptural exegesis, aphorisms, science writing, philosophic reflection, and recipes.

70   Various media also abound. Judith Darrow's project on the fresco 70
includes several original paintings in a style that might be called post-modern gothic. Kobernik's project on Spring is very nearly a coffee table book with many photographs and drawings and an elegant design, as well as a lovely, floral smell. Nearly all of Jan Harris' project on blue is displayed in blue, on blue. The Grand Canyon project includes music, as does the project on blue, and many others. Videos are also common. Project containers are often interesting. We have received projects in folders, books, albums, boxes, crates, ovens, and even the back of a pickup truck. The project on blue comes in a binder covered with a blue suit. Eric Hutchinson's project on train travel is contained in its own kerchief-and-pole hobo bag. McGeorge's project on belly dancing comes wrapped in a beautiful scarf.

Some of the projects include strong elements of parody, often with serious intent: Sherri Edvalson's "A Feminist Education for Barbie" explores the effectiveness of gender theory and pedagogy in a continually sexist culture; it is enacted through a series of mock assignments for various courses and contained in a Barbie bookbag. Sue Ruth's EmpTV Guide, which is written in the form of a mock *TV Guide,* includes substantial research on television programming and cultural criticism, as well as scripts for mock commercials and Barnie's appearance on the Home Shopping Network. The project shows us locked into a media culture from which even parody cannot quite grant us escape.

In the midst of a grand variety of possible subjects, purposes, and forms, choices must be made. In his project on Houdini, Randy Kromwall saw and wanted to show intensity, obsession, awe, and passion in the magician's relationship to one of his most famous and dangerous tricks, the Water Torture Cell. Kromwall crafted a discourse that is part dialogue, part interior monologue, part lyric poem. The machine speaks, claiming that it is loved, and Houdini answers: "Yes, I love you / But you also terrify me. . . ." Kromwall gives his project a sensational tone and circus-like aura through the use of gothic type and several colorful posters advertising Houdini.

In her project on theories of good and evil, Judy Cornish used genres and media creatively to represent the ways in which her sources, and Cornish herself, have seen the two forces interlocking, and even becoming one. Her project design employed only black, white, and gray for its many images from high art and pop culture. Cornish made some images from scratch, and processed others into collages and striking juxtapositions. Among her writings is a dialogue in which the Kenpo concept of "push/pull," a way of absorbing violence, is explicated by a master and absorbed by a student, physically and spiritually. At the end, a provisional peace is realized when master and student redirect violence in a dance of acceptance.

In a reflective essay we typically assign at the end of a project, Cornish writes that her work on good and evil grew from her own hard life choices, which have made her question whether she was "good" or "evil," or if these words refer to anything real. Her project makes use of views on good and evil from writers of various time periods and cultures, including Toni Morrison, John Barth, Niccolo Machiavelli, and Kitaro Nishida. Cornish has told us that her personal connection to the material not only prompted the project, but pushed her toward doing more research and writing, even after she had clearly gone far beyond the requirements of the assignment. She was intellectually exploring a question that she was also urgently living.

75   A similar personal impetus motivates many of our students' projects, and sometimes leads them to work beyond the project. For Michelle Skow, a project on the Japanese American Internment grew into a larger capstone project, to which she has continued to add, even now that she has graduated. Skow realized that her own identity was deeply entwined with her grandparents' experience during the Internment. In her reflective essay, she wrote:

> The Japanese American Internment experience is something my grandparents rarely discuss. When they do, they refer to their internment as "camp"—a euphemism for unlawful incarceration. Both claim to remember little of what happened during this time, even though my grandma was eleven and my grandpa was fourteen. . . . I have urged them to share, in-depth, this part of their lives with me, but they cling tightly to their vow of silence. I cannot say I disagree with their desire to forgive and forget, but I feel a part of me is missing.

Skow's project became an act of historical memory and re-creation. It begins dramatically, with a stark copy of the internment order (see Figure 1).[13] The project also includes: a conventional historical narrative about the Internment; found texts, such as James Masao Mitsui's

CCC 51:3 / FEBRUARY 2000

Figure 1: Executive Order No. 9066 as it appeared in 1942. The full text is repeated in Note 13.

poems written from photographs; Skow's own poems; diary entries written by Skow from the point of view of her grandparents during the Internment; photographs; and a poster announcing Executive Order 9066, the Internment order.

At times, we are taken to the camps; at other times, we are looking back at them. Gradually, Skow comes to better understand not only the Internment, but also her older relatives' attitude about it. She writes:

> I want to forget Okasan as she sits,
> Silently crocheting doily after doily,
> Tablecloth after tablecloth.
> Her nymph-like hands, cracked and withered
> From the burning sun and stinging dust.
> Working consciously, stitching a contract of silence:
> Never forsake, never look back, never forget.

She has circled back to her grandmother's silence, with a new understanding. But not a full one. Skow followed up her first "multiproject" with another on first generation Japanese Americans that grew into a capstone for her English/History double major. Now that she has graduated, she continues to tell us about new reading and writing that she has done, including essays on her "third generation" cultural heritage, and more writings from her grandparents' point of view. She says that she sees herself trying to mesh the first-generation world view and her own.

As well as asking students to write reflectively about (and, often, within) their projects, we also ask students to refract, to think about projects deflected from the original, threads left hanging, questions remaining, or questions not yet asked.[14] Several of our students have followed Skow in creating linked projects. Michael McClure began with an autobiographic project modeled after Gregory Ulmer's concept of "mystory," held in a trunk full of texts and objects supposedly recovered in an archeological dig.[15] McClure followed this project with another on the artist Joseph Cornell, who made art in and from boxes, cases, and trunks. McClure's project includes a Cornellesque box of found and made objects, including an old gold watch, and several expository, interpretive, and creative writings, including a meditation on archeological time in Cornell's work.

80   These projects continue to evolve in the minds of their viewers/   80
readers as well as their makers. We return to them again and again,

trying to understand them in full, but also finding pleasure in knowing that we will not, that they will remain fertile mysteries. This is an experience far different from reading modernist research papers, where all meanings are to be made immediately clear, and the product is considered acceptable in large measure because it follows the rules. In multi-writing, "rules" are few. Students are shown some of the earlier projects, then asked to do something better. We assess them according to what they demonstrate as researchers, writers, and thinkers. We ask them to find a variety of sources, show us some of their range and depth as a rhetor, and reach for a philosophic understanding of their subject and their own project that will allow the work to hang together and make each piece part of the same web.

Less Efficiency, More Mystery

It would be possible, perhaps even desirable, to deconstruct the progression we have presented. One could easily cast the alternatives listed above as simply a series of possibilities to be mixed and matched, as supplements of, or replacements for, the modernist research paper. It might be quite sound pedagogically, for instance, to ask students to write a research paper, then a research argument, essay, or multi-writing research project; or to continue teaching the research paper at the 100-level, and then move on to alternative methods later; or to use alternative methods in introductory courses to get students started researching with fervor, and then require the research paper as they progress toward graduation. Such methods would satisfy consciences that believe the modernist paper ought still to be taught, but also allow students valuable new experiences.

For our purposes, however, establishing a progression is vital, for it shows the purpose and nature of research writing changing to meet the demands of a fluid world of complex relationships. If we want to describe a fixed world as others have described it, the modernist research paper will do. The research argument allows us to move beyond exposition of the unchanging to inscribe a human world continually remade by argument, in which research supports the will to stake and defend a claim. The personal research paper allows an inward turn from this culture of conflict, asking its writer to explore and mediate personal conflicts, contradictions, and questions.

The research essay provides an important reconnection with the social scene of writing, taking as its purpose the personal exploration of an issue or theme of collective concern. The essay can be seen as a discourse of the question, in which a variety of genres of writing are used to wander the terrain of a subject matter through which the writer may have tread before, but which she or he cannot claim to finally "know." The research essay thus foregrounds a shift in priorities—begun in the research argument and personal research paper—away from claims to, or descriptions of, verifiable knowledge, and toward a more open stance on the part of writers aware of uncertainty and contingency.

The multi-writing research project makes visible use of possibilities implicit in the research essay. Here, the trail of a question or questions leads through a range of connected material, including different genres of writing and, in some cases, different media, disciplines, and cultures. The maker of the multi-writing project is a collector, but not in the way of Muensterberger's collector/possessor. Instead, the intent here is to lay out a portion of what is potentially an inexhaustible, and radically open, network, to which the project's maker, and its readers/viewers, can add. One can imagine an infinite multi-writing which would call into its fold, bit by bit, all of discourse. Even the other methods of research writing—the research paper, the research argument, the personal research paper, the research essay—would be subsumed by this syncretic, ravenous multi-text.

85   Are we arguing that facts are useless, or that the discourses of expository intent, such as the modernist research paper, be abandoned? No. We are suggesting, however, that facts and expository writing have limits; they allow only certain types of inquiry to take place. What we envision, finally, is a discourse that will not have limits, that will allow for various kinds and levels of inquiry to echo, question, and deepen one another. Cornish's Kenpo scene may end with a brief bit of peace, but her project on good and evil settles nothing. Theories are both upheld and negated, as they challenge, question, and dance with one another. And yet, something important has happened. A student, an intellectual, a person has (re-)engaged an important, open question—one of the fascinations/terrors/joys through which she shapes, repeatedly and anew, her examined life.

Above all, we want our students to view mystery as a source of inquiry, research, and writing. Mystery is an academic value; what good would an institute of inquiry be if everything was already known? A collective appreciation of mystery can also be a basis for revising the academy, making it truly a place of free inquiry, where the unknown is approached from many directions, using a variety of ways of thinking, writing, and making. In this academy, we envision the research writer learning many traditions of inquiry and discourse, while also learning to use these traditions syncretically in the composition classroom. Here, students can begin to write the eclectic and multiple texts of their learning; they can, in singer Sarah McLachlan's oxymoronic words, mix craft and inspiration, and "build a mystery."

Notes

1. James E. Ford notes that the 1995 volume he edited, *Teaching the Research Paper: From Theory to Pedagogy, from Research to Writing,* is the first book on research paper instruction. His introduction provides additional counts: only 2 sessions on research writing have been presented at the MLA Convention, only 1 published bibliography has appeared on the subject (1). Further "[Research paper instruction] has been ignored in the periodic overview of the profession conducted by the MLA, NCTE, and CEA. . . . The annual and semiannual bibliographies published in the major writing journals omit it completely" (2). This inattention is striking, especially given Ford's estimate that 56 percent of first-year composition teachers devote an average of 29 percent of their time to research paper instruction (1–2).

2. In Oregon, for instance, the research paper is most often taught in the third of a three-course sequence in first-year writing.

3. See Covino's *Forms of Wondering: A Dialogue of Writing,* for Writers, a textbook on writing enacted through a series of dialogic forms. For Covino's re-reading of the Western rhetorical and philosophic tradition as a series of wonderings, see *The Art of Wondering.*

4. See Kundera's *The Art of the Novel.*

5. Of course, the practices of the modern academy were exclusionary—sexist, racist, and classist. Still, the direction of the academy at this stage was, roughly, toward greater inclusion.

6. Historian Daniel J. Boorstin identifies seeking as the great communal human act: ". . . While the finding, the belief that we have found the Answer, can separate us and make us forget our humanity, it is the seeking that continues to bring us together" (1). Philosopher Steven R. L. Clark brings together seeking and saying: ". . . the pursuit of knowledge through the exchange of ideas is something that we must assume we have been about since we were talking beasts" (4).

7. For examples of nomadic thought, see especially Deleuze and Guattari's *A Thousand Plateaus: Capitalism and Schizophrenia.*

8. Bauman identifies this reenactment with postmodernity, seeing it as a way of relating to the world that comes after the tragic history of modernism, in

which power-supported structures of cultural meaning are repeatedly erected only to be demolished.

9. A work such as Sharon Crowley and Debra Hawhee's *Ancient Rhetorics for Contemporary Students,* while not nominally a research-writing text, could be helpful in showing students the range of argumentative strategies.

10. James Berlin's "Contemporary Composition: The Major Pedagogical Theories" and Lester Faigley's "Competing Theories of Process: A Critique and a Proposal" brand Macrorie's work "expressionist." Berlin argues that expressionist pedagogies typically encourage students to use writing to reach toward a deep, personal truth. While students in expressionist classrooms often work together, the purpose of this collaboration is for students to help each other come to realizations that are finally individual. Expressionist practices are thus reminiscent of Platonic dialectics.

In Textual Carnivals, Susan Miller carries the critique of expressionism further, suggesting that such pedagogic strategies perpetuate the dominant order by enacting writing as an individual act, separate from social concerns and constraints.

Expressionist discourse fares better, however, in Geoffrey Sirc's "Never Mind the Tagmemics; Where's the Sex Pistols?" Here, Macrorie is cast as something of a punk compositionist, whose work is finally devalued because it does not ask students to bow to the dominant discursive order of academic convention.

11. If our suggestions of the value of wondering and the uses of mystery seem to suggest a purely humanistic or philosophic viewpoint on research writing, consider an episode of *Nova* in which scientists confront the thrilling mysteries of the planet Venus. Venus, these scientists say, was traditionally thought to be very similar to Earth, close in size and, probably, composition. It was even thought that Venus might have oceans and rich oil deposits. Data from various probes, however, suggest not only that Venus is not like Earth, but that things happen there that could not happen on Earth, at least given our current understanding of natural processes and laws. The Earths surface, for instance, is thought (and verifiably proven) to have been made over time, through the mechanics of volcanic eruption and plate tectonics. The surface of Venus appears to be all one age. By Earthly standards, this can't be.

12. For more on using multi-writing to meet proficiency standards, see "Multi-Genre Writing and State Standards," an article in the *Oregon English Journal,* which we wrote with high school teachers Tom Lovell, Jennifer Pambrun, and John Scanlan.

13. The text of Executive Order No. 9066 is as follows:

Instructions to All Persons of Japanese Ancestry Living in the Following Area:

All that portion of the City and County of San Francisco, State of California, lying generally west of the north-south line established by Junipero Serra Boulevard, Worchester Avenue, and Nineteenth Avenue, and lying generally north of the east-west line established by California Street, to the intersection of Market Street, and thence on Market Street to San Francisco Bay.

All Japanese persons, both alien and non-alien, will be evacuated from the above designated area by 12:00 o'clock noon Tuesday, April 7, 1942.

No Japanese person will be permitted to enter or leave the above described area after 8:00 A.M., Thursday, April 2, 1942, without obtaining special permission from the Provost Marshall at the Civil Control Station located at:

1701 Van Ness Avenue
San Francisco, California

The Civil Control Station is equipped to assist the Japanese population affected by this evacuation in the following ways:

1. Give advice and instructions on the evacuation.
2. Provide services with respect to the management, leasing, sale, storage or other disposition of most kinds of property including: real estate, business and professional equipment, buildings, household goods, boats, automobiles, livestock, etc.
3. Provide temporary residence elsewhere for all Japanese in family groups.
4. Transport persons and a limited amount of clothing and equipment to their new residence, as specified below.

The Following Instructions Must Be Observed:

1. A responsible member of each family, preferably the head of the family, or the person in whose name most of the property is held, and each individual living alone, will report to the Civil Control Station to receive further instructions. This must be done between 8:00 A.M. and 5:00 P.M., Thursday, April 2, 1942, or between 8:00 A.M. and 5:00 P.M., Friday, April 3, 1942.
2. Evacuees must carry with them on departure for the Reception Center, the following property:
   (a) Bedding and linens (no mattress) for each member of the family;
   (b) Toilet articles for each member of the family,
   (c) Extra clothing for each member of the family;
   (d) Sufficient knives, forks, spoons, plates, bowls and cups for each member of the family;
   (e) Essential personal effects for each member of the family.

All items carried will be securely packaged, tied and plainly marked with the name of the owner and numbered in accordance with instructions received at the Civil Control Station.

The size and number of packages are limited to that which can be carried by the individual or family group.

No contraband items as described in paragraph 6, Public Proclamation No. 3, Headquarters Western Defense Command and Fourth Army, dated March 24, 1942, will be carried.

3. The United States Government through its agencies will provide for the storage at the sole risk of the owner of the more substantial household items, such as iceboxes, washing machines, pianos and other heavy furniture. Cooking utensils and other small items will be accepted if crated, packed and plainly marked with the name and address of the owner. Only one name and address will be used by a given family.

4. Each family and individual living alone, will be furnished transportation to the Reception Center. Private means of transportation will not be utilized. All instructions pertaining to the movement will be obtained at the Civil Control Station.

Go to the Civil Control Station at 1701 Van Ness Avenue, San Francisco, California, between 8:00 A.M. and 5:00 P.M., Thursday, April 2, 1942, or between 8:00 A.M. and 5:00 P.M., Friday, April 3, 1942, to receive further instructions.

J. L. DeWITT
Lieutenant General, U. S. Army, Commanding

14. A similar view of revision as refraction is held by Nancy Welch in *Getting Restless*. Welsh argues that composition teachers have failed to ask questions such as "something missing, something else?" in responding to student drafts, instead conceiving of revision mainly as a way to narrow foci, correct inappropriate tones, and achieve clarity. For Welch, revision should strive not to eliminative dissonance, but instead use it as "the start of a reproductive struggle that can lead to a change of direction, a change of thesis, a real re-envisioning of the text, its meaning and intentions" (30).

15. Ulmer presents "mystory" as a writing-after-video that combines personal, professional, and historic elements and utilizes the jump-cut logic of television. Ulmer's own mystory, "Derrida at Little Bighorn," can be seen as a work of personal and public research writing for the electronic age.

Works Cited

Ackerman, Diane. *A Natural History of the Senses*. New York: Random House, 1990.

Anzaldúa, Gloria. *Borderlands/La Frontera: The New Mestiza*. San Francisco: Aunt Lute Books, 1991.

Ballenger, Bruce. *The Curious Researcher. A Guide to Writing Research Papers*. Boston: Allyn and Bacon, 1994.

Barthelme, Donald. "Not-Knowing." *The Art of the Essay*. Ed. Lydia Fakundiny. Boston: Houghton Mifflin, 1991, 485–97.

Bartholomae, David. "Inventing the University." *When a Writer Can't Write: Studies in Writer's Block and Other Composing-Process Problems.* Ed. Mike Rose. New York: Guilford P, 1985. 134–65.

Bauman, Zygmunt. *Intimations of Postmodernity.* London: Routledge, 1992.

Berlin, James. "Contemporary Composition: The Major Pedagogical Theories." *College English* 44 (1982): 343–48.

Boorstin, Daniel J. *The Seekers: The Story of Man's Continuing Quest to Understand His World.* New York. Random House, 1998.

Booth, Wayne C., Gregory G. Colomb, and Joseph M. Williams. *The Craft of Research.* Chicago: U of Chicago P, 1995.

Canby, Henry S., et al. *English Composition in Theory and Practice,* 3rd ed. New York: Macmillan, 1933.

Clark, Steven R. L. "Ancient Philosophy." *The Oxford History of Western Philosophy.* Ed. Anthony Kenny. Oxford: Oxford UP, 1994. 1–54.

Connors, Robert J. *Composition-Rhetoric: Backgrounds, Theory, and Pedagogy.* Pittsburgh: U of Pittsburgh P, 1997.

Covino. William A. *The Art of Wondering: A Revisionist Return to the History of Rhetoric.* Portsmouth, NH: Heinemann, 1988.

———. *Forms of Wondering: A Dialogue of Writing, for Writers.* Portsmouth, NH: Heinemann, 1990.

Cowan, James. *A Mapmaker's Dream: The Meditations of Fra Mauro, Cartographer to the Court of Venice.* New York: Warner, 1996.

Crowley, Sharon, and Debra Hawhee. *Ancient Rhetorics for Contemporary Students.* 2nd ed. Boston: Allyn and Bacon, 1999.

Davis, Robert L., Tom Lovell, Jennifer Pambrun, John Scanlan, and Mark Shadle. "Multi-Genre Writing and State Standards. *Oregon English Journal* 20.2 (1988): 5–10.

Deleuze, Gilles, and Félix Guattari. *A Thousand Plateaus: Capitalism and Schizophrenia.* Trans. Brian Massumi. Minneapolis: U of Minnesota P, 1987.

Elkins, James. *The Object Stares Back: On the Nature of Seeing.* New York: Simon and Schuster, 1996.

Faigley, Lester. "Competing Theories of Process: A Critique and a Proposal." *College English* 48 (1986): 527–42.

Fakundiny, Lydia. "On Approaching the Essay." *The Art of the Essay.* Ed. Lydia Fakundiny. Boston: Houghton Mifflin, 1991. 1–19.

Ford, James E. "Introduction: The Need for *The Research Paper.*" *Teaching the Research Paper: From Theory to Practice, from Research to Writing.* Ed. James E. Ford. Metuchen, NJ: Scarecrow, 1995. 1–5.

Ford, James E., and Dennis R. Perry. "Research Paper Instruction in Undergraduate Writing Programs: National Survey." *College English* 44 (1982): 825–31.

Griffin, Susan. "The Red Shoes." *The Eros of Everyday Life: Essays on Ecology, Gender, and Society.* New York: Doubleday, 1995. 161–76.

Halpern, Daniel, ed. *Who's Writing This?: Notations on the Authorial I, with Self-Portraits.* Hopewell, NJ: Ecco P, 1995.

Heilker, Paul. *The Essay: Theory and Pedagogy for an Active Form.* Urbana, IL: NCTE, 1996.

Jolliffe, David A. *Inquiry and Genre: Writing to Learn in College.* Boston: Allyn and Bacon, 1999.

Kafka, Franz. *The Castle.* Trans. Edwin and Willa Muir. New York: Knopf, 1941.

Kinneavy, James. *A Theory of Discourse.* Englewood Cliffs, NJ: Prentice-Hall, 1971.

Klein, Julie Thompson. *Interdisciplinarity: History, Theory and Practice.* Detroit: Wayne State UP, 1990.

Kundera, Milan. *The Art of the Novel.* Trans. Linda Asher. New York: Grove P, 1988.

Lanham, Richard. *The Electronic Word: Democracy, Technology, and the Arts.* Chicago: U of Chicago P, 1993.

Larson, Richard L. "The 'Research Paper' in the Writing Course: A Non-Form of Writing." *College English* 44 (1982): 811–16.

Macrorie, Ken. *The I-Search Paper.* Portsmouth, NH: Heinemann, 1988.

Miller, Susan. *Textual Carnivals: The Politics of Composition.* Carbondale: Southern Illinois UP, 1991.

Muensterberger, Werner. *Collecting: An Unruly Passion: Psychological Perspectives.* Princeton, NJ: Princeton UP, 1994.

Olson, Charles. *The Special View of History.* Berkeley: Oyez, 1970.

Ondaatje, Michael. *The Collected Works of Billy the Kid.* New York: Norton, 1974.

Owens, Derek. "Composition as the Voicing of Multiple Fictions." *Into the Field: Sites of Composition Studies.* Ed. Anne Ruggles Gere. New York: MLA, 1993. 159–75.

Posusta, Steven. *Don't Panic: The Procrastinator's Guide to Writing an Effective Term Paper (You know who you are).* Santa Barbara: Bandanna, 1996.

Romano, Tom. *Writing with Passion: Life Stories, Multiple Genres.* Portsmouth, NH: Heinemann, 1995.

Russell, David R. *Writing in the Academic Disciplines 1870–1990: A Curricular History.* Carbondale: Southern Illinois UP, 1991.

Sanders, Scott Russell. *The Paradise of Bombs.* Athens: U of Georgia P, 1987.

———. "The Singular First Person." *Sewanee Review* 96 (1988): 658–72.

Schwegler, Robert E., and Linda K. Shamoon. "The Aims and Process of the Research Paper." *College English* 44 (1982): 817–24.

Seyler, Dorothy U. *Doing Research: The Complete Research Paper Guide.* 2nd ed. Boston: McGraw-Hill, 1999.

Sirc, Geoffrey. "Never Mind the Tagmemics: Where's the Sex Pistols?" *College Composition and Communication* 48 (1997): 9–29.

Ulmer, Gregory. *Teletheory: Grammatology in the Age of Video.* New York: Routledge, 1989.

Veit, Richard. *Research: The Student's Guide to Writing Research Papers.* 2nd ed. Boston; Allyn and Bacon, 1998.

"Venus Unveiled." *Nova.* PBS. Oct. 17, 1995.

Welch, Nancy. *Getting Restless: Rethinking Revision in Writing Instruction.* Portsmouth, NH: Heinemann-Boynton/Cook, 1997.

Wolverton, S. F. "Professional Scullery." *Educational Review* 60 (1920): 407.

Zeldin, Theodore. *An Intimate History of Humanity.* New York: Harper, 1996.

The Future Isn't What It Used to Be: Student Competencies for the 21st Century

Sheryl L. Day and Mark A. Koorland

Sheryl L. Day is a visiting assistant professor at Florida State University, Tallahassee, with specialization in teacher preparation, providing services to postsecondary students with disabilities, and assistive technology. Mark A. Koorland is a professor and chair of special education at FSU-T with specialization in applied behavior analysis, teacher education, and learning disabilities.

From the onset, the focus of American education has been to acquire a core of commonly held knowledge. That is, education has provided instruction for remembering knowledge from distinct content areas (e.g., the parts of speech, the quadratic equation). Until recently, an emphasis on "learning to remember" satisfied the needs of employers and contributed to increased work opportunities for the average person (Philippi, 1989). A shift in the competencies students will need to succeed in the world of work has begun, and the traditional goals of the educational system no longer match the needs of the consumer (i.e., the business community). Approaching the 21st century and a very different labor market means education must change to keep pace with the new information/service age economy and to meet employer requirements for a qualified work force.

In September of 1989, President Bush and the nation's governors agreed to six national goals in education to be achieved by the year

Reprinted from *Contemporary Education* 69, no. 1 (1997), Indiana State University.

2000. These goals, focusing on students' abilities to demonstrate the knowledge and skills necessary to compete in a global economy, represent a new educational strategy. America 2000 intends to transform our schools into organizations committed to producing skilled graduates as the norm and not as the exception. To attain the America 2000 goals, the Secretary's Commission on Achieving Necessary Skills (SCANS) prepared a report on the demands of the workplace. The Commission began its inquiry in May, 1990. Results drawn from interviews with business owners, unions, workers, and supervisors found that good jobs increasingly depend on people who can put knowledge to work (Secretary's Commission on Achieving Necessary Skills [SCANS], 1991).

As a result of demographic changes and technological advances, the workplace is subject to constant change. According to Coopers and Lybrand (1996), in a recent survey of the chief executive officers of 434 product and service companies, 47% cited the reduced availability of skilled trained workers as a potential barrier to company growth. If the supply of new workers suitable for entry-level work is dwindling, employers may draw increasingly from the ranks of the less qualified. Subsequently, more workers in the future may come from groups whose development has historically been neglected (Carnevale, 1989). Already outside the economic mainstream because of poor skills, this group and others will have to acquire an educational foundation appropriate for building broader and more sophisticated skills.

"Workers now have to manage their work stations, schedule their time, think about quality, solve problems, and apply their skills to new technologies" (Daggett, 1992, p. 1). What impact will a need for new and different skills have on students with academic and/or behavioral deficiencies? By developing a functional description of characteristics and performance expectancies for all students entering the next century, recommendations can be made regarding the specific barriers that exist for individuals requiring special education services. The purpose of this educational futures literature review, employing content analysis, is to determine essential skills for functioning in an increasingly sophisticated 21st century work environment. Additionally, this review will examine implications for those with special needs and provide recommendations for successful acquisition of essential skills by students with disabilities.

Data Collection

Benjamin's Work

5   To identify future educational trends and construct an educational   5
guide for the coming years, Benjamin (1988) analyzed the literature
and offered recommendations for change. He cited fourteen themes,
within 209 documents published between 1974–1987. We analyzed
Benjamin's (1988) themes for essential student skills.

Secretary's Commission on Achieving Necessary Skills

The widely acknowledged SCANS report concludes that effective job
performance consists of five competencies and three foundation skills.
These eight essential skills and competencies for all students apply
equally to individuals moving directly from high school to work and
to those pursuing a college education (SCANS, 1991). All SCANS
competencies essential to workplace success appear in related articles
subsequently reviewed here.

Additional Sources

Twenty-five additional sources were obtained using descriptors such as
educational trends, education work relationship, and outcomes of education. Examination of the reference lists of previous related research
provided additional sources.

Method

Content analysis, an ethnographic approach, was applied to the
reviewed literature. Budd, Thorp, and Donohew (cited in Benjamin,
1988) define content analysis as a "systematic technique for analyzing
message content and message handling" (p. 286). Competency categories emerged out of the data and were not preestablished or imposed
on the data. This ethnographic approach was combined with the constant comparative analysis method. The constant comparative method
can be described as a series of steps, "analysis and data collection occur
in a pulsating fashion where the analysis keeps doubling back to more
data collection and coding" (Glaser and Strauss, 1967, p. 27).

All literature for this review was read independently by two reviewers to establish reliable classification of the category types. A reliability index is provided to describe between reader consistency for placing data into categories. Interrater agreement for this review is .81.

10   Competencies appearing two or fewer times in the literature (e.g.,   10
being a specialist, having knowledge of global history) were excluded from further analysis. Two separate categories of competencies, life long learner and learning to learn, were eventually collapsed into one—life long learning. The results are presented by citation frequency (e.g., "higher level thinking" and "interpersonal communication" appear first because references to these competencies are most frequent) in Table 2. Example subcompetencies a student should be able to perform are also shown.

Results

High Frequency Competencies

The need for higher level thinking skills was cited across 18% of the reviewed material. Because of the nature of future society, cited authors believe that students must be able to use logic to draw conclusions from available information. Students must problem solve, apply rules and principles to new situations, and use questioning, inquiry, and the scientific process (Benjamin, 1988; Cawelti, 1989; Hall, 1993; Philippi, 1989).

The futures literature contains equivalent percentages of references to interpersonal communication skills and to skills of higher level thinking. These authors predict a growing need for individuals who collaborate with team members to make decisions, demonstrate appropriate social interactions, and have "peopling" skills. Individuals in this category must accept and give criticism and feedback (Brandhorst, 1990; Carnevale, 1989; Shane, 1989).

Moderate Frequency Competencies

Once associated with management or high level employees, decision making skills, cited across 8% of the review sources, are now believed to be basic requirements in the workplace. If this notion is correct, in order to meet future employer needs, students must learn to specify goals, make judgments, generate alternatives, and evaluate and choose best alternatives (Edgar, 1988; Fennick, Peters, & Guyon, 1993; U.S. Department of Labor, Department of Education, 1988).

The futures literature contained references to communicating skills at moderate frequency. Fundamental communication is employing language effectively in a variety of contexts, using technology to communicate through networking and responding appropriately in written and oral forms (Kortering & Elrod, 1992; Met, 1989; Oaks & Pedras, 1992).

Self managing skills are essential for the future according to 7% of the citations. As workers and students assume additional responsibility, predictions indicate that they will need to set goals, carry them through, display intrapersonal understanding, and evaluate their own work (Brant, 1989; Hall, 1993; Lawlor, 1993; SCANS, 1991).

Increased contact with people from other cultures, and the need to shift jobs frequently in various sectors of the economy led educational futurists to cite ability to cope with diversity as important across 6% of the citations. Various authors believe students need to work effectively in multicultural settings, adapt in times of change, and accept change as inevitable, using change to advantage (Benjamin, 1988; Cain & Taber, 1987; Levin & Rumberger, 1989).

Information managing skills are believed essential across 6% of the citations. One reason is the U.S. economic base has shifted from industrial manufacturing to service and information. To manage information, students must be able to access information, manipulate content in order to extend relationships, and interpret and apply information (Philippi, 1989; Pope, 1993; SCANS, 1991).

The world of work is increasingly complex and requires workers to understand their own work in the context of others. Six percent of references indicated a need for students to acquire knowledge of systems, such as understanding and predicting relationships, recognizing discrete tasks as parts of the coherent whole, and suggesting improvements to existing systems (Brandhorst, 1990; The Carnegie Forum, 1986; SCANS, 1991).

Because skills and knowledge become obsolete much more rapidly than in the past, life long learning was cited as critical for future employees. To prepare for the rapid changes of the future, the writers cited in this review believe that students should acquire knowledge and skills needed to learn effectively, access a greater variety of educational resources, and continue education throughout various life stages (Lawlor, 1993; Philippi, 1989; Pope, 1993; U.S. Department of Labor, Department of Education, 1988).

Low Frequency Competencies

20 Mathematics use in the workplace exceeds the traditional basics of num-   20
ber concepts and computation skill. Five percent of literature pointed
to a need for higher proficiency levels in math. Competent individuals use math concepts to reason and interpret data, use graphs and
charts to report quantitative information, and use quantitative data
to construct logical explanations of real world situations (The Carnegie
Forum, 1986; Lawlor, 1993; Philippi, 1989; SCANS, 1991).

Using writing in a functional context to produce organized readable products will always be critical to success in some job positions.
When job requirements involve written products, writing exceeds all
others as the skill requiring improvement among those newly hired
by American companies (The Olsten Corporation, 1993). Students
working in such positions need written communication skills, especially using language appropriate to the subject matter and audience
(Fennick, Peters, & Guyon, 1993; Pope, 1993; SCANS, 1991).

Workplace applications of reading can be considered "reading to
do." Reading permits locating information and using higher level thinking strategies to problem solve. Students need to employ reading skills
to perform a job task by locating, understanding, and interpreting written information (Manning, 1993; SCANS, 1991; U.S. Department of
Labor, Department of Education, 1988).

Discussion

Twelve competencies students will need to move successfully into the
world of 21st century work were found in the literature. The authors
cited in this literature review opine that future performance standards
reflect a reversal of the value of workplace specialization and job functions requiring rigidly defined skills. Success in the future will require
general skills. Future workers will need to be highly skilled, flexible,
and self-aware. They will have to think like generalists to solve problems by drawing solutions from information in a variety of fields.

Curiously, few specific references were found concerning the impact
of tomorrow's competencies on workers with disabilities. Some authors
do recommend general educational innovations, assistance for "the
other half" (i.e., students not seeking postsecondary education, an
apprenticeship, or the military), and assistance for those "disadvantaged" who are struggling for jobs, or to avoid displacement by more

skilled workers. Recommendations, centering on what and how we teach, include restructuring secondary programs to include early career exploration, learning job skills in the workplace, rather than in the classroom, and providing increased opportunities for students to develop interpersonal skills, leadership abilities, and communication skills. (Benjamin, 1988; Carnevale, 1989; Philippi, 1989).

25   Although unintended to address the acquisition of specific skills, 25
certain reform strategies of the special education reform agenda could better prepare students with disabilities to acquire skills believed essential for the future. An example is inclusive schooling to accommodate students of varying abilities and cultural backgrounds. Such schooling practices would likely provide students with increased opportunities to cope with diversity and build interpersonal communication skills. Also, improvement of teacher training programs and teachers better prepared to perform in reformed school settings should benefit students in gaining essential skills. And, assistive technology should play a central role in curricular reform. Such technology can help students to acquire higher level thinking, communication, and self-management skills.

Future research in this area could examine the extent that school reform addresses skills needed for the future. If students are not provided opportunities to practice and learn collaborative skills, make judgments, use language effectively, and write within functional contexts, they will be unprepared for the future's demands. The restructuring of our educational system is underway. The degree to which educational reform in special education ensures mastering skills for the future will determine how prepared learners with disabilities are for the challenges of the new economic era.

Table 1 Summary of Educational Futures Literature

Identifying Number	Authors (date)	Publication Type
1	Benjamin (1988)	Dissertion
2	Brandhorst (1990)	Journal article
3	Brant (1989)	Journal article
4	Cain & Taber (1987)	Journal article
5	The Carnegie forum (A Nation Prepared) (1986)	Private organization report
6	Carnevale (1989)	Journal article
7	Cawelti (1989)	Journal article
8	Dede (1989)	Journal article
9	Edgar (1988)	Journal article

Table 1 Summary of Educational Futures Literature *(cont.)*

Identifying Number	Authors (date)	Publication Type
10	Fennick, Peters, & Guyon (1993)	Journal article
11	Hall (1993)	Journal article
12	Kortering & Elrod (1992)	Journal article
13	Lawlor (1993)	Newspaper article
14	Levin & Rumberger (1989)	Government publication
15	Manning (1993)	Newspaper article
16	Mecklenburger (1993)	Journal article
17	Met (1989)	Journal article
18	Oaks & Pedras (1992)	Journal article
19	The Olsten Corp. (1993)	Private organization report
20	Philippi (1989)	Government publication
21	Pope (1993)	Journal article
22	SCANS (1991)	Government publication
23	Shane (1989)	Journal article
24	Steen (1989)	Journal article
25	Stone (1990)	Journal article
26	U.S. Dept. Labor/Ed (1988) (The Bottom Line)	Government publication
27	WORKFORCE 2000 (1987)	Private organization report

Table 2 Competency categories By Citation Frequency (a)

Referenced	Category	Example of competency Competency [a]
	High Frequency	
1, 3, 5, 6, 7, 8, 9, 10, 11, 14, 16, 20, 21, 22, 25, 26, 27,	1. Higher Level Thinking	Problem Solve
1, 2, 3, 6, 7, 8, 10, 14, 17, 18, 20, 21, 22, 23, 24, 26, 27	2. Interpersonal Communication	Collaborate with team members to make decisions
	Moderate Frequency	
1, 5, 6, 9, 10, 14, 22, 26,	3. Decision Making	Make judgments
1, 6, 12, 17, 18, 20, 23, 25	4. Communicating effectively	Use language
3, 6, 10, 11, 13, 14, 22	5. Self Managing	Set goals and carry them through
1, 3, 4, 14, 21, 26	6. Coping With Diversity	Work effectively in multicultural society
1, 14, 20, 21, 22, 26	7. Managing Information	Access information
1, 2, 5, 6, 17, 22	8. Systems Knowledge	Understand and predict relationships
5, 13, 20, 21, 22, 26	9. Life Long Learning	Acquire knowledge/skills needed to learn effectively
	Low Frequency	
5, 13, 19, 22, 24	10. Higher Level Math	Use logic to reason and interpret data
5, 10, 21, 22, 23	11. Writing	Use writing in a functioning context
6, 15, 22 23, 26	12. Reading	Read to "do" (rather than to "remember")

Table 2 Competency categories By Citation Frequency (a) (*cont.*)

Referenced	Example of competency Competency[a]
	High Frequency
1, 3, 5, 6, 7, 8, 9, 10, 11 14, 16, 20, 21, 22, 25, 26, 27,	Use scientific process
1, 2, 3, 6, 7, 8, 10, 14, 17,	Give and accept criticism, feedback
18, 20, 21, 22, 23, 24, 26, 27	**Moderate Frequency**
1, 5, 6, 9, 10, 14, 22, 26,	Determine learning goals and methods of attainment
1, 6, 12, 17, 18, 20, 23, 25	Use technology to communication through networking
3, 6, 10, 11, 13, 14, 22	Display intrapersonal understanding
1, 3, 4, 14, 21, 26	Adapt and be flexible in times of change
1, 14, 20, 21, 22, 26	Interpret and apply information
1, 2, 5, 6, 17, 22	Suggest improvements
5, 13, 20, 21, 22, 26	Contribute to society
	Low Frequency
5, 13, 19, 22, 24	Use spreadsheets and statistical programs
5, 10, 21, 22, 23	Organize and write clear readable products
6, 15, 22,	Use readily available job print
23, 26	material (manual, graphs)

[a] See Table 1 for literature source and corresponding identifying numbers

References

Benjamin, J. S. (1988). The future isn't what it use to be: A content analysis of the educational futures and educational reform report literatures with recommendations for public school policy (Doctoral dissertation, Indiana University, 1988). *Dissertation Abstracts International*, 49, 07A.

Brandhorst, A. R. (1990). Teaching 21st century citizenship: Social psychological foundations. *Theory and Research in Social Education*, 18, 157–188.

Brant, R. (1989). On liberal education for tomorrow's world: A conversation with Douglas Heath. *Educational Leadership*, 47, 37–40.

Cain, R., & Taber, D. (1987). *Educating Disabled People For The 21st Century*. Boston, MA: College Hill Press.

The Carnegie Forum on Education and the Economy. (1986). *A Nation Prepared: Teachers for the 21st Century*. Washington, DC.

Carnevale, A. P., Gainer, L. J., Meltzer, A. S., & Holland, S. L. (1989). *Workplace basics: The Skills Employers Want*. Alexandria, VA: The American Society for Training and Development.

Cawelti, G (1989). Designing high schools for the future. *Educational Leadership*, 47, 30–35.

Coopers & Lybrand. (1996). *Total Quality Management Service Survey*. Arlington, VA.

Daggett, W. R. (1992). Job skills of 90's requires new educational model for ALL students. *Liaison Bulletin*, 18(5) 1–2.

Dede, C. (1989). The evolution of information technology: Implications for curriculum. *Educational Leadership*, 47, 23–26.

Edgar, E. (1988). Employment as an outcome for mildly handicapped students: Current status and future directions. *Focus on Exceptional Children*, 21, 1–7.

Fennick, R., Peters, M., & Guyon, L. (1993). Solving problems in 21st century academic and workplace writing. *English Journal*, 82, 46–53.

Fields, M. J., & Postetter, D. (Eds.). (1993, November). *Leading and Managing for Performance: An Examination of Challenges Confronting Special Education*. (Available from [National Association of State Directors of Special Education, Inc. 1800 Diagonal Road, Suite 320 King Street Station I Alexandria, VA 22314]).

Glaser, B. & Strauss, A. (1967). *The Discovery of Grounded Theory: Strategies for Qualitative Research*. New York: Aldine Publishing Company.

Hall, C.E. (1993). The work force of the future: Multiethnic, multicultural. *Tech Directions*, 52, 18–20.

Kortering, L. J., & Elrod, G. F. (1992). Programs for adolescents with mild handicaps: Evaluating where we are and contemplating change. *Career Development for Exceptional Individuals*, 14, 145–157.

Lawlor, J. (1993, December 1). Working in the 90's: Where the jobs are. *USA Today*, 1, 2B.

Levin, H. M. & Rumberger, R.W. (1989). *Schooling for the modern workplace*. (CE Report No. CE 054-082). Washington, DC: Commission on Workforce Quality and Labor Market Efficiency. (NTIS No. 99-94756-75-008-04).

Manning, A. (1993, October 20). Workplace classes help employees raise the bottom line. *USA Today*, 6D.

Mecklenburger, J. (1993). The next generation of America's schools. *National Forum*, 74, 40–43.

Met, M. (1989). Which foreign languages should students learn? *Educational Leadership*, 47, 54–58.

Oaks, M. M. & Pedras, M. J. (1992). A catalyst for curriculum integration: Technology education. *The Technology Teacher*, 52, 11–14.

The Olsten Corporation. (1993). *Skills for success (The Olsten Forum on Human Resource Issues and Trends)* New York: Author.

Philippi, J. W. (1989). *Facilitating the flow of information between the business and education communities*. (CE Report No. CE 054-095). Washington, DC: Commission on Workforce Quality and Labor Market Efficiency. (NTIS No. 99-9-3372-75-014-04).

Pope, C. A. (1993). Our time has come: English for the 21st century. *English Journal*, 82, 38–41.

Secretary's Commission on Achieving Necessary Skills, U.S. Department of Labor, (1991). *What work requires of schools: A SCANS report for America 2000.* Washington, DC: U.S. Department of Labor.

Shane, H. G. (1989). Educated foresight for the 1990s. *Educational Leadership*, 47, 4–6.

Steen, L. A. (1989). Teaching mathematics for tomorrow's world. *Educational Leadership*, 47, 18–22.

Stone, R. D. (1990). A challenge: Education in the 21st century. *The Technology Teacher*, 50, 14–15.

U.S. Department of Labor, Department of Education. (1988). *The Bottom Line.* Washington, DC: U.S. Government Printing Office.

Woodward, J. (1992). *Workforce 2000 and the mildly handicapped: Identifying emerging issues and trends in technology for special education* (Contract No. HS90008001). Washington, DC: OSERS.

WORKFORCE 2000: Work and Workers for the 21st Century. (1987). Indianapolis, IN: Hudson Institution.

Soft Sciences Are Often Harder than Hard Sciences

Jared Diamond

Why should we be concerned about "a dogfight among intellectuals," one in which a mathematician succeeds in blocking a highly regarded political scientist from membership in the National Academy of Sciences (NAS)? Jared Diamond, a member of the NAS, sees a threat in store for all of us if experts in the hard sciences continue to be ignorant of the rather different challenges in the so-called soft sciences, which include sociology, political science, and areas of psychology, as well as other fields. Diamond is convinced that soft science requires researchers to work harder to develop the controls necessary for testing their hypotheses. From Diamond's perspective, respect for their work—especially as it addresses human behavior—is critical to the survival of the human race.

A professor of physiology at the University of California, Los Angeles, School of Medicine, Diamond has pursued research that spans the hard and soft sciences. In 1999, he was awarded the National Medal of Science for his uncommon ability to write about important scientific issues for the public and for his groundbreaking research in applying Darwinian theory to the fields of human history, physiology, ecology, and conservation biology. Diamond's public writings include regular contributions to both Nature *and* Discover *magazines. One of his major conservation efforts was to design a comprehensive nature-reserve system for Indonesian New Guinea. He is widely known for his Pulitzer Prize–winning book,* Guns, Germs, and Steel: The Fates of Human Societies *(1997), which examines 13,000 years of human development and behavior.*

Reprinted from *Discover*, by permission of the author.

Diamond's most recent book is Collapse: How Societies Choose to Fail or Succeed *(2005)*.

In addition to his NAS membership, Diamond has been elected to the American Academy of Arts and Sciences and the American Philosophical Society. He has also received the MacArthur Foundation Fellowship, known as the "genius grant."

The following essay was originally published in 1987, as an opinion piece in Discover.

The overall correlation between frustration and instability [in 62 countries of the world] was 0.50.

—SAMUEL HUNTINGTON, professor of government, Harvard

This is utter nonsense. How does Huntington measure things like social frustration? Does he have a social-frustration meter? I object to the academy's certifying as science what are merely political opinions.

—SERGE LANG, professor of mathematics, Yale

What does it say about Lang's scientific standards that he would base his case on twenty-year-old gossip? . . . a bizarre vendetta . . . a madman . . .

—Other scholars, commenting on Lang's attack

1   For those who love to watch a dogfight among intellectuals supposedly above such things, it's been a fine dogfight, well publicized in *Time* and elsewhere. In one corner, political scientist and coauthor of *The Crisis of Democracy,* Samuel Huntington. In the other corner, mathematician and author of *Diophantine Approximation on Abelian Varieties with Complex Multiplication,* Serge Lang. The issue: whether Huntington should be admitted, over Lang's opposition, to an academy of which Lang is a member. The score after two rounds: Lang 2, Huntington 0, with Huntington still out.

Lang *vs.* Huntington might seem like just another silly blood-letting in the back alleys of academia, hardly worth anyone's attention. But this particular dogfight is an important one. Beneath the name calling, it has to do with a central question in science: Do the so-called soft sciences, like political science and psychology, really constitute science at all, and do they deserve to stand beside "hard sciences," like chemistry and physics?

The arena is the normally dignified and secretive National Academy of Sciences (NAS), an honor society of more than 1,500 leading American scientists drawn from almost every discipline. NAS's annual election of about sixty new members begins long before each year's spring meeting, with a multistage evaluation of every prospective candidate by members expert in the candidate's field. Challenges of candidates by the membership assembled at the annual meeting are rare, because candidates have already been so thoroughly scrutinized by the appropriate experts. In my eight years in NAS, I can recall only a couple of challenges before the Lang-Huntington episode, and not a word about those battles appeared in the press.

At first glance, Huntington's nomination in 1986 seemed a very unlikely one to be challenged. His credentials were impressive: president of the American Political Science Association; holder of a named professorship at Harvard; author of many widely read books, of which one, *American Politics: The Promise of Disharmony*, got an award from the Association of American Publishers as the best book in the social and behavioral sciences in 1981; and many other distinctions. His studies of developing countries, American politics, and civilian-military relationships received the highest marks from social and political scientists inside and outside NAS. Backers of Huntington's candidacy included NAS members whose qualifications to judge him were beyond question, like Nobel Prize–winning computer scientist and psychologist Herbert Simon.

5   If Huntington seemed unlikely to be challenged, Lang was an even   5 more unlikely person to do the challenging. He had been elected to the academy only a year before, and his own specialty of pure mathematics was as remote as possible from Huntington's specialty of comparative political development. However, as *Science* magazine described it, Lang had previously assumed for himself "the role of a sheriff of scholarship, leading a posse of academics on a hunt for error," especially in the political and social sciences. Disturbed by what he saw as the use of "pseudomathematics" by Huntington, Lang sent all NAS members several thick mailings attacking Huntington, enclosing photocopies of letters describing what scholar A said in response to scholar B's attack on scholar C, and asking members for money to help pay

the postage and copying bills. Under NAS rules, a candidate challenged at an annual meeting is dropped unless his candidacy is sustained by two-thirds of the members present and voting. After bitter debates at both the 1986 and 1987 meetings, Huntington failed to achieve the necessary two-thirds support.

Much impassioned verbiage has to be stripped away from this debate to discern the underlying issue. Regrettably, a good deal of the verbiage had to do with politics. Huntington had done several things that are now anathema in U.S. academia: He received CIA support for some research; he did a study for the State Department in 1967 on political stability in South Vietnam; and he's said to have been an early supporter of the Vietnam War. None of this should have affected his candidacy. Election to NAS is supposed to be based solely on scholarly qualifications; political views are irrelevant. American academics are virtually unanimous in rushing to defend academic freedom whenever a university president or an outsider criticizes a scholar because of his politics. Lang vehemently denied that his opposition was motivated by Huntington's politics. Despite all those things, the question of Huntington's role with respect to Vietnam arose repeatedly in the NAS debates. Evidently, academic freedom means that outsiders can't raise the issue of a scholar's politics but other scholars can.

It's all the more surprising that Huntington's consulting for the CIA and other government agencies was an issue, when one recalls why NAS exists. Congress established the academy in 1863 to act as official adviser to the U. S. government on questions of science and technology. NAS in turn established the National Research Council (NRC), and NAS and NRC committees continue to provide reports about a wide range of matters, from nutrition to future army materials. As is clear from any day's newspaper, our government desperately needs professionally competent advice, particularly about unstable countries, which are one of Huntington's specialties. So Huntington's willingness to do exactly what NAS was founded to do—advise the government— was held against him by some NAS members. How much of a role his politics played in each member's vote will never be known, but I find it unfortunate that they played any role at all.

I accept, however, that a more decisive issue in the debates involved perceptions of the soft sciences—e.g., Lang's perception that Huntington used pseudomathematics. To understand the terms soft and hard science, just ask any educated person what science is. The answer you get will probably involve several stereotypes: Science is something done in a laboratory, possibly by people wearing white coats and holding test tubes; it involves making measurements with instruments, accurate to several decimal places; and it involves controlled, repeatable experiments in which you keep everything fixed except for one or a few things that you allow to vary. Areas of science that often conform well to these stereotypes include much of chemistry, physics, and molecular biology. These areas are given the flattering name of hard science, because they use the firm evidence that controlled experiments and highly accurate measurements can provide.

We often view hard science as the only type of science. But science (from the Latin *scientia*—knowledge) is something much more general, which isn't defined by decimal places and controlled experiments. It means the enterprise of explaining and predicting—gaining knowledge of—natural phenomena, by continually testing one's theories against empirical evidence. The world is full of phenomena that are intellectually challenging and important to understand, but that can't be measured to several decimal places in labs. They constitute much of ecology, evolution, and animal behavior; much of psychology and human behavior; and all the phenomena of human societies, including cultural anthropology, economics, history, and government.

10   These soft sciences, as they're pejoratively termed, are more difficult to study, for obvious reasons. A lion hunt or revolution in the third world doesn't fit inside a test tube. You can't start it and stop it whenever you choose. You can't control all the variables; perhaps you can't control *any* variable. You may even find it hard to decide what a variable is. You can still use empirical tests to gain knowledge, but the types of tests used in the hard sciences must be modified. Such differences between the hard and soft sciences are regularly misunderstood by hard scientists, who tend to scorn soft sciences and reserve special contempt for the social sciences. Indeed, it was only in the early 1970s that NAS, confronted with the need to offer the government competent advice about social problems, began to admit social scientists at all. Huntington had the misfortune to become a touchstone of this widespread misunderstanding and contempt.

While I know neither Lang nor Huntington, the broader debate over soft versus hard science is one that has long fascinated me, because I'm among the minority of scientists who work in both areas. I began my career at the hard pole of chemistry and physics, then took my PhD in membrane physiology, at the hard end of biology. Today I divide my time equally between physiology and ecology, which lies at the soft end of biology. My wife, Marie Cohen, works in yet a softer field, clinical psychology. Hence I find myself forced every day to confront the differences between hard and soft science. Although I don't agree with some of Lang's conclusions, I feel he has correctly identified a key problem in soft science when he asks, "How does Huntington measure things like social frustration? Does he have a social-frustration meter?" Indeed, unless one has thought seriously about research in the social sciences, the idea that anyone could measure social frustration seems completely absurd.

The issue that Lang raises is central to any science, hard or soft. It may be termed the problem of how to "operationalize" a concept. (Normally I hate such neologistic jargon, but its a suitable term in this case.) To compare evidence with theory requires that you measure the ingredients of your theory. For ingredients like weight or speed it's clear what to measure, but what would you measure if you wanted to understand political instability? Somehow, you would have to design a series of actual operations that yield a suitable measurement—i.e., you must operationalize the ingredients of theory.

Scientists do this all the time, whether or not they think about it. I shall illustrate operationalizing with four examples from my and Marie's research, progressing from hard science to softer science.

Let's start with mathematics, often described as the queen of the sciences. I'd guess that mathematics arose long ago when two cave women couldn't operationalize their intuitive concept of "many." One cave woman said, "Let's pick this tree over here, because it has many bananas." The other cave woman argued, "No, let's pick that tree over there, because it has more bananas." Without a number system to operationalize their concept of "many," the two cave women could never prove to each other which tree offered better pickings.

15   There are still tribes today with number systems too rudimentary   15
to settle the argument. For example, some Gimi villagers with whom I worked in New Guinea have only two root numbers, *iya* = 1 and *rarido* = 2, which they combine to operationalize somewhat larger numbers: 4 = *rarido-rarido*, 7 =*rarido-rarido-rarido-iya*, etc. You call imagine what it would be like to hear two Gimi women arguing about whether to climb a tree with 27 bananas or one with 18 bananas.

Now let's move to chemistry, less queenly and more difficult to operationalize than mathematics but still a hard science. Ancient philosophers speculated about the ingredients of matter, but not until the eighteenth century did the first modern chemists figure out how to measure these ingredients. Analytical chemistry now proceeds by identifying some property of a substance of interest, or of a related substance into which the first can be converted. The property must be one that can be measured, like weight, or the light the substance absorbs, or the amount of neutralizing agent it consumes.

For example, when my colleagues and I were studying the physiology of hummingbirds, we knew that the little guys liked to drink sweet nectar, but we would have argued indefinitely about how sweet sweet was if we hadn't operationalized the concept by measuring sugar concentrations. The method we used was to treat a glucose solution with an enzyme that liberates hydrogen peroxide, which reacts (with the help of another enzyme) with another substance called dianisidine to make it turn brown, whereupon we measured the brown color's intensity with an instrument called a spectrophotometer. A pointer's deflection on the spectrophotometer dial let us read off a number that provided an operational definition of sweet. Chemists use that sort of indirect reasoning all the time, without anyone considering it absurd.

My next-to-last example is from ecology, one of the softer of the biological sciences, and certainly more difficult to operationalize than chemistry. As a bird watcher, I'm accustomed to finding more species of birds in a rain forest than in a marsh. I suspect intuitively that this has something to do with a marsh being a simply structured habitat, while a rain forest has a complex structure that includes shrubs, lianas, trees of all heights, and crowns of big trees. More complexity means more niches for different types of birds. But how do I operationalize the idea of habitat complexity, so that I can measure it and test my intuition?

Obviously, nothing I do will yield as exact an answer as in the case where I read sugar concentrations off a spectrophotometer dial. However, a pretty good approximation was devised by one of my teachers, the ecologist Robert MacArthur, who measured how far a board at a certain height above the ground had to be moved in a random direction away from an observer standing in the forest (or marsh) before it became half obscured by the foliage. That distance is inversely proportional to the density of the foliage at that height. By repeating the measurement at different heights, MacArthur could calculate how the foliage was distributed over various heights.

20   In a marsh all the foliage is concentrated within a few feet of the   20
ground, whereas in a rain forest it's spread fairly equally from the ground to the canopy. Thus the intuitive idea of habitat complexity is

operationalized as what's called a foliage height diversity index, a single number. MacArthur's simple operationalization of these foliage differences among habitats, which at first seemed to resist having a number put on them, proved to explain a big part of the habitats' differences in numbers of bird species. It was a significant advance in ecology.

For the last example let's take one of the softest sciences, one that physicists love to deride: clinical psychology. Marie works with cancer patients and their families. Anyone with personal experience of cancer knows the terror that a diagnosis of cancer brings. Some doctors are more frank with their patients than others, and doctors appear to withhold more information from some patients than from others. Why?

Marie guessed that these differences might be related to differences in doctors' attitudes toward things like death, cancer, and medical treatment. But how on earth was she to operationalize and measure such attitudes, convert them to numbers, and test her guesses? I can imagine Lang sneering "Does she have a cancer-attitude meter?"

Part of Marie's solution was to use a questionnaire that other scientists had developed by extracting statements from sources like tape-recorded doctors' meetings and then asking other doctors to express their degree of agreement with each statement. It turned out that each doctor's responses tended to cluster in several groups, in such a way that his responses to one statement in a cluster were correlated with his responses to other statements in the same cluster. One cluster proved to consist of expressions of attitudes toward death, a second cluster consisted of expressions of attitudes toward treatment and diagnosis, and a third cluster consisted of statements about patients' ability to cope with cancer. The responses were then employed to define attitude scales, which were further validated in other ways, like testing the scales on doctors at different stages in their careers (hence likely to have different attitudes). By thus operationalizing doctors' attitudes, Marie discovered (among other things) that doctors most convinced about the value of early diagnosis and aggressive treatment of cancer are the ones most likely to be frank with their patients.

In short, all scientists, from mathematicians to social scientists, have to solve the task of operationalizing their intuitive concepts. The book by Huntington that provoked Lang's wrath discussed such operationalized concepts as economic well-being, political instability, and social and economic modernization. Physicists have to resort to very indirect (albeit accurate) operationalizing in order to "measure" electrons. But the task of operationalizing is inevitably more difficult and less exact in the soft sciences, because there are so many uncontrolled variables. In the four examples I've given, number of bananas and concentration of sugar can be measured to more decimal places than can habitat complexity and attitudes toward cancer.

25   Unfortunately, operationalizing lends itself to ridicule in the social   25
sciences, because the concepts being studied tend to be familiar ones that all of us fancy we're experts on. Anybody, scientist or no, feels entitled to spout forth on politics or psychology, and to heap scorn on what scholars in those fields write. In contrast, consider the opening sentences of Lang's paper *Diophantine Approximation on Abelian Varieties with Complex Multiplication:* "Let A be an abelian variety defined over a number field K. We Suppose that A is embedded in projective space. Let A_K be the group of points on A rational over K." How many people feel entitled to ridicule these statements while touting their own opinions about abelian varieties?

No political scientist at NAS has challenged a mathematical candidate by asking "How, does he measure things like 'many'? Does he have a many-meter? Such questions would bring gales of laughter over the questioner's utter ignorance of mathematics. It seems to me that Lang's question "How does Huntington measure things like social frustration?" betrays an equal ignorance of how the social sciences make measurements.

The ingrained labels "soft science" and "hard science" could be replaced by hard (i.e., difficult) science and easy science, respectively. Ecology and psychology and the social sciences are much more difficult and, to some of us, intellectually more challenging than mathematics and chemistry. Even if NAS were just an honorary society, the intellectual challenge of the soft sciences would by itself make them central to NAS.

But NAS is more than an honorary society; it's a conduit for advice to our government. As to the relative importance of soft and hard science for humanity's future, there can be no comparison. It matters little whether we progress with understanding the diophantine approximation. Our survival depends on whether we progress with understanding how people behave, why some societies become frustrated, whether their governments tend to become unstable, and how political leaders make decisions like whether to press a red button. Our National Academy of Sciences will cut itself out of intellectually challenging areas of science, and out of the areas where NAS can provide the most needed scientific advice, if it continues to judge social scientists from a posture of ignorance.

Why Write . . . Together?

Lisa Ede and Andrea Lunsford

When Lisa Ede and Andrea Lunsford—professors of writing and rhetoric—cowrote "Why Write . . . Together?" (1983), they had already collaborated on two other articles. At the time, they acknowledged that their different styles, as both people and writers, created difficulties they didn't encounter when each of them wrote alone. Yet over the twenty years since their first round of collaborations, they have continued to work together on articles, books, conference presentations, and talks on campuses across the country.

Collaborative writing itself became a scholarly interest for both Ede and Lunsford, to the extent that they are considered to be among the foremost experts in the study and practice of collaboration, in professional as well as in academic writing. They were among the first in their field to recognize that university students are taught to write almost exclusively as individuals, even though most move into professions that require a substantial amount of coauthorship. As promoters of collaborative writing, Ede and Lansford explore the situations in which two (or more) heads are better than one.

Lisa Ede is professor of English and director of the Center for Writing and Learning at Oregon State University. Andrea Lansford taught at the University of British Columbia and then was for many years professor of English at Ohio State University. She is currently professor of English and director of the Program for Writing and Rhetoric at Stanford University. Among Ede and Lunsford's many collaborative projects, the most notable in this context is their detailed study of joint authorship in academic and professional worlds, Singular Texts, Plural Authors: Perspectives on Collaborative Writing *(1990). The article presented here offers Lansford and Ede's early—and prescient—thoughts on the role of collaboration; it was published in the January 1983 issue of* Rhetoric Review.

Reprinted from *Rhetoric Review* 1, no 2, by permission of Taylor and Francis.

1   It was 10:00 P.M. We had just spent another twelve-hour day work-   1
ing on our paper. Lisa was settling into a chair with a hot toddy.
Andrea was shoving off for a shower. We were grumpy, tired, full of
self-pity; this was the third day we had worked at such a pace. Only
one day remained before Lisa had to begin the eight-hour trek from
Andrea's home in Vancouver to her own in Corvallis. We had to finish
a draft of the paper, our first joint writing project, the next day.

All at once—we both remember it this way—Lisa sat upright and
announced: "Andrea takes a shower every night; Lisa takes one every morning." Since the meaning of this toddy-stimulated statement was hardly
self-evident, Lisa went on to explain that suddenly the significance of all
our differences, of which this was just one example, seemed clear. How
could two such opposite people ever hope to write a paper—together?

Warming to the silliness of the topic, we began to list all the ways
we differ. Andrea showers every night; Lisa, every morning. Andrea
drinks only iced tea, even at breakfast; Lisa drinks only the hottest of
hot tea. Andrea hates milk and most dairy products; they form a sta-
ple of Lisa's diet. Andrea always wears her hair pulled back; Lisa gets
a headache from even the thought of a single barrette. Andrea is a metic-
ulous housekeeper; Lisa, so-so at best.

As the list of opposites grew, we felt a giddy sense of relief. No
wonder the past few days had been so trying. Two such contrary, often
downright cantankerous, people should have *expected* trouble. The
struggle began to make sense: not just our personalities but our composing processes and, to a lesser degree, our styles, differed radically.
After all, didn't Lisa love dashes, sprinkling them liberally through her
prose, while Andrea seldom used them? Andrea preferred long paragraphs; Lisa's were usually shorter. Lisa wrote at a desk or (in a pinch)
at a table; Andrea worked sitting cross-legged on the floor or on the
bed. Andrea was a sprinter; she liked to write a draft straight through,
as quickly as possible, revising and typing later. Lisa worked more
slowly, dividing a paper into small sections, revising and typing as
she went.

5   We decided that night that if we ever did complete our joint   5
essay, we would someday explore the mystery—or the madness—of
coauthorship. Since that time, we have coauthored two other articles
and have several joint projects in mind. Thus, while we continue individual research efforts, our status as sometime coauthors seems assured.
Somehow, despite the difficulties, we not only manage to write essays
together, but actually like doing so. And, as we have worked together,

the question that arose that night—how can two people with different interests, personalities, habits, and composing processes together write one essay?—has expanded into many questions. This article is a brief anecdotal response to some of those questions. In it, we wish to sketch the outlines of the process of coauthorship as we have come to understand it, to set forth the advantages and disadvantages we encountered, and to pose a series of questions which we hope will be explored in future research.

In our experience, coauthorship has meant the two of us creating one text—together. We discovered and thought through ideas together, talked through almost every section and draft of the papers together, and often wrote drafts by talking and then recording directly. Such is not always the case. Indeed, our use of the term is probably atypical. More typically, no doubt, two authors contribute separate sections, which are then put together. Only at that point do the coauthors revise the whole text, and even in revising authors may work separately. In this way, people can coauthor articles without ever being together or doing any writing together. This second form of coauthorship may best describe the kind of academic writing done by, say, a professor and a student, or the kind done by many researchers in science. It may also describe coauthorship in much professional and business writing. Yet a third concept covered by the blanket term *coauthorship* is that of group writing. It is not unusual, especially in business, for a number of people to contribute to a single text. The head of the writing division for an international mining corporation recently told us that as many as fifteen people contribute sections to their annual report. Subsequently, four or five of those people come together to revise the entire report, which generally goes through a dozen drafts.

We believe that important distinctions exist among these types of coauthorship and, indeed, that other types of coauthorship can be identified. Since our experience has been primarily of the first type, however—that of conceiving, drafting, and revising a text together—we will concentrate on that concept and will use the term *coauthorship* in this essay to refer to this type of writing together.

We are also here referring only to academic writing. The essays we have coauthored have all been addressed to those in our field, readers of *College Composition and Communication, College English,* and rhetoric journals. In that sense, we have gone into each project with a clear sense of audience, medium of publication, and purpose (although we could, of course, easily misjudge our audience or medium or alter our purposes).

As with much academic writing, we began by working within only our own time constraints. But as so often is the case, this internal control soon gave way to external pressures. An invitation to speak at a conference was accepted; an article was solicited for a journal or committed to a book—and suddenly the external pressure to write on demand appeared. In this important regard, that of writing on demand, much academic writing may be closer to professional writing than we usually consider it to be. But in other ways, the genres vary markedly. As writers of an article for *Rhetoric Review,* for instance, we have a different kind of control over shape and substance than we would if we were writing an annual report for a mining company. As with the various types of coauthorship, we think these generic distinctions are important ones that need to be explored. While we hope to pursue these questions in the future, we are speaking here not of business or professional writing, but only of the academic genre with which we are all so familiar.

So what is this process of coauthoring an academic paper? We've drawn boxes and arrows, spirals and loops, but will offer no schematized representation of the process we have experienced. If you can imagine the words *talk ... write ... talk ... read ... talk ... write ... talk ... read ...* written in a large looping spiral—that comes closest to a description of the process as we know it. We wish especially to emphasize the frequency and proportion of *talking* in this process.

10   As we noted earlier, each of our projects grew out of a particular   10 rhetorical situation: We were constrained by a broad topic and by a medium of publication and an audience. Within those guidelines, our first and longest talks occurred. These early talks were characterized by a lot of foolishness (Why not claim that the concept of audience simply doesn't exist? or, How about writing a dialogue between Aristotle and Wittgenstein?), fantasy (What if we could visit Kenneth Burke for a month?), and unfocused rambling (Where do you suppose we've put our notes on those ten articles? What do you think is the best reading for *krisis*?)* In our first project, these talks helped us sound the depths of our topic and, most importantly, discover the enormity of what we did not know. Intensive periods of reading and research fol-

---

krisis: A classical Greek term etymologically related to the verb *krinō,* "to pull apart or separate." The word *krisis* means an agreed-upon choice or judgment. Lunsford and Ede's choice of *krisis* as an example is interesting in that the coauthors themselves must make a choice or judgment about their reading of the term.

lowed, as did more and more talking, trading of notes, and posing of yet more unanswered questions. All told, this first coauthored essay took us six months, during which we met four times for two- to four-day writing sessions. These sessions were pressure-filled, frustrating—and very exciting. For one of them, we met half-way between our homes, in Seattle, and worked for two-and-a-half days in a hotel room, distracted only by the person trying unsuccessfully to "tidy up" around the stacks of books, articles, and drafts, and by our husbands, who insisted on reporting on all the fun they were having while we worked. We estimate writing and talking time in these sessions to be almost equal, with more time given to writing in the last session and more to talk in the earlier ones. At the end of each session the process of talk . . . write . . . talk . . . read . . . talk . . . write . . . talk . . . read . . . left us tired but exhilarated. And in each case the process produced a draft, one we could take back home, work on, and talk about in our frequent phone calls. We have kept every draft, all our notes, and some protocols from each of our projects, but we do not wish to turn this into a full-blown case study of our admitted idiosyncrasies. Rather, we wish to turn to a brief discussion of how coauthoring altered our individual writing processes.

Most noticeable, as we have mentioned, was the much larger proportion of talking together about our research and writing. Papers written singly have never been completely silent affairs; we talk to others about our work or ask colleagues to read and discuss essays or drafts with us. But never had either of us (both prodigious talkers to begin with) ever talked so much or for so long while writing a paper. This talking, in fact, seemed to be a necessary part of coauthoring, one that made our writing more productive and efficient. Nor is this result surprising. Our "talks," after all, gave us the constant benefits of dialectic, the traditional counterpart of rhetoric.

Coauthorship effected a second, less pleasurable change in our ordinary writing processes. All academic writers are accustomed to the pressure of deadlines, but in single authorship these deadlines are more or less manageable. Coauthorship presented us with completely rigid time-schedules and hence with more pressure than either of us was used to working under: If we had only two-and-a-half days to work together, then we had to come up with a text at that very time. Or else.

We also noted shifts in our usual revision strategies. In the first place, neither of us was accustomed to having *talk* serve as the basis for a majority of the revisions we made. When writing alone, writers usually revise while or after reading. We found also that our individual revising strategies differed substantially: Lisa generally revises and types each section as it is drafted; Andrea favors long periods of staring into space during which she composes various alternative drafts in her head before beginning a long burst of writing. Editing strategies were equally affected. In the coauthored articles, we found ourselves attending much more closely to quotation format and footnote citations in our early drafts than we would ordinarily have done. We were concerned to get the citations exactly right, since our resources were split up between us and our two libraries. Going back to find a missing source would be much more difficult than usual.

These changes in revision strategies reflect, we believe, a change in the rhetorical situations coauthors work within; they must cooperate and collaborate at every turn. Coauthorship, then, demands flexibility and compromise, traits single writers can often eschew. For us, this changed situation meant giving up some of our cherished stylistic tics—like Lisa's dashes—or a favored revision strategy.

15   The spirit of cooperation and compromise necessary to coauthor-   15
ship helped us identify two additional ways in which our customary experience with writing was changed. As of this writing, we feel less ego involvement with the pieces we have coauthored than those we have written alone. Hence, we have a greater distance front the work. At this point, we cannot report whether coauthorship gives us more—or less—confidence in the written product. But the questions of confidence and of ego-involvement raise a number of issues, some of which we will address in the concluding section of this essay. Most importantly, we found that coauthoring led us to alter our normal problem-solving styles. In spite of the tendency to work on writing and revising a paper one small section at a time, Lisa's basic approach to problems is broad and synthetic; she ordinarily begins by casting a very wide net. Andrea, on the other hand, approaches problems analytically, narrowing and drawing out implications, searching for closure almost at once. Working as coauthors identified this difference in approach for us, and led us to balance the two styles continually against one another. As a result, one often felt we were circling endlessly, spinning our wheels, while the other alternatively felt we were roaring hell-bent toward our conclusion.

Such changes obviously require significant accommodation and compromise, which can be seen as either advantages or disadvantages of coauthorship. Had we not finally decided on the former, we would not be writing this now. Many others, in similar situations and with similar interests, might choose differently. Indeed, some time in the future our own circumstances or any of a number of other internal or external changes could prompt us to decide that the advantages of coauthorship no longer outweigh the disadvantages. Coauthorship, as we have pointed out, makes the whole process of writing more difficult in some ways. (Perhaps our worst moment occurred one afternoon in Seattle when Lisa revised the mid section of our first project three times—requiring Andrea to change the following pages, which she was working on at the time, substantially every time.) Those problems were offset for us, however, by the stimulation of working with someone who shares the same interests. Even more important to us was the strong sense that in some writing situations we were more likely to achieve a better understanding, generate potentially richer and fresher ideas, and develop a stronger overall argument than we might have done working alone. (We specify "some writing situations" to emphasize that we chose the projects on which we collaborated carefully and for a number of particular reasons; as we have noted, we continued to work on independent research efforts during this period.)

We felt, in short, a kind of synergism when we worked together. This synergisim, the sense that by combining our efforts we could in some instances achieve more together than alone, carried us through some difficult times. But other factors also played a role. Although we knew before we began writing together that we differed in our composing habits and stylistic preferences, we each shared a respect for the other's abilities. Also, each of us knew the other was a person on whom we could count, once committed, to complete a project no matter how much or how violently we differed. Finally, we *wanted* to work together, both because we are friends (who now can deduct the expenses for all the trips we would have taken anyway) and because we feel that collaboration and collegiality are ideals much discussed but little practiced in academic life.

Although we have gone into some detail about our relationship as coauthors, we have by no means given a full accounting of the ups and downs, ins and outs, arguments and counter-arguments involved in working together. (For a while we planned to include process footnotes such as [1]"Believe it or not, Andrea put this dash in here"; or [7]"At this point, Lisa *begged* to be able to type what we had written.") We hope in future research to investigate further the concepts and kinds of coauthorship and the implications coauthoring may hold for our field. In the meantime, we would very much like to hear from other coauthors about their experiences writing with others. Because Andrea lives in the land of lost mail, please write to Lisa. We hope shortly to begin a more formal gathering of data about coauthoring in various disciplines and professions. Even this brief exploration, however, has raised a number of questions which we believe need to be addressed.

(1) What specific features distinguish the processes of co- or group-authoring from those of single authorship? Are these features the same for the three types of coauthorship described above? Can these features of process be linked to any features of the resulting products? In short, how can we best *define* coauthorship?

20　　(2) Is there a limit to how many people can write together? Are　20 projects such as the *Oxford English Dictionary,* Bible, *Short Title Catalogue,* elaborate computer programs, encyclopedias—all often involving more than 100 authors—examples of coauthorship? That is to say, what are the parameters of coauthorship?

(3) In what ways, if any, does co- or group-authorship affect the way we view the traditional rhetor-audience relationship?

(4) How does technology affect the processes of coauthoring? In our experience, writing together would have been much more difficult and much slower without the telephone, xerox, and self-correcting typewriter. Had we each had word processors at home and a computer link, what other differences might we have noted?

(5) What epistemological implications does coauthorship hold for traditional notions of creativity and originality? Our own strong sense that two may create ideas that neither would have reached alone argues for the value of dialectic as invention.

(6) How might the ethics of coauthorship be examined and defined? We spoke earlier of noting less ego involvement in our coauthored pieces. Perhaps this factor is related to our sense of shared responsibility: If we are wrong, at least we are wrong together. But in cases of group authorship, where does the responsibility lie? Who stands behind the words of a report written by fifteen people? As group authorship becomes more and more the norm in some genres, such questions gather urgency.

25　　(7) Is the emphasis on or weight of various cognitive and rhetor-　25 ical strategies different when coauthoring than when writing alone? As we noted, many of our customary revision strategies were altered by the process of coauthorship, and the rhetorical situation, which demanded collaboration and compromise, strongly affected our usual processes.

(8) Finally, we were led to think most seriously of the pedagogical implications of coauthorship. What do we know as a discipline about the advantages or disadvantages of having students participate in co- or group-writing? If advantages do exist, don't they in some ways contradict our profession's traditional insistence on students' working alone? And perhaps most importantly, do we have ways to teach students to adjust readily to co- or group-writing tasks?

Although this whimsical report of our experiences as coauthors is severely limited, perhaps serving best to raise questions, the issue of co- and group-authorship in general is not of limited or peripheral significance. As a rule, writers in the humanities have tended to ignore coauthorship, both in writing and in teaching, while colleagues in the sciences and the professions have long used it as a major mode. In view of this anomaly, the images of the lonely writer in a garret, or students hunched against the solitary ordeal of writing proficiency examinations, seem particularly inappropriate. We are, after all, most often responsible for teaching those who go into science and the professions how to write. And when we consider that these students are going into jobs already making use of rapidly developing computer technology, which holds such potential significance for coauthoring, the question for both writers and teachers may be not "Why write together?" but "Why NOT write together?"

On Dumpster Diving

Lars Eighner

Lars Eighner (1948–) became homeless in the 1980s after losing a job and being unable to find another immediately. He had been a student at the University of Texas at Austin before this, at which time he had been thrown out of his mother's house for being gay. While homeless he wrote stories and articles for magazines when he was able to find a typewriter to use and stay in one place long enough to write. He remained homeless for about three years, caring for and traveling with his dog, Lizbeth. In 1993 he published Travels with Lizbeth: Three Years on the Road and on the Streets, *an autobiographical account of that period which is in turns humorous, philosophical, and a good narrative. The following essay is an excerpted chapter from that book. Eighner's writing is successful because of the unabashedly honest and self-aware way he takes on his subject and opens his reader to a new world—here, the contents of trash dumpsters.*

This chapter was composed while the author was homeless. The present tense has been preserved.

1   Long before I began Dumpster diving I was impressed with Dumpsters, enough so that I wrote the Merriam-Webster research service to discover what I could about the word *Dumpster.* I learned from them that it is a proprietary word belonging to the Dempsey Dumpster company. Since then I have dutifully capitalized the word, although it was lowercased in almost all the citations Merriam-Webster photocopied for me. Dempsey's word is too apt. I have never heard these things called anything but Dumpsters. I do not

know anyone who knows the generic name for these objects. From time to time I have heard a wino or hobo give some corrupted credit to the original and call them Dipsy Dumpsters.

I began Dumpster diving about a year before I became homeless.

I prefer the word *scavenging* and use the word *scrounging* when I mean to be obscure. I have heard people, evidently meaning to be polite, use the word *foraging*, but I prefer to reserve that word for gathering nuts and berries and such which I do also according to the season and the opportunity. *Dumpster diving* seems to me to be a little too cute and, in my case, inaccurate because I lack the athletic ability to lower myself into the Dumpsters as the true divers do, much as their increased profit.

I like the frankness of the word *scavenging*, which I can hardly think of without picturing a big black snail on an aquarium wall. I live from the refuse of others. I am a scavenger. I think it a sound and honorable niche, although if I could I would naturally prefer to live the comfortable consumer life, perhaps—and only perhaps—as a slightly less wasteful consumer, owing to what I have learned as a scavenger.

5   While Lizbeth and I were still living in the shack on Avenue B as my   5
savings ran out, I put almost all my sporadic income into rent. The necessities of daily life I began to extract from Dumpsters. Yes, we ate from them. Except for jeans, all my clothes came from Dumpsters. Boom boxes, candles, bedding, toilet paper, a virgin male love doll, medicine, books, a typewriter, dishes, furnishings, and change, sometimes amounting to many dollars—I acquired many things from the Dumpsters.

I have learned much as a scavenger. I mean to put some of what I have learned down here, beginning with the practical art of Dumpster diving and proceeding to the abstract.

What is safe to eat?

After all, the finding of objects is becoming something of an urban art. Even respectable employed people will sometimes find something tempting sticking out of a Dumpster or standing beside one. Quite a number of people, not all of them of the bohemian type, are willing to brag that they found this or that piece in the trash. But eating from Dumpsters is what separates the dilettanti from the professionals. Eating safely from the Dumpsters involves three principles: using the senses and common sense to evaluate the conditions of the found materials, knowing the Dumpsters of a given area and checking them regularly, and seeking always to answer the question "Why was this discarded?"

Perhaps everyone who has a kitchen and a regular supply of groceries has, at one time or another, made a sandwich and eaten half of it before discovering mold on the bread or got a mouthful of milk before realizing the milk had turned. Nothing of the sort is likely to happen to a Dumpster diver because he is constantly reminded that most food is discarded for a reason. Yet a lot of perfectly good food can be found in Dumpsters.

10 Canned goods, for example, turn up fairly often in the Dumpsters 10 I frequent. All except the most phobic people would be willing to eat from a can, even if it came from a Dumpster. Canned goods are among the safest of foods to be found in Dumpsters but are not utterly foolproof.

Although very rare with modern canning methods, botulism is a possibility. Most other forms of food poisoning seldom do lasting harm to a healthy person, but botulism is most certainly fatal and often the first symptom is death. Except for carbonated beverages, all canned goods should contain a slight vacuum and suck air when first punctured. Bulging, rusty, and dented cans and cans that spew when punctured should be avoided, especially when the contents are not very acidic or syrupy.

Heat can break down the botulin, but this requires much more cooking than most people do to canned goods. To the extent that botulism occurs at all, of course, it can occur in cans on pantry shelves as well as in cans from Dumpsters. Need I say that home-canned goods are simply too risky to be recommended

From time to time one of my companions, aware of the source of my provisions, will ask, "Do you think these crackers are really safe to eat?" For some reason it is most often the crackers they ask about.

This question has always made me angry. Of course I would not offer my companion anything I had doubts about. But more than that, I wonder why he cannot evaluate the condition of the crackers for himself. I have no special knowledge and I have been wrong before. Since he knows where the food comes from, it seems to me he ought to assume some of the responsibility for deciding what he will put in his mouth. For myself I have few qualms about dry foods such as crackers, cookies, cereal, chips, and pasta if they are free of visible contaminates and still dry and crisp. Most often such things are found in the original packaging, which is not so much a positive sign as it is the absence of a negative one.

15   Raw fruits and vegetables with intact skins seem perfectly safe to   15 me, excluding of course the obviously rotten. Many are discarded for minor imperfections that can be pared away. Leafy vegetables, grapes, cauliflower, broccoli, and similar things may be contaminated by liquids and may be impractical to wash.

Candy, especially hard candy, is usually safe if it has not drawn ants. Chocolate is often discarded only because it has become discolored as the cocoa butter de-emulsified. Candying, after all, is one method of food preservation because pathogens do not like very sugary substances.

All of these foods might be found in any Dumpster and can be evaluated with some confidence largely on the basis of appearance. Beyond these are foods that cannot be correctly evaluated without additional information.

I began scavenging by pulling pizzas out of the Dumpster behind a pizza delivery shop. In general, prepared food requires caution, but in this case I knew when the shop closed and went to the Dumpster as soon as the last of the help left.

Such shops often get prank orders; both the orders and the products made to fill them are called *bogus*. Because help seldom stays long at these places, pizzas are often made with the wrong topping, refused on delivery for being cold, or baked incorrectly. The products to be discarded are boxed up because inventory is kept by counting boxes: A boxed pizza can be written off; an unboxed pizza does not exist.

20   I never placed a bogus order to increase the supply of pizzas and   20 I believe no one else was scavenging in this Dumpster. But the people in the shop became suspicious and began to retain their garbage in the shop overnight. While it lasted I had a steady supply of fresh, sometimes warm pizza. Because I knew the Dumpster I knew the source of the pizza, and because I visited the Dumpster regularly I knew what was fresh and what was yesterday's.

The area I frequent is inhabited by many affluent college students. I am not here by chance; the Dumpsters in this area are very rich. Students throw out many good things, including food. In particular they tend to throw everything out when they move at the end of a semester, before and after breaks, and around midterm, when many of them despair of college. So I find it advantageous to keep an eye on the academic calendar.

Students throw food away around breaks because they do not know whether it has spoiled or will spoil before they return. A typical discard is a half jar of peanut butter. In fact, nonorganic peanut butter does not require refrigeration and is unlikely to spoil in any reasonable time. The student does not know that, and since it is Daddy's money, the student decides not to take a chance. Opened containers require caution and some attention to the question. "Why was this discarded?" But in the case of discards from student apartments, the answer may be that the item was thrown out through carelessness, ignorance, or wastefulness. This can sometimes be deduced when the item is found with many others, including some that are obviously perfectly good.

Some students, and others, approach defrosting a freezer by chucking out the whole lot. Not only do the circumstances of such a find tell the story, but also the mass of frozen goods stays cold for a long time and items may be found still frozen or freshly thawed.

Yogurt, cheese, and sour cream are items that are often thrown out while they are still good. Occasionally I find a cheese with a spot of mold, which of course I just pare off, and because it is obvious why such a cheese was discarded, I treat it with less suspicion than an apparently perfect cheese found in similar circumstances. Yogurt is often discarded, still sealed, only because the expiration date on the carton had passed. This is one of my favorite finds because yogurt will keep for several days, even in warm weather.

25   Students throw out canned goods and staples at the end of semesters and when they give up college at midterm. Drugs, pornography, spirits, and the like are often discarded when parents are expected—Dad's day, for example. And spirits also turn up after big party weekends, presumably discarded by the newly reformed. Wine and spirits, of course, keep perfectly well even once opened, but the same cannot be said of beer.

My test for carbonated soft drinks is whether they still fizz vigorously. Many juices or other beverages are too acidic or too syrupy to cause much concern, provided they are not visibly contaminated. I have discovered nasty molds in vegetable juices, even when the product was found under its original seal; I recommend that such products be decanted slowly into a clear glass. Liquids always require some care. One hot day I found a large jug of Pat O'Brien's Hurricane mix. The jug had been opened, but it was still ice cold. I drank three large glasses before it became apparent to me that someone had added the rum to the mix, and not a little rum. I never tasted the rum, and by the time I began to feel the effects I had already ingested a very large quantity of the beverage. Some divers would have considered this a boon, but being suddenly intoxicated in a public place in the early afternoon is not my idea of a good time.

I have heard of people maliciously contaminating discarded food and even handouts, but mostly I have heard of this from people with vivid imaginations who have had no experience with the Dumpsters themselves. Just before the pizza shop stopped discarding its garbage at night, jalapeños began showing up on most of the discarded pizzas. If indeed this was meant to discourage me it was a wasted effort because I am native Texan.

For myself, I avoid game, poultry, pork, and egg-based foods, whether I find them raw or cooked. I seldom have the means to cook what I find, but when I do I avail myself of plentiful supplies of beef, which is often in very good condition. I suppose fish becomes disagreeable before it becomes dangerous. Lizbeth is happy to have any such thing that is past its prime and, in fact, does not recognize fish as food until it is quite strong.

Home leftovers, as opposed to surpluses from restaurants, are very often bad. Evidently, especially among students, there is a common type of personality that carefully wraps up even the smallest leftover and shoves it into the back of the refrigerator for six months or so before discarding it. Characteristic of this type are the reused jars and margarine tubs to which the remains are committed. I avoid ethnic foods I am unfamiliar with. If I do not know what it is supposed to look like when it is good, I cannot be certain I will be able to tell if it is bad.

30   No matter how careful I am I still get dysentery at least once a   30 month, oftener in warm weather. I do not want to paint too romantic a picture. Dumpster diving has serious drawbacks as a way of life.

I learned to scavenge gradually, on my own. Since then I have initiated several companions into the trade. I have learned that there is a predictable series of stages a person goes through in learning to scavenge.

At first the new scavenger is filled with disgust and self-loathing. He is ashamed of being seen and may lurk around, trying to duck behind things, or he may try to dive at night. (In fact, most people instinctively look away from a scavenger. By skulking around, the novice calls attention to himself and arouses suspicion. Diving at night is ineffective and needlessly messy.)

Every grain of rice seems to be a maggot. Everything seems to stink. He can wipe the egg yolk off the found can, but he cannot erase from his mind the stigma of eating garbage.

That stage passes with experience. The scavenger finds a pair of running shoes that fit and look and smell brand-new. He finds a pocket calculator in perfect working order. He finds pristine ice cream, still frozen, more than he can eat or keep. He begins to understand: People throw away perfectly good stuff, a lot of perfectly good stuff.

35   At this stage, Dumpster shyness begins to dissipate. The diver, 35 after all, has the last laugh. He is finding all manner of good things that are his for the taking. Those who disparage his profession are the fools, not he.

He may begin to hang on to some perfectly good things for which he has neither a use nor a market. Then he begins to take note of the things that are not perfectly good but are nearly so. He mates a Walkman with broken earphones and one that is missing a battery cover. He picks up things that he can repair.

At this stage he may become lost and never recover. Dumpsters are full of things of some potential value to someone and also of things that never have much intrinsic value but are interesting. All the Dumpster divers I have known come to the point of trying to acquire everything they touch. Why not take it, they reason, since it is all free? This is, of course, hopeless. Most divers come to realize that they must restrict themselves to items of relatively immediate utility. But in some cases the diver simply cannot control himself. I have met several of these pack-rat types. Their ideas of the values of various pieces of junk verge on the psychotic. Every bit of glass may be a diamond, they think, and all that glisters, gold.

I tend to gain weight when I am scavenging. Partly this is because I always find far more pizza and doughnuts than water-packed tuna, nonfat yogurt, and fresh vegetables. Also I have not developed much faith in the reliability of Dumpsters as a food source, although it has been proven to me many times. I tend to eat as if I have no idea where my next meal is coming from. But mostly I just hate to see food go to waste and so I eat much more than I should. Something like this drives the obsession to collect junk.

As for collecting objects, I usually restrict myself to collecting one kind of small object at a time, such as pocket calculators, sunglasses, or campaign buttons. To live on the street I must anticipate my needs to a certain extent: I must pick up and save warm bedding I find in August because it will not be found in Dumpsters in November. As I have no access to health care, I often hoard essential drugs, such as antibiotics and antihistamines. (This course can be recommended only to those with some grounding in pharmacology. Antibiotics, for example, even when indicated are worse than useless if taken in insufficient amounts.) But even if I had a home with extensive storage space, I could not save everything that might be valuable in some contingency.

40   I have proprietary feelings about my Dumpsters. As I have mentioned, it is no accident that I scavenge from ones where good finds are common. But my limited experience with Dumpsters in other areas suggests to me that even in poorer areas, Dumpsters, if attended with sufficient diligence, can be made to yield a livelihood. The rich students discard perfectly good kiwifruit; poorer people discard perfectly good apples. Slacks and Polo shirts are found in the one place; jeans and T-shirts in the other. The population of competitors rather than the affluence of the dumpers most affects the feasibility of survival by scavenging. The large number of competitors is what puts me off the idea of trying to scavenge in places like Los Angeles. 40

Curiously, I do not mind my direct competition, other scavengers, so much as I hate the can scroungers.

People scrounge cans because they have to have a little cash. I have tried scrounging cans with an able-bodied companion. Afoot a can scrounger simply cannot make more than a few dollars a day. One can extract the necessities of life from the Dumpsters directly with far less effort than would be required to accumulate the equivalent value in cans. (These observations may not hold in places with container redemption laws.)

Can scroungers, then, are people who must have small amounts of cash. These are drug addicts and winos, mostly the latter because the amounts of cash are so small. Spirits and drugs do, like all other commodities, turn up in Dumpsters and the scavenger will from time to time have a half bottle of a rather good wine with his dinner. But the wino cannot survive on these occasional finds; he must have his daily dose to stave off the DTs. All the cans he can carry will buy about three bottles of Wild Irish Rose.

I do not begrudge them the cans, but can scroungers tend to tear up the Dumpsters, mixing the contents and littering the area. They become so specialized that they can see only cans. They earn my contempt by passing up change, canned goods, and readily hockable items.

45   There are precious few courtesies among scavengers. But it is common practice to set aside surplus items: pairs of shoes, clothing, canned goods, and such. A true scavenger hates to see good stuff go to waste, and what he cannot use he leaves in good condition in plain sight.

Can scroungers lay waste to everything in their path and will stir one of a pair of good shoes to the bottom of a Dumpster, to be lost or ruined in the muck. Can scroungers will even go through individual garbage cans, something I have never seen a scavenger do.

Individual garbage cans are set out on the public easement only on garbage days. On other days going through them requires trespassing close to a dwelling. Going through individual garbage cans without scattering litter is almost impossible. Litter is likely to reduce the public's tolerance of scavenging. Individual cans are simply not as productive as Dumpsters; people in houses and duplexes do not move so often and for some reason do not tend to discard as much useful material. Moreover, the time required to go through one garbage can that serves one household is not much less than the time required to go through a Dumpster that contains the refuse of twenty apartments.

But my strongest reservation about going through individual garbage cans is that this seems to me a very personal kind of invasion to which I would object if I were a householder. Although many things in Dumpsters are obviously meant never to come to light, a Dumpster is somehow less personal.

I avoid trying to draw conclusions about the people who dump in the Dumpsters I frequent. I think it would be unethical to do so, although I know many people will find the idea of scavenger ethics too funny for words.

50   Dumpsters contain bank statements, correspondence, and other documents, just as anyone might expect. But there are also less obvious sources of information. Pill bottles, for example. The labels bear the name of the patient, the name of the doctor, and the name of the drug. AIDS drugs and antipsychotic medicines, to name but two groups, are specific and are seldom prescribed for any other

disorders. The plastic compacts for birth-control pills usually have complete label information.

Despite all of this sensitive information, I have had only one apartment resident object to my going through the Dumpster. In that case it turned out the resident was a university athlete who was taking bets and who was afraid I would turn up his wager slips.

Occasionally a find tells a story. I once found a small paper bag containing some unused condoms, several partial tubes of flavored sexual lubricants, a partially used compact of birth-control pills, and the torn pieces of a picture of a young man. Clearly she was through with him and planning to give up sex altogether.

Dumpster things are often sad—abandoned teddy bears, shredded wedding books, despaired-of sales kits. I find many pets lying in state in Dumpsters. Although I hope to get off the streets so that Lizbeth can have a long and comfortable old age, I know this hope is not very realistic. So I suppose when her time comes she too will go into a Dumpster. I will have no better place for her. And after all, it is fitting, since for most of her life her livelihood has come from the Dumpster. When she finds something I think is safe that has been spilled from a Dumpster, I let her have it. She already knows the route around the best ones. I like to think that if she survives me she will have a chance of evading the dog catcher and of finding her sustenance on the route.

Silly vanities also come to rest in the Dumpsters. I am a rather accomplished needleworker. I get a lot of material from the Dumpsters. Evidently sorority girls, hoping to impress someone, perhaps themselves, with their mastery of a womanly art, buy a lot of embroider-by-number kits, work a few stitches horribly, and eventually discard the whole mess. I pull out their stitches, turn the canvas over, and work an original design. Do not think I refrain from chuckling as I make gifts from these kits.

55 I find diaries and journals. I have often thought of compiling a book of literary found objects. And perhaps I will one day. But what I find is hopelessly commonplace and bad without being, even unconsciously, camp. College students also discard their papers. I am horrified to discover the kind of paper that now merits an A in an undergraduate course. I am grateful, however, for the number of good books and magazines the students throw out.

In the area I know best I have never discovered vermin in the Dumpsters, but there are two kinds of kitty surprise. One is alley cats whom I meet as they leap, claws first, out of Dumpsters. This is especially thrilling when I have Lizbeth in tow. The other kind of kitty surprise is a plastic garbage bag filled with some ponderous, amorphous mass. This always proves to be used cat litter.

City bees harvest doughnut glaze and this makes the Dumpster at the doughnut shop more interesting. My faith in the instinctive wisdom of animals is always shaken whenever I see Lizbeth attempt to catch a bee in her mouth, which she does whenever bees are present. Evidently some birds find Dumpsters profitable, for birdie surprise is almost as common as kitty surprise of the first kind. In hunting season all kinds of small game turn up in Dumpsters, some of it, sadly, not entirely dead. Curiously, summer and winter, maggots are uncommon.

The worst of the living and near-living hazards of the Dumpsters are the fire ants. The food they claim is not much of a loss, but they are vicious and aggressive. It is very easy to brush against some surface of the Dumpster and pick up half a dozen or more fire ants, usually in some sensitive area such as the underarm. One advantage of bringing Lizbeth along as I make Dumpster rounds is that, for obvious reasons, she is very alert to ground-based fire ants. When Lizbeth recognizes a fire-ant infestation around our feet, she does the Dance of the Zillion Fire Ants. I have learned not to ignore this warning from Lizbeth, whether I perceive the tiny ants or not, but to remove ourselves at Lizbeth's first pas de bourrée. All the more so because the ants are the worst in the summer months when I wear flip-flops if I have them. (Perhaps someone will misunderstand this. Lizbeth does the Dance of the Zillion Fire Ants when she recognizes more fire ants than she cares to eat, not when she is being bitten. Since I have learned to react promptly, she does not get bitten at all. It is the isolated patrol of fire ants that falls in Lizbeth's range that deserves pity. She finds them quite tasty.)

By far the best way to go through a Dumpster is to lower yourself into it. Most of the good stuff tends to settle at the bottom because it is usually weightier than the rubbish. My more athletic companions have often demonstrated to me that they can extract much good material from a Dumpster I have already been over.

60   To those psychologically or physically unprepared to enter a 60 Dumpster, I recommend a stout stick, preferably with some barb or hook at one end. The hook can be used to grab plastic garbage bags. When I find canned goods or other objects loose at the bottom of a

Dumpster, I lower a bag into it, roll the desired object into the bag, and then hoist the bag out—a procedure more easily described than executed. Much Dumpster diving is a matter of experience for which nothing will do except practice.

Dumpster diving is outdoor work, often surprisingly pleasant. It is not entirely predictable; things of interest turn up every day and some days there are finds of great value. I am always very pleased when I can turn up exactly the thing I most wanted to find. Yet in spite of the element of chance, scavenging more than most other pursuits tends to yield returns in some proportion to the effort and intelligence brought to bear. It is very sweet to turn up a few dollars in change from a Dumpster that has just been gone over by a wino.

The land is now covered with cities. The cities are full of Dumpsters. If a member of the canine race is ever able to know what it is doing, then Lizbeth knows that when we go around to the Dumpsters, we are hunting. I think of scavenging as a modern form of self-reliance. In any event, after having survived nearly ten years of government service, where everything is geared to the lowest common denominator, I find it refreshing to have work that rewards initiative and effort. Certainly I would be happy to have a sinecure again, but I am no longer heartbroken that I left one.

I find from the experience of scavenging two rather deep lessons. The first is to take what you can use and let the rest go by. I have come to think that there is no value in the abstract. A thing I cannot use or make useful, perhaps by trading, has no value however rare or fine it may be. I mean useful in a broad sense—some art I would find useful and some otherwise.

I was shocked to realize that some things are not worth acquiring, but now I think it is so. Some material things are white elephants that eat up the possessor's substance. The second lesson is the transience of material being. This has not quite converted me to a dualist, but it has made some headway in that direction. I do not suppose that ideas are immortal, but certainly mental things are longer lived than other material things.

65   Once I was the sort of person who invests objects with sentimental value. Now I no longer have those objects, but I have the sentiments yet.

Many times in our travels I have lost everything but the clothes I was wearing and Lizbeth. The things I find in Dumpsters, the love letters and rag dolls of so many lives, remind me of this lesson. Now I hardly pick up a thing without envisioning the time I will cast it aside. This I think is a healthy state of mind. Almost everything I have now has already been cast out at least once, proving that what I own is valueless to someone.

Anyway, I find my desire to grab for the gaudy bauble has been largely sated. I think this is an attitude I share with the very wealthy—we both know there is plenty more where what we have came from. Between us are the rat-race millions who nightly scavenge the cable channels looking for they know not what.

I am sorry for them.

Who Shot Mohammed al-Dura?

James Fallows

James Fallows is a national correspondent for The Atlantic *and the author of* Looking at the Sun *(1994),* Breaking the News *(1996), and* Free Flight *(2001). His article about the postwar future of Iraq, "The Fifty-first State?" appeared in the November 2002* Atlantic.

The image of a boy shot dead in his helpless father's arms during an Israeli confrontation with Palestinians has become the Pietà of the Arab world. Now a number of Israeli researchers are presenting persuasive evidence that the fatal shots could not have come from the Israeli soldiers known to have been involved in the confrontation. The evidence will not change Arab minds—but the episode offers an object lesson in the incendiary power of an icon

1   The name Mohammed al-Dura is barely known in the United States. Yet to a billion people in the Muslim world it is an infamous symbol of grievance against Israel and—because of this country's support for Israel—against the United States as well.

Al-Dura was the twelve-year-old Palestinian boy shot and killed during an exchange of fire between Israeli soldiers and Palestinian demonstrators on September 30, 2000. The final few seconds of his life, when he crouched in terror behind his father, Jamal, and then slumped to the ground after bullets ripped through his torso, were captured by a television camera and broadcast around the world. Through repetition they have become as familiar and significant to Arab and Islamic viewers as photographs of bombed-out Hiroshima are to the people of Japan—or as footage of the crumbling World Trade Center

Reprinted by permission from *The Atlantic*, June 2003.

is to Americans. Several Arab countries have issued postage stamps carrying a picture of the terrified boy. One of Baghdad's main streets was renamed The Martyr Mohammed Aldura Street. Morocco has an al-Dura Park. In one of the messages Osama bin Laden released after the September 11 attacks and the subsequent U.S. invasion of Afghanistan, he began a list of indictments against "American arrogance and Israeli violence" by saying, "In the epitome of his arrogance and the peak of his media campaign in which he boasts of 'enduring freedom,' Bush must not forget the image of Mohammed al-Dura and his fellow Muslims in Palestine and Iraq. If he has forgotten, then we will not forget, God willing."

But almost since the day of the episode evidence has been emerging in Israel, under controversial and intriguing circumstances, to indicate that the official version of the Mohammed al-Dura story is not true. It now appears that the boy cannot have died in the way reported by most of the world's media and fervently believed throughout the Islamic world. Whatever happened to him, he was not shot by the Israeli soldiers who were known to be involved in the day's fighting— or so I am convinced, after spending a week in Israel talking with those examining the case. The exculpatory evidence comes not from government or military officials in Israel, who have an obvious interest in claiming that their soldiers weren't responsible, but from other sources. In fact, the Israel Defense Forces, or IDF, seem to prefer to soft-pedal the findings rather than bring any more attention to this gruesome episode. The research has been done by a variety of academics, ex-soldiers, and Web-loggers who have become obsessed with the case, and the evidence can be cross-checked.

No "proof" that originates in Israel is likely to change minds in the Arab world. The longtime Palestinian spokesperson Hanan Ashrawi dismissed one early Israeli report on the topic as a "falsified version of reality [that] blames the victims." Late this spring Said Hamad, a spokesman at the PLO office in Washington, told me of the new Israeli studies, "It does not surprise me that these reports would come out from the same people who shot Mohammed al-Dura. He was shot of course by the Israeli army, and not by anybody else." Even if evidence that could revise the understanding of this particular death were widely accepted (so far it has been embraced by a few Jewish groups in Europe and North America), it would probably have no effect on the underlying hatred and ongoing violence in the region. Nor would evidence that clears Israeli soldiers necessarily support the overarching Likud policy of sending soldiers to occupy territories and protect settlements. The Israelis still looking into the al-Dura case do not all endorse Likud occupation policies. In fact, some strongly oppose them.

5   The truth about Mohammed al-Dura is important in its own right, because this episode is so raw and vivid in the Arab world and so hazy, if not invisible, in the West. Whatever the course of the occupation of Iraq, the United States has guaranteed an ample future supply of images of Arab suffering. The two explosions in Baghdad markets in the first weeks of the war, killing scores of civilians, offered an initial taste. Even as U.S. officials cautioned that it would take more time and study to determine whether U.S. or Iraqi ordnance had caused the blasts, the Arab media denounced the brutality that created these new martyrs. More of this lies ahead. The saga of Mohammed al-Dura illustrates the way the battles of wartime imagery may play themselves out.

The harshest version of the al-Dura case from the Arab side is that it proves the ancient "blood libel"—Jews want to kill gentile children—and shows that Americans count Arab life so cheap that they will let the Israelis keep on killing. The harshest version from the Israeli side is that the case proves the Palestinians' willingness to deliberately sacrifice even their own children in the name of the war against Zionism. In Tel Aviv I looked through hour after hour of videotape in an attempt to understand what can be known about what happened, and what it means.

The Day

The death of Mohammed al-Dura took place on the second day of what is now known as the second intifada, a wave of violent protests throughout the West Bank and Gaza. In the summer of 2000 Middle East peace negotiations had reached another impasse. On September 28 of that year, a Thursday, Ariel Sharon, then the leader of Israel's Likud Party but not yet Prime Minister, made a visit to the highly contested religious site in Jerusalem that Jews know as the Temple Mount and Muslims know as Haram al-Sharif, with its two mosques. For Palestinians this was the trigger—or, in the view of many Israelis, the pretext—for the expanded protests that began the next day.

On September 30 the protest sites included a crossroads in the occupied Gaza territory near the village of Netzarim, where sixty families of Israeli settlers live. The crossroads is a simple right-angle intersection of two roads in a lightly developed area. Three days earlier a roadside bomb had mortally wounded an IDF soldier there. At one corner of the intersection were an abandoned warehouse, two six-story office buildings known as the "twin towers," and a two-story building. (These structures and others surrounding the crossroads have since been torn down.) A group of IDF soldiers had made the two-story building their outpost, to guard the road leading to the Israeli settlement.

Diagonally across the intersection was a small, ramshackle building and a sidewalk bordered by a concrete wall. It was along this wall that Mohammed al-Dura and his father crouched before they were shot. (The father was injured but survived.) The other two corners of the crossroads were vacant land. One of them contained a circular dirt berm, known as the Pita because it was shaped like a pita loaf. A group of uniformed Palestinian policemen, armed with automatic rifles, were on the Pita for much of the day.

10   Early in the morning of Saturday, September 30, a crowd of Pales-   10
tinians gathered at the Netzarim crossroads. TV crews, photographers, and reporters from many news agencies, including Reuters, AP, and the French television network France 2, were also at the ready. Because so many cameras were running for so many hours, there is abundant documentary evidence of most of the day's events—with a few strange and crucial exceptions, most of them concerning Mohammed al-Dura.

"Rushes" (raw footage) of the day's filming collected from these and other news organizations around the world tell a detailed yet confusing story. The tapes overlap in some areas but leave mysterious gaps in others. No one camera, of course, followed the day's events from beginning to end; and with so many people engaged in a variety of activities simultaneously, no one account could capture everything. Gabriel Weimann, the chairman of the communications department at the University of Haifa, whose book *Communicating Unreality* concerns the media's distorting effects, explained to me on my visit that the footage in its entirety has a "*Rashomon* effect." Many separate small dramas seem to be under way. Some of the shots show groups of young men walking around, joking, sitting and smoking and appearing to enjoy themselves. Others show isolated moments of intense action, as protesters yell and throw rocks, and shots ring out from various directions. Only when these vignettes are packaged together as a conventional TV news report do they seem to have a narrative coherence.

Off and on throughout the morning some of the several hundred Palestinian civilians at the crossroads mounted assaults on the IDF outpost. They threw rocks and Molotov cocktails. They ran around waving the Palestinian flag and trying to pull down an Israeli flag near the outpost. A few of the civilians had pistols or rifles, which they occasionally fired; the second intifada quickly escalated from throwing rocks to using other weapons. The Palestinian policemen, mainly in the Pita area, also fired at times. The IDF soldiers, according to Israeli spokesmen, were under orders not to fire in response to rocks or other thrown objects. They were to fire only if fired upon. Scenes filmed throughout the day show smoke puffing from the muzzles of M-16s pointed through the slits of the IDF outpost.

To watch the raw footage is to wonder, repeatedly, What is going on here? In some scenes groups of Palestinians duck for cover from gunfire while others nonchalantly talk or smoke just five feet away. At one dramatic moment a Palestinian man dives forward clutching his leg, as if shot in the thigh. An ambulance somehow arrives to collect him exactly two seconds later, before he has stopped rolling from the momentum of his fall. Another man is loaded into an ambulance—and, in footage from a different TV camera, appears to jump out of it again some minutes later.

At around 3:00 P.M. Mohammed al-Dura and his father make their first appearance on film. The time can be judged by later comments from the father and some journalists on the scene, and by the length of shadows in the footage. Despite the number of cameras that were running that day, Mohammed and Jamal al-Dura appear in the footage of only one cameraman—Talal Abu-Rahma, a Palestinian working for France 2.

Jamal al-Dura later said that he had taken his son to a used-car market and was on the way back when he passed through the crossroads and into the crossfire. When first seen on tape, father and son are both crouched on the sidewalk behind a large concrete cylinder, their backs against the wall. The cylinder, about three feet high, is referred to as "the barrel" in most discussions of the case, although it appears to be a section from a culvert or a sewer system. On top of the cylinder is a big paving stone, which adds another eight inches or so of protection. The al-Duras were on the corner diagonally opposite the Israeli outpost. By hiding behind the barrel they were doing exactly what they should have done to protect themselves from Israeli fire.

Many news accounts later claimed that the two were under fire for forty-five minutes, but the action captured on camera lasts a very brief time. Jamal looks around desperately. Mohammed slides down behind him, as if to make his body disappear behind his father's. Jamal clutches a pack of cigarettes in his left hand, while he alternately waves and cradles his son with his right. The sound of gunfire is heard, and four bullet holes appear in the wall just to the left of the pair. The father starts yelling. There is another burst. Mohammed goes limp and falls forward across his father's lap, his shirt stained with blood. Jamal, too, is hit, and his head starts bobbling. The camera cuts away. Although France 2 or its cameraman may have footage that it or he has chosen not to release, no other visual record of the shooting or its immediate aftermath is known to exist. Other Palestinian casualties of the day are shown being evacuated, but there is no known on-tape evidence of the boy's being picked up, tended to, loaded into an ambulance, or handled in any other way after he was shot.

The footage of the shooting is unforgettable, and it illustrates the way in which television transforms reality. I have seen it replayed at least a hundred times now, and on each repetition I can't help hoping that this time the boy will get himself down low enough, this time the shots will miss. Through the compression involved in editing the footage for a news report, the scene acquired a clear story line by the time European, American, and Middle Eastern audiences saw it on television: Palestinians throw rocks. Israeli soldiers, from the slits in their outpost, shoot back. A little boy is murdered.

What is known about the rest of the day is fragmentary and additionally confusing. A report from a nearby hospital says that a dead boy was admitted on September 30, with two gun wounds to the left side of his torso. But according to the photocopy I saw, the report also says that the boy was admitted at 1:00 P.M.; the tape shows that Mohammed was shot later in the afternoon. The doctor's report also notes, without further explanation, that the dead boy had a cut down his belly about eight inches long. A boy's body, wrapped in a Palestinian flag but with his face exposed, was later carried through the streets to a burial site (the exact timing is in dispute). The face looks very much like Mohammed's in the video footage. Thousands of mourners lined the route. A BBC TV report on the funeral began, "A Palestinian boy has been martyred." Many of the major U.S. news organizations reported that the funeral was held on the evening of September 30, a few hours after the shooting. Oddly, on film the procession appears to take place in full sunlight, with shadows indicative of midday.

The Aftermath

Almost immediately news media around the world began reporting the tragedy. Print outlets were generally careful to say that Mohammed al-Dura was killed in "the crossfire" or "an exchange of fire" between Israeli soldiers and Palestinians. *The New York Times*, for instance, reported that he was "shot in the stomach as he crouched behind his father on the sidelines of an intensifying battle between Israeli and Palestinian security forces." But the same account included Jamal al-Dura's comment that the fatal volley had come from Israeli soldiers. Jacki Lyden said on NPR's *Weekend All Things Considered* that the boy had been "caught in crossfire." She then interviewed the France 2 cameraman, Talal Abu-Rahma, who said that he thought the Israelis had done the shooting.

> ABU-RAHMA: I was very sad. I was crying. And I was remembering my children. I was afraid to lose my life. And I was sitting on my knees and hiding my head, carrying my camera, and I was afraid from the Israeli to see this camera, maybe they will think this is a weapon, you know, or I am trying to shoot on them. But I was in the most difficult situation in my life. A boy, I cannot save his life, and I want to protect myself.

20   LYDEN: Was there any attempt by the troops who were firing to cease   20
fire to listen to what the father had to say? Could they even see what they were shooting at?

> ABU-RAHMA: Okay. It's clear it was a father, it's clear it was a boy over there for ever who [presumably meaning "whoever"] was shooting on them from across the street, you know, in front of them. I'm sure from that area, I'm expert in that area, I've been in that area many times. I know every [unintelligible] in that area. Whoever was shooting, he got to see them, because that base is not far away from the boy and the father. It's about a hundred and fifty meters [about 500 feet].

On that night's broadcast of *ABC World News Tonight*, the correspondent Gillian Findlay said unambiguously that the boy had died "under Israeli fire." Although both NBC and CBS used the term "cross-fire" in their reports, videos of Israeli troops firing and then the boy dying left little doubt about the causal relationship. Jamal al-Dura never wavered in his view that the Israelis had killed his son. "Are you sure they were Israeli bullets?" Diane Sawyer, of ABC News, asked him in an interview later that year. "I'm a hundred percent sure," he replied, through his translator. "They were Israelis." In another interview he told the Associated Press, "The bullets of the Zionists are the bullets that killed my son."

By Tuesday, October 3, all doubt seemed to have been removed. After a hurried internal investigation the IDF concluded that its troops were probably to blame. General Yom-Tov Samia, then the head of the IDF's Southern Command, which operated in Gaza, said, "It could very much be—this is an estimation—that a soldier in our position, who has a very narrow field of vision, saw somebody hiding behind a cement block in the direction from which he was being fired at, and he shot in that direction." General Giora Eiland, then the head of IDF operations, said on an Israeli radio broadcast that the boy was apparently killed by "Israeli army fire at the Palestinians who were attacking them violently with a great many petrol bombs, rocks, and very massive fire."

The further attempt to actually justify killing the boy was, in terms of public opinion, yet more damning for the IDF. Eiland said, "It is known that [Mohammed al-Dura] participated in stone throwing in the past." Samia asked what a twelve-year-old was doing in such a dangerous place to begin with. Ariel Sharon, who admitted that the footage of the shooting was "very hard to see," and that the death was "a real tragedy," also said, "The one that should be blamed is only the one . . . that really instigated all those activities, and that is Yasir Arafat."

Palestinians, and the Arab-Islamic world in general, predictably did not agree. Sweatshirts, posters, and wall murals were created showing the face of Mohammed al-Dura just before he died. "His face, stenciled three feet high, is a common sight on the walls of Gaza," Matthew McAllester, of *Newsday,* wrote last year. "His name is known to every Arab, his death cited as the ultimate example of Israeli military brutality." In modern warfare, Bob Simon said on CBS's *60 Minutes,* "one picture can be worth a thousand weapons," and the picture of the doomed boy amounted to "one of the most disastrous setbacks Israel has suffered in decades." Gabriel Weimann, of Haifa University, said that when he first heard of the case, "it made me sick to think this was done in my name." Amnon Lord, an Israeli columnist who has investigated the event, told me in an e-mail message that it was important "on the mythological level," because it was "a framework story, a paradigmatic event," illustrating Israeli brutality. Dan Schueftan, an Israeli strategist and military thinker, told me that the case was uniquely damaging. He said, "[It was] the ultimate symbol of what the Arabs want to think: the father is trying to protect his son, and the satanic Jews—there is no other word for it—are trying to kill him. These Jews are people who will come to kill our children, because they are not human."

25   Two years after Mohammed al-Dura's death his stepmother, Amal, became pregnant with another child, the family's eighth. The parents named him Mohammed. Amal was quoted late in her pregnancy as saying, "it will send a message to Israel: 'Yes, you've killed one, but God has compensated for him. You can't kill us all.'"

Second Thoughts

In the fall of last year Gabriel Weimann mentioned the Mohammed al-Dura case in a special course that he teaches at the Israeli Military Academy, National Security and Mass Media. Like most adults in Israel, Weimann, a tall, athletic-looking man in his early fifties, still performs up to thirty days of military-reserve duty a year. His reserve rank is sergeant, whereas the students in his class are lieutenant colonels and above.

To underscore the importance of the media in international politics, Weimann shows some of his students a montage of famous images from past wars: for World War II the flag raising at Iwo Jima; for Vietnam the South Vietnamese officer shooting a prisoner in the head and the little girl running naked down a path with napalm on her back. For the current intifada, Weimann told his students, the lasting iconic image would be the frightened face of Mohammed al-Dura.

One day last fall, after he discussed the images, a student spoke up. "I was there," he said. "We didn't do it."

"Prove it," Weimann said. He assigned part of the class, as its major research project, a reconsideration of the evidence in the case. A surprisingly large amount was available. The students began by revisiting an investigation undertaken by the Israeli military soon after the event.

30   Shortly after the shooting General Samia was contacted by Nahum Shahaf, a physicist and engineer who had worked closely with the

IDF on the design of pilotless drone aircraft. While watching the orig-inal news broadcasts of the shooting Shahaf had been alarmed, like most viewers inside and outside Israel. But he had also noticed an appar-ent anomaly. The father seemed to be concerned mainly about a threat originating on the far side of the barrel behind which he had taken shelter. Yet when he and his son were shot, the barrel itself seemed to be intact. What, exactly, did this mean?

Samia commissioned Shahaf and an engineer, Yosef Duriel, to work on a second IDF investigation of the case. "The reason from my side is to check and clean up our values," Samia later told Bob Simon, of CBS. He said he wanted "to see that we are still acting as the IDF." Shahaf stressed to Samia that the IDF should do whatever it could to preserve all physical evidence. But because so much intifada activity continued in the Netzarim area, the IDF demolished the wall and all related struc-tures. Shahaf took one trip to examine the crossroads, clad in body armor and escorted by Israeli soldiers. Then, at a location near Beersheba, Sha-haf, Duriel, and others set up models of the barrel, the wall, and the IDF shooting position, in order to re-enact the crucial events.

Bullets had not been recovered from the boy's body at the hospi-tal, and the family was hardly willing to agree to an exhumation to re-examine the wounds. Thus the most important piece of physical evi-dence was the concrete barrel. In the TV footage it clearly bears a mark from the Israeli Bureau of Standards, which enabled investigators to determine its exact dimensions and composition. When they placed the equivalent in front of a concrete wall and put mannequins repre-senting father and son behind it, a conclusion emerged: soldiers in the Israeli outpost could not have fired the shots whose impact was shown on TV. The evidence was cumulative and reinforcing. It involved the angle, the barrel, the indentations, and the dust.

Mohammed al-Dura and his father looked as if they were shel-tering themselves against fire from the IDF outpost. In this they were successful. The films show that the barrel was between them and the Israeli guns. The line of sight from the IDF position to the pair was blocked by concrete. Conceivably, some other Israeli soldier was pres-ent and fired from some other angle, although there is no evidence of this and no one has ever raised it as a possibility; and there were Pales-tinians in all the other places, who would presumably have noticed the presence of additional IDF troops. From the one location where Israeli soldiers are known to have been, the only way to hit the boy would have been to shoot through the concrete barrel.

This brings us to the nature of the barrel. Its walls were just under two inches thick. On the test range investigators fired M-16 bullets at a similar barrel. Each bullet made an indentation only two fifths to four fifths of an inch deep. Penetrating the barrel would have required multiple hits on both sides of the barrel's wall. The videos of the shooting show fewer than ten indentations on the side of the barrel facing the IDF, indicating that at some point in the day's exchanges of fire the Israelis did shoot at the barrel. But photographs taken after the shooting show no damage of any kind on the side of the barrel facing the al-Duras—that is, no bullets went through.

35   Further evidence involves the indentations in the concrete wall. 35
The bullet marks that appear so ominously in the wall seconds before the fatal volley are round. Their shape is significant because of what it indicates about the angle of the gunfire. The investigators fired volleys into a concrete wall from a variety of angles. They found that in order to produce a round puncture mark, they had to fire more or less straight on. The more oblique the angle, the more elongated and skidlike the hole became.

The dust resulting from a bullet's impact followed similar rules. A head-on shot produced the smallest, roundest cloud of dust. The more oblique the angle, the larger and longer the cloud of dust. In the video of the shooting the clouds of dust near the al-Duras' heads are small and round. Shots from the IDF outpost would necessarily have been oblique.

In short, the physical evidence of the shooting was in all ways inconsistent with shots coming from the IDF outpost—and in all ways consistent with shots coming from someplace behind the France 2 cameraman, roughly in the location of the Pita. Making a positive case for who might have shot the boy was not the business of the investigators hired by the IDF. They simply wanted to determine whether the soldiers in the outpost were responsible. Because the investigation was overseen by the IDF and run wholly by Israelis, it stood no chance of being taken seriously in the Arab world. But its fundamental point—that the concrete barrel lay between the outpost and the boy, and no bullets had gone through the barrel—could be confirmed independently from news footage.

It was at this point that the speculation about Mohammed al-Dura's death left the realm of geometry and ballistics and entered the world of politics, paranoia, fantasy, and hatred. Almost as soon as the second IDF investigation was under way, Israeli commentators started questioning its legitimacy and Israeli government officials distanced themselves from its findings. "It is hard to describe in mild terms the stupidity of this bizarre investigation," the liberal newspaper *Ha'aretz* said in an editorial six weeks after the shooting. The newspaper claimed that Shahaf and Duriel were motivated not by a need for dispassionate inquiry but by the belief that Palestinians had staged the whole shooting. (Shahaf told me that he began his investigation out of curiosity but during the course of it became convinced that the multiple anomalies indicated a staged event.) "The fact that an organized body like the IDF, with its vast resources, undertook such an amateurish investigation—almost a pirate endeavor—on such a sensitive issue, is shocking and worrying," *Ha'aretz* said.

As the controversy grew, Samia abbreviated the investigation and subsequently avoided discussing the case. Most government officials, I was told by many sources, regard drawing any further attention to Mohammed al-Dura as self-defeating. No new "proof" would erase images of the boy's death, and resurrecting the discussion would only ensure that the horrible footage was aired yet again. IDF press officials did not return any of my calls, including those requesting to interview soldiers who were at the outpost.

So by the time Gabriel Weimann's students at the Israeli Military Academy, including the one who had been on the scene, began looking into the evidence last fall, most Israelis had tried to put the case behind them. Those against the Likud policy of encouraging settlements in occupied territory think of the shooting as one more illustration of the policy's cost. Those who support the policy view Mohammed al-Dura's death as an unfortunate instance of "collateral damage," to be weighed against damage done to Israelis by Palestinian terrorists. Active interest in the case was confined mainly to a number of Israelis and European Jews who believe the event was manipulated to blacken Israel's image. Nahum Shahaf has become the leading figure in this group.

Shahaf is a type familiar to reporters: the person who has given himself entirely to a cause or a mystery and can talk about its ramifications as long as anyone will listen. He is a strongly built man of medium height, with graying hair combed back from his forehead. In photos he always appears stern, almost glowering, whereas in the time I spent with him he seemed to be constantly smiling, joking, having fun. Shahaf is in his middle fifties, but like many other scientists and engineers, he has the quality of seeming not quite grown up. He used to live in California, where, among other pursuits, he worked as a hang-gliding instructor. He moves and gesticulates with a teenager's lack of self-consciousness about his bearing. I liked him.

Before getting involved in the al-Dura case, Shahaf was known mainly as an inventor. He was only the tenth person to receive a medal from the Israeli Ministry of Science, for his work on computerized means of compressing digital video transmission. "But for two and a half years I am spending time only on the al-Dura case," he told me. "I left everything for it, because I believe that this is most important." When I arrived at his apartment, outside Tel Aviv, to meet him one morning, I heard a repeated sound from one room that I assumed was from a teenager's playing a violent video game. An hour later, when we walked into that room—which has been converted into a video-research laboratory, with multiple monitors, replay devices, and computers—I saw that it was one mob scene from September 30, being played on a continuous loop.

Shahaf's investigation for the IDF showed that the Israeli soldiers at the outpost did not shoot the boy. But he now believes that everything that happened at Netzarim on September 30 was a ruse. The boy on the film may or may not have been the son of the man who held him. The boy and the man may or may not actually have been shot. If shot, the boy may or may not actually have died. If he died, his killer may or may not have been a member of the Palestinian force, shooting at him directly. The entire goal of the exercise, Shahaf says, was to manufacture a child martyr, in correct anticipation of the damage this would do to Israel in the eyes of the world—especially the Islamic world. "I believe that one day there will be good things in common between us and the Palestinians," he told me. "But the case of Mohammed al-Dura brings the big flames between Israel and the Palestinians and Arabs. It brings a big wall of hate. They can say this is the proof, the ultimate proof, that Israeli soldiers are boy-murderers. And that hatred breaks any chance of having something good in the future."

The reasons to doubt that the al-Duras, the cameramen, and hundreds of onlookers were part of a coordinated fraud are obvious. Shahaf's evidence for this conclusion, based on his videos, is essentially an accumulation of oddities and unanswered questions about the chaotic events of the day. Why is there no footage of the boy after he was shot? Why does he appear to move in his father's lap, and to clasp a hand over his eyes after he is supposedly dead? Why is one Palestinian policeman wearing a Secret Service-style earpiece in one ear? Why is another Palestinian man shown waving his arms and yelling at others, as if "directing" a dramatic scene? Why does the funeral appear—based on the length of shadows—to have occurred before the apparent time of the shooting? Why is there no blood on the father's shirt just after they are shot? Why did a voice that seems to be that of the France 2 cameraman yell, in Arabic, "The boy is dead" before he had been hit? Why do ambulances appear instantly for seemingly everyone else and not for al-Dura?

45   A handful of Israeli and foreign commentators have taken up Shahaf's cause. A Web site called masada2000.org says of the IDF's initial apology, "They acknowledged guilt, for never in their collective minds would any one of them have imagined a scenario whereby Mohammed al-Dura might have been murdered by his *own* people . . . a cruel plot staged and executed by Palestinian sharp-shooters and a television cameraman!" Amnon Lord, writing for the magazine *Makor Rishon,* referred to a German documentary directed by Esther Schapira that was "based on Shahaf's own decisive conclusion" and that determined "that Muhammad Al-Dura was not killed by IDF gunfire at Netzarim junction." "Rather," Lord continued, "the Palestinians, in cooperation with foreign journalists and the UN, arranged a well-staged production of his death." In March of this year a French writer, Gérard Huber, published a book called *Contre expertise d'une mise en scène* (roughly, *Re-evaluation of a Re-enactment*). It, too, argues that the entire event was staged. In an e-mail message to me Huber said that before knowing of Shahaf's studies he had been aware that "the images of little Mohammed were part of the large war of images between Palestinians and Israelis." But until meeting Shahaf, he said, "I had not imagined that it involved a fiction"—a view he now shares. "The question of 'Who killed little Mohammed?'" he said, "has become a screen to disguise the real question, which is: 'Was little Mohammed actually killed?'"

The truth about this case will probably never be determined. Or, to put it more precisely, no version of truth that is considered believable by all sides will ever emerge. For most of the Arab world, the rights and wrongs of the case are beyond dispute: an innocent boy was murdered, and his blood is on Israel's hands. Mention of contrary evidence or hypotheses only confirms the bottomless dishonesty of the guilty parties—much as Holocaust-denial theories do in the Western world. For the handful of people collecting evidence of a staged event, the truth is also clear, even if the proof is not in hand. I saw Nahum Shahaf lose his good humor only when I asked him what he thought explained the odd timing of the boy's funeral, or the contradictions in eyewitness reports, or the other loose ends in the case. "I don't 'think,' I know!" he said several times. "I am a physicist. I work from the evidence." Schapira had collaborated with him for the German documentary and then produced a film advancing the "minimum" version of his case, showing that the shots did not, could not have, come from the IDF outpost. She disappointed him by not embracing the maximum version—the all-encompassing hoax—and counseled him not to talk about a staged event unless he could produce a living boy or a cooperative eyewitness. Shahaf said that he still thought well of her, and that he was not discouraged. "I am only two and a half years into this work," he told me. "It took twelve years for the truth of the Dreyfus case to come out."

For anyone else who knows about Mohammed al-Dura but is not in either of the decided camps—the Arabs who are sure they know what happened, the revisionists who are equally sure—the case will remain in the uncomfortable realm of events that cannot be fully explained or understood. "Maybe it was an accidental shooting," Gabriel Weimann told me, after reading his students' report, which, like the German documentary, supported the "minimum" conclusion— the Israeli soldiers at the outpost could not have killed the boy. (He could not show the report to me, he said, on grounds of academic confidentiality.) "Maybe even it was staged—although I don't think my worst enemy is so inhuman as to shoot a boy for the sake of publicity. Beyond that, I do not know." Weimann's recent work involves the way that television distorts reality in attempting to reconstruct it, by putting together loosely related or even random events in what the viewer imagines is a coherent narrative flow. The contrast between the confusing, contradictory hours of raw footage from the Netzarim crossroads and the clear, gripping narrative of the evening news reports assembled from that footage is a perfect example, he says.

The significance of this case from the American perspective involves the increasingly chaotic ecology of truth around the world. In Arab and Islamic societies the widespread belief that Israeli soldiers shot this boy has political consequences. So does the belief among some Israelis and Zionists in Israel and abroad that Palestinians will go to any lengths to smear them. Obviously, these beliefs do not create the basic tensions in the Middle East. The Israeli policy of promoting settlements in occupied territory, and the Palestinian policy of terror, are deeper obstacles.

There would never have been a showdown at the Netzarim crossroads, or any images of Mohammed al-Dura's shooting to be parsed in different ways, if there were no settlement nearby for IDF soldiers to protect. Gabriel Weimann is to the left of Dan Schueftan on Israel's political spectrum, but both believe that Israel should end its occupation. I would guess that Nahum Shahaf thinks the same thing, even though he told me that to preserve his "independence" as a researcher, he wanted to "isolate myself from any kind of political question."

The images intensify the self-righteous determination of each side. If anything, modern technology has aggravated the problem of mutually exclusive realities. With the Internet and TV, each culture now has a more elaborate apparatus for "proving," dramatizing, and disseminating its particular truth.

50   In its engagement with the Arab world the United States has 50 assumed that what it believes are noble motives will be perceived as such around the world. We mean the best for the people under our control; stability, democracy, prosperity, are our goals; why else would we have risked so much to help an oppressed people achieve them? The case of Mohammed al-Dura suggests the need for much more modest assumptions about the way other cultures—in particular today's embattled Islam—will perceive our truths.

The "Banking" Concept of Education

Paulo Freire

Most of us have had learning experiences driven by what Paulo Freire calls the "banking" concept of education—the teacher, as the authority, "deposits" knowledge into students. Freire (pronounced "Fr-air-ah") believes that learning should instead be driven by inquiry involving dialogue between teachers and students, in which teachers become students and students become teachers. To submit to the "banking" concept, says Freire, is to capitulate to those in power, who control learning in order to maintain the status quo. Freire proposes displacing "banking" with "problem-posing" education, a process of seeing reality in terms of our relationship to the world. It is through this process that students are liberated, by "becoming more fully human."

Freire's approach to education was deeply influenced by his work with adults living in the impoverished urban and rural areas of Brazil. A native of Brazil, Freire was drawn to education after university studies in law, philosophy, and the psychology of language. In addition to reading extensively in education, he absorbed the writings of Marx as well as Catholic intellectuals. Working through government and university organizations, he developed a "pedagogy of the oppressed," for the purpose of giving marginalized people the power to shape their own lives. His approach encouraged political action during a time when competing reform movements in Brazil challenged those in positions of military and economic power. The effectiveness, and consequent threat, of Freire's work led to his exile from Brazil after a 1964 military coup.

Reprinted from *Pedagogy of the Oppressed,* by permission of the Continuum International Publishing Group.

*Exile gave Freire the opportunity to continue develop-
ing and spreading the practice of his pedagogy, first in
Chile, then as a teacher and fellow at Harvard University,
and eventually through the World Council of Churches in
Geneva, Switzerland. After sixteen years in exile, Freire re-
turned to Brazil as a faculty member at the University of Sao
Paulo. In his capacity as minister of education for the city of
Sao Paulo, he later led in the reform of Brazil's schools.*

*Worldwide, Freire is regarded as one of the central fig-
ures in educational philosophy and practice. His books include* Education as the Practice of Freedom *(1967);*
Pedagogy of the Oppressed *(1970), the source of the following selection;* Education for Critical Consciousness
(1973); and The Politics of Education *(1985). Freire
died in 1997 at the age of seventy-five.*

1   A careful analysis of the teacher-student relationship at any level,   1
inside or outside the school, reveals its fundamentally *narrative*
character. This relationship involves a narrating Subject (the
teacher) and patient, listening objects (the students). The contents,
whether values or empirical dimensions of reality, tend in the process of
being narrated to become lifeless and petrified. Education is suffering
from narration sickness.

The teacher talks about reality as if it were motionless, static, compartmentalized, and predictable. Or else he expounds on a topic completely alien to the existential experience of the students. His task is
to "fill" the students with the contents of his narration—contents which
are detached from reality, disconnected from the totality that engendered
them and could give them significance. Words are emptied of their
concreteness and become a hollow, alienated, and alienating verbosity.

The outstanding characteristic of this narrative education, then,
is the sonority of words, not their transforming power. "Four times
four is sixteen; the capital of Pará is Belém." The student records, mem-
orizes, and repeats these phrases without perceiving what four times
four really means, or realizing the trite significance of "capital" in the
affirmation "the capital of Pará is Belém," that is, what Belém means
for Pará and what Pará means for Brazil.

Narration (with the teacher as narrator) leads the students to memorize mechanically the narrated content. Worse yet, it turns them into

"containers," into "receptacles" to be "filled" by the teacher. The more completely she fills the receptacles, the better a teacher she is. The more meekly the receptacles permit themselves to be filled, the better students they are.

5   Education thus becomes an act of depositing, in which the stu-   5
dents are the depositories and the teacher is the depositor. Instead of communicating, the teacher issues communiqués and makes deposits which the students patiently receive, memorize, and repeat. This is the "banking" concept of education, in which the scope of action allowed to the students extends only as far as receiving, filing, and storing the deposits. They do, it is true, have the opportunity to become collectors or catalogers of the things they store. But in the last analysis, it is the people themselves who are filed away through the lack of creativity, transformation, and knowledge in this (at best) misguided system. For apart from inquiry, apart from the praxis, individuals cannot be truly human. Knowledge emerges only through invention and reinvention, through the restless, impatient, continuing, hopeful inquiry human beings pursue in the world, with the world, and with each other.

In the banking concept of education, knowledge is a gift bestowed by those who consider themselves knowledgeable upon those whom they consider to know nothing. Projecting an absolute ignorance onto others, a characteristic of the ideology of oppression, negates education and knowledge as processes of inquiry. The teacher presents himself to his students as their necessary opposite; by considering their ignorance absolute, he justifies his own existence. The students, alienated like the slave in the Hegelian dialectic*, accept their ignorance as justifying the teacher's existence—but, unlike the slave, they never discover that they educate the teacher.

The raison d'être† of libertarian education, on the other hand, lies in its drive towards reconciliation. Education must begin with the solution of the teacher-student contradiction, by reconciling the poles of the contradiction so that both are simultaneously teachers *and* students.

This solution is not (nor can it be) found in the banking concept. On the contrary, banking education maintains and even stimulates the

---

Hegelian dialectic: The dynamic model of nature and mind offered by German philosopher Georg Wilhelm Friedrich Hegel (1770–1831), where a thesis comes into tension with an antithesis leading toward further synthesis.
†*raison d'être*: Reason for being.

contradiction through the following attitudes and practices, which mirror oppressive society as a whole:

a. the teacher teaches and the students are taught;
b. the teacher knows everything and the students know nothing;
c. the teacher thinks and the students are thought about;
d. the teacher talks and the students listen—meekly;
e. the teacher disciplines and the students are disciplined;
f. the teacher chooses and enforces his choice, and the students comply;
g. the teacher acts and the students have the illusion of acting through the action of the teacher;
h. the teacher chooses the program content, and the students (who were not consulted) adapt to it;
i. the teacher confuses the authority of knowledge with his or her own professional authority, which she and he sets in opposition to the freedom of the students;
j. teacher is the Subject of the learning process, while the pupils are mere objects.

It is not surprising that the banking concept of education regards men as adaptable, manageable beings. The more students work at storing the deposits entrusted to them, the less they develop the critical consciousness which would result from their intervention in the world as transformers of that world. The more completely they accept the passive role imposed on them, the more they tend simply to adapt to the world as it is and to the fragmented view of reality deposited in them.

The capability of banking education to minimize or annul the students' creative power and to stimulate their credulity serves the interests of the oppressors, who care neither to have the world revealed nor to see it transformed. The oppressors use their "humanitarianism" to preserve a profitable situation. Thus they react almost instinctively against any experiment in education which stimulates the critical facilities and is not content with a partial view of reality but always seeks out the ties which link one point to another and one problem to another.

Indeed, the interests of the oppressors lie in "changing the consciousness of the oppressed, not the situation which oppresses them"[1] for the more the oppressed can be led to adapt to that situation, the more easily they can be dominated. To achieve this end, the oppressors use the banking concept of education in conjunction with a paternalistic social action apparatus, within which the oppressed receive the euphemistic title of "welfare recipients." They are treated as individual cases, as marginal persons who deviate from the general configuration of a "good, organized, and just" society. The oppressed are regarded as the pathology of the healthy society, which must therefore adjust these "incompetent and lazy" folk to its own patterns by changing their mentality. These marginals need to be "integrated," "incorporated" into the healthy society that they have "forsaken."

The truth is, however, that the oppressed are not "marginals," are not people living "outside" society. They have always been "inside"— inside the structure which made them "beings for others." The solution is not to "integrate" them into the structure of oppression, but to transform that structure so that they can become "beings for themselves." Such transformation, of course, would undermine the oppressors' purposes; hence their utilization of the banking concept of education to avoid the threat of student *conscientização*.*

The banking approach to adult education, for example, will never propose to students that they critically consider reality. It will deal instead with such vital questions as whether Roger gave green grass to the goat, and insist upon the importance of learning that, on the contrary, Roger gave green grass to the rabbit. The "humanism" of the banking approach masks the effort to turn women and men into automatons—the very negation of their ontological vocation to be more fully human.

Those who use the banking approach, knowingly or unknowingly (for there are innumerable well-intentioned bank-clerk teachers who do not realize that they are serving only to dehumanize), fail to perceive that the deposits themselves contain contradictions about reality. But, sooner or later, these contradictions may lead formerly passive students to turn against their domestication and the attempt to domesticate reality. They may discover through existential experience that their present of life is irreconcilable with their vocation to become fully human. They may perceive through their relations with reality that reality is really a *process*, undergoing constant transformation. If men and women are searchers and their ontological vocation is humanization, sooner or later they may perceive the contradiction in which

---

conscientização: The ability to perceive social, political, and economic contradictions, and to act against the oppressive elements of reality.

banking education seeks to maintain them, and then engage themselves in the struggle for their liberation.

15   But the humanist, revolutionary educator cannot wait for this pos-   15
sibility to materialize. From the outset, her efforts must coincide with those of the students to engage in critical thinking and the quest for mutual humanization. His efforts must be imbued with a profound trust in people and their creative power. To achieve this, they must be partners of the students in their relations with them.

The banking concept does not admit to such partnership—and necessarily so. To resolve the teacher-student contradiction, to exchange the role of depositor, prescriber, domesticator, for the role of student among students would be to undermine the power of oppression and serve the cause of liberation.

Implicit in the banking concept is the assumption of a dichotomy between human beings and the world: a person is merely *in* the world, not *with* the world or with others; the individual is spectator, not re-creator. In this view, the person is not a conscious being (*corpo con-sciente*); he or she is rather the possessor of *a* consciousness: an empty "mind" passively open to the reception of deposits of reality from the world outside. For example, my desk, my books, my coffee cup, all the objects before me—as bits of the world which surrounds me—would be "inside" me, exactly as I am inside my study right now. This view makes no distinction between being accessible to consciousness and entering consciousness. The distinction, however, is essential: The objects which surround me are simply accessible to my consciousness, not located within it. I am aware of them, but they are not inside me.

It follows logically from the banking notion of consciousness that the educator's role is to regulate the way the world "enters into" the students. The teacher's task is to organize a process which already occurs spoutaneously, to "fill" the students by making deposits of informa-tion which he or she considers to constitute true knowledge.[2] And since people "receive" the world as passive entities, education should make them more passive still, and adapt them to the world. The edu-cated individual is the adapted person, because she or he is better "fit" for the world. Translated into practice, this concept is well suited to the purposes of the oppressors, whose tranquillity rests on how well people fit the world the oppressors have created, and how little they question it.

The more completely the majority adapt to the purposes which the dominant minority prescribe for them (thereby depriving them of the right to their own purposes), the more easily the minority can continue to prescribe. The theory and practice of banking education serve this end quite efficiently. Verbalistic lessons, reading requirements,[3] the methods for evaluating "knowledge," the distance between the teacher and the taught, the criteria for promotion: Everything in this ready-to-wear approach serves to obviate thinking.

20   The bank-clerk educator does not realize that there is no true security in his hypertrophied role, that one must seek to live *with* others in solidarity. One cannot impose oneself, nor even merely, coexist with one's students. Solidarity requires true communication, and the concept by which such an educator is guided fears and proscribes communication.

Yet only through communication can human life hold meaning. The teacher's thinking is authenticated only by the authenticity of the students' thinking. The teacher cannot think for her students, nor can she impose her thought on them. Authentic thinking, thinking that is concerned about *reality,* does not take place in ivory-tower isolation, but only in communication. If it is true that thought has meaning only when generated by action upon the world, the subordination of students to teachers becomes impossible.

Because banking education begins with a false understanding of men and women as objects, it cannot promote the development of what Fromm calls "biophily," but instead produces its opposite: "necrophily."

> While life is characterized by growth in a structured, functional manner, the necrophilous person loves all that does not grow, all that is mechanical. The necrophilous person is driven by the desire to transform the organic into the inorganic, to approach life mechanically, as if all living persons were things. . . . Memory, rather than experience: having, rather than being, is what counts. The necrophilous person can relate to an object—a flower or a person—only if he possesses it; hence a threat to his possession is a threat to himself, if he loses possession he loses contact with the world. . . . he loses control, and in the act of controlling he kills life.[4]

Oppression—overwhelming control—is necrophilic; it is nourished by love of death, not life. The banking concept of education, which serves the interests of oppression, is also necrophilic. Based on a mechanistic, static, naturalistic, spatialized view of consciousness, it transforms students into receiving objects. It attempts to control thinking and action, leads women and men to adjust to the world, and inhibits their creative power.

When their efforts to act responsibly are frustrated, when they find themselves unable to use their faculties, people suffer. "This suffering due to impotence is rooted in the very fact that the human equilibrium has been disturbed."[5] But the inability to act which causes people's anguish also causes them to reject their impotence, by attempting

> . . . to restore [their] capacity to act. But can [they], and how? One way is to submit to and identify with a person or group having power. By this symbolic participation in another person's life, [men have] the illusion of acting, when in reality [they] only submit to and become part of those who act.[6]

25 Populist manifestations perhaps best exemplify this type of behavior by the oppressed, who, by identifying with charismatic leaders, come to feel that they themselves are active and effective. The rebellion they express as they emerge in the historical process is motivated by that desire to act effectively. The dominant elites consider the remedy to be more domination and repression, carried out in the name of freedom, order, and social peace (that is, the peace of the elites). Thus they can condemn—logically, from their point of view—"the violence of a strike by workers and [can] call upon the state in the same breath to use violence in putting down the strike."

Education as the exercise of domination stimulates the credulity of students, with the ideological intent (often not perceived by educators) of indoctrinating them to adapt to the world of oppression. This accusation is not made in the naive hope that the dominant elites will thereby simply abandon the practice. Its objective is to call the attention of true humanists to the fact that they cannot use banking educational methods in the pursuit of liberation, for they would only negate that very pursuit. Nor may a revolutionary society inherit these methods from an oppressor society. The revolutionary society which practices banking education is either misguided or mistrusting of people. In either event, it is threatened by the specter of reaction.

Unfortunately, those who espouse the cause of liberation are themselves surrounded and influenced by the climate which generates the banking concept, and often do not perceive its true significance or its dehumanizing power. Paradoxically, then, they utilize this same instrument of alienation in what they consider an effort to liberate. Indeed, some "revolutionaries" brand as "innocents," "dreamers," or even "reactionaries" those who would challenge this educational practice. But one does not liberate people by alienating them. Authentic liberation—the process of humanization—is not another deposit to be made in men. Liberation is it praxis: the action and reflection of men and women upon their world in order to transform it. Those truly committed to the cause of liberation can accept neither the mechanistic concept of consciousness as an empty vessel to be filled, nor the use of banking methods of domination (propaganda, slogans—deposits) in the name of liberation.

Those truly committed to liberation must reject the banking concept in its entirety, adopting instead a concept of women and men as conscious beings, and consciousness as consciousness intent upon the world. They must abandon the educational goal of deposit-making and replace it with the posing of the problems of human beings in their relations with the world. "Problem-posing" education, responding to the essence of consciousness—*intentionality*—rejects communiqués and embodies communications. It epitomizes the special characteristic of consciousness: being *conscious of*, not only as intent on objects but as turned in upon itself in a Jasperian* "split"—consciousness as consciousness *of* consciousness.

Liberating education consists in acts of cognition, not transferrals of information. It is a learning situation in which the cognizable object (far from being the end of the cognitive act) intermediates the cognitive actors—teacher on the one hand and students on the other. Accordingly, the practice of problem-posing education entails at the outset that the teacher-student contradiction be resolved. Dialogical relations—indispensable to the capacity of cognitive actors to cooperate in perceiving the same cognizable object—are otherwise impossible.

30   Indeed, problem-posing education, which breaks with the vertical 30
patterns characteristic of banking education, can fulfill its function as

---

Jasperian: Karl Jaspers (1883–1969), a German psychiatrist and philosopher who had a strong influence on modern technology, psychiatry, and philosophy.

the practice of freedom only if it can overcome the above contradiction. Through dialogue, the teacher-of-the-students and the students-of-the-teacher cease to exist and a new term emerges: teacher-student with students-teachers. The teacher is no longer merely the-one-who-teaches but one who is himself taught in dialogue with the students, who in turn while being taught also teach. They become jointly responsible for a process in which all grow. In this process, arguments based on "authority" are no longer valid; in order to function, authority must be *on the side of* freedom, not *against* it. Here, no one teaches another, nor is anyone self-taught. People teach each other, mediated by the world, by the cognizable objects which in banking education are "owned" by the teacher.

The banking concept (with its tendency to dichotomize every-thing) distinguishes two stages in the action of the educator. During the first, he cognizes a cognizable object while he prepares his lessons in his study or his laboratory; during the second, he expounds to his students about that object. The students are not called upon to know, but to memorize the contents narrated by the teacher. Nor do the students practice any act of cognition, since the object towards which that act should be directed is the property of the teacher rather than a medium evoking the critical reflection of both teacher and students. Hence in the name of the "preservation of culture and knowledge" we have a system which achieves neither true knowledge nor true culture.

The problem-posing method does not dichotomize the activity of the teacher-student: She is not "cognitive" at one point and "narra-tive" at another. She is always "cognitive," whether preparing a pro-ject or engaging in dialogue with the students. He does not regard cognizable objects as his private property, but as the object of reflec-tion by himself and the students. In this way, the problem-posing edu-cator constantly re-forms his reflections in the reflection of the students. The students—longer docile listeners—are now critical coinvestigators in dialogue with the teacher. The teacher presents the material to the students for their consideration, and reconsiders her earlier consider-ations as the students express their own. The role of the problem-posing educator is to create, together with the students, the conditions under which knowledge at the level of the *doxa* is superseded by true knowl-edge, at the level of the *logos*.

Whereas banking education anesthetizes and inhibits creative power, problem-posing education involves a constant unveiling of reality. The former attempts to maintain the *submersion* of consciousness; the latter strives for the *emergence* of consciousness and *critical intervention* in reality.

Students, as they are increasingly posed with problems relating to themselves in the world and with the world, will feel increasingly challenged and obliged to respond to that challenge. Because they apprehend the challenge as interrelated to other problems within a total context, not as a theoretical question, the resulting comprehension tends to be increasingly critical and thus constantly less alienated. Their response to the challenge evokes new challenges, followed by new understandings; and gradually the students come to regard themselves as committed.

35 Education as the practice of freedom—as opposed to education as 35 the practice of domination—denies that man is abstract, isolated, independent, and unattached to the world; it also denies that the world exists as a reality apart from people. Authentic reflection considers neither abstract man nor the world without people, but people in their relations with the world. In these relations consciousness and world are simultaneous: Consciousness neither precedes the world nor follows it.

> La conscience et le monde sent donnés d'un même coup: extérieur par essence à la conscience, le monde est, par essence relatif à elle.[8]

In one of our culture circles in Chile, the group was discussing (based on a codification) the anthropological concept of culture. In the midst of the discussion, a peasant who by banking standards was completely ignorant said: "Now I see that without man there is no world." When the educator responded: "Let's say, for the sake of argument, that all the men on earth were to die, but that the earth itself remained, together with trees, birds, animals, rivers, seas, the stars . . . wouldn't all this be a world?" "Oh no," the peasant replied emphatically. "There would be no one to say: 'This is a world.'"

The peasant wished to express the idea that there would be lacking the consciousness of the world which necessarily implies the world of consciousness. *I* cannot exist without a *non-I*. In turn, the *not-I* depends on that existence. The world which brings consciousness into existence becomes the world *of* that consciousness. Hence, the previously cited affirmation of Sartre: *"La conscience et le monde sont donnés d'un même coup."*

As women and men, simultaneously reflecting on themselves and on the world, increase the scope of their perception, they begin to direct their observations towards previously inconspicuous phenomena:

> In perception properly so-called, as an explicit awareness [*Gewahren*], I am turned towards the object, to the paper, for instance. I apprehend it as being this here and now. The apprehension is a singling out, every object having a background in experience. Around and about the paper lie books, pencils, inkwell, and so forth, and these in a certain sense are also "perceived," perceptually there, in the "field of intuition"; but whilst I was turned towards the paper there was no turning in their direction, nor any apprehending of them, not even in a secondary sense. They appeared and yet were not singled out, were not posited on their own account. Every perception of a thing has such a zone of background intuitions or background awareness, if "intuiting" already includes the state of being turned towards, and this also is a "conscious experience," or more briefly a "consciousness of" all indeed that in point of fact lies in the co-perceived objective background.[9]

That which had existed objectively but had not been perceived in its deeper implications (if indeed it was perceived at all) begins to "stand out," assuming the character of a problem and therefore of challenge. Thus, men and women begin to single out elements from their "background awareness" and to reflect upon them. These elements are now objects of their consideration, and, as such, objects of their action and cognition.

In problem-posing education, people develop their power to perceive critically *the way they exist* in the world *with which* and *in which* they find themselves; they come to see the world not as a static reality, but as a reality in process, in transformation. Although the dialectical relations of women and men with the world exist independently of how these relations are perceived (or whether or not they are perceived at all), it is also true that the form of action they adopt is to a large extent a function of how they perceive themselves in the world. Hence, the teacher-student and the students-teachers reflect simultaneously on themselves and the world without dichotomizing this reflection from action, and thus establish an authentic form of thought and action.

Once again, the two educational concepts and practices under analysis come into conflict. Banking education (for obvious reasons) attempts, by mythicizing reality, to conceal certain facts which explain the way human beings exist in the world; problem-posing education sets itself the task of demythologizing. Banking education resists dialogue; problem-posing education regards dialogue as indispensable to the act of cognition which unveils reality. Banking education treats students as objects of assistance; problem-posing education makes them critical thinkers. Banking education inhibits creativity and domesticates (although it cannot completely destroy) the *intentionality* of consciousness by isolating consciousness from the world, thereby denying people their ontological and historical vocation of becoming more fully human. Problem-posing education bases itself on creativity and stimulates true reflection and action upon reality; thereby responding to the vocation of persons as beings who are authentic only when engaged in inquiry and creative transformation. In sum: Banking theory and practice, as immobilizing and fixating forces, fail to acknowledge men and women as historical beings; problem-posing theory and practice take the people's historicity as their starting point.

Problem-posing education affirms men and women as beings in the process of *becoming*—as unfinished, uncompleted beings in and with a likewise unfinished reality. Indeed, in contrast to other animals who are unfinished, but not historical, people know themselves to be unfinished; they are aware of their incompletion. In this incompletion and this awareness lie the very roots of education as an exclusively human manifestation. The unfinished character of human beings and the transformational character of reality necessitate that education be an ongoing activity.

Education is thus constantly remade in the praxis. In order to *be,* it must *become.* Its "duration" (in the Bergsonian* meaning of the word) is found in the interplay of the opposites *permanence* and *change.* The banking method emphasizes permanence and becomes reactionary; problem-posing education—which accepts neither a "well-behaved" present nor a predetermined future—roots itself in the dynamic present and becomes revolutionary.

Bergsonian: Henri-Louis Bergon (1859–1941), a French philosopher influential in the first half of the twentieth century.

Problem-posing education is revolutionary futurity. Hence, it is prophetic (and, as such, hopeful). Hence, it corresponds to the historical nature of humankind. Hence, it affirms women and men as beings who transcend themselves, who move forward and look ahead, for whom immobility represents a fatal threat, for whom looking at the past must only be a means of understanding more clearly what and who they are so that they can more wisely build the future. Hence, it identifies with the movement which engages people as beings aware of their incompletion—a historical movement which has its point of departure, its Subjects and its objective.

45 The point of departure of the movement lies in the people themselves. But since people do not exist apart from the world, apart from reality, the movement must begin with the human-world relationship. Accordingly, the point of departure must always be with men and women in the "here and now," which constitutes the situation within which they are submerged, from which they emerge, and in which they intervene. Only by starting from this situation—which determines their perception of it—can they begin to move. To do this authentically they must perceive their state not as fated and unalterable, but merely as limiting—and therefore challenging.

Whereas the banking method directly or indirectly reinforces men's fatalistic perception of their situation, the problem-posing method presents this very situation to them as a problem. As the situation becomes the object of their cognition, the naive or magical perception which produced their fatalisim gives way to perception which is able to perceive itself even as it perceives reality, and can thus be critically objective about that reality.

A deepened consciousness of their situation leads people to apprehend that situation as a historical reality susceptible of transformation. Resignation gives way to the drive for transformation and inquiry, over which men feel themselves to be in control. If people, as historical beings necessarily engaged with other people in a movement of inquiry, did not control that movement, it would be (and is) a violation of their humanity. Any situation in which some individuals prevent others from engaging in the process of inquiry is one of violence. The means used are not important; to alienate human beings from their own decision-making is to change them into objects.

This movement of inquiry must be directed towards humanization—the people's historical vocation. The pursuit of full humanity, however, cannot be carried out in isolation or individualism, but only in fellowship and solidarity; therefore it cannot unfold in the antagonistic relations between oppressors and oppressed. No one can be authentically human while he prevents others from being so. Attempting *to be more* human, individualistically, leads to *having more,* egotistically, a form of dehumanization. Not that it is not fundamental to *have* in order *to be* human. Precisely because it *is* necessary, some men's *having* must not be allowed to constitute an obstacle to others' *having,* must not consolidate the power of the former to crush the latter.

Problem-posing education, as a humanist and liberating praxis, posits as fundamental that the people subjected to domination must fight for their emancipation. To that end, it enables teachers and students to become Subjects of the educational process by overcoming authoritarianism and an alienating intellectualism; it also enables people to overcome their false perception of reality. The world—no longer something to be described with deceptive words—becomes the object of that transforming action by men and women which results in their humanization.

50   Problem-posing education does not and cannot serve the interests of the oppressor. No oppressive order could permit the oppressed to begin to question: Why? While only a revolutionary society can carry out this education in systematic terms, the revolutionary leaders need not take full power before they can employ the method. In the revolutionary process, the leaders cannot utilize the banking method as an interim measure, justified on grounds of expediency, with the intention of *later* behaving in a genuinely revolutionary fashion. They must be revolutionary— that is to say, dialogical—from the outset.   50

Notes

1. Simone de Beauvoir, *La pensée de droite, aujourd'hui* (Paris); ST, *El pensamiento político de la derecha* (Buenos Aires, 1963), p. 34.

2. This concept corresponds to what Sartre calls the "digestive" or "nutritive" concept of education, in which knowledge is "fed" by the teacher to the students to "fill them out." See Jean-Paul Sartre, "Une idée fundamentale de la phénomenologie de Husserl: L'intentionalité," *Situations* I (Paris, 1947).

3. For example, some professors specify in their reading lists that a book should be read from pages 10 to 15—and do this to "help" their students!

4. Eric Fromm, *The Heart of Man* (New York. 1966), p. 41.

5. Ibid., p. 31.

6. Ibid.

7. Reinhold Neibuhr, *Moral Man and Immoral Society* (New York, 1960), p. 130.

8. Sartre, op. cit., p. 32. [The passage is obscure but could be read as "Consciousness and the world are given simultaneously: The outside world as it enters consciousness is relative to our ways of perceiving it."—Editor's note]

9. Edmund Husserl, *Ideas—General Introduction to Pure Phenomenology* (London, 1969), pp. 105–06.

Other Voices, Other Rooms

Gerald Graff

A professor at the University of Illinois at Chicago, Gerald Graff has made a career of seeking coherence through controversy. His hotly debated book, Literature against Itself: Literary Ideas in Modern Society *(1979), argues against trends in literary criticism that have driven academic research for some years. "Other Voices, Other Rooms" is taken from* Beyond the Culture Wars: How Teaching the Conflicts Can Revitalize American Education *(1992), which challenges institutional structures and ideological stances that discourage dialogue within the academy.* Beyond the Culture Wars *won the American Book Award in 1993.*

From his vantage point as a teacher of undergraduates, Graff views the curriculum, especially the general-education curriculum, as disjointed and confusing. The "cognitive dissonance" undergraduates experience could be the source of a deeper, more coherent education, Graff believes, if the intellectual and cultural debates that drive academic research were brought into the classroom. "Contrast," says Graff, "is fundamental to understanding, for no subject, idea, or text is an island." Although such contrasts can sometimes be brought into the classroom by exceptional teachers, Graff is convinced that the surer source is an institutional atmosphere and structure that encourages dialogue among scholars.

For Graff the goal is not consensus, but the kind of coherence that is won through genuine and explicit conversation: "One of the oddest things about the university is that it calls itself a community of scholars yet organizes its curriculum in a way that conceals the links of the community from those who are not already aware of them."

Reprinted from *Beyond the Culture Wars: How Teaching the Conflicts Can Revitalize American Education* (1993), W.W. Norton & Company.

1   An undergraduate tells of an art history course in which the instruc-   1
      tor observed one day, "As we now know, the idea that knowl-
      edge can be objective is a positivist myth that has been exploded
by postmodern thought." It so happens the student is concurrently enrolled
in a political science course in which the instructor speaks confidently
about the objectivity of his discipline as if it had not been "exploded" at
all. What do you do? the student is asked. "What else can I do?" he says.
"I trash objectivity in art history, and I presuppose it in political science."

   A second undergraduate describes a history teacher who makes a
point of stressing the superiority of Western culture in developing the
ideas of freedom, democracy, and free-market capitalism that the rest
of the world is now rushing to imitate. She also has a literature teacher
who describes such claims of Western supremacy as an example of the
hegemonic ideology by which the United States arrogates the right to
police the world. When asked which course she prefers, she replies,
"Well, I'm getting an A in both."

   To some of us these days, the moral of these stories would be that
students have become cynical relativists who care less about convictions than about grades and careers. In fact, if anything is surprising,
it is that more students do not behave in this cynical fashion, for the
established curriculum encourages it. The disjunction of the curriculum is a far more powerful source of relativism than any doctrine
preached by the faculty.

   One of the oddest things about the university is that it calls itself
a community of scholars yet organizes its curriculum in a way that conceals the links of the community from those who are not already aware
of them. The courses being given at any moment on a campus represent any number of rich potential conversations within and across the
disciplines. But since students experience these conversations only as
a series of monologues, the conversations become actual only for the
minority who can reconstruct them on their own. No self-respecting
educator would deliberately design a system guaranteed to keep students dependent on the whim of the individual instructor. Yet this is
precisely the effect of a curriculum composed of courses that are not
in dialogue with one another.

Ships in the Night

5   The problem deepens when teachers are further apart. A student today   5
    can go from a course in which the universality of Western culture is

taken for granted (and therefore not articulated) to a course in which it is taken for granted (and therefore not articulated) that such claims of universality are fallacious and deceptive. True, for the best students the resulting cognitive dissonance is no great problem. The chance to try on a variety of clashing ideas, to see what they feel like, is one of the most exciting opportunities an education can provide; it can be especially rewarding for students who come to the university with already developed skills at summarizing and weighing arguments and synthesizing conflicting positions on their own. Many students, however, become confused or indifferent and react as the above two students did by giving their teachers whatever they seem to want even though it is contradictory.

Then, too, when their teachers' conflicting perspectives do not enter into a common discussion, students may not even be able to infer what is wanted. Like everyone else, teachers tend to betray their crucial assumptions as much in what they do not say, what they take to go without saying, as in what they say explicitly. To students who are not at home in the academic intellectual community, the significance of these silences and exclusions is likely to be intimidating, if it does not elude them entirely.

Furthermore, in an academic environment in which there is increasingly less unspoken common ground, it may not even be clear to students that their teachers are in conflict, for different words may be used by several teachers for the same concepts or the same words for different concepts. If students do not know that "positivism" has in some quarters become a derogatory buzzword for any belief in objectivity, they may not become aware that the art history and political science teachers in the above example are in disagreement. A student who goes from one humanist who speaks of "traditional moral themes" to another who speaks of "patriarchal discursive practices" may not become aware that the two teachers are actually referring to the same thing. Students in such cases are being exposed to some of the major cultural debates of their time, but in a way that makes it difficult to recognize them *as* debates.

Note, too, that the instructors in these situations are protected by the insularity of their classrooms, which makes it unnecessary, if not impossible, for them to confront the challenges to their assumptions that would be represented by their colleagues. Professors do not expect such immunity from peer criticism when they publish their work or appear at professional conferences. It is only in the classroom that such immunity is taken for granted as if it were a form of academic freedom. Since students enjoy no such protection, one can hardly blame them if they, too, protect themselves by compartmentalizing the contradictions to which they are exposed, as my first student did when he became an objectivist in one course and all antiobjectionist on the other.

I recall a semester late in college when I took a course in modern poetry taught by a New Critic, a follower of T. S. Eliot, and a course in seventeenth-century English literature taught by an older scholar who resented Eliot and the New Critics, who had attacked John Milton for his grandiloquence and lack of irony. Three days a week between ten and eleven I listened with dutiful respect to the New Critic's theories of irony and paradox, and between eleven and twelve I listened with dutiful respect to the argument that these New Critical theories had no application whatsoever to Milton, Dryden, and their contemporaries. What was really odd, however, is that I hardly focused at the time on the fact that my two teachers were in disagreement.

10   Was I just ridiculously slow to comprehend the critical issues that were at stake? Perhaps so, but since no one was asking me to think about the relationship between the two courses, I did not. If my teachers disagreed, this was their business—a professional dispute that did not concern me. Each course was challenging enough on its own terms, and to have raised the question of how they related would have only risked needlessly multiplying difficulties for myself. Then, too, for me to ask my teachers about their differences might have seemed impertinent and ill-mannered—who was I to impugn their authority? Only later did it dawn on me that studying different centuries and clashing theories without having them brought together had made things much *harder* since it removed the element of contrast.

Contrast is fundamental to understanding, for no subject, idea, or text is an island. In order to become intelligible "in itself," it needs to be seen in its relation to other subjects, ideas, and texts. When this relation of interdependence is obscured because different courses do not communicate, subjects, ideas, and texts become harder to comprehend, if not unintelligible. We think we are making things simpler for students by abstracting periods, texts, and authors from their relationships with other periods, texts, and authors so that we can study them closely in a purified space. But the very act of isolating an object from its contrasting background and relations makes it hard to grasp. Since we cannot talk about everything all at once, subjects do have to be distinguished and to that extent isolated from one another. But this isolation does not have to preclude connections and relations. It is hard to grasp the modernity of modern literature unless one can compare it with something that is not modern.

That is why teachers in modern periods need nonmodernists (and vice versa) in order to make their subjects intelligible to their students, just as teachers who defend the culture of the West need the teachers who criticize it (and vice versa). Without the criticisms, after all, there would be no need to defend the West to begin with. Insofar as neither a defense nor a critique of tradition makes sense apart from the dialogue these positions are engaged in, a curriculum which removes that dialogue from view defeats the goals of traditionalists and revisionists alike. It is true that fundamental conflicts like these may turn out to be nonnegotiable. But no one knows this in advance, and even if a dispute proves to be nonnegotiable, to learn that this is the case is not worthless.

I noted earlier that among the factors that make academic culture more confusing today than in the past is not only that there is more controversy but that there is even controversy about what can legitimately be considered controversial. Traditionalists are often angry that there should even *be* a debate over the canon, while revisionists are often angry that there should even be a debate over "political correctness," or the relevance of ideology and politics to their subjects. A recent feminist critic says she finds it "astonishing" that it still needs repeating at this late date that "the perspective assumed to be 'universal' which has dominated knowledge . . . has actually been male and culture-bound."[1] Since the feminist argument, however, is that we still fail to see how culture-bound our thinking is, it is hard to see why this critic should be astonished that she still needs to make the point. Another political critic writes that "we are perhaps already weary of the avalanche of papers, books, and conferences entitled 'The Politics of X,' and we have recently begun to question that most hallowed of all political slogans on the left, 'everything is political.'"[2] Yet the idea of politics that this critic and her audience are already "weary of" is one that most people have not yet encountered and might well find incomprehensible. The "advanced" academic and the layperson (or the traditional academic) are so far apart that what is already old news to one has not yet become intelligible to the other.

Imagine how this affects students who, at the moment they are negotiating the difficult transition from the lay culture to the academic culture, must also negotiate the unpredictable and unfathomable discrepancies between academic departments and factions. When there is no correlation of the different discourses to which students are exposed, it becomes especially difficult for them to infer which assumptions are safe and which are likely to be challenged. The problem is that knowledge of what is and is not considered potentially or legitimately controversial cannot be learned a priori; you cannot get it out of E. D. Hirsch's *Dictionary of Cultural Literacy.* Such knowledge comes only through interaction with a community, and that interaction is precisely what is prevented by a disconnected system of courses. Then, too, assumptions about what is and is not potentially controversial tend to change from one moment to the next and one subcommunity to the next, and they are changing at a faster rate today than in the past.

15   Thomas S. Kuhn in *The Structure of Scientific Revolutions* describes   15 moments of crisis or "paradigm shift" in the sciences, when "a law that cannot be demonstrated to one group of scientists may . . . seem intuitively obvious to another."[3] The fate of Kuhn's own book is an interesting case in point. Even as his sociological account of scientific paradigm change has been treated as virtual holy writ by many literary theorists (for a while it seemed almost obligatory to begin every book or essay with a respectful bow to Kuhn), his work has often been ignored or dismissed by scientists and philosophers in reducing scientific discovery to "mob psychology." As the controversy over Kuhn has revealed, both the literati and the scientists have remained largely walled up within their clashing assumptions about objectivity, the smugness of which might have been punctured had these parties been forced to argue with each other in their teaching. This mutual smugness has persisted in the sniper fire that continues to be exchanged over the concept of objectivity and the extent to which knowledge is independent of the social situation of the knower; revisionists sneer at the concept and traditionalists sneer at the very idea of questioning it.

The question neither group seems to ask is what it must be like to be a student caught in the crossfire between these conflicting views of objectivity, each one prone to present itself as "intuitively obvious" and uncontroversial. A rhetoric scholar, Gregory Colomb, has studied the disorientation experienced by a bright high school graduate who, after doing well in a humanities course as a freshman at the University of Chicago, tried to apply her mastery to a social science course, only to come up with a grade of C.[4] Imagine trying to write an academic paper when you sense that almost anything you say can be used against you and that the intellectual moves that got you an A in existentialist philosophy may get you a C minus and a dirty look in Skinnerian behaviorism.

Consider the fact that the passive voice that is so standard in sociology writing ("it will be contended in this paper . . .") has been perennially rebuked in English courses.[5] Or consider something so apparently trivial as the convention of using the present tense to describe actions in literature and philosophy and the past tense to describe them in history. Plato *says* things in literary and philosophical accounts while in historical accounts he *said* them. Experienced writers become so accustomed to such tense shifting that it seems a simple matter, but it reflects deep-rooted and potentially controversial differences between disciplines. Presumably, Plato speaks in the present in literary and philosophical contexts because ideas there are considered timeless; only when we move over to history does it start to matter that the writer is dead.[6] We English teachers write "tense shift" in the margin when student writers betray uncertainty about this convention, but how do we expect them to "get" it when they pass from the very different time zones of history and philosophy/English with no engagement of the underlying issues?

One of the most frequent comments teachers make on student papers is "What's your evidence?" But nobody would ever finish a piece of writing if it were necessary to supply evidence for everything being said, so in order to write, one must acquire a sense of which statements have to be supported by evidence (or further argument) and which ones a writer can get away with because they are already taken for granted by the imagined audience. What happens, then, when a writer has no way of knowing whether an assumption that he or she got away with with audience A will also be conceded by audience B? It is no wonder that students protect themselves from the insecurity of such a situation by "psyching out" each course as it comes—and then forgetting about it as soon as possible after the final exam in order to clear their minds for the seemingly unrelated demands of the next set of courses.

It is only ideas and reasoning processes but the recall of basic information as well that figure to be impaired by disjunctive curricular organization. To use the jargon of information theory, an information system that is experienced as an unrelated series of signals will be weak in the kind of redundancy that is needed for information to be retained. Faced with a curriculum overloaded with data and weak in redundancy, students may find it difficult to know which items of information they are supposed to remember. Then, too, a student may be exposed to the same information in several courses while failing to recognize it as "the same," since it is contextualized differently in each course. When students fail to identify a cultural literacy item on a test, the problem may be not that they don't know the information but that they don't know they know it; they may have learned it in a context whose relevance to the test question they don't recognize. What is learned seems so specific to a particular course that it is difficult for students to see its application beyond.

20   The critic Kenneth Burke once compared the intellectual life of a   20
culture to a parlor in which different guests are forever dropping in and out. As the standard curriculum represents the intellectual life, however, there is no parlor; the hosts congregate in separate rooms with their acolytes and keep their differences and agreements to themselves. Making one's way through the standard curriculum is rather like trying to comprehend a phone conversation by listening at only one end.[7] You can manage it up to a point, but this is hardly the ideal way to do it.

To venture a final comparison, it is as if you were to try to learn the game of baseball by being shown a series of rooms in which you see each component of the game separately: pitchers going through their windups in one room; hitters swinging their bats in the next; then infielders, outfielders, umpires, fans, field announcers, ticket scalpers, broadcasters, hot-dog vendors, and so on. You see them all in their different roles, but since you see them separately you get no clear idea of what the game actually looks like or why the players do what they do. No doubt you would come away with a very imperfect understanding of baseball under these conditions. Yet it does not seem far-fetched to compare these circumstances with the ones students face when they are exposed to a series of disparate courses, subjects, and perspectives and expected not only to infer the rules of the academic-intellectual game but to play it competently themselves.

The Declaration of Independence

Thomas Jefferson

Thomas Jefferson (1743–1826) was born in Virginia in a well-to-do land-owning family. He graduated from the College of William and Mary and then studied law. When he was elected at age 26 to the Virginia legislature, he had already begun forming his revolutionary views. As a delegate to the Second Continental Congress in 1775, he was the principal writer of the Declaration of Independence, which was adopted on July 4, 1776. After the Revolution he was Governor of Virginia from 1775 to 1777. From then until 1801, when he was elected the third President of the United States, Jefferson served in various federal positions, including secretary of state and ambassador to France. Jefferson was influential as an advocate of democracy in the early years of the United States, although his ideas were more typical of the eighteenth century "enlightened man" than original. The Declaration of Independence shows his ideas and style as well as those of the times and remains not merely an important historical document but also an eloquent statement of the founding principles of this country.

1   When in the course of human events, it becomes necessary for one people to dissolve the political bands which have connected them with another, and to assume among the powers of the earth, the separate and equal station to which the Laws of Nature and of Nature's God entitle them, a decent respect to the opinions of mankind requires that they should declare the causes which impel them to the separation.

We hold these truths to be self-evident, that all men are created equal, that they are endowed by their Creator with certain inalienable rights, that among these are life, liberty, and the pursuit of happiness. That to secure these rights, governments are instituted among men, deriving their just powers from the consent of the governed. That whenever any form of government becomes destructive of these ends, it is the right of the people to alter or to abolish it, and to institute new government, laying its foundation on such principles and organizing its powers in such form, as to them shall seem most likely to effect their safety and happiness. Prudence, indeed, will dictate that governments long established should not be changed for light and transient causes; and accordingly all experience hath shown, that mankind are more disposed to suffer, while evils are sufferable, than to right themselves by abolishing the forms to which they are accustomed. But when a long train of abuses and usurpations, pursuing invariably the same object, evinces a design to reduce them under absolute despotism, it is their right, it is their duty, to throw off such government, and to provide new guards for their future security. Such has been the patient sufferance of these Colonies; and such is now the necessity which constrains them to alter their former systems of government. The history of the present King of Great Britain is a history of repeated injuries and usurpations, all having in direct object the establishment of an absolute tyranny over these States. To prove this, let facts be submitted to a candid world.

He has refused his assent to laws, the most wholesome and necessary for the public good.

He has forbidden his Governors to pass laws of immediate and pressing importance, unless suspended in their operation till his assent should be obtained; and when so suspended, he has utterly neglected to attend to them.

5   He has refused to pass other laws for the accommodation of large   5
districts of people, unless those people would relinquish the right of representation in the legislature, a right inestimable to them and formidable to tyrants only.

He has called together legislative bodies at places unusual, uncomfortable, and distant from the depository of their public records, for the sole purpose of fatiguing them into compliance with his measures.

He has dissolved representative houses repeatedly, for opposing with manly firmness his invasions on the rights of the people.

He has refused for a long time, after such dissolutions, to cause others to be elected; whereby the legislative powers, incapable of annihilation, have returned to the people at large for their exercise; the State remaining in the meantime exposed to all the dangers of invasion from without and convulsions within.

He has endeavoured to prevent the population of these states; for that purpose obstructing the laws for naturalization of foreigners; refusing to pass others to encourage their migration hither, and raising the conditions of new appropriations of lands.

10 He has obstructed the administration of justice, by refusing his assent to laws for establishing judiciary powers.

He has made judges dependent on his will alone, for the tenure of their offices, and the amount and payment of their salaries.

He has erected a multitude of new offices, and sent hither swarms of officers to harass our people, and eat out their substance.

He has kept among us, in times of peace, standing armies without the consent of our legislatures.

He has affected to render the military independent of and superior to the civil power.

15 He has combined with others to subject us to a jurisdiction foreign of our constitution, and unacknowledged by our laws; giving his assent to their acts of pretended legislation:

For quartering large bodies of armed troops among us:

For protecting them, by a mock trial, from punishment for any murders which they should commit on the inhabitants of these States:

For cutting off our trade with all parts of the world:

For imposing taxes on us without our consent:

20 For depriving us in many cases of the benefits of trial by jury:

For transporting us beyond seas to be tried for pretended offences:

For abolishing the free system of English laws in a neighbouring Province, establishing therein an arbitrary government, and enlarging its boundaries so as to render it at once an example and fit instrument for introducing the same absolute rule into these Colonies:

For taking away our Charters, abolishing our most valuable laws, and altering fundamentally the forms of our governments:

For suspending our own legislatures, and declaring themselves invested with power to legislate for us in all cases whatsoever.

25 He has abdicated government here, by declaring us out of his protection and waging war against us.

He has plundered our seas, ravaged our coasts, burnt our towns, and destroyed the lives of our people.

He is at this time transporting large armies of foreign mercenaries to complete the works of death, desolation, and tyranny, already begun with circumstances of cruelty and perfidy scarcely parallelled in the most barbarous ages, and totally unworthy the head of a civilized nation.

He has constrained our fellow citizens taken captive on the high seas to bear arms against their country, to become the executioners of their friends and brethren, or to fall themselves by their hands.

He has excited domestic insurrections amongst us, and has endeavoured to bring on the inhabitants of our frontiers, the merciless Indian savages, whose known rule of warfare, is an undistinguished destruction of all ages, sexes, and conditions.

30   In every stage of these oppressions we have petitioned for redress   30 in the most humble terms: our repeated petitions have been answered only by repeated injury. A prince whose character is thus marked by every act which may define a tyrant is unfit to be the ruler of a free people.

Nor have we been wanting in attention to our British brethren. We have warned them from time to time of attempts by their legislature to extend an unwarrantable jurisdiction over us. We have reminded them of the circumstances of our emigration and settlement here. We have appealed to their native justice and magnanimity, and we have conjured them by the ties of our common kindred to disavow these usurpations, which would inevitably interrupt our connections and correspondence. They too have been deaf to the voice of justice and of consanguinity. We must, therefore, acquiesce in the necessity, which denounces our separation, and hold them, as we hold the rest of mankind, enemies in war, in peace friends.

We, therefore, the Representatives of the United States of America, in General Congress assembled, appealing to the Supreme Judge of the world for the rectitude of our intentions, do, in the name, and by authority of the good people of these Colonies, solemnly publish and declare, That these United Colonies are, and of right ought to be, Free and Independent States; that they are absolved from all allegiance to the British Crown, and that all political connection between them and the state of Great Britain, is and ought to be totally dissolved; and that as Free and Independent States, they have full power to levy war, conclude peace, contract alliances, establish commerce, and to do all other acts and things which Independent States may of right do. And for the support of this declaration, with a firm reliance on the protection of Divine Providence, we mutually pledge to each other our lives, our fortunes, and our sacred honor.

Personality and Individual Writing Processes

George H. Jensen
John K. DiTiberio

George H. Jensen is Assistant Professor in the Division of Developmental Studies at Georgia State University in Atlanta. He has published essays in Proof *and* MBTI News. *John K. DiTiberio is a Staff Psychologist at the Counseling Service, University of Illinois at Chicago. He has published essays in the* Journal of College Student Personnel *and* MBTI News; *he is the current editor of* MBTI News.

[1] Though composition theorists concur that writing should be taught as a process, they seem to agree little on the nature of that process. Pearl G. Aldrich, in a recent article in this journal, surveyed the writing habits of business executives and concluded that their writing suffered from inadequate planning: "These responses, therefore, showed that the majority of these, and presumably other, adult writers seem not to know the value of deciding in advance of writing what their purpose, audience, and point will be."[1] Peter Elbow, on the other hand, feels that writers often become blocked by too much planning. He advises: "Write fast. Don't waste any time or energy on how to organize it, what to start with, paragraphing, wording, spelling, grammar, or any other matters of presentation. Just get things down helter-skelter."[2] Both authors describe distinctly different writing processes that apparently work for them, but what would happen if Aldrich were a student in Elbow's class or Elbow a student in Aldrich's class? To state the question more generally, how can we teach a classroom full of individuals, each of whom needs to approach the process of writing in his or her own way?

Three possible approaches to the problem can be suggested. We

Reprinted from *College Composition and Communication* 35, no. 3 (1983), by permission of the National Council of Teachers of English.

can advise all students to write as we do and teach a single writing process. The process will, if we are lucky, work for some students. It will, however, not work for others, for it will force them to write in a way that will fail to draw upon their strengths. Or we can suggest that students try a variety of approaches, as W. Ross Winterowd does when discussing outlines: "Some writers prepare detailed outlines before they begin to write, but most don't. Most writers use some kind of brief outline or notes, but some writers don't. You just can't generalize. However, outlines can be useful."[3] Winterowd's approach is preferable, but it also has limitations. If students feel confused about how to write an essay, will such open-ended advice confuse them further? If students rigidly cling to ineffective writing processes, will teachers be reluctant to suggest a new approach? Will teachers of writing become as ineffective as permissive parents?

A third approach is to develop an understanding of how people differ and how these differences affect the writing process. We can then more effectively individualize writing instruction. In recent years, various conceptual systems for identifying learning styles have been introduced into the classroom.[4] Some teachers have thus discovered practical tools for understanding differences in how students learn and how they function best. One such system, which we feel can also explain many variations in individual writing processes, will be presented here.

Jung's Theory of Psychological Types

Teachers often hesitate to use personality theory to improve their instruction, perhaps with good reason. Armchair psychologists who use labels loosely, sometimes vengefully, are dangerous and too plentiful. We do not encourage their proliferation. However, a conceptual framework that identifies personality types or learning styles can, if used judiciously, provide teachers with valuable insight into how students differ. For this purpose, we believe that the system that C. G. Jung presented in *Psychological Types*[5] and that Isabel Myers later refined[6] holds promise for improving instruction and research in the field of composition.

5   Jung's system is promising for several reasons. It has a solid grounding in a theory of personality and yet can be understood and used, when appropriate caution is observed, by teachers not formally trained in psychology. Second, the system humanistically appreciates differences. It does *not* label some people as adequate and others as inadequate. Third, when applied to education, the system can help teachers

to understand why individual students are having difficulties. The theory identifies important aspects of learning style that have already been applied to reading skills, study skills, and academic motivation.[7] It has also proven useful for increasing retention of at least one group of at-risk students.[8] Finally, the Myers-Briggs Type Indicator (MBTI),[9] which will be discussed later, has been found useful in other fields of research and can be easily incorporated into research on composition. Teachers and researchers should receive training before using the MBTI. Yet, even if teachers do not administer the instrument, the theoretical model presented in this article can still have a profound effect on how they teach.

The typology of personality consists of four bi-polar dimensions, each of which represents opposing psychological processes: Extraversion-Introversion (ways of focusing one's energy), Sensing—Intuition (ways of perceiving), Thinking—Feeling (ways of making decisions), and Judging—Perceiving (ways of approaching tasks in the outer world). The theory behind the dimensions can be explained with the metaphor of handedness. Though we have two hands and use each every day, we begin at an early age to use one of them more frequently. Consequently, the preferred hand develops more quickly and adequately. Similarly, we begin at an early age to prefer one psychological process of each bi-polar scale over the other, e.g., extraversion over introversion. Though we all use extraversion and introversion each day, we come to feel more comfortable with one and use it more frequently. Thus, that preferred process matures more rapidly. Since our unpreferred process matures more slowly and may even remain undeveloped, we are often less competent and feel more awkward when using it.

Our development as individuals, learners and writers comes as we gradually learn to employ both our preferred and our unpreferred processes. Myers believed that healthy personality development consists of learning to use our preferences progressively more expertly, but not rigidly or exclusively.[10] It is important, she believed, to develop our unpreferred psychological processes as a supplement.

In a perception analogous to Myers' statement about development of personality, we have observed that writers can perform better and with less anxiety when they employ primarily their preferred processes in early stages, while still generating ideas, and then use their unpreferred processes in later stages to round out their writing. Writers become anxious or emotionally blocked when they overuse one process to the neglect of its opposite (e.g., use feeling to the neglect of thinking), or when they fail to use the strengths of their preferences, which

Myers would call their individual gifts.[11] If teachers deliver the same advice to all students, they may, despite good intentions, render more harm than good. Then students will begin to write as the teachers wish, not necessarily as they write best.

Setting for our Observations

Our early reading of Jung and Myers suggested hypotheses about how an individual's personality might be related to his or her writing process. Since then, we have clarified and refined these hypotheses at both the University of Illinois at Chicago and Georgia State University in the following settings:

1. A thesis support group. At a weekly meeting, graduate students discuss difficulties that they are having in writing their theses. Participants take the MBTI, and the results are used to help explain writing blocks and suggest remedies. To date, twenty-five students have participated in the group.
2. Workshops on approaches to writing, designed to develop prewriting strategies and reduce writing blocks. The participants' personality types are used to explain the cognitive processes behind writing blocks and to suggest methods for overcoming these blocks. To date, seventy-seven students and university staff have participated.
3. A writing clinic. Students who seek writing instruction through the Academic Skills Program, a division of the University of Illinois at Chicago Counseling Service, are administered the MBTI. The instructor uses the results to help the student to develop an effective writing process, reduce writing anxiety, and overcome writing blocks. To date, thirty-one students have taken the MBTI and discussed their writing processes and essays with a writing instructor.
4. A developmental writing program. Since beginning initial drafts of this paper, the senior author has begun reaching classes for developmental students at Georgia State University. The model has been found useful with eighty-two undergraduates to relieve writing anxiety and specific writing blocks, and to provide remedial instruction in writing.

10   In all of these settings, students reported that knowledge of their personality type and how it relates to writing helped to reduce writing   10

anxiety and overcome writing blocks. However, the findings should be viewed cautiously until tested experimentally.

Extraversion-Introversion

The first dimension of Jung's system identifies a person's general orientation toward life. "Extraverts" (Jung's spelling is preserved here) predominantly focus their energy outward toward interacting with people and things. They tend to value outer experience (talking and acting) so highly that they often leap into tasks with little planning, then rely on trial and error to complete the task. Since they spend more time dealing with outer experience rather than inner experience (reflecting and observing), they think most clearly and develop more ideas while in action or in conversation. "Introverts" predominantly focus their energy inward through consideration and contemplation. More cautious about the outer world, they anticipate and reflect before becoming involved with it, in order to avoid errors. They think best and develop more ideas when alone, uninterrupted by people and events.

Classroom teachers who allow for discussion and activity with other students meet the extraverts' need for doing. Those that give advance notice and time for reflection ("wait time") allow introverts to consider before becoming involved in activities or discussions. Estimates of both the general American population and the average public school classroom suggest that there are between two and three extraverts for every introvert.[12] Teachers, however, are more evenly balanced between the two.[13]

As predicted by theory, the extraverts with whom we have worked write with little planning, though they often feel guilty about not writing from outlines. They sometimes describe their writing process as "quick and dirty" or the "easy way." They tend to generate ideas best from talking about the topic, interviewing others, or presenting an extemporaneous report. Extraverts often find freewriting a good method for developing ideas, for they think better when writing quickly, impulsively, and uncritically. Their pauses while writing are more frequently instances of an inability to generate ideas rather than moments of productive planning. They also benefit from talking the subject out or, as Peter Elbow suggests, from writing about having nothing to write about. Some even "write" better by speaking their first drafts into a tape recorder.

If expected to perform traditional prewriting strategies, such as outlining or tagmemic analysis, most extraverts we have observed do so more easily *after* writing a first draft as a means of clarifying rather than generating ideas. Discussing drafts seems to help them both to realize the need for revision and to understand what needs to be revised. Some may not revise unless they receive oral feedback. They are blocked less frequently when they can allow their first drafts to be relatively unfocused, filled with a wide range of data or ideas. In later drafts, they can more easily bring balance to their writing by selecting the most important ideas or data from the first draft and writing about each in greater depth.

15   A member of our thesis support group exemplifies the difficulties 15 that many extraverts have with writing. One of her first comments in the group was that she disliked writing because of the isolation and the lack of oral feedback. Writing seemed too isolated a process for her, and she often became blocked. Her blocks, interestingly, were usually overcome by some form of extraverted activity, not by contemplation or planning. She developed the structure for the first draft of her thesis by preparing for and presenting a talk on the topic. She overcame another block by writing an abstract for a later talk. After reading her first draft, her advisor heard her present her findings at a campus symposium. He told her that he understood the oral presentation better than the written version. The talk and her advisor's oral feedback helped her to reevaluate her first draft, focus it, and make appropriate revisions.

In our experience, introverts generally have less difficulty with writing than extraverts, perhaps because they tend to follow the composing process as it is traditionally taught. Their basic writing process often follows the prewriting-writing-rewriting pattern. They generally want most of their ideas clarified before writing. They can and should be encouraged to develop ideas while writing, but they tend to find writing easier when much of the essay is written mentally before they put pen to paper. After they start to write, they pause frequently to plan further or to anticipate the direction of the essay. They may become dissatisfied with a first sentence or transition not because it is poorly written but because they are unsure about where it is leading. They tend to write alone, asking for advice reluctantly and then perhaps only from close friends or during private sessions with a teacher. Because introverts usually generate their ideas in isolation, we have found that their essays can be improved if they revise to connect their ideas with lived experience, perhaps by adding descriptions of experiences, as an extravert would tend to do naturally.

The introvert's writing difficulties, though seemingly less frequent, can be equally frustrating. After six years of research and planning, an introvert in our thesis support group still had difficulty writing his thesis because he wanted to have practically every word thought out before putting anything on paper. He had, with only moderate difficulty, written many graduate school papers in this way. With the longer and more complex Ph.D. thesis, however, he became locked into his introversion and did little but plan. Introverts blocked by too much reflection can be encouraged to write, at least temporarily, in a more extraverted way, to leap into writing even without planning and discover their meaning as they write. They may, thus, achieve a more productive balance between introverted planning and extraverted activity.

Sensing—Intuition

"Sensing" and "intuition" represent alternative ways of perceiving or taking in information. Sensing involves the direct and conscious use of seeing, hearing, tasting, smelling, or touching to record carefully the particulars of one's environment. Intuition involves the use of impressions, hunches, and the imagination to perceive patterns, relationships, and configurations. Sensing types are often described as concrete, detail-oriented, practical and matter-of-fact, while intuitives are seen as abstract, idea-oriented, and imaginative. But the distinction between the two is clearer when we focus less on the behaviors and character traits and more on the perceptual processes underlying them.

Both factual data and theoretical concepts may be employed by each type, but with different emphasis. In telling a story, the starting point for sensing types is a solid grounding in reality: they begin with what happened, when, to whom, and, in sequence, how it occurred. In contrast, intuitives are likely to report first what the sensing type saves for last (or neglects): the meaning behind the event in the context of other similar events. For them, details and examples are mundane unless fitted into a conceptual scheme. At times, they may overlook them entirely, caught up in the inspiration of their idea.

20   In school work, detailed and factual material that is concretely ver-   20
ifiable suits sensing types; abstractions and conceptual complexities stimulate intuitives. Sensing types enjoy putting to use what they have learned; intuitive types like new learning just because it is different. Soundness of understanding is a value to the sensing; quickness of

understanding and originality are sought by intuitives. Sensors re-check data to insure certainty. Intuitives trust first impressions and hunches. Because of these differences, Myers discovered that sensing types experience more difficulty in learning to read, taking tests (especially standardized, timed tests), and meeting other traditional standards of academic achievement. But it is important to note that Myers believes this difficulty is not related to their competence as much as it is to how they are taught.[14] For example, intuitive teachers often fail to provide sensing types with the concrete examples that they need in order to understand concepts.

As with extraverts, sensing types have been estimated to outnumber intuitives at least two to one in the general American population and in public school classrooms. Teachers are more evenly balanced between the two, but more intuitive teachers are found in higher education.[15]

In our experience, sensing types write to the best of their ability when given explicit, detailed, and specific instructions. General directions may lead them to become blocked unless they ask the instructor for clarification or in some way translate the directions into a precise and complete set of expectations. One sensing type who was receiving help from an intuitive instructor in our writing clinic complained: "When I came in here, I thought that you were going to tell me exactly how to improve my writing." He wanted the instructor to give him a clear, step-by-step procedure for improving his writing. Certainly, this sensing student needs to learn that writing is more than following rules and that good writing cannot be programmed. On the other hand, the intuitive instructor would probably have been more effective with this student if he had given detailed instructions and concrete advice on how to generate and organize ideas. Our experience has shown that clear and specific expectations in the early stages of instruction provide sensing students a sound base from which they are more likely, in later contacts, to respond imaginatively to open-ended assignments. Conversely, intuitives pay more careful attention to regulations if they know their original ideas do have an outlet for expression.

When preparing to write, sensing types collect large amounts of data, for each fact seems equally important. Their first drafts similarly tend to be a recording of facts not always clearly related to a central theme or idea. They may find writing easier when given a specific framework to follow, such as the five-paragraph essay. If over-anxious, they may try to apply such patterns too rigidly. They may become blocked when they can only think of four paragraphs, or when they have six and cannot make them fit the pattern. Even during a first draft, sensing types attend closely to mechanics and often view revising as merely "correcting" or proofreading. When revising, they may need to be encouraged to explain, as an intuitive would naturally, the implications of their data or ideas by adding or rewriting topic sentences, thesis statements, or summaries.

Sensing types are usually at their best dealing with concrete information, but preferably in sequential step-by-step fashion. They therefore can become overwhelmed by too large a set of data. A sensing type in our thesis support group found it difficult to know which facts to include in his initial draft. In part because of his anxiety about the "correct" way to prepare a thesis, each piece of collected data held an importance of its own simply because it was factual. The criteria that he had initially developed for inclusion or exclusion of such data struck him as arbitrary. Exasperated, he settled on the only solution that seemed reasonable: he would include as many details as possible and let his advisor decide what to cut. We suggested that he include only the details needed to replicate the study and talked about how to apply this criterion. He then felt that he better understood what his committee was likely to expect.

25   Intuitive types, on the other hand, write best when given general instructions from which they can create their own goals. Developing a unique approach to the topic seems to be an important part of their prewriting, but they can become blocked by their need for originality. Several intuitives with whom we have worked become blocked while struggling to find an original way to write a commonplace memorandum. At their best, intuitives generate ideas almost unconsciously and write quickly, letting one idea trigger another with little attention to mechanics. Their first drafts may contain only ideas and generalities unsupported by concrete examples, which are left for later drafts or neglected entirely. When revising, they need to resolve unnecessary complexities, check their facts, correct mechanical errors, and clarify their ideas by supplying concrete examples.

One intuitive member of our thesis support group said that the more she reads, the more complex her topic becomes and the more she is confused. She explained the escalating complexity of her ideas by saying, "Things can become fuzzy very quickly." Unless these complexities are resolved, usually by verifying the theories with illustrations (i.e., applying them to a concrete situation), the writing of intuitive types may be confusing and difficult to read, as in the treatises of many brilliant but obscure philosophers.

As with introverts, intuitives with whom we have worked in general have less difficulty with writing than sensing types. Because words and phrases are abstract representations of reality, they are more naturally interesting to intuitives, who become intrigued by symbolic and often subtle meanings implied but not always explicitly stated. Sensing types' difficulties with writing often emerge from a lack of development of what for them is a less preferred process: the quick intuitive grasp of the possible, recognition of the intangible, and adept "reading between the lines." In contrast, writing difficulties for intuitives frequently relate to their tendency to define unclearly the problem they are discussing, and to neglect illustrative examples of the perspective they are describing.

Thinking—Feeling

"Thinking" and "feeling" describe how one makes evaluations, judgments, and decisions. Thinking types prefer to make decisions on the basis of objective criteria. They want to do what is right, even if feelings are hurt or group harmony is disrupted. They excel at the process of categorizing, whether facts and details or ideas. Feeling types prefer to make decisions on the basis of subjective factors, such as their personal values, the values of others involved, and the effect of the decision on group harmony. They excel at the process of facilitating interpersonal relationships.

In schools, thinking types tend to be particularly motivated when an assignment engages their mind analytically and is presented with a clear and logical rationale, and when they are treated fairly. Feeling types tend to be particularly motivated when given special encouragement and when projects relate to what they care most about. Certainly all students will be inclined to perform better when invited both to achieve an objective understanding of the material and to become personally invested in its application. The balance needed varies according to the type of student. An absence of the former invitation would most seriously hinder thinking types, and of the latter invitation, feeling types.

30　　In general public school classrooms, thinking and feeling types　30 appear in roughly equal numbers, with percentages among males tending slightly toward thinking and among females toward feeling. In part because there are more females among school teachers, feeling types tend to predominate in this group.[16] McCaulley found that academic GPA's were higher among high school students whose preference on this dimension was clear and unimbivalent, whether toward thinking or feeling.[17]

Unless assigned topics for writing are presented with clear objective performance standards, thinking types may view the writing project as a meaningless academic exercise and become blocked. They usually organize their ideas or findings into categories or clearly formulated organizational structures. They also tend to focus on the clarity of content rather than on whether or not the audience will find it interesting. As a result, their first drafts may read as dry academic treatises or outlines in which key points are numbered. To achieve a balance, they may need to enliven their writing with vivid, personal examples when revising.

If feeling types do not select a topic that they can relate to their personal values, they may become blocked. What is most important to them in writing is to connect with another human being through their communication. When writing, they tend to focus more on how their audience may react to their writing than on content and organization. At times, therefore, they may be excessively concerned that their audience may be bored or that their ideas are inadequate. They may likewise become stalled by searching for just the right phrase or wording to capture the reader's attention. We have found that, because their concern for impact is often greater than their concern for content, feeling types may need, when revising, to clarify their thoughts or improve their organization.

Thinking and feeling types differ most strikingly as writers in how they approach organization. Thinking types usually follow an outline or an organizational pattern. They will then use the outline to make decisions, including material specified in the outline and excluding material not in the outline. Without this structure, they lack the objective criteria so important to them for making organizational decisions as they write. As an example, one thinking type wrote the following in response to a comment that her essay was unorganized: "I found it hard to write this paper. I would not think of any pattern that I (could) do. I believe I could have developed my paper more. I realize I put certain sentences out of order."

Feeling types, who base decisions more on personal values, may develop outlines or search for organizational patterns, but are less likely to follow them closely. One feeling type said that she makes outlines but uses them for only a paragraph or two. Then, once she begins to discover what she really wants to say, she ignores the outline and follows the flow of her own personal thought process. In addition to following the "flow" of their thoughts, organically developing structure from their own reactions to the subject matter, many feeling types may also make organizational decisions by trying to anticipate the audience's reaction to what they are writing. For example, if they feel that the audience needs more examples at a particular point, they will include them. If they feel that the audience will be bored by too many examples, they will exclude them. Outlines can seem too constraining to these writers. Another feeling type described her writing process with the following analogy: "Writing is like a summer breeze in that it cools your senses by releasing your thoughts and feelings. It allows a person to 'let themselves go' and let the pen and paper take total control of mind and hand. Writing is freedom and freedom is beautiful."

35   The strengths of "thinking" writers tend to include a natural gift   35 for incisive critical analysis, logical organization of content, and brevity of expression. At times, however, they may dogmatically state beliefs as if universally held, and may fail to provide warmth or human interest in their writing.

"Feeling" writers, in contrast, are more inclined to write from the heart, giving a personal flavor to their essays. Since they prefer subjective to objective processes in organizing their writing, they may at times understate a point of controversy affecting someone they care about, or overstate a message of personal conviction.

Judging-Perceiving

"Judging" and "perceiving" describe how individuals approach tasks in the outer world. Judging types tend to structure the outer world in a way that will lead them to get things done. They select projects that can be completed, formulate problems in a way that will enable them to be solved, and work on tasks, usually only one at a time, until finished. They tend to be decisive. Perceiving types are willing to leave the outer world unstructured, or tasks unfinished, so that they might better understand those tasks and the world around them. They are more inquisitive than decisive. Quickly made decisions narrow their field of vision, so they attempt to maintain a flexible perspective to be open to new information or ideas.

In schools, unexpected emergencies and last-minute information on a research project can disturb the judging types' need for order unless they allow time in their schedules to deal with the unexpected. Flexibility and spontaneity are the way of life for perceiving types, who need to be given deadlines to nudge them toward closure. Judging and perceiving types appear in roughly equal numbers in the general population, but classroom teaching and especially school administration attract more of the planful judging types.[18] Likewise, most health professions involving delivery of service include larger numbers of judging types; investigative research fields instead draw more inquisitive perceiving types.[19] School GPA's in subjects where productivity is important often are found to be higher among judging types.[20]

In our experience with writers, judging types tend to limit their topics quickly and set goals that are manageable. Before writing, they usually devote time to what Flower and Hayes call process goals (how to get things done),[21] which ideally include plans to stop at key intervals to analyze and revise objectives. Much of their writing process reflects their need to complete the first draft expediently. They tend to make stylistic and organizational decisions quickly, sometimes arbitrarily. Their quickly written first drafts are often shorter than later ones. When revising, they need to reevaluate decisions that have been made hastily or arbitrarily, to consider more thoroughly the implications of their data or ideas, and to expand their writing to clarify or qualify bluntly worded statements.

40   Judging types' need to complete tasks helps them to finish writing projects, but it may also create blocks. Several judging types with whom we have worked said that they frequently begin to write before they have finished their research. If they have not gathered enough information to generate adequate ideas, the draft proceeds slowly and painfully. And even though they are blocked, they may force themselves to stare at a blank sheet of paper. Writing becomes easier for them when they learn to put a stalled project aside to finish the research or generate more ideas.   40

judging types may also adhere to their plans too rigidly. A judging type with whom we worked developed, early in the process, a schedule for writing a graduate research paper. He then followed his plan without evaluating or revising it. He realized only a few days before the assignment was due that the topic he had selected was simply unworkable. To avoid being locked into unproductive plans, judging types need to allow time in their plans so that they can be spontaneous.

They need to stop writing at key intervals, and reevaluate and perhaps revise their process goals.

Perceiving types, in our experience, tend to select broad topics and
dive into reading without narrowing their focus. They discover a multitude of interesting possibly-related studies in a literature search, without knowing clearly what they will do with the information they gather.
Because they are curious and inquisitive, their topics may be limited
only as the deadline approaches. How effectively they limit their topic
will determine whether they finish the assignment at the last minute,
late, or at all. Even if the subject is appropriately focused, they may
delay writing because there is always one more paper or book to read.
They become blocked when trying to decide between one of two
approaches or if they feel that they do not know enough to begin
writing. As a perceiving type in our thesis support group said: "Data
collection is easy; writing about it is hard."

Perceiving types may also have difficulty dividing the essay into
sections, and may thus believe they need a large block of time before
they can begin to write. When writing, they pause more frequently
than judging types, not to reflect or anticipate as an introvert does, but
to take in numerous alternatives. Their first drafts tend to be long
and thorough but also too inclusive. When revising, they usually need
to cut down the length of the paper or to refocus its direction.

When at their best, perceiving types write essays that are comprehensive and well thought out. They may, however, not believe their work
to be adequately thorough. They tend to be perfectionistic, not about
mechanics as a sensing type might, but about wanting to include enough
background or related material. They often feel that, even in a short
paper, they must write everything that could possibly be written about
the topic. A perceiving type in our thesis support group, who was also
an introvert, feared that his committee would criticize his thesis for being
too short, that they would ask for more information or explanations.
Not surprisingly, once he finally submitted a rough draft of the introduction, his advisor's only suggestion was that he cut the length.

Interaction of the Dimensions

45 On its simplest level, Jung's typology consists of the four bi-polar dimen- 45
sions just described. The second layer of complexity arises when the
preferences combine to create sixteen possible types as illustrated below
on Figure 1.

	SENSING (S) TYPES		INTUITIVE (N) TYPES		
INTROVERTS (I)	ISTJ	ISFJ	INFJ	INTJ	JUDGING (J) TYPES
	ISTP	ISFP	INFP	INTP	PERCEIVING (P) TYPES
	ESTP	ESFP	ENFP	ENTP	
EXTRAVERTS (E)	ESTJ	ESFJ	ENFJ	ENTJ	JUDGING TYPES
	THINKING (T) TYPES	FEELING (F) TYPES		THINKING TYPES	

Figure 1.

The sixteen types represent an interaction—rather than a simple combination—of the dimensions. If the dimensions were merely combined, one would expect an introverted-intuitive-thinking-judging type (INTJ) to be very similar to an introverted-sensing-thinking-judging type (ISTJ). But although the two differ on only one descriptor out of four, the one on which they differ is the decisive (in the words of Jung and Myers the "dominant") dimension. The difference is more influential in producing contrasting behavior than the similarities are in producing similar behavior. The greatest strength of the one is the most visible weakness of the other, and vice versa. The limited scope of this article permits neither a description of all sixteen types nor an explanation of how a given type's preferences interact. Though an understanding of the separate dimensions as described here can broaden teachers' understanding of how individual writers differ, it is important to acknowledge that the personality constructs have more complexity than we were able to describe.[22]

The Myers-Briggs Type Indicator

The Myers-Briggs Type Indicator (MBTI) can help researchers to identify a writer's personality type. It is a measure of one's expressed preferences on each of the four dimensions discussed above. It is not, however, a performance test and does not measure how well people use their preferred processes. Form G of the MBTI (emerging from forty years of development through earlier forms) is a 126-item pencil-and-paper inventory. Its reliability and validity compare favorably to those of other such instruments.[23]

All pencil-and-paper inventories, however, have shortcomings and can be easily misused. The MBTI is one of the most benign of psychological instruments, since it was designed to identify the strengths and gifts of each type. Nevertheless, results from the MBTI can be misused if those administering and interpreting them attach primarily negative connotations to certain types. It is difficult for some to accept that all types have different but equally valid ways of dealing with the world. Training in the uses of psychological tests and the MBTI in particular is important if teachers, researchers, and clinicians are to appreciate the subtleties of the instrument. The Center for Applications of Psychological Type offers training workshops for administering and interpreting the MBTI.[24]

50   Though results from the MBTI may eventually provide valuable   50 information for composition teachers, we are not suggesting that teachers should test or label students wholesale. The MBTI should first be used in research to validate the observational findings presented in this article and to explore other related topics.

Implications for Research

The MBTI needs to be used to investigate the relationship between personality and writing in at least five areas:

1. We need hard data on how each MBTI dimension affects writing. The findings reported in this article only begin to show the effects of each dimension. Our work reported here, as noted, is basically an observational study. It needs to be replicated and the results analyzed systematically. The interaction of the four bi-polar scales of the MBTI also needs to be studied, for the sixteen personality types can potentially identify sixteen different writing processes.
2. The effect of teaching styles on writing instruction can be researched using the MBTI. DeNovellis and Lawrence have reported that MBTI preferences relate to teaching style,[25] but we do not yet understand how they specifically affect the teaching of composi-

tion. We have observed that writers function best when early drafts draw upon their preferred MBTI processes and later drafts draw upon unpreferred modes to round out the writing. If this finding is supported by research, then it can provide the writing teacher with a system for delivering the appropriate intervention for an individual writer at a particular point in his or her writing process. We suspect that teachers in general may tend to advise students to write as they (the teachers) do, instead of adapting their advice to the needs of different students. We further suspect that a lack of match between writing teachers' preferences and those of their students is not the most critical variable; lack of understanding of the richness and usefulness of individual differences is, we believe, of more profound importance regardless of one's type. Research is needed to confirm or disconfirm these hypotheses.

3. Writers of different ages and writers with varying levels of writing experience should be studied to see if the MBTI can help to explain some features of the development of writing ability. Our experience suggests that all types can and do write well. We suspect that writers become more skillful when they develop and mature both their preferred and unpreferred processes. Young writers, who may still be developing the preferred processes of their personality, may find it difficult to write in a way that requires them to use their unpreferred processes. We believe that writers should not be encouraged to develop their unpreferred processes until they have first developed the preferred. Pending further research, this must remain tentative advice.

4. The conceptual system of Jung and Myers can probably tell us a great deal about how teachers evaluate writing. According to theory, sensory teachers would tend to focus on facts, mechanics, and how well the student followed directions. Intuitive teachers are likely to focus on ideas and creativity. Schiff's initial examination of the MBTI and teachers' assessment of students' writing confirms the theory, but needs to be replicated and extended.[26]

5. We also need to re-evaluate current research methodology. In research on pausing, for example,[27] measuring the length and frequency of pauses may have more meaning if the effect of personality type on frequency of pauses is considered. Introverts naturally pause more than extraverts; perceiving types do so more than judging types. An extraverted-judging type who pauses frequently may

very well be blocked, but an introverted-perceiving type, with the same number of pauses, may be productively planning or considering options. Other applications of the theory of personality types to research on composing processes might prove fruitful.

Conclusion

Whether or not teachers have results of the MBTI for their students, the theoretical model described in this article can have a profound effect on how they think about and teach writing. If they know this model, teachers of composition can, at the very least, look for and be more accepting of legitimate differences in how students write, and can recognize how their own personality type may differ from those of their students. They should also begin to realize that a weakness in a student's writing is often associated with a contrasting strength. Though a student may sometimes neglect topic sentences and summaries, he or she may be observant of details and write excellent descriptive prose. Though another student may neglect mechanics, his or her writing may contain very fresh and new ideas. With or without MBTI results, an understanding of sensing and intuition as different ways of perceiving can help teachers to deal with such diversity. They can then, in an accepting and supportive way, help students move first from their strengths as writers to develop the skills that they need to improve.

Notes

1. Pearl G. Aldrich, "Adult Writers: Some Reasons for Ineffective Writing on the Job," *CCC,* 33 (October, 1982), 286.

2. Peter Elbow, *Writing With Power* (New York: Oxford, 1981), p. 27.

3. W. Ross Winterowd, *The Contemporary Writer* (New York: Harcourt, Brace, Jovanovich, 1975), p. 61.

4. James W. Keefe, ed., *Student Learning Styles and Brain Behavior* (Reston, VA: National Association of Secondary School Principals, 1982).

5. C. G. Jung, *Psychological Types* (New York: Harcourt, Brace, 1923).

6. Isabel B. Myers, *Gifts Differing* (Palo Alto, CA: Consulting Psychologists Press, 1980).

7. Mary H. McCaulley, *The Myers-Briggs Type Indicator and the Teaching-Learning Process* (Gainesville, FL: Center for Applications of Psychological Type, 1974).

8. Isabel B. Myers, *Relation of Psychological Type to Dropout in Nursing* (Gainesville, FL: Center for Applications of Psychological Type, 1964).

9. Isabel B. Myers, *The Myers-Briggs Type Indicator: Manual* (Palo Alto, CA: Consulting Psychologists Press, 1962).

10. Myers, *Gifts Differing*, p. 182.

11. George H. Jensen and John K. DiTiberio, "The MBTI and Writing Blocks," *MBTI News*, (Spring, 1983), 14–15.

12. Gordon Lawrence, *People Types and Tiger Stripes: A Practical Guide to Learning Styles* (Gainesville, FL: Center for Applications of Psychological Type, 1982), p. 39.

13. Jeffrey L. Hoffman and Marianne Betkouski, "A Summary of Myers-Briggs Type Indicator Research Applications in Education," *Research in Psychological Type*, 3 (1981), 4-41.

14. Myers, *Gifts Differing*, pp. 147–156.

15. Lawrence, *People Types*, p. 39.

16. Lawrence, *People Types*, p. 39.

17. Mary H. McCaulley, "Type and Education," unpublished manuscript.

18. Lawrence, *People Types*, p. 39.

19. Mary H. McCaulley, *Application of the Myers-Briggs Type Indicator to Medicine and Other Health Professions* (Gainesville, FL: Center for Applications of Psychological Type, 1978).

20. Mary H. McCaulley and Frank L. Netter, *Psychological Type Differences in Education* (Gainesville, FL: Center for Applications of Psychological Type, 1974).

21. Linda Flower and John R. Hayes, "A Cognitive Process Theory of Writing," *CCC*, 32 (December, 1981), 377–381.

22. For more information on how the dimensions interact see Myers, *Gifts Differing*, pp. 17–25 and 83–116.

23. Norman D. Sundberg, "The Myers-Briggs Type Indicator," in *The Sixth Mental Measurements Yearbook*, ed. O. K. Buros (Highland Park, NJ: The Gryphon Press, 1970), pp. 1126–7.

24. The Center for Applications of Psychological Type, Inc. is a nonprofit organization providing training, research consultation, scoring services and publications pertaining to the MBTI, located at 2720 N.W. 6th Street, Suite A, Gainesville, FL 32601.

25. R. DeNovellis and Gordon Lawrence, "Correlations of Teacher Personality Variables and Classrooms Observation Data," paper presented at the American Educational Research Association, Chicago, 1974.

26. Peter M. Schiff, "Writing Styles and Teaching Styles," paper presented at the Conference on English Education, Anaheim, CA, 1981.

27. Ann Matsuhashi, "Pausing and Planning: The Tempo of Written Discourse Production," *Research in the Teaching of English,* 15 (May, 1981), 113–134.

A Case of Assisted Suicide

Jack Kevorkian

Jack Kevorkian (1928–) was born in Pontiac, Michigan. A graduate of the University of Michigan medical school with a specialty in pathology (1952), Kevorkian has become one of the most well-known proponents of euthanasia because of the many "assisted suicides" he has attended. Kevorkian's active involvement in euthanasia began in 1990, when a 54-year-old woman diagnosed with Alzheimer's disease died after using his home-built "suicide machine" or "death machine." Since that time, Kevorkian—also called "Dr. Death" by some in the media—has facilitated numerous euthanasia deaths, all the while fighting court injunctions, murder charges, legislative bans on assisted suicide, and the loss of his license to practice medicine in California and Michigan. He has admitted to assisting in at least 130 deaths and served prison time for administering fatal drug injections to a patient with Lou Gehrig's disease. Kevorkian's publications include the article "The Last Fearsome Taboo: Medical Aspects of Planned Death" in Medicine and Law *(1988) and the book* Prescription: Medicide *(1991). In this excerpt from* Prescription: Medicide, *Kevorkian describes the first use of his so-called "death machine" and advances his reasons for using it.*

1   A mid the flurry of telephone calls in the fall of 1989 was one from a man in Portland, Oregon, who learned of my campaign from an item in *Newsweek* (November 13, 1989). Ron Adkins's rich, baritone, matter-of-fact voice was tinged with a bit of expectant anxiety as he calmly explained the tragic situation of his beloved wife. Janet Adkins was a remarkable, accomplished, active

woman—wife, mother, grandmother, revered friend, teacher, musician, mountain climber, and outdoorsperson—who, for some time, had noticed (as did her husband) subtle and gradually progressive impairment of her memory. The shock of hearing the diagnosis of Alzheimer's disease four months earlier was magnified by the abrupt and somewhat callous way her doctor announced it. The intelligent woman knew what the diagnosis portended, and at that instant decided she would not live to experience the horror of such a death.

Knowing that Janet was a courageous fighter, Ron and their three sons pleaded with her to reconsider and at least give a promising new therapy regimen a try. Ron explained to me that Janet was eligible to take part in an experimental trial using the newly developed drug Tacrine® or THA at the University of Washington in Seattle. I concurred that Janet should enroll in the program because any candidate for the Mercitron must have exhausted every potentially beneficial medical intervention, no matter how remotely promising.

I heard nothing more from the Adkinses until April 1990. Ron called again, after Janet and he saw me and my device on a nationally televised talk show. Janet had entered the experimental program in January, but it had been stopped early because the new drug was ineffective. In fact, her condition got worse; and she was more determined than ever to end her life. Even though from a physical standpoint Janet was not imminently terminal, there seemed little doubt that mentally she was—and, after all, it is one's mental status that determines the essence of one's existence. I asked Ron to forward to me copies of Janet's clinical records, and they corroborated what Ron had said.

I then telephoned Janet's doctor in Seattle. He opposed her planned action and the concept of assisted suicide in general. It was his firm opinion that Janet would remain mentally competent for at least a year (but from Ron's narrative I concluded that her doctor's opinion was wrong and that time was of the essence). Because Janet's condition was deteriorating and there was nothing else that might help arrest it, I decided to accept her as the first candidate—a qualified, justifiable candidate if not "ideal"—and well aware of the vulnerability to criticism of picayune and overly emotional critics.

A major obstacle was finding a place to do it. Because I consider medicide to be necessary, ethical, and legal, there should be nothing furtive about it. Another reason to pursue the practice above-board is to avert the harrassment or vindictiveness of litigation. Consequently, when searching for a suitable site I always explained that I planned to assist a suffering patient to commit suicide. That posed no problem for helping a Michigan resident in his or her own residence. But it was a different matter for an out-of-state guest who must rent temporary quarters.

And I soon found out how difficult a matter it could be. My own apartment could not be used because of lease constraints, and the same was true of my sister's apartment. I inquired at countless motels, funeral homes, churches of various denominations, rental office buildings, clinics, doctors' offices for lease, and even considered the futile hope of renting an emergency life-support ambulance. Many owners, proprietors, and landlords were quite sympathetic but fearful and envisioned the negative public reaction that could seriously damage and even destroy their business enterprises. In short, they deemed it bad for public relations. More dismaying yet was the refusal of people who are known supporters and active campaigners for euthanasia to allow Janet and me the use of their homes.

Finally, a friend agreed to avail us of his modest home in Detroit; I immediately contacted Ron to finalize plans. My initial proposal was to carry out the procedure at the end of May 1990, but Ron and Janet preferred to avoid the surge of travel associated with the Memorial Day weekend. The date was postponed to Monday, June 4th.

In the meantime, my friend was warned by a doctor, in whom he confided, not to make his home available for such a purpose. Soon thereafter the offer was quickly withdrawn. With the date set and airline tickets having been purchased by Janet, Ron, and a close friend of Janet's, I had to scamper to find another site. The device required an electrical outlet, which limited the possibilities.

I had made a Herculean effort to provide a desirable, clinical setting. Literally and sadly, there was "no room at the inn." Now, having been refused everywhere I applied, the *only alternative* remaining was my 1968 camper and a suitable campground.

10   As expected, the owners of a commercial site refused permission,   10 even though they were sympathetic to the proposed scheme. They then suggested the solution by recommending that I rent space at a public camping site not too far away. The setting was pleasant and idyllic.

As with many other aspects of this extraordinary event, I was aware of the harsh criticism that would be leveled at the use of a "rusty old van." In the first place, the twenty-two-year-old body may have been rusting on the outside, but its interior was very clean, orderly, and comfortable. I have slept in it often and not felt degraded. But carping critics missed the point: the essence and significance of the event are far more important than the splendor of the site where it takes place. If critics are thus deluded into denouncing the exit from existence under these circumstances, then why not the same delusional denunciation of entrance into existence when a baby is, of necessity, born in an old taxicab? On the contrary, the latter identical scenario seems to arouse only feelings of sentimental reverence and quaint joy.

But the dishonesty doesn't stop there. I have been repeatedly criticized for having assisted a patient after a short personal acquaintance of two days. Overlooked or ignored is my open avowal to be the first practitioner in this country of a new and as yet officially unrecognized specialty. Because of shameful stonewalling by her own doctors, Janet was forced to refer herself to me. And acting as a unique specialist, of necessity self-proclaimed, solitary, and independent, I was obligated to scrutinize Janet's clinical records and to consult with her personal doctor. The latter's uncooperative attitude (tacitly excused by otherwise harsh critics) impaired but did not thwart fulfillment of my duties to a suffering patient and to my profession.

It is absurd even to imply, let alone to protest outright, that a medical specialist's competence and ethical behavior are contingent upon some sort of time interval, imposed arbitrarily or by fiat. When a doctor refers a patient for surgery, in many cases the surgical specialist performs his *ultimate* duty after personal acquaintance with the patient from a mere hour or two of prior consultation (in contrast to my having spent at least twelve hours in personal contact with Janet). In a few instances the surgeon operates on a patient seen for the first time on the operating table—and anesthetized to unconsciousness.

Moreover, in sharp contrast to the timorous, secretive, and even deceitful intention and actions of other medical euthanasists on whom our so-called bioethicists now shower praise, I acted openly, ethically, legally, with complete and uncompromising honesty, and—even more important—I remained in personal attendance during the second most meaningful medical event in a patient's earthly existence. Were he alive today, it's not hard to guess what Hippocrates would say about all this.

15　　　My two sisters, Margo and Flora, and I met with Ron, Janet, and　15
Janet's close friend Carroll Rehmke in their motel room on Saturday

afternoon, 2 June 1990. After getting acquainted through a few minutes of conversation, the purpose of the trip was thoroughly discussed.
I had already prepared authorization forms signifying Janet's intent,
determination, and freedom of choice, which she readily agreed to
sign. Here again, while she was resolute in her decision, and absolutely
mentally competent, her impaired memory was apparent when she
needed her husband's assistance in forming the cursive letter "A." She
could print the letter but not write it, and the consent forms required
that her signature be written. So her husband showed her on another
piece of paper how to form the cursive "A," and Janet complied. At
this time, Ron and Carroll also signed a statement attesting to Janet's
mental competence. Following this signing session, I had Flora videotape my interview with Janet and Ron. The forty-five-minute taping
reinforced my own conviction that Janet was mentally competent but
that her memory had failed badly. However, the degree of memory
failure led me to surmise that within four to six months she would be
too incompetent to qualify as a candidate. It should be pointed out
that in medical terms loss of memory does not automatically signify
mental incompetence. Any rational critic would concede that a mentally sound individual can be afflicted with even total amnesia.

Around 5:30 P.M. that same day all six of us had dinner at a well-
known local restaurant. Seated around the same table for many hours,
our conversation covered many subjects, including the telling of jokes.
Without appearing too obvious, I constantly observed Janet's behavior and assessed her moods as well as the content and quality of her
thoughts. There was absolutely no doubt that her mentality was intact
and that she was not the least depressed over her impending death. On
the contrary, the only detectable anxiety or disquieting demeanor was
among the rest of us to a greater or lesser degree. Even in response to
jokes, Janet's appropriately timed and modulated laughter indicated
clear and coherent comprehension. The only uneasiness or distress she
exhibited was due to her embarrassment at being unable to recall
aspects of the topic under discussion at the time. And that is to be
expected of intelligent, sensitive, and diligent individuals.

We left the restaurant at 12:30 A.M. Sunday. Janet and Ron enjoyed their last full day by themselves.

At 8:30 A.M. the next day, Monday, 4 June 1990, I drove into a
rented space at Groveland Park in north Oakland County, Michigan.
At the same time, my sisters drove to the motel to fetch Janet, who
had composed (and submitted to my sister) a brief and clear note re-

iterating her genuine desire to end her life and exonerating all others in this desire and the actual event. For the last time, Janet took tearful leave of her grieving husband and Carroll, both of whom were inconsolable. It was Janet's wish that they not accompany her to the park.

The day began cold, damp, and overcast. I took a lot of time in setting up the Mercitron and giving it a few test runs. In turning to get a pair of pliers in the cramped space within the van, I accidentally knocked over the container of thiopental solution, losing a little over half of it. I was fairly sure that the remainder was enough to induce and maintain adequate unconsciousness, but I chose not to take the risk. I drove the forty-five miles home and got some more.

20   In the meantime, at about 9:30 A.M. my sisters and Janet had arrived at the park. They were dismayed to learn of the accidental spill and opted to accompany me on the extra round trip, which required two and one-half hours. We reentered the park at approximately noontime. Janet remained in the car with Margo while Flora helped me with minor tasks in the van as I very carefully prepared and tested the Mercitron. Everything was ready by about 2:00 P.M., and Janet was summoned.   20

She entered the van alone through the open sliding side door and lay fully clothed on the built-in bed covered with freshly laundered sheets. Her head rested comfortably on a clean pillow. The windows were covered with new draperies. With Janet's permission I cut small holes in her nylon stockings at the ankles, attached ECG electrodes to her ankles and wrists, and covered her body with a light blanket. Our conversation was minimal. In accordance with Janet's wish, Flora read to her a brief note from her friend Carroll, followed by a reading of the Lord's prayer. I then repeated my earlier instructions to Janet about how the device was to be activated, and asked her to go through the motions. In contrast to my sister and me, Janet was calm and outwardly relaxed.

I used a syringe with attached needle to pierce a vein near the frontal elbow area of her left arm. Unfortunately, her veins were delicate and fragile; even slight movement of the restrained arm caused the needle to penetrate through the wall of the vein resulting in leakage. Two more attempts also failed, as did a fourth attempt on the right side. Finally an adequate puncture was obtained on the right arm. (It was reassuring to me to learn later that doctors in Seattle had had similar difficulty with her veins.)

The moment had come. With a nod from Janet I turned on the ECG and said, "Now." Janet hit the Mercitron's switch with the outer edge of her palm. In about ten seconds her eyelids began to flicker and droop. She looked up at me and said, "Thank you, thank you." I replied at once as her eyelids closed, "Have a nice trip." She was unconscious and perfectly still except for two widely spaced and mild coughs several minutes later. Agonal complexes in the ECG tracing indicated death due to complete cessation of blood circulation in six minutes.

It was 2:30 P.M. Suddenly—for the first time that cold, dank day—warm sunshine bathed the park.

Letter from Birmingham Jail

Martin Luther King, Jr.

Martin Luther King, Jr. (1929–1968) was born in Atlanta, Georgia. The son and grandson of Baptist ministers, he attended Moorhouse College, Crozer Theological Seminary, and Boston University where he received a Ph.D. (1955) and met his future wife, Coretta Scott. King's active involvement in the civil rights movement began in 1955, when he led a boycott of segregated buses in Montgomery, Alabama. From the mid 1950s until he was shot and killed in Memphis, Tennessee, while supporting striking city workers, King organized boycotts, sit-ins, mass demonstrations, and other protest activities. As a black civil rights leader, King was arrested, jailed, stoned, stabbed, and beaten; his house was bombed; he was placed under secret surveillance by Federal Bureau of Investigation (FBI) director J. Edgar Hoover; and in 1966 he was awarded the Nobel Peace Prize. Through his leadership—always underscored by his nonviolent beliefs—King's name has become synonymous with the watersheds of the civil rights movement in the United States: Rosa Parks; the Southern Christian Leadership Conference (which King founded); Selma, Alabama; the Civil Rights Act; the Voting Rights Act; and the 1963 civil rights march on Washington, D. C. His published works include Strength to Love *(1963) and* Conscience for Change *(1967). This essay—published in a revised form in* Why We Can't Wait *(1964)—is King's stern response to eight clergymen from Alabama who were asking civil rights activists to give up public demonstrations in Birmingham, Alabama, and turn to the courts. Read the clergymen's public statement first, then King's detailed rebuttal (printed here as it appeared originally). Keep in mind that King wrote these words four months before he delivered his famous "I Have a Dream" speech during the August 1963 civil rights march on Washington; after long years of activism, he was clearly impatient with the slow progress of the civil rights movement.*

Public Statement by Eight Alabama Clergymen

(April 12, 1963)

1   We the undersigned clergymen are among those who, in January, issued "An Appeal for Law and Order and Common Sense," in dealing with racial problems in Alabama. We expressed understanding that honest convictions in racial matters could properly be pursued in the courts, but urged that decisions of those courts should in the meantime be peacefully obeyed.

Since that time there had been some evidence of increased forbearance and a willingness to face facts. Responsible citizens have undertaken to work on various problems which cause racial friction and unrest. In Birmingham, recent public events have given indication that we all have opportunity for a new constructive and realistic approach to racial problems.

However, we are now confronted by a series of demonstrations by some of our Negro citizens, directed and led in part by outsiders. We recognize the natural impatience of people who feel that their hopes are slow in being realized. But we are convinced that these demonstrations are unwise and untimely.

We agree rather with certain local Negro leadership which has called for honest and open negotiation of racial issues in our area. And we believe this kind of facing of issues can best be accomplished by citizens of our own metropolitan area, white and Negro, meeting with their knowledge and experience of the local situation. All of us need to face that responsibility and find proper channels for its accomplishment.

5   Just as we formerly pointed out that "hatred and violence have no sanction in our religious and political traditions," we also point out that such actions as incite to hatred and violence, however technically

peaceful those actions may be, have not contributed to the resolution of our local problems. We do not believe that these days of new hope are days when extreme measures are justified in Birmingham.

We commend the community as a whole, and the local news media and law enforcement officials in particular, on the calm manner in which these demonstrations have been handled. We urge the public to continue to show restraint should the demonstrations continue, and the law enforcement officials to remain calm and continue to protect our city from violence.

We further strongly urge our own Negro community to withdraw support from these demonstrations, and to unite locally in working peacefully for a better Birmingham. When rights are consistently denied, a cause should be pressed in the courts and in negotiations among local leaders, and not in the streets. We appeal to both our white and Negro citizenry to observe the principles of law and order and common sense.

Signed by:

C.C. J. CARPENTER, D.D., LL.D., *Bishop of Alabama*

JOSEPH A. DURICK, D.D., *Auxiliary Bishop, Diocese of Mobile, Birmingham*

RABBI MILTON L. GRAFMAN, *Temple Emanu-El, Birmingham, Alabama*

BISHOP PAUL HARDIN, *Bishop of the Alabama-West Florida Conference of the Methodist Church*

BISHOP NOLAN B. HARMON, *Bishop of the North Alabama Conference of the Methodist Church*

GEORGE M. MURRAY, D.D., LL.D., *Bishop Coadjutor, Episcopal Diocese of Alabama*

EDWARD V. RAMAGE, *Moderator, Synod of the Alabama Presbyterian Church in the United States*

EARL STALLINGS, *Pastor, First Baptist Church, Birmingham, Alabama*

Letter from Birmingham Jail

MARTIN LUTHER KING, JR.
Birmingham City Jail
April 16, 1963

Bishop C. C. J. Carpenter
Bishop Joseph A. Durick
Rabbi Milton L. Grafman
Bishop Paul Hardin
Bishop Nolan B. Harmon
The Rev. George M. Murray
The Rev. Edward V. Ramage
The Rev. Earl Stallings

My dear Fellow Clergymen,

While confined here in the Birmingham City Jail, I came across your recent statement calling our present activities "unwise and untimely." Seldom, if ever, do I pause to answer criticism of my work and ideas. If I sought to answer all of the criticisms that cross my desk, my secretaries would be engaged in little else in the course of the day and I would have no time for constructive work. But since I feel that you are men of genuine good will and your criticisms are sincerely set forth, I would like to answer your statement in what I hope will be patient and reasonable terms.

I think I should give the reason for my being in Birmingham, since you have been influenced by the argument of "outsiders coming in." I have the honor of serving as president of the Southern Christian Leadership Conference, an organization operating in every Southern state with headquarters in Atlanta, Georgia. We have some eighty-five affiliate organizations all across the South—one being the Alabama Christian Movement for Human Rights. Whenever necessary and possible we share staff, educational, and financial resources with our affiliates. Several months ago our local affiliate here in Birmingham invited us to be on call to engage in a nonviolent direct action program if such were deemed necessary. We readily consented, and when the hour came we lived up to our promises. So I, along with several members of my staff, am here, because I was invited here. I am here because I have basic organizational ties here.

10   But more basically, I am in Birmingham because injustice is here. 10
Just as the eighth century prophets left their little villages and carried
their "thus saith the Lord" far beyond the boundaries of their home
town, and just as the Apostle Paul left his little village of Tarsus and
carried the gospel of Jesus Christ to practically every hamlet and city
of the Greco-Roman world, I too am compelled to carry the gospel of
freedom beyond my particular home town. Like Paul, I must constantly respond to the Macedonian call for aid.

Moreover, I am cognizant of the interrelatedness of all communities and states. I cannot sit idly by in Atlanta and not be concerned
about what happens in Birmingham. Injustice anywhere is a threat to
justice everywhere. We are caught in an inescapable network of mu-
tuality, tied in a single garment of destiny. Whatever affects one directly affects all indirectly. Never again can we afford to live with the
narrow, provincial "outside agitator" idea. Anyone who lives inside the
United States can never be considered an outsider anywhere in this
country.

You deplore the demonstrations that are presently taking place in
Birmingham. But I am sorry that your statement did not express a
similar concern for the conditions that brought the demonstrations
into being. I am sure that each of you would want to go beyond the
superficial social analyst who looks merely at effects, and does not
grapple with underlying causes. I would not hesitate to say that it is
unfortunate that so-called demonstrations are taking place in Birmingham at this time, but I would say in more emphatic terms that it
is even more unfortunate that the white power structure of this city
left the Negro community with no other alternative.

In any nonviolent campaign there are four basic steps: (1) collection of the facts to determine whether injustices are alive; (2) negotiation; (3) self-purification; and (4) direct action. We have gone
through all of these steps in Birmingham. There can be no gainsaying
of the fact that racial injustice engulfs this community. Birmingham
is probably the most thoroughly segregated city in the United States.
Its ugly record of police brutality is known in every section of this
country. Its unjust treatment of Negroes in the courts is a notorious
reality. There have been more unsolved bombings of Negro homes and
churches in Birmingham than any city in this nation. These are the
hard, brutal, and unbelievable facts. On the basis of these conditions,
Negro leaders sought to negotiate with the city fathers. But the political leaders consistently refused to engage in good faith negotiation.

Then came the opportunity last September to talk with some of the leaders of the economic community. In these negotiating sessions certain promises were made by the merchants—such as the promise to remove the humiliating racial signs from the stores. On the basis of these promises Rev. Shuttlesworth and the leaders of the Alabama Christian Movement for Human Rights agreed to call a moratorium on any type of demonstrations. As the weeks and months unfolded we realized that we were the victims of a broken promise. The signs remained. As in so many experiences of the past we were confronted with blasted hopes, and the dark shadow of a deep disappointment settled upon us. So we had no alternative except that of preparing for direct action, whereby we would present our very bodies as a means of laying our case before the conscience of the local and national community. We were not unmindful of the difficulties involved. So we decided to go through a process of self-purification. We started having workshops on nonviolence and repeatedly asked ourselves the questions, "Are you able to accept blows without retaliating?" "Are you able to endure the ordeals of jail?"

15   We decided to set our direct action program around the Easter   15
season, realizing that with the exception of Christmas, this was the largest shopping period of the year. Knowing that a strong economic withdrawal program would be the by-product of direct action, we felt that this was the best time to bring pressure on the merchants for the needed changes. Then it occurred to us that the March election was ahead, and so we speedily decided to postpone action until after election day. When we discovered that Mr. Connor was in the run-off, we decided again to postpone so that the demonstrations could not be used to cloud the issues. At this time we agreed to begin our nonviolent witness the day after the run-off.

This reveals that we did not move irresponsibly into direct action. We too wanted to see Mr. Connor defeated; so we went through postponement after postponement to aid in this community need. After this we felt that direct action could be delayed no longer.

You may well ask, "Why direct action? Why sit-ins, marches, etc.? Isn't negotiation a better path?" You are exactly right in your call for negotiation. Indeed, this is the purpose of direct action. Nonviolent direct action seeks to create such a crisis and establish such creative tension that a community that has constantly refused to negotiate is forced to confront the issue. It seeks so to dramatize the issue that it can no longer be ignored. I just referred to the creation of tension as a part of the work of the nonviolent resister. This may sound rather shocking. But I must confess that I am not afraid of the word tension. I have earnestly worked and preached against violent tension, but there is a type of constructive nonviolent tension that is necessary for growth. Just as Socrates felt that it was necessary to create a tension in the mind so that individuals could rise from the bondage of myths and half-truths to the unfettered realm of creative analysis and objective appraisal, we must see the need of having nonviolent gadflies to create the kind of tension in society that will help men rise from the dark depths of prejudice and racism to the majestic heights of understanding and brotherhood. So the purpose of the direct action is to create a situation so crisis-packed that it will inevitably open the door to negotiation. We, therefore, concur with you in your call for negotiation. Too long has our beloved Southland been bogged down in the tragic attempt to live in monologue rather than dialogue.

One of the basic points in your statement is that our acts are untimely. Some have asked, "Why didn't you give the new administration time to act?" The only answer that I can give to this inquiry is that the new administration must be prodded about as much as the outgoing one before it acts. We will be sadly mistaken if we feel that the election of Mr. Boutwell will bring the millennium to Birmingham. While Mr. Boutwell is much more articulate and gentle than Mr. Connor, they are both segregationists dedicated to the task of maintaining the status quo. The hope I see in Mr. Boutwell is that he will be reasonable enough to see the futility of massive resistance to desegregation. But he will not see this without pressure from the devotees of civil rights. My friends, I must say to you that we have not made a single gain in civil rights without determined legal and nonviolent pressure. History is the long and tragic story of the fact that privileged groups seldom give up their privileges voluntarily. Individuals may see the moral light and voluntarily give up their unjust posture; but as Reinhold Niebuhr has reminded us, groups are more immoral than individuals.

We know through painful experience that freedom is never voluntarily given by the oppressor; it must be demanded by the oppressed. Frankly I have never yet engaged in a direct action movement that was "well timed," according to the timetable of those who have not suffered unduly from the disease of segregation. For years now I have heard the

word "Wait!" It rings in the ear of every Negro with a piercing familiarity. This "wait" has almost always meant "never." It has been a tran-
quilizing thalidomide, relieving the emotional stress for a moment,
only to give birth to an ill-formed infant of frustration. We must come
to see with the distinguished jurist of yesterday that "justice too long
delayed is justice denied." We have waited for more than three hundred and forty years for our constitutional and God-given rights. The
nations of Asia and Africa are moving with jet-like speed toward the
goal of political independence, and we still creep at horse and buggy
pace toward the gaining of a cup of coffee at a lunch counter.

20   I guess it is easy for those who have never felt the stinging darts of   20
segregation to say wait. But when you have seen vicious mobs lynch
your mothers and fathers at will and drown your sisters and brothers at
whim; when you have seen hate filled policemen curse, kick, brutalize,
and even kill your black brothers and sisters with impunity; when you
see the vast majority of your twenty million Negro brothers smothering
in an air-tight cage of poverty in the midst of an affluent society; when
you suddenly find your tongue twisted and your speech stammering as
you seek to explain to your six-year-old daughter why she can't go to the
public amusement park that has just been advertised on television, and
see tears welling up in her little eyes when she is told that Funtown is
closed to colored children, and see the depressing clouds of inferiority
begin to form in her little mental sky, and see her begin to distort her
little personality by unconsciously developing a bitterness toward white
people; when you have to concoct an answer for a five-year-old son asking in agonizing pathos: "Daddy, why do white people treat colored
people so mean?"; when you take a cross country drive and find it necessary to sleep night after night in the uncomfortable corners of your
automobile because no motel will accept you; when you are humiliated
day in and day out by nagging signs reading "white" and "colored";
when your first name becomes "nigger" and your middle name becomes
"boy" (however old you are) and your last name becomes "John," and
when your wife and mother are never given the respected title "Mrs.";
when you are harried by day and haunted by night by the fact that you
are a Negro, living constantly at tip-toe stance never quite knowing what
to expect next, and plagued with inner fears and outer resentments;
when you are forever fighting a degenerating sense of "nobodiness";——
then you will understand why we find it difficult to wait. There comes
a time when the cup of endurance runs over, and men are no longer

willing to be plunged into an abyss of injustice where they experience the bleakness of corroding despair. I hope, sirs, you can understand our legitimate and unavoidable impatience.

You express a great deal of anxiety over our willingness to break laws. This is certainly a legitimate concern. Since we so diligently urge people to obey the Supreme Court's decision of 1954 outlawing segregation in the public schools, it is rather strange and paradoxical to find us consciously breaking laws. One may well ask, "How can you advocate breaking some laws and obeying others?" The answer is found in the fact that there are two types of laws. There are *just* laws and there are *unjust* laws. I would be the first to advocate obeying just laws. One has not only a legal but moral responsibility to obey just laws. Conversely, one has a moral responsibility to disobey unjust laws. I would agree with Saint Augustine that "An unjust law is no law at all."

Now what is the difference between the two? How does one determine when a law is just or unjust? A just law is a man-made code that squares with the moral law or the law of God. An unjust law is a code that is out of harmony with the moral law. To put it in the terms of Saint Thomas Aquinas, an unjust law is a human law that is not rooted in eternal and natural law. Any law that uplifts human personality is just. Any law that degrades human personality is unjust. All segregation statutes are unjust because segregation distorts the soul and damages the personality. It gives the segregator a false sense of superiority and the segregated a false sense of inferiority. To use the words of Martin Buber, the great Jewish philosopher, segregation substitutes an "I-it" relationship for the "I-thou" relationship, and ends up relegating persons to the status of things. So segregation is not only politically, economically, and sociologically unsound, but it is morally wrong and sinful. Paul Tillich has said that sin is separation. Isn't segregation an existential expression of man's tragic separation, an expression of his awful estrangement, his terrible sinfulness? So I can urge men to obey the 1954 decision of the Supreme Court because it is morally right, and I can urge them to disobey segregation ordinances because they are morally wrong.

Let us turn to a more concrete example of just and unjust laws. An unjust law is a code that a majority inflicts on a minority that is not binding on itself. This is *difference* made legal. On the other hand a just law is a code that a majority compels a minority to follow that it is willing to follow itself. This is *sameness* made legal.

Let me give another explanation. An unjust law is a code inflicted upon a minority which that minority had no part in enacting or creating because they did not have the unhampered right to vote. Who can say the legislature of Alabama which set up the segregation laws was democratically elected? Throughout the state of Alabama all types of conniving methods are used to prevent Negroes from becoming registered voters and there are some counties without a single Negro registered to vote despite the fact that the Negro constitutes a majority of the population. Can any law set up in such a state be considered democratically structured?

25   These are just a few examples of unjust and just laws. There are   25
some instances when a law is just on its face but unjust in its application. For instance, I was arrested Friday on a charge of parading without a permit. Now there is nothing wrong with an ordinance which requires a permit for a parade, but when the ordinance is used to preserve segregation and to deny citizens the First Amendment privilege of peaceful assembly and peaceful protest, then it becomes unjust.

I hope you can see the distinction I am trying to point out. In no sense do I advocate evading or defying the law as the rabid segregationist would do. This would lead to anarchy. One who breaks an unjust law must do it *openly, lovingly* (not hatefully as the white mothers did in New Orleans when they were seen on television screaming "nigger, nigger, nigger") and with a willingness to accept the penalty. I submit that an individual who breaks a law that conscience tells him is unjust, and willingly accepts the penalty by staying in jail to arouse the conscience of the community over its injustice, is in reality expressing the very highest respect for law.

Of course there is nothing new about this kind of civil disobedience. It was seen sublimely in the refusal of Shadrach, Meshach, and Abednego to obey the laws of Nebuchadnezzar because a higher moral law was involved. It was practiced superbly by the early Christians who were willing to face hungry lions and the excruciating pain of chopping blocks, before submitting to certain unjust laws of the Roman Empire. To a degree academic freedom is a reality today because Socrates practiced civil disobedience.

We can never forget that everything Hitler did in Germany was "legal" and everything the Hungarian freedom fighters did in Hungary was "illegal." It was "illegal" to aid and comfort a Jew in Hitler's Germany. But I am sure that, if I had lived in Germany during that time, I would have aided and comforted my Jewish brothers even though it was illegal. If I lived in a communist country today where certain principles dear to the Christian faith are suppressed, I believe I would openly advocate disobeying those antireligious laws.

I must make two honest confessions to you, my Christian and Jewish brothers. First I must confess that over the last few years I have been gravely disappointed with the white moderate. I have almost reached the regrettable conclusion that the Negroes' great stumbling block in the stride toward freedom is not the White Citizens' "Counciler" or the Ku Klux Klanner, but the white moderate who is more devoted to "order" than to justice; who prefers a negative peace which is the absence of tension to a positive peace which is the presence of justice; who constantly says "I agree with you in the goal you seek, but I can't agree with your methods of direct action;" who paternalistically feels that he can set the timetable for another man's freedom; who lives by the myth of time and who constantly advises the Negro to wait until a "more convenient season." Shallow understanding from people of good will is more frustrating than absolute misunderstanding from people of ill will. Lukewarm acceptance is much more bewildering than outright rejection.

30   I had hoped that the white moderate would understand that law 30 and order exist for the purpose of establishing justice, and that when they fail to do this they become the dangerously structured dams that block the flow of social progress. I had hoped that the white moderate would understand that the present tension in the South is merely a necessary phase of the transition from an obnoxious negative peace, where the Negro passively accepted his unjust plight, to a substance-filled positive peace, where all men will respect the dignity and worth of human personality. Actually, we who engage in nonviolent direct action are not the creators of tension. We merely bring to the surface the hidden tension that is already alive. We bring it out in the open where it can be seen and dealt with. Like a boil that can never be cured as long as it is covered up but must be opened with all its pus-flowing ugliness to the natural medicines of air and light, injustice must likewise be exposed, with all of the tension its exposing creates, to the light of human conscience and the air of national opinion before it can be cured.

In your statement you asserted that our actions, even though peaceful, must be condemned because they precipitate violence. But can this assertion be logically made? Isn't this like condemning the robbed man because his possession of money precipitated the evil act of robbery? Isn't this like condemning Socrates because his unswerving commitment to truth and his philosophical delvings precipitated the misguided popular mind to make him drink the hemlock? Isn't this like condemning Jesus because His unique God consciousness and never-ceasing devotion to His will precipitated the evil act of crucifixion? We must come to see, as federal courts have consistently affirmed, that it is immoral to urge an individual to withdraw his efforts to gain his basic constitutional rights because the quest precipitates violence. Society must protect the robbed and punish the robber.

I had also hoped that the white moderate would reject the myth of time. I received a letter this morning from a white brother in Texas which said: "All Christians know that the colored people will receive equal rights eventually, but is it possible that you are in too great of a religious hurry? It has taken Christianity almost 2,000 years to accomplish what it has. The teachings of Christ take time to come to earth." All that is said here grows out of a tragic misconception of time. It is the strangely irrational notion that there is something in the very flow of time that will inevitably cure all ills. Actually time is neutral. It can be used either destructively or constructively. I am coming to feel that the people of ill will have used time much more effectively than the people of good will. We will have to repent in this generation not merely for the vitriolic words and actions of the bad people, but for the appalling silence of the good people. We must come to see that human progress never rolls in on wheels of inevitability. It comes through the tireless efforts and persistent work of men willing to be co-workers with God, and without this hard work time itself becomes an ally of the forces of social stagnation.

We must use time creatively, and forever realize that the time is always ripe to do right. Now is the time to make real the promise of democracy, and transform our pending national elegy into a creative psalm of brotherhood. Now is the time to lift our national policy from the quicksand of racial injustice to the solid rock of human dignity.

You spoke of our activity in Birmingham as extreme. At first I was rather disappointed that fellow clergymen would see my nonviolent efforts as those of the extremist. I started thinking about the fact that I stand in the middle of two opposing forces in the Negro community. One is a force of complacency made up of Negroes who, as a result of long years of oppression, have been so completely drained of self-respect and a sense of "somebodiness" that they have adjusted to segregation, and of a few Negroes in the middle class who, because of a degree of academic and economic security, and because at points they profit by segregation, have unconsciously become insensitive to the problems of the masses. The other force is one of bitterness and hatred and comes perilously close to advocating violence. It is expressed in the various black nationalist groups that are springing up over the nation, the largest and best known being Elijah Muhammad's Muslim movement. This movement is nourished by the contemporary frustration over the continued existence of racial discrimination. It is made up of people who have lost faith in America, who have absolutely repudiated Christianity, and who have concluded that the white man is an incurable "devil." I have tried to stand between these two forces saying that we need not follow the "do-nothingism" of the complacent or the hatred and despair of the black nationalist. There is the more excellent way of love and nonviolent protest. I'm grateful to God that, through the Negro church, the dimension of nonviolence entered our struggle. If this philosophy had not emerged I am convinced that by now many streets of the South would be flowing with floods of blood. And I am further convinced that if our white brothers dismiss us as "rabble rousers" and "outside agitators"—those of us who are working through the channels of nonviolent direct action—and refuse to support our nonviolent efforts, millions of Negroes, out of frustration and despair, will seek solace and security in black nationalist ideologies, a development that will lead inevitably to a frightening racial nightmare.

35   Oppressed people cannot remain oppressed forever. The urge for 35 freedom will eventually come. This is what has happened to the American Negro. Something within has reminded him of his birthright of freedom; something without has reminded him that he can gain it. Consciously and unconsciously, he has been swept in by what the Germans call the *Zeitgeist*, and with his black brothers of Africa, and his brown and yellow brothers of Asia, South America, and the Caribbean, he is moving with a sense of cosmic urgency toward the promised land of racial justice. Recognizing this vital urge that has engulfed the Negro community, one should readily understand public demonstrations. The Negro has many pent-up resentments and latent frustrations. He has to get them out. So let him march sometime; let him have his prayer pilgrimages to the city hall; understand why he must have sit-ins and freedom rides. If his repressed emotions do not come out in these nonviolent ways, they will come out in ominous expressions of violence. This is not a threat; it is a fact of history. So I

have not said to my people, "Get rid of your discontent." But I have tried to say that this normal and healthy discontent can be channeled through the creative outlet of nonviolent direct action. Now this approach is being dismissed as extremist. I must admit that I was initially disappointed in being so categorized.

But as I continued to think about the matter I gradually gained a bit of satisfaction from being considered an extremist. Was not Jesus an extremist in love? "Love your enemies, bless them that curse you, pray for them that despitefully use you." Was not Amos an extremist for justice— "Let justice roll down like waters and righteousness like a mighty stream." Was not Paul an extremist for the gospel of Jesus Christ— "I bear in my body the marks of the Lord Jesus." Was not Martin Luther an extremist— "Here I stand; I can do none other so help me God." Was not John Bunyan an extremist— "I will stay in jail to the end of my days before I make a butchery of my conscience." Was not Abraham Lincoln an extremist— "This nation cannot survive half slave and half free." Was not Thomas Jefferson an extremist— "We hold these truths to be self evident that all men are created equal." So the question is not whether we will be extremist but what kind of extremist will we be. Will we be extremists for hate or will we be extremists for love? Will we be extremists for the preservation of injustice or will we be extremists for the cause of justice? In that dramatic scene on Calvary's hill three men were crucified. We must never forget that all three were crucified for the same crime—the crime of extremism. Two were extremists for immorality, and thus fell below their environment. The other, Jesus Christ, was an extremist for love, truth, and goodness, and thereby rose above His environment. So, after all, maybe the South, the nation, and the world are in dire need of creative extremists.

I had hoped that the white moderate would see this. Maybe I was too optimistic. Maybe I expected too much. I guess I should have realized that few members of a race that has oppressed another race can understand or appreciate the deep groans and passionate yearnings of those that have been oppressed, and still fewer have the vision to see that injustice must be rooted out by strong, persistent, and determined action. I am thankful, however, that some of our white brothers have grasped the meaning of this social revolution and committed themselves to it. They are still all too small in quantity, but they are big in quality. Some like Ralph McGill, Lillian Smith, Harry Golden, and James Dabbs have written about our struggle in eloquent, prophetic, and understanding terms. Others have marched with us down nameless streets of the South. They have languished in filthy, roach-infested jails, suffering the abuse and brutality of angry police-men who see them as "dirty nigger lovers." They, unlike so many of their moderate brothers and sisters, have recognized the urgency of the moment and sensed the need for powerful "action" antidotes to com-bat the disease of segregation.

Let me rush on to mention my other disappointment. I have been so greatly disappointed with the white Church and its leadership. Of course there are some notable exceptions. I am not unmindful of the fact that each of you has taken some significant stands on this issue. I commend you, Rev. Stallings, for your Christian stand on this past Sunday, in welcoming Negroes to your worship service on a nonseg-regated basis. I commend the Catholic leaders of this state for inte-grating Springhill College several years ago.

But despite these notable exceptions I must honestly reiterate that I have been disappointed with the Church. I do not say that as one of those negative critics who can always find something wrong with the Church. I say it as a minister of the gospel, who loves the Church; who was nurtured in its bosom; who has been sustained by its spiritual blessings and who will remain true to it as long as the cord of life shall lengthen.

40   I had the strange feeling when I was suddenly catapulted into the leadership of the bus protest in Montgomery several years ago that we would have the support of the white Church. I felt that the white minis-ters, priests, and rabbis of the South would be some of our strongest allies. Instead, some have been outright opponents, refusing to understand the freedom movement and misrepresenting its leaders; all too many others have been more cautious than courageous and have remained silent be-hind the anesthetizing security of stained glass windows.   40

In spite of my shattered dreams of the past, I came to Birming-ham with the hope that the white religious leadership of the commu-nity would see the justice of our cause and, with deep moral concern, serve as the channel through which our just grievances could get to the power structure. I had hoped that each of you would understand. But again I have been disappointed.

I have heard numerous religious leaders of the South call upon their worshippers to comply with a desegregation decision because it is the law, but I have longed to hear white ministers say follow this decree because integration is morally right and the Negro is your brother. In the midst of blatant injustices inflicted upon the Negro, I have watched white churches stand on the sideline and merely mouth pious irrelevancies and sanctimonious trivialities. In the midst of a mighty struggle to rid our nation of racial and economic injustice, I have heard so many ministers say, "Those are social issues with which the Gospel has no real concern," and I have watched so many churches commit themselves to a completely otherworldly religion which made a strange distinction between body and soul, the sacred and the secular.

So here we are moving toward the exit of the twentieth century with a religious community largely adjusted to the status quo, standing as a tail light behind other community agencies rather than a headlight leading men to higher levels of justice.

I have travelled the length and breadth of Alabama, Mississippi, and all the other Southern states. On sweltering summer days and crisp autumn mornings I have looked at her beautiful churches with their spires pointing heavenward. I have beheld the impressive outlay of her massive religious education buildings. Over and over again I have found myself asking: "Who worships here? Who is their God? Where were their voices when the lips of Governor Barnett dripped with words of interposition and nullification? Where were they when Governor Wallace gave the clarion call for defiance and hatred? Where were their voices of support when tired, bruised, and weary Negro men and women decided to rise from the dark dungeons of complacency to the bright hills of creative protest?"

45   Yes, these questions are still in my mind. In deep disappointment, 45 I have wept over the laxity of the Church. But be assured that my tears have been tears of love. There can be no deep disappointment where there is not deep love. Yes, I love the Church; I love her sacred walls. How could I do otherwise? I am in the rather unique position of being the son, the grandson, and the great grandson of preachers. Yes, I see the Church as the body of Christ. But, oh! How we have blemished and scarred that body through social neglect and fear of being nonconformists.

There was a time when the Church was very powerful. It was during that period when the early Christians rejoiced when they were deemed worthy to suffer for what they believed. In those days the Church was not merely a thermometer that recorded the ideas and principles of popular opinion; it was a thermostat that transformed the mores of society. Wherever the early Christians entered a town the power structure got disturbed and immediately sought to convict them for being "disturbers of the peace" and "outside agitators." But they went on with the conviction that they were a "colony of heaven" and had to obey God rather than man. They were small in number but big in commitment. They were too God-intoxicated to be "astronomically intimidated." They brought an end to such ancient evils as infanticide and gladiatorial contest.

Things are different now. The contemporary Church is so often a weak, ineffectual voice with an uncertain sound. It is so often the arch-supporter of the status quo. Far from being disturbed by the presence of the Church, the power structure of the average community is consoled by the Church's silent and often vocal sanction of things as they are.

But the judgment of God is upon the Church as never before. If the Church of today does not recapture the sacrificial spirit of the early Church, it will lose its authentic ring, forfeit the loyalty of millions, and be dismissed as an irrelevant social club with no meaning for the twentieth century. I am meeting young people every day whose disappointment with the Church has risen to outright disgust.

Maybe again I have been too optimistic. Is organized religion too inextricably bound to the status quo to save our nation and the world? Maybe I must turn my faith to the inner spiritual Church, the church within the Church, as the true *ecclesia* and the hope of the world. But again I am thankful to God that some noble souls from the ranks of organized religion have broken loose from the paralyzing chains of conformity and joined us as active partners in the struggle for freedom. They have left their secure congregations and walked the streets of Albany, Georgia, with us. They have gone through the highways of the South on torturous rides for freedom. Yes, they have gone to jail with us. Some have been kicked out of their churches and lost the support of their bishops and fellow ministers. But they have gone with the faith that right defeated is stronger than evil triumphant. These men have been the leaven in the lump of the race. Their witness has been the spiritual salt that has preserved the true meaning of the Gospel in these troubled times. They have carved a tunnel of hope through the dark mountain of disappointment.

50   I hope the Church as a whole will meet the challenge of this decisive hour. But even if the Church does not come to the aid of justice, I have no despair about the future. I have no fear about the outcome of our struggle in Birmingham, even if our motives are

presently misunderstood. We will reach the goal of freedom in Birmingham and all over the nation, because the goal of America is freedom. Abused and scorned though we may be, our destiny is tied up with the destiny of America. Before the pilgrims landed at Plymouth, we were here. Before the pen of Jefferson etched across the pages of history the majestic words of the Declaration of Independence, we were here. For more than two centuries our foreparents labored in this country without wages; they made cotton "king"; and they built the homes of their masters in the midst of brutal injustice and shameful humiliation—and yet out of a bottomless vitality they continued to thrive and develop. If the inexpressible cruelties of slavery could not stop us, the opposition we now face will surely fail. We will win our freedom because the sacred heritage of our nation and the eternal will of God are embodied in our echoing demands.

I must close now. But before closing I am impelled to mention one other point in your statement that troubled me profoundly. You warmly commended the Birmingham police force for keeping "order" and "preventing violence." I don't believe you would have so warmly commended the police force if you had seen its angry violent dogs literally biting six unarmed, nonviolent Negroes. I don't believe you would so quickly commend the policemen if you would observe their ugly and inhuman treatment of Negroes here in the city jail; if you would watch them push and curse old Negro women and young Negro girls; if you would see them slap and kick old Negro men and young Negro boys; if you will observe them, as they did on two occasions, refuse to give us food because we wanted to sing our grace together. I'm sorry that I can't join you in your praise for the police department.

It is true that they have been rather disciplined in their public handling of the demonstrators. In this sense they have been rather publicly "nonviolent." But for what purpose? To preserve the evil system of segregation. Over the last few years I have consistently preached that nonviolence demands that the means we use must be as pure as the ends we seek. So I have tried to make it clear that it is wrong to use immoral means to attain moral ends. But now I must affirm that it is just as wrong, or even more so, to use moral means to preserve immoral ends. Maybe Mr. Connor and his policemen have been rather publicly nonviolent, as Chief Pritchett was in Albany, Georgia, but they have used the moral means of nonviolence to maintain the immoral end of flagrant racial injustice. T. S. Eliot has said that there is no greater treason than to do the right deed for the wrong reason.

I wish you had commended the Negro sit-inners and demonstrators of Birmingham for their sublime courage, their willingness to suffer, and their amazing discipline in the midst of the most inhuman provocation. One day the South will recognize its real heroes. They will be the James Merediths, courageously and with a majestic sense of purpose, facing jeering and hostile mobs and the agonizing loneliness that characterizes the life of the pioneer. They will be old, oppressed, battered Negro women, symbolized in a seventy-two year old woman of Montgomery, Alabama, who rose up with a sense of dignity and with her people decided not to ride the segregated buses, and responded to one who inquired about her tiredness with ungrammatical profundity: "My feets is tired, but my soul is rested." They will be young high school and college students, young ministers of the gospel and a host of the elders, courageously and nonviolently sitting in at lunch counters and willingly going to jail for conscience sake. One day the South will know that when these disinherited children of God sat down at lunch counters they were in reality standing up for the best in the American dream and the most sacred values in our Judeo-Christian heritage, and thus carrying our whole nation back to great wells of democracy which were dug deep by the founding fathers in the formulation of the Constitution and the Declaration of Independence.

Never before have I written a letter this long (or should I say a book?). I'm afraid that it is much too long to take your precious time. I can assure you that it would have been much shorter if I had been writing from a comfortable desk, but what else is there to do when you are alone for days in the dull monotony of a narrow jail cell other than write long letters, think strange thoughts, and pray long prayers!

55   If I have said anything in this letter that is an overstatement of the   55
truth and is indicative of an unreasonable impatience, I beg you to forgive me. If I have said anything in this letter that is an understatement of the truth and is indicative of my having a patience that makes me patient with anything less than brotherhood, I beg God to forgive me.

I hope this letter finds you strong in the faith. I also hope that circumstances will soon make it possible for me to meet each of you, not as an integrationist or a civil rights leader, but as a fellow clergyman and a Christian brother. Let us all hope that the dark clouds of racial prejudice will soon pass away and the deep fog of misunderstanding will be lifted from our fear-drenched communities and in some not too distant tomorrow the radiant stars of love and brotherhood will shine over our great nation with all of their scintillating beauty.

Yours for the cause of
Peace and Brotherhood
MARTIN LUTHER KING, JR.

Learning the Language

Perri Klass

Perri Klass (1958–) was born to American parents in Trinidad and earned her M. D. from Harvard in 1986, going on to become a pediatrician. She has been writing and publishing widely while pursuing her medical career. Her fiction includes two novels, Recombinations *(1985) and* Other Women's Children *(1990), and a collection of short stories,* I Am Having an Adventure *(1986). She published a collection of autobiographical essays,* A Not Entirely Benign Procedure *(1987) about her experience in medical school. The following selection, "Learning the Language," is excerpted from that book. Klass is sensitive to uses of language and understands how language affects thinking. As you read this essay, think about other special groups who also use language in unique ways.*

1   "**M**rs. Tolstoy is your basic LOL in NAD, admitted for a soft rule-out MI," the intern announces. I scribble that on my patient list. In other words, Mrs. Tolstoy is a Little Old Lady in No Apparent Distress who is in the hospital to make sure she hasn't had a heart attack (rule out a Myocardial Infarction). And we think it's unlikely that she has had a heart attack (a *soft* rule-out).

If I learned nothing else during my first three months of working in the hospital as a medical student, I learned endless jargon and abbreviations. I started out in a state of primeval innocence, in which I didn't even know that "s̄ CP, SOB, N/V" meant "without chest pain, shortness of breath, or nausea and vomiting." By the end I took the abbreviations so much for granted that I would complain to my

Reprinted from *Not an Entirely Benign Procedure*, by permission of Elaine Markson Literary Agency. Copyright © 1987 by Perri Klass.

mother the English professor, "And can you believe I had to put down three NG tubes last night?"

"You'll have to tell me what an NG tube is if you want me to sympathize properly," my mother said. NG, nasogastric—isn't it obvious?

I picked up not only the specific expressions but also the patterns of speech and the grammatical conventions; for example, you never say that a patient's blood pressure fell or that his cardiac enzymes rose. Instead, the patient is always the subject of the verb: "He dropped his pressure." "He bumped his enzymes." This sort of construction probably reflects the profound irritation of the intern when the nurses come in the middle of the night to say that Mr. Dickinson has disturbingly low blood pressure. "Oh, he's gonna hurt me bad tonight," the intern might say, inevitably angry at Mr. Dickinson for dropping his pressure and creating a problem.

5   When chemotherapy fails to cure Mrs. Bacon's cancer, what we say is, "Mrs. Bacon failed chemotherapy."   5

"Well, we've already had one hit today, and we're up next, but at least we've got mostly stable players on our team." This means that our team (group of doctors and medical students) has already gotten one new admission today, and it is our turn again, so we'll get whoever is admitted next in emergency, but at least most of the patients we already have are fairly stable, that is, unlikely to drop their pressures or in any other way get suddenly sicker and hurt us bad. Baseball metaphor is pervasive. A no-hitter is a night without any new admissions. A player is always a patient—a nitrate player is a patient on nitrates, a unit player is a patient in the intensive care unit, and so on, until you reach the terminal player.

It is interesting to consider what it means to be winning, or doing well, in this perennial baseball game. When the intern hangs up the phone and announces, "I got a hit," that is not cause for congratulations. The team is not scoring points; rather, it is getting hit, being bombarded with new patients. The object of the game from the point of view of the doctors, considering the players for whom they are already responsible, is to get as few new hits as possible.

This special language contributes to a sense of closeness and professional spirit among people who are under a great deal of stress. As a medical student, I found it exciting to discover that I'd finally cracked the code, that I could understand what doctors said and wrote, and could use the same formulations myself. Some people seem to become enamored of the jargon for its own sake, perhaps because they are so deeply thrilled with the idea of medicine, with the idea of themselves as doctors.

I knew a medical student who was referred to by the interns on the team as Mr. Eponym because he was so infatuated with eponymous terminology, the more obscure the better. He never said "capillary pulsations" if he could say "Quincke's pulses." He would lovingly tell over the multinamed syndromes—Wolff-Parkinson-White, Lown-Ganong-Levine, Schönlein-Henoch—until the temptation to suggest Schleswig-Holstein or Stevenson-Kefauver or Baskin-Robbins became irresistible to his less reverent colleagues.

10 And there is the jargon that you don't ever want to hear yourself using. You know that your training is changing you, but there are certain changes you think would be going a little too far. 10

The resident was describing a man with devastating terminal pancreatic cancer. "Basically he's CTD," the resident concluded. I reminded myself that I had resolved not to be shy about asking when I didn't understand things. "CTD?" I asked timidly.

The resident smirked at me. "Circling The Drain."

The images are vivid and terrible. "What happened to Mrs. Melville?"

"Oh, she boxed last night." To box is to die, of course.

15 Then there are the more pompous locutions that can make the beginning medical student nervous about the effects of medical training. A friend of mine was told by his resident, "A pregnant woman with sickle-cell represents a failure of genetic counseling." 15

Mr. Eponym, who tried hard to talk like the doctors, once explained to me, "An infant is basically a brainstem preparation." The term "brainstem preparation," as used in neurological research, refers to an animal whose higher brain functions have been destroyed so that only the most primitive reflexes remain, like the sucking reflex, the startle reflex, and the rooting reflex.

And yet at other times the harshness dissipates into a strangely elusive euphemism. "As you know, this is a not entirely benign procedure," some doctor will say, and that will be understood to imply agony, risk of complications, and maybe even a significant mortality rate.

The more extreme forms aside, one most important function of medical jargon is to help doctors maintain some distance from their patients. By reformulating a patient's pain and problems into a language that the patient doesn't even speak, I suppose we are in some sense taking those pains and problems under our jurisdiction and also reducing their emotional impact. This linguistic separation between doctors and patients allows conversations to go on at the bedside that are unintelligible to the patient. "Naturally, we're worried about adeno-CA," the intern can say to the medical student, and lung cancer need never be mentioned.

I learned a new language this past summer. At times it thrills me to hear myself using it. It enables me to understand my colleagues, to communicate effectively in the hospital. Yet I am uncomfortably aware that I will never again notice the peculiarities and even atrocities of medical language as keenly as I did this summer. There may be specific expressions I manage to avoid, but even as I remark them, promising myself I will never use them, I find that this language is becoming my professional speech. It no longer sounds strange in my ears—or coming from my mouth. And I am afraid that as with any new language, to use it properly you must absorb not only the vocabulary but also the structure, the logic, the attitudes. At first you may notice these new and alien assumptions every time you put together a sentence, but with time and increased fluency you stop being aware of them at all. And as you lose that awareness, for better or for worse, you move closer and closer to being a doctor instead of just talking like one.

From Silence to Words: Writing as Struggle

Min-zhan Lu

Min-zhan Lu (1946–) was born in China. Lu, who grew up speaking English as well as a number of Chinese dialects, has taught composition and literary criticism at Drake University. She has published both academic articles related to composition issues and articles about her life in China. This article, published in College English *in 1987, relates Lu's challenges acquiring literacy in both China and the United States and how those challenges have affected her writing and teaching.*

Imagine that you enter a parlor. You come late. When you arrive, others have long preceded you, and they are engaged in a heated discussion. . . . You listen for a while, until you decide that you have caught the tenor of the argument; then you put in your oar. Someone answers; you answer him; another comes to your defense; another aligns himself against you, to either the embarrassment or gratification of your opponent, depending upon the quality of your ally's assistance. However, the discussion is interminable. The hour grows late, you must depart. And you do depart, with the discussion still vigorously in progress.

—*Kenneth Burke, The Philosophy of Literary Form*

Men are not built in silence, but in word, in work, in action-reflection.

—*Paulo Freire, Pedagogy of the Oppressed*

From *College English*, April, 1987. Copyright © 1987 by the National Council of Teachers of English.

1

My mother withdrew into silence two months before she 1 died. A few nights before she fell silent, she told me she regretted the way she had raised me and my sisters. I knew she was referring to the way we had been brought up in the midst of two conflicting worlds—the world of home, dominated by the ideology of the Western humanistic tradition, and the world of a society dominated by Mao Tse-tung's Marxism. My mother had devoted her life to our education, an education she knew had made us suffer political persecution during the Cultural Revolution. I wanted to find a way to convince her that, in spite of the persecution, I had benefited from the education she had worked so hard to give me. But I was silent. My understanding of my education was so dominated by memories of confusion and frustration that I was unable to reflect on what I could have gained from it.

This paper is my attempt to fill up that silence with words, words I didn't have then, words that I have since come to by reflecting on my earlier experience as a student in China and on my recent experience as a composition teacher in the United States. For in spite of the frustration and confusion I experienced growing up caught between two conflicting worlds, the conflict ultimately helped me to grow as a reader and writer. Constantly having to switch back and forth between the discourse of home and that of school made me sensitive and self-conscious about the struggle I experienced every time I tried to read, write, or think in either discourse. Eventually, it led me to search for constructive uses for such struggle.

From early childhood, I had identified the differences between home and the outside world by the different languages I used in each. My parents had wanted my sisters and me to get the best education they could conceive of—Cambridge. They had hired a live-in tutor, a Scot, to make us bilingual. I learned to speak English with my parents, my tutor, and my sisters. I was allowed to speak Shanghai dialect only with the servants. When I was four (the year after the Communist Revolution of 1949), my parents sent me to a local private school where I learned to speak, read, and write in a new language—Standard Chinese, the official written language of New China.

In those days I moved from home to school, from English to Standard Chinese to Shanghai dialect, with no apparent friction. I spoke each language with those who spoke the language. All seemed quite "natural"—servants spoke only Shanghai dialect because they were servants; teachers spoke Standard Chinese because they were teachers;

languages had different words because they were different languages. I thought of English as my family language, comparable to the many strange dialects I didn't speak but had often heard some of my classmates speak with their families. While I was happy to have a special family language, until second grade I didn't feel that my family language was any different than some of my classmates' family dialects.

5   My second grade homeroom teacher was a young graduate from a missionary school. When she found out I spoke English, she began to practice her English on me. One day she used English when asking me to run an errand for her. As I turned to close the door behind me, I noticed the puzzled faces of my classmates. I had the same sensation I had often experienced when some stranger in a crowd would turn on hearing me speak English. I was more intensely pleased on this occasion, however, because suddenly I felt that my family language had been singled out from the family languages of my classmates. Since we were not allowed to speak any dialect other than Standard Chinese in the classroom, having my teacher speak English to me in class made English an official language of the classroom. I began to take pride in my ability to speak it.

This incident confirmed in my mind what my parents had always told me about the importance of English to one's life. Time and again they had told me of how my paternal grandfather, who was well versed in classic Chinese, kept losing good-paying jobs because he couldn't speak English. My grandmother reminisced constantly about how she had slaved and saved to send my father to a first-rate missionary school. And we were made to understand that it was my father's fluent English that had opened the door to his success. Even though my family had always stressed the importance of English for my future, I used to complain bitterly about the extra English lessons we had to take after school. It was only after my homeroom teacher had "sanctified" English that I began to connect English with my education. I became a much more eager student in my tutorials.

What I learned from my tutorials seemed to enhance and reinforce what I was learning in my classroom. In those days each word had one meaning. One day I would be making a sentence at school: "The national flag of China is red." The next day I would recite at home, "My love is like a red, red rose." There seemed to be an agreement between the Chinese "red" and the English "red," and both corresponded to the patch of color printed next to the word. "Love" was my love for my mother at home and my love for my "motherland" at school; both "loves" meant how I felt about my mother. Having two loads of homework forced me to develop a quick memory for words and a sensitivity to form and style. What I learned in one language carried over to the other. I made sentences such as, "I saw a red, red rose among the green leaves," with both the English lyric and the classic Chinese lyric—red flower among green leaves—running through my mind, and I was praised by both teacher and tutor for being a good student.

Although my elementary schooling took place during the fifties, I was almost oblivious to the great political and social changes happening around me. Years later, I read in my history and political philosophy textbooks that the fifties were a time when "China was making a transition from a semi-feudal, semi-capitalist, and semi-colonial country into a socialist country," a period in which "the Proletarians were breaking into the educational territory dominated by Bourgeois Intellectuals." While people all over the country were being officially classified into Proletarians, Petty-bourgeois, National-bourgeois, Poor-peasants, and Intellectuals, and were trying to adjust to their new social identities, my parents were allowed to continue the upper middle-class life they had established before the 1949 Revolution because of my father's affiliation with British firms. I had always felt that my family was different from the families of my classmates, but I didn't perceive society's view of my family until the summer vacation before I entered high school.

First, my aunt was caught by her colleagues talking to her husband over the phone in English. Because of it, she was criticized and almost labeled a Rightist. (This was the year of the Anti-Rightist movement, a movement in which the Intellectuals became the target of the "socialist class-struggle.") I had heard others telling my mother that she was foolish to teach us English when Russian had replaced English as the "official" foreign language. I had also learned at school that the American and British Imperialists were the arch-enemies of New China. Yet I had made no connection between the arch-enemies and the English our family spoke. What happened to my aunt forced the connection on me. I began to see my parents' choice of a family language as an anti-Revolutionary act and was alarmed that I had participated in such an act. From then on, I took care not to use English outside home and to conceal my knowledge of English from my new classmates.

10   Certain words began to play important roles in my new life at the   10
junior high. On the first day of school, we were handed forms to fill
out with our parents' class, job, and income. Being one of the few people not employed by the government, my father had never been officially classified. Since he was a medical doctor, he told me to put him
down as an Intellectual. My homeroom teacher called me into the office a couple of days afterwards and told me that my father couldn't
be an Intellectual if his income far exceeded that of a Capitalist. He
also told me that since my father worked for Foreign Imperialists, my
father should be classified as an Imperialist Lackey. The teacher looked
nonplussed when I told him that my father couldn't be an Imperialist
Lackey because he was a medical doctor. But I could tell from the way
he took notes on my form that my father's job had put me in an unfavorable position in his eyes.

The Standard Chinese term "class" was not a new word for me.
Since first grade, I had been taught sentences such as, "The Working
class are the masters of New China." I had always known that it was
good to be a worker, but until then, I had never felt threatened for not
being one. That fall, "class" began to take on a new meaning for me.
I noticed a group of Working-class students and teachers at school. I
was made to understand that because of my class background, I was
excluded from that group.

Another word that became important was "consciousness." One
of the slogans posted in the school building read, "Turn our students
into future Proletarians with socialist consciousness and education!"
For several weeks we studied this slogan in our political philosophy
course, a subject I had never had in elementary school. I still remember the definition of "socialist consciousness" that we were repeatedly
tested on through the years: "Socialist consciousness is a person's political soul. It is the consciousness of the Proletarians represented by
Marxist Mao Tse-tung thought. It takes expression in one's action, language, and lifestyle. It is the task of every Chinese student to grow up
into a Proletarian with a socialist consciousness so that he can serve
the people and the motherland." To make the abstract concept accessible to us, our teacher pointed out that the immediate task for
students from Working-class families was to strengthen their socialist consciousnesses. For those of us who were from other class
backgrounds, the task was to turn ourselves into Workers with socialist consciousnesses. The teacher never explained exactly how we were

supposed to "turn" into Workers. Instead, we were given samples of the ritualistic annual plans we had to write at the beginning of each term. In these plans, we performed "self-criticism" on our consciousnesses and made vows to turn ourselves into Workers with socialist consciousnesses. The teacher's division between those who did and those who didn't have a socialist consciousness led me to reify the notion of "consciousness" into a thing one possesses. I equated this intangible "thing" with a concrete way of dressing, speaking, and writing. For instance, I never doubted that my political philosophy teacher had a socialist consciousness because she was from a steelworker's family (she announced this the first day of class) and was a party member who wore grey cadre suits and talked like a philosophy textbook. I noticed other things about her. She had beautiful eyes and spoke Standard Chinese with such a pure accent that I thought she should be a film star. But I was embarrassed that I had noticed things that ought not to have been associated with her. I blamed my observation on my Bourgeois consciousness.

At the same time, the way reading and writing were taught through memorization and imitation also encouraged me to reduce concepts and ideas to simple definitions. In literature and political philosophy classes, we were taught a large number of quotations from Marx, Lenin, and Mao Tse-tung. Each concept that appeared in these quotations came with a definition. We were required to memorize the definitions of the words along with the quotations. Every time I memorized a definition, I felt I had learned a word: "The national red flag symbolizes the blood shed by Revolutionary ancestors for our socialist cause"; "New China rises like a red sun over the eastern horizon." As I memorized these sentences, I reduced their metaphors to dictionary meanings: "red" meant "Revolution" and "red sun" meant "New China" in the "language" of the Working class. I learned mechanically but eagerly. I soon became quite fluent in this new language.

As school began to define me as a political subject, my parents tried to build up my resistance to the "communist poisoning" by exposing me to the "great books"—novels by Charles Dickens, Nathaniel Hawthorne, Emily Brontë, Jane Austen, and writers from around the turn of the century. My parents implied that these writers represented how I, their child, should read and write. My parents replaced the word "Bourgeois" with the word "cultured." They reminded me that I was in school only to learn math and science. I needed to pass the other courses to stay in school, but I was not to let the "Red doctrines" corrupt my mind. Gone were the days when I could innocently write, "I saw the red, red rose among the green leaves," collapsing, as I did, English and Chinese cultural traditions. "Red" came to mean Revolution at school, "the Commies" at home, and adultery in *The Scarlet Letter.* Since I took these symbols and metaphors as meanings natural to people of the same class, I abandoned my earlier definitions of English and Standard Chinese as the language of home and the language of school. I now defined English as the language of the Bourgeois and Standard Chinese as the language of the Working class. I thought of the language of the Working class as someone else's language and the language of the Bourgeois as my language. But I also believed that, although the language of the Bourgeois was my real language, I could and would adopt the language of the Working class when I was at school. I began to put on and take off my Working class language in the same way I put on and took off my school clothes to avoid being criticized for wearing Bourgeois clothes.

15   In my literature classes, I learned the Working-class formula for reading. Each work in the textbook had a short "Author's Biography": "X X X, born in 19—in the province of X X X, is from a Worker's family. He joined the Revolution in 19—. He is a Revolutionary realist with a passionate love for the Party and Chinese Revolution. His work expresses the thoughts and emotions of the masses and sings praise to the prosperous socialist construction on all fronts of China." The teacher used the "Author's Biography" as a yardstick to measure the texts. We were taught to locate details in the texts that illustrated these summaries, such as words that expressed Workers' thoughts and emotions or events that illustrated the Workers' lives.

I learned a formula for Working-class writing in the composition classes. We were given sample essays and told to imitate them. The theme was always about how the collective taught the individual a lesson. I would write papers about labor-learning experiences or school-cleaning days, depending on the occasion of the collective activity closest to the assignment. To make each paper look different, I dressed it up with details about the date, the weather, the environment, or the appearance of the Master-worker who had taught me "the lesson." But as I became more and more fluent in the generic voice of the Working-class Student, I also became more and more self-conscious about the language we used at home.

For instance, in senior high we began to have English classes ("to study English for the Revolution," as the slogan on the cover of the textbook said), and I was given my first Chinese-English dictionary. There I discovered the English version of the term "class-struggle." (The Chinese characters for a school "class" and for a social "class" are different.) I had often used the English word "class" at home in sentences such as, "So and so has class," but I had not connected this sense of "class" with "class-struggle." Once the connection was made, I heard a second layer of meaning every time someone at home said a person had "class." The expression began to mean the person had the style and sophistication characteristic of the bourgeoisie. The word lost its innocence. I was uneasy about hearing that second layer of meaning because I was sure my parents did not hear the word that way. I felt that therefore I should not be hearing it that way either. Hearing the second layer of meaning made me wonder if I was losing my English.

My suspicion deepened when I noticed myself unconsciously merging and switching between the "reading" of home and the "reading" of school. Once I had to write a report on *The Revolutionary Family,* a book about an illiterate woman's awakening and growth as a Revolutionary through the deaths of her husband and all her children for the cause of the Revolution. In one scene the woman deliberated over whether or not she should encourage her youngest son to join the Revolution. Her memory of her husband's death made her afraid to encourage her son. Yet she also remembered her earlier married life and the first time her husband tried to explain the meaning of the Revolution to her. These memories made her feel she should encourage her son to continue the cause his father had begun.

I was moved by this scene. "Moved" was a word my mother and sisters used a lot when we discussed books. Our favorite moments in novels were moments of what I would now call internal conflict, moments which we said "moved" us. I remember that we were "moved" by Jane Eyre when she was torn between her sense of ethics, which compelled her to leave the man she loved, and her impulse to stay with the only man who had ever loved her. We were also moved by Agnes in *David Copperfield* because of the way she restrained her love for David so that he could live happily with the woman he loved. My standard method of doing a book report was to model it on the review by the Publishing Bureau and to dress it up with detailed quotations from the book. The review of *The Revolutionary Family* emphasized the woman's Revolutionary spirit. I decided to use the scene that had moved me to illustrate this point. I wrote the report the night before it was due. When I had finished, I realized I couldn't possibly hand it in. Instead of illustrating her Revolutionary spirit, I had dwelled on her internal conflict, which could be seen as a moment of weak sentimentality that I should never have emphasized in a Revolutionary heroine. I wrote another report, taking care to illustrate the grandeur of her Revolutionary spirit by expanding on a quotation in which she decided that if the life of her son could change the lives of millions of sons, she should not begrudge his life for the cause of Revolution. I handed in my second version but kept the first in my desk.

20   I never showed it to anyone. I could never show it to people out- 20
side my family, because it had deviated so much from the reading enacted by the jacket review. Neither could I show it to my mother or sisters, because I was ashamed to have been so moved by such a "Revolutionary" book. My parents would have been shocked to learn that I could like such a book in the same way they liked Dickens. Writing this book report increased my fear that I was losing the command over both the "language of home" and the "language of school" that I had worked so hard to gain. I tried to remind myself that, if I could still tell when my reading or writing sounded incorrect, then I had retained my command over both languages. Yet I could no longer be confident of my command over either language because I had discovered that when I was not careful—or even when I was—my reading and writing often surprised me with its impurity. To prevent such impurity, I became very suspicious of my thoughts when I read or wrote. I was always asking myself why I was using this word, how I was using it, always afraid that I wasn't reading or writing correctly. What confused and frustrated me most was that I could not figure out why I was no longer able to read or write correctly without such painful deliberation.

I continued to read only because reading allowed me to keep my thoughts and confusion private. I hoped that somehow, if I watched myself carefully, I would figure out from the way I read whether I had really mastered the "languages." But writing became a dreadful chore. When I tried to keep a diary, I was so afraid that the voice of school might slip in that I could only list my daily activities. When I wrote for school, I worried that my Bourgeois sensibilities would betray me.

The more suspicious I became about the way I read and wrote, the more guilty I felt for losing the spontaneity with which I had learned to "use" these "languages." Writing the book report made me feel that my reading and writing in the "language" of either home or school could not be free of the interference of the other. But I was unable to acknowledge, grasp, or grapple with what I was experiencing, for both my parents and my teachers had suggested that, if I were a good student, such interference would and should not take place. I assumed that once I had "acquired" a discourse, I could simply switch it on and off every time I read and wrote as I would some electronic tool. Furthermore, I expected my readings and writings to come out in their correct forms whenever I switched the proper discourse on. I still regarded the discourse of home as natural and the discourse of school alien, but I never had doubted before that I could acquire both and switch them on and off according to the occasion.

When my experience in writing conflicted with what I thought should happen when I used each discourse, I rejected my experience because it contradicted what my parents and teachers had taught me. I shied away from writing to avoid what I assumed I should not experience. But trying to avoid what should not happen did not keep it from recurring whenever I had to write. Eventually my confusion and frustration over these recurring experiences compelled me to search for an explanation: how and why had I failed to learn what my parents and teachers had worked so hard to teach me?

I now think of the internal scene for my reading and writing about *The Revolutionary Family* as a heated discussion between myself, the voices of home, and those of school. The review on the back of the book, the sample student papers I came across in my composition classes, my philosophy teacher—these I heard as voices of one group. My parents and my home readings were the voices of an opposing group. But the conversation between these opposing voices in the internal scene of my writing was not as polite and respectful as the parlor scene Kenneth Burke has portrayed (see epigraph). Rather, these voices struggled to dominate the discussion, constantly incorporating, dismissing, or suppressing the arguments of each other, like the battles between the hegemonic and counter-hegemonic forces described in Raymond Williams' *Marxism and Literature* (108–14).

25   When I read *The Revolutionary Family* and wrote the first version of my report, I began with a quotation from the review. The voices of both home and school answered, clamoring to be heard. I tried to listen to one group and turn a deaf ear to the other. Both persisted. I negotiated my way through these conflicting voices, now agreeing with one, now agreeing with the other. I formed a reading out of my interaction with both. Yet I was afraid to have done so because both

home and school had implied that I should speak in unison with only one of these groups and stand away from the discussion rather than participate in it.

My teachers and parents had persistently called my attention to the intensity of the discussion taking place on the external social scene. The story of my grandfather's failure and my father's success had from my early childhood made me aware of the conflict between Western and traditional Chinese cultures. My political education at school added another dimension to the conflict; the war of Marxist-Maoism against them both. Yet when my parents and teachers called my attention to the conflict, they stressed the anxiety of having to live through China's transformation from a semi-feudal, semi-capitalist, and semi-colonial society to a socialist one. Acquiring the discourse of the dominant group was, to them, a means of seeking alliance with that group and thus of surviving the whirlpool of cultural currents around them. As a result, they modeled their pedagogical practices on this utilitarian view of language. Being the eager student, I adopted this view of language as a tool for survival. It came to dominate my understanding of the discussion on the social and historical scene and to restrict my ability to participate in that discussion.

To begin with, the metaphor of language as a tool for survival led me to be passive in my use of discourse, to be a bystander in the discussion. In Burke's "parlor," everyone is involved in the discussion. As it goes on through history, what we call "communal discourses"— arguments specific to particular political, social, economic, ethnic, sexual, and family groups—form, re-form and transform. To use a discourse in such a scene is to participate in the argument and to contribute to the formation of the discourse. But when I was growing up, I could not take on the burden of such an active role in the discussion. For both home and school presented the existent conventions of the discourse each taught me as absolute laws for my action. They turned verbal action into a tool, a set of conventions produced and shaped prior to and outside of my own verbal acts. Because I saw language as a tool, I separated the process of producing the tool from the process of using it. The tool was made by someone else and was then acquired and used by me. How the others made it before I acquired it determined and guaranteed what it produced when I used it. I imagined that the more experienced and powerful members of the community were the ones responsible for making the tool. They were the ones who participated in the discussion and fought with opponents.

When I used what they made, their labor and accomplishments would ensure the quality of my reading and writing. By using it, I could survive the heated discussion. When my immediate experience in writing the book report suggested that knowing the conventions of school did not guarantee the form and content of my report, when it suggested that I had to write the report with the work and responsibility I had assigned to those who wrote book reviews in the Publishing bureau, I thought I had lost the tool I had earlier acquired.

Another reason I could not take up an active role in the argument was that my parents and teachers contrived to provide a scene free of conflict for practicing my various languages. It was as if their experience had made them aware of the conflict between their discourse and other discourses and of the struggle involved in reproducing the conventions of any discourse on a scene where more than one discourse exists. They seemed convinced that such conflict and struggle would overwhelm someone still learning the discourse. Home and school each contrived a purified space where only one discourse was spoken and heard. In their choice of textbooks, in the way they spoke, and in the way they required me to speak, each jealously silenced any voice that threatened to break the unison of the scene. The homogeneity of home and of school implied that only one discourse could and should be relevant in each place. It led me to believe I should leave behind, turn a deaf ear to, or forget the discourse of the other when I crossed the boundary dividing them. I expected myself to set down one discourse whenever I took up another just as I would take off or put on a particular set of clothes for school or home.

Despite my parents' and teachers' attempts to keep home and school discrete, the internal conflict between the two discourses continued whenever I read or wrote. Although I tried to suppress the voice of one discourse in the name of the other, having to speak aloud in the voice I had just silenced each time I crossed the boundary kept both voices active in my mind. Every "I think . . . " from the voice of home or school brought forth a "However . . . " or a "But. . ." from the voice of the opponents. To identify with the voice of home or school, I had to negotiate through the conflicting voices of both by restating, taking back, qualifying my thoughts. I was unconsciously doing so when I did my book report. But I could not use the interaction comfortably and constructively. Both my parents and my teachers had implied that my job was to prevent that interaction from happening. My sense of having failed to accomplish what they had taught silenced me.

30   To use the interaction between the discourses of home and school constructively, I would have to have seen reading or writing as a process in which I worked my way towards a stance through a dialectical process of identification and division. To identify with an ally, I would have to have grasped the distance between where he or she stood and where I was positioning myself. In taking a stance against an opponent, I would have to have grasped where my stance identified with the stance of my allies. Teetering along the "wavering line of pressure and counter-pressure" from both allies and opponents, I might have worked my way towards a stance of my own (Burke, *A Rhetoric of Motives*, 23). Moreover, I would have to have understood that the voices in my mind, like the participants in the parlor scene, were in constant flux. As I came into contact with new and different groups of people or read different books, voices entered and left. Each time I read or wrote, the stance I negotiated out of these voices would always be at some distance from the stances I worked out in my previous and my later readings or writings.

I could not conceive such a form of action for myself because I saw reading and writing as an expression of an established stance. In delineating the conventions of a discourse, my parents and teachers had synthesized the stance they saw as typical for a representative member of the community. Burke calls this the stance of a "god" or the "prototype"; Williams calls it the "official" or "possible" stance of the community. Through the metaphor of the survival tool, my parents and teachers had led me to assume I could automatically reproduce the official stance of the discourse I used. Therefore, when I did my book report on *The Revolutionary Family*, I expected my knowledge of the official stance set by the book review to ensure the actual stance of my report. As it happened, I began by trying to take the official stance of the review. Other voices interrupted. I answered back. In the process, I worked out a stance approximate but not identical to the official stance I began with. Yet the experience of having to labor to realize my knowledge of the official stance or to prevent myself from wandering away from it frustrated and confused me. For even though I had been actually reading and writing in a Burkean scene, I was afraid to participate actively in the discussion. I assumed it was my role to survive by staying out of it.

Not long ago, my daughter told me that it bothered her to hear her friend "talk wrong." Having come to the United States from China with little English, my daughter has become sensitive to the way English, as spoken by her teachers, operates. As a result, she has amazed her teachers with her success in picking up the language and in adapting to life at school. Her concern to speak the English taught in the classroom "correctly" makes her uncomfortable when she hears people using "ain't" or double negatives, which her teacher considers "improper." I see in her the me that had eagerly learned and used the discourse of the Working class at school. Yet while I was torn between the two conflicting worlds of school and home, she moves with seeming ease from the conversations she hears over the dinner table to her teacher's words in the classroom. My husband and I are proud of the good work she does at school. We are glad she is spared the kinds of conflict between home and school I experienced at her age. Yet as we watch her becoming more and more fluent in the language of the classroom, we wonder if, by enabling her to "survive" school, her very fluency will silence her when the scene of her reading and writing expands beyond that of the composition classroom.

For when I listen to my daughter, to students, and to some composition teachers talking about the teaching and learning of writing, I am often alarmed by the degree to which the metaphor of a survival tool dominates their understanding of language as it once dominated my own. I am especially concerned with the way some composition classes focus on turning the classroom into a monological scene for the students' reading and writing. Most of our students live in a world similar to my daughter's, somewhere between the purified world of the classroom and the complex world of my adolescence. When composition classes encourage these students to ignore those voices that seem irrelevant to the purified world of the classroom, most students are often able to do so without much struggle. Some of them are so adept at doing it that the whole process has for them become automatic.

However, beyond the classroom and beyond the limited range of these students' immediate lives lies a much more complex and dynamic social and historical scene. To help these students become actors in such a scene, perhaps we need to call their attention to voices that may seem irrelevant to the discourse we teach rather than encourage them to shut them out. For example, we might intentionally complicate the classroom scene by bringing into it discourses that stand at varying distances from the one we teach. We might encourage students to explore ways of practicing the conventions of the discourse they are learning by negotiating through these conflicting voices. We could also encourage them to see themselves as responsible for forming or transforming as well as preserving the discourse they are learning.

35   As I think about what we might do to complicate the external and internal scenes of our students' writing, I hear my parents and teachers saying: "Not now. Keep them from the wrangle of the marketplace until they have acquired the discourse and are skilled at using it." And I answer: "Don't teach them to 'survive' the whirlpool of crosscurrents by avoiding it. Use the classroom to moderate the currents. Moderate the currents, but teach them from the beginning to struggle." When I think of the ways in which the teaching of reading and writing as classroom activities can frustrate the development of students, I am almost grateful for the overwhelming complexity of the circumstances in which I grew up. For it was this complexity that kept me from losing sight of the effort and choice involved in reading or writing with and through a discourse.

References

Burke, Kenneth. *The Philosophy of Literary Form: Studies in Symbolic Action.* 2nd ed. Baton Rouge: Louisiana State UP, 1967.

———. *A Rhetoric of Motives.* Berkeley: U of California P, 1969.

Freire, Paulo. *Pedagogy of the Oppressed.* Trans. M. B. Ramos. New York: Continuum, 1970.

Williams, Raymond. *Marxism and Literature.* New York: Oxford UP, 1977.

From Outside, In

Barbara Mellix

Each one of us, at varying points in life and career, will find ourselves moving, as in the title of this essay, "From Outside, In." This entry can also be, in some sense, a leave-taking, and as such can involve several communities. It also may involve complicated relationships between language and power and may require a new awareness of what is "proper" in each community. No easy move, this stepping "from outside, in." It forces us to rethink who we are and may prompt us to discover both the limits and the re-sourcefulness of language.

Raised in Greeleyville, South Carolina, Barbara Mellix draws on her own vexed relationship to multiple languages and communities in this essay, published in the Georgia Review *in 1987. The essay recounts her experiences from early childhood through her first college writing courses that she took as a working mother. Mellix went on to receive her MFA in creative writing in 1986 from the University of Pittsburgh. In addition to teaching writing in the English department at the University of Pittsburgh, she serves as executive assistant dean in the College of Arts and Sciences, where she edits the college's alumni magazine.*

1 Two years ago, when I started writing this paper, trying to bring order out of chaos, my ten-year-old daughter was suffering from an acute attack of boredom. She drifted in and out of the room complaining that she had nothing to do, no one to "be with" because none of her friends were at home. Patiently I explained that I was working on something special and needed peace and quiet, and I suggested that she paint, read, or work with her computer. None of these interested her. Finally, she pulled up a chair to my desk and watched me, now and then heaving long, loud sighs. After two or three minutes (nine

Reprinted by permission from *Georgia Review* 41, no. 2.

or ten sighs), I lost my patience. "Looka here, Allie," I said, "you are too old for this kinda carryin' on. I done told you this is important. You wronger than dirt to be in here haggin' me like this and you know it. Now git on outta here and leave me off before I put my foot all the way down."

I was at home, alone with my family, and my daughter understood that this way of speaking was appropriate in that context. She knew, as a matter of fact, that it was almost inevitable; when I get angry at home, I speak some of my finest, most cherished black English. Had I been speaking to my daughter in this manner in certain other environments, she would have been shocked and probably worried that I had taken leave of my sense of propriety.

Like my children, I grew up speaking what I considered two distinctly different languages—black English and standard English (or as I thought of them then, the ordinary everyday speech of "country" coloreds and "proper" English)—and in the process of acquiring these languages, I developed an understanding of when, where, and how to use them. But unlike my children. I grew up in a world that was primarily black. My friends, neighbors, minister, teachers—almost everybody I associated with every day—were black. And we spoke to one another in our own special language: *That sho is a pretty dress you got on. If she don' soon leave me off I'm gon tell her head a mess. I was so mad I could'a pissed a blue rod. He all the time trying to low-rate somebody. Ain't that just about the nastiest thing you ever set ears on?*

Then there were the "others," the "proper" blacks, transplanted relatives and one-time friends who came home from the city for weddings, funerals, and vacations. To these we spoke standard English. "Ain't?" my mother would yell at me when I used the term in the presence of "others." "You *know* better than that." And I would hang my head in shame and say the "proper" word.

5   I remember one summer sitting in my grandmother's house in   5
Greeleyville, South Carolina, when it was full of the chatter of city relatives who were home on vacation. My parents sat quietly, only now and then volunteering a comment or answering a question. My mother's face took on a strained expression when she spoke. I could see that she was being careful to say just the right words in just the right way. Her voice sounded thick, muffled. And when she finished speaking, she would lapse into silence, her proper smile on her face. My father was more articulate, more aggressive. He spoke quickly, his words sharp and clear. But he held his proud head higher, a signal that he, too, was uncomfortable. My sisters and brothers and I stared at our aunts,

uncles, and cousins, speaking only when prompted. Even then, we hesitated, formed our sentences in our minds, then spoke softly, shyly.

My parents looked small and anxious during those occasions, and I waited impatiently for our leave-taking when we would mock our relatives the moment we were out of their hearing. "Reeely," we would say to one another, flexing our wrists and rolling our eyes, "how dooo you stan' this heat? Chile, it just too hyooo-mid for words." Our relatives had made us feel "country," and that was our way of regaining pride in ourselves while getting a little revenge in the bargain. The words bubbled in our throats and rolled across our tongues, a balming.

As a child I felt this same doubleness in uptown Greeleyville where the whites lived. "Ain't that a pretty dress you're wearing!" Toby, the town policeman, said to me one day when I was fifteen. "Thank you very much," I replied, my voice barely audible in my own ears. The words felt wrong in my mouth, rigid, foreign. It was not that I had never spoken that phrase before—it was common in black English, too—but I was extremely conscious that this was an occasion for proper English. I had taken out my English and put it on as I did my church clothes, and I felt as if I were wearing my Sunday best in the middle of the week. It did not matter that Toby had not spoken grammatically correct English. He was white and could speak as he wished. I had something to prove. Toby did not.

Speaking standard English to whites was our way of demonstrating that we knew their language and could use it. Speaking it to standard-English-speaking blacks was our way of showing them that we, as well as they, could "put on airs." But when we spoke standard English, we acknowledged (to ourselves and to others—but primarily to ourselves) that our customary way of speaking was inferior. We felt foolish, embarrassed, somehow diminished because we were ashamed to be our real selves. We were reserved, shy in the presence of those who owned and/or spoke *the* language.

My parents never set aside time to drill us in standard English. Their forms of instruction were less formal. When my father was feeling particularly expansive, he would regale us with tales of his exploits in the outside world. In almost fluent English, complete with dialogue and flavored with gestures and embellishment, he told us about his attempt to get a haircut at a white barbershop; his refusal to acknowledge one of the town merchants until the man addressed him as "Mister"; the time he refused to step off the sidewalk uptown to let some whites pass; his airplane trip to New York City (to visit a sick relative) during which the stewardess and porters—recognizing that he was a "gentleman"—addressed him as "Sir." I did not realize then—nor, I think, did my father—that he was teaching us, among other things, standard English and the relationship between language and power.

10   My mother's approach was different. Often, when one of us said, "I'm gon wash off my feet," she would say, "And what will you walk on if you wash them off?" Everyone would laugh at the victim of my mother's "proper" mood. But it was different when one of us children was in a proper mood. "You think you are so superior," I said to my oldest sister one day when we were arguing and she was winning. "Superior!" my sister mocked. "You mean I am acting 'biggidy'?" My sisters and brothers sniggered, then joined in teasing me. Finally, my mother said, "Leave your sister alone. There's nothing wrong with using proper English." There was a half-smile on her face. I had gotten "uppity," had "put on airs" for no good reason. I was at home, alone with the family, and I hadn't been prompted by one of my mother's proper moods. But there was also a proud light in my mother's eyes; her children were learning English very well.

        Not until years later, as a college student, did I begin to understand our ambivalence toward English, our scorn of it, our need to master it, to own and be owned by it—an ambivalence that extended to the public-school classroom. In our school, where there were no whites, my teachers taught standard English but used black English to do it. When my grammar-school teachers wanted us to write, for example, they usually said something like, "I want y'all to write five sentences that make a statement. Anybody get done before the rest can color." It was probably almost those exact words that led me to write these sentences in 1953 when I was in the second grade:

> The white clouds are pretty.
> There are only 15 people in our room.
> We will go to gym.
> We have a new poster.
> We may go out doors.

Second grade came after "Little First" and "Big First," so by then I knew the implied rules that accompanied all writing assignments. Writing was an occasion for proper English. I was not to write in the way we spoke to one another: The white clouds pretty; There ain't but 15 people in our room; We going to gym; We got a new poster; We can go out in the yard. Rather I was to use the language of "other": clouds *are*, there *are*, we *will*, we *may*.

My sentences were short, rigid, perfunctory, like the letters my mother wrote to relatives:

Dear Papa,
How are you? How is Mamie? Fine I hope. We are fine. We will come to see you Sunday. Cousin Ned will give us a ride.
    Love,
    Daughter

The language was not ours. It was something from outside us, something we used for special occasions.

15   But my coloring on the other side of that second-grade paper is 15
different. I drew three hearts and a sun. The sun has a smiling face that radiates and envelops everything it touches. And although the sun and its world are enclosed in a circle, the colors I used—red, blue, green, purple, orange, yellow, black—indicates that I was less restricted with drawing and coloring than I was with writing standard English. My valentines were not just red. My sun was not just a yellow ball in the sky.

By the time I reached the twelfth grade, speaking and writing standard English had taken on new importance. Each year about half of the newly graduated seniors of our school moved to large cities— particularly in the North—to live with relatives and find work. Our English teacher constantly corrected our grammar: "Not 'ain't,' but 'isn't.'" We seldom wrote papers, and even those few were usually plot summaries of short stories. When our teacher returned the papers, she usually lectured on the importance of using standard English: "I *am*; you *are*; he, she, or it *is*," she would say, writing on the chalkboard as she spoke. "How you gon git a job talking about 'I is,' or 'I isn't' or 'I ain't'?"

In Pittsburgh, where I moved after graduation, I watched my aunt and uncle—who had always spoken standard English when in Greeleyville— switch from black English to standard English to a mixture of the two, according to where they were or who they were with. At home and with certain close relatives, friends, and neighbors, they spoke black English. With those less close, they spoke a mixture. In public and with strangers, they generally spoke standard English.

In time, I learned to speak standard English with ease and to switch smoothly from black to standard or a mixture, and back again. But no matter where I was, no matter what the situation or occasion, I continued to write as I had in school:

Dear Mommie,
How are you? How is everybody else? Fine I hope. I am fine. So are
Aunt and Uncle. Tell everyone I said hello. I will write again soon.
   Love,
   Barbara

At work, at a health insurance company, I learned to write letters to customers. I studied form letters and letters written by coworkers, memorizing the phrases and the ways in which they were used. I dictated:

Thank you for your letter of January 5. We have made the
changes in your coverage you requested. Your new premium
will be $150 every three months. We are pleased to have
been of service to you.

20 In a sense, I was proud of the letters I wrote for the company: They 20
were proof of my ability to survive in the city, the outside world—an
indication of my growing mastery of English. But they also indicate
that writing was still mechanical for me, something that didn't require
much thought.

Reading also became a more significant part of my life during those
early years in Pittsburgh. I had always liked reading, but now I devoted
more and more of my spare time to it. I read romances, mysteries, popular novels. Looking back, I realized that the books I liked best were
simple, unambiguous: good versus bad and right versus wrong with
right rewarded and an wrong punished, mysteries unraveled and all set
right in the end. It was how I remembered life in Greeleyville.

Of course I was romanticizing. Life in Greeleyville had not been
so very uncomplicated. Back there I had been—first as a child, then
as a young woman with limited experience in the outside world—
living in a relatively closed-in society. But there were implicit and
explicit principles that guided our way of life and shaped our relationships with one another and the people outside—principles that a
newcomer would find elusive and baffling. In Pittsburgh, I had matured,
become more experienced: I had worked at three different jobs, associated with a wider range of people, married, had children. This new
environment with different prescripts for living required that I speak

standard English much of the time, and slowly, imperceptibly, I had ceased seeing a sharp distinction between myself and "others." Reading romances and mysteries, characterized by dichotomy, was a way of shying away from change, from the person I was becoming.

But that other part of me—that part which took great pride in my ability to hold a job writing business letters—was increasingly drawn to the new developments in my life and the attending possibilities, opportunities for even greater change. If I could write letters for a nationally known business, could I not also do something better, more challenging, more important? Could I not, perhaps, go to college and become a school teacher? For years, afraid and a little embarrassed, I did no more than imagine this different me, this possible me. But sixteen years after coming north, when my younger daughter entered kindergarten, I found myself unable—or unwilling—to resist the lure of possibility. I enrolled in my first college course: Basic Writing, at the University of Pittsburgh.

For the first time in my life, I was required to write extensively about myself. Using the most formal English at my command, I wrote these sentences near the beginning of the term:

> One of my duties as a homemaker is simply picking up after others. A day seldom passes that I don't search for a mislaid toy, book, or gym shoe, etc. I change the Ty-D-Bol, fight "ring around the collar," and keep our laundry smelling "April fresh." Occasionally, I settle arguments between my children and suggest things to do when they're bored. Taking telephone messages for my oldest daughter is my newest and sometimes most aggravating chore. Hanging the toilet paper is my most insignificant.

25 My concern was to use "appropriate" language, to sound as if I belonged 25 in a classroom. But I felt separate from the language—as if it did not and could not belong to me. I couldn't think and feel genuinely in that language, couldn't make it express what I thought and felt about being a housewife. A part of me resented, among other things, being judged by such things as the appearance of my family's laundry and toilet bowl, but in that language I could only imagine and write about a conventional housewife.

For the most part, the remainder of the term was a period of adjustment, a time of trying to find my bearings as a student in a college composition class, to learn to shut out my black English whenever I composed, and to prevent it from creeping into my formulations; a time for trying to grasp the language of the classroom and reproduce it in my prose; for trying to talk about myself in that language, reach others through it. Each experience of writing was like standing naked and revealing my imperfection, my "otherness." And each new assignment was another chance to make myself over in language, reshape myself, make myself "better" in my rapidly changing image of a student in a college composition class.

But writing became increasingly unmanageable as the term progressed, and by the end of the semester, my sentences sounded like this:

> My excitement was soon dampened, however, by what seemed like a small voice in the back of my head saying that I should be careful with my long awaited opportunity. I felt frustrated and this seemed to make it difficult to concentrate.

There is a poverty of language in these sentences. By this point, I knew that the clichéd language of my Housewife essay was unacceptable, and I generally recognized trite expressions. At the same time, I hadn't yet mastered the language of the classroom, hadn't yet come to see it as belonging to me. Most notable is the lifelessness of the prose, the apparent absence of a person behind the words. I wanted those sentences—and the rest of the essay—to convey the anguish of yearning to, at once, become something more and yet remain the same. I had the sensation of being split in two, part of me going into a future the other part didn't believe possible. As that person, the student writer at that moment, I was essentially mute. I could not—in the process of composing—use the language of the old me, yet I couldn't imagine myself in the language of "others."

I found this particularly discouraging because at midsemester I had been writing in a much different way. Note the language of this introduction to an essay I had written then, near the middle of the term:

> Pain is a constant companion to the people in "Footwork." Their jobs are physically damaging. Employers are insensitive to their feelings and in many cases add to their problems. The general public wounds them further by treating them with disgrace because of what they do for a living. Although the workers are as diverse as they are similar, there is a definite link between them. They suffer a great deal of abuse.

30   The voice here is stronger, more confident, [with] appropriate terms 30
like "physically damaging," "wounds them further," "insensitive,"
"diverse"—terms I couldn't have imagined using when writing about
my own experience—shaping them into sentences like "Although the
workers are as diverse as they are similar, there is a definite link between
them." And there is the sense of a personality behind the prose, someone who sympathizes with the workers. "The general public wounds
them further by treating them with disgrace because of what they do
for a living."

What causes these differences? I was, I believed, explaining other
people's thoughts and feelings, and I was free to move about in the language of "others" so long as I was speaking *of* others. I was unaware
that I was transforming into my best classroom language my own
thoughts and feelings about people whose experiences and ways of
speaking were in many ways similar to mine.

The following year, unable to turn back or to let go of what had
become something of an obsession with language (and hoping to catch
and hold the sense of control that had eluded me in Basic Writing), I
enrolled in a research writing course. I spent most of the term learning how to prepare for and write a research paper. I chose sex education as my subject and spent hours in libraries, searching for
information, reading, taking notes. Then (not without messiness and
often demoralizing frustration) I organized my information into categories, wrote a thesis statement, and composed my paper—a series
of paragraphs and quotations spaced between carefully constructed
transitions. The process and results felt artificial, but as I would later
come to realize I was passing through a necessary stage. My sentences
sounded like this:

> This reserve becomes understandable with examination of
> who the abusers are. In an overwhelming number of cases,
> they are people the victims know and trust. Family mem-
> bers, relatives, neighbors, and close family friends commit
> seventy-five percent of all reported sex crimes against chil-
> dren, and parents, parent substitutes, and relatives are the
> offenders in thirty to eighty percent of all reported cases.
> While assault by strangers does occur, it is less common,
> and is usually a single episode. But abuse by family mem-
> bers, relatives, and acquaintances may continue for an
> extended period of time. In cases of incest, for example,

children are abused repeatedly for an average of eight years. In such cases, "the use of physical force is rarely necessary because of the child's trusting, dependent relationship with the offender. The child's cooperation is often facilitated by the adult's position of dominance, an offer of material goods, a threat of physical violence or a misrepresentation of moral standards."

The completed paper gave me a sense of profound satisfaction, and I read it often after my professor returned it. I know now that what I was pleased with was the language I used and the professional voice it helped me maintain. "Use better words," my teacher had snapped at me one day after reading the notes I'd begun accumulating from my research, and slowly I began taking on the language of my sources. In my next set of notes, I used the word "vacillating"; my professor applauded. And by the time I composed the final draft, I felt at ease with terms like "overwhelming number of cases," "single episode," and "reserve," and I shaped them into sentences similar to those of my "expert" sources.

If I were writing the paper today, I would of course do some things differently. Rather than open with an anecdote—as my teacher suggested—I would begin simply with a quotation that caught my interest as I was researching my paper (and which I scribbled, without its source, in the margin of my notebook): "Truth does not do so much good in the world as the semblance of truth does evil." The quotation felt right because it captured what was for me the central idea of my essay—an idea that emerged gradually during the making of my paper—and expressed it in a way I would like to have said it. The anecdote, a hypothetical situation I invented to conform to the information in the paper, felt forced and insincere because it represented—to a great degree—my teacher's understanding of the essay, *her* idea of what in it was most significant. Improving upon my previous experiences with writing, I was beginning to think and feel in the language I used, to find my own voices in it, to sense that how one speaks influences how one means. But I was not yet secure enough, comfortable enough with the language to trust my intuition.

35   Now that I know that to seek knowledge, freedom, and autonomy   35
means always to be in the concentrated process of becoming—always to be venturing into new territory, feeling one's way at first, then getting one's balance, negotiating, accommodating, discovering one's self

in ways that previously defined "others"—I sometimes get tired. And I ask myself why I keep on participating in this highbrow form of violence, this slamming against perplexity. But there is no real futility in the question, no hint of that part of the old me who stood outside standard English, hugging to herself a disabling mistrust of a language she thought could not represent a person with her history and experience. Rather, the question represents a person who feels the consequences of her education, the weight of her possibilities as teacher and writer and human being, a voice in society. And I would not change that person, would not give back the good burden that accompanies my growing expertise, my increasing power to shape myself in language and share that self with "others."

"To speak," says Frantz Fanon, "means to be in a position to use a certain syntax, to grasp the morphology of this or that language, but it means above all to assume a culture, to support the weight of civilization."[1] To write means to do the same, but in a more profound sense. However, Fanon also says that to achieve mastery means to "get" in a position of power, to "grasp," to "assume." This I have learned both as a student and subsequently as a teacher—can involve tremendous emotional and psychological conflict for those attempting to master academic disclosure. Although as a beginning student writer I had a fairly good grasp of ordinary spoken English and was proficient at what Labov calls "code-switching" (and what John Baugh in *Black Street Speech* terms "style shifting"), when I came face to face with the demands of academic writing, I grew increasingly self-conscious, constantly aware of my status as a black and a speaker of one of the many black English vernaculars— a traditional outsider. For the first time, I experienced my sense of doubleness as something menacing, a built-in enemy. Whenever I turned inward for salvation, the balm so available during my childhood, I found instead this new fragmentation which spoke to me in many voices. It was the voice of my desire to prosper, but at the same time it spoke of what I had relinquished and could not regain: a safe way of being, a state of powerlessness which exempted me from responsibility for who I was and might be. And it accused me of betrayal, of turning away from blackness. To recover balance, I had to take on the language of the academy, the language of "others." And to do that, I had to learn to imagine myself as a part of the culture of that language, and therefore someone free to manage that language, to take liberties with it. Writing and rewriting, practicing, experimenting, I came to comprehend more fully the generative power of language. I discovered—with the help of some especially sensitive teachers—that through writing one can continually bring new selves into being, each with new responsibilities and difficulties, but also with new possibilities. Remarkable power, indeed. I write and continually give birth to myself.

Note

1. *Black Skin, White Masks* (1952; rpt. New York: Grove Press, 1967), pp. 17–18.

The Maker's Eye: Revising Your Own Manuscripts

Donald M. Murray

Donald M. Murray (1924–2006), born in Boston, spent most of his life writing, editing, and teaching writing. He published fiction, poetry, and a variety of nonfiction. He was an editor for Time *magazine and in 1954 won a Pulitzer Prize for editorial writing. His textbooks on writing include* Writing for Your Readers, A Writer Teaches Writing, Write to Learn, Read to Write, *and* The Craft of Revision. *The following essay was published in the journal* The Writer *in 1973. As you read about how Murray approached revision, think about your own writing and revising habits.*

1   When students complete a first draft, they consider the job of writing done—and their teachers too often agree. When professional writers complete a first draft, they usually feel that they are at the start of the writing process. When a draft is completed, the job of writing can begin.

That difference in attitude is the difference between amateur and professional, inexperience and experience, journeyman and craftsman. Peter F. Drucker, the prolific business writer, calls his first draft "the zero draft"—after that he can start counting. Most writers share the feeling that the first draft, and all of those which follow, are opportunities to discover what they have to say and how best they can say it.

To produce a progression of drafts, each of which says more and says it more clearly, the writer has to develop a special kind of reading skill. In school we are taught to decode what appears on the page as finished writing. Writers, however, face a different category of possibility and responsibility when they read their own drafts. To them the words on the page are never finished. Each can be changed and rearranged, can set off a chain reaction of confusion or clarified meaning. This is a different kind of reading, which is possibly more difficult and certainly more exciting.

Writers must learn to be their own best enemy. They must accept the criticism of others and be suspicious of it; they must accept the praise of others and be even more suspicious of it. Writers cannot depend on others. They must detach themselves from their own pages so that they can apply both their caring and their craft to their own work.

5   Such detachment is not easy. Science fiction writer Ray Bradbury   5
supposedly puts each manuscript away for a year to the day and then rereads it as a stranger. Not many writers have the discipline or the time to do this. We must read when our judgment may be at its worst, when we are close to the euphoric moment of creation.

Then the writer, counsels novelist Nancy Hale, "should be critical of everything that seems to him most delightful in his style. He should excise what he most admires, because he wouldn't thus admire it if he weren't . . . in a sense protecting it from criticism." John Ciardi, the poet, adds, "The last act of the writing must be to become one's own reader. It is, I suppose, a schizophrenic process, to begin passionately and to end critically, to begin hot and to end cold; and, more important, to be passion-hot and critic-cold at the same time."

Most people think that the principal problem is that writers are too proud of what they have written. Actually, a greater problem for most professional writers is one shared by the majority of students. They are overly critical, think everything is dreadful, tear up page after page, never complete a draft, see the task as hopeless.

The writer must learn to read critically but constructively, to cut what is bad, to reveal what is good. Eleanor Estes, the children's book author, explains: "The writer must survey his work critically, coolly, as though he were a stranger to it. He must be willing to prune, expertly and hard-heartedly. At the end of each revision, a manuscript may look . . . worked over, torn apart, pinned together, added to, deleted from, words changed and words changed back. Yet the book must maintain its original freshness and spontaneity."

Most readers underestimate the amount of rewriting it usually takes to produce spontaneous reading. This is a great disadvantage to the student writer, who sees only a finished product and never watches the craftsman who takes the necessary step back, studies the work carefully, returns to the task, steps back, returns, steps back, again and again. Anthony Burgess, one of the most prolific writers in the English-speaking world, admits, "I might revise a page twenty times." Roald Dahl, the popular children's writer, states, "By the time I'm nearing the end of a story, the first part will have been reread and altered and corrected at least 150 times. . . . Good writing is essentially rewriting. I am positive of this."

10   Rewriting isn't virtuous. It isn't something that ought to be done.   10 It is simply something that most writers find they have to do to discover what they have to say and how to say it. It is a condition of the writer's life.

There are, however, a few writers who do little formal rewriting, primarily because they have the capacity and experience to create and review a large number of invisible drafts in their minds before they approach the page. And some writers slowly produce finished pages, performing all the tasks of revision simultaneously, page by page, rather than draft by draft. But it is still possible to see the sequence followed by most writers most of the time in rereading their own work.

Most writers scan their drafts first, reading as quickly as possible to catch the larger problems of subject and form, then move in closer and closer as they read and write, reread and rewrite.

The first thing writers look for in their drafts is information. They know that a good piece of writing is built from specific, accurate, and interesting information. The writer must have an abundance of information from which to construct a readable piece of writing.

Next writers look for *meaning* in the information. The specifics must build a pattern of significance. Each piece of specific information must carry the reader toward meaning.

15   Writers reading their own drafts are aware of *audience.* They put   15 themselves in the reader's situation and make sure that they deliver information which a reader wants to know or needs to know in a manner which is easily digested. Writers try to be sure that they anticipate and answer the questions a critical reader will ask when reading the piece of writing.

Writers make sure that the *form* is appropriate to the subject and the audience. Form, or genre, is the vehicle which carries meaning to the reader, but form cannot be selected until the writer has adequate information to discover its significance and an audience which needs or wants that meaning.

Once writers are sure the form is appropriate, they must then look at the *structure,* the order of what they have written. Good writing is built on a solid framework of logic, argument, narrative, or motivation which runs through the entire piece of writing and holds it together. This is the time when many writers find it most effective to outline as a way of visualizing the hidden spine by which the piece of writing is supported.

The element on which writers may spend a majority of their time is *development.* Each section of a piece of writing must be adequately developed. It must give readers enough information so that they are satisfied. How much information is enough? That's as difficult as asking how much garlic belongs in a salad. It must be done to taste, but most beginning writers underdevelop, underestimating the reader's hunger for information.

As writers solve development problems, they often have to consider questions of *dimension.* There must be a pleasing and effective proportion among all the parts of the piece of writing. There is a continual process of subtracting and adding to keep the piece of writing in balance.

20 Finally, writers have to listen to their own voices. *Voice* is the force 20 which drives a piece of writing forward. It is an expression of the writer's authority and concern. It is what is between the words on the page, what glues the piece of writing together. A good piece of writing is always marked by a consistent, individual voice.

As writers read and reread, write and rewrite, they move closer and closer to the page until they are doing line-by-line editing. Writers read their own pages with infinite care. Each sentence, each line, each clause, each phrase, each word, each mark of punctuation, each section of white space between the type has to contribute to the clarification of meaning.

Slowly the writer moves from word to word, looking through language to see the subject. As a word is changed, cut, or added, as a construction is rearranged, all the words used before that moment and all those that follow that moment must be considered and reconsidered.

Writers often read aloud at this stage of the editing process, muttering or whispering to themselves, calling on the ear's experience with language. Does this sound right—or that? Writers edit, shifting back and forth from eye to page to ear to page. I find I must do this careful editing in short runs, no more than fifteen or twenty minutes at a stretch, or I become too kind with myself. I begin to see what I hope is on the page, not what actually is on the page.

This sounds tedious if you haven't done it, but actually it is fun. Making something right is immensely satisfying, for writers begin to learn what they are writing about by writing. Language leads them to meaning, and there is the joy of discovery, of understanding, of making meaning clear as the writer employs the technical skills of language.

25   Words have double meanings, even triple and quadruple meanings. Each word has its own potential for connotation and denotation. And when writers rub one word against the other, they are often rewarded with a sudden insight, an unexpected clarification.

The maker's eye moves back and forth from word to phrase to sentence to paragraph to sentence to phrase to word. The maker's eye sees the need for variety and balance, for a firmer structure, for a more appropriate form. It peers into the interior of the paragraph, looking for coherence, unity, and emphasis, which make meaning clear.

I learned something about this process when my first bifocals were prescribed. I had ordered a larger section of the reading portion of the glass because of my work, but even so, I could not contain my eyes within this new limit of vision. And I still find myself taking off my glasses and bending my nose towards the page, for my eyes unconsciously flick back and forth across the page, back to another page, forward to still another, as I try to see each evolving line in relation to every other line.

When does this process end? Most writers agree with the great Russian writer Tolstoy, who said, "I scarcely ever reread my published writings, if by chance I come across a page, it always strikes me: all this must be rewritten; this is how I should have written it."

The maker's eye is never satisfied, for each word has the potential to ignite new meaning. This article has been twice written all the way through the writing process, and it was published four years ago. Now it is to be republished in a book. The editors make a few small suggestions, and then I read it with my maker's eye. Now it has been re-edited, re-revised, re-read, re-re-edited, for each piece of writing to the writer is full of potential and alternatives.

30   A piece of writing is never finished. It is delivered to a deadline, torn out of the typewriter on demand, sent off with a sense of accomplishment and shame and pride and frustration. If only there were a couple more days, time for just another run at it, perhaps then . . .

A Lapse in Standards: Linking Standards-Based Reform with Student Achievement

Bill Nave, Edward Meich, and Frederick Mosteller

Bill Nave received a doctorate in education from Harvard University and serves as director for research and evaluation for TERC (the combined initials of the organizations' founding members), an education research and development organization. Edward Miech, who also received an education doctorate from Harvard, is the founder and CEO of EdSite, an organization devoted to educational reform. Frederick Mosteller is professor emeritus of mathematical statistics at Harvard with a distinguished record in the scholarship of his field. In this article, the authors address a controversial question among public and legislative commentators on education: is testing a good way to improve education?

Little empirical evidence supports or refutes the existence of a causal link between standards and enhanced student learning. In its absence, the authors articulate five "theories of action," discuss a study that proposes one such concrete mechanism, and present two small case studies that suggest how standards can affect student learning in day-to-day practice.

1   David Hornbeck, until recently superintendent of schools in   1
Philadelphia, is a true believer. He believes that high academic standards will lead 95% of Philadelphia's public

---

"A Lapse in Standards" by Bill Nave, Edward Miech, and Frederick Mosteller, published in *Phi Delta Kappan*, October 2000. Reprinted with permission by *Phi Delta Kappan*.

school students to achieve a rating of "proficient" on the standardized Stanford Achievement Test (SAT 9) by the year 2008.[1] Critics wonder how that's possible in a city where 80% of the students live in poverty.[2]

How does Hornbeck think this will work? What's his "theory of action"?[3] He suggests that students need somebody to believe in them. Communicating high expectations for all students conveys to them that you believe that they can meet the standards. Says Hornbeck, "If you don't have real faith that every child can succeed, [failure] becomes a self-fulfilling prophecy."[4]

Is faith in students enough? What mechanisms actually link the act of raising standards with improved student achievement? Little empirical evidence supports or refutes the existence of a causal link between standards and enhanced student learning. In its absence, we articulate here five "theories of action" by which standards might improve student achievement, We also discuss a study that proposes one such concrete mechanism, and we present two small case studies that suggest how standards can affect student learning in day-to-day practice.

Definitions

We begin with brief definitions of the different types of standards that reformers have proposed to raise student achievement. The most commonly discussed standards are content standards, performance standards, and opportunity-to-learn standards.[5]

Content standards. Sometimes called curriculum frameworks, content standards define the specific subject matter that students are expected to master.[6] For example, the National Council of Teachers of Mathematics (NCTM) has created a comprehensive set of K–12 mathematics content standards and has taken the next step of suggesting teaching methods that can support students' learning the prescribed content.[7]

The process of creating content standards can be complex. The Consortium for Policy Research in Education (CPRE) has analyzed the standards-setting process in five states and three national curriculum projects and has offered a set of nine suggestions to guide those who would set standards.[8]

Performance standards. The notion of performance standards covers one or more of three ideas: 1) how students will demonstrate mastery of the content defined by the content standards (e.g., by solving a set of math word problems and explaining the process of solution); 2) the degree of mastery expected in a student's performance (e.g., a certain percentage correct on an assessment with given content), and 3) the proportion of students in a school expected to perform at or above a specified level.[9]

Opportunity-to-learn standards. Such standards require that students have adequate resources (e.g., supplies, textbooks, good teachers) available before they are penalized for failing to attain the standards set for them. Vermont's supreme court, for example, ruled in 1997 that it was the state's responsibility to provide for all Vermont students "substantially equal access" to a high-quality basic education, and this means a more equitable funding mechanism. Included in Vermont's new education funding law is a set of statewide performance standards. Progress toward meeting those standards is to be assessed and reported to the public annually.[10]

Other kinds of standards mentioned less frequently include certification standards and world-class standards. Certification standards define the minimum requirements for a candidate to obtain a teaching credential. World-class standards are based on the curriculum and the expectations for students in industrialized countries that score well on international exams.[11]

Empirical Evidence For Standards-Based Reform

The standards-based reform movement is relatively new, and we found few empirical studies of the impact of any of the types of standards on schools and students. Most empirical studies evaluated implementation. For example, a typical study examined how faithfully the standards-based Kentucky Education Reform Act (KERA) was being implemented across the state.[12]

We found one empirical study that demonstrated a link between the adoption of high performance standards and improvement in student achievement.[13] This study examined student motivation and achievement in the Regents earth science classes of one high school teacher in rural New York. The school district had decided to place a much larger proportion of its ninth graders in the more demanding Regents earth science classes than in the less rigorous non-Regents version, where students with a history of low science achievement in the eighth grade had previously been placed. During three school years, beginning in 1987, the percentage of freshmen in Regents earth science classes increased from 40% to 70%.

For one particularly difficult unit of study, all students in this teacher's Regents classes were told that they had to achieve 100% on the unit test, which included the creation of a detailed water budget for a specific locale.[14] Students who did not score 100% the first time could ask for extra study aids, peer tutoring, or extra tutoring from the teacher during lunch hour, study hall, or before or after school. Thus students were required to continue to work on the unit on their own time until they achieved the perfect score, which all but one of them eventually did (71 of 72 students in the three classes).[15]

The researchers explored how students understood their success in this science unit and concluded that students came to attribute their success to their own effort and motivation, whereas at the beginning of the school year they had attributed their degree of success in science classes to factors outside their control, such as lack of natural ability.

This modest study is by no means definitive. It was quite small—one teacher, three classes of students, one school—and lasted only a few weeks. However, it raises a number of intriguing questions. Is this change in the students' attribution of success from extrinsic factors (natural ability in science) to intrinsic factors (motivation and effort) one mechanism—one "theory of action"—that can guide standards-based reformers in implementing their reforms and guide researchers in evaluating such efforts?

Possible Mechanisms Linking Standards and Achievement

15   The effectiveness of the standards-based movement in raising student   15
achievement is still an open question. Given the small size of the research base, another approach to thinking about standards-based reforms involves articulating theories of action about how such reforms might work. What plausible mechanisms could link higher standards to improved student learning? If we had a sufficiently detailed theory of action that explained how standards could influence student achievement, then evaluations could focus closely on this hypothesized causal chain, with its particular expectations and assumptions, to see what happens when the new standards are put into practice.[16]

For example, advocates of standards-based reform might subscribe to one or more of the following five theories of action about how standards might improve student achievement. These examples of theories of action have been greatly simplified for purposes of illustration and do not purport to reflect the opinions of any particular person or group (including the authors of this article). A detailed theory of action might combine several of these simplified scenarios. We follow these hypothetical scenarios with two examples—mini case studies—of the outcome of standards-based reforms in two schools.

1. *Use ambitious, uniform expectations to inspire students to achieve at higher levels.* Those who subscribe to this theory see the problem of low student achievement as stemming from an environment in which many students settle into predictable patterns of achievement: the high performers continue to perform at high levels, the average performers continue to perform at average levels, and the low performers continue to perform at low levels. Proponents of this theory believe that student performance relates directly to the images students have internalized of themselves as learners, as they attribute success in the classroom to innate ability or to effort and perseverance.

These advocates argue that creating a set of common, ambitious standards for all students will disrupt these self-fulfilling prophecies by demonstrating to students that they *are* capable of achieving at high levels when they work hard and persist. We have already connected this theory of action to Hornbeck's push for high standards in Philadelphia and to the improved achievement in earth science reported in the rural New York school.

2. *Use ambitious, uniform expectations to inspire teachers to believe that their students can achieve at higher levels.* Adherents of this theory of action believe that many teachers mentally label students according to initial impressions, test scores, reports from other teachers, and other information. Because teacher expectations can exert a powerful positive or negative influence on the achievement of individual students, they link low student achievement to the low expectations teachers hold for many groups of students. They argue that implementing common, ambitious standards for all students will induce teachers to believe that all their students can achieve at high levels and that student success in school should be attributed to effort rather than to predetermined, "fixed" ability levels. Again, Hornbeck's

assertion that high standards will communicate to Philadelphia's students that "we believe in them" spells out high expectations for all students and sets an example for teachers to follow.

20   Does students' achievement improve when their teachers expect more of them? The well-known field trial of teacher expectations, *Pygmalion in the Classroom,* and the many follow-up studies on teacher expectations seem to support this theory of action.[17] In the *Pygmalion* study, teachers were informed that the results of a test designed to predict "academic blooming" identified several of their students (actually randomly chosen) as potential 'bloomers'. Many of the students thus identified did in fact improve academically—more so than peers who were not so identified. Robert Rosenthal and Lenore Jacobson attributed the student improvements to higher teacher expectations.

In addition, researchers found evidence of the influence of teacher expectations in a national field trial that measured the effects of standardized testing in Ireland. Student achievement moved in the direction of teacher expectations, whether those expectations were higher or lower than students' initial achievement levels.[18]

3. *Use a big stick to wake up and challenge unmotivated students.* Adherents of this theory of action believe that low student achievement results from an overall lack of effort on the part of students. They believe that a majority of students merely put in their time at school before going off to watch television or engage in other activities that are not especially rigorous or intellectually challenging. Advocates of this theory argue that introducing high-stakes tests and meaningful consequences (both positive and negative) will spur students to reorder their priorities, take school more seriously, and improve their academic achievement. Those advocates believe that U.S. students are capable of matching or surpassing the achievement of students in other nations, given the proper standards and incentives.

Do students respond positively to the threat of negative sanctions? One common school policy that currently embodies this theory of action is the requirement that high school students maintain a minimum grade-point average in order to participate in varsity athletics. A few states have discontinued such policies because they resulted in more dropouts rather than in higher grades for student athletes. The National Collegiate Athletic Association also has a policy requiring high school graduates to have a minimum high school grade-point average and to achieve a minimum score on a college admission test in order to be eligible for athletic scholarships or to participate in intercollegiate sports as freshmen.[19]

4. *Use a big stick to wake up and challenge unmotivated teachers.* Those who subscribe to this theory of action see the problem of low student achievement as partly caused by a lack of effort on the part of teachers. Advocates of this theory argue that incentives for recognizing and rewarding excellent teaching are weak at present, since teachers are on the same salary schedule regardless of their classroom performance. They believe that the majority of teachers fall far short of their potential as effective practitioners, because this system of compensation ignores sometimes large differences in the quality of classroom teaching. Holding teachers accountable for the performance of their students on standards-based assessments, say advocates of this theory, will motivate teachers to improve the achievement of their students by improving their teaching, especially if the teachers' jobs are on the line.

25   Does the threat of getting fired (or the threat of other substantial negative sanctions) motivate teachers to improve their teaching? Some education policies that appear to incorporate this theory of action are reconstitution, state takeovers of educationally troubled districts, and accreditation proceedings. Reconstitution uses a radical step to improve student achievement in underperforming schools: reassign or release the entire faculty and bring in a new principal and new teaching staff.[20] Sometimes schools are notified that they are "on probation" or "under consideration" for reconstitution if student achievement or other factors do not improve by a certain date.

On another level, some states have adopted policies that allow them to take over underperforming school districts. For example, New Jersey's department of education took over the Jersey City school district in an effort to improve educational opportunities for the district's children.[21]

Finally, almost all public high schools periodically undergo a regional accreditation process in which a team of outside educators conducts an in-depth review of a school's facilities and operations. Schools that do not pass the initial review sometimes receive additional time to address issues and problems that the accreditation team feels are serious and require swift resolution.

5. *Use a collaborative process when setting standards to increase stakeholder investment in improving teaching and learning.* Advocates

of this theory view the problem of low student achievement as stemming from schools with programs that are too broad to enjoy widespread support from the community. A collaborative process for setting content standards will allow teachers, administrators, parents, students, and community members to become more invested in schools and student achievement through their active involvement in choosing what is important in the curriculum. This community engagement around a common set of ambitious standards will align teachers and parents, as well as other constituencies, behind a general expectation of high levels of student achievement.

Does community involvement improve student learning? Reforms that incorporate this theory of action include site-based decision making and the School Development Program, commonly known as the Comer schools project after its founder, Yale psychiatrist Dr. James Comer. In a Comer school, various members of a school community work together to improve the climate of a school to better support student learning. The teams include parents, teachers, social workers, medical workers, and mental health workers. Student learning in some Comer schools has improved dramatically.[22]

30   As an example of wide community involvement in setting content 30 standards, the state of Maine has engaged in a decade-long process of including thousands of teachers and community members in an ongoing discussion of what Maine high school students should know and be able to do when they graduate, no matter what town they live in. This process has resulted in the creation of Maine's Common Core of Learning in 1992, the adoption by the state legislature of Maine's *Learning Results* in 1997, and the alignment of the state's annual assessment of fourth-, eighth-, and 11th-grade students with the *Learning Results* document. Communities across the state continue to engage in local discussions about how to bring their curricula and teaching into alignment with the high expectations outlined in *Learning Results*.[23]

Standards-Based Reform In Philadelphia

How might these theories of action apply to an ongoing, ambitious standards-based reform? Based on an interview one of us conducted with Hornbeck and on documents from the Philadelphia School District, we derived the following seven steps from Hornbeck's theory of action in Philadelphia.[24]

1. *Hold high expectations for all students, including those from groups that have historically not performed well in school—low-income students, racial- or language-minority students, and students with disabilities.* "Expectations are far more than attitudes. Their enormous power derives from the fact that they generate behaviors on the part of individuals and policies and practices on the part of institutions. These behaviors, policies, and practices create self-fulfilling prophecies."[25]

2. *Create content and performance standards that apply to all students; then create a K–12 curriculum guide based on those standards.* A committee of 117 Philadelphia teachers worked on the curriculum framework documents, which include sections on seven core learning areas and six sets of competencies that cut across the learning areas. The introduction to these documents explains the constructivist theory of learning that undergirds the work, and each curriculum page includes a specific content standard, related benchmarks, specific concepts or skills related to the standard, examples of work students might do to meet that standard, classroom assessment suggestions, teacher resources, suggested instructional strategies, and final assessment strategies.

3. *Place the curriculum guide in the hands of teachers and provide professional development time for them to become familiar with its contents.* Teachers received the part of the three-volume curriculum frameworks corresponding to their grade level during January 1998. Each volume is more than an inch thick and is contained in a large loose-leaf binder. When the volume is open on a table, it is more than three feet wide. Hornbeck budgeted for professional development time for teachers to begin working with the frameworks as soon as they received them, but the way this time was used differed widely from school to school, depending on various local factors.

4. *Expect teachers to incorporate the guide into their lesson planning.* This expectation grows out of the second theory of action described above.

5. *Expect students to learn more from these new lessons and classroom experiences.* The underlying premise for this sort of expectation is the first theory of action described above.

6. *Expect these students to perform better on the districts standardized test.* Hornbeck reports that 232 of 259 schools showed improvement in the standardized test scores and other measures after the first year the standards were in place.

7. *Hold principals accountable for classroom-by-classroom improvements in student achievement.* This expectation applies the "big stick" theory of action to principals.

Mini Case Studies

Examples from the teaching experience of one of us—Nave's 25 years of teaching so-called at-risk students—suggest two possibilities for what content and performance standards might took like in classroom practice. The first example is in some ways similar to the New York study we cited.

40　　For eight years, Nave taught all four core academic subjects to 40 groups of 20 low-achieving high school freshmen in a self-contained classroom. He required students to complete every assignment in every subject with at least 80% mastery before they earned credit for the assignment. The students used study halls, lunch periods, and time before and after school to continue working on the assignments until they achieved a satisfactory outcome. When necessary, Nave visited the homes of students to secure the support of parents. Eventually, most of the students began working harder on the assignments the first time. They told turn that they were tired of spending so much time in school when their friends were hanging out at the mall. This outcome is similar to that of the New York study in that the students changed their study habits, thereby achieving better work the first time they attempted an assignment.

The second example comes from a public high school for dropouts, a school Nave helped design and taught in for five years. At the River Valley School in Turner, Maine, students earned a regular high school diploma, not a GED (General Education Development) certificate. Curriculum for the school was derived from the written curriculum of the local high school, except that the teachers added to the depth and breadth of that curriculum by requiring mastery of more content knowledge than was indicated by the original high school's curriculum document.

In addition, as with the self-contained class, students earned no credit on an assignment until they had mastered at least 80% of the content. The teachers informed students of these extra requirements when they applied for admission to the school, inviting them to return to the local high school from which they had withdrawn if they didn't wish to work harder for a diploma.

The school offered a major incentive for the students to stay: "credit by objective." As soon as a student demonstrated 80% mastery of all the curriculum for a course, the student earned a high school credit for the course and was not required to put in a certain number of hours of seat time. Therefore, the amount of time it took students to earn a diploma was entirely in their hands: the more they studied, the faster they mastered the coursework. The teachers were essentially tutors and resource specialists for these students.

It didn't take long for the students to catch on, especially after the first group of students set the tone and created the culture of working hard for themselves—not for someone else, as had been the case for many of them in the regular high school. Most students reported that they had never worked so hard in school. Nearly all confided that they had never read an entire book, cover to cover, as was required as part of their first English credit. The experience of the River Valley School demonstrates that students can indeed be inspired by high and uniform expectations.

Conclusions and Suggestions

45 Standards-based reforms might improve student achievement, but 45 little research definitely linking the two is available. Anecdotal evidence provides some small, classroom-based "existence proofs" of the connection between higher standards and better student achievement. The study in New York, albeit limited in scope, provides a tantalizing glimpse of a mechanism by which standards can lead to enhanced student learning.

We recommend that all advocates of standards-based reform outline the mechanisms by which their particular strategies might improve student achievement so that further research can be used to refine such theories of action and, ultimately, so that a theory-based evaluation design can examine the links in the hypothesized causal chain. We hope to see the growth of a substantial body of research in the next few years providing evidence of how and when various types of standards-based reforms lead to improved student achievement.

Endnotes

1. Philadelphia is using the SAT 9, a relatively recent version of the test that includes "performance" questions requiring open-ended responses from

students—for example, explaining why they solved a math problem in a particular way.

2. Michael Grunwald, "Philadelphia Puts School Chief to Test," *Boston Globe*, 19 October 1997, p. A-1.

3. Chris Argyris and Donald Schön, *Organizational Learning: A Theory of Action Perspective* (Reading, Mass.: Addison-Wesley, 1978).

4. Grunwald, p. A-22,

5. Linda Darling-Hammond, "National Standards and Assessments: Will They Improve Education?," *American Journal of Education*, August 1994, pp. 478–510; "The Push for New Standards Provokes Hope and Fear—and Both Are Justified," *Harvard Education Letter*, September/October 1993, pp. 1–3, 5; Anne C. Lewis, "An Overview of the Standards Movement," *Phi Delta Kappan*, June 1995, pp. 744–50; and Milbrey W. McLaughlin and Lorrie A. Shepard, "Improving Education Through Standards-Based Reform: A Report by the National Academy of Education Panel on Standards-Based Education Reform," ERIC ED 387 867, 1995.

6. David Cohen, "What Standards for National Standards?," *Phi Delta Kappan*, June 1995, pp. 751–57.

7. *Curriculum and Evaluation Standards for School Mathematics* (Reston, Va.: National Council of Teachers of Mathematics, 1989); and *Professional Standards for Teaching Mathematics* (Reston, Va.: National Council of Teachers of Mathematics, 1991). Revised standards were published in the spring of 2000.

8. The five states are Vermont, Kentucky, New York, California, and South Carolina, and the three projects are the National Council of Teachers of Mathematics' standards, the College Board's Advanced Placement program, and the National Science Foundation's programs of the 1950s and 1960s. For details, see "Developing Content Standards: Creating a Process for Change," *CPRE Policy Brief*, ERIC ED 362 981, October 1993.

9. For a detailed examination of how the National Assessment of Educational Progress determines its performance standards, see *Setting Performance Standards for Student Achievement: A Report of the National Academy of Education Panel on the Evaluation of the NAEP Trial State Assessments: An Evaluation of the 1992 Achievement Levels* (Stanford, Calif.: National Academy of Education, 1993).

10. *Act 60: Vermont's Equal Educational Opportunity Act: Your Handbook* (Montpelier: Vermont Department of Taxes, 1997).

11. Lewis, op. cit.

12. *A Review of the Research on the Kentucky Education Reform Act 1995* (Frankfort: Kentucky Institute for Education Research, February 1996).

13. James D. Allen and Anne Dietrich, "Student Differences in Attribution and Motivation Toward the Study of High School Regents Earth Science," paper presented at the annual meeting of the American Educational Research Association, Chicago, 1991, ERIC ED 338 482.

14. The researchers selected this unit because the concepts were likely to be new to all the students. Thai is, few students were likely to have had any past experience with the process of tracing the flow of water through a specific locale or using knowledge of rainfall amounts, soil moisture retention limits, relation of evapotranspiration to temperature regimes, and so on. Therefore, all students began this unit on a "level playing field."

15. At the end of the school year, 12 previously low-achieving students also earned passing scores on the demanding Regents exam for the entire course, thus earning Regents credit for the course.

16. This is an example of what Carol Weiss describes as "theory-based evaluation." See Carol H. Weiss, *Bringing Theory-Based Evaluation Within Our Means* (Cambridge, Mass.: Harvard Project on Schooling and Children, 1997).

17. Robert Rosenthal and Lenore Jacobson, *Pygmalion in the Classroom: Teacher Expectation and Pupils' Intellectual Development* (New York: Holt, Rinehart & Winston, 1968); and Robert Rosenthal, "Interpersonal Expectancy Effects: A 30-Year Perspective," *Current Directions in Psychological Science*, December 1994, pp. 176–79.

18. Thomas Kellaghan, George F. Madaus, and Peter W. Airasian, *The Effects of Standardized Testing* (Boston: Kluwer-Nijhoff Publishing, 1982).

19. Center for the Study of Athletics, *Summary Results from the 1987–88 National Study of Intercollegiate Athletes* (Palo Alto. Calif.: American Institute for Research, Studies of Intercollegiate Athletics, Report No. 1, 1988).

20. Caroline Hendrie, "Reconstitution Gaining New Momentum," *Education Week*, 24 September 1997, P. 1.

21. For a case study of this takeover, see Margaret Dolan, "State Takeover of a Local District in New Jersey: A Case Study," ERIC ED 345 370, 1992.

22. James P. Comer et al., *Rallying the Whole Village: The Comer Process for Reforming Education* (New York: Teachers College Press, 1996).

23. One of us (Nave) has been involved with various components of this process since 1990.

24. Nave conducted a phone interview with Hornbeck on 24 March 1998. See also *Children Achieving* (Philadelphia: School District of Philadelphia, 1995); and *Curriculum Frameworks*, 3 vols. (Philadelphia: School District of Philadelphia, 1998). These volumes cover grades K–4, 5–8, and 9–12.

25. *Children Achieving*, p. I–1.

Politics and the English Language

George Orwell

George Orwell is the pen name used by the British author Eric Blair (1903–1950). Orwell was born in the Indian village of Motihari, near Nepal, where his father was stationed in the Civil Service. India was then part of the British Empire. From 1907 to 1922 Orwell lived in England, returning to India and Burma and a position in the Imperial Police, which he held until 1927. Thereafter he lived in England, Paris, Spain, and elsewhere, writing on a wide range of topics. He fought in the Spanish Civil War and was actively engaged in several political movements, always against totalitarianism of any kind. He is best known today for two novels of political satire: Animal Farm *(1945) and* 1984 *(1949). He was also a prolific journalist and essayist, with his essays collected in five volumes. He wrote "Politics and the English Language" shortly after the end of World War II, at a time when patriotic fervor was very strong in the Allied countries such as England the United States, while Marxist ideology was growing elsewhere. Orwell was particularly sensitive to the use of language for political purposes, which he saw as a special instance of a more general corruption of the English language. In the 50 years since this was written, many of the phrases Orwell writes about have dropped from common use, so you may have difficulty understanding some of his examples. Nonetheless, his general points will be quite clear, and you will be able to find contemporary analogues to his examples.*

1   ost people who bother with the matter at all would admit   1
 M that the English language is in a bad way, but it is generally
        assumed that we cannot by conscious action do anything
about it. Our civilization is decadent and our language—so the argument runs—must inevitably share in the general collapse. It follows
that any struggle against the abuse of language is a sentimental archaism, like preferring candles to electric light or hansom cabs to air-
planes. Underneath this lies the half-conscious belief that language is
a natural growth and not an instrument which we shape for our own
purposes.

Now, it is clear that the decline of a language must ultimately have
political and economic causes: it is not due simply to the bad influence of this or that individual writer. But an effect can become a cause,
reinforcing the original cause and producing the same effect in an intensified form, and so on indefinitely. A man may take to drink because he feels himself to be a failure, and then fail all the more
completely because he drinks. It is rather the same thing that is happening to the English language. It becomes ugly and inaccurate because our thoughts are foolish, but the slovenliness of our language
makes it easier for us to have foolish thoughts. The point is that the
process is reversible. Modern English, especially written English, is full
of bad habits which spread by imitation and which can be avoided if
one is willing to take the necessary trouble. If one gets rid of these
habits one can think more clearly, and to think clearly is a necessary
first step towards political regeneration: so that the fight against bad
English is not frivolous and is not the exclusive concern of professional
writers. I will come back to this presently, and I hope that by that time
the meaning of what I have said here will have become clearer. Meanwhile, here are five specimens of the English language as it is now habitually written.

These five passages have not been picked out because they are especially bad—I could have quoted far worse if I had chosen—but because they illustrate various of the mental vices from which we now
suffer. They are a little below the average, but are fairly representative samples. I number them so that I can refer back to them when
necessary:

"(1) I am not, indeed, sure whether it is not true to say that the
Milton who once seemed not unlike a seventeenth-century Shelley
had not become, out of an experience ever more bitter in each year,

more alien (sic) *to the founder of that Jesuit sect which nothing could induce him to tolerate."*

Professor Harold Laski (Essay in *Freedom of Expression*).

"(2) Above all, we cannot play ducks and drakes with a native battery of idioms which prescribes such egregious collocations of vocables as the Basic put up with *for* tolerate *or* put at a loss *for* bewilder.*"*

Professor Lancelot Hogben (*Interglossa*).

"(3) On the one side we have the free personality: by definition it is not neurotic, for it has neither conflict nor dream. Its desires, such as they are, are transparent, for they are just what institutional approval keeps in the forefront of consciousness; another institutional pattern would alter their number and intensity; there is little in them that is natural, irreducible, or culturally dangerous. But on the other side, *the social bond itself is nothing but the mutual reflection of these self-secure integrities. Recall the definition of love. Is not this the very picture of a small academic? Where is there a place in this hall of mirrors for either personality or fraternity?"*

Essay on psychology in *Politics* (New York).

"(4) All the 'best people' from the gentlemen's clubs, and all the frantic fascist captains, united in common hatred of Socialism and bestial horror of the rising tide of the mass revolutionary movement, have turned to acts of provocation, to foul incendiarism, to medieval legends of poisoned wells, to legalize their own destruction of proletarian organizations, and rouse the agitated petty-bourgeoisie to chauvinistic fervor on behalf of the fight against the revolutionary way out of the crisis."

Communist pamphlet.

"(5) If a new spirit is to be infused into this old country, there is one thorny and contentious reform which must be tackled, and that is the humanization and galvanization of the B.B.C. Timidity here will bespeak cancer and atrophy of the soul. The heart of Britain may be sound and of strong beat, for instance, but the British lion's roar at present is like that of Bottom in Shakespeare's Midsummer Night's Dream—*as gentle as any sucking dove. A virile new Britain cannot continue indefinitely to be traduced in the eyes or rather ears, of the world by the effete languors of Langham Place,*

brazenly masquerading as 'standard English'. When the Voice of Britain is heard at nine o'clock, better far and infinitely less ludicrous to hear aitches honestly dropped than the present priggish, inflated, inhibited, school-ma'amish arch braying of blameless bashful mewing maidens!"

Letter in *Tribune.*

Each of these passages has faults of its own, but, quite apart from avoidable ugliness, two qualities are common to all of them. The first is staleness of imagery: the other is lack of precision. The writer either has a meaning and cannot express it, or he inadvertently says something else, or he is almost indifferent as to whether his words mean anything or not. This mixture of vagueness and sheer incompetence is the most marked characteristic of modern English prose, and especially of any kind of political writing. As soon as certain topics are raised, the concrete melts into the abstract and no one seems able to think of turns of speech that are not hackneyed: prose consists less and less of words chosen for the sake of their meaning, and more and more of phrases tacked together like the sections of a prefabricated henhouse. I list below, with notes and examples, various of the tricks by means of which the work of prose-construction is habitually dodged:

Dying Metaphors

5   A newly invented metaphor assists thought by evoking a visual image,   5
while on the other hand a metaphor which is technically "dead" (e.g. *iron resolution*) has in effect reverted to being an ordinary word and can generally be used without loss of vividness. But in between these two classes there is a huge dump of worn-out metaphors which have lost all evocative power and are merely used because they save people the trouble of inventing phrases for themselves. Examples are: *Ring the changes on, take up the cudgels for, toe the line, ride roughshod over, stand shoulder to shoulder with, play into the hands of, no axe to grind, grist to the mill, fishing in troubled waters, on the order of the day, Achilles' heel, swan song, hotbed.* Many of these are used without knowledge of their meaning (what is a "rift," for instance?), and incompatible metaphors are frequently mixed, a sure sign that the writer is not interested in what he is saying. Some metaphors now current have been twisted out of their original meaning without those who use them even being aware of the fact. For example, *toe the line* is sometimes written *tow*

the line. Another example is *the hammer and the anvil,* now always used with the implication that the anvil gets the worst of it. In real life it is always the anvil that breaks the hammer, never the other way about: a writer who stopped to think what he was saying would be aware of this, and would avoid perverting the original phrase.

Operators or Verbal False Limbs

These save the trouble of picking out appropriate verbs and nouns, and at the same time pad each sentence with extra syllables which give it an appearance of symmetry. Characteristic phrases are: *render inoperative, militate against, make contact with, be subjected to, give rise to, give grounds for, have the effect of, play a leading part (role) in, make itself felt, take effect, exhibit a tendency to, serve the purpose of, etc., etc.* The keynote is the elimination of simple verbs. Instead of being a single word, such as *break, stop, spoil, mend, kill,* a verb becomes a *phrase,* made up of a noun or adjective tacked on to some general-purposes verb such as *prove, serve, form, play, render.* In addition, the passive voice is wherever possible used in preference to the active, and noun constructions are used instead of gerunds (*by examination of* instead of *by examining*). The range of verbs is further cut down by means of the *-ize* and *de-* formation, and the banal statements are given an appearance of profundity by means of the *not un-* formation. Simple conjunctions and prepositions are replaced by such phrases as *with respect to, having regard to, the fact that, by dint of, in view of, in the interests of, on the hypothesis that;* and the ends of sentences are saved from anticlimax by such resounding commonplaces as *greatly to be desired, cannot be left out of account, a development to be expected in the near future, deserving of serious consideration, brought to a satisfactory conclusion,* and so on and so forth.

Pretentious Diction

Words like *phenomenon, element, individual* (as noun), *objective, categorical, effective, virtual, basic, primary, promote, constitute, exhibit, exploit, utilize, eliminate, liquidate,* are used to dress up simple statements and give an air of scientific impartiality to biased judgments. Adjectives like *epoch-making, epic, historic, unforgettable, triumphant, age-old, inevitable, inexorable, veritable,* are used to dignify the sordid processes of international politics, while writing that aims at glorifying war usually takes on an archaic color, its characteristic words being: *realm, throne, chariot, mailed fist, trident, sword, shield, buckler, banner, jackboot, clarion.* Foreign words and expressions such as *cul de sac, ancien régime, deus ex machina, mutatis mutandis, status quo, gleichschaltung, weltanschauung,* are used to give an air of culture and elegance. Except for the useful abbreviations *i.e., e.g.,* and *etc.,* there is no real need for any of the hundreds of foreign phrases now current in English. Bad writers, and especially scientific, political and sociological writers, are nearly always haunted by the notion that Latin or Greek words are grander than Saxon ones, and unnecessary words like *expedite, ameliorate, predict, extraneous, deracinated, clandestine, subaqueous* and hundreds of others constantly gain ground from their Anglo-Saxon opposite numbers. The jargon peculiar to Marxist writing (*hyena, hangman, cannibal, petty bourgeois, these, gentry, lacquey, flunkey, mad dog, White Guard,* etc.) consists largely of words and phrases translated from Russian, German or French; but the normal way of coining a new word is to use a Latin or Greek root with the appropriate affix and, where necessary, the *-ize* formation. It is often easier to make up words of this kind (*deregionalize, impermissible, extramarital, non-fragmentory* and so forth) than to think up the English words that will cover one's meaning. The result, in general, is an increase in slovenliness and vagueness.

Meaningless Words

In certain kinds of writing, particularly in art criticism and literary criticism, it is normal to come across long passages which are almost completely lacking in meaning. Words like *romantic, plastic, values, human, dead, sentimental, natural, vitality,* as used in art criticism, are strictly meaningless in the sense that they not only do not point to any discoverable object, but are hardly ever expected to do so by the reader. When one critic writes, "The outstanding feature of Mr. X's work is its living quality", while another writes, "The immediately striking thing about Mr. X's work is its peculiar deadness", the reader accepts this as a simple difference of opinion. If words like *black* and *white* were involved, instead of the jargon words *dead* and *living,* he would see at once that language was being used in an improper way. Many political words are similarly abused. The word *Fascism* has now no meaning except in so far as it signifies "something not desirable." The words *democracy, socialism, freedom, patriotic, realistic, justice,* have each of them several different meanings which cannot be reconciled with one another. In the case of a word like *democracy*, not only is there no agreed definition, but the attempt to make one is resisted from all sides. It is almost universally felt that when we call a country democratic we are praising it: consequently the defenders of every kind of régime claim that it is a democracy, and fear that they might have to stop using the word if it were tied down to any one meaning. Words of this kind are often used in a consciously dishonest way. That is, the person who uses them has his own private definition, but allows his hearer to think he means something quite different. Statements like *Marshal Pétain was a true patriot, The Soviet Press is the freest in the world, The Catholic Church is opposed to persecution,* are almost always made with intent to deceive. Other words used in variable meanings, in most cases more or less dishonestly, are: *class, totalitarian, science, progressive, reactionary, bourgeois, equality.*

Now that I have made this catalogue of swindles and perversions, let me give another example of the kind of writing that they lead to. This time it must of its nature be an imaginary one. I am going to translate a passage of good English into modern English of the worst sort. Here is a well-known verse from *Ecclesiastes:*

> *"I returned and saw under the sun, that the race is not to the swift, nor the battle to the strong, neither yet bread to the wise, nor yet riches to men of understanding, nor yet favour to men of skill; but time and chance happeneth to them all."*

10 Here it is in modern English: 10

> *"Objective consideration of contemporary phenomena compels the conclusion that success or failure in competitive activities exhibits no tendency to be commensurate with innate capacity, but that a considerable element of the unpredictable must invariably be taken into account."*

This is a parody, but not a very gross one. Exhibit (3), above, for instance, contains several patches of the same kind of English. It will be seen that I have not made a full translation. The beginning and ending of the sentence follow the original meaning fairly closely, but in the middle the concrete illustrations—race, battle, bread—dissolve into the vague phrase "success or failure in competitive activities." This had to be so, because no modern writer of the kind I am discussing—no one capable of using phrases like "objective consideration of contemporary phenomena"—would ever tabulate his thoughts in that precise and detailed way. The whole tendency of modern prose is away from concreteness. Now analyze these two sentences a little more closely. The first contains forty-nine words but only sixty syllables, and all its words are those of everyday life. The second contains thirty-eight words of ninety syllables: eighteen of its words are from Latin roots, and one from Greek. The first sentence contains six vivid images, and only one phrase ("time and chance") that could be called vague. The second contains not a single fresh, arresting phrase, and in spite of its ninety syllables it gives only a shortened version of the meaning contained in the first. Yet without a doubt it is the second kind of sentence that is gaining ground in modern English. I do not want to exaggerate. This kind of writing is not yet universal, and outcrops of simplicity will occur here and there in the worst-written page. Still, if you or I were told to write a few lines on the uncertainty of human fortunes, we should probably come much nearer to my imaginary sentence than to the one from *Ecclesiastes*.

As I have tried to show, modern writing at its worst does not consist in picking out words for the sake of their meaning and inventing images in order to make the meaning clearer. It consists in gumming together long strips of words which have already been set in order by someone else, and making the results presentable by sheer humbug. The attraction of this way of writing is that it is easy. It is easier—even quicker, once you have the habit—to say *In my opinion it is a not unjustifiable assumption* that than to say *I think*. If you use ready-made phrases, you not only don't have to hunt about for words; you also don't have to bother with the rhythms of your sentences, since these phrases are generally so arranged as to be more or less euphonious. When you are composing in a hurry—when you are dictating to a stenographer, for instance, or making a public speech—it is natural to fall into a pretentious, Latinized style. Tags like *a consideration which we should do well to bear in mind* or *a conclusion to which all of us would readily assent* will save many a sentence from coming down with a bump. By using stale metaphors, similes and idioms, you save much mental effort, at the cost of leaving your meaning vague, not only for your reader but for yourself. This is the significance of mixed metaphors. The sole aim of a metaphor is to call up a visual image. When these images clash—as in *The Fascist octopus has sung its swan song, the jackboot is thrown into the melting pot*—it can't be taken as certain that the writer is not seeing a mental image of the objects he is naming; in other words he is not really thinking. Look again at the examples I gave at the beginning of this essay. Professor Laski (1) uses five negatives in fifty-three words. One of these is superfluous, making nonsense of the whole passage, and in addition there is the slip *alien* for akin, making further nonsense, and several avoidable pieces of clumsiness which increase the general vagueness. Professor Hogben (2) plays ducks and drakes with a battery which is able to write prescriptions, and, while disapproving of the everyday phrase *put up with,* is unwilling to look *egregious* up in the dictionary and see what it means. (3), if one takes an uncharitable attitude towards it, is simply meaningless: probably one could work out its intended meaning by reading the whole of the article in which it occurs. In (4), the writer knows more or less what he wants to say, but an accumulation of stale phrases chokes him like tea leaves blocking a sink. In (5), words and meaning have almost parted company. People who write in this manner usually have a general emotional meaning—they dislike one thing and want to express solidarity with another—but they are not interested in the detail of what they are saying. A scrupulous writer, in every sentence that he writes, will ask himself at least four questions, thus: What am I trying to say? What words will express it? What image or idiom will make it clearer? Is this image fresh enough to have an effect? And he will probably ask himself two more: Could I put it more shortly? Have I said anything that is avoidably ugly? But you are not obliged to go to all this trouble. You can shirk it by simply throwing your mind open and letting the ready-made phrases come crowding in. They will construct your sentences for you—even think your thoughts for you, to a certain extent—and at need they will perform the important service of partially concealing your meaning even from yourself. It is at this point that the special connection between politics and the debasement of language becomes clear.

In our time it is broadly true that political writing is bad writing. Where it is not true, it will generally be found that the writer is some kind of rebel, expressing his private opinions and not a "party line." Orthodoxy, of whatever colour, seems to demand a lifeless, imitative style. The political dialects to be found in pamphlets, leading articles, manifestos, White Papers and the speeches of under-secretaries do, of course, vary from party to party, but they are all alike in that one almost never finds in them a fresh, vivid, home-made turn of speech. When one watches some tired hack on the platform mechanically repeating the familiar phrases—*bestial atrocities, iron heel, bloodstained tyranny, free peoples of the world, stand shoulder to shoulder*—one often has a curious feeling that one is not watching a live human being but some kind of dummy: a feeling which suddenly becomes stronger at moments when the light catches the speaker's spectacles and turns them into blank discs which seem to have no eyes behind them. And this is not altogether fanciful. A speaker who uses that kind of phraseology has gone some distance towards turning himself into a machine. The appropriate noises are coming out of his larynx, but his brain is not involved as it would be if he were choosing his words for himself. If the speech he is making is one that he is accustomed to make over and over again, he may be almost unconscious of what he is saying, as one is when one utters the responses in church. And this reduced state of consciousness, if not indispensable, is at any rate favorable to political conformity.

In our time, political speech and writing are largely the defence of the indefensible. Things like the continuance of British rule in India, the Russian purges and deportations, the dropping of the atom bombs on Japan, can indeed be defended, but only by arguments which are too brutal for most people to face, and which do not square with the professed aims of political parties. Thus political language has to consist largely of euphemism, question-begging and sheer cloudy vagueness. Defenceless villages are bombarded from the air, the inhabitants driven out into the countryside, the cattle machine-gunned, the huts set on fire with incendiary bullets: this is called *pacification*. Millions of peasants are robbed of their farms and sent trudging along the roads with no more than they can carry: this is called *transfer of population* or *rectification of frontiers*. People are imprisoned for years without trial, or shot in the back of the neck or sent to die of scurvy in Arctic lumber camps: this is called *elimination of unreliable elements*. Such phraseology is needed if one wants to name things without calling up mental pictures of them. Consider for instance some comfortable English professor defending Russian totalitarianism. He cannot say outright, "I believe in killing off your opponents when you can get good results by doing so." Probably, therefore, he will say something like this:

15   "While freely conceding that the Soviet régime exhibits certain 15 features which the humanitarian may be inclined to deplore, we must, I think, agree that a certain curtailment of the right to political opposition is an unavoidable concomitant of transitional periods, and that the rigors which the Russian people have been called upon to undergo have been amply justified in the sphere of concrete achievement."

The inflated style is itself a kind of euphemism. A mass of Latin words falls upon the facts like soft snow, blurring the outlines and covering up all the details. The great enemy of clear language is insincerity. When there is a gap between one's real and one's declared aims, one turns as it were instinctively to long words and exhausted idioms, like a cuttlefish squirting out ink. In our age there is no such thing as "keeping out of politics." All issues are political issues, and politics itself is a mass of lies, evasions, folly, hatred and schizophrenia. When the general atmosphere is bad, language must suffer. I should expect to find—this is a guess which I have not sufficient knowledge to verify—that the German, Russian and Italian languages have all deteriorated in the last ten to fifteen years, as a result of dictatorship.

But if thought corrupts language, language can also corrupt thought. A bad usage can spread by tradition and imitation, even among people who should and do know better. The debased language that I have been discussing is in some ways very convenient. Phrases like *a not unjustifiable assumption, leaves much to be desired, would serve no good purpose, a consideration which we should do well to bear in mind,* are a continuous temptation, a packet of aspirins always at one's elbow. Look back through this essay, and for certain you will find that I have again and again committed the very faults I am protesting against. By this morning's post I have received a pamphlet dealing with conditions in Germany. The author tells me that he "felt impelled" to write it. I open it at random, and here is almost the first sentence that I see: "(The Allies) have an opportunity not only of achieving a radical transformation of Germany's social and political structure in such a way as to avoid a nationalistic reaction in Germany itself, but at the same time of laying the foundations of a cooperative and unified Europe." You see, he "feels impelled" to write—feels, presumably, that he has something new to say—and yet his words, like cavalry horses answering the bugle, group themselves automatically into the familiar dreary pattern. This invasion of one's mind by ready-made phrases (*lay the foundations, achieve a radical transformation*) can only be prevented if one is constantly on guard against them, and every such phrase anaesthetizes a portion of one's brain.

I said earlier that the decadence of our language is probably curable. Those who deny this would argue, if they produced an argument at all, that language merely reflects existing social conditions, and that we cannot influence its development by any direct tinkering with words and constructions. So far as the general tone or spirit of a language goes, this may be true, but it is not true in detail. Silly words and expressions have often disappeared, not through any evolutionary process but owing to the conscious action of a minority. Two recent examples were *explore every avenue* and *leave no stone unturned,* which were killed by the jeers of a few journalists. There is a long list of fly-blown metaphors which could similarly be got rid of if enough people would interest themselves in the job; and it should also be possible to laugh the *not un-* formation out of existence, to reduce the amount of Latin and Greek in the average sentence, to drive out foreign phrases and strayed scientific words, and, in general, to make pretentiousness unfashionable. But all these are minor points. The defence of the English language implies more than this, and perhaps it is best to start by saying what it does not imply.

To begin with it has nothing to do with archaism, with the salvaging of obsolete words and turns of speech, or with the setting up of a "standard English" which must never be departed from. On the contrary, it is especially concerned with the scrapping of every word or idiom which has outworn its usefulness. It has nothing to do with correct grammar and syntax, which are of no importance so long as one makes one's meaning clear, or with the avoidance of Americanisms, or with having what is called a "good prose style." On the other hand it is not concerned with fake simplicity and the attempt to make written English colloquial. Nor does it even imply in every case preferring the Saxon word to the Latin one, though it does imply using the fewest and shortest words that will cover one's meaning. What is above all needed is to let the meaning choose the word, and not the other way about. In prose, the worst thing one can do with words is to surrender to them. When you think of a concrete object, you think wordlessly, and then, if you want to describe the thing you have been visualizing you probably hunt about till you find the exact words that seem to fit. When you think of something abstract you are more inclined to use words from the start, and unless you make a conscious effort to prevent it, the existing dialect will come rushing in and do the job for you, at the expense of blurring or even changing your meaning. Probably it is better to put off using words as long as possible and get one's meaning as clear as one can through pictures or sensations. Afterwards one can choose—not simply accept—the phrases that will best cover the meaning, and then switch round and decide what impression one's words are likely to make on another person. This last effort of the mind cuts out all stale or mixed images, all prefabricated phrases, needless repetitions, and humbug and vagueness generally. But one can often be in doubt about the effect of a word or a phrase, and one needs rules that one can rely on when instinct fails. I think the following rules will cover most cases:

(i) Never use a metaphor, simile or other figure of speech which you are used to seeing in print.
(ii) Never use a long word where a short one will do.
(iii) If it is possible to cut a word out, always cut it out.
(iv) Never use the passive where you can use the active.
(v) Never use a foreign phrase, a scientific word or a jargon word if you can think of an everyday English equivalent.
(vi) Break any of these rules sooner than say anything outright barbarous.

20   These rules sound elementary, and so they are, but they demand a deep change of attitude in anyone who has grown used to writing in the style now fashionable. One could keep all of them and still write bad English, but one could not write the kind of stuff that I quoted in those five specimens at the beginning of this article.

I have not here been considering the literary use of language, but merely language as an instrument for expressing and not for concealing or preventing thought. Stuart Chase and others have come near to claiming that all abstract words are meaningless, and have used this as a pretext for advocating a kind of political quietism. Since you don't know what Fascism is, how can you struggle against Fascism? One need not swallow such absurdities as this, but one ought to recognize that the present political chaos is connected with the decay of language, and that one can probably bring about some improvement by starting at the verbal end. If you simplify your English, you are freed from the worst follies of orthodoxy. You cannot speak any of the necessary dialects, and when you make a stupid remark its stupidity will be obvious, even to yourself. Political language—and with variations this is true of all political parties, from Conservatives to Anarchists—is designed to make lies sound truthful and murder respectable, and to give an appearance of solidity to pure wind. One cannot change this all in a moment, but one can at least change one's own habits, and from time to time one can even, if one jeers loudly enough, send some worn-out and useless phrase—some *jackboot, Achilles' heel, hotbed, melting pot, acid test, veritable inferno* or other lump of verbal refuse—into the dustbin where it belongs.

Shooting an Elephant
George Orwell

George Orwell is the pen name used by the British author Eric Blair (1903–1950). Orwell was born in the Indian village of Motihari, near Nepal, where his father was stationed in the Civil Service. India was then part of the British Empire; Orwell's grandfather too had served the Empire in the Indian Army. From 1907 to 1922 Orwell lived in England, returning to India and Burma and a position in the Imperial Police, which he held until 1927. This is the period about which he writes in "Shooting an Elephant." Thereafter he lived in England, Paris, Spain, and elsewhere, writing on a wide range of topics. He fought in the Spanish Civil War and was actively engaged in several political movements, always against totalitarianism of any kind. He is best known today for two novels of political satire: Animal Farm *(1945) and* 1984 *(1949). He was also a prolific journalist and essayist, with his essays collected in five volumes. "Shooting an Elephant" was first published in 1936 and later collected in a book of the same name in 1950. Note that Orwell is writing as an older, wiser man about events that took place when he was in his early twenties some two decades previously. This combined perspective of the young man experiencing the incident and the older man looking back on it is part of the rich reading experience.*

1   In Moulmein, in Lower Burma, I was hated by large numbers of people—the only time in my life that I have been important enough for this to happen to me. I was sub-divisional police officer of the town, and in an aimless, petty, kind of way anti-European feel-

From *Shooting an Elephant and Other Essays* by George Orwell. Published by Harcourt Brace and Company. Harcourt Brace and Company and Heath & Co., Ltd.

ing was very bitter. No one had the guts to raise a riot, but if a European woman went through the bazaars alone somebody would probably spit betel juice over her dress. As a police officer I was an obvious target and was baited whenever it seemed safe to do so. When a nimble Burman tripped me up on the football field and the referee (another Burman) looked the other way, the crowd yelled with hideous laughter. This happened more than once. In the end the sneering yellow faces of young men that met me everywhere, the insults hooted after me when I was at a safe distance, got badly on my nerves. The young Buddhist priests were the worst of all. There were several thousand of them in the town and none of them seemed to have anything to do except stand on street corners and jeer at Europeans.

All this was perplexing and upsetting. For at that time I had already made up my mind that imperialism was an evil thing and the sooner I chucked up my job and got out of it the better. Theoretically—and secretly, of course—I was all for the Burmese and all against their oppressors, the British. As for the job I was doing, I hated it more bitterly than I can perhaps make clear. In a job like that you see the dirty work of Empire at close quarters. The wretched prisoners huddling in the stinking cages of the lock-ups, the grey, cowed faces of the long-term convicts, the scarred buttocks of the men who had been flogged with bamboos—all these oppressed me with an intolerable sense of guilt. But I could get nothing into perspective. I was young and ill-educated and I had had to think out my problems in the utter silence that is imposed on every Englishman in the East. I did not even know that the British Empire is dying, still less did I know that it is a great deal better than the younger empires that are going to supplant it. All I knew was that I was stuck between my hatred of the empire I served and my rage against the evil-spirited little beasts who tried to make my job impossible. With one part of my mind I thought of the British Raj as an unbreakable tyranny, as something clamped down, in *saecula saeculorum*, upon the will of prostrate peoples; with another part I thought that the greatest joy in the world would be to drive a bayonet into a Buddhist priest's guts. Feelings like these are the normal by-products of imperialism; ask any Anglo-Indian official, if you can catch him off duty.

One day something happened which in a roundabout way was enlightening. It was a tiny incident in itself, but it gave me a better glimpse than I had had before of the real nature of imperialism—the real motives for which despotic governments act. Early one morning the sub-inspector at a police station the other end of the town rang me up on the 'phone and said that an elephant was ravaging the bazaar. Would I please come and do something about it? I did not know what I could do, but I wanted to see what was happening and I got on to a pony and started out. I took my rifle, an old .44 Winchester and much too small to kill an elephant, but I thought the noise might be useful *in terrorem*. Various Burmans stopped me on the way and told me about the elephant's doings. It was not, of course, a wild elephant, but a tame one which had gone "must." It had been chained up, as tame elephants always are when their attack of "must" is due, but on the previous night it had broken its chain and escaped. Its mahout, the only person who could manage it when it was in that state, had set out in pursuit, but had taken the wrong direction and was now twelve hours' journey away, and in the morning the elephant had suddenly reappeared in the town. The Burmese population had no weapons and were quite helpless against it. It had already destroyed somebody's bamboo hut, killed a cow and raided some fruit-stalls and devoured the stock; also it had met the municipal rubbish van and, when the driver jumped out and took to his heels, had turned the van over and inflicted violence upon it.

The Burmese sub-inspector and some Indian constables were waiting for me in the quarter where the elephant had been seen. It was a very poor quarter, a labyrinth of squalid bamboo huts, thatched with palm-leaf, winding all over a steep hillside. I remember that it was a cloudy, stuffy, morning at the beginning of the rains. We began questioning the people as to where the elephant had gone and, as usual, failed to get any definite information. That is invariably the case in the East; a story always sounds clear enough at a distance, but the nearer you get to the scene of events the vaguer it becomes. Some of the people said that the elephant had gone in one direction, some said that he had gone in another, some professed not even to have heard of any elephant. I had almost made up my mind that the whole story was a pack of lies, when we heard yells a little distance away. There was a loud, scandalized cry of "Go away, child! Go away this instant!" and an old woman with a switch in her hand came round the corner of a hut, violently shooing away a crowd of naked children. Some more women followed, clicking their tongues and exclaiming; evidently there was something that the children ought not to have seen. I rounded the hut and saw a man's dead body sprawling in the mud. He was an Indian, a black Dravidian coolie, almost naked, and he could not have been dead many minutes. The people said that the elephant had come suddenly upon him round the corner of the hut, caught him with its trunk, put its foot on his back and ground him into the earth. This was the rainy season and the ground was soft, and his face had scored a trench a foot deep and a couple of yards long. He was lying on his belly with arms crucified and head sharply twisted to one side. His face was coated with mud, the eyes wide open, the teeth bared and grinning with an expression of unendurable agony. (Never tell me, by the way, that the dead look peaceful. Most of the corpses I have seen looked devilish.) The friction of the great beast's foot had stripped the skin from his back as neatly as one skins a rabbit. As soon as I saw the dead man I sent an orderly to a friend's house nearby to borrow an elephant rifle. I had already sent back the pony, not wanting it to go mad with fright and throw me if it smelt the elephant.

5   The orderly came back in a few minutes with a rifle and five cartridges, and meanwhile some Burmans had arrived and told us that the elephant was in the paddy fields below, only a few hundred yards away. As I started forward practically the whole population of the quarter flocked out of the houses and followed me. They had seen the rifle and were all shouting excitedly that I was going to shoot the elephant. They had not shown much interest in the elephant when he was merely ravaging their homes, but it was different now that he was going to be shot. It was a bit of fun to them, as it would be to an English crowd; besides they wanted the meat. It made me vaguely uneasy. I had no intention of shooting the elephant—I had merely sent for the rifle to defend myself if necessary—and it is always unnerving to have a crowd following you. I marched down the hill, looking and feeling a fool, with the rifle over my shoulder and an evergrowing army of people jostling at my heels. At the bottom, when you got away from the huts, there was a metalled road and beyond that a miry waste of paddy fields a thousand yards across, not yet ploughed but soggy from the first rains and dotted with coarse grass. The elephant was standing eight yards from the road, his left side towards us. He took not the slightest notice of the crowd's approach. He was tearing up bunches of grass, beating them against his knees to clean them and stuffing them into his mouth.

I had halted on the road. As soon as I saw the elephant I knew with perfect certainty that I ought not to shoot him. It is a serious matter to shoot a working elephant—it is comparable to destroying a huge and costly piece of machinery—and obviously one ought not to do it if it can possibly be avoided. And at that distance, peacefully eating, the elephant looked no more dangerous than a cow. I thought then and I think now that his attack of "must" was already passing off; in which case he would merely wander harmlessly about until the mahout came back and caught him. Moreover, I did not in the least want to shoot him. I decided that I would watch him for a little while to make sure that he did not turn savage again, and then go home.

But at that moment I glanced round at the crowd that had followed me. It was an immense crowd, two thousand at the least and growing every minute. It blocked the road for a long distance on either side. I looked at the sea of yellow faces above the garish clothes—faces all happy and excited over this bit of fun, all certain that the elephant was going to be shot. They were watching me as they would watch a conjurer about to perform a trick. They did not like me, but with the magical rifle in my hands I was momentarily worth watching. And suddenly I realized that I should have to shoot the elephant after all. The people expected it of me and I had got to do it; I could feel their two thousand wills pressing me forward, irresistibly. And it was at this moment, as I stood there with the rifle in my hands, that I first grasped the hollowness, the futility of the white man's dominion in the East. Here was I, the white man with his gun, standing in front of the unarmed native crowd—seemingly the leading actor of the piece; but in reality I was only an absurd puppet pushed to and fro by the will of those yellow faces behind. I perceived in this moment that when the white man turns tyrant it is his own freedom that he destroys. He becomes a sort of hollow, posing dummy, the conventionalized figure of a sahib. For it is the condition of his rule that he shall spend his life in trying to impress the "natives," and so in every crisis he has got to do what the "natives" expect of him. He wears a mask, and his face grows to fit it. I had got to shoot the elephant. I had committed myself to doing it when I sent for the rifle. A sahib has got to act like a sahib; he has got to appear resolute, to know his own mind and do definite things. To come all that way, rifle in hand, with a thousand people marching at my heels, and then to trail feebly away, having done nothing—no, that was impossible. The crowd would laugh at me. And my whole life, every white man's life in the East, was one long struggle not to be laughed at.

But I did not want to shoot the elephant. I watched him beating his bunch of grass against his knees, with that preoccupied grandmotherly air that elephants have. It seemed to me that it would be murder to shoot him. At that age I was not squeamish about killing animals, but I had never shot an elephant and never wanted to. (Somehow it always seems worse to kill a *large* animal.) Besides, there was the beast's owner to be considered. Alive, the elephant was worth at least a hundred pounds; dead, he would only be worth the value of his tusks, five pounds, possibly. But I had got to act quickly. I turned to some experienced-looking Burmans who had been there when we arrived, and asked them how the elephant had been behaving. They all said the same thing: he took no notice of you if you left him alone, but he might charge if you went too close to him.

It was perfectly clear to me what I ought to do. I ought to walk up to within, say, twenty-five yards of the elephant and test his be-havior. If he charged, I could shoot; if he took no notice of me, it would be safe to leave him until the mahout came back. But also I knew that I was going to do no such thing. I was a poor shot with a rifle and the ground was soft mud into which one would sink at every step. If the elephant charged and I missed him, I should have about as much chance as a toad under a steam-roller. But even then I was not thinking particularly of my own skin, only of the watchful yellow faces behind. For at that moment, with the crowd watching me, I was not afraid in the ordinary sense, as I would have been if I had been alone. A white man mustn't be frightened in front of "natives"; and so, in general, he isn't frightened. The sole thought in my mind was that if anything went wrong those two thousand Burmans would see me pursued, caught, trampled on and reduced to a grinning corpse like that Indian up the hill. And if that happened it was quite probable that some of them would laugh. That would never do. There was only one alternative. I shoved the cartridges into the magazine and lay down on the road to get a better aim.

10   The crowd grew very still, and a deep, low, happy sigh, as of people 10 who see the theatre curtain go up at last, breathed from innumerable throats. They were going to have their bit of fun after all. The rifle was a beautiful German thing with cross-hair sights. I did not then know that in shooting an elephant one would shoot to cut an imaginary bar running from ear-hole to ear-hole. I ought, therefore, as the elephant was sideways on, to have aimed straight at his ear-hole; actually I aimed several inches in front of this, thinking the brain would be fur-ther forward.

When I pulled the trigger I did not hear the bang or feel the kick— one never does when a shot goes home—but I heard the devilish roar of glee that went up from the crowd. In that instant, in too short a time, one would have thought, even for the bullet to get there, a mysterious, terrible change had come over the elephant. He neither stirred nor fell, but every line of his body had altered. He looked suddenly stricken, shrunken, immensely old, as though the frightful impact of the bullet had paralysed him without knocking him down. At last, after what seemed a long time—it might have been five seconds, I dare say—he sagged flabbily to his knees. His mouth slobbered. An enormous senility seemed to have settled upon him. One could have imagined him thousands of years old. I fired again into the same spot. At the second shot he did not collapse but climbed with desperate slowness to his feet and stood weakly upright, with legs sagging and head drooping. I fired a third time. That was the shot that did for him. You could see the agony of it jolt his whole body and knock the last remnant of strength from his legs. But in falling he seemed for a moment to rise, for as his hind legs collapsed beneath him he seemed to tower upward like a huge rock toppling, his trunk reaching skywards like a tree. He trumpeted, for the first and only time. And then down he came, his belly towards me, with a crash that seemed to shake the ground even where I lay.

I got up. The Burmans were already racing past me across the mud. It was obvious that the elephant would never rise again, but he was not dead. He was breathing very rhythmically with long rattling gasps, his great mound of a side painfully rising and falling. His mouth was wide open—I could see far down into caverns of pale pink throat. I waited a long time for him to die, but his breathing did not weaken. Finally I fired my two remaining shots into the spot where I thought his heart must be. The thick blood welled out of him like red velvet, but still he did not die. His body did not even jerk when the shots hit him, the tortured breathing continued without a pause. He was dying, very slowly and in great agony, but in some world remote from me where not even a bullet could damage him further. I felt that I had got to put an end to that dreadful noise. It seemed dreadful to see the great beast lying there, powerless to move and yet powerless to die, and not even to be able to finish him. I sent back for my small rifle and poured shot after shot into his heart and down his throat. They seemed to make no impression. The tortured gasps continued as steadily as the ticking of a clock.

In the end I could not stand it any longer and went away. I heard later that it took him half an hour to die. Burmans were bringing dahs and baskets even before I left, and I was told they had stripped his body almost to the bones by the afternoon.

Afterwards, of course, there were endless discussions about the shooting of the elephant. The owner was furious, but he was only an Indian and could do nothing. Besides, legally I had done the right thing, for a mad elephant has to be killed, like a mad dog, if its owner fails to control it. Among the Europeans opinion was divided. The older men said I was right, the younger men said it was a damn shame to shoot an elephant for killing a coolie, because an elephant was worth more than any damn Coringhee coolie. And afterwards I was very glad that the coolie had been killed; it put me legally in the right and it gave me a sufficient pretext for shooting the elephant. I often wondered whether any of the others grasped that I had done it solely to avoid looking a fool.

Workers

Richard Rodriguez

*Richard Rodriguez (1944–) was born in San Francisco. A
child of Mexican immigrants, Rodriguez spoke Spanish
until he went to a Catholic school at age 6. As a youth, he
delivered newspapers and worked as a gardener. Rodriguez
received a B.A. from Stanford University, an M.A. from
Columbia University, and a Ph.D. in English Renaissance
literature from the University of California at Berkeley, and
attended the Warburg Institute in London on a Fulbright
fellowship. A noted prose stylist, Rodriguez has worked as a
teacher, journalist, and educational consultant, in addition
to writing, lecturing, and appearing frequently on the Public Broadcast System (PBS) program,* The MacNeil-Lehrer
News Hour. *Rodriguez's books include* Hunger of Memory: The Education of Richard Rodriguez *(1982), a collection of autobiographical essays;* Mexico's Children
(1990); and Days of Obligation: An Argument With My
Mexican Father *(1992), which was nominated for a National Book Award. In addition, he has been published in*
The American Scholar, Change, College English,
Harper's, Mother Jones, Reader's Digest, *and* Time. *Not
unfamiliar with controversy, Rodriguez often speaks out
against affirmative action and bilingual education. The
following essay, which appeared in* Hunger of Memory, *reveals lessons Rodriguez learned about his choices in life and
Mexican migrant workers who have none.*

1   It was at Stanford, one day near the end of my senior year, that a   1
friend told me about a summer construction job he knew was
available. I was quickly alert. Desire uncoiled within me. My
friend said that he knew I had been looking for summer employment.

He knew I needed some money. Almost apologetically he explained: It was something I probably wouldn't be interested in, but a friend of his, a contractor, needed someone for the summer to do menial jobs. There would be lots of shoveling and raking and sweeping. Nothing too hard. But nothing more interesting either. Still, the pay would be good. Did I want it? Or did I know someone who did?

I did. Yes, I said, surprised to hear myself say it.

In the weeks following, friends cautioned that I had no idea how hard physical labor really is. ("You only *think* you know what it is like to shovel for eight hours straight.") Their objections seemed to me challenges. They resolved the issue. I became happy with my plan. I decided, however, not to tell my parents. I wouldn't tell my mother because I could guess her worried reaction. I would tell my father only after the summer was over, when I could announce that, after all, I did know what "real work" is like.

The day I met the contractor (a Princeton graduate, it turned out), he asked me whether I had done any physical labor before. "In high school, during the summer," I lied. And although he seemed to regard me with skepticism, he decided to give me a try. Several days later, expectant, I arrived at my first construction site. I would take off my shirt to the sun. And at last grasp desired sensation. No longer afraid. At last become like a *bracero*. "We need those tree stumps out of here by tomorrow," the contractor said. I started to work.

5   I labored with excitement that first morning—and all the days   5
after. The work was harder than I could have expected. But it was never as tedious as my friends had warned me it would be. There was too much physical pleasure in the labor. Especially early in the day, I would be most alert to the sensations of movement and straining. Beginning around seven each morning (when the air was still damp but the scent of weeds and dry earth anticipated the heat of the sun), I would feel my body resist the first thrusts of the shovel. My arms, tightened by sleep, would gradually loosen; after only several minutes, sweat would gather in beads on my forehead and then—a short while later—I would feel my chest silky with sweat in the breeze. I would return to my work. A nervous spark of pain would fly up my arm and settle to burn like an ember in the thick of my shoulder. An hour, two passed. Three. My whole body would assume regular movements; my shoveling would be described by identical, even movements. Even later in the day, my enthusiasm for primitive sensation would survive the heat and the dust and the insects pricking my back. I would strain

wildly for sensation as the day came to a close. At three-thirty, quitting time, I would stand upright and slowly let my head fall back, luxuriating in the feeling of tightness relieved.

Some of the men working nearby would watch me and laugh. Two or three of the older men took the trouble to teach me the right way to use a pick, the correct way to shovel. "You're doing it wrong, too fucking hard," one man scolded. Then proceeded to show me— what persons who work with their bodies all their lives quickly learn— the most economical way to use one's body in labor.

"Don't make your back do so much work," he instructed. I stood impatiently listening, half listening, vaguely watching, then noticed his work-thickened fingers clutching the shovel. I was annoyed. I wanted to tell him that I enjoyed shoveling the wrong way. And I didn't want to learn the right way. I wasn't afraid of back pain. I liked the way my body felt sore at the end of the day.

I was about to, but, as it turned out, I didn't say a thing. Rather it was at that moment I realized that I was fooling myself if I expected a few weeks of labor to gain me admission to the world of the laborer. I would not learn in three months what my father had meant by "real work." I was not bound to this job; I could imagine its rapid conclusion. For me the sensations were to be feared. Fatigue took a different toll on their bodies—and minds.

It was, I know, a simple insight. But it was with this realization that I took my first step that summer toward realizing something even more important about the "worker." In the company of carpenters, electricians, plumbers, and painters at lunch, I would often sit quietly, observant. I was not shy in such company. I felt easy, pleased by the knowledge that I was casually accepted, my presence taken for granted by men (exotics) who worked with their hands. Some days the younger men would talk and talk about sex, and they would howl at women who drove by in cars. Other days the talk at lunchtime was subdued; men gathered in separate groups. It depended on who was around. There were rough, good-natured workers. Others were quiet. The more I remember that summer, the more I realize that there was no single *type* of worker. I am embarrassed to say I had not expected such diversity. I certainly had not expected to meet, for example, a plumber who was an abstract painter in his off hours and admired the work of Mark Rothko. Nor did I expect to meet so many workers with college diplomas. (They were the ones who were not surprised that I intended to enter graduate school in the fall.) I suppose what I really want to say here is painfully obvious, but I must say it nevertheless: The men of that summer were middle-class Americans. They certainly didn't constitute an oppressed society. Carefully completing their work sheets; talking about the fortunes of local football teams; planning Las Vegas vacations; comparing the gas mileage of various makes of campers—they were not *los pobres* my mother had spoken about.

10   On two occasions, the contractor hired a group of Mexican aliens.   10
They were employed to cut down some trees and haul off debris. In all, there were six men of varying age. The youngest in his late twenties; the oldest (his father?) perhaps sixty years old. They came and they left in a single old truck. Anonymous men. They were never introduced to the other men at the site. Immediately upon their arrival, they would follow the contractor's directions, start working—rarely resting—seemingly driven by a fatalistic sense that work which had to be done was best done as quickly as possible.

I watched them sometimes. Perhaps they watched me. The only time I saw them pay me much notice was one day at lunchtime when I was laughing with the other men. The Mexicans sat apart when they ate, just as they worked by themselves. Quiet. I rarely heard them say much to each other. All I could hear were their voices calling out sharply to one another, giving directions. Otherwise, when they stood briefly resting, they talked among themselves in voices too hard to overhear.

The contractor knew enough Spanish, and the Mexicans—or at least the oldest of them, their spokesman—seemed to know enough English to communicate. But because I was around, the contractor decided one day to make me his translator. (He assumed I could speak Spanish.) I did what I was told. Shyly I went over to tell the Mexicans that the *patrón* wanted them to do something else before they left for the day. As I started to speak, I was afraid with my old fear that I would be unable to pronounce the Spanish words. But it was a simple instruction I had to convey. I could say it in phrases.

The dark sweating faces turned toward me as I spoke. They stopped their work to hear me. Each nodded in response. I stood there. I wanted to say something more. But what could I say in Spanish, even if I could have pronounced the words right? Perhaps I just wanted to engage them in small talk, to be assured of their confidence, our familiarity. I thought for a moment to ask them where in Mexico they were from. Something like that. And maybe I wanted to tell them (a lie, if need be) that my parents were from the same part of Mexico.

I stood there.

15   Their faces watched me. The eyes of the man directly in front of 15
me moved slowly over my shoulder, and I turned to follow his glance
toward *el patrón* some distance away. For a moment I felt swept up by
that glance into the Mexicans' company. But then I heard one of them
returning to work. And then the others went back to work. I left them
without saying anything more.

    When they had finished, the contractor went over to pay them in
cash. (He later told me that he paid them collectively—"for the job,"
though he wouldn't tell me their wages. He said something quickly
about the good rate of exchange "in their own country.") I can still
hear the loudly confident voice he used with the Mexicans. It was the
sound of the *gringo* I had heard as a very young boy. And I can still
hear the quiet, indistinct sounds of the Mexican, the oldest, who
replied. At hearing that voice I was sad for the Mexicans. Depressed
by their vulnerability. Angry at myself. The adventure of the summer
seemed suddenly ludicrous. I would not shorten the distance I felt
from *los pobres* with a few weeks of physical labor. I would not become
like them. They were different from me.

    After that summer, a great deal—and not very much really—
changed in my life. The curse of physical shame was broken by the
sun; I was no longer ashamed of my body. No longer would I deny
myself the pleasing sensations of my maleness. During those years
when middle-class black Americans began to assert with pride, "Black
is beautiful," I was able to regard my complexion without shame. I am
today darker than I ever was as a boy. I have taken up the middle-class
sport of long-distance running. Nearly every day now I run ten or fifteen miles, barely clothed, my skin exposed to the California winter
rain and wind or the summer sun of late afternoon. The torso, the soccer player's calves and thighs, the arms of the twenty-year-old I never
was, I possess now in my thirties. I study the youthful parody shape
in the mirror: the stomach lipped tight by muscle; the shoulders
rounded by chin-ups; the arms veined strong. This man. A man. I
meet him. He laughs to see me, what I have become.

    The dandy. I wear double-breasted Italian suits and custom-made
English shoes. I resemble no one so much as my father—the man
pictured in those honeymoon photos. At that point in life when he
abandoned the dandy's posture, I assume it. At the point when my
parents would not consider going on vacation, I register at the Hotel
Carlyle in New York and the Plaza Athenée in Paris. I am as taken by

the symbols of leisure and wealth as they were. For my parents, however, those symbols became taunts, reminders of all they could not achieve in one lifetime. For me those same symbols are reassuring reminders of public success. I tempt vulgarity to be reassured. I am filled with the gaudy delight, the monstrous grace of the nouveau riche.

In recent years I have had occasion to lecture in ghetto high schools. There I see students of remarkable style and physical grace. (One can see more dandies in such schools than one ever will find in middle-class high schools.) There is not the look of casual assurance I saw students at Stanford display. Ghetto girls mimic high-fashion models. Their dresses are of bold, forceful color; their figures elegant, long; the stance theatrical. Boys wear shirts that grip at their overdeveloped muscular bodies. (Against a powerless future, they engage images of strength.) Bad nutrition does not yet tell. Great disappointment, fatal to youth, awaits them still. For the moment, movements in school hallways are dancelike, a procession of postures in a sexual masque. Watching them, I feel a kind of envy. I wonder how different my adolescence would have been had I been free. . . . But no, it is my parents I see—their optimism during those years when they were entertained by Italian grand opera.

20   The registration clerk in London wonders if I have just been to   20
Switzerland. And the man who carries my luggage in New York guesses the Caribbean. My complexion becomes a mark of my leisure. Yet no one would regard my complexion the same way if I entered such hotels through the service entrance. That is only to say that my complexion assumes its significance from the context of my life. My skin, in itself, means nothing. I stress the point because I know there are people who would label me "disadvantaged" because of my color. They make the same mistake I made as a boy, when I thought a disadvantaged life was circumscribed by particular occupations. That summer I worked in the sun may have made me physically indistinguishable from the Mexicans working nearby. (My skin was actually darker because, unlike them, I worked without wearing a shirt. By late August my hands were probably as tough as theirs.) But I was not one of *los pobres*. What made me different from them was an attitude of *mind*, my imagination of myself.

I do not blame my mother for warning me away from the sun when I was young. In a world where her brother had become an old man in his twenties because he was dark, my complexion was something to worry about. "Don't run in the sun," she warns me today. I run. In the end, my father was right—though perhaps he did not know how right or why—to say that I would never know what real work is. I will never know what he felt at his last factory job. If tomorrow I worked at some kind of factory, it would go differently for me. My long education would favor me. I could act as a public person—able to defend my interests, to unionize, to petition, to speak up—to challenge and demand. (I will never know what real work is.) I will never know what the Mexicans knew, gathering their shovels and ladders and saws.

Their silence stays with me now. The wages those Mexicans received for their labor were only a measure of their disadvantaged condition. Their silence is more telling. They lack a public identity. They remain profoundly alien. Persons apart. People lacking a union obviously, people without grounds. They depend upon the relative good will or fairness of their employers each day. For such people, lacking a better alternative, it is not such an unreasonable risk.

Their silence stays with me. I have taken these many words to describe its impact. Only: the quiet. Something uncanny about it. Its compliance. Vulnerability. Pathos. As I heard their truck rumbling away, I shuddered, my face mirrored with sweat. I had finally come face to face with *los pobres*.

Entering the Conversation

Mike Rose

If you walked out the back door of 9116 South Vermont and across our narrow yard, you would run smack into those four single-room rentals and, alongside them, an old wooden house-trailer. The trailer had belonged to Mrs. Jolly, the woman who sold us the property. It was locked and empty, and its tires were flat and fused into the asphalt driveway. Rusted dairy cases had been wedged in along its sides and four corners to keep it balanced. Two of its eight windows were broken, the frames were warped, and the door stuck. I was getting way too old to continue sharing a room with my mother, so I began to eye that trailer. I decided to refurbish it. It was time to have a room of my own.

Lou Minton had, by now, moved in with us, and he and I fixed the windows and realigned the door. I painted the inside by combining what I could find in our old shed with what I could afford to buy: The ceiling became orange, the walls yellow, the rim along the windows flat black. Lou redid the wiring and put in three new sockets. I got an old record player from the secondhand store for five dollars. I had Roy Herweck, the illustrator of our high school annual, draw women in mesh stockings and other objets d'redneck art on the yellow walls, and I put empty Smirnoff and Canadian Club bottles on the ledges above the windows. I turned the old trailer into the kind of bachelor digs a seventeen-year-old in South L.A. would fancy. My friends from high school began congregating there. When she could, my mother would make us a pot of spaghetti or pasta fasul'. And there was a clerk across the street at Marty's Liquor who would sell to us: We would run back across Vermont Avenue laughing and clutching our bags and seal ourselves up in the trailer. We spun fantasies about the waitress at the Mexican restaurant and mimicked our teachers and caught touchdown passes and, in general, dreamed our way through

Reprinted from *Lives on the Boundary: A Moving Account of the Struggles and Achievements of America's Educationally Underprepared* (1989), Free Press, a division of Simon and Schuster.

adolescence. It was a terrible time for rock 'n' roll—Connie Francis and Bobby Rydell were headliners in 1961—so we found rhythm and blues on L.A.'s one black station, played the backroom ballads of troubadour Oscar Brand, and discovered Delta and Chicago blues on Pacifica's KPFK:

> I'm a man
> I'm a full-grown man

As I fell increasingly under Mr. MacFarland's spell, books began replacing the liquor bottles above the windows: *The Trial* and *Waiting for Godot* and *No Exit* and *The Stranger*. Roy sketched a copy of the back cover of *Exile and the Kingdom,* and so the pensive face of Albert Camus now looked down from that patch of wall on which a cartoon had once pressed her crossed legs. My mother found a quilt that my grandmother had sewn from my father's fabric samples. It was dark and heavy, and I would lie under it and read Rimbaud and not understand him and feel very connected to the life I imagined Jack Mac-Farland's life to be: a subterranean ramble through Bebop and breathless poetry and back-alley revelations.

In 1962, John Connor moved into dank, old Apartment 1. John had also grown up in South L.A., and he and I had become best friends. His parents moved to Oregon, and John—who was a good black-top basketball player and an excellent student—wanted to stay in Los Angeles and go to college. So he rented an apartment for forty dollars a month, and we established a community of two. Some nights, John and I and Roy the artist and a wild kid named Gaspo would drive into downtown L.A.—down to where my mother had waited fearfully for a bus years before—and roam the streets and feel the excitement of the tenderloin: the flashing arrows, the blue-and-orange beer neon, the burlesque houses, the faded stairwell of Roseland—which we would inch up and then run down—brushing past the photos of taxi dancers, glossy and smiling in a glass display. Cops would tell us to go home, and that intensified this bohemian romance all the more.

5   About four months after John moved in, we both entered Loyola   5
University. Loyola is now coeducational; its student center houses an Asian Pacific Students Association, Black Student Alliance, and Chicano Resource Center; and its radio station, KXLU, plays the most untamed rock 'n' roll in Los Angeles. But in the early sixties, Loyola was pretty much a school for white males from the middle and upper

middle class. It was a sleepy little campus—its undergraduate enroll-ment was under two thousand—and it prided itself on providing spir-itual as well as intellectual guidance for its students: Religion and Christian philosophy courses were a required part of the curriculum. It defined itself as a Catholic intellectual community—promotional brochures relied on phrases like "the social, intellectual, and spiritual aspects of our students"—and made available to its charges small classes, a campus ministry, and thirty-six clubs (the Chess Club, Economics Society, Fine Arts Circle, Debate Squad, and more). There were also six fraternities and a sports program that included basketball, base-ball, volleyball, rugby, soccer, and crew. Loyola men, it was assumed, shared a fairly common set of social and religious values, and the uni-versity provided multiple opportunities for them to develop their minds, their spirits, and their social networks. I imagine that parents sent their boys to Loyola with a sigh of relief: God and man strolled together out of St. Robert Bellarmine Hall and veered left to Sacred Heart Chapel. There was an occasional wild party at one of the off-campus fraternity houses, but, well, a pair of panties in the koi pond was not on a par with crises of father and violence against the state.

John and I rattled to college in his '53 Plymouth. Loyola Boule-vard was lined with elms and maples, and as we entered the campus we could see the chapel tower rising in the distance. The chapel and all the early buildings had been constructed in the 1920s and were white and separated by broad sweeps of very green grass. Palm trees and stone pines grew in rows and clumps close to the buildings, and long concrete walkways curved and angled and crossed to connect everything, proving that God, as Plato suspected, is always doing geometry.

Most freshman courses were required, and I took most of mine in St. Robert Bellarmine Hall. Saint Robert was a father of the church who wrote on papal power and censored Galileo: The ceiling in his hallway was high, and dim lights hung down from it. The walls were beige up to about waist level, then turned off-white. The wood trim was dark and worn. The floor combined brown linoleum with brown and black tile. Even with a rush of students, the building maintained its dignity. We moved through it, and its old, clanking radiators warmed us as we did, but it was not a warmth that got to the bone. I remem-ber a dream in which I climbed up beyond the third floor—up thin, narrow stairs to a bell tower that held a small, dusky room in which a priest was playing church music to a class of shadows.

My first semester classes included the obligatory theology and ROTC and a series of requirements: biology, psychology, speech, logic, and a language. I went to class and usually met John for lunch: We'd bring sandwiches to his car and play the radio while we ate. Then it was back to class, or the library, or the student union for a Coke. This was the next step in Jack MacFarland's plan for me—and I did okay for a while. I had learned enough routines in high school to act like a fairly typical student, but—except for the historical sketch I received in Senior English—there wasn't a solid center of knowledge and assurance to all this. When I look back through notes and papers and various photographs and memorabilia, I begin to remember what a disengaged, half-awake time it really was. I'll describe two of the notebooks I found. The one from English is a small book, eight by seven, and only eleven pages of it are filled. The notes I did write consist of book titles, dates of publication, names of characters, pointless summaries of books that were not on our syllabus and that I had never read ("*The Alexandria Quartet:* 5 or 6 characters seen by different people in different stages of life"), and quotations from the teacher ("Perception can bring sorrow.") The notes are a series of separate entries. I can't see any coherence. My biology lab notes are written on green-tint quadrille. They, too, are sparse. There is an occasional poorly executed sketch of a tiny organism or of a bone and muscle structure. Some of the formulas and molecular models sit isolated on the page, bare of any explanatory discussion. The lecture notes are fragmented; a fair number of sentences remain incomplete.

By the end of the second semester my grades were close to dipping below a C average, and since I had been admitted provisionally, that would have been that. Jack MacFarland had oriented me to Western intellectual history and had helped me develop my writing, but he had worked with me for only a year, and I needed more than twelve months of his kind of instruction. Speech and Introductory Psychology presented no big problems. General Biology had midterm and final examinations that required a good deal of memorizing, and I could do that, but the textbook—particularly the chapter covered in the second semester—was much, much harder than what I read in high school, and I was so ill-adept in the laboratory that I failed that portion of the class. We had to set up and pursue biological problems, not just memorize—and at the first sign of doing rather than memorizing, I would automatically assume the problem was beyond me and distance myself from it. Logic, another requirement, spooked me with its syllogisms and Venn diagrams—they were just a step away from more formal mathematics—so I memorized what I could and squirmed around the rest. Theology was god-awful; ROTC was worse. And Latin, the language I elected on the strength of Jack MacFarland's one piece of bad advice, had me suffocating under the dust of a dead civilization. Freshman English was taught by a frustrated novelist with glittering eyes who had us, among other things, describing the consumption of our last evening's meal using the images of a battlefield.

10   I was out of my league.   10

Faculty would announce office hours. If I had had the sense, I would have gone, but they struck me as aloof and somber men, and I felt stupid telling them I was . . . well—stupid. I drifted through the required courses, thinking that as soon as these requirements were over, I'd never had to face anything even vaguely quantitative again. Or anything to do with foreign languages. Or ROTC. I fortified myself with defiance: I worked up an imitation of the old priest who was my Latin teacher, and I kept my ROTC uniform crumpled in the greasy trunk of John's Plymouth.

Many of my classmates came from and lived in a world very different from my own. The campus literary magazine would publish excerpts from the journals of upperclassmen traveling across Europe, standing before the Berlin Wall or hiking through olive groves toward Delphi. With the exception of one train trip back to Altoona, I had never been out of Southern California, and this translated, for me, into some personal inadequacy. Fraternities seemed exclusive and a little strange. I'm not sure why I didn't join any of Loyola's three dozen societies and clubs, though I do know that things like the Debate Squad were way too competitive. Posters and flyers and squibs in the campus newspaper gave testament to a lot of connecting activity, but John and I pretty much kept to ourselves, ragging on the "Loyola man," reading the literary magazine aloud with a French accent, simultaneously feeling contempt for and exclusion from a social life that seemed to work with the mystery and enclosure of the clockwork in a music box.

It is an unfortunate fact of our psychic lives that the images that surround us as we grow up—no matter how much we may scorn them later—give shape to our deepest needs and longings. Every year Loyola men elected a homecoming queen. The queen and her princesses were students at the Catholic sister schools: Marymount, Mount St. Mary's, St. Vincent's. They had names like Corinne and Cathy, and they came from the Sullivan family or the Mitchells or the Ryans. They were taught to stand with toe to heel, their smiles were inviting, and the photographer's flash illuminated their eyes. Loyola men met them at fraternity parties and mixers and "CoEd Day," met them according to rules of manner and affiliation and parental connection as elaborate as a Balinese dance. John and I drew mustaches on their photographs, but something about them reached far back into my life.

Growing up in South L.A. was certainly not a conscious misery. My neighborhood had its diversions and its mysteries, and I felt loved and needed at home. But all in all there was a dreary impotence to the years, and isolation, and a deep sadness about my father. I protected myself from the harsher side of it all through a life of the mind. And while that interior life included spaceships and pink chemicals and music and the planetary moons, it also held the myriad television images of the good life that were piped into my home: Robert Young sitting down to dinner, Ozzie Nelson tossing the football with his sons, the blond in a Prell commercial turning toward the camera. The images couldn't have been more trivial—all sentimental phosphorescence— but as a child tucked away on South Vermont, they were just about the only images I had of what life would be without illness and dead ends. I didn't realize how completely their message had seeped into my being, what loneliness and sorrow was being held at bay—didn't realize it until I found myself in the middle of Loyola's social life without a guidebook, feeling just beyond the superficial touch of the queen and her princesses, those smiling incarnations of a television promise. I scorned the whole silly show and ached to be embraced by one of these mythic females under the muted light of a paper moon.

15   So I went to school and sat in class and memorized more than under- 15 stood and whistled past the academic graveyard. I vacillated between the false potency of scorn and feelings of ineptitude. John and I would get in his car and enjoy the warmth of each other and laugh and head down the long strip of Manchester Boulevard, away from Loyola, away from the palms and green, green lawns, back to South L.A. We'd throw the ball in the alley or lag pennies on Vermont or hit Marty's Liquor. We'd leave much later for a movie or a football game at Mercy High or the terrible safety of downtown Los Angeles. Walking, then, past the *discotecas* and pawnshops, past the windows full of fried chicken and yellow lamps, past the New Follies, walking through hustlers and lost drunks and prostitutes and transvestites with rouge the color of bacon—

stopping, finally, before the musty opening of a bar where two silhouettes moved around a pool table as though they were underwater.

I don't know what I would have found if the flow of events hadn't changed dramatically. Two things happened. Jack MacFarland privately influenced my course of study at Loyola, and death once again ripped through our small family.

The coterie of MacFarland's students—Art Mitz, Mark Dever, and me—were still visiting our rumpled mentor. We would stop by his office or his apartment to mock our classes and the teachers and all that "'Loyola man' bullshit." Nobody had more appreciation for burlesque than Jack MacFarland, but I suppose he saw beneath our caustic performances and knew we were headed for trouble. Without telling us, he started making phone calls to some of his old teachers at Loyola—primarily to Dr. Frank Carothers, the chairman of the English Department—and, I guess, explained that these kids needed to be slapped alongside the head with a good novel. Dr. Carothers volunteered to look out for us and agreed to some special studies courses that we could substitute for a few of the more traditional requirements, courses that would enable us to read and write a lot under the close supervision of a faculty member. In fact, what he promised were tutorials—and that was exceptional, even for a small college. All this would start up when we returned from summer vacation. Our sophomore year, Jack MacFarland finally revealed, would be different.

When Lou Minton rewired the trailer, he rigged a phone line from the front house: A few digits and we could call each other. One night during the summer after my freshman year, the phone rang while I was reading. It was my mother and she was screaming. I ran into the house to find her standing in the kitchen hysterical—both hands pressed to her face—and all I could make out was Lou's name. I didn't see him in the front of the house, so I ran back through the kitchen to the bedroom. He had fallen back across the bed, a hole right at his sideburn, his jaw still quivering. They had a fight, and some ugly depth of pain convulsed within him. He left the table and walked to the bedroom. My mother heard the light slam of a .22. Nothing more.

That summer seems vague and distant. I can't remember any specifics, though I had to take care of my mother and handle the affairs of the house. I probably made do by blunting a good deal of what I saw and navigating with intuitive quadrants. But though I cannot remember details, I do recall feelings and recognitions: Lou's suicide came to represent the sadness and dead time I had protected myself against, the personal as well as public oppressiveness of life in South Los Angeles. I began to see that my escape to the trailer and my isolationist fantasies of the demimonde would yield another kind of death, a surrender to the culture's lost core. An alternative was somehow starting to take shape around school and knowledge. Knowledge seemed . . . was it empowering? No, that's a word I would use now. Then I felt freed, as if I were untying fetters. There simply were times when the pain and confusion of that summer would give way to something I felt more than I knew: a lightness to my body, an ease in breathing. Three or four months later I took an art history course, and one day during a slide show on Gothic architecture I felt myself rising up within the interior light of Mont-Saint-Michel. I wanted to be released from the despair that surrounded me on South Vermont and from my own troubled sense of exclusion.

20   Jack MacFarland had saved me at one juncture—caught my fancy   20
and revitalized my mind—what I felt now was something further, some tentative recognition that an engagement with ideas could foster competence and lead me out into the world. But all this was very new and fragile, and given what I know now, I realize how easily it could have been crushed. My mother, for as long as I can remember, always added onto any statement of intention—hers or others'—the phrase *se vuol Dio,* if God wants it. The fulfillment of desire, no matter how trivial, required the blessing of the gods, for the world was filled with threat. "I'll plant the seeds this weekend," I might say. "Se vuol Dio," she would add. *Se vuol Dio.* The phrase expressed several lifetimes of ravaged hope: my grandfather's lost leg, the failure of the Rose Spaghetti House, my father laid low, Lou Minton, the landscapes of South L.A. *Se vuol Dio.* For those who live their lives on South Vermont, tomorrow doesn't beckon to be defined from a benign future. It's up to the gods, not you, if any old thing turns out right. I carried within me no history of assurances that what I was feeling would lead to anything.

Because of its size and because of the kind of teacher who is drawn to small liberal arts colleges, Loyola would turn out to be a very good place for me. For even with MacFarland's yearlong tour through ideas and language, I was unprepared. English prose written before the twentieth century was difficult, sometimes impossible, for me to comprehend. The kind of reasoning I found in logic was very foreign. My writing was okay, but I couldn't hold a candle to Art Mitz or Mark Dever or to those boys who came from good schools. And my fears about science and mathematics prevailed: Pereira Hall, the Math and Engineering Building, was only forty to fifty yards from the rear entrance to the English Department but seemed an unfriendly mirage, a malevolent castle floating in the haze of a mescaline dream.

We live, in America, with so many platitudes about motivation and self-reliance and individualism—and myths spun from them, like those of Horatio Alger—that we find it hard to accept the fact that they are serious nonsense. To live your early life on the streets of South L.A.—or Homewood or Spanish Harlem or Chicago's South Side or any one of hundreds of other depressed communities—and to journey up through the top levels of the American educational system will call for support and guidance at many, many points along the way. You'll need people to guide you into conversations that seem foreign and threatening. You'll need models, lots of them, to show you how to get at what you don't know. You'll need people to help you center yourself in your own developing ideas. You'll need people to watch out for you. There is much talk these days about the value of a classical humanistic education, a call for an immersion in the humanities, a return to the great books. These appeals raise lots of suspicions, for such curricula have traditionally served to exclude working-class people from the classroom. It doesn't, of necessity, have to be that way. The teachers that fate and Jack MacFarland's crisis intervention sent my way worked at making the humanities truly human. What transpired between us was the essence of humane liberal education, and it enabled me to move far beyond the cognitive charade of my freshman year.

———

From the midpoint of their freshman year, Loyola students had to take one philosophy course per semester: Logic, Philosophy of Nature, Philosophy of Man, General Ethics, Natural Theology, and so on. Logic was the first in the series, and I had barely gotten a C. The rest of the courses looked like a book fair of medieval scholasticism with the mold scraped off the bindings, and I dreaded their advent. But I was beginning my sophomore year at a time when the best and brightest of the Jesuit community were calling for an intellectually panoramic, socially progressive Catholicism, and while this lasted, I reaped the benefits. Sections of the next three courses I had to take would be taught by a young man who was studying for the priesthood and who was, himself, attempting to develop a personal philosophy that incorporated the mind and the body as well as the spirit.

Mr. Johnson could have strolled off a Wheaties box. Still in his twenties and a casting director's vision of those good looks thought to be all-American, Don Johnson had committed his very considerable intelligence to the study and teaching of philosophy. Jack MacFarland had introduced me to the Greeks, to Christian scholasticism, eighteenth-century deism, and French existentialism, but it was truly an introduction, a curtsy to that realm of the heavens where the philosophers dwell. Mr. Johnson provided a fuller course. He was methodical and spoke with vibrance and made connections between ancients and moderns with care. He did for philosophy what Mr. MacFarland had done for literary history: He gave me a directory of key names and notions.

25   We started in a traditional way with the Greek philosophers who   25 preceded Socrates—Thales, Heraclitus, Empedocles—and worked our way down to Kant and Hegel. We read a little Aquinas, but we also read E. A. Burtt's *The Metaphysical Foundations of Modern Science,* and that gave me entry to Kepler, Copernicus, Galileo (which I was then spelling *Galelao*), and Newton. As he laid out his history of ideas, Mr. Johnson would consider aloud the particular philosophical issue involved, so we didn't, for example, simply get an outline of what Hegel believed, but we watched and listened as Don Johnson reasoned like Hegel and then raised his own questions about the Hegelian scheme. He was a working philosopher, and he was thinking out loud in front of us.

The Metaphysical Foundations of Modern Science was very tough going. It assumed not only a familiarity with Western thought but, as well, a sophistication in reading a theoretically rich argument. It was, in other words, the kind of book you encounter with increased frequency as you move through college. It combined the history of mathematics and science with philosophical investigation, and when I tried to read it, I'd end up rescanning the same sentences over and over, not understanding them, and, finally, slamming the book down on the desk—swearing at this golden boy Johnson and angry with myself. Here's a typical passage, one of the many I marked as being hopeless:

> We begin now to glimpse the tremendous significance of what these fathers of modern science were doing, but let us continue with our questions. What further specific metaphysical doctrines was Kepler led to adopt as a consequence of this notion of what constitutes the real world? For one thing, it led him to appropriate in his own way the distinction between primary and secondary qualities, which

had been noted in the ancient world by the atomist and skeptical schools, and which was being revived in the sixteenth century in varied form by such miscellaneous thinkers as Vives, Sanchez, Montaigne, and Campanella. Knowledge as it is immediately offered the mind through the senses is obscure, confused, contradictory, and hence untrustworthy; only those features of the world in terms of which we get certain and consistent knowledge open before us what is indubitably and permanently real. Other qualities are not real qualities of things, but only signs of them. For Kepler, of course, the real qualities are those caught up in this mathematical harmony underlying the world of the senses, and which, therefore, have a causal relation to the latter. *The real world is a world of quantitative characteristics only; its differences are differences of number alone.*

I couldn't get the distinction that was being made between primary and secondary qualities, and I certainly didn't have the background that would enable me to make sense of Burtt's brief historical survey: from "atomist and skeptical schools [to] . . . Campanella." It is clear from the author's italics that the last sentence of the passage is important, so I underlined it, but because Burtt's discussion is built on a rich intellectual history that I didn't know, I was reading words but not understanding text. I was the human incarnation of language-recognition computer programs: able to record the dictionary meanings of individual words but unable to generate any meaning out of them.

"What," I asked in class, "are primary and secondary qualities? I don't get it." And here Don Johnson was very good. "The answer," he said, "can be found in the passage itself. I'll go back through it with you. Let's start with primary and secondary qualities. If some qualities are primary and others secondary, which do you think would be most important?"

"Primary?"

30   "Right. Primary qualities. Whatever they are. Now let's turn to   30 Kepler, since Kepler's the subject of this passage. What is it that's more important to Kepler?"

I pause and say tentatively, "Math." Another student speaks up, reading from the book: "Quantitative characteristics."

"All right. So primary qualities, for Kepler, are mathematical, quantitative. But we still don't know what this primary and secondary opposition really refers to, do we? Look right in the middle of the paragraph. Burtt is comparing mathematical knowledge to the immediate knowledge provided by—what?"

My light bulb goes on: "The senses."

"There it is. The primary-secondary opposition is the opposition between knowledge gained by pure mathematical reasoning versus knowledge gained through our five senses."

35   We worked with *The Metaphysical Foundations of Modern Science*   35
for some time, and I made my way slowly through it. Mr. Johnson was helping me develop an ability to read difficult texts—I was learning how to reread critically, how to tease out definitions and basic arguments. And I was also gaining confidence that if I stayed with material long enough and kept asking questions, I would get it. That assurance proved to be more valuable than any particular body of knowledge I learned that year.

For my second semester, I had to take Philosophy of Man, and it was during that course that Mr. Johnson delivered his second gift. We read Gabriel Marcel and Erich Fromm, learning about phenomenology and social criticism. We considered the human animal from an anthropological as well as philosophical perspective. And we read humanistic psychologist Abraham Maslow's *Toward a Psychology of Being*. Maslow wrote about "the 'will to health,' the urge to grow, the pressure of self-actualization, the quest for one's identity." The book had a profound effect on me. Six months before, Lou Minton's jaw quivered as if to speak the race's deepest sorrow, and through the rest of that summer I could only feel in my legs and chest some fleeting assurance that the world wasn't a thin mask stretched over nothingness. Now I was reading an articulation of that vague, hopeful feeling. Maslow was giving voice to some delicate possibility within me, and I was powerfully drawn to it. Every person is, in part, "'his own project' and makes himself." I had to know more, so I called Mr. Johnson up and asked if I could visit with him. "Sure," he said, and invited me to campus. So one Saturday morning I took a series of early buses and headed west.

Mr. Johnson and the other initiates to the priesthood lived in an old white residence hall on the grassy east edge of campus, and the long walk up Loyola Boulevard was quiet and meditative: Birds were flying tree to tree and a light breeze was coming in off Playa del Rey. I walked up around the gym, back behind Math-Engineering to his quarters, a simple one-story building with those Spanish curves that seem simultaneously thick and weightless. The sun had warmed the stucco. A window by the door was open, and a curtain had fluttered out. I rang the bell and heard steps on a hardwood floor. Mr. Johnson opened the door and stepped out. He was smiling and his eyes were attentive in the light . . . present . . . there. They said, "Come, let's talk."

Dr. Frank Carothers taught what is generally called the sophomore survey, a yearlong sequence of courses that introduces the neophyte English major to the key works in English literary history. Dr. Carothers was tall and robust. He wore thick glasses and a checkered bow tie and his hairline was male Botticelli, picking up somewhere back beyond his brow. As the year progressed, he spread English literary history out in slow time across the board, and I was introduced to people I'd never heard of: William Langland, a medieval acolyte who wrote the dream-vision *Piers Plowman;* the sixteenth-century poet Sir Thomas Wyatt; Elizabethan lyricists with peculiar names like Orlando Gibbons and Tobias Hume (the author of the wondrous suggestion that tobacco "maketh lean the fat men's tumour"); the physician Sir Thomas Browne; the essayist Joseph Addison; the biographer James Boswell; the political philosopher Edmund Burke, whose prose I could not decipher; and poets Romantic and Victorian (Shelley and Rossetti and Algernon Charles Swinburne). Some of the stuff was invitingly strange ("Pallid and pink as the palm of the flag-flower . . ."), some was awfully hard to read, and some was just awful. But Dr. Carothers laid it all out with his reserved passion, drew for us a giant conceptual blueprint onto which we could place other courses, other books. He was precise, thorough, and rigorous. And he started his best work once class was over.

Being a professor was, for Frank Carothers, a profoundly social calling: He enjoyed the classroom, and he seemed to love the more informal contacts with those he taught, those he once taught, and those who stopped by just to get a look at this guy. He stayed in his office until about four each afternoon, leaning back in us old swivel chair, hands clasped behind his head, his bow tie tight against his collar. He had strong opinions, and he'd get irritated if you missed class, and he sometimes gave quirky advice—but there he'd be shaking his head sympathetically as students poured out their troubles. It was pure and primary for Frank Carothers: Teaching allowed him daily to fuse the joy he got from reading literature—poetry especially—with his deep pleasure in human community. What I saw when I was around him—

and I hung out in his office from my sophomore year on—was very different from the world I had been creating for myself, a far cry from my withdrawal into an old house trailer with a silent book.

40   One of Dr. Carothers's achievements was the English society. The   40
English Society had seventy-eight members, and that made it just about the biggest organization on campus: jocks, literati, C-plus students, frat boys, engineers, mystics, scholars, profligates, bullies, geeks, Republicans—all stood side by side for group pictures. The English Society sponsored poetry readings, lectures, and card games, and best of all, barbecues in the Carotherses' backyard. We would caravan out to Manhattan Beach to be greeted by Betsy, the youngest of seven Carothers children, and she'd walk us back to her father who, wrapped now in an apron, was poking coals or unscrewing the tops from jugs of red wine.

Vivian Carothers, a delicate, soft-spoken woman, would look after us and serve up trays of cheese and chips and little baked things. Students would knock on the redwood gate all through the late afternoon, more and more finding places for themselves among flowers and elephant ears, patio furniture, and a wizened pine. We would go on way past sunset, talking to Dr. Carothers and to each other about books and sports and currently despised professors, sometimes letting off steam and sometimes learning something new. And Frank Carothers would keep us fed, returning to the big, domed barbecue through the evening to lift the lid and add hamburgers, the smoke rising off the grill and up through the telephone lines stretching like the strings of Shelley's harp over the suburbs of the South Bay.

When I was learning my craft at Jack MacFarland's knee, I continually misused words and wrote fragments and run-on sentences and had trouble making my pronouns agree with whatever it was that preceded them. I also produced sentences like these:

> Some of these modern-day Ramses are inherent of their wealth, others are self-made.

> An exhibition of will on the part of the protagonist enables him to accomplish a subjective good (which is an element of tragedy, namely: the protagonist does not fully realize the objective wrong that he is doing. He feels objectively justified if not completely right.)

I was struggling to express increasingly complex ideas, and I couldn't get the language straight: Words, as in my second sentence on tragedy, piled up like cars in a serial wreck. I was encountering a new language—the language of the academy—and was trying to find my way around in it. I have some more examples, written during my first year and a half at Loyola. There was inflated vocabulary:

> I conjectured that he was the same individual who had arrested my attention earlier.

> In his famed speech, "The American Scholar," Ralph Waldo Emerson posed several problems that are particularly germane to the position of the young author.

There were cliches and mixed and awkward metaphors:

> In 1517, when Luther nailed his 95 theses to the door of Wittenburg Cathedral, he unknowingly started a snowball rolling that was to grow to tremendous reprocussions.

45 And there was academic melodrama: 45

> The vast realm of the cosmos or the depths of a man's soul hold questions that reason flounders upon, but which can be probed by the peculiar private insight of the seer.

Pop grammarians and unhappy English teachers get a little strange around sentences like these. But such sentences can be seen as marking a stage in linguistic growth. Appropriating a style and making it your own is difficult, and you'll miss the mark a thousand times along the way. The botched performances, though, are part of it all, and developing writers will grow through them if they are able to write for people who care about language, people who are willing to sit with them and help them as they struggle to write about different things. That is what Ted Erlandson did for me.

Dr. Erlandson was one of the people who agreed to teach me and my Mercy High companions a seminar—a close, intensive course that would substitute for a larger, standard offering like Introduction to Prose Literature. He was tall and lanky and had a long reddish brown beard and lectured in a voice that was basso and happy. He was a strong lecturer and possessed the best memory for fictional detail I'd ever witnessed. And he cared about prose. The teachers I had during my last three years at Loyola assigned a tremendous amount of writing. But it was Ted Erlandson who got in there with his pencil and worked on my style. He would sit me down next to him at his big desk, sweep books and pencils across the scratched veneer, and go back over the sentences he wanted me to revise.

He always began by reading the sentence out loud: "Camus ascented to a richer vision of life that was to characterize the entirety of his work." Then he would fiddle with the sentence, talking and looking up at me intermittently to comment or ask questions: "'Ascent'. That sounds like 'assent', I know, but look it up, Mike." He'd wait while I fluttered the dictionary. "Now, 'the entirety of his work' . . . try this instead: 'his entire work.' Let's read it. 'Camus assented to a richer vision of life that would characterize his entire work.' Sounds better, doesn't it?"

And another sentence. "'Irregardless of the disastrous ending of *Bread and Wine,* it must be seen as an affirmative work.' 'Irregardless' . . . people use it all the time, but 'regardless' will do just fine. Now, I think this next part sounds a little awkward; listen: 'Regardless of the disastrous ending of *Bread and Wine,* it . . .' Hear that? Let's try removing the 'of' and the 'it': 'Regardless of the disastrous ending, *Bread and Wine* must be seen as an affirmative work.' Hmmm. Better, I think."

50 And so it would go. He rarely used grammatical terms, and he 50 never got technical. He dealt with specific bits of language: "Try this here" or "Here's another way to say it." He worked as a craftsman works, with particulars, and he shuttled back and forth continually between print and voice, making me breathe my prose, making me hear the language I'd generated in silence. Perhaps he was more directive than some would like, but, to be truthful, direction was what I needed. I was easily frustrated, and it didn't take a lot to make me doubt myself. When teachers would write "no" or "awkward" or "rewrite" alongside the sentences I had worked so hard to produce, I would be peeved and disappointed. "Well, what the hell *do* they want?" I'd grumble to no one in particular. So Ted Erlandson's linguistic parenting felt just right: a modeling of grace until it all slowly, slowly began to work itself into the way I shaped language.

When Father Albertson lectured, he would stand pretty much in one spot slightly to the left or right of center in front of us. He tended to hold his notes or a play or a critical study in both hands, releasing one to emphasize a point with a simple gesture. He was tall and thin, and his voice was soft and tended toward monotone. When he spoke, he looked very serious, but when one of us responded with any kind of intelligence, a little smile would come over his face. Jack MacFarland had told me that it was Clint Albertson's Shakespeare course that would knock my socks off.

For each play we covered, Father Albertson distributed a five- to ten-page list of questions to ask ourselves as we read. These study questions were of three general types.

The first type was broad and speculative and was meant to spark reflection on major characters and key events. Here's a teaser on *Hamlet:*

> Would you look among the portrait-paintings by Raphael, or Rembrandt, or Van Gogh, or El Greco, or Rouault for an ideal representation of Hamlet? Which painting by which of these men do you think most closely resembles your idea of what Hamlet should look like?

The second type focused on the details of the play itself and were very specific. Here are two of the thirty-eight he wrote for *As You Like It:*

> ACT I, SCENE 2
>
> How is Rosalind distinguished from Celia in this scene? How do you explain the discrepancy between the Folio version of lines 284–287 and Act I, scene 3, line 117?
>
> ACT II, SCENES 4–6:
>
> It has been said these scenes take us definitely out of the world of reality into a world of dream. What would you say are the steps of the process by which Shakespeare brings about this illusion?

55   The third kind of question required us to work with some historical   55
or critical study. This is an example from the worksheet on *Romeo and Juliet:*

> Read the first chapter of C. S. Lewis's *Allegory of Love,* "Courtly Love." What would you say about Shakespeare's concept of love in relation to what Lewis presents as the traditional contradictory concepts in medieval literature of "romantic love" vs. "marriage."

Father Albertson had placed over 150 books on the reserve shelf in the library, and they ranged from intellectual history to literary criticism to handbooks on theater production. I had used a few such "secondary sources" to quote in my own writing since my days with Jack

MacFarland, but this was the first time a teacher had so thoroughly woven them into a course. Father Albertson would cite them during lectures as naturally as though he were recalling a discussion he had overheard. He would add his own opinions and, since he expected us to form opinions, would ask us for ours.

I realize that this kind of thing—the close, line-by-line examination, the citing of critical opinion—has given rise to endless parodies of the academy: repressed schoolmen clucking along in the land of lost language. It certainly can be that way. But the Clint Albertson, all the learning furthered my comprehension of the play. His questions forced me to think carefully about Shakespeare's choice of words, about the crafting of a scene, about the connections between language and performance. I had to read very, very closely, leaning over the thin Formica desk in the trailer, my head cupped in my hands with my two index fingers in my ears to blot out the noise from the alley behind me. There were times when no matter how hard I tried, I wouldn't get it. I'd close the book, feeling stupid to my bones, and go find John. Over then to the liquor store, out into the night. The next day I would visit Father Albertson and tell him I was lost, ask him why this stuff was so damned hard. He'd listen and ask me to tell him why it made me so angry. I'd sputter some more, and then he'd draw me to the difficult passage, slowly opening the language up, helping me comprehend a distant, stylized literature, taking it apart, touching it.

I would then return to a classroom where a historically rich conversation was in progress. Other readers of Shakespeare—from Samuel Johnson to the contemporary literary critic Wylie Sypher—were given voice by Father Albertson, and we were encouraged to enter the dialogue, to consider, to take issue, to be seated amid all that potentially intimidating shoptalk. We were shown how to summarize an opinion, argue with it, weave it into our own interpretations. Nothing is more exclusive than the academic club: its language is highbrow, it has fancy badges, and it worships tradition. It limits itself to a few participants who prefer to take to each other. What Father Albertson did was bring us inside the circle, nudging us out into the chatter, always just behind us, whispering to try this step, then this one, encouraging us to feel the moves for ourselves.

———————

Those four men collectively gave me the best sort of liberal education, the kind longed for in the stream of blue-ribbon reports on the humanities that now cross my desk. I developed the ability to read closely, to persevere in the face of uncertainty and ask questions of what I was reading—not with downcast eyes, but freely, aloud, realizing there is no such thing as an open book. My teachers modeled critical inquiry and linguistic precision and grace, and they provided various cognitive maps for philosophy and history and literature. They encouraged me to make connections and to enter into conversations—present and past—to see what talking a particular kind of talk would enable me to do with a thorny philosophical problem or a difficult literary text. And it was all alive. It transpired in backyards and on doorsteps and inside offices as well as in the classroom. I could smell their tobacco and see the nicks left by their razors. They liked books and ideas, and they liked to talk about them in ways that fostered growth rather than established dominance. They lived their knowledge. And maybe because of that their knowledge grew in me in ways that led back out to the world. I was developing a set of tools with which to shape a life.

60   I continued to take courses from my four mentors, and as I moved 60
through my last two years, I found other teachers who kept the fire going as well: the progressive theologian Paul Hilsdale, the psychologist Carlo Weber, Father Trame—a historian who had us writing papers and exams every other week—the philosophers Gary Schouborg and Norbert Rigali. It was an exciting time for me, full of hope and promise. But I would not be telling the whole story if I didn't admit that with the deep satisfaction of growth came a mix of disturbance and fear.

I began noticing dates of birth and of death. Keats wrote "Ode to a Nightingale" when he was twenty-four. F. Scott Fitzgerald had two novels under his belt by his thirtieth year. A writer's best work, Fitzgerald once said, was produced by the time he was thirty. I became obsessed with impossible comparisons. Jacques Barzun started writing the 375-page *Darwin, Marx, Wagner* in his late twenties. Maslow published his first articles when he was twenty-four. And on. And on. As long as I stayed half-awake intellectually, there was no tension, no failed attempts at mastery, no confrontation with my limits. But now I was trying hard, and I could see how limited I was. It would be quite a while before I could relax into the gifts I did possess, but in the meantime, birthdates, printings, and copyrights all ticked off like some ruthless gauge of my own dim ability.

I lived a life of choice and possibility during the weekdays and then returned every evening to South Vermont. One day in the middle of my junior year, I lay down on the couch in the living room and could not get up. The TV and the table, John and my mother seemed distant, and I was cold and afraid, as if there were some indeterminate sickness all through me. I pulled my knees to my chest. My mother didn't know what to do, so she brought me blankets and a pillow. I stayed there for two days, getting up only to eat, returning quickly to keep the fear at bay, curling up again, bringing the blankets close again. Finally, I asked John to drive me out to see Dr. Metzger, the young Kaiser physician who had ministered to my father during his last year.

Dr. Metzger sat across from me and listened, ten or so years older than me, round faced, a goatee, serious. I couldn't express what it was that was making me feel cold and shaky, just that I was scared and didn't know what to do about it. He encouraged me to talk, and I did—talked about the last few years and Lou Minton and my own imagined infirmity. He leaned forward and told me that I have to move, that my mother would be okay, that she was strong and could manage. It was simple: Move. I would have to move away from South Vermont.

By the time John and I got home, I was feeling better, and within a few days I was back to normal. Dr. Metzger had released something, and eventually I would move. . . . I knew that I had to. I thought maybe I could move once I finished up at Loyola.

65   Those last years saw a gradual shift from the somnambulance and   65
uncertain awakenings of my earlier time in college. I was involved, and I was meeting with success. And success carried with it its own challenges and threats, its own fears and its own further promises. Perhaps the best way to give you a sense of the texture of these years is to offer a few vignettes, a few clips from the footage that runs through my mind as I sit at my typewriter. I'll begin with one that occurred a month or so after I returned from Dr. Metzger's office.

The third course I took from Mr. Johnson was General Ethics. I was a junior and the class was a mix of juniors and seniors. One of the seniors was Brian Kelly. Brian was Loyola's pride—he was handsome, reflective, and gifted, and, by the time he graduated, he would win the triple crown of graduate fellowships: the Woodrow Wilson, the Danforth, and the Rhodes. A remarkable feat.

A course like General Ethics turns on the question of the existence of universal needs and values, and Mr. Johnson's bent was to look to anthropologists rather than theologians to provide the base for the course. He thought it might be a good idea to introduce the class to the issues by setting up a mock debate, one in which the first speaker would argue for the presence of ethical universals (like incest taboos) and the other speaker would support a strict cultural relativism. He asked me and Brian to conduct this piece of pedagogical theater, each of us collaborating beforehand and presenting the two sides of the argument.

Brian and I worked for two or three weeks, sharing materials and agreeing on methods of presentation. The debate came, and I went first, setting out the various anthropological evidence I could find in favor of ethical universals. Then I turned the podium over to Brian and sat down. He rose to the podium and knocked me flat. He couldn't check his combative instincts and discharged a formidable debater's arsenal: He spoke condescendingly. He questioned my sources and the way I reasoned with them. He brought in material I hadn't seen before. I was dumbstruck. This was big-time, no-holds-barred academic debate, and I was going down for the count. When it came my turn to respond to Brian, I repeated mechanically some of the things I had said earlier, but I couldn't reason with any flair. I was flushed with anger and humiliation, and my mouth dried up and my tongue felt as if it belonged to someone else.

More than a year after the debate with Brian, I won the Blenkiron Award for excellence in English—a plaque and a hundred dollars from one of Loyola's benefactors. Ted Erlandson was by then the chairman of English, and he presided over the ceremony. My name was called, and I walked to the podium. He shook my hand and offered me the plaque. As I was walking back and reading the inscription, I saw that the engraver had made a mistake: *Rose* was spelled *Ruse*. Ruse. A wily subterfuge. A trick. The plaque was returned and made right, of course, but the joke still went down. A peek from behind the curtain. A wink in the hall of mirrors. Was I the real thing or not?

70 One of the many people I met at the crossroads of Frank Carothers's 70 office was Mike Casey. Casey was usually clad in strong opinion and a thin corduroy jacket. He edited *El Playano,* the campus literary magazine John and I used to lampoon in the old Plymouth. But I started liking Casey, and when he asked me to join the magazine, I put sarcasm behind me and signed on. I worked as an assistant for a semester, and that was fun. Casey promoted me to associate editor, and, at the end of my junior year, he and Dr. Carothers—the magazine's faculty advisor—chose me to be editor. They took a chance. Unlike the other two candidates, I had no experience with high school newspapers

or annuals, and all I had done at Loyola was publish, at Casey's suggestion, a stuffy essay on Samuel Beckett and an intellectual exercise that passed for a poem.

El Playano had a small office on the second floor of the student center and was published three times a year. I learned about editing, and, because the magazine had a staff of six, I learned something about management. Students submitted stories and poems, and my editors and I would sit around an old wooden desk and make our decisions. I would then meet with the writers, trying to articulate things about style or plot that I was just coming to understand myself. Then came preparation of manuscripts, pasteup, design, printing, and proofreading, and the exciting day when my assistant editors and I drove to the printers to pick up boxloads of magazines.

We distributed *El Playano* across the campus: walking into the student union, the bookstore, the library, into departments and offices, into solemn places, given entrance with our magazines, probably too loud, like miners back from a long dig slapping bundles onto the assayer's counter. I had responsibilities: timetables, deadlines. I instituted subscriptions for alumni. I made pronouncements, this from my first issue: "Good writing is essential to good learning." I got us an interview with Ray Bradbury. I scouted and found some talented freshman writers. I was on the inside oiling a few gears:

> Now I'm a man
> I made 21

Every year Loyola sponsored a lecture for the faculty and the alumni. Students were not invited. The speaker for 1965–66 was the distinguished French philosopher and playwright, Gabriel Marcel. Mr. Johnson had told me about Marcel's *Homo Viator,* man the traveler, and I wanted to hear him speak. I sneaked into the auditorium through the exit at the north corridor and nestled in about halfway down the aisle. Mr. Johnson was just finishing his introduction. He turned to the left wing and announced Gabriel Marcel. The applause began, and a tiny, bent man scuttled out across the stage. He used a cane and tried to walk fast and his hips bobbed like pistons gone awry. He was white haired and looked to be seventy. Several times from wing to a desk at center stage he glanced out at the audience to acknowledge the applause. He was smiling—a happy smile, a smile that counterposed his body, all missteps and wild angles.

The auditorium was fairly small, so I could see Marcel's face clearly. I understood only bits and pieces of his speech—which was an attempt to distinguish his philosophy from existentialism—but it was not the text of the speech that pulled me in, it was the delivery. Once this old and crippled man settled into the safe confines of chair and desk, age and infirmity receded. His voice was strong and steady and his eyes were bright. He spoke with conviction and wit, and, for those moments anyway, it seemed that I was witnessing the pure mind that Yeats longed for. When Marcel hobbled out, he was "a tattered coat upon a stick," but when he spoke I saw a body transformed, a promise that an aged person need not be "a paltry thing"—that a life of the mind can bring with it at least momentary deliverance, an athletics of the spirit.

75 After my poor freshman year, my grades started their ascent. I did 75
increasingly well through my sophomore year and managed to get all A's as a junior. That sort of rise, combined with my work on the campus literary magazine, made me a contender for a fellowship to graduate school. Loyola had a faculty committee charged with preparing promising seniors for fellowship applications, and they contacted me.

I could get strong letters from my teachers, but the committee believed that a further letter from an influential nonacademic—an industrialist or a judge or a legislator—would help my case, particularly with the more prestigious awards. I didn't know any such person, so they set out to have me meet a few people who were part of the wealthy Catholic network.

The first man who interviewed me was the president of an oil company with a branch in Los Angeles. His office was on Wilshire Boulevard near downtown, and when the secretary escorted me in, I entered a world of dark wood and leather and brass. I sat in a chair that took me deep into it. Across a wide expanse of mahogany sat a man in his fifties. He was pale and his white hair was perfectly trimmed and he wore a navy blue suit. He began asking me about my studies, speaking slowly and seemingly from someplace very far away. There was an ornate rifle mounted on the wall behind him. I talked about literature and philosophy and about the literary magazine, and he watched me. He asked several other questions and then shifted in his chair to ask me what I thought of the currently volatile Free Speech Movement. I said a few things in favor of the movement—academic bureaucracy, relevance, the kind of thing you'd expect—and something very quick happened to his face. The next question—one about a priest he knew at Loyola—was asked while he looked into his hands, which were lying, palms up and crossed, on his desk top. Then he thanked me, and the secretary—as if by magic—came through the door, smiled, and walked me out.

A week or so later, I was invited to join the dean and several faculty members at their lunch with a visiting speaker, a former member of the State Department under Jack Kennedy. I was seated across from the man just as the salads were arriving. I introduced myself, and he acknowledged the introduction and began to eat. He leaned over his plate, looking up when spoken to. I asked a few things about the Kennedys—superficial questions, for at that time in my life I had a *Reader's Digest* knowledge of the particulars of working politics. He answered briefly—not rude but not engaged—and returned to his food. Separate body parts were energized—an arm moving up and out from his side, fingers working away like a typist's on chicken amandine— but his face remained jowly and passive. His eyes were flat. When the watermelon arrived, he cut wedges with the knife in his right hand and spit the seeds into the fist of his left. Then he slowly opened his fist to run the palm over the edge of his plate, depositing the seeds.

I have no idea if either man wrote me a letter.

But this is a story with a happy ending. Not all my encounters with the world of academic gamesmanship were so chilly. Father Albertson encouraged me to play a long shot and apply for the big three— the Wilson, Danforth, and Rhodes—and I was lucky enough to get an interview for the Danforth. The Danforth Foundation, a philanthropic organization based in Saint Louis, leaned toward candidates who were planning a career in college teaching. The fellowships were prestigious: Your college had to nominate you, and 120 winners would be chosen from the 2,000 or so nominees.

My interview was set for nine o'clock in the Statler Hilton near downtown L.A. The buses were running late, and I had to transfer twice and sprint through the faded opulence of the Hilton's broad lobby. David Tyack was a historian from Reed College, and he greeted me at the door of his room and we sat by a window in the sun. Just the two of us. Tyack was a young man, academic, tweedy, but humane and engaging. We talked for over an hour about the philosophy I had been reading for Mr. Johnson, about the literary magazine, about my difficult first year at Loyola. I remember on moment particularly: me leaning forward into a stream of sunlight, my elbows on my knees, hands out, describing Gabriel Marcel's walk across the stage.

One year of good grades could never stack up against the best of the Danforth applicants, but Tyack wrote a strong report, and I received an honorable mention from the Danforth Foundation. A month or so later I got word from UCLA that I was awarded full support for three years of graduate study. Like those red A-minuses on Jack Mac-Farland's papers, the Danforth honorable mention read like a certification of ability. And I'd be going to UCLA. Good Lord. Four years before, I couldn't have shaken out their doormat.

I had promised to meet some friends at Mr. Pockets, a pool hall and pizzeria on Lincoln Boulevard close to Loyola. It was late in the evening, and I was finishing up the layout on the last issue of the magazine. I locked up the office and walked out of the student center into a thick fog. The lights from St. Robert's were out, and the lamps on Loyola Boulevard looked like big tufts of cotton stuck high up on invisible poles. I walked along the boulevard past the library; with its foyer lights left on, it seemed a glowing, fuzzy block floating back in the trees.

I was thinking about the magazine. About particular stories and how much I liked it, felt part of it, how hard it was going to be to leave it. A song lyric started drifting in and out of my thoughts:

> Me and my cat named dog.
> We're walking high against the fog . . .

85   I couldn't see more than a few feet in front of me, but the air was 85 moist and it felt good to breathe it. The magazine. I started singing the lyric aloud, its silliness blending with the bittersweetness of parting. I was well past the library when my foot caught something. A white cloth on the ground. I bent over and picked a large pair of men's undershorts off the tip of my shoe. What story is this? I wondered, and kept walking, thinking, finally, about the bar and the friends waiting for me there, finding the song again, singing it louder now and twirling the underwear in rhythmic snaps over my head.

Writing Around Rules

Mike Rose

"No one writes effortlessly," Mike Rose suggests. "Our com-
posing is marked by pauses, false starts, gnawing feelings of
inadequacy, crumpled paper." When pauses, false starts, and
anxiety block a writer, however, the results can be disastrous.
Mike Rose was born in Los Angeles, studied at the Univer-
sity of California at Los Angeles, and wrote his dissertation
on "writer's block." He has written articles in professional
journals, published Writer's Block: The Cognitive Dimension *(1983),* Lives on the Boundary *(1989), and* Possible
Lives: The Promise of Education in America *(1995).*

In this selection, Rose cites examples of student writers
who have problems writing—not because they are espe-
cially anxious about writing, but because they follow cer-
tain "rules" too rigidly. As you read this essay, see if you
recognize yourself in any of these case studies.

I.

Here's Liz, a junior English major, at work on a paper for a college
course: she has been given a two-page case study and must analyze it
using the ideas contained in a second, brief handout. She has about
one hour to complete her assignment. As she reads and rereads the
handouts, she scribbles notes to herself in the margins. Liz is doing
what most effective writers would do with such materials: paraphras-
ing the main points in the passages, making connections among them,
recording associations to other pertinent knowledge. But a closer look
at these interpretive notes reveals something unusual: Liz seems to be
editing them as she goes along, cleaning them up as though they were
final copy. In one of her notes she jots down the phrase "is saying
that not having creative work is the. . . ." She stops, thinks for a
moment, and changes "is the" to "causes." (Later on, explaining this

---

Reprinted from *Patterns in Action*, Second Edition.

change, she'll comment that "you're not supposed to have passive verbs.") She then replaces "is saying" with "says," apparently following her directive about passive voice, but later changes it again, noting that "says" is "too colloquial." Liz pauses after this editing and looks up—she has forgotten what she initially was trying to capture in her writing. "That happens a lot," she says.

Liz was one of the many college students I studied over a two-and-one-half-year period (*Writer's Block: The Cognitive Dimension*). The purpose of my study was to try to gain insight into what causes some young writers to compose with relative fluency and what leads others to experience more than their fair share of blocks, dead ends, conflicts, and the frustrations of the blank page. What I uncovered was a whole array of problems that I would label as being primarily *cognitive* rather than primarily *emotional* in nature. That is, many students were engaging in self-defeating composing behaviors not because they had some deep-seated fear of revealing their thoughts or of being evaluated or because of some longstanding aversion to writing, but rather because they had somehow learned a number of rules, planning strategies, or assumptions about writing that limited rather than enhanced their composing. We saw Liz lose her train of thought by adhering too rigidly to stylistic rules when she should have been scribbling ideas freely in order to discover material for her essay. Let me offer two further vignettes that illustrate some of the other cognitive difficulties I uncovered.

Tyrrell, also a junior English major, says he doesn't like to sketch out any sort of plan or draft of what he's going to write. He'll think about his topic, but his pen usually won't touch paper until he begins writing the one, and only, draft he'll produce. As he writes, he pauses frequently and at length to make all sorts of decisions about words, ideas, and rhetorical effects. In short, he plans his work as he goes along. There's nothing inherently wrong with writing this way, but where difficult assignments involving complex materials are concerned, it helps to sketch out a few ideas, some direction, a loose organizational structure before beginning to write. When a coworker and I studied Tyrrell's composing, we noted the stylistic flourishes in his essay, but also its lack of direction. As my colleague noted, "[His] essay bogs down in description and in unexplained abstractions." Perhaps the essay would have had more direction if Tyrrell had roughed out a few ideas before composing his one and only draft. Why didn't he do so? Consider his comment on planning:

> [Planning] is certainly not spontaneous and a lot of the times it's not even really what you feel because it becomes very mechanical. It's almost like—at least I feel—it's diabolical, you know, because . . . it'll sacrifice truth and real feelings that you have.

Tyrrell assumes that sketching out a plan before writing, somehow violates the spontaneity of composing: to plan dooms one to write mechanical, unemotional prose. Yet, while too much planning may sometimes make the actual writing a joyless task, it is also true that most good writing is achieved through some kind of prefiguring, most often involving pen and paper. Such planning does not necessarily subvert spontaneity; in fact, since it reduces the load on the writer's immediate memory, it might actually free one to be more spontaneous, to follow the lead of new ideas as they emerge. Tyrrell's assumption, then, is inaccurate. By recognizing only this one path to spontaneity, he is probably limiting his effectiveness as a writer and, ironically, may be reducing his opportunities to be spontaneous.

5   Gary is an honors senior in biochemistry. When I observed him,   5
he spent over half of his writing time meticulously analyzing each sentence of the assignment's reading passage on one of the handouts. He understood the passage and the assignment well enough but wanted to make sure the passage was sufficiently broken down to be of use when he composed his essay. As Gary conducted this minute analysis, he wrote dozens and dozens of words and phrases across the handouts. He then summarized these words and phrases in a list of six items. He *then* tried to condense all six items into a thesis sentence:

> I have concepts . . . and my task here is to say what is being said about all of those all at once.

Gary's method was, in this case, self-defeating. He worked in too precise a fashion, generating an unwieldy amount of preliminary material, which he didn't seem to be able to rank or thin out—and he was unable to focus his thinking in a single thesis sentence. Gary's interpretive and planning strategies were inappropriately elaborate, and they were inflexible. It was not surprising that when Gary's hour was up, he had managed to write only three disconnected sentences. Not really an essay at all.

But what about the students who weren't stymied, who wrote with relative fluency? They too talked of rules and assumptions and displayed planning strategies. The interesting thing, though, is that their rules were more flexible; that is, a rule seemed to include conditions under which it ought and ought not to be used. The rules weren't absolutes, but rather statements about what one might do in certain writing situations. Their assumptions, as well, were not absolute and they tended to enhance composing, opening up rather than restricting possibilities. And their planning strategies tended to be flexible and appropriate to the task. Fluent writers had their rules, strategies, and assumptions, but they were of a different kind from those of the blocked writers.

What to do? One is tempted to urge the blocked writers to clear their minds of troubling rules, plans, and assumptions. In a few cases, that might not be such a bad idea. But what about Liz's preoccupation with passive constructions? Some degree of concern about casting one's language in the active voice is a good thing. And Gary's precise strategies? It would be hard to imagine good academic writing that isn't preceded by careful analysis of one's materials. Writers need the order and the guidance that rules, strategies, and assumptions provide. The answer to Liz's, Tyrrell's, and Gary's problems, then, lies in altering their approaches to make them more conditional, adaptive, and flexible. Let me explain further. For the sake of convenience, I'll focus on rules, though what I'll say has application to the assumptions we develop and the planning strategies we learn.

II.

Writing is a phenomenally complex learned activity. To write in a way that others can understand we must employ a large and complicated body of conventions. We learn from our parents or earliest teachers that script, in English, goes left to right straight across the page. We learn about letter formation, spelling, sentence structure, and so on. Some of this information we absorb more or less unconsciously through reading, and some of it we learn formally as guidelines, as directives . . . as rules.

10   And there are all kinds of rules. Some tell us how to format our   10
writing (for example, when to capitalize, how to paragraph, how to footnote). There are grammar rules (for example, "Make a pronoun agree in number with its antecedent"). There are preferences concerning style that are often stated as rules ("Avoid passive voice"). There are

usage rules ("*That* always introduces restrictive clauses; *which* can introduce both restrictive and nonrestrictive clauses"). There are rules that tell us how to compose ("Before you begin writing, decide on your thesis and write it down in a single declarative sentence"). The list goes on and on. Some of these rules make sense; others are confusing, questionable, or contradictory. Fortunately, we assimilate a good deal of the information they contain gradually by reading other writers, by writing ourselves, or by simply being around print. Therefore, we can confirm or alter or reject them from experience.

But all too often the rules are turned into absolutes. And that's where the trouble begins. Most rules about writing should not be expressed (in textbooks), stored (in our minds), or enacted (on the page) as absolutes, as mathematical, unvarying directives. True, a few rules apply in virtually all situations (for example, certain formatting rules or capitalization rules). But most rules do not. Writing rules, like any rules about language, have a history and have a time and place. They are highly context-bound.

Should you always, as some textbooks suggest, place your thesis sentence at the beginning of your first paragraph or, as others suggest, work up to it and place it at the end of the paragraph? Well, the answer is that both injunctions are right . . . and wrong. Students writing essay exams would be well-advised to demonstrate their knowledge and direct the reader's attention as soon as possible. But the writer who wants to evoke a mood might offer a series of facts and events that gradually lead up to a thesis sentence. The writing situation, the rhetorical purpose, and the nature of the material one is working with will provide the answer. A single-edged rule cannot.

How about our use of language usage rules? Certainly there's a right and a wrong here? Again, not quite. First of all, there's a time in one's writing to worry about such things. Concern yourself with questions of usage too early in your composing and you'll end up like Liz, worrying about the minutiae of language while your thought fades to a wisp. Second, the social consequences of following or ignoring such rules vary widely depending on whether you're writing formal or informal prose. Third, usage rules themselves have an evolutionary history: we aren't obliged to follow some of the rules that turn-of-the-century writers had to deal with, and our rules will alter and even disappear as the English language moves on in time. No, there are no absolutes here either.

Well, how about some of the general, commonsense rules about the very act of writing itself? Certainly, rules like "Think before you write" ought to be followed? Again, a qualification is in order. While it certainly is good advice to think through ideas before we record them for others to see, many people, in fact, use writing as a way of thinking. They make major decisions *as* they write. There are times when it's best to put a piece of writing aside and ponder, but there are also times when one ought to keep a pen in hand and attempt to resolve a conceptual tangle by sketching out what comes to mind. Both approaches are legitimate.

15   I'll stop here. I hope I've shown that it's difficult to make hard   15
and fast statements about the structure, the language, or the composing of an essay. Unfortunately, there's a strong push in our culture to make absolute statements about writing, especially where issues of style and usage are concerned. But I hope by now the reader of this essay believes that most rules about writing—about how to do it, about how it should be structured, about what words to use—are not absolute, and should be taught and enacted in a flexible, context-dependent way. Given certain conditions, you follow them; given other conditions you modify or suspend them. A teacher may insist that a young writer follow a particular dictum in order to learn a pattern, but there must come a time when the teacher extends the lesson and explains when the dictum is and isn't appropriate.

Professors, Students, and the Syllabus

Sharon Rubin

When Sharon Rubin was assistant dean for undergraduate studies at the University of Maryland, she reviewed dozens of syllabi as part of the process of approving general-education courses. She learned that for most courses, the syllabus presented an incomplete, often confusing, picture of what students could expect. From this evidence she came to the conclusion that "the inadequate syllabus is a symptom of a larger problem—the lack of communication between teachers and students" (par. 8).

"Professors, Students, and the Syllabus" proposes a "place of meeting," sought by students and faculty alike. For Rubin, the answers to the questions a syllabus should address add up to the message that teachers want their students to master the material.

After her assistant deanship at the University of Maryland, Rubin became dean of liberal arts at Salisbury University, part of the University of Maryland system. She continued her work as an administrator at Ramapo College of New Jersey, where she served as the vice president for academic affairs. At Ramapo College, she returned to teaching and is currently professor of American studies in the School of American and International Studies.

1 For the past two years I've been sitting in on the meetings of a committee charged with approving courses for the University of Maryland's general-education program. Very often the committee members leave those meetings mystified and exasperated. It's not that the courses proposed are inadequate; it's just that the syllabi submitted with the proposals are so often virtually impossible to decode.

I've listened while a faculty member from a related discipline has tried to guess what a syllabus might possibly mean. I've seen carefully worded letters from the dean requesting clarification—and then looked on as the committee has tried to relate a three-page response to the original syllabus. The committee has even developed a new cover sheet for all proposals, which requests detailed information about objectives and asks for samples of test questions and paper assignments. Yet sufficiently informative syllabi are still so rare that when one appears it elicits audible sighs of relief around the conference table.

The syllabi our committee gets are not much different from the ones I've picked up at conferences or seen attached to grant proposals. In other words, I don't believe the problem is local or idiosyncratic; rather, it seems to be basic to the teaching endeavor. We keep forgetting that what we know—about our disciplines, about our goals, about out teaching methods—is not known (or agreed upon) by everyone. We seem to assume that our colleagues and our students will intuitively be able to reconstruct the creature we see in our mind's eye from the few bones we give them in the syllabus.

The worst syllabi seem to fall into one of two categories.

5   The "listers" merely specify which books or chapters will be read   5 during which weeks, without a hint about the principles behind the selection. The most puzzling of this type assign chapters in the textbooks in an order considerably different from the order intended by the authors. At best, such modification gives students the impression that the teacher is improving on the original organization for some as yet unrevealed purpose, at worst, it gives students the idea that one order is no less logical or coherent than another, and that all parts are interchangeable and equally valid.

The "scolders" give brief descriptions of content and lengthy sets of instruction detailing what will happen if a student comes in late or leaves early, hands in a paper after the deadline, misses an exam, fails to follow the rules for margins and double-spacing, does not participate in class discussion. The scolders often sound more like lawyers than professors. Undoubtedly the syllabus as legal document has evolved because so often students demand that their teachers provide a set of rules, probably to give the students something concrete to cling to as they struggle with the content of the course. If even sophisticated scholars fall into the trap of equating quantitative data with significance, it's not surprising that students mistake the rules for the meaning.

Here are some questions our committee often finds unanswered even in wonderful syllabi for wonderful courses:

- Why should a student want to take this course? How does it make a difference as part of the discipline? How does it fit into the general-education program?
- What are the objectives of the course? Where does it lead, intellectually and practically? Students should be able to find out what they will know by the end of the course, and also what they will be able to do better afterward than before. Is the purpose of the course to increase their problem-solving abilities, improve their communication skills, sharpen their understanding of moral ambiguities, allow them to translate knowledge from one context to another? Why are the objectives important, and how will different parts of the course help students accomplish those objectives?
- What are the prerequisites? Students should be given some idea about what they should already know and what skills they should already have before taking the course, so they can realistically assess their readiness. Will they be expected to know how to compare and contrast, to analyze and synthesize, or will they be taught those skills during the course?
- Why do the parts of the course come in the order they do? Most syllabi note the order in which topics will be discussed, but make no attempt to explain the way the professor has chosen to organize the course. Sections of the syllabus are usually titled, but only infrequently are questions provided for students to help them put the reading assignments and homework into context.
- Will the course be primarily lectures, discussions, or group work? When a percentage of the grade is for "class participation," what does the professor expect from the students—regular attendance? questions? answers to questions? Will the students be given alternative ways to achieve success in the class, based on different learning styles?
- What is the purpose of the assignments? Students are frequently told how much an assignment will "count" and how many pages long it must be, but they are rarely given any idea about what it will demand of them or what the goal is. Will students be required to describe, discuss, analyze, provide evidence, criticize, defend, compare, apply? To what end? If students are expected to present a project before the class, are the criteria for an excellent presentation made clear?

- What will the tests test?—memory? understanding? ability to synthesize? To present evidence logically? To apply knowledge in a new context?
- Why have the books been chosen? What is their relative importance in the course and in the discipline? Is the emphasis in the course on primary or secondary materials and why?

"Well," you may say, "the syllabus isn't the course—everything will be made clear as the semester progresses." Or, "I can't ask my overworked secretary to type a twelve-page syllabus." Or, "Students are interested only in the numbers—of books, of pages to read, of written assignments, of questions on the exam." Or, "A syllabus with all that information is too static—it doesn't allow me the flexibility to be creative on the spur of the moment." Maybe those are relevant objections—and maybe they are excuses for badly thought-out, hurriedly patched-together efforts. Whatever the rationale, I believe that the inadequate syllabus is a symptom of a larger problem—the lack of communication between teachers and students.

Most of the latest reports on undergraduate education have in common the criticism that faculty members and the students no longer seem to be connecting. Our students do not seem to be involved in learning, they say. We seem to have lost the ability to create a shared community of values; we have substituted diversity for coherence and cannot find our way back to integrating principles. However, these reports all seem to ignore a very real wish among students and faculty members to find a place of meeting.

10   In 1982–83, Lee Knefelkamp of the University of Maryland asked   10
217 faculty members at eight colleges what they worried about most the first day of class. Their three most common concerns were, "Will the students get involved?" "Will they like me?" "Will the class work well as a class?"

When 157 students at those institutions responded to the same question, their three most common concerns were, "Will I be able to do the work?" "Will I like the professor?" "Will I get along with my classmates?"

The notion of relationship between teachers and students and material to be learned is clear in the answers from both groups. However, when the faculty members were asked what they thought students worried about the first day of class, they responded, "Will I get a good grade?" "Will the work be hard?" "Will the class be interesting?" When the students were asked what they thought teachers worried about, they generally couldn't answer the question at all.

The survey showed that there was a real desire on the part of both students and teacher for connectedness, but neither group realized that the other shared that desire. If the participants on both sides don't understand how to develop their relationship, learning will be diminished.

The syllabus is a small place to start bringing students and faculty members back together, of course, and its improvement is not the revolutionary gesture that curriculum reform seems to be. But if students could be persuaded that we are really interested in their understanding the material we offer, that we support their efforts to master it, and that we take their intellectual struggles seriously, they might respond by becoming more involved in our courses, by trying to live up to our expectations, and by appreciating our concern.

15   Then the real work of learning can begin.   15

Conversational Ballgames
Nancy Sakamoto

Student Journal Responses

My brother was thinking of becoming a Hare Krishna and invited me and my mom to attend one of their feasts at "the temple." We went. We had to sit on the floor, which was OK. We got there early, and as it got closer to the time set for the beginning of the festivities, more and more people came. Soon it was so crowded, we were packed in like slabs of bacon in an Oscar Mayer package. Besides having to contend with so many people, Mom and I were encircled by people from India. I've always thought of Americans as fairly friendly people, but our experience with the Indians led me to believe that Americans are pretty cold fish. The festivities started and even more people crowded in. Then Mom and I noticed we were being used as chair backs. Several people were leaning against us. They didn't seem to care that we were complete strangers. It was getting hotter and hotter and I was getting more and more uncomfortable having so many strange bodies pressed up against me. Then I saw my mom remove an Indian man's hand from her calf. He had been using Mom as a bolster to prop himself up. That was it—I couldn't stand it anymore! We got up and left. I couldn't believe how uncomfortable that made me.

My mom is Japanese—that makes me 1/2 Japanese. Last summer my cousins Zeshiko and Yoko visited us from Japan. Talking to them was very interesting. I know Japanese a little bit, enough to get by if I were to suddenly become lost in Japan. But nonetheless speaking with my two cousins opened my eyes quite a bit. Japanese is a passive language. So whenever they spoke (Yoko, the younger one could speak a little bit of English), they put it in the passive. That drove me nuts. But then I realized how English must sound to Japanese—very straightforward and pushy. Western. Anyway, that experience made me see things in a new light.

Reprinted from *Polite Fictions* (1982), Kinseido Publishing Company, Ltd.

Nancy Sakamoto is an American woman married to a Japanese man. Her essay, which originally appeared in Polite Fictions *(1982), indicates that she has lived in both cultures and taught English to Japanese students. Her topic— how conversing in a foreign language requires learning about cultural expectations—is increasingly important as Americans become more aware of dramatic differences in cultures around the world: East European men may kiss each other when they meet; Latins may be late for a meeting without intending insult; Americans' loud voices may seem rude and obnoxious to Asians; and Arabs may converse with their faces only ten inches apart—an uncomfortably close distance for most Americans.*

"Conversational Ballgames" explains how different cultural expectations distinguish North American from Japanese conversations. Sakamoto compares conversations to different kinds of games. For Americans, talking is like playing tennis or volleyball, whereas for the Japanese, talking is more like bowling. As you read her essay, see if her comparison of the rules of conversation and the rules of a game helps to illustrate different cultural "rules for the game."

Conversational Ballgames

1   After I was married and had lived in Japan for a while, my Japanese gradually improved to the point where I could take part in simple conversations with my husband and his friends and family. And I began to notice that often, when I joined in, the others would look startled, and the conversational topic would come to a halt. After this happened several times, it became clear to me that I was doing something wrong. But for a long time, I didn't know what it was.

Finally, after listening carefully to many Japanese conversations, I discovered what my problem was. Even though I was speaking Japanese, I was handling the conversation in a Western way.

Japanese-style conversations develop quite differently from Western-style conversations. And the difference isn't only in the languages. I realized that just as I kept trying to hold Western-style conversations even when I was speaking Japanese, so my English students kept trying to hold Japanese-style conversations even when they were speaking

English. We were unconsciously playing entirely different conversational ballgames.

A Western-style conversation between two people is like a game of tennis. If I introduce a topic, a conversational ball, I expect you to hit it back. If you agree with me, I don't expect you simply to agree and do nothing more. I expect you to add something—a reason for agreeing, another example, or an elaboration to carry the idea further. But I don't expect you always to agree. I am just as happy if you question me, or challenge me, or completely disagree with me. Whether you agree or disagree, your response will return the ball to me.

And then it is my turn again. I don't serve a new ball from my original starting line. I hit your ball back again from where it has bounded. I carry your idea further, or answer your questions or objections, or challenge or question you. And so the ball goes back and forth, with each of us doing our best to give it a new twist, an original spin, or a powerful smash.

And the more vigorous the action, the more interesting and exciting the game. Of course, it one of us gets angry, it spoils the conversation, just as it spoils a tennis game. But getting excited is not at all the same as getting angry. After all, we are not trying to hit each other. We are trying to hit the ball. So long as we attack only each other's opinions and do not attack each other personally, we don't expect anyone to get hurt. A good conversation is supposed to be interesting and exciting.

If there are more than two people in the conversation, then it is like doubles in tennis, or like volleyball. There's no waiting in line. Whoever is nearest and quickest hits the ball, and if you step back, someone else will hit it. No one stops the game to give you a turn. You're responsible for taking your own turn. But whether it's two players or a group, everyone does his best to keep the ball going, and no one person has the ball for very long.

A Japanese-style conversation, however, is not at all like tennis or volleyball. It's like bowling. You wait for your turn. And you always know your place in line. It depends on such things as whether you are older or younger, a close friend or a relative stranger to the previous speaker, in a senior or junior position, and so on.

When your turn comes, you step up to the starting line with your bowling ball, and carefully bowl it. Everyone else stands back and watches politely, murmuring encouragement. Everyone waits until the ball has reached the end of the alley and watches to see if it knocks down all the pins, or only some of them, or none of them. There is a pause, while everyone registers your score.

10　　　Then, after everyone is sure that you have completely finished your turn, the next person in line steps up to the same starting line, with a different ball. He doesn't return your ball, and he does not begin from where your ball stopped. There is no back and forth at all. All the balls run parallel. And there is always a suitable pause between turns. There is no rush, no excitement, no scramble for the ball.

No wonder everyone looked startled when I took part in Japanese conversations. I paid no attention to whose turn it was and kept snatching the ball halfway down the alley and throwing it back at the bowler. Of course the conversation died. I was playing the wrong game.

This explains why it is almost impossible to get a Western-style conversation or discussing going with English students in Japan. I used to think that the problem was their lack of English language ability. But I finally came to realize that the biggest problem is that they, too, are playing the wrong game.

Whenever I serve a volleyball, everyone just stands back and watches it fall, with occasional murmurs of encouragement. No one hits it back. Everyone waits until I call on someone to take a turn. And when that person speaks, he doesn't hit my ball back. He serves a new ball. Again, everyone just watches it fall.

So I call on someone else. This person does not refer to what the previous speaker has said. He also serves a new ball. Nobody seems to have paid any attention to what anyone else has said. Everyone begins again from the same starting line, and all the balls run parallel. There is never any back and forth. Everyone is trying to bowl with a volleyball.

15　　　Now that you know about the difference in the conversational ball-games, you may think that all your troubles are over. But if you have been trained all your life to play one game, it is no simple matter to switch to another, even if you know the rules. Knowing the rules is not at all the same thing as playing the game.

Even now, during a conversation in Japanese I will notice a startled reaction and belatedly realize that once again I have rudely interrupted by instinctively trying to hit back the other person's bowling ball. It is no easier for me to "just listen" during a conversation, than it is for my Japanese students to "just relax" when speaking with foreigners. Now I can truly sympathize with how hard they must find it to try to carry on a Western-style conversation.

Revision Strategies of Student Writers and Experienced Adult Writers

Nancy Sommers

A lthough various aspects of the writing process have been studied extensively of late, research on revision has been notably
absent. The reason for this, I suspect, is that current models of
the writing process have directed attention away from revision. With few
exceptions, these models are linear; they separate the writing process into
discrete stages. Two representative models are Gordon Rohman's suggestion that the composing process moves from prewriting to writing to
rewriting and James Britton's model of the writing process as a series of
stages described in metaphors of linear growth, conception—incubation—
production.[1] What is striking about these theories of writing is that
they model themselves on speech: Rohman defines the writer in a way
that cannot distinguish him from a speaker ("A writer is a man who . . .
puts [his] experience into words in his own mind"—p. 15); and Britton bases his theory of writing on what he calls (following Jakobson)
the "expressiveness" of speech.[2] Moreover, Britton's study itself follows
the "linear model" of the relation of thought and language in speech proposed by Vygotsky, a relationship embodied in the linear movement
"from the motive which engenders a thought to the shaping of the
thought, *first* in inner speech, *then* in meanings of words, and *finally*

Reprinted from *College Composition and Communications* 31, no. 4, by permission of
the author.

Nancy Sommers, formerly Director of Composition at the University of Oklahoma,
is now Adjunct Assistant Professor at New York University. She has taught writing at
Boston University, the Harvard Graduate School of Business Administration, and the
Polaroid Corporation. An NCTE Promising Researcher for her studies of the processes
of revising, she is writing a research monograph on revision.

in words" (quoted in Britton, p. 40). What this movement fails to take into account in its linear structure—"first . . . then . . . finally"—is the recursive shaping of thought by language; what it fails to take into account is *revision*. In these linear conceptions of the writing process revision is understood as a separate stage at the end of the process—a stage that comes after the completion of a first or second draft and one that is temporally distinct from the prewriting and writing stages of the process.[3]

The linear model bases itself on speech in two specific ways. First of all, it is based on traditional rhetorical models, models that were created to serve the spoken art of oratory. In whatever ways the parts of classical rhetoric are described, they offer "stages" of composition that are repeated in contemporary models of the writing process. Edward Corbett, for instance, describes the "five parts of a discourse"—*inventio, dispositio, elocutio, memoria, pronuntiatio*—and, disregarding the last two parts since "after rhetoric came to be concerned mainly with written discourse, there was no further need to deal with them,"[4] he produces a model very close to Britton's conception [*inventio*], incubation [*dispositio*], production [*elocutio*]. Other rhetorics also follow this procedure, and they do so not simply because of historical accident. Rather, the process represented in the linear model is based on the irreversibility of speech. Speech, Roland Barthes says, "is irreversible":

> "A word cannot be retracted, except precisely by saying that one retracts it. To cross out here is to add: if I want to erase what I have just said, I cannot do it without showing the eraser itself (I must say: *'or rather . . .' 'I expressed myself badly . . .'*); paradoxically, it is ephemeral speech which is indelible, not monumental writing. All that one can do in the case of a spoken utterance is to tack on another utterance."[5]

What is impossible in speech is *revision:* like the example Barthes gives, revision in speech is an afterthought. In the same way, each stage of the linear model must be exclusive (distinct from the other stages) or else it becomes trivial and counterproductive to refer to these junctures as "stages."

By staging revision after enunciation, the linear models reduce revision in writing, as in speech, to no more than an afterthought. In this way such models make the study of revision impossible. Revision, in Rohman's model, is simply the repetition of writing; or to pursue Britton's organic metaphor, revision is simply the further growth of what is already there, the "preconceived" product. The absence of research on revision, then, is a function of a theory of writing which makes revision both superfluous and redundant, a theory which does not distinguish between writing and speech.

5   What the linear models do produce is a parody of writing. Isolating revision and then disregarding it plays havoc with the experiences composition teachers have of the actual writing and rewriting of experienced writers. Why should the linear model be preferred? Why should revision be forgotten, superfluous? Why do teachers offer the linear model and students accept it? One reason, Barthes suggests, is that "there is a fundamental tie between teaching and speech," while "writing begins at the point where speech becomes *impossible*."[6] The spoken word cannot be revised. The possibility of revision distinguishes the written text from speech. In fact, according to Barthes, this is the essential difference between writing and speaking. When we must revise, when the very idea is subject to recursive shaping by language, then speech becomes inadequate. This is a matter to which I will return, but first we should examine, theoretically, a detailed exploration of what student writers as distinguished from experienced adult writers *do* when they write and rewrite their work. Dissatisfied with both the linear model of writing and the lack of attention to the process of revision, I conducted a series of studies over the past three years which examined the revision processes of student writers and experienced writers to see what role revision played in their writing processes. In the course of my work the revision process was redefined as *a sequence of changes in a composition—changes which are initiated by cues and occur continually throughout the writing of a work.*

Methodology

I used a case study approach. The student writers were twenty freshmen at Boston University and the University of Oklahoma with SAT verbal scores ranging from 450–600 in their first semester of composition. The twenty experienced adult writers from Boston and Oklahoma City included journalists, editors, and academics. To refer to the two groups, I use the terms *student writers* and *experienced writers* because the principal difference between these two groups is the amount of experience they have had in writing.

Each writer wrote three essays, expressive, explanatory, and persuasive, and rewrote each essay twice, producing nine written products in draft and final form. Each writer was interviewed three times after the final revision of each essay. And each writer suggested revisions for a composition written by an anonymous author. Thus extensive written and spoken documents were obtained from each writer.

The essays were analyzed by counting and categorizing the changes made. Four revision operations were identified: deletion, substitution, addition, and reordering. And four levels of changes were identified: word, phrase, sentence, theme (the extended statement of one idea). A coding system was developed for identifying the frequency of revision by level and operation. In addition, transcripts of the interviews in which the writers interpreted their revisions were used to develop what was called a *scale of concerns* for each writer. This scale enabled me to codify what were the writer's primary concerns, secondary concerns, tertiary concerns, and whether the writers used the same scale of concerns when revising the second or third drafts as they used in revising the first draft.

Revision Strategies of Student Writers

Most of the students I studied did not use the terms *revision* or *rewriting*. In fact, they did not seem comfortable using the word *revision* and explained that revision was not a word they used, but the word their teachers used. Instead, most of the students had developed various functional terms to describe the type of changes they made. The following are samples of these definitions:

> *Scratch Out and Do Over Again:* "I say scratch out and do over, and that means what it says. Scratching out and cutting out. I read what I have written and I cross out a word and put another word in; a more decent word or a better word. Then if there is somewhere to use a sentence that I have crossed out, I will put it there."
>
> *Reviewing:* "Reviewing means just using better words and eliminating words that are not needed. I go over and change words around."
>
> *Reviewing:* "I just review every word and make sure that everything is worded right. I see if I am rambling; I see if I can put a better word in or leave one out. Usually when I read what I have written, I say to myself, 'that word is so bland or so trite,' and then I go and get my thesaurus."

Redoing: "Redoing means cleaning up the paper and cross-ing out. It is looking at something and saying, no that has to go, or no, that is not right."

Marking Out: "I don't use the word rewriting because I only write one draft and the changes that I make are made on top of the draft. The changes that I make are usually just marking out words and putting different ones in."

Slashing and Throwing Out: "I throw things out and say they are not good. I like to write like Fitzgerald did by inspi-ration, and if I feel inspired then I don't need to slash and throw much out."

10   The predominant concern in these definitions is vocabulary. The students understand the revision process as a rewording activity. They do so because they perceive words as the unit of written discourse. That is, they concentrate on particular words apart from their role in the text. Thus one student quoted above thinks in terms of dictionar-ies, and, following the eighteenth century theory of words parodied in *Gulliver's Travels,* he imagines a load of things carried about to be exchanged. Lexical changes are the major revision activities of the stu-dents because economy is their goal. They are governed, like the lin-ear model itself, by the Law of Occam's razor that prohibits logically needless repetition: redundancy and superfluity. Nothing governs speech more than such superfluities; speech constantly repeats itself precisely because spoken words, as Barthes writes, are expendable in the cause of communication. The aim of revision according to the students' own description is therefore to clean up speech; the redundancy of speech is unnecessary in writing, their logic suggests, because writing, unlike speech, can be reread. Thus one student said, "Redoing means clean-ing up the paper and crossing out." The remarkable contradiction of cleaning by marking might, indeed, stand for student revision as I have encountered it.

The students place a symbolic importance on their selection and rejection of words as the determiners of success or failure for their com-positions. When revising, they primarily ask themselves: can I find a better word or phrase? A more impressive, not so cliched, or less hum-drum word? Am I repeating the same word or phrase too often? They approach the revision process with what could be labeled as a "the-saurus philosophy of writing"; the students consider the thesaurus a harvest of lexical substitutions and believe that most problems in their essays can be solved by rewording. What is revealed in the students' use of the thesaurus is a governing attitude toward their writing: that the meaning to be communicated is already there, already finished, already produced, ready to be communicated, and all that is necessary is a better word "rightly worded." One student defined revision as "redoing"; "redoing" meant "just using better words and eliminating words that are not needed." For the students, writing is translating: the thought to the page, the language of speech to the more formal language of prose, the word to its synonym. Whatever is translated, an original text already exists for students, one which need not be discovered or acted upon, but simply communicated.[7]

The students list repetition as one of the elements they most worry about. This cue signals to them that they need to eliminate the repetition either by substituting or deleting words or phrases. Repetition occurs, in large part, because student writing imitates—transcribes—speech: attention to repetitious words is a manner of cleaning speech. Without a sense of the developmental possibilities of revision (and writing in general) students seek, on the authority of many textbooks, simply to clean up their language and prepare to type. What is curious, however, is that students are aware of lexical repetition, but not conceptual repetition. They only notice the repetition if they can "hear" it; they do not diagnose lexical repetition as symptomatic of problems on a deeper level. By rewording their sentences to avoid the lexical repetition, the students solve the immediate problem, but blind themselves to problems on a textual level; although they are using different words, they are sometimes merely restating the same idea with different words. Such blindness, as I discovered with student writers, is the inability to "see" revision as a process: the inability to "re-view" their work again, as it were, with different eyes, and to start over.

The revision strategies described above are consistent with the students' understanding of the revision process as requiring lexical changes but not semantic changes. For the students, the extent to which they revise is a function of their level of inspiration. In fact, they use the word *inspiration* to describe the ease or difficulty with which their essay is written, and the extent to which the essay needs to be revised. If students feel inspired, if the writing comes easily, and if they don't get stuck on individual words or phrases, then they say that they cannot see any reason to revise. Because students do not see revision as an activity in which they modify and develop perspectives and ideas, they feel that if they know what they want to say, then there is little reason for making revisions.

The only modification of ideas in the students' essays occurred when they tried out two or three introductory paragraphs. This results, in part, because the students have been taught in another version of the linear model of composing to use a thesis statement as a controlling device in their introductory paragraphs. Since they write their introductions and their thesis statements even before they have really discovered what they want to say, their early close attention to the thesis statement, and more generally the linear model, function to restrict and circumscribe not only the development of their ideas, but also their ability to change the direction of these ideas.

15   Too often as composition teachers we conclude that students do 15 not willingly revise. The evidence from my research suggests that it is not that students are unwilling to revise, but rather that they do what they have been taught to do in a consistently narrow and predictable way. On every occasion when I asked students why they hadn't made any more changes, they essentially replied, "I knew something larger was wrong, but I didn't think it would help to move words around." The students have strategies for handling words and phrases and their strategies helped them on a word or sentence level. What they lack, however, is a set of strategies to help them identify the "something larger" that they sensed was wrong and work from there. The students do not have strategies for handling the whole essay. They lack procedures or heuristics to help them reorder lines of reasoning or ask questions about their purposes and readers. The students view their compositions in a linear way as a series of parts. Even such potentially useful concepts as "unity" or "form" are reduced to the rule that a composition, if it is to have form, must have an introduction, a body, and a conclusion, or the sum total of the necessary parts.

The students decide to stop revising when they decide that they have not violated any of the rules for revising. These rules, such as "Never begin a sentence with a conjunction" or "Never end a sentence with a preposition," are lexically cued and rigidly applied. In general, students will subordinate the demands of the specific problems of their text to the demands of the rules. Changes are made in compliance with abstract rules about the product, rules that quite often do not apply to the specific problems in the text. These revision strategies are teacher-based, directed towards a teacher-reader who expects compliance with rules—with pre-existing "conceptions"—and who will only examine parts of the composition (writing comments about those parts in the margins of their essays) and will cite any violations of rules in those parts. At best the students see their writing altogether passively through the eyes of former teachers or their surrogates, the textbooks, and are bound to the rules which they have been taught.

Revision Strategies of Experienced Writers

One aim of my research has been to contrast how student writers define revision with how a group of experienced writers define their revision processes. Here is a sampling of the definitions from the experienced writers:

> *Rewriting:* "It is a matter of looking at the kernel of what I have written, the content, and then thinking about it, responding to it, making decisions, and actually restructuring it."

> *Rewriting:* "I rewrite as I write. It is hard to tell what is a first draft because it is not determined by time. In one draft, I might cross out three pages, write two, cross out a fourth, rewrite it, and call it a draft. I am constantly writing and rewriting. I can only conceptualize so much in my first draft—only so much information can be held in my head at one time; my rewriting efforts are a reflection of how much information I can encompass at one time. There are levels and agenda which I have to attend to in each draft."

> *Rewriting:* "Rewriting means on one level, finding the argument, and on another level, language changes to make the argument more effective. Most of the time I feel as if I can go on rewriting forever. There is always one part of a piece that I could keep working on. It is always difficult to know at what point to abandon a piece of writing. I like this idea that a piece of writing is never finished, just abandoned."

> *Rewriting:* "My first draft is usually very scattered. In rewriting, I find the line of argument. After the argument is resolved, I am much more interested in word choice and phrasing."

> *Revising:* "My cardinal rule in revising is never to fall in love with what I have written in a first or second draft. An idea,

sentence, or even a phrase that looks catchy, I don't trust. Part of this idea is to wait a while. I am much more in love with something after I have written it than I am a day or two later. It is much easier to change anything with time."

Revising: "It means taking apart what I have written and putting it back together again. I ask major theoretical questions of my ideas, respond to those questions, and think of proportion and structure, and try to find a controlling metaphor. I find out which ideas can be developed and which should be dropped. I am constantly chiseling and changing as I revise."

The experienced writers describe their primary objective when revising as finding the form or shape of their argument. Although the metaphors vary, the experienced writers often use structural expressions such as "finding a framework," "a pattern," or "a design" for their argument. When questioned about this emphasis, the experienced writers responded that since their first drafts are usually scattered attempts to define their territory, their objective in the second draft is to begin observing general patterns of development and deciding what should be included and what excluded. One writer explained, "I have learned from experience that I need to keep writing a first draft until I figure out what I want to say. Then in a second draft, I begin to see the structure of an argument and how all the various sub-arguments which are buried beneath the surface of all those sentences are related." What is described here is a process in which the writer is both agent and vehicle. "Writing," says Barthes, unlike speech, "develops like a seed, not a line,"[8] and like a seed it confuses beginning and end, conception and production. Thus, the experienced writers say their drafts are "not determined by time," that rewriting is a "constant process," that they feel as if (they) "can go on forever." Revising confuses the beginning and end, the agent and vehicle; it confuses, *in order to find*, the line of argument.

After a concern for form, the experienced writers have a second objective: a concern for their readership. In this way, "production" precedes "conception." The experienced writers imagine a reader (reading their product) whose existence and whose expectations influence their revision process. They have abstracted the standards of a reader and this reader seems to be partially a reflection of themselves and functions as a critical and productive collaborator—a collaborator who has yet to love their work. The anticipation of a reader's judgment causes a feeling of dissonance when the writer recognizes incongruities between intention and execution, and requires these writers to make revisions on all levels. Such a reader gives them just what the students lacked: new eyes to "re-view" their work. The experienced writers believe that they have learned the causes and conditions, the product, which will influence their reader, and their revision strategies are geared towards creating these causes and conditions. They demonstrate a complex understanding of which examples, sentences, or phrases should be included or excluded. For example, one experienced writer decided to delete public examples and add private examples when writing about the energy crisis because "private examples would be less controversial and thus more persuasive." Another writer revised his transitional sentences because "some kinds of transitions are more easily recognized as transitions than others." These examples represent the type of strategic attempts these experienced writers use to manipulate the conventions of discourse in order to communicate to their reader.

20   But these revision strategies are a process of more than communication; they are part of the process of *discovering meaning* altogether. Here we can see the importance of dissonance; at the heart of revision is the process by which writers recognize and resolve the dissonance they sense in their writing. Ferdinand de Saussure has argued that meaning is differential or "diacritical," based on differences between terms rather than "essential" or inherent qualities of terms. "Phonemes," he said, "are characterized not, as one might think, by their own positive quality but simply by the fact that they are distinct."[9] In fact, Saussure bases his entire *Course in General Linguistics* on these differences, and such differences are dissonant; like musical dissonances which gain their significance from their relationship to the "key" of the composition which itself is determined by the whole language, specific language (parole) gains its meaning from the system of language (langue) of which it is a manifestation and part. The musical composition—a "composition" of parts—creates its "key" as in an over-all structure which determines the value (meaning) of its parts. The analogy with music is readily seen in the compositions of experienced writers: both sorts of composition are based precisely on those structures experienced writers seek in their writing. It is this complicated relationship between the parts and the whole in the work of experienced writers which destroys the linear model; writing cannot develop "like a line" because each addition or deletion is a reordering of the whole. Explicating Saus-

sure, Jonathan Culler asserts that "meaning depends on difference of meaning."[10] But student writers constantly struggle to bring their essays into congruence with a predefined meaning. The experienced writers do the opposite: they seek to discover (to create) meaning in the engagement with their writing, in revision. They seek to emphasize and exploit the lack of clarity, the differences of meaning, the dissonance, that writing as opposed to speech allows in the possibility of revision. Writing has spatial and temporal features not apparent in speech—words are recorded in space and fixed in time—which is why writing is susceptible to reordering and later addition. Such features make possible the dissonance that both provokes revision and promises, from itself, new meaning.

For the experienced writers the heaviest concentration of changes is on the sentence level, and the changes are predominantly by addition and deletion. But, unlike the students, experienced writers make changes on all levels and use all revision operations. Moreover, the operations the students fail to use—reordering and addition—seem to require a theory of the revision process as a totality—a theory which, in fact, encompasses the *whole* of the composition. Unlike the students, the experienced writers possess a nonlinear theory in which a sense of the whole writing both precedes and grows out of an examination of the parts. As we saw, one writer said he needed "a first draft to figure out what to say," and "a second draft to see the structure of an argument buried beneath the surface." Such a "theory" is both theoretical and strategical; once again, strategy and theory are conflated in ways that are literally impossible for the linear model. Writing appears to be more like a seed than a line.

Two elements of the experienced writers' theory of the revision process are the adoption of a holistic perspective and the perception that revision is a recursive process. The writers ask: what does my essay as a *whole* need for form, balance, rhythm, or communication. Details are added, dropped, substituted, or reordered according to their sense of what the essay needs for emphasis and proportion. This sense, however, is constantly in flux as ideas are developed and modified; it is constantly "re-viewed" in relation to the parts. As their ideas change, revision becomes an attempt to make their writing consonant with that changing vision.

The experienced writers see their revision process as a recursive process—a process with significant recurring activities—with different levels of attention and different agenda for each cycle. During the first revision cycle their attention is primarily directed towards narrowing the topic and delimiting their ideas. At this point, they are not as concerned as they are later about vocabulary and style. The experienced writers explained that they get closer to their meaning by not limiting themselves too early to lexical concerns. As one writer commented to explain her revision process, a comment inspired by the summer 1977 New York power failure: "I feel like Con Edison cutting off certain states to keep the generators going. In first and second drafts, I try to cut off as much as I can of my editing generator, and in a third draft, I try to cut off some of my idea generators, so I can make sure that I will actually finish the essay." Although the experienced writers describe their revision process as a series of different levels or cycles, it is inaccurate to assume that they have only one objective for each cycle and that each cycle can be defined by a different objective. The same objectives and sub-processes are present in each cycle, but in different proportions. Even though these experienced writers place the predominant weight upon finding the form of their argument during the first cycle, other concerns exist as well. Conversely, during the later cycles, when the experienced writers' primary attention is focused upon stylistic concerns, they are still attuned, although in a reduced way, to the form of the argument. Since writers are limited in what they can attend to during each cycle (understandings are temporal), revision strategies help balance competing demands on attention. Thus, writers can concentrate on more than one objective at a time by developing strategies to sort out and organize their different concerns in successive cycles of revision.

It is a sense of writing as discovery—a repeated process of beginning over again, starting out new—that the students failed to have. I have used the notion of dissonance because such dissonance, the incongruities between intention and execution, governs both writing and meaning. Students do not see the incongruities. They need to rely on their own internalized sense of good writing and to see their writing with their "own" eyes. Seeing in revision—seeing beyond hearing—is at the root of the word *revision* and the process itself; current dicta on revising blind our students to what is actually involved in revision. In fact, they blind them to what constitutes good writing altogether. Good writing disturbs: it creates dissonance. Students need to seek the dissonance of discovery, utilizing in their writing, as the experienced writers do, the very difference between writing and speech—the possibility of revision.

Notes

1. D. Gordon Rohman and Albert O. Wlecke, "Pre-writing: The Construction and Application of Models for Concept Formation in Writing," Cooperative Research Project No. 2174, U.S. Office of Education, Department of Health, Education, and Welfare; James Britton, Anthony Burgess, Nancy Martin, Alex McLeod, Harold Rosen, *The Development of Writing Abilities (11–18)* (London: Macmillan Education, 1975).

2. Britton is following Roman Jakobson, "Linguistics and Poetics," in T. A. Sebeok, *Style in Language* (Cambridge, Mass: MIT Press, 1960).

3. For an extended discussion of this issue see Nancy Sommers, "The Need for Theory in Composition Research," *College Composition and Communication,* 30 (February, 1979), 46–49.

4. *Classical Rhetoric for the Modern Student* (New York: Oxford University Press, 1965), p. 27.

5. Roland Barthes, "Writers, Intellectuals, Teachers," in *Image-Music-Text,* trans. Stephen Heath (New York: Hill and Wang, 1977), pp. 190–191.

6. "Writers, Intellectuals, Teachers," p. 190.

7. Nancy Sommers and Ronald Schleifer, "Means and Ends: Some Assumptions of Student Writers," *Composition and Teaching,* II (in press).

8. *Writing Degree Zero* in *Writing Degree Zero and Elements of Semiology,* trans. Annette Lavers and Colin Smith (New York: Hill and Wang, 1968), p. 20.

9. *Course in General Linguistics,* trans. Wade Baskin (New York, 1966), p. 119.

10. Jonathan Culler, *Saussure* (Penguin Modern Masters Series; London: Penguin Books, 1976), p. 70.

Acknowledgment: The author wishes to express her gratitude to Professor William Smith, University of Pittsburgh, for his vital assistance with the research reported in this article and to Patrick Hays, her husband, for extensive discussions and critical editorial help.

Men and Women Use Different Approaches in Classroom Discussion

Deborah Tannen

*Deborah Tannen is professor of linguistics at George-
town University and author of the best-selling* You Just
Don't Understand: Women and Men in Conversation
(William E. Morrow & Company, 1990).

1 When I researched and wrote my latest book, *You Just Don't
Understand: Women and Men in Conversation,* the furthest
thing from my mind was reevaluating my teaching strategies.
But that has been one of the direct benefits of having written the book.

The primary focus of my linguistic research always has been the
language of everyday conversation. One facet of this is conversational
style: how different regional, ethnic, and class backgrounds, as well as
age and gender, result in different ways of using language to communicate. *You Just Don't Understand* is about the conversational styles of
women and men. As I gained more insight into typically male and
female ways of using language, I began to suspect some of the causes
of the troubling facts that women who go to single-sex schools do
better in later life, and that when young women sit next to young
men in classrooms, the males talk more. This is not to say that all
men talk in class, nor that no women do. It is simply that a greater percentage of discussion time is taken by men's voices.

The research of sociologists and anthropologists such as Janet Lever,
Marjorie Harness Goodwin, and Donna Eder has shown that girls and
boys learn to use language differently in their sex-separate peer groups.

Reprinted from *The Chronicle of Higher Education* 37, no. 40 (June 19, 1991), by permission of the author. Reprinted in *The Princeton Anthology of Writing: Favorite Pieces*
by the Ferris/McGraw Writers at Princeton, ed. by John McPhee and Carol Rigolot,
Princeton University Press, 2001.

Typically, a girl has a best friend with whom she sits and talks, frequently telling secrets. It's the telling of secrets, the fact and the way that they talk to each other, that makes them best friends. For boys, activities are central: Their best friends are the ones they do things with. Boys also tend to play in larger groups that are hierarchical. High-status boys give orders and push low-status boys around. So boys are expected to use language to seize center stage: by exhibiting their skill, displaying their knowledge, and challenging and resisting challenges.

These patterns have stunning implications for classroom interaction. Most faculty members assume that participating in class discussion is a necessary part of successful performance. Yet speaking in a classroom is more congenial to boys' language experience than to girls', since it entails putting oneself forward in front of a large group of people, many of whom are strangers and at least one of whom is sure to judge speakers' knowledge and intelligence by their verbal display.

5   Another aspect of many classrooms that makes them more hospitable to most men than to most women is the use of debate-like formats as a learning tool. Our educational system, as Walter Ong argues persuasively in his book *Fighting for Life* (Cornell University Press, 1981), is fundamentally male in that the pursuit of knowledge is believed to be achieved by ritual opposition: public display followed by argument and challenge. Father Ong demonstrates that ritual opposition— what he calls "adversativeness" or "agonism"— is fundamental to the way most males approach almost any activity. (Consider, for example, the little boy who shows he likes a little girl by pulling her braids and shoving her.) But ritual opposition is antithetical to the way most females learn and like to interact. It is not that females don't fight, but that they don't fight for fun. They don't ritualize opposition.

Anthropologists working in widely disparate parts of the world have found contrasting verbal rituals for women and men. Women in completely unrelated cultures (for example, Greece and Bali) engage in ritual laments: spontaneously produced rhyming couplets that express their pain, for example, over the loss of loved ones. Men do not take part in laments. They have their own, very different verbal ritual: a contest, a war of words in which they vie with each other to devise clever insults.

When discussing these phenomena with a colleague, I commented that I see these two styles in American conversation: Many women bond by talking about troubles, and many men bond by exchanging playful insults and put-downs, and other sorts of verbal sparring. He exclaimed: "I never thought of this, but that's the way I teach: I have students read an article, and then I invite them to tear it apart. After we've torn it to shreds, we talk about how to build a better model."

This contrasts sharply with the way I teach: I open the discussion of readings by asking, "What did you find useful in this? What can we use in our own theory building and our own methods?" I note what I see as weaknesses in the author's approach, but I also point out that the writer's discipline and purposes might be different from ours. Finally, I offer personal anecdotes illustrating the phenomena under discussion and praise students' anecdotes as well as their critical acumen.

These different teaching styles must make our classrooms wildly different places and hospitable to different students. Male students are more likely to be comfortable attacking the readings and might find the inclusion of personal anecdotes irrelevant and "soft." Women are more likely to resist discussion they perceive as hostile, and, indeed, it is women in my classes who are most likely to offer personal anecdotes.

10   A colleague who read my book commented that he had always   10 taken for granted that the best way to deal with students' comments is to challenge them; this, he felt it was self-evident, sharpens their minds and helps them develop debating skills. But he had noticed that women were relatively silent in his classes, so he decided to try beginning discussion with relatively open-ended questions and letting comments go unchallenged. He found, to his amazement and satisfaction, that more women began to speak up.

Though some of the women in his class clearly liked this better, perhaps some of the men liked it less. One young man in my class wrote in a questionnaire about a history professor who gave students questions to think about and called on people to answer them: "He would then play devil's advocate . . . i.e., he debated us. . . . That class really sharpened me intellectually. . . . We as students do need to know how to defend ourselves." This young man valued the experience of being attacked and challenged publicly. Many, if not most, women would shrink from such "challenge," experiencing it as public humiliation.

A professor at Hamilton College told me of a young man who was upset because he felt his class presentation had been a failure. The professor was puzzled because he had observed that class members had listened attentively and agreed with the student's observations. It turned out that it was this very agreement that the student interpreted as failure: Since no one had engaged his ideas by arguing with him, he felt they had found them unworthy of attention.

So one reason men speak in class more than women is that many of them find the "public" classroom setting more conducive to speaking, whereas most women are more comfortable speaking in private to a small group of people they know well. A second reason is that men are more likely to be comfortable with the debate-like form that discussion may take. Yet another reason is the different attitudes toward speaking in class that typify women and men.

Students who speak frequently in class, many of whom are men, assume that it is their job to think of contributions and try to get the floor to express them. But many women monitor their participation not only to get the floor but to avoid getting it. Women students in my class tell me that if they have spoken up once or twice, they hold back for the rest of the class because they don't want to dominate. If they have spoken a lot one week, they will remain silent the next. These different ethics of participation are, of course, unstated, so those who speak freely assume that those who remain silent have nothing to say, and those who are reining themselves in assume that the big talkers are selfish and hoggish.

15   When I looked around my classes, I could see these differing ethics 15
and habits at work. For example, my graduate class in analyzing conversation had 20 students, 11 women and 9 men. Of the men, four were foreign students: two Japanese, one Chinese, and one Syrian. With the exception of the three Asian men, all the men spoke in class at least occasionally. The biggest talker in the class was a woman, but there were also five women who never spoke at all, only one of whom was Japanese. I decided to try something different.

I broke the class into small groups to discuss the issues raised in the readings and to analyze their own conversational transcripts. I devised three ways of dividing the students into groups: one by the degree program they were in, one by gender, and one by conversational style, as closely as I could guess it. This meant that when the class was grouped according to conversational style, I put Asian students together, fast talkers together, and quiet students together. The class split into groups six times during the semester, so they met in each grouping twice. I told students to regard the groups as examples of interactional data and to note the different ways they participated in the different groups. Toward the end of the term, I gave them a questionnaire asking about their class and group participation.

I could see plainly from my observation of the groups at work that women who never opened their mouths in class were talking away in the small groups. In fact, the Japanese woman commented that she found it particularly hard to contribute to the all-woman group she was in because "I was overwhelmed by how talkative the female students were in the female-only group." This is particularly revealing because it highlights that the same person who can be "oppressed" into silence in one context can become the talkative "oppressor" in another. No one's conversational style is absolute; everyone's style changes in response to the context and others' styles.

Some of the students (seven) said they preferred the same-gender groups; others preferred the same-style groups. In answer to the question "Would you have liked to speak in class more than you did?" six of the seven who said Yes were women; the one man was Japanese. Most startlingly, this response did not come only from quiet women; it came from women who had indicated they had spoken in class never, rarely, sometimes, and often. Of the 11 students who said the amount they had spoken was fine, 7 were men. Of the four women who checked "fine," two added qualifications indicating it wasn't completely fine: One wrote in "maybe more," and one wrote, "I have an urge to participate but often feel I should have something more interesting/relevant/wonderful/intelligent to say!!"

I counted my experiment a success. Everyone in the class found the small groups interesting, and no one indicated he or she would have preferred that the class not break into groups. Perhaps most instructive, however, was the fact that the experience of breaking into groups, and of talking about participation in class, raised everyone's awareness about classroom participation. After we had talked about it, some of the quietest women in the class made a few voluntary contributions, though sometimes I had to insure their participation by interrupting the students who were exuberantly speaking out.

20   Americans are often proud that they discount the significance of cultural differences: "We are all individuals," many people boast. Ignoring such issues as gender and ethnicity becomes a source of pride: "I treat everyone the same." But treating people the same is not equal treatment if they are not the same.

The classroom is a different environment for those who feel comfortable putting themselves forward in a group than it is for those who find the prospect of doing so chastening, or even terrifying. When a professor asks, "Are there any questions?," students who can formulate statements the fastest have the greatest opportunity to respond.

Those who need significant time to do so have not really been given a chance at all, since by the time they are ready to speak, someone else has the floor.

In a class where some students speak out without raising hands, those who feel they must raise their hands and wait to be recognized do not have equal opportunity to speak. Telling them to feel free to jump in will not make them feel free; one's sense of timing, of one's rights and obligations in a classroom, are automatic, learned over years of interaction. They may be changed over time, with motivation and effort, but they cannot be changed on the spot. And everyone assumes his or her own way is best. When I asked my students how the class could be changed to make it easier for them to speak more, the most talkative woman said she would prefer it if no one had to raise hands, and a foreign student said he wished people would raise their hands and wait to be recognized.

My experience in this class has convinced me that small-group interaction should be part of any class that is not a small seminar. I also am convinced that having the students become observers of their own interaction is a crucial part of their education. Talking about ways of talking in class makes students aware that their ways of talking affect other students, that the motivations they impute to others may not truly reflect others' motives, and that the behaviors they assume to be self-evidently right are not universal norms.

The goal of complete equal opportunity in class may not be attainable, but realizing that one monolithic classroom-participation structure is not equal opportunity is itself a powerful motivation to find more-diverse methods to serve diverse students—and every classroom is diverse.